Lecture Notes in Artificial Intelligence   1325

Subseries of Lecture Notes in Computer Science
Edited by J. G. Carbonell and J. Siekmann

Lecture Notes in Computer Science

Edited by G. Goos, J. Hartmanis and J. van Leeuwen

Springer
Berlin
Heidelberg
New York
Barcelona
Budapest
Hong Kong
London
Milan
Paris
Santa Clara
Singapore
Tokyo

Zbigniew W. Raś   Andrzej Skowron   (Eds.)

Foundations of Intelligent Systems

10th International Symposium, ISMIS'97
Charlotte, North Carolina, USA
October 15-18, 1997
Proceedings

Springer

Series Editors

Jaime G. Carbonell, Carnegie Mellon University, Pittsburgh, PA, USA
Jörg Siekmann, University of Saarland, Saarbrücken, Germany

Volume Editors

Zbigniew W. Raś
University of North Carolina, Department of Computer Science
9201 University City Boulevard, Charlotte, NC 28223, USA
E-mail: ras@uncc.edu

Andrzej Skowron
University of Warsaw, Institute of Mathematics
Banacha 2, 02-097 Warsaw, Poland
E-mail: skowron@mimuw.edu.pl

Cataloging-in-Publication Data applied for

Die Deutsche Bibliothek - CIP-Einheitsaufnahme

Foundations of intelligent systems : 10th international symposium ;
proceedings / ISMIS '97, Charlotte, North Carolina, USA, October
15 - 18, 1997. Z. W. Ras ; A. Skowron (ed.). - Berlin ; Heidelberg ;
New York ; Barcelona ; Budapest ; Hong Kong ; London ; Milan ;
Paris ; Santa Clara ; Singapore ; Tokyo : Springer, 1997
   (Lecture notes in computer science ; Vol. 1325 : Lecture notes in
   artificial intelligence)
   ISBN 3-540-63614-5

CR Subject Classification (1991): I.2, H.5, F.4.1, H.3.3

ISBN 3-540-63614-5 Springer-Verlag Berlin Heidelberg New York

Typesetting: Camera ready by author
SPIN 10545727   06/3142 – 5 4 3 2 1 0   Printed on acid-free paper

Preface

This volume contains the papers selected for presentation at the Tenth International Symposium on Methodologies for Intelligent Systems - ISMIS'97, held in Charlotte, North Carolina, October 15-18, 1997. The symposium was hosted by UNC-Charlotte and sponsored by the Oak Ridge National Laboratory, First Union National Bank, University of Warsaw, UNC-Charlotte, and others.

ISMIS is a conference series that was started in 1986 in Knoxville, Tennessee. Since then it has been held in Charlotte (North Carolina), Knoxville (Tennessee), Torino (Italy), Trondheim (Norway), and Zakopane (Poland).

The Program Committee selected the following major areas for ISMIS'97:
- Approximate Reasoning
- Evolutionary Computation
- Intelligent Information Systems
- Knowledge Representation and Integration
- Learning and Knowledge Discovery
- Logic for Artificial Intelligence
- Methodologies

The contributed papers were selected from 117 full draft papers by the following Program Committee: Luigia Carlucci Aiello, Alan Biermann, Jacques Calmet, Wesley Chu, Robert Demolombe, Jon Doyle, Attilio Giordana, Diana Gordon, Mirsad Hadzikadic, Jiawei Han, David Hislop, Janusz Kacprzyk, Willi Kloesgen, Yves Kodratoff, Alberto Martelli, Robert Meersman, Zbigniew Michalewicz, Ryszard Michalski, Ephraim Nissan, Lin Padgham, Rohit Parikh, Lynne Parker, Gregory Piatetsky-Shapiro, Francois Pin (Program Co-Chair), Henri Prade, Luc De Raedt, Lorenza Saitta, Erik Sandewall, Yoav Shoham, Andrzej Skowron (Program Co-Chair), Richmond Thomason, Shusaku Tsumoto, S.K. Michael Wong, Jing Xiao, Carlo Zaniolo, Gian Piero Zarri, Maria Zemankova, and Jan M. Zytkow. Additionally, we acknowledge the help in reviewing the papers from: Lawrence Cavedon, Jianhua Chen, David Chiu, Jutta Eusterbrock, Jerzy Grzymala-Busse, Bozena Kostek, Marzena Kryszkiewicz, Neil Murray, Xumin Nie, Olga Pons, Henryk Rybinski, Roman Swiniarski, Stan Szpakowicz, Les Sztandera, Christel Vrain, Anita Wasilewska, Hans Weigand, Alicja Wieczorkowska, and Wojtek Ziarko.

The Symposium was organized by the Computer Science Department, UNC-Charlotte. The Organizing Committee consisted of I.I. Ageenko, B. Bachman, M. Hadzikadic, K. Harber, M. Klopotek, M.S. Narasimha, Z.W. Ras (chair), J. Senyszyn, and M. Szymanowska. Z.W. Ras was the general chair of the Symposium.

We wish to express our thanks to Alan Biermann, Jaime Carbonell, Wesley Chu, Michael Lowry, and Gregory Piatetsky-Shapiro who presented the invited talks at the symposium. We would like to express our appreciation to the sponsors of the symposium and to all who submitted papers for presentation and publication in the proceedings. Special thanks are due to Alfred Hofmann of Springer-Verlag for his help and support.

July, 1997   Z.W. Raś, A. Skowron

Table of Contents

Session 7B   Logic for AI

Goal-Oriented Multimedia Dialogue with Variable Initiative

Alan W. Biermann, Curry Guinn, Michael S. Fulkerson, Greg A. Keim, Zheng Liang, Douglas M. Melamed, Krishnan Rajagopalan

Duke University, Durham, NC 27708, USA

Abstract. A dialogue algorithm is described that executes Prolog-style rules in an attempt to achieve a goal. The algorithm selects paths in the proof in an attempt to achieve success and proves subgoals on the basis of internally available information where possible. Where "missing axioms" are discovered, the algorithm interacts with the user to solve subgoals, and it uses the received information from the user to attempt to complete the proof. A multimedia grammar codes messages sent to and received from the user into a combination of speech, text, and voice tokens. This theory is the result of a series of dialog projects implemented in our laboratory. These will be described including statistics that measure their levels of success.

1 Problem Solving and Subdialogues

When two individuals collaborate to solve a problem, they undertake a variety of behaviors to enable a fast and efficient convergence to a goal. They reason individually to find a sequence of actions that will achieve success and if they are successful, the problem will be solved directly. The reasoning, however, could uncover obstacles and they may then communicate to try to address them. One participant may see a solution to the problem if a specific issue can be solved and bring that to the attention of the other. The other may be able to provide the needed support but may respond with other subproblems to be faced. They hand back and forth subproblems related to the global goal and solutions to them as they find them. If a sufficient set of the subgoals is solved, the global one will be solved also and the interaction will terminate with success.

The problematic subgoals are thus the ones that generate most interactions. We will call the set of interactions related to a given subgoal a *subdialogue*, and every problem solving dialogue seems to be an amalgamation of such subdialogues. Thus we do not see a problem solving dialogue as a linear coverage from beginning to end. Rather we see it as a light footed dance in the space of mentionable topics with almost every step aimed at a problematic subgoal.

The concept of subdialogues as constituents of dialogue has been studied widely. For example, Grosz and Sidner [5] call them *segments* and they give an analysis of dialogue phenomena in terms of a three part model. Specifically, they define the *intentional structure* to be the reasoning mechanism that supports the interaction, the *attentional structure* to be the representation of current and recent subtopics within the dialogue, and the *linguistic structure* to be the syntax of the interaction. As another example, Allen et al. [1] have developed a blackboard architecture for processing subdialogues and give extensive examples of their use in discourse understanding . Reichman [9] developed a somewhat grammatical view of discourse which she analyzed in terms of "context spaces," a construction analogous to our subdialogues.

A theory of subdialogues must account for a variety of phenomena. There must be a way to decide when to open a subdialogue, and each participant must decide whether or not to follow the lead of the other participant. That is, the question of who has the *initiative* [10] must be decided and this may require some negotiation. A decision must be made within a subdialogue as to what is an appropriate question or answer to transmit to the partner and how to present it. This may include reference to a *user model* [7]. Sentence processing will necessarily reference the context of the subdialogue for the purposes of noun phrase resolution and other meaning linkages. The subdialogue context will make it possible to correct errors in the recognition of incoming speech. *Metastatements* must be made from time to time announcing the beginning and end of significant parts of the session, giving the session status, and otherwise encouraging collaboration and keeping the partners in synchronism.

An example of a problem solving dialogue appears in Figure 1. This illustrates the usage of the Duke Programming Tutor as a student discovers she has forgotten to include quotes around the strings to be printed. All interactions are spoken except where noted. The subdialogues are marked; the top level subdialogue aimed at teaching the student a set of concepts in programming is listed as subdialogue 1; the specific interactions aimed at finding the remaining error and at getting instruction on the writeln statement are listed as subdialogues 2 and 3.

The collection of mechanisms that enable participation in problem solving dialogue constitutes a theory of such dialogue [1, 3, 5, 6, 9, 10, 11, 13]. This paper will overview such a theory, describe several implementations, and give data concerning its capabilities in sessions with human beings. For an overview of the literature on computer aided instruction, see [12].

2   A Theory of Dialogue for Machine Implementation

The issue is how to build a machine that can participate in problem solving dialogue. The theory begins with a problem solving mechanism; it is a Prolog-style theorem prover [6, 10, 11] that can operate on a Horn clause database to infer goals in the application domain of interest. The system begins with a top level goal and attempts to prove that the goal is true using rules from the database[1]. If it succeeds, the system will announce that the goal is achieved and no significant dialogue will occur. If it fails, it will look for subgoals that would help complete the proof. Then it will consult its user model to determine whether

---

[1] The system does not use traditional Prolog depth-first search left to right processing. It selects paths using domain and dialogue criteria.

All interactions by student and computer are spoken except where noted. The subdialogues are indicated by integers.

The interaction has proceeded to the point where everything is correct except that there are no quotes around the strings that are to be printed.

Student	*I need more help.*	1
Computer	THE WRITELN STATEMENT IS NOT CORRECT. (Figure 2)	2
Student	*Explain writeln.*	3
Computer	THE WRITELN STATEMENT IS USED WHEN YOU WANT TO OUTPUT SOME VALUE ONTO THE SCREEN DURING THE EXECUTION OF THE PROGRAM.	3
Student	*Okay.*	3
Computer	TO USE THE WRITELN STATEMENT, YOU HAVE TO TYPE IN THE FOLLOWING. (Figure 3)	3
Student	*What's wrong with my program?*	1
Computer	THE WRITELN STATEMENT IS NOT DONE YET.	2
Student	*I do not understand.*	2
Computer	THERE IS SOMETHING MISSING HERE. (Figure 4)	2
Student	*I do not understand.*	2
Computer	YOU NEED TO ADD AN APOSTROPHE HERE.	2
Student	{Oh.} [Student inserts two missing quotes in each writeln statement.] *Okay.*	2
Computer	CONGRATULATIONS. YOUR PROGRAM IS CORRECT NOW.	1

Fig. 1. A spoken language and graphics dialogue between a student and the machine.

any failed subgoals may be approachable by the user. Upon finding a needed subgoal that may be within the user's repertoire, it will initiate a subdialogue to try to achieve that subgoal. This interaction may involve the discovery of additional subgoals and their associated subdialogues, it may be interrupted by user initiated subdialogues, and a complex and highly fragmented interaction may ensue. The system controls flow continually, of course, to guide the session to ultimately solve the global goal.

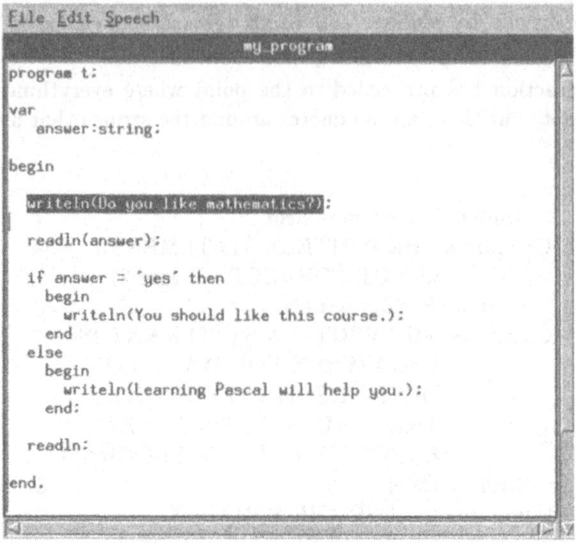

Fig. 2. "THE WRITELN STATEMENT IS NOT CORRECT."

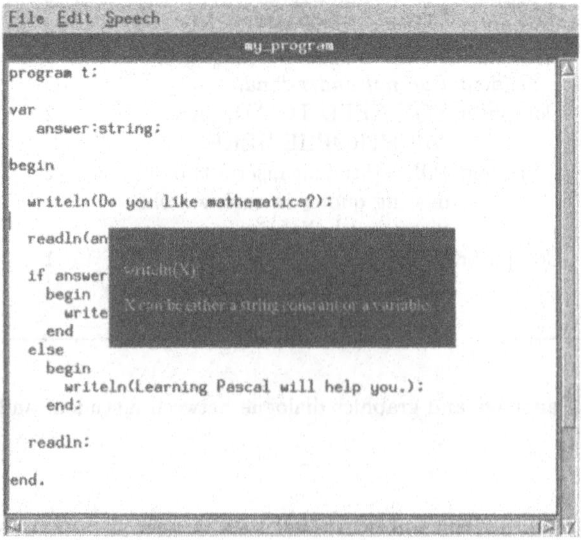

Fig. 3. "TO USE THE WRITELN STATEMENT, YOU HAVE TO TYPE IN THE FOLLOWING:"

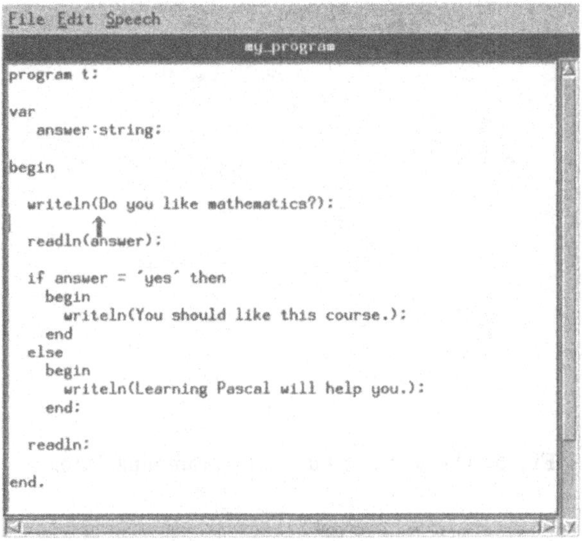

Fig. 4. "THERE IS SOMETHING MISSING HERE."

All of this can be illustrated by showing the design of our Duke Programming Tutor which is aimed at teaching a set of concepts to a student. The highest level goal is that the student understand the set of concepts and its subgoals are those concepts. This is shown in Figure 5. The subgoals below any specific concept are its constituents and this decomposition proceeds to a very low level, the atomic concepts in the current domain. An important subgoal in the proof tree is that the user be able to do an example program. The tutorial session proceeds by selecting subgoals that the user model says are appropriate for this user at this time and then initiating dialogue to address them.

Suppose, for example, that the user has been asked to write an example program and has typed in the code shown in Figure 2. (In order to serve a specific course currently being taught at Duke, the system teaches Pascal.) The system compares this program with a model and creates a Prolog description of what the user has typed. The system then attempts to prove that the program is correct using this synthesized set of rules. The theorem proving tree is shown in Figure 6.

It turns out that this program has an error in the writeln statements; the single quotes around the text to be printed are missing. Theorem proving proceeds down the tree and discovers that none of the following subgoals can be achieved: **exerciseprog**, **body**, **writeln**, **leftquote**. So it can undertake a subdialogue to try to achieve one of these subgoals.

But the system must not initiate an iteraction without consulting the user model. It must decide what subgoal is reasonable to attempt. It must not use

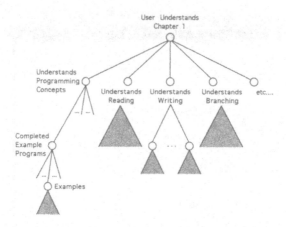

Fig. 5. The goal tree for the Programming Tutor.

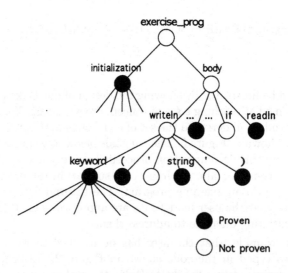

Fig. 6. The theorem proving tree for the student's example program.

vocabulary or concepts that are outside the user's repertoire. Also it should not address the user at a level far below his or her capabilities. For example, this tutor is initially to be used in the first weeks of the course when much emphasis is at the statement level of the code. So the user model would allow reference to statement level concepts and below: `writeln`, `leftquote`. The system could then choose the highest level one, `writeln`, and send it to the user: "THE WRITELN STATEMENT IS NOT CORRECT" (with highlighting). On the other hand, a first day student would not be familiar with the concept of a statement and might have to receive coaching at the character or word level: "YOU NEED TO ADD AN APOSTROPHE HERE" (with a displayed arrow). A more expert student (at a level we are not working with at this time) might be able to handle concepts like a sort routine or a hash function computation. For such a student, references at the statement level would be quite inappropriate unless higher level coaching failed.

For the purposes of the current example, let us examine the system behavior after the statement "THE WRITELN STATEMENT IS NOT CORRECT" (with highlighting). Here are the possible user responses:

Correct repair The user might see the error in the code and edit the program until the error is fixed. This result would yield a revision to the Prolog representation of Figure 6 and would show the failed nodes related to this error now repaired. The theorem proving would continue to try to show that the exercise program is correct and look for other failure points in the proof.

Additional questioning The student might fail to understand the recent output. Either the user model was incorrect or the student just needs more help. Here the system steps to a level lower in the theorem proving tree and gives another output: "THERE IS SOMETHING MISSING HERE" (with a graphic arrow).

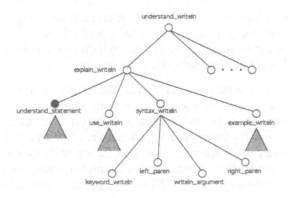

Fig. 7. Proving the assertion that the user understands writeln.

Related remarks The student may give an assertion or ask a question related to the recent output. For example, the response might be to ask a general question about the particular construction at hand: "*Explain writeln.*" Here the system does a nearest neighbor search of expected meanings in the current context and tries to find a local meaning with a syntax that is near (in the Hamming distance sense) to the user's utterance. If it finds such, it makes a corresponding entry in the Prolog database and computes its appropriate answer.

In the current tutorial example, the dialogue algorithm attempts to prove explain_writeln and fails. Figure 7 shows the knowledge base for the writeln statement. The same mechanism as described above governs processing. We will assume the predicate understand_statement has been proved through earlier interactions; the user knows what a statement is. Next the system examines use_writeln, checks that the user model allows the interaction, and then enunciates "THE WRITELN STATEMENT IS USED WHEN YOU WANT TO OUTPUT SOME VALUE ONTO THE SCREEN DURING THE EXECUTION OF THE PROGRAM." If the user indicates understanding with "*okay*" or some paraphrase of it, the assertion use_writeln will go into the database and control will return to the dialogue system. It will continue the proof of explain_writeln by enunciating the predicate syntax_writeln. If the user indicates lack of understanding at this point, then the subgoals below syntax_writeln will be enunciated to the user: "THE SYNTAX OF THE WRITELN STATEMENT RE-QUIRES THAT YOU FIRST TYPE THE KEYWORD WRITELN", "YOU THEN HAVE TO TYPE A LEFT PARENTHESIS, '(' ", and so forth. Assuming all of these receive positive confirmation from the user, syntax_writeln will be proven and control can return to the dialogue machine. If any of them fails, they could conceivably be decomposed to lower level concepts and their associated explanations.

Unrelated remarks The user may assert something that does not relate to the subgoal in any direct way. The system has a priority list of other subgoals and proceeds to search them in order for a (low Hamming distance) match with the incoming utterance. Upon finding one, its behaviors will proceed as described in the previous case. If no match is found, the system can ask for a repeat of the assertion or follow its own initiative for the next step.

Metastatements Metastatements [6] are defined to be assertions above or about the dialogue. They are not part of the information exchange needed to solve the problem but rather refer to what has just been done, what should be done next, or how the interaction is proceeding. They serve the purpose synchronizing the interaction, maintaining morale for the participants, and directing attention to key issues. Our system has few abilities to handle such statements from the user. But if the user says "*Please repeat,*" the system responds appropriately.

In summary, the dialogue system has a top level algorithm that cycles through the steps described above. Its functioning is approximated by the algorithm shown in Figure 8.

3 Communication with the Reasoning System

The internal representation for the purposes of reasoning is in terms of logical predicates. The external form is in terms of spoken sentences, graphical objects (pointers or highlighting, in our case), and displayed text. A translation [4, 8] is needed between the two forms so that the user can communicate with the

```
Attempt proof of top level goal.
If success then halt.
While top level goal is not achieved:
        Select failed subgoal
                If system has initiative, its own scoring will govern choice.
                If user has initiative, the choice will follow user's selection.
        If selected subgoal is approachable as indicated by user model:
                Engage in subdialogue.
                Enter results into database.
```

Fig. 8. The dialogue algorithm.

internal system. This section will describe a type of multimedia grammar that can do this translation successfully.

The grammar is based upon a set of operators which manage the syntax and semantics of the language. A given multimedia communication is accounted for by a sequence of these operators as will be described here.

An operator will have five constituents:

 a. a name
 b. an applicability criterion
 c. a syntactic form
 d. a semantic form
 e. a complexity

An example such operator is the noun-line operator associated with the noun "line." It has the following five constituents:

 a. noun-line,
 b. initializes a noun phrase,
 c. "line" (spoken),
 d. collect all objects of type line from the input stream,
 e. 1

The usage of this operator can be illustrated by applying it to the program in Figure 2. That is, we could begin constructing a noun phrase with the spoken word "line" and the associated semantics would collect all of the lines in the input stream. If the program in Figure 2 is the input, then the semantics of noun-line would be as shown in Figure 9(a). The collected objects are those items delineated by square brackets.

Another operator corresponds to the use of spoken ordinal words such as "first" or "tenth."

a. ordinal,
b. previous operator should be a noun or adjective,
c. the spoken ordinal word appended to the left of the phrase,
d. collect the specified single object,
e. 1

We can apply this operator instantiated at "fifth" to the result of the noun-line operator in Figure 9(a) to obtain the object in Figure 5(b). It counts through the square bracketed objects until its finds the fifth one. It sends that to the output stream.

In a similar fashion, a variety of operators can be constructed for other parts of speech. Without further discussion, we note that the complete noun phrase "the ninth character in the fifth line" can be easily accounted for as shown in Figure 9. The semantics resolve to the single object [D] which is, in fact, the ninth character in the fifth line of the original program. The complexity of this operator sequence is 7.

An example of an operator for the spoken article "this" accompanied by an appropriately aimed arrow on the screen is as follows:

a. art-pointer
b. the previous operator should be a noun or adjective,
c. "this" (spoken with an arrow aimed at the designated item),
d. collect the specified object,
e. 1

It is easy to see how this operator can be used instead of some of the others listed above to account for these forms instead of the one shown in Figure 9:

"the ninth character in this line" (with graphics arrow) complexity $= 6$
"this character" (with graphics arrow)   complexity $= 2$

Thus there are many syntactic forms capable of expressing a given meaning and the purpose of the complexity computation is to narrow the search to only a few forms one of which will be most appropriate for defining the target meaning for the utterance.

The mechanism of the complexity computation gives the system the ability to adapt its communications to the current situation being encountered. For example, a normal user operating in a typical environment might appropriately receive a lot of speech communications with graphics aids as described here. However, if the situation changed so the user was distracted from seeing the screen, the complexities of the graphics outputs could be increased greatly to filter them out of the communications. In another situation, the ambient noise could become intolerable so that spoken communications cease to function successfully. In this case, spoken outputs could be rated as highly complex and they would be filtered from the outputs.

In general, we allow the full power of a programming language in the syntax and semantics slots for the operators. Thus the syntax could be coded to operate a mechanical arm or adjust the expression on a simulated face. However, our own usage has included only spoken and displayed words and graphics arrows or highlighting of one kind or another.

Certainly, this mechanism is capable of processing full sentences, but we omit the additional discussion here.

Notice also that our mechanism works both as a generator of communications or as a recognizer of them. This can be illustrated by re-examining the generation described above. As a generator, one begins with the program in Figure 2 and tries to find a way to specify a particular [D]. Here one searches the space of operators for a sequence that specifies that [D] and a side effect is one of the syntactic forms given above. As a recognizer, one begins with the example program and a syntax such as "the ninth character in the fifth line." Here we search for the sequence of operators that creates the syntax and a side effect is a computation of the meaning which is that certain [D].

While the system can function in both directions, our recent implementation has used it only in the generation mode. We have a theory of error correction for speech input in the context of subdialogues that we have not been able to combine with the multimedia grammars. This is illustrated in Figure 10 which shows in the rightmost column a series of expected meanings after the machine utterance "THE WRITELN STATEMENT IS NOT CORRECT." These expectations come from the contexts described above: correct repair, additional questions, related remarks, and so forth. Associated with each meaning is a set of possible syntactic forms as shown in the second column. The incoming utterance, which typically will contain misrecognition, is shown on the left in Figure 10 and the computation is to find the syntax that is closest to one of the syntactic forms of the second column. The distance is a Hamming-like computation with heavier weighting for the more important words. This process is highly related to what is referred to in the literature as *plan recognition* [2].

4 Variable Initiative

If one participant has the major knowledge related to a subgoal, efficiency requires that that individual control the interaction. However, when the current subgoal is complete, the other participant may have the more complete knowledge of some new subgoal so control should be returned. Only if these changes are made quickly to account, at every instant, for where the initiative should be will the dialogue move forward at its best speed.

In realistic situations, the case is not always as clear cut. One participant might seem to have slightly more knowledge at a given time but, in fact, be willing to yield the initiative if the other makes a strong assertion. Thus variable initiative is the most general and useful feature. A system may be strongly directive and always follow its own selection of subdialogues without regard for the inputs from the partner. It may be weakly directive and proceed similarly but with the option of accepting partner goals if they are strongly asserted. It may be mildly passive and follow the partner specified goals except where it

```
[program t;]
[var]
[      answer:string;]
[begin]
[writeln(Do you like mathematics?);]
[readln(answer);]
[if answer = 'yes' then]
[      begin]
[      writeln(You should like this course.);]
[      end]
[else]
[      begin]
[      writeln(Learning Pascal will help you.);]
[      end;]
[readln;]
[end.]
```

(a) Semantics for the syntax "line."   Complexity = 1

`[writeln(Do you like mathematics?);]`

(b) Semantics for the syntax "fifth line."   Complexity = 2

`[writeln(Do you like mathematics?);]`

(c) Semantics for the syntax "the fifth line."   Complexity = 3

`writeln(Do you like mathematics?);`

(d) Semantics for the syntax "in the fifth line."   Complexity = 4

`[w] [r] [i] [t] [e] [l] [n] [(] [D] [o] [ ] [y] [o] [u] [ ]....`

(e) Semantics for the syntax "character in the fifth line."   Complexity = 5

`[D]`

(f) Semantics for the syntax "ninth character in the fifth line."   Complexity = 6

`[D]`

(g) Semantics for the syntax "the ninth character in the fifth line." Complexity = 7

Fig. 9. The operator sequence for the syntax "the ninth character in the fifth line."

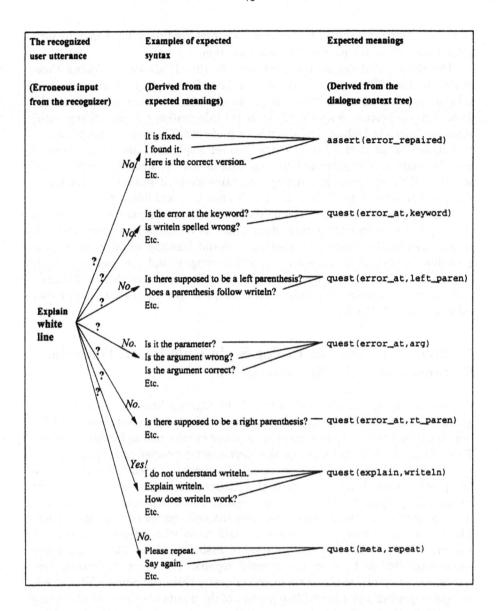

The recognized user utterance	Examples of expected syntax	Expected meanings
(Erroneous input from the recognizer)	(Derived from the expected meanings)	(Derived from the dialogue context tree)

It is fixed.
I found it.
No. Here is the correct version.
Etc.
→ assert(error_repaired)

Is the error at the keyword?
No. Is writeln spelled wrong?
Etc.
→ quest(error_at, keyword)

Is there supposed to be a left parenthesis?
No. Does a parenthesis follow writeln?
Etc.
→ quest(error_at, left_paren)

Explain white line

No. Is it the parameter?
Is the argument wrong?
Is the argument correct?
Etc.
→ quest(error_at, arg)

No. Is there supposed to be a right parenthesis?
Etc.
→ quest(error_at, rt_paren)

Yes! I do not understand writeln.
Explain writeln.
How does writeln work?
Etc.
→ quest(explain, writeln)

No. Please repeat.
Say again.
Etc.
→ quest(meta, repeat)

Fig. 10. Error correction in the context of expected meanings. The system finds the best match using a modified Hamming distance criterion between the incoming recognized speech and the allowed syntactic versions of the expected meanings.

finds very strong reasons for following its own preferred path. Or it may be very passive and follow the partner without exception.

The theory of dialogue described here [6, 10, 11] allows for coding these behaviors. First, the system must have methods for selecting its preferred next subgoal. A reasonable way to do this is to use heuristic information from the domain in conjunction with locally available information to rank all suggested subgoals. Then the highest ranking ones are preferred. The system then selects its best choice for the next subgoal. When the user responds, however, the decision must be made as to whether to follow the user or to more strongly assert its own selection. If the system is in a strongly directive mode, it will tend to not follow the user's preference and if it is in a passive mode, it will follow the user.

Guinn [6] has developed a scheme that maintains real numbers on the nodes of the proof tree indicating their desirability as subgoals to be examined. It uses its user model to estimate whether it should take the initiative on a given desirable subgoal. If it chooses to take that subgoal and the user objects, it enunciates the major branches of the subtree that cause it to choose that tree. (This is called negotiation.) This is an attempt to get the user to accept that subgoal and to follow it.

5   Some Examples of Prolog-Style Rule-Based Dialogue Systems and their Characteristics

Our project constructed a system called the Circuit-Fixit-Shoppe [10, 11] to gain experience with the ideas described above. This system used speech only for both input and output and contained a database of information for circuit repair. The system used a Verbex 6000 speaker-dependent connected-speech recognition system with a small vocabulary grammar (125 words). It used a Dectalk system for speech output. It had four levels of initiative which were set manually. The circuit being repaired was set up on a Radio Shack experimenter's board so that the user could easily make measurements and change the existing wiring. The system was tested with a series of eight users who attempted a total of 141 circuit repairs and who spoke a total of 2840 utterances. The experimental sessions resulted in 84 percent successful repairs. The input utterances were spoken to the system at the average rate of nearly three per minute. The speech recognizer perfectly recognized 50.0 percent of the inputs but the error correction system using the context and nearest neighbor strategies raised the recognition up to 81.5 percent. The system was tested at two levels of initiative, directive and mildly passive. The main difference between the two modes was that the sessions were much longer involving more and shorter spoken inputs when the system was in directive mode. In this mode, the system tended to force the user through long sequences of steps that he or she would have preferred to skip. With the system in the mildly passive mode, the users tended to use longer sentences and move much more rapidly to a solution to each problem.

A second system [6] was built to test ideas related to mixed initiative and negotiation. This system had a new dialogue algorithm that had been proven

	Without Mixed Init. and Neg.	*With* Mixed Init. and Neg.
Execution Time (sec.)	93	47
Number of Utterances	41.4	28.1
Branches Explored	6.2	3.3

Fig. 11. Averages for execution time, number of utterances, and number of branches explored below a node for solving 206 problems with and without mixed initiative and negotiation features.

to be mathematically correct. It was implemented without any translation to external media; that is, its only essential language was the predicate calculus language of its theorem proving system. The system was analyzed and tested with three new features: an automatic initiative setting feature, a negotiation feature, and a summary feature that enables the system to explain to its partner a failed reasoning chain to prevent its recurrence. The system was tested by setting up two copies of itself, each with a different portion of a total database of facts. Then the two copies of the system were allowed to carry out a dialogue by passing predicates back and forth until the dialogue goal was proven. The table in Figure 11 shows the execution times, number of utterances, and average number of branches explored below a node for solving 206 problems when the features are turned off and on. The graphs show that efficiency nearly doubled on several dimensions when the mixed initiative and negotiation features were turned on.

More recently, our project has implemented the Duke Programming Tutor system as described above. This system has the complete reasoning and multimedia capabilities described and was tested in a prototype version in September, 1995 by eleven students in a first course in computer science. All eleven students were able to use the system successfully on their assignments although one did not finish in the specified time period. The average length of the dialogues was about 16 minutes, during which students spoke an average of 28 utterances (1.78 utterances per minute). The word error rate was about 15 percent.

6 Summary

Dialogue theory is the implementing technology for speech and general multimedia interactive systems. It asserts that efficient convergence to a goal involves the discovery of obstacles to its achievement and the immediate addressing of them. This leads to subdialogues and the many jumps from one to another as the problem solving process goes forward.

A dialogue system is built around a reasoning mechanism, in our case an executive for Prolog-style rules. The dialogue is driven by the theorem proving steps; specifically, most interactions address the failures to complete the proof. The communications between the system and the outside world require a translation mechanism that can convert between the internal predicate calculus and the multimedia external forms.

Once the structure of the system has been created, one can find ways to include many capabilities such as user modeling, variable initiative, negotiation, expectation to error correct speech and many others.

7 Acknowledgment

This work is supported by Office of Naval Research Grant No. N00014-94-1-0938, National Science Foundation Grant No. IRI-92-21842, and a grant from the Research Triangle Institute which is funded by the Army Research Office.

References

1. J. Allen, S. Guez, L. Hoebel, E. Hinkelman, K. Jackson, A. Kyburg, and D. Traum. The discourse system project. Technical Report 317, University of Rochester, 1989.

2. J. F. Allen and C. R. Perrault. Analyzing intention in dialogues. *Artificial Intelligence*, 15(3):143–178, 1980.

3. J. F. Allen, L. K. Schubert, G. Ferguson, P. Heeman, C. H. Hwang, T. Kato, M. Light, N. G. Martin, B. W. Miller, M. Poesio, and D. R. Traum. The TRAINS project: A case study in building a conversational planning agent. *Journal of Experimental and Theoretical AI*, 7:7–48, 1995.

4. S.K. Feiner and K.R. McKeown. Coordinating text and graphics in explanation generation. In *Proceedings of the 8th National Conference on Artficial Intelligence*, volume I, pages 442–449. AAAI Press/The MIT Press, 1990.

5. Barbara J. Grosz and Candace L. Sidner. Attention, intentions, and the structure of discourse. *Computational Linguistics*, 12(3):175–204, Sep 1986.

6. Curry I. Guinn. *Meta-Dialogue Behaviors: Improving the Efficiency of Human-Machine Dialogue–A Computational Model of Variable Inititive and Negotiation in Collaborative Problem-Solving*. PhD thesis, Duke University, 1995.

7. Alfred Kobsa and Wolfgang Wahlster, editors. *User Models in Dialog Systems*. Springer-Verlag, Berlin, 1989.

8. M.T. Maybury, editor. *Intelligent Multimedia Interfaces*. AAAI/MIT Press, 1993.

9. R. Reichman. *Getting computers to talk like you and me*. The MIT Press, Cambridge, Mass., 1985.

10. Ronnie W. Smith and D. Richard Hipp. *Spoken Natural Language Dialog Systems: A Practical Approach*. Oxford University Press, 1994.

11. Ronnie W. Smith, D. Richard Hipp, and Alan W. Biermann. An arctitecture for voice dialog systems based on prolog-style theorem proving. *Computational Linguistics*, 21(3):281–320, September 1995.

12. Etienne Wenger. *Artificial Intelligence and Tutoring Systems*. Morgan Kaufmann Publishers, Inc., Los Altos, CA, 1987.

13. S. R. Young, A. G. Hauptmann, W. H. Ward, E. T. Smith, and P. Werner. High level knowledge sources in usable speech recognition systems. *Communications of the ACM*, pages 183–194, August 1989.

Knowledge-Based Image Retrieval
with Spatial and Temporal Constructs
(Invited Paper)

Wesley W. Chu, Alfonso F. Cárdenas, and Ricky K. Taira

University of Califoria, Los Angeles, CA 90095

{wwc,cardenas}@cs.ucla.edu, rtaira@mail.rad.ucla.edu

Abstract

A knowledge-based approach to retrieve medical images by feature and content with spatial and temporal constructs is developed. Selected objects of interest in a medical image (e.g. x-ray, MR image) are segmented, and contours are generated from these objects. Features (e.g. shape, size, texture) and content (e.g. spatial relationships among objects) are extracted and stored in a feature and content database. Knowledge about image features can be expressed as a hierarchical structure called a Type Abstraction Hierarchy (TAH). The high-level nodes in the TAH represent more general concepts than low-level nodes. Thus, traversing along TAH nodes allows approximate matching by feature and content if an exact match is not available. TAHs can be generated automatically by clustering algorithms based on feature values in the databases and hence are scalable to large collections of image features. Further, since TAHs are generated based on user classes and applications, they are context- and user-sensitive.

A knowledge-based semantic image model is proposed which consists of four layers (raw data layer, feature and content layer, schema layer, and knowledge layer) to represent the various aspects of an image objects' characteristics. The model provides a mechanism for accessing and processing spatial, evolutionary, and temporal queries.

A knowledge-based spatial temporal query language (KSTL) has developed which extends ODMG's OQL and supports approximate matching of feature and content, conceptual terms, and temporal logic predicates. Furthe: a visual query language has been developed that accept point-click-and-drag visual iconic input on the screen which is then translated into KSTL. User models are introduced to provide default parameter values for specifying query conditions.

We have implemented a Knowledge-Based Medical Database System (KMeD) at UCLA, and currently under evaluation by the medical staff. The results from this research should be applicable to other multimedia information systems as well.

*This work is supported in part by the National Science Foundation Scientific Database Initiative Grant IRI9116849, and also in part by ARPA contract F30602-94-C-0207

1   Introduction

A new generation of intelligent database systems must emerge, in order to effectively disseminate, integrate, retrieve, correlate, and visualize multimedia medical information. Many medical Picture Archiving and Communication Systems (PACS) [HT92] have several terabytes of image data on-line, yet utilization of data for research and teaching is very limited. Search engines for medical images are needed that can support content-based image retrieval. Exactly matched content-based retrieval will almost never yield any answer; further, it is especially difficult when the task involves searching for image data that contain imprecise descriptors. To illustrate some of these difficulties, consider the following queries:

Query 1   Find patients with similar lesions to that of patient with ID "P000-01" based on their shape and locations.

Query 2   Find patients treated either by Dr. Smith or Jones whose lesions exhibit a decrease in size by at least 50% for every scheduled examination.

Query 3   Find African-American patients with similar post-therapy lesion development to the image sequence shown on the screen.

Some of the problems that must be addressed include: 1) How do we communicate these natural language queries to a computer system? Conventional database query languages are limited in their expressibility, especially concerning fuzzy correlations (e.g. in the vicinity of), spatial concepts (e.g. INSIDE, NEARBY, FAR AWAY), and temporal concepts (e.g. size doubled since initial diagnosis); 2) What methods are used to match cases stored within the raw image repository (e.g. PACS) to the conditions specified in the user query? The system needs to be able to mimic the response of a trained expert in the medical field. That is, the system must know of all subclasses of a specified object (e.g. a malignant tumor[1] could be an adenocarcinoma, or any number of other cancerous growths), reference variations (e.g. synonyms, lexical variants, abbreviations, etc.), conceptual terms (e.g. large, small), and context sensitive terms (e.g. SIMILAR TO); 3) How does the system intelligently relax certain constraints when no exact query solutions exist? For example, in order for the system to find a solution, it may need to relax the shape of the mass from spherical to elliptical; 4) What kind of user interface is suitable for users? A flexible user interface is required to allow the user to express the query and navigate through the presented query solutions. The user requires tools to visualize the presented answers in a specific format.

---

[1]In this paper, the terms *tumor*, *lesion*, *neoplasm*, and *adenocarcinoma* are used interchangably

In this paper, Section 2 presents the four-layered knowledge-based semantic image model for representing medical images with spatial and temporal features. Section 3 presents the language for specifying visual query with temporal and spatial constructs. Section 4 discusses the translation of the visual query expression into the knowledge-based spatial and temporal query language (KSTL) which can be implemented as extension of ODMG's OQL. Section 5 discusses the knowledge-based query answering for approximate matching images with features and contents via relaxation. The data flow and system architecture is presented in Section 6.

2 Knowledge-Based Semantic Temporal Image Model

Currently, images cannot be easily or effectively retrieved due to the lack of a comprehensive data model that captures the structured abstractions and knowledge that are needed for image retrieval. To remedy such shortcomings, predicates should contain semantic (e.g. INSIDE, FAR_AWAY, etc.), conceptual (e.g. large, small, etc.), and *similar-to* terms in order to retrieve medical images by feature and content. The *similar-to* operators allow users to retrieve images close to the target image based on a prespecified set of features.

An image model is proposed which consists of a Raw Data Layer (RDL), Feature and Content Layer (FCL), a Schema Layer (SL), and a Knowledge Layer (KL). Figure 1 illustrates the four-layered modeling for brain lesions.

2.1 Raw Data Layer

The Raw Data Layer stores the actual pixel-level image data in the database. Its main function is to abstract from the rest of the model encoding techniques such as compression, encryption, or special formatting. When images are accessed from the Raw Data Layer, they are translated by the RDL into a canonical image format. Therefore, image data formatting is uniform at any layer above the Raw Data Layer, with low-level concerns such as compression algorithms effectively hidden and autonomous from the higher-level components of the system.

2.2 Feature and Content Layer

At the Feature and Content Layer, we store image features such as contours, spatial relationship characteristics, and temporal sequences. The contours can be segmented manually, semi-automatically (using techniques like active contours [DV+93] and liquid transforms in [NB+93]), or automatically [LTSK95, WLK92, WA+95] depending on the contrast and sep-

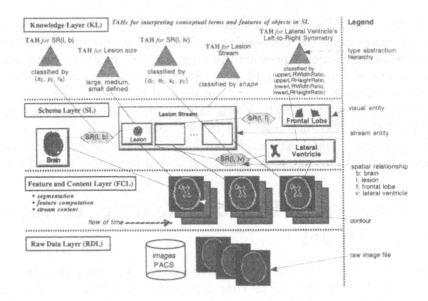

Figure 1: An example representation of brain lesions. SR(l, b), SR(l, lv), and SR(l, f) represent the spatial relationships of lesion and brain, lesion and lateral ventricle, and lesion and frontal lobe, respectively. The lesion stream entity represents a temporal sequence of lesions.

arability of the image objects. Raw image segmentation will be provided by the radiologists [LTSK95]. The segmented contours are used to compute spatial and temporal features, after which they are integrated into the proposed model for querying images by content and feature.

2.2.1 Spatial Feature Computation

Shape Modeling Image objects in medical images are often complex in shape and require detailed comparison on specific portions. Thus, we propose a decomposition approach to describe an object's shape. A object with a complex shape is first decomposed into context-dependent substructures. The decomposition is based on the fundamental line and curve segments identified by the generated $\psi - s$ function from the chain code of the object contours [MA79]. These decomposed fundamental lines and curves are then matched to a shape model of the specific objects. These models encapsulate the "part-of" knowledge between the lines and curves that constitute the object model. The shape models are used to identify and verify contoured objects that conform to the general expected object shapes. They are also used to locate key landmark features to aid in further feature analysis. Instance data is matched to model data using an interpretation tree that utilizes unary and binary spatial constraints [Gri90].

Spatial Relationship Modeling In modeling spatial relationships, existing semantic constructs such as *overlap* and *separate* [Fra88, CYD88] are insufficient to fully represent spatial relationships among objects [HCT96]. Additional detailed variations on spatial relationships should be captured in spatial relationship modeling. To distinguish images based on *similar* spatial relationships, relevant spatial relationship features are specified by domain experts. For example, the spatial relationship for a lesion that is near another object can be captured using the distance of the centroids of the two contours on the x-axis and y-axis, the angle of coverage (the angle for viewing a contour from the centroid of another contour), and the ratio of area to classify the spatial relationship [HCT96].

These computed features will be classified automatically with clustering algorithms into type abstraction hierarchies (TAH) (see Section 2.4) and conceptual terms are annotated at the TAH nodes to enable image querying via conceptual predicates.

2.3 Schema Layer

In the Schema Layer, we construct a database schema that represents the entities and spatial relationships among objects based on the extracted shape and spatial relationship features from object contours in the Feature and Content Layer. Other entities in this layer capture the temporal and evolutionary aspects of the database.

2.3.1 Visual Entities

Objects in an image are represented in the Schema Layer as *visual entities* (VEs). Instances of VEs consist of conventional attributes (e.g. patient ID, date, doctor name, etc.) in the raw data layer as well as visual attributes (e.g. shape, size, texture, etc.) of object contours in the Feature and Content Layer. *Spatial relationships* among entities can also be represented in the schema, as shown in Figure 2.

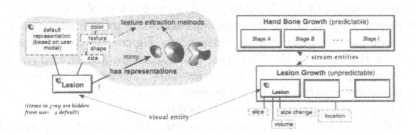

Figure 2: Visual notation of visual entities and streams, used in both schema diagrams and the visual query language.

VEs maintain a list of canonical visual representations derived from actual images. Their features and content are extracted by the methods described in Section 2.2.

2.3.2 Stream Entities

Multiple versions of an object over a period of time (for example, the stages undergone by a tumor during the cancer process of a particular patient) can be linked to form a *stream entity* for that time period.

A stream is a sequence of ordered objects [DC97] which can be classified into *simple streams* and *composite streams*. The ordered objects in a simple stream are all regular objects, and a composite stream may have other streams as its contained objects. A composite stream is composed spatially or temporally from simple streams by *composition constructors*, such as synchronization, concatenation, and evolutionary constructors [CIT94]. Composite streams allow cross-sectional views across streams of different data to be viewed and queried at the same time (Figure 2).

2.4 Knowledge Layer

We propose to classify image shapes and spatial relationship features into a hierarchical structure known as a type abstraction hierarchy (TAH) [CC94]. The attributes used for classification are context and user sensitive, and are specified initially by the user when generating the TAHs. Spatial concepts are represented as feature value ranges. Higher nodes in the TAH represent more generalized concepts (i.e. wider range of feature values) than that of the lower nodes (i.e. narrower range of the feature values). TAH nodes generated based on shape features can be labeled with conceptual terms (e.g. large, small, etc.), and TAH nodes generated based on spatial relationship features can be labeled with semantic spatial relationship terms (e.g. near by, far away). The value ranges and the corresponding relaxation error are represented at each TAH node. Relaxation error is the expected pairwise feature distance between members in a TAH node. Hence the error is a measure of the closeness of the images under this node. Images under the same TAH node have similar characteristics with respect to a set of features and thus all of the images under the same TAH node can be considered as similar (see Figure 3). By traversing up and down the nodes in the TAH (i.e. generalization and specialization of features in the TAH, respectively), we are able to select the best node that approximately matches the target feature values. Therefore, this provides a way to process queries with *similar-to* operators.

TAH can be automatically generated via MDISC clustering algorithm [CCHY96] which classify images with shapes and/or spatial relationships. A TAH generated based on spatial relationship features is shown in Figure 3.

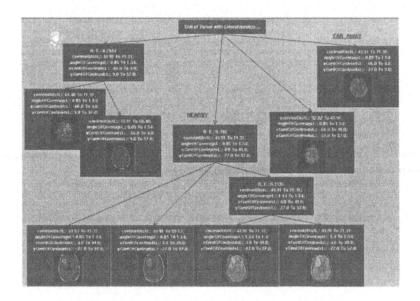

Figure 3: A type abstraction hierarchy classifies MR images based on the spatial relationship of tumors and lateral ventricle. The attributes used in the TAH are context and user sensitive, and may be pre-specified by the user.

In addition, an ontology of spatial relationship terms (Figure 4) is used to guide the generation and labeling of TAH nodes. Similar listings of commonly used terms for shapes have been developed jointly with domain experts (e.g. radiologists). Users may edit the TAH by deleting and moving TAH nodes to satisfy the users' desired representation.

We can thus derive features from contoured objects and classify all of their images into a TAH structure based on these features. The TAHs can be used for visual query interpretation and knowledge-based query processing. A TAH directory will be developed which can be indexed on TAH characteristics (e.g. attributes used, context, user type) to retrieve TAHs for reuse.

Visual entities, spatial relationships, and stream entities in the Schema Layer are linked to TAHs in the Knowledge Layer to provide preset values for conceptual terms and relaxed ranges (see Figure 1). This knowledge is used for modifying and relaxing a user's query input into the approximate or relaxed query conditions.

2.5 User Model

User models maintain profiles of object matching preferences and relaxation control policies for different user classes (Figure 5). The user model consists of lists of image objects, features representing the objects and spa-

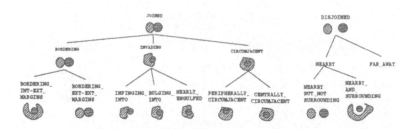

Figure 4: An ontology for semantic spatial relationship operators for topological categories between two objects with the representative icons shown.

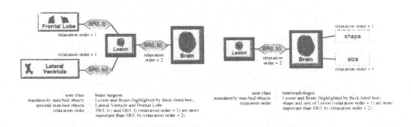

Figure 5: Example of user models for two user classes for retrieving images with a brain lesion.

tial relationships, object matching policies, and policies for relaxing query conditions when no satisfactory answer is found. When object matching and relaxation control policies are not explicitly specified by the user during a query, such information may be obtained from the corresponding user model to guide the relaxation of query constraints. Objects in the user model are divided into *mandatorily matched objects* which must be matched with the query context for the user model, and *optionally matched objects* which provide guidance for additional matched features to enhance the query constraints.

For example, in studying images with lesion(s), a typical concern of brain surgeons are lesion locations and their spatial relationships with other objects in the brain, while the concerns of brain radiologists include shape, size, and location of lesions in the brain (Figure 5).

When visual query is used to query similar images, the VE identifies the objects of interest as well as the user class. The knowledge-based query processor dynamically matches user models based on the identified objects and user class in the VE to provide the information required for knowledge-based query answering (e.g. features of similarity and relaxation policy). Thus, the VE and user model can be used to customize query processing for different types of users.

3 Visual Query Language

The visual query language, M Query language [DC97], is an extension from the PICQUERY+ language [CIT+93]. A subset of the notation for the language is shown in Figure 6, and is based on a combined entity-relationship and object-oriented data model that we have designed [DC97].

VE (visual entity) boxes contain any visual entities being queried (Figure 7). When the user wishes to ask a visual query, the VEs involved are selected and placed within a VE box to show their relative appearance, positioning, and sizing. The query processor interprets this box as a query predicate which constrains n-tuples of VEs to those n-tuples that are visually similar to the arrangement in the box (where n is the number of VEs placed in the box).

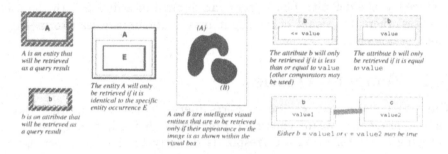

Figure 6: Visual query language notation.

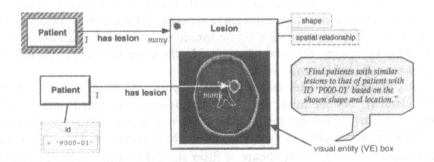

Figure 7: Visual query expression for Query 1.

3.1 Visual Image Queries

In general, predicates are formed by placing values (alphanumeric or image) inside the entities or attributes for which they are intended to match. A comparison operator (such as =, >, and <) may be entered to specify particular types of comparisons. When a value is entered into an attribute, entity, or visual box without an explicit comparator, the system defaults the comparison to SIMILAR_TO.

In Figure 7, the desired similarity is based on the shape of the tumor and its spatial relationship with the lateral ventricle, as specified by shape and spatial relationship attributes. An exact match is desired for the patient ID, so an "=" is explicitly entered in the id attribute, while the VE box arrangement of a brain, lateral ventricle, and tumor implies a similarity comparison.

When the visual query is executed, the features of the visual entities in the query are extracted and compared based on the indicated attributes. The user can specify other similarity measures by opening a menu that describes other descriptors, such as size and roundness for the shape category, location for the distance category, angle of coverage for the nearness category, etc. Otherwise, the object matching policies in the user model are used as the default. The system can engage in a dialog with the user in cases where the visual query input may ambiguously lead to multiple query statements.

3.2 Temporal Queries

Our visual query language also supports querying of stream entities. Based on the proposed stream construct previously defined, our approach to querying this form of data corresponds directly to the user's perception of that data — as a sequence of events or data points in time, which we represent in our system as a temporal descriptive pattern.

Streams are drawn as a sequence of stream elements, enclosed by an overall stream box. Ellipses may be added in between actual stream element boxes to show that additional stream elements may exist. Time flows from left to right in this representation, so the leftmost box within a stream represents the first element of the stream, the rightmost box represents the last element, etc.

If a predicate or filter is applicable to only one element (i.e. just the first element, last element, etc.), the predicate is attached only to that element's box. If the filter is intended for a range of elements, then the predicate is attached to the set of ellipses which corresponds to that range of elements. Finally, if a predicate or filter should be applied to all elements in that stream, it is attached not to an individual stream element, but to the overall stream box. The user can edit the contents of the stream box (i.e. arrange where ellipses appear, determine how many element boxes are within the stream, add numeric time constraints, etc.) to suit the needs of the query.

Figure 8 illustrates a sample stream query. The query combines elements from our previous PICQUERY+ work with the new visual language. The predicate (size change $\leq$ -50%) in Figure 8 is attached to the Le-

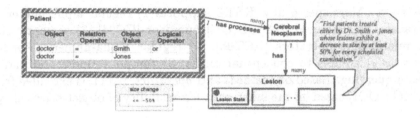

Figure 8: Visual query expression for Query 2.

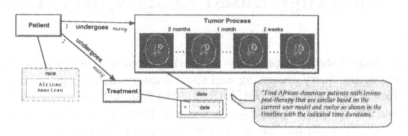

Figure 9: Visual query expression for Query 3.

sion box, and so must be true for all Lesion States within the stream. The predicates in Figure 9 are VE boxes representing individual elements of the Tumor Process stream, and are applied to the stream elements whose time stamps fall within the specified ranges above the VE boxes. Solving this query involves translating the visual query into an algebraic form (Section 4), which can then be solved by our proposed knowledge-based query processor.

Tumor size change after treatment (specified by date) can also be represented by a stream of MR images with time durations (Figure 9). Using our proposed knowledge-based query processing technique, we are able to retrieve an approximately matched sequence in the image database.

Attributes such as size change may also be queried on a conceptual level (i.e. size change is stable or shows little change) if such concepts are specified in the knowledge base in terms of actual values or value ranges.

4 Knowledge-Based Spatial and Temporal Query Language (KSTL)

To process an MQuery expression, we need to translate it into a statement in the Knowledge-based Spatial and Temporal Language (KSTL). KSTL is an object-oriented query language extended from OQL[Cat96] with stream constructs. More specifically, KSTL supports 1) regular alpha-numerical operators, 2) *similar_to* [BASED_ON] operator [CC94], 3) semantic spatial relationship operators [HCT96], 4) regular alpha-numerical operators with references to conceptual terms, 5) temporal operators, and 6) stream querying. Based on *methods* and *operators*, KSTL is extended from ODMG's OQL based on the inhererant extensibility of object-oriented system.

5 Knowledge-Based Image Query Answering

A knowledge-based image query answering approach is used to resolve the conceptual query answering and spatial query answering (i.e., method *described_As* and operator *SIMILAR_TO BASED_ON* are processed). The methods for temporal querying are mainly direct time point comparison [TCG+93]; thus can be directly implemented as OQL methods.

Knowledge-based query answering consists of the following three phases (Figure 10).

Query Analysis and Feature Selection Based on the target image, query context, and user class, the system analyzes and selects the relevant features and spatial relationships for knowledge-based content matching. A user model will be consulted to derive the matching and relaxation policy.

Knowledge-based Content Matching Spatial relationship and conceptual terms in the query are used to select the appropriate TAH from the TAH directory for query modification. For queries with *similar-to* operators, features and spatial relationships of the target images and user class are used for selecting the TAH(s). For queries with semantic spatial relationship operators and/or conceptual terms, the labels on the TAH node are used for matching the conceptual terms. The images under the TAH nodes are the images satisfied by the conceptual term (see Figure 3). After this phase, the knowledge required for resolving the conceptual terms (e.g. TAHs and matched user model) are attached with the query.

Query Execution and Relaxation Query conditions are modified based on the value ranges of the matched TAH nodes for semantic spatial relationship operators and conceptual terms. For the *similar-to* operator, the selected TAHs are traversed until a TAH node is reached whose value range is closest to the target image (see Figure 3). The value ranges in the parent TAH nodes of the matched TAH node can be used to replace the similar-to conditions. Thus, the query is transformed into a regular query (i.e. without containing conceptual terms) and can be sent to the commercially available OQL query processor to retrieve answers where the OQL

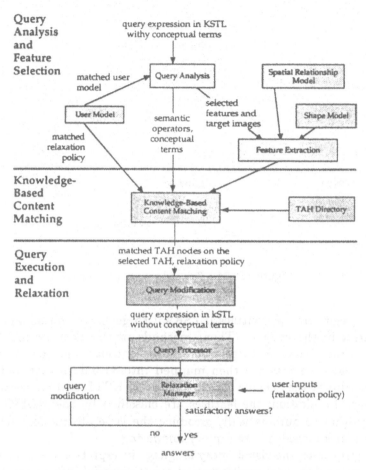

Figure 10: The flow diagram of knowledge-based query processing.

query optimizer will optimize the queries since, after the query modification, the proposed OQL extention does not violate the OQL syntax and its declarative nature. This process of relaxation by query modification may be repeated until the set of returned answers match the user requirements. (e.g. number of similar images, relaxation error, etc. [CC94]). The returned images can be ranked based on a specific measure (e.g. their *relaxation error (RE)* with the target image) [CCHY96].

6 Data Flow and System Architecture

Figure 11 illustrates the overall flow and key elements of our proposed system. Our raw data set will be images stored in the UCLA Picture Archiving and Communication System [HT92]. These images will be sent

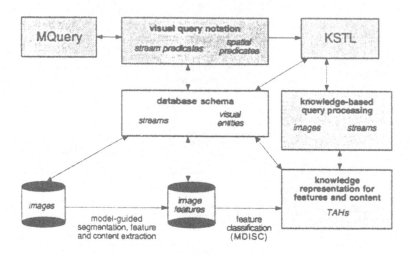

Figure 11: Data flow and system architecture.

through segmentation routines [LTSK95] to generate contours of objects
of interest in the images. Then, methods in the Feature and Content
Layer extract image features from these contours and spatial relationships. These features are then mapped into visual entities and spatial
relationships at the Schema Layer, for use by KSTL and our visual query
language. In addition, the features are classified by the MDISC clustering algorithm to automatically produce the type abstraction hierarchies
required for knowledge-based query answering.

At query time, the visual query language interprets a user's query input
on the screen (physical positions and other pictorial information). Based
on query notation and the database schema, the interpreter maps the user's
input into appropriate query conditions. The translated query conditions
and terms are used to formulate KSTL statements. The knowledge-based
query processing parses the KSTL statement then uses type abstraction
hierarchies for approximate matching of features and content to derive
answers. The query result is returned back to the graphical user interface
for presentation and visualization.

7   Comparison with Other On-Going Re-
search

Pixel matching methods employed for content-based retrieval are time-
consuming and of limited practical use since little of the image object
semantics is explicitly modeled. QBIC [NB+93] uses global shape features
such as area and circularity to retrieve similarly shaped objects. How-

ever, due to the limited precision of global shape features [Lev85], such an approach has limited expressiveness for answering queries with conceptual terms and predicates. Thus, we used a decomposition approach to describe the specific shape features of interested objects.

Statistical approaches can be used to retrieve similar images by relaxing a certain percentage of the standard deviation of the feature values (e.g., VIMS [BPJ93]), However, the same amount of relaxation is applied throughout the distribution, and thus is insensitive to the position of the operating point. Moreover, many image features are based on multiple attributes. Using standard deviation to to retrieve similar feature values lacks the consideration of correlation among different attributes.

Retrieving image by feature has been studied recently [CIT94, ACF$^+$93, CCT95]. However, matching features exactly is difficult. Therefore, it is essential to use a cooperative answering technique [CCHY96] to provide approximate matching of features. Previously proposed cooperative database systems used the rule based approach [CD89], and therefore are not scalable. In our approach, knowledge is structurally represented at different levels of abstraction by the type abstraction hierarchy, and can be automatically generated from relational databases for both numerical and non-numerical data. Our knowledge acquisition algorithm uses the technique of unsupervised *conceptual clustering* [MS83, CCHY96]. In order to provide spatial relaxations of image features, we have extended this knowledge representation into spatial domain.

In previous cooperative systems, no relaxation control facilities were provided for the relaxation process nor the quality of the answer. Our system provides a cost model to optimizing the relaxation and includes handling of feature relaxation control for image data.

Current research in multimedia databases tackles individual components of the overall multimedia database problem. Models exist for representing image, sound, or video data [GBT93], and query languages for retrieving images by content have also been developed [NB$^+$93]. Modeling and query languages over conventional alphanumeric databases has also been progressing [MK93]. However, to support the multimedia medical database requirements of our system, we need to support combined alphanumeric and multimedia requirements. The visual query language, MQuery, supports knowledge-based temporal and spatial query answering.

8 Conclusions

In this paper, we presented techniques for image retrieval by feature and content with temporal, spatial, and conceptual constructs. Innovative techniques include: 1) a four-layered integrated spatial and temporal data model that characterizes low-level image features (such as raw image data, and contours), abstract semantic image representations (including image objects and streams), and generic domain knowledge; 2) automatic feature analysis and classification for knowledge-based query answering; 3) development of a visual query language, *MQuery*, which is used to formulate queries with temporal, spatial, and conceptual image predicates; and 4) techniques for translating the visual query language into a textual query language, and Knowledge-based Spatial Temporal query Language (KSTL) which extends ODMG's OQL query language.

We have implemented a Knowledge-Based Medical Database System (KMeD) at UCLA, and the staff in the medical school is currently evaluating its functionality and effectiveness. The evaluation feedback will be useful in improving the system and providing further research directions.

9 Acknowledgements

The development of KMeD is a team effort. We would like to thank the development and implementation effort of J. Dionisio for the M query language, C. Hsu for the development of knowledge-based query processing system, and the domain knowledge consultation from Dr. D. R. Aberle of the UCLA Radiological Science Department.

References

[ACF+93] M. Arya, W. Cody, C. Faloutsos, J. Richardson, and A. Toga. QBISM: A prototype 3-D medical image database system. *Bulletin of the Technical Committee on Data Engineering*, 16(1):38–42, March 1993.

[BPJ93] J. R. Bach, S. Paul, and R. Jain. A visual information management system for the interactive retrieval of faces. *IEEE Transaction on Knowledge and Data Engineering*, Oct 1993.

[Cat96] R. G. G. Cattell, editor. *The Object Database Standard: ODMG - 93 (Release 1.2)*. Morgan Kaufmann, 1996.

[CC94] W. W. Chu and Q. Chen. A structured approach for cooperative query answering. *IEEE Transactions on Knowledge and Data Engineering*, 6(5), Oct 1994.

[CCHY96] W. W. Chu, K. Chiang, C. C. Hsu, and H. Yau. An error-based conceptual clustering method for providing approximate query answers. *Communications of ACM, Virtual Extension Edition (http://www.acm.org/cacm/extension)*, December 1996.

[CCT95] W. W. Chu, A. F. Cardenas, and R. K. Taira. KMeD: A knowledge-based multimedia medical distributed database system. *Information Systems*, 20(2):75–96, 1995.

33

[CD89]   F. Cuppens and R. Demolombe. How to recognize interesting topics to provide cooperative answering. *Information Systems.* 14(2):163–173, 1989.

[CIT+93]   A. F. Cardenas, I. T. Ieong, R. K. Taira, et al. The knowledge-based object-oriented PICQUERY+ language. *IEEE Trans. on Knowledge and Data Engineering*, 5(4):644–657, August 1993.

[CIT94]   W. W. Chu, T. Ieong, and R. Taira. A semantic modeling approach for image retrieval by content. *The VLDB Journal.* 3(4):445–478, Oct. 1994.

[CYD88]   S. K. Chang, C. W. Yan, and D. C. Dimitroff. An intelligent image database system. *IEEE Transaction on Software Engineering*, May 1988.

[DC97]   J. D. N. Dionisio and A. F. Cardenas. A unified data model for representing multimedia, timeline, and simulation data, 1997. To appear in *IEEE Transactions on Knowledge and Data Engineering.*

[DV+93]   D. Daneels, D. Van Campenhout, et al. Interactive outlineing: An improved approach using active contours. In *Image and Video Storage and Retrieval, SPIE*, 1993.

[Fra88]   Frank. PSQL: Pictorial spatial query language. *IEEE Transaction on Software Engineering*, May 1988.

[GBT93]   S. Gibbs, C. Breiteneder, and D. Tsichritzis. Data modeling of time-based media. In D. Tsichritzis, editor, *Visual Objects*, pages 1–22. Centre Universitaire d'Informatique, Université de Genève, 1993.

[Gri90]   W. Grimson. *Object Recognition by Computer: the role of Geometric Constraints.* MIT Press, MIT, MA, 1990.

[HCT96]   C. C. Hsu, W. W. Chu, and R. K. Taira. A knowledge-based approach for retrieving images by content. IEEE Transaction on Knowledge and Data Engineering, August 1996.

[HT92]   H. K. Huang and R. K. Taira. Infrastructure design of a picture archiving and communication system. *American Journal of Roentgenology*, 158:743–749, 1992.

[Lev85]   M. D. Levine. *Vision in Man and Machine.* McGraw Hill Publishing Co., Inc., 1985.

[LTSK95]   B. J. Liu, R. K. Taira, J. Shim, and P. Keaton. Automatic segmentation of bones from digital hand radiographs. In *Proceedings of the SPIE: Medical Imaging Image Processing*, volume 2434, pages 659–669, February 1995.

[MA79]   W. N. Martin and J. K. Aggarwal. Computer analysis of dynamic scenes containing currilinear figures. *Pattern Recognition*, 11:169–178, 1979.

[MG95]   R. Mehrotra and J. Gary. Similar-shape retrieval in shape data management. *IEEE Computer*, Sep 1995.

[MK93]   L. Mohan and R. L. Kashyap. A visual query language for graphical interaction with schema-intensive databases. *IEEE Transactions on Knowledge and Data Engineering*, 5(5):843–858, October 1993.

[MS83]   R. S. Michalski and R. E. Stepp. Learning from observation: Conceptual clustering. In R. S. Michalski, J. G. Carbonell, and T. M. Mitchell, editors, *Machine Learning*, volume 1. Margan Kaufmann Publishers, Inc., 1983.

[NB⁺93]   Wayne Niblack, R. Barber, et al. The qbic project: Querying images by content using color, texture, and shape. In *Storage and Retrieval for Images and Video Databases, SPIE*, 1993.

[SHB93]   M. Sonka, V. Hlavac, and R. Boyle. *Image, Processing, Analysis and Machine Vision*, volume 1. Chapman & Hall Computing, 1993.

[TCG⁺93] A. Tansel, J. Clifford, S. Gadia, S. Jajodia, A. Segev, and R. Snodgrass, editors. *Temporal Databases*. The Benjamin/Cummings Publishing Company, Inc., 1993.

[WA⁺95]   R. Wasserman, R. Acharya, et al. Multimodality tumor delineation via fuzzy fusion and deformable modelling. In *Proceedings of the SPIE, Medical Image: Image Processing*, 1995.

[WLK92]   A. J. Worth, S. Lehar, and D. N. Kennedy. A recurrent cooperative/competitive field for segmentation of magnetic resonance brain images. *IEEE Transactions on Knowledge and Data Engineering*, 4(2):156–161, April 1992.

Verification and Validation of AI Systems that Control Deep-Space Spacecraft

Michael Lowry, Klaus Havelund, and John Penix

Computational Sciences Division
NASA Ames Research Center
M.S. 269-2
Moffett Field, CA 94035

Abstract. NASA is developing technology for the next generation of deep-space robotic spacecraft, with the aim of enabling new types of missions and radically reducing costs. One technology under development is Autonomy: highly capable spacecraft that perform significant scientific missions with little or no commanding and monitoring from Earth. Artificial Intelligence provides a basis for autonomy technology, but raises issues of verification and validation outside the scope of empirical testing technology for conventionally commanded spacecraft. This paper describes research towards extending formal methods verification techniques for the mathematical verification of AI systems controlling deep-space spacecraft. This paper first overviews a planned space mission called DS-1 which includes an AI-based autonomy experiment. It then describes part of this AI system called the executive, which includes an 'intelligent' operating system based on goal-oriented constructs. The paper then describes focused research on applying and extending model-checking technology for verifying both the core services of the executive and the concurrent task programs run by the executive.

1 NASA's New Millennium Program

The successful landing of Mars Pathfinder on Independence day (July 4, 1997) signalled a new era in man's exploration of the solar system: faster, better, and cheaper. The Mars Pathfinder project was completed in four years, delivered widely sampled geological data from a mobile rover and cost just $250 million (1997) dollars. In contrast, the two Viking missions of twenty years ago took over eight years to develop, delivered data from fixed landers and orbiters, and cost over $3 billion (1997) dollars. The Mars pathfinder project took advantage of off-the-shelf technology to reduce development costs.

NASA is preparing for an order-of-magnitude expanded space exploration program in the next decade within the constraints of a flat-lined budget. One key aspect of this plan is the New Millennium program: a series of technology validation flights whose objective is to accelerate the flight-qualification of new spacecraft technology. For example, new generations of radiation-hardened microprocessors, based on commercial designs, will be flight-qualified in New Millennium missions. Up to now the functional performance of space-qualified hardware has often lagged a decade or more behind commercial hardware. New Millennium will greatly accelerate the space-hardening and space qualification of new technology. This will reduce development costs for subsequent science-oriented missions and enhance the technology base for these missions. The New Millennium program is also aimed towards decreasing operations costs while enhancing science return.

Operations costs are largely determined by two factors: launch weight and personnel. Microelectronics and other miniaturization technology can greatly reduce the launch weight of a deep-space robotic spacecraft. This alone can save hundreds of millions of dollars by reducing the size of the required launch rocket; for example, from a Space Shuttle to a Titan rocket to a Delta rocket. Personnel costs are the second major factor in operations costs, with missions such as Voyager requiring hundreds of non-science personnel at the peak of encounters to monitor the health of spacecraft subsystems, sequence the commands executed by the spacecraft, and navigate.

2 Deep-Space 1 and AI-Based Autonomy

As one of its objectives, the New Millennium program is seeking to reduce non-science personnel costs by an order of magnitude through automation technology. The ultimate objective of the automation technology is spacecraft autonomy: deep-space robotic spacecraft that navigate themselves, monitor their own health, monitor the status of mission goals, and take appropriate corrective actions. Autonomous spacecraft will be commanded at the level of mission goals rather than traditional spacecraft sequences, the latter being roughly equivalent to macro-assembler programs for embedded systems. This will be accomplished by extending the feedback loops which on today's spacecraft operate only at the low level of servo-mechanisms (e.g., maintaining attitude control) to feedback loops which operate all the way up to science goals. In addition to greatly reducing operations costs, autonomous spacecraft will also enable new kinds of missions that cannot be accomplished through light-time delayed remote control, such as comet landings.

The first New Millennium mission is Deep-Space 1 (DS-1), which currently includes plans for an asteroid rendezvous, a Mars fly-by, and a comet fly-by. Critical technology being tested includes an ion propulsion system (IPS) and on-board optical navigation. Another experiment is the flight-testing an AI-based control system called Remote Agent (RA), the first towards the goal of spacecraft autonomy. The remote agent has three subsystems: a planner which decomposes goals into task-nets and then sequences tasks along a time-line according to precedence constraints and resource constraints; an executive which concurrently executes these tasks; and a next-generation fault detection and recovery system called MIR. The executive subsystem and MIR provide the feedback loops at higher levels. The executive subsystem combines features of multithreaded operating systems with AI languages based on sub-goaling, such as Prolog and MRS. This paper describes research aimed at formal verification of the executive subsystem.

3 Analytic Verification Effort

A major concern for spacecraft engineers and mission planners is verification and validation of advanced software architectures such as the remote agent. Traditional approaches to verification and validation include extensive testing and manual review. Furthermore, traditional spacecraft *sequences* - that is, command sequences to control a spacecraft - are time-stamped, straight-line programs that are reviewed by engineering teams from each spacecraft subsystem. For example, the thermal team will review a sequence to check for overheating, the power system team will review a sequence to check for safety of the electrical system. Each command is time-stamped to execute at a particular time, down to millisecond precision. More flexible methods for commanding a spacecraft are controversial - even minimal extensions such as *conditional sequencing*, where the execution timing of a command depends on the spacecraft's environment. An example would be a command to wait until the spacecraft comes out of the shadow of a planet before turning the solar panels towards the sun. Traditionally, all feedback loops above the level of servo-mechanisms go through ground manual control, with human-in-the-loop verification. Verification and validation is a major obstacle in accepting more autonomous architectures.

As an adjunct to the regular testing effort for DS-1, an effort among several NASA centers to apply formal methods to verifying and debugging DS-1 is being pursued. In previous NASA formal method studies the software being analyzed was developed in a waterfall process, with relatively long phases for requirements and design (months to years). This allowed plenty of time for formal methods practitioners to exercise their analysis tools and feedback their results to requirements analysts. In contrast, the DS-1 software has been developed through the spiral model [1]. The spiral model is an iterative software development process with four or more distinct phases for each turn of the spiral: requirements, design, coding, and testing. In contrast to the one-shot waterfall model, the spiral model provides iterative feedback on requirements and design through testing and validation of earlier turns of the spiral. It is a process well-suited to developing novel architectures where there is substantial initial uncertainty on requirements and designs. However, it results in highly time-compressed phases. In the case of DS-1, each turn of the spiral has lasted two to three months, and each phase of each spiral lasts just a matter of weeks. This presents a substantial challenge to formal methods efforts, stressing automation over labor-intensive manual methods.

The NASA-wide effort is being called analytic verification, to stress its complementing empirical validation efforts and to highlight its foundation in mathematical approaches to software engineering. We believe this name is also more informative to the spacecraft engineers and mission planners than the name 'formal methods'. As part of this analytic verification effort, our team at NASA Ames is pursuing formal verification of part of the remote agent. The technology we are developing stresses model-checking over interactive theorem-proving, because the former is much more automated than the latter. The long-term goal of our effort is to make our technology directly usable by the design and development team, as low-overhead tools. In the interim, we are our own users, providing feedback from our efforts to the design and development team.

4 Executive Core Services

The executive subsystem of the remote agent is conceptually composed of two layers: a set of core services that implement a robust operating system for executing concurrent tasks, and a set of mission-specific task programs. The language in which both layers are written is an extension of Lisp called the Executive Sequencing Language (ESL), principally authored by Eran Gatt of JPL. ESL is defined through a set of Lisp macros. ESL code operates in a multi-threaded Lisp.

In this section we overview one aspect of the executive that will serve as examples of the formal verification techniques described in section 5: the *with-maintained-properties* construct in the core executive system. Section 6 describes an example task program for thrusting with the ion propulsion system, which will serve as examples for the abstraction techniques described in subsequent sections.

The services provided by the core executive system, such as those provided by the *with-maintained-properties* construct described below, provide an API (application programming interface) for defining task programs that achieve diverse goals such as acquiring images and changing trajectory. These programs are executed concurrently in order to achieve the token nets generated by the planner. For the purposes of this paper, assume that each token in the token net corresponds to the invocation of a task program in the executive, with the appropriate parameters. The core services of the executive include as a subset those of an operating system for managing a queue of jobs, which must be assigned resources and synchronized according to their concurrency constraints. The executive keeps an agenda of tasks (jobs) which are broken down into sequences of commands; the executive activates and suspends these tasks. The resources are typically states of a device, more generally, resources are *properties*. A property is any value that is controlled and monitored. The executive differs from a standard operating system in at least two respects: the extensive support for monitoring and recovering from property violations - leading to robust execution, and the high level of abstraction provided by goal-oriented AI constructs.

4.1 Maintaining Properties during Task Execution

This subsection describes the architecture implemented in the executive for assigning and monitoring properties required by task programs for successful execution. The analytic verification and debugging of this architecture is described in the next section. The primitive construct that invokes these services is the *(with-maintained-properties* **prop body***)* construct (implemented as a Lisp macro), which takes as parameters a set of properties and the body of a task program. The specification of this construct is that it guarantees the properties while the body is executing. By having the properties managed in this manner, the task programs can focus on sequencing activities without worrying about maintaining and monitoring the values of the maintained properties.

Further constructs are built using the *with-maintained-properties* construct. For example, the *(with-selected-device* **class** **(do-activity)***)* construct selects a device of the class, achieves its ready-state, and then locks the properties of that ready-state and maintains them with the assistance of MIR while it does the activity. This ESL construct is used within the DS-1 executive to maintain properties of devices, which are physical objects on the spacecraft. There are classes of devices which are defined to have various properties. A task can select a device and execute with the knowledge that the desired state of this device is being maintained by the system. Further constructs built using the *with-maintained-properties* construct are used to maintain states during sequencing. For example, thrusting in the ion propulsion system is controlled by creating a thrusting state predicate and associating it with the property IPS-THRUSTING.

The basic architecture in which *with-maintained-properties* operates is a collection of concurrent tasks that require specific values of certain properties in order to execute correctly. If a property value become false, then the associated tasks should be suspended while action is taken to re-achieve the property. Tasks must also be coordinated so they do not require conflicting values of properties. The following are some of the basic protocol requirements for this architecture whose analytic verification and debugging is described in section 5:

1. A task wanting a property to have a specific value subscribes to the property. To coordinate multiple tasks wanting property values, the properties are locked during *subscription*. Property locks are used to coordinate tasks so that they do not try to achieve different values for a single property at the same time. Mutually exclusive access to the locks is guaranteed by placing the code for locking within a critical section. The subscription process can have three outcomes for a task:

1a. No other task is subscribing to that lock, in which case the subscription is successful, this task becomes the owner of the lock, and *snarfs* the property.

1b. Some other task already owns lock, and the values that the two tasks want the property to have are compatible. In this case the task successfully subscribes to the lock but does not become the lock's owner - it is a secondary subscriber. It also *snarfs* the property.

1c. Some other task is subscribing to the lock and the values are incompatible. In this case the subscription FAILS.

2. The owner of a lock, after successfully subscribing, attempts to actually make the property true by calling the **achieve** method on the property. All secondary subscribers wait for the property to be achieved by the owner. If the owner's attempt to achieve the property fails, then all of the lock's subscribers **fail**.

3. Once a lock property has been achieved, the lock's subscribers, which were waiting for the owner to achieve the property, are signaled and continue to run. The body of these tasks are executed.

4. If a locked property becomes false (is violated) during execution of a body (through events exogenous to the executive, such as device failures), signal this loss, suspend execution of the body, and attempt to recover the property. Maintained property violations are detected by a daemon. This daemon will attempt to restore or recover violated properties, using recovery actions that are either explicitly stated in the task definition, or default recovery actions that can involve invocation of MIR. If the recovery action is not successful, then all tasks which have snarfed the property are aborted.

5. When a task terminates, either normally or aborted, it unsubscribes to all properties it has snarfed. If the owner of a locked property unsubscribes to the property, then ownership is passed to the next task subscribing to the property. If there are no further tasks subscribing to the property, then the lock on the property is released.

The next section describes a simple error trace found through analytic verification that violates requirement 5 and then a more complex error trace that violates requirement 4.

5 Analytic Verification of Executive Core Services

This section describes ongoing work to verify and debug key components of the core services of the executive. An abstracted model of the Lisp code was manually developed of the implementation for locking, snarfing, and releasing properties. This model includes the *with-maintained-properties* construct described in the previous section. The model was written in PROMELA, the language for the model-checker SPIN [2]. Even this highly abstracted model was at the limits of computational complexity for large workstations (i.e., a workstation with 268MB of memory).

Model-checking is a formal methods technique for verifying and debugging concurrent or real-time systems modeled as interacting finite state machines. Given a model and a property, a model-checker searches for *traces* of the model that violate the property. Properties can be invariants, temporal properties (i.e., defined through model operators such as *eventually*), or in the case of real-time model-checkers, metric time constraints defined through linear relations. A trace is an interleaved sequence of states (or dually, transitions) of the finite state machines. Model checkers differ from simulators in that they explore all possible traces, in other words all realizable paths through the reachability graph. They also enable checking much richer concurrency properties than is typical of simulators. Some model checkers are similar to theorem-provers in that they manipulate symbolic descriptions of the transition relation. However, model-checkers do not perform induction, which typically needs to be guided manually in real-world verification proofs. Trading off from this deficiency, they are completely automatic, and thus more practical for verification in a spiral development process.

Different model checkers provide different languages for defining the interacting finite state machines. The PROMELA language is a C-like language with facilities for creating processes and for interprocess communication through buffered channels. SPIN compiles a PROMELA model into a C program which is then run to find error traces. To formulate the model of the executive core services in PROMELA, a number of trade-offs had to be made. For example, the spring 1997 release of PROMELA did not directly support procedures. Modeling procedure calls as process invocations led to state explosions, a subsequent attempt at modeling procedure calls as macro calls avoided the state explosion but required careful separation of variable names. Neither the precise details of our abstracted PROMELA model nor the various trade-offs are enumerated in this paper. However, the reader should be aware that formulating computationally tractable models of complex systems requires expertise, artistry, and experimentation.[1]

This section focuses on two subtle bugs that were found regarding the protocol requirements described in section 4. These bugs were first found through error traces of our abstracted PROMELA model and then confirmed in the executive Lisp code. The designers of the executive believe these bugs would not have been detected through means other than formal verification. Empirical testing would not have uncovered these bugs because they arise only in a multithreaded environment, and only in unusual circumstances that are unlikely to arise during testing. Model-checking is able to find these bugs because it considers all possible interleavings of concurrent processes.

We should first note that the executive has performed well under empirical testing, and moreover we have been able to analytically verify that the implementation satisfies various requirements. For example, the following requirements have been verified, in the abstracted PROMELA model, of the property protocols described in section 4:

1. If a property is snarfed by a task, it can only be snarfed by another task if the property values are compatible (requirement 1b).
2. When a task terminates normally, it releases all locks (requirement 5, normal termination).

The verification of these requirements was achieved by placing invariants in the model at the appropriate locations, and running the model over all interleavings to demonstrate that there are no traces where the invariants are violated.

The subtle bugs which have been found through model-checking concern traces in abnormal situations, for example, where a property is violated in a situation that was not considered by the executive design team. The first bug is demonstrated by an error trace where a task may abort without releasing its property locks. The *with-maintained-property* construct uses the Lisp construct *unwind-protect* to provide a wrapper around the execution of the body. This ensures that errors signalled during the execution of the body (e.g., an error signalled because a locked property is violated) are caught and han-

---

1. The authors thank Gerard Holzmann, the creator of SPIN, for his advise and help.

dled by recovery procedures. However, after the body is executed, the *with-maintained-property* construct exits the *unwind-protect* wrapper and executes code to release the locks. If after the *unwind-protect* wrapper is exited a property violation occurs, and then the daemon which monitors property violations wakes up, it will signal an error. Because this error occurs outside the dynamic context of an *unwind-protect*, the error falls through and causes the task to be aborted - whether or not the release locks code has been fully executed.

This error trace was communicated to the development team, resulting in experiments with a critical section being placed in the *with-maintained-property* construct around the code to release locks. This prevents any other thread from executing (including the daemon monitoring property violations) when any instance of *with-maintained-properties* enters the release-locks section of code. This still leaves an even more unlikely (by over an order of magnitude) error trace that was found through model-checking: a property violation occurs exactly at the point where the *unwind-protect* wrapper is exited and the gap before the critical section for release locks is entered. The best means of handling this unlikely error trace is not obvious, because it is necessary to be conservative in creating critical sections of code. Excluding other threads from executing can itself lead to timing bugs. This brief overview of this error trace illustrates the nature of the interactions between the analytic verification team and the executive development team, and also the subtle nature of concurrency bugs.

An even more subtle error trace concerns the interaction of the internal operation of the daemon which monitors the properties and the code for achieving property locks. Simplified versions of the Lisp code for both, circa the spring of 1997, are given below in Algol-like notation, preceded by explanations. The simplified versions are sufficient for understanding the nature of the error trace, and for understanding how the verification technology is applied to AI programming constructs.

The maintain-properties-daemon is an infinite loop, and is normally sleeping. First it checks the locks data structure; if there is an inconsistency with the database for the actual property values, it invokes recovery procedures. Then it determines whether there has been any new memory-event occurrences (induced by an external event) or snarf-event occurrences (induced by a task snarfing a property). If not, it goes back to sleep until a memory-event or snarf-event occurs. Hence, if no event occurs for a while, then the damon will not perform check-locks.

```
maintain-properties-daemon
loop-forever do
        if check-locks
            do-automatic-recovery;
        if not(changed? (memory-event-count + pl-snarf-event-count))
            then wait-for(memory-event or snarf-event);
    od
```

The **achieve-lock-property** routine is called within the dynamic scope of a task, which is the value of $this-task. This routine is called after a task successfully snarfs a property-lock; the routine is called with the lock as a parameter. If the task is the owner, then it first achieves the property and then sets the achieved-field to boolean TRUE. If the task is not the owner of the lock, it waits for the property to be achieved.

```
achieve-lock-properties (lock)
    p = property-lock-property(lock);
    if owner(lock) = $this-task then do
        achieve p;
        property-lock-achieved?(lock) = TRUE;
        od
    else wait-for(p);
```

An error trace arises in the SPIN model for the following requirement, which is part of requirement 4 listed in the previous section. In contrast to the previous requirements, which were formulated as invariants, this requirement is formulated as a temporal property:

> If a task relies on some property to hold, and the database is modified
> such that it no longer holds, then the task will eventually terminate,
> either by itself or by an abort from the daemon.

The error trace is summarized by the following sequence of events which refer to the interaction between the environment, the daemon, the **achieve-lock-properties** routine, and multiple tasks:

1. A task calls **snarf-property-locks**, becomes the owner of the lock, and then calls **achieve-lock-properties**. In the call of the latter, first achieve is called (because the task is the owner of the lock). After this succeeds, but before the achieved-value is set to TRUE, the task is suspended (put to sleep) by the executive. That is, the property has been achieved, but the achieved-field in the property lock has not yet been set to TRUE. (A second task is activated by the executive and starts to run).

2. The database is now modified by the environment in such a way that it becomes inconsistent with the property lock just created by the first task. This causes a memory event.

3. The daemon is awakened. The daemon starts looking for an inconsistency, but finds none since the achieved-field has not been set yet. Specifically, check-locks signals an inconsistency only if the achieved-field is set to TRUE. Hence, the daemon discovers nothing and goes back to sleep.

4. The first task is awakened and finishes executing the **achieve-lock-properties**. It assigns TRUE to the achieved-field of the lock, and continues execution as if everything is consistent.

5. Unless another memory-event or snarf-event occurs, the daemon remains asleep. The task is not stopped, and continues executing (if it is an infinite loop, perhaps indefinitely) even though properties it depends on are not valid.

This error trace could be eliminated through a critical region in the **achieve-lock-properties** routine. However, it also reinforces a known design flaw of the spring 1997 implementation of the executive: there can be a significant time lag between a property being violated and a task being informed of the violation. Prior to model-checking, it was not known that this time lag could be indefinite. This significant time lag is being eliminated in the design of the next version of the executive by changing where the property lock daemon resides and when it is invoked.

This section has overviewed aspects of the analytic verification and debugging of the DS-1 remote agent executive. It demonstrates that formal methods technology, specifically model-checking, which has been successfully applied in the past to verification and debugging of digital hardware, communication protocols, and operating system protocols; can be extended to the verification and debugging of AI-based concurrent systems. However, it has not described the manual effort in hand translating the Lisp code to the language of a model-checker (e.g., PROMELA), the much more considerable effort in abstracting the model so it is computationally tractable even for a large workstation. This required manual effort has made it somewhat difficult to stay current with the executive design and development team working under the rapid spiral model. Nonetheless, we have made a contribution to the overall verification effort for the DS-1 remote agent.

6 Executive Task Programs

This section and the next section together describe research towards automating the abstraction of AI programs for computationally tractable model-checking. The context for this research is verification of the task-specific executive programs, which run on top of the API provided by the core executive services.

The task-specific programs need to be verified both against the goals they are meant to achieve as well as the constraints they cannot violate while executing. A subclass of these constraints are *flight rules* which are formulated by experts to guide the safe operation of the spacecraft. One class of flight rules have the form that a class of events never occur in states satisfying particular predicates:

[never] state-predicate -> event

In other words, the event should only occur in states that satisfy the negation of the state-predicate. An example of such a flight rule concerns the requirements for the spacecraft to have directional control over the propulsion. The Engine Gimbal Actuator (EGA) must be activated to provide directional control over the thrust vector. Thus one implication of the requirement is the following flight rule: the EGA must be on whenever the attitude control system (ACS) is in Thrust Vector Control (TVC) mode. This can be formulated as two rules, which together are equivalent to the constraint that a time interval in which the ACS is in TVC mode is contained by a time interval when the EGA is on:

[never] EGA-off -> turn-on-TVC-mode
[never] TVC-mode-on -> turn-off-EGA

The executive controls devices such as the EGA and the ACS by broadcasting messages to processes that subscribe (listen) to particular classes of messages, these processes implement the low-level device control protocols. Thus from the viewpoint of the task-specific executive programs, flight rules such as the one above are equivalent to predicates on the state in which particular messages are allowed to be sent by the executive.

The rest of this section describes a procedure within the executive task program that achieves a thrust level of the ion propulsion system. It contains a call to change the ACS into TVC-mode. It is a simplified version of the procedure as it existed in the spring of 1997. The part of the procedure which sends out a message to the ACS is the subroutine call **change-acs-mode**.

```
to-achieve-IPS-THRUSTING (level)
   if (ips-thrusting-state-p or ips-standby-state-p)
     then do
         check-type( level, ips-thrust-level-type);
         command-with-mir-confirmation(send_fsc_ips_set_thrust_level(level));
         wait-for(memory-event(ips-state = steady-state and thrust-level = level));
         with-guardian(warp-safe (monitor(ips-thrust-duration-achieved))),
                                          change-acs-mode(tvc_mode));
     od
     else do
         achieve (ips-standby-state);
         achieve (ips-thrusting(level));
     od
```

The procedure first checks that the IPS is either in a thrusting state or a standby state. If neither (the else clause), it first achieves a standby state, and then tries to achieve the thrusting level. Otherwise (the then clause), it performs a sequence of steps that do not themselves change whether the EGA is turned on. These commands instead set-up and monitor the thrust-level given as parameter. Finally, the ACS is switched to TVC-mode.

Note that this procedure does not itself guarantee that the EGA is turned on when the ACS is switched to TVC-mode. (In fact, achieving IPS standby-mode turns the EGA off.) Thus the existence of a possible error trace for the flight rule is not excluded by the code in this procedure, but rather depends on the context in which this procedure is called. However, the program is more complicated than need be to determine whether or not there is an error trace. The superfluous steps can greatly increase the number of interleavings during model-checking.

7 Abstraction-based Verification

Model-checking is an attractive method for verifying flight rules, specifically that state constraints (invariants) are satisfied at those points in the code where messages are broadcast. However, the executive task descriptions are moderately complex (tens to hundreds of pages), and have a large state space. The code described in section 6 is only a small part of the overall program to control the IPS. This makes it computationally infeasible as a general methodology to run a model-checker on a direct translation of the ESL programs. But for each flight rule, only a small portion of the program is relevant. However, given the number of flight rules, manually abstracting a model of the task programs for each flight rule is not cost effective. Thus we are developing automated abstraction methods for generating reduced models. As applied to the code described in section 6, the abstraction methods would yield the simplified program below with respect to the EGA constraint:

```
to-achieve-IPS-THRUSTING (level)
   if (ips-thrusting-state-p or ips-standby-state-p)
     then do
         change-acs-mode(tvc_mode);
     od
     else do
         achieve (ips-standby-state);
         achieve (ips-thrusting(level));
     od
```

7.1 WP-Based Program Slicing

Program slicing [4,5] is a technique to extract a partial program that is equivalent to an original program over a subset of the program variables. The input to a traditional slicing algorithm is a program and a designated subset of variables, the output of the slicing algorithm is a partial program that for every program execution has identical values assigned to the designated subset of variables upon program termination. The key idea of slicing algorithms is to work backwards from the program end-point, keeping statements that have an effect on the designated variables and removing statements that have no effect. As the algorithm works backwards over the program statements, additional variables might be added to the designated set if they have occur in expressions which modify the designated set.

The concept of program slicing can be extended to abstract ESL programs for the purpose of model checking. However, instead of slicing with respect to variables, the programs are sliced with respect to state predicates, starting from a statement which contains the operation(s) which are required to only be executed in particular states. In other words, the programs are sliced with respect to a never property of the form described in section 6. The partial program that is generated from such a never property has the following guarantee: its error traces for the never property are in direct correspondence to the error traces of the original program. This is called WP-program slicing, as the algorithm is defined using Dijkstra's weakest-precondition calculus. In the example above, the slicing begins at the statement which changes the ACS to TVC-mode.

Two rules for this slicing calculus are described. **Slice** takes a code-sequence terminated by a statement, and a state predicate, and returns a reduced code-sequence. It determines where it can substitute the IDLE statement without affecting error traces by calculating when a statement "passes through" a state predicate. This occurs when the weakest precondition is the same as the state predicate. The IDLE statements can later be removed.

The slicing rule for straight-line sequences is:

Slice({code-sequence ; statement} , state-predicate) ->
If WP(statement, state-predicate) = state-predicate
   then {Slice(code-sequence,state-predicate); IDLE}
   else {Slice(code-sequence,WP(state-predicate,statement)) ; statement}

The rule states that IDLE can be substituted for a statement if the statement has no effect on the state predicate. Otherwise, the weakest precondition of the state-predicate is substituted for the state-predicate and slicing continues backwards. A more elaborate calculus would allow substituting a simpler statement that had the same weakest precondition.

The rule for conditionals requires the definition of a weakest predicate reduction:

Definition R is a *predicate reduction* of Q by P iff R & P => Q

Definition R is a *weakest predicate reduction* (WPR) of Q by P iff for any S which is a predicate reduction of Q by P, S => R

The rule for conditionals is defined on the following pattern:
Slice({code-sequence; if P then *then-statement* else *else-statement*}, Q)

Let *then-WP* = WP(*then-statment, Q*)
Let *else-WP* = WP(*else-statment, Q*)

Let *reduced-then-WP* = WPR(*P,then-WP*)
Let *reduced-else-WP* = WPR(not(*P*),*else-WP*)

Note that when the condition P implies *then-WP*, the IDLE statement can be substituted for *then-statement*. In other words, the *then-statement* is executed only in a context where it will not generate an error trace. Define *reduced-then-statement* as IDLE when P implies *then-WP*, otherwise it is the same as *then-statement*. Similarly, when not(*P*) implies *else-WP*, the IDLE statement can be substituted for *else-statement*. Define *reduced-else-statement* accordingly.

The rule for slicing conditionals can now be defined:
Slice({code-sequence; if P then *then-statement* else *else-statement*}, Q) ->

{Slice(code-sequence, (*P* and *reduced-then-WP*) or (not(*P*) and *reduced-else-WP*)))
; if P then *reduced-then-statement* else *reduced-else-statement*}

Note that the weakest precondition for the conditional is composed of reduced weakest preconditions for the then-statement and the else-statement.

7.2 Future Research on Abstraction-based Verification

Future work will include a full calculus for WP-slicing of ESL constructs. Many of the ESL constructs such as *with-maintained-properties* greatly simplify WP-slicing. In other words, the API provided by core executive services is designed to simplify ensuring that requirements and constraints for task program execution are met. For example, *with-maintained-properties* is specified to guarantee that properties are achieved and maintained throughout the execution of the body. The weakest precondition of the body for a state-predicate implied by these properties is simply **true**.

Another method under investigation for abstracting ESL task programs is equivalence-based abstract interpretation.WP-program slicing can substantially reduce the size of programs. However, it does not reduce the size of the full state space, defined as the product of the number of values that can be assigned to each program variable. By reducing some state transitions to IDLE, WP-program slicing reduces the number of reachable states, defined as the subset of the state space that can be reached through sequences of valid transitions from the initial state. Nonetheless, non-symbolic model-checking is required to enumerate all the possible reachable values for each program variable, even if many of these values result in equivalent traces with respect to an invariant or temporal property.

The state space can be greatly reduced by merging equivalent values, and redefining the operations according to the equivalence classes. Mapping values to equivalence classes and operations to abstracted operations over the equivalence classes is a type of *abstract interpretation*, [3]. Abstract interpretation is defined as a homomorphism from the concrete domain of values and operations in a programming language to an abstract domain, typically with values ordered in a lattice and abstracted operations defined through lattice operations (e.g., meet and join). Abstract interpretation is often applied through fixed mappings for various types of analysis used in compiler optimization, such as dead code detection.

In this ongoing research, we are applying abstract interpretation through dynamically determined mappings to reduce the state space for model-checking. To date, we have only considered mappings based on explicit values: discrete enumerated values and convex intervals over the real numbers. The method is similar to WP-based program slicing: starting from an operation constrained by a flight rule, the state space is merged into one equivalence class. Walking backwards through the code from this operation, this one equivalence class is then recursively partitioned into distinct classes according to those states satisfying the weakest precondition for each statement. At worst, the original state space is regenerated.

8 Summary

Verification technology is important for next generation of autonomous spacecraft. This paper has described ongoing work in applying and extending formal methods techniques, specifically model-checking, to the verification of an AI-based autonomy architecture. The paper presented examples of the core services provided by the DS-1 remote agent executive and task programs executed by the executive. Verification and debugging of the core services protocol requirements through model-checking were described. The paper then described on-going research to automate the abstraction of task programs in order to enable model-checking of flight rules and other requirements.

Acknowledgments

This research was supported by NASA Code S and NASA Code Q . We wish to thank our colleagues at other NASA centers participating in the analytic verification effort for DS-1 for their helpful suggestions in this research. We wish also to thank various members of the model-checking research community for their advise.

References

1. B. W. Boehm: A Sprial Modle of Software Development and Enhancement. *ACM Sigsoft Software Eng. Notes 11(4):22-42.*
2. G. J. Holzmann: The Model Checker SPIN, *IEEE Transactions on Software Engineering.* Vol 23, No. 5, May 1997.
3. N. Jones, C. Gomard,and P. Sestoft: *Partial Evaluation and Automatic Program Generation,* ed. C.A.R. Hoare, Prentice Hall, 1993.
4. B. Korel and J. Laski: Dynamic Slicing of Computer Programs, *J. Systems Software.* Vol 13, 1990, pp 187-195.
5. M. Weiser: Program Slicing, *Proc. Fifth International Conference on Software Engineering,* 1981, pp. 439-449.

Data Mining and Knowledge Discovery: The Third Generation

Gregory Piatetsky-Shapiro

Knowledge Stream Partners, Cambridge MA, USA
gps@kdnuggets.com

Abstract. This paper examines the current trends in business applications of data mining and knowledge discovery systems. The focus is on newly emerging "Third Generation" data mining systems, which are solution-oriented and integrate smoothly with existing business systems.

Keywords: Data Mining, Knowledge Discovery, Industrial Applications, Knowledge Discovery Process, Third Generation

1 Extended Abstract

The first generation of data mining and knowledge discovery systems arose from academic research and was technology driven (Fayyad et al 1996). These systems usually performed classification or clustering, and relied upon a particular technique, such as decision trees (e.g. C4.5, KnowledgeSeeker), neural networks (BrainMaker, SNNS) or nearest neighbours. These systems were adopted by early proponents of data mining – data analysts, statisticians – all those who had sufficient expertise and understanding of the process of data analysis to be able to use those tools.

The first generation of data mining tools was in many ways a significant advance over the traditional statistical tools such as linear or logistic regression, especially for noisy and non-linear problems such as credit approval or fraud detection.

However, the first generation data mining tools were oriented towards the expert and required an in-depth understanding of their various parameters. They also required extensive preprocessing to convert existing data into their formats and postprocessing to interpret the results. A further problem was that these tools only supported one discovery task, e.g. classification. However, to solve a specific problem, such as fraud detection, the analyst frequently needed to do other types of data analysis (find clusters in data, visualize them, find rules to discriminate between clusters, find new clusters, and so on).

The second generation of data mining tools provided better support for the knowledge discovery process. Typically, they integrated several discovery methods, including clustering, classification, and visualization, and provided database connectivity allowing easy import and export of data to and from databases. Examples of such tools include Clementine, IDIS Data Mining Suite, Darwin, and IBM Intelligent Miner.

However, while these tools are powerful, they are still oriented towards the power data analyst rather than the business end user. These tools solve the data analysis problem, and not the business problem that the end users want to solve.

In the process of solving the specific problems, many companies have built a domain-specific shell around their data mining tools. These shells have led to the development of vertical customized tools oriented towards specific business problems. Examples of such tools include HNC Eagle(tm), a Card Merchant Risk Management system used by banks to detect fraud and prevent attrition, and IBM Advanced Scout, which analyzes NBA game statistics and finds patterns of play that coaches can use right away.

We argue that these "Third Generation" tools hold the biggest promise to make useful discoveries and examine existing tools and applications in several sectors, including banking, finance, and insurance.

We look at the steps of knowledge discovery process and the outline features that would be desirable in the future tools. Finally, we discuss the challenges for the further progress in research and development in data mining and knowledge discovery.

Acknowledgments: I am very grateful to Steve Gallant for his comments on this abstract.

2 References

Fayyad, U., Piatetsky-Shapiro, G., Smyth, P., and Uthurusamy, R. 1996. Advances in Knowledge Discovery and Data Mining, Cambridge, MA: AAAI/MIT Press.

Piatetsky-Shapiro, G., Knowledge Discovery Mine: Siftware page, www.kdnuggets.com/siftware.html

Embedding Prioritized Circumscription in Logic Programs

Jianhua Chen
Computer Science Department
Louisiana State University
Baton Rouge, LA 70803, USA
E-mail: jianhua@bit.csc.lsu.edu

Abstract

In this paper, we present a method for embedding prioritized circumscription of a clausal theory into general disjunctive logic programs (GDP) with negation as failure in the head. In recent works, Sakama and Inoue show that parallel circumscription can be embedded in GDP. They also show that prioritized circumscription of a clausal theory can be represented in the framework of GDP extended with priorities. In our method, the priorities of minimization in the circumscription policy are translated into the syntactical form of logic program rules, and the models of the circumscription are precisely captured by the stable models of the program. Thus we show that prioritized circumscription can be directly embedded in GDP without extending the GDP logic programming framework. This result further asserts the expressive power of the class of general disjunctive programs and supports its use for knowledge representation in Artificial Intelligence.

1   Introduction

Circumscription [16] is a powerful formalism for modeling common-sense, non-monotonic reasoning. The close relationships between circumscription and various forms of logic programming have been investigated by a number of researchers and many significant results have been reported in the literature. Reiter [21] indicated that circumscription in Horn theories with all predicates minimized implies Clark's predicate completion semantics. Kundu and Chen [8] showed that circumscription for a sub-class of first-order clausal theories can be expressed as a modified form of predicate completion. Lifschitz [9] established the connection between the closed-world assumption (CWA) semantics in logic programming

*Work supported in part by NSF grant IRI-9409370 and LEQSF grant LEQSF(RF/95-97) RDA-37

and circumscription in a first-order theory with all predicates minimized. Lifschitz [11] and Przymusinski [18] characterized the perfect model semantics for stratified (disjunctive) logic programs by prioritized circumscription. Gelfond, Przymusinska and Przymusinski [6] further investigated several forms of generalized CWA's and their connections with circumscription. Circumscription has also been related to default logic [20], autoepistemic logic [17], the logic of minimal belief and negation as failure (MBNF) [12], and to the stable model semantics of disjunctive programs.

Several works have been reported in the literature which translate circumscriptive theories into logic programs. There are several advantages of doing the translation. First, computing circumscription is usually difficult because in general the circumscription of a first order theory involves second-order quantifiers. By embedding circumscription in a logic program, one can get around this problem by using the proof procedures readily available in logic programming to answer queries to circumscription. This will complement other existing works on computing circumscription [8, 10, 19]. Second, the translation of circumscription into logic programs will shed insight on the expressive power of logic programming languages as tools for knowledge representation. Finally the embedding of circumscriptive theories may also enhance our understanding of the logic program semantics through a characterization by circumscription.

Gelfond and Lifschitz [4] presented a method for embedding prioritized circumscription in normal logic programs. Their method requires that the theory must be stratifiable and without fixed predicates and that each clause in the theory contains at most one literal from the varied predicates. Sakama and Inoue [2] showed that parallel circumscription of first order clausal theories can be embedded in general disjunctive logic programs with negation as failure in the head (GDP). More recently, they presented [3] a framework of prioritized logic programming (PLP) and show that several forms of non-monotonic reasoning such as abduction, default reasoning and prioritized circumscription can be represented in the PLP framework. The study about prioritized circumscription is important for representing common-sense knowledge, because prioritized circumscription is a more expressive form of circumscription which allows the specification of different priorities for minimizing the predicates involved.

In this paper, we present an embedding of prioritized circumscription into GDP, i.e., general disjunctive logic programs with negation as failure in the head. We consider only the *Herbrand models* of circumscriptive theories throughout this paper, which amounts to adopting both the *unique name assumption* and the *domain closure assumption*, when considering only *function-free* first-order theories. Our method is inspired by the embedding in [2] and it extends the ideas there in order to handle the priorities. Similar to [3], we do not place restrictions on the existence of fixed and varying predicates. This makes our method quite general. On the other hand, our method provides a *direct* embedding of prioritized circumscription into GDP, which is in contrast to [3] where the semantics of GDP has to be extended with the notion of priorities in order to capture prioritized circumscription. In our translation, the priorities of the predicates to be minimized are represented by the syntactical forms of the resulting program rules, and the stable model semantics for GDP is sufficient to represent the prioritized circumscription. Thus our method further asserts the expressive power of the class of GDP's and supports the application of GDP's as knowledge representation tools.

The rest of this paper is organized as follows. In Section 2, we briefly review the notion of general disjunctive logic programs with negation as failure in the head, and the notion of prioritized circumscription. In Section 3, we show our method of embedding and prove the correctness of it. In Section 4, we relate prioritized circumscription with MBNF, the logic of minimal beliefs and negation as failure [12], and with AE-logic (autoepistemic logic) [17]. We conclude in Section 5. For simplicity, throughout the paper we consider only first-order logic programs and theories without function symbols. Due to space limit, most of the proofs are omitted which can be found in the full version of the paper.

2 General Disjunctive Programs and Prioritized Circumscription

2.1 General Disjunctive Programs

A general disjunctive logic program (GDP) π considered in this paper is a collection of rules of the following form:

$$A_1| \cdots |A_l|notA_{l+1}| \cdots |notA_k \leftarrow B_1, \cdots, B_m, notB_{m+1}, \cdots, notB_n. \quad (1)$$

Here each of the A_i's and the B_j's is an atom, $k \geq l \geq 0$, $n \geq m \geq 0$, "not" denotes *negation as failure*. By convention, we call the disjunction of the A_i's (and the $notA_i$'s) on the left hand side of the arrow the *head* of the rule, whereas the conjunction on the right hand side the *body* of the rule. Note that rules of the above form are more general than the ordinary disjunctive logic programs in that we allow negation as failure (the $notA_j$'s) to appear in the head of a rule. This increases the expressive power of logic programs for representing commonsense knowledge, as [2] showed. If a program rule (1) above contains variables in its predicates, the rule is effectively an abbreviation of all ground rules obtained from (1) by replacing the variables with the constants occurring in π. Note that for each rule of the form (1), there is a corresponding (universally quantified) clause in first-order logic which is of the form

$$A_1 \vee \cdots \vee A_l \vee \neg A_{l+1} \vee \cdots \vee \neg A_k \vee \neg B_1 \vee \cdots \vee \neg B_m \vee B_{m+1} \vee \cdots \vee B_n. \quad (2)$$

An interpretation I of a program π is a set of ground atoms from the *Herbrand Base* of π. We say that I satisfies a program rule of the form (1) if I satisfies every ground instance of (1). The satisfaction of a ground rule (1) by I means that I satisfies the corresponding ground clause (2), i.e., either $\{A_1, \cdots, A_l, B_{m+1}, \cdots, B_n\} \cap I \neq \emptyset$ or $\{A_{l+1}, \cdots, A_k, B_1, \cdots, B_m\} \cap I = \emptyset$.

The stable model semantics of a GDP is defined in two steps. Let I be an interpretation and let π be a program without any occurrence of negation as failure. We say that I is a stable model of π if I is a *minimal* interpretation satisfying π. Now let π be any GDP. We define the *reduct* of π with respect to I, denoted as π^I, as follows. A ground rule of the form $A_1 | \cdots | A_l \leftarrow B_1, \cdots, B_m$ belongs to π^I if and only if there is a ground rule of the form (1) in π such that $\{A_{l+1}, \cdots, A_k\} \subseteq I$ and $\{B_{m+1}, \cdots, B_n\} \cap I = \emptyset$. I is a stable model of π if and only if I is a stable model of π^I.

The class of general disjunctive programs outlined above is a proper subset of the class of General Extended Disjunctive Programs (GEDP) which was initially proposed by Lifschitz and Woo [14] as a subset of the MBNF logic, and further developed and investigated by Inoue and Sakama. The class of GEDP programs is an extension of the class of EDP programs with classical negations proposed by Gelfond and Lifschitz [5], in that GEDP allows negation as failure in the head of program rules. In a series of studies [7, 2, 3], Inoue and Sakama have investigated the GEDP's, their expressive power as knowledge representation tools, their relationships with other non-monotonic logics, and the query-answering procedures for GEDP's. These studies show that GEDP's are more expressive than the ordinary logic programs in that they can represent knowledge in situations where the notion of minimality of models is too strong. A distinctive feature of the GEDP's is that it can have non-minimal models. The class of GDP's also has this characteristics.

2.2 Prioritized Circumscription

Circumscription [16] is a powerful non-monotonic reasoning formalism, which is based on the notion of minimal models. Let Δ be a first-order theory and let P, Z be disjoint subsets of the predicates occurring in Δ. Let Q be the set of the rest of the predicates in Δ. The parallel circumscription $CIRC(\Delta; P; Z)$ is defined as a second-order theory

$$CIRC(\Delta;\ P;\ Z) = \Delta(P, Z) \wedge \forall P', Z'[(\Delta(P', Z') \wedge P' \to P) \to (P' = P)]$$

Here P', Z' are tuples of predicates which are of the same arity as that of the predicates in P and Z, respectively, $P' \to P$ is the abbreviation of the conjunction $\forall x \bigwedge_j [P_j(x) \to P_j'(x)]$, where $P_j \in P$ and $P_j' \in P'$. Semantically, the models M of $CIRC(\Delta; P; Z)$ are the so-called PZ_minimal (also denoted as (P, Z)_minimal) models, in that the extensions for the P predicates in M are *minimal* among the models of Δ which agrees with M on extensions for predicates in Q. We denote by M_P the extension of the P predicates in M, i.e., M_P is the set of ground atoms in M with predicates in P; similarly, M_Q is the extension of the Q predicates in M. The sets of predicates P and Z define a preference relation "$\leq_{PZ}$" among models of Δ: for two models M and N of Δ, we have $M \leq_{PZ} N$ if and only if $M_Q = N_Q$ and $M_P \subseteq N_P$. If $M \leq_{PZ} N$ but $N \not\leq_{PZ} M$, we say that M is strictly preferred to N, denoted as $M <_{PZ} N$. Thus the PZ_minimal models of Δ, which are all models of $CIRC(\Delta; P; Z)$, are all minimal elements under the preference relation $\leq_{PZ}$.

Prioritized circumscription is a generalization of parallel circumscription, which allows the specification of priorities in the minimization of predicates. In this case, the predicates in P are partitioned into disjoint sets $P_1, \cdots, P_t$, and the predicates in P_j will have higher priorities than those in P_k to be minimized for

$k > j$. Syntactically, the prioritized circumscription is defined as a conjunction of a number of parallel circumscriptions:

$CIRC(\Delta; P_1 > P_2 > \cdots > P_t; Z) =$
$CIRC(\Delta; P_1; \bigcup_{j>1} P_j \cup Z) \wedge CIRC(\Delta; P_2; \bigcup_{j>2} P_j \cup Z) \wedge \cdots \wedge CIRC(\Delta; P_t; Z)$

Semantically, a model M of Δ is a model of $CIRC(\Delta; P_1 > P_2 > \cdots > P_t; Z)$ if and only if M is $(P_1, P_2 \cup \cdots \cup P_t \cup Z)$_minimal, and $(P_2, P_3 \cup \cdots \cup P_t \cup Z)$_minimal, $\cdots$, and (P_t, Z)_minimal. Prioritized circumscription can characterize the perfect model semantics for stratified disjunctive and normal programs.

3 Embedding Prioritized Circumscription in Disjunctive Programs

In this section, we present the embedding of prioritized circumscription in GDP and show a one-to-one correspondence between the models of the circumscription and the stable models of the resulting program.

To facilitate the presentation, we need to introduce the following notations. Let Δ be a first-order clausal theory and let P, Q, Z respectively be the sets of predicates in Δ to be minimized, fixed and varied. Let $P = P_1 \cup P_2 \cup \cdots \cup P_t$ be the partition of P which defines the minimization priorities of the predicates in P. We define the collections of predicates Q_j, Z_j for $1 \leq j \leq t$ as follows. $Q_j = Q \cup \bigcup_{i<j} P_i$ and $Z_j = Z \cup \bigcup_{i>j} P_i$. We say that a clause C is a P^+Q clause if every literal occurring in C is from a predicate in $P \cup Q$, and the predicate in P occurs in C only positively. Similarly we define the notion of a $P_j{}^+Q_j$ clause. We denote by $P_j{}^+Q_j(\Delta)$ the collection of $P_j{}^+Q_j$ clauses C which satisfy the following two conditions:

1. $\Delta \vdash C$, i.e., C is in $Th(\Delta)$, the deductive closure of Δ.

2. C is a *minimal* clause in $Th(\Delta)$, i.e., if there is another clause C' in $Th(\Delta)$ which θ-subsumes C, then C θ-subsumes C' as well.

Now we are ready to define the embedding of prioritized circumscriptions in GDP.

Definition 1 Given a first-order function-free clausal theory Δ, the priorities $P_1 > P_2 > \cdots > P_t$, and the varied predicates Z, the GDP program $\pi = \pi(\Delta)$ corresponding to $CIRC(\Delta; P_1 > \cdots > P_t; Z)$ is defined to be

$\pi(\Delta) = \pi_{sft} \cup \pi_1 \cup \cdots \cup \pi_t \cup \pi_{qz}$,

where each of the programs is obtained as follows: First, for each clause

$$p_1 \vee \cdots \vee p_r \vee \neg p_{r+1} \vee \cdots \vee \neg p_m \vee q_1 \vee \cdots \vee q_s \vee$$
$$\neg q_{s+1} \vee \cdots \vee \neg q_n \vee z_1 \vee \cdots \vee z_u \vee \neg z_{u+1} \vee \cdots \vee \neg z_w \qquad (3)$$

in Δ, where $p_i \in P$, $q_j \in Q$ and $z_k \in Z$, π_{sft} contains the program rule

$$q_1 | \cdots | q_s | z_1 | \cdots | z_u \leftarrow q_{s+1}, \cdots, q_n, z_{u+1}, \cdots, z_w, p_{r+1}, \cdots, p_m, notp_1, \cdots, notp_r. \qquad (4)$$

Second, for each clause

$$p_1 \vee \cdots \vee p_r \vee q_1 \vee \cdots \vee q_s \vee \neg q_{s+1} \vee \neg q_n \qquad (5)$$

in $P_j^+ Q_j(\Delta)$, where $p_i \in P_j$ and $q_i \in Q_j$, $1 \leq j \leq t$, π_j contains a program rule

$$p_1| \cdots |p_r|q_1| \cdots |q_s \leftarrow q_{s+1}, \cdots, q_n. \qquad (6)$$

Finally, for each predicate $q \in Q$ and $z \in Z$, the program π_{qz} contains the program rules

$$q|notq \leftarrow \quad and \quad z|notz \leftarrow . \qquad (7)$$

The next few lemmas set the stage for proving the correctness of our embedding.

Lemma 1 ((Lemma 3.5 in [2].) Let Δ be a first-order clausal theory and let M be a model of Δ. M is PZ_minimal if and only if $M_P \cup M_Q$ is a P_minimal model of $P^+Q(\Delta)$.

Corollary 1 Let $CIRC(\Delta; P_1 > P_2 > \cdots > P_t; Z)$ be a prioritized circumscription of Δ. Let M be a model of Δ. Then M is (P_j, Z_j)_minimal if and only if $M_{P_j} \cup M_{Q_j}$ is a P_j_minimal model of $P_j^+ Q_j(\Delta)$.

Let Δ be a first-order, function-free clausal theory and let P, Z be two disjoint set of predicates occurring in Δ. Let M be a model of Δ. We define, as in [2], the related theory Δ^{M_P} as follows: A ground clause

$$\neg p_{r+1} \vee \cdots \vee \neg p_m \vee q_1 \vee \cdots \vee q_s \vee \neg q_{s+1} \vee \cdots \vee \neg q_n \vee z_1 \vee \cdots \vee z_u \vee \neg z_{u+1} \vee \cdots \vee \neg z_w \qquad (8)$$

belongs to Δ^{M_P} if and only if the related clause (3) is in Δ and $\{p_1, \cdots, p_r\} \cap M_P = \emptyset$.

Lemma 2 ((Lemma 3.6 in [2].) Let M be a PZ_minimal model of Δ. Then $M_Q \cup M_Z$ is a P_minimal model of Δ^{M_P}.

Now we are ready to present the main result of the paper.

Theorem 1 Let $CIRC(\Delta; P_1 > P_2 > \cdots > P_t; Z)$ be a prioritized circumscription of Δ. Let π be the associated GDP program obtained from Δ by the translation specified in Definition (1). Let M be an interpretation. M is a model of $CIRC(\Delta; P_1 > P_2 > \cdots > P_t; Z)$ if and only if M is a stable model of π.

Proof Let M be a model of $CIRC(\Delta; P_1 > P_2 > \cdots > P_t; Z)$. The program π^M can be written as

$$\pi^M = \pi_{sft}^{M_P} \cup \pi_1 \cup \cdots \cup \pi_t \cup \pi_{qz}^{M_Q \cup M_Z}$$

Further simplifying, we get

$$\pi^M = \pi_{sft}^{M_P} \cup \pi_1 \cup \cdots \cup \pi_t \cup M_Q \cup M_Z.$$

Clearly, M satisfies each π_j for $1 \leq j \leq t$ and $M_Q \cup M_Z$. Also, according to Lemma 2, $M_Q \cup M_Z$ is a P_minimal model of Δ^{M_P} and hence $M_Q \cup M_Z$ satisfies $\pi_{sft}^{M_P}$ as well. Thus M satisfies π^M. The results in Lemma 1 and Corollary 1 show that $M_P \cup M_Q$ is a minimal set satisfying $\pi_1 \cup \pi_2 \cup \cdots \cup \pi_t \cup M_Q$. Thus M is a minimal set of ground atoms satisfying π^M. This shows that M is a stable model of the program π.

Now assume that M is a stable model of the program π. We show that M is a model of the prioritized circumscription. First we show that M is a model of Δ. Clearly M satisfies the theory Δ^{M_P} and thus it satisfies the associated clause (3) in Δ. For each clause C in Δ which does not have associated clause (8) in Δ^{M_P}, M_P contains a ground atom p_j which occurs positively in C. Thus, M is a model of Δ. Since $M_P \cup M_Q$ is a minimal set satisfying $\pi_1 \cup \pi_2 \cup \cdots \cup \pi_t \cup M_Q$, it is easy to see from the syntactical form of the rules in π_j, $1 \leq j \leq t$, that $M_{P_j} \cup M_{Q_j}$ is a P_j-minimal set satisfying π_j. It follows that $M_{P_j} \cup M_{Q_j}$ is a P_j-minimal model of $P_j^+ Q_j(\Delta)$ for $1 \leq j \leq t$. By Corollary 1, M is (P_j, Z_j)-minimal for $1 \leq j \leq t$, and thus M is a model of the prioritized circumscription. $\quad\Box$

4 Relating Prioritized Circumscription with MBNF Logic and AE Logic

The class of general disjunctive programs (GDP) is a sub-class of the class of general extended disjunctive programs (GEDP), which can be viewed as the "logic programming" part of the MBNF logic. The MBNF logic [12] is a very powerful and expressive modal logic, which involves two modal operators "**B**" (for minimal belief) and "*not*" (for negation as failure). Lifschitz has shown that MBNF can be used as a general logical framework for non-monotonic reasoning in the sense that various non-monotonic formalisms such as default logic, circumscription, and several forms of logic programming can be embedded in MBNF. For more details about MBNF logic, see [12].

The existing works that embed circumscription in MBNF consider only parallel circumscription. Our method of embedding prioritized circumscription in GDP will readily lead to the embedding of prioritized circumscription in MBNF. The key connection is that every GEDP π can be mapped to an MBNF theory $\sigma(\pi)$, and there is a one-to-one correspondence between the answer sets (stable models) of π and the MBNF models of $\sigma(\pi)$.

The notion of an answer set for a general extended disjunctive program π is defined in a way similar to the notion of stable model for a GDP, except that an answer set may contain literals which are (classical) negations of ground atoms. This is natural, considering that a GEDP π may include classical negation in any program rules: A GEDP π is a collection of rules of the form

$$L_1| \cdots |L_r|notL_{r+1}| \cdots |notL_m \leftarrow L_{m+1}, \cdots, L_s, notL_{s+1}, \cdots, notL_n. \quad (9)$$

Given a GEDP π, the related MBNF theory $\sigma(\pi)$ is obtained by mapping each rule of the form (9) to an MBNF clause of the form

$$\mathbf{B}L_1 \vee \cdots \vee \mathbf{B}L_r \vee notL_{r+1} \vee \cdots \vee notL_m \vee$$
$$\neg\mathbf{B}L_{m+1} \vee \cdots \vee \neg\mathbf{B}L_s \vee \neg notL_{s+1} \vee \cdots \vee \neg notL_n. \quad (10)$$

For an answer set M of a GEDP π, we use $Mod(M)$ to denote the set of interpretations $\{I: I \models L_j$ for each $L_j \in M\}$. Note that when π is a GDP, an answer set (stable model) M of π is a set of ground atoms, and thus $Mod(M)$ in this case is the set of all interpretations which agree with M on truth value assignment for atoms in M. For example, if $M = \{p, q\}$ and the language of the program π has two other ground atoms r and s, then $Mod(M) = \{\{p, q\}, \{p, q, r\}, \{p, q, s\}, \{p, q, r, s\}\}$. Noticing that the models of an MBNF theory are sets of interpretations, the following lemma is straightforward [14].

Lemma 3 Let π be a GEDP and $\sigma(\pi)$ be its associated MBNF theory. Then a set of interpretations S is an MBNF model of $\sigma(\pi)$ if and only if $S = Mod(M)$ for some answer set M of π.

Theorem 2 Let Δ be a first-order clausal theory and let $CIRC(\Delta; P_1 > P_2 > \cdots > P_t; Z)$ be a prioritized circumscription of Δ, and $\pi(\Delta)$ be the GDP program associated with the prioritized circumscription. let $\sigma(\pi(\Delta))$ be the MBNF theory associated with $\pi(\Delta)$. Then a set S of interpretations is an MBNF model of $\sigma(\pi(\Delta))$ if and only if $S = Mod(M)$ for some model M of $CIRC(\Delta; P_1 > P_2 > \cdots > P_t; Z)$.

The autoepistemic logic (AE logic) [17] is another important non-monotonic modal logic (with one modal operator "**B**"), which has been related to many other non-monotonic formalisms. The connection between MBNF and AE Logic has been made in [1], which in turn gives rise to results that embed GEDP into AE logic. The same embedding of GEDP into AE logic is also obtained in [13, 15]. From the result of this paper, it is straightforward to relate the prioritized circumscription $CIRC(\Delta; P_1 > P_2 > \cdots > P_t; Z)$ with AE logic. For a GEDP π, we define the related AE logic theory $AE(\pi)$ as a collection of AE formulas obtained by mapping each program rule of the form (9) to the formula

$$(L_1 \wedge \mathbf{B}L_1) \vee \cdots \vee (L_r \wedge \mathbf{B}L_r) \vee notL_{r+1} \vee \cdots \vee notL_m \vee$$
$$\neg(L_{m+1} \wedge \mathbf{B}L_{m+1}) \vee \cdots \vee \neg(L_s \wedge \mathbf{B}L_s) \vee \neg notL_{s+1} \vee \cdots \vee \neg notL_n. \quad (11)$$

In AE logic, formulas may contain the modal operator "**B**". Modal-free formulas are called *objective*. The notion of *stable expansions* plays an important semantic role. An AE theory Δ is said to entail a formula ϕ if $\mathbf{B}\phi$ is in every stable expansion of Δ. A set of formulas Γ is a stable expansion of Δ if Γ satisfies the fixed point equation

$$\Gamma = Th(\Delta \cup \{\mathbf{B}\phi : \phi \in \Gamma\} \cup \{\neg\mathbf{B}\psi : \psi \notin \Gamma\}) \quad (12)$$

Associated with each stable expansion Γ of Δ, we define a set of interpretations $S_\Gamma = \{I: I \models \phi$ for any objective $\phi \in \Gamma\}$. A set of interpretations S is called an AE model of Δ if $S = S_\Gamma$ for a stable expansion Γ of Δ. The following theorem is now straightforward.

Theorem 3 Let Δ be a first-order clausal theory and let $CIRC(\Delta; P_1 > P_2 > \cdots > P_t; Z)$ be a prioritized circumscription of Δ, and $\pi(\Delta)$ be the GDP program associated with the prioritized circumscription. Let $AE(\pi(\Delta))$ be the AE logic theory associated with $\pi(\Delta)$. Then a set S of interpretations is an AE model of $AE(\pi(\Delta))$ if and only if $S = Mod(M)$ for some model M of $CIRC(\Delta; P_1 > P_2 > \cdots > P_t; Z)$.

5 Conclusions

In this paper, we present an embedding of prioritized circumscription into general disjunctive logic programs with negation as failure in the head. Our embedding is direct in the sense that there is no need to augment the stable model semantics for GDP with priorities in order to capture prioritized circumscription. This further asserts the expressive power of GDP with negation as failure in the head and supports using GDP as knowledge representation tools for Artificial Intelligence. The results of this paper also lead to embeddings of prioritized circumscription into the MBNF logic and AE logic.

References

[1] J. Chen, Minimal Knowledge + Negation as Failure = Only Knowing (sometimes). *Proceedings of the 2nd International Workshop on Logic Programming and Non-monotonic Reasoning*, June 1993, pp. 132-150.

[2] C. Sakama, K. Inoue, Embedding Circumscriptive Theories in General Disjunctive Programs, *Proceedings of the 3rd International Workshop on Logic Programming and Non-monotonic Reasoning*, June 1995, pp. 344-357.

[3] C. Sakama, K. Inoue, Representing Priorities in Logic Programs, *Proceedings of the 1996 Joint International Conference and Symposium on Logic Programming*, pp. 82-96.

[4] M. Gelfond and V. Lifschitz, Compiling Circumscriptive Theories in Logic Programs, *Proceedings of 2nd International Workshop on Nonmonotonic Reasoning*, 1988, LNAI 346, pp. 74-99.

[5] M. Gelfond and V. Lifschitz, Classical Negation in Logic Programs and Disjunctive Databases. *New Generation Computing*, **9** (1991), pp. 365-385.

[6] M. Gelfond, H. Przymusinska, and T. Przymusinski, On the Relationship between Circumscription and Negation as Failure, *Artificial Intelligence*, **38** (1989), pp. 75-94.

[7] K. Inoue, C. Sakama, On Positive Occurrences of Negation as Failure, *Proceedings of KR'94*, pp. 293-304.

[8] S. Kundu and J. Chen, A New Class of Theories for Which Circumscription Can Be Obtained via The Predicate Completion. *Journal of Experimental and Theoretical AI*, **8** (1996), pp. 191-205.

[9] V. Lifschitz, Closed World Databases and Circumscription, *Artificial Intelligence*, **27** (1985), pp. 229-235.

[10] V. Lifschitz, Computing Circumscription, *Proceedings of IJCAI-85*, pp. 121-127.

[11] V. Lifschitz, On the Declarative Semantics of Logic Programs with Negation, In *Foundations of Deductive Databases and Logic Programming* (J. Minker ed.), Morgan Kaufmann, 1988, pp. 177-192.

[12] V. Lifschitz, Minimal Belief and Negation As Failure. *Artificial Intelligence*, **70** (1-2), 1994, pp. 53-72.

[13] V. Lifschitz, G. Schwarz, Extended Logic Programs as Autoepistemic Theories, *Proceedings of the 2nd International Workshop on Logic Programming and Non-monotonic Reasoning*, June 1993, pp. 101-114.

[14] V. Lifschitz, T. Woo, Answer Sets in General Nonmonotonic Reasoning (preliminary report), *Proceedings of KR'92*, pp. 603-614.

[15] W. Marek and M. Truszczynski, Reflexive Autoepistemic Logic and Logic Programming, *Proceedings of the 2nd International Workshop on Logic Programming and Non-monotonic Reasoning*, June 1993, pp. 115-131.

[16] J. McCarthy, Circumscription - A Form of Non-monotonic Reasoning, *Artificial Intelligence* **13** (1-2), 1980, pp. 27-39.

[17] R. Moore, Semantical Considerations on Nonmonotonic Logic, *Artificial Intelligence*, **25** (1), 1985, pp. 75-94.

[18] T. Przymusinski, On the Declarative Semantics of Deductive Databases and Logic Programs, In *Foundations of Deductive Databases and Logic Programming* (J. Minker ed.), Morgan Kaufmann, 1988, pp. 193-216.

[19] T. Przymusinski, An Algorithm to Compute Circumscription, *Artificial Intelligence*, **38** (1989), pp. 49-73.

[20] R. Reiter, A Logic for Default Reasoning, *Artificial Intelligence*, **13** (1-2), 1980, pp. 81-132.

[21] R. Reiter, Circumscription Implies Predicate Completion (sometimes), *Proceedings of AAAI'82*, pp. 418-420.

Extending Temporal Logic for Capturing Evolving Behaviour

Stefan Conrad & Gunter Saake

Universität Magdeburg, FIN-ITI
Postfach 4120, D-39016 Magdeburg, Germany
{conrad|saake}@iti.cs.uni-magdeburg.de

Abstract. The known approaches to object specification based on first-order temporal logic fail in capturing the often occurring need to change the dynamic behaviour of a system during lifetime of that system. Usually all possible behaviours have to be described in advance, i.e. at specification time. Therefore, we here present an extension going beyond first-order temporal logic. Now, it becomes possible to specify ways of dynamically changing the behaviour of a system during lifetime. This can be done by giving each object an additional (non-first-order) attribute. The value of this attribute contains a set of first-order formulas being the currently valid behaviour specification. In addition, this approach can easily be extended for introducing a way of default reasoning.

1 Motivation

In the area of information systems, temporal logic is a widely accepted means to specify dynamic behaviour of objects. This is due to the fact that information systems (as a generalization of database systems) are state-based systems for which the state-based approach of temporal logic is obviously appropriate.

Currently, the (temporal) specification of information systems has become a popular research area based on a clean and well-understood theory (cf. e.g. [KM89, FM91]). Several specification languages like ALBERT [DDP93], LCM [FW93], OBLOG [SSE87], and TROLL [JSHS96] have been developed for supporting the specification of objects and their dynamic behaviour based on temporal or dynamic logics.

Of course there are other formal approaches to specifying dynamic behaviour of objects. For instance, conditional term rewriting is another way of describing object behaviour. The specification language Maude is based on a conditional term rewriting semantics [Mes93].

However, all approaches to specifying information systems assume that the dynamic behaviour of the system and its parts is totally known at specification time. In addition, once specified the behaviour is fixed for the entire life (or run) time of the information system. This restriction seems not to be adequate for a large number of typical information system applications. Because of the long life (or run) time of information systems changes of the dynamic behaviour are often required within the lifetime of a system.

This research has been supported in part by the European Commission through Esprit ModelAge (No. 8319), ASPIRE (No. 22704) and FIREworks (No. 23531).

Typical examples for such changes of the dynamic behaviour are given in information systems for libraries and banks: For a library it may happen that the rules for borrowing and returning books change in order to avoid too much administrative work in writing reminders. Due to changes of laws (or bank rules) it could become necessary to change the computation of yearly interests or to restrict the evolution of an account in some way. These changes are modifications of axioms describing the dynamic behaviour of the system. In consequence, we have to find a framework for describing evolving specifications where we can specify the evolution of first-order dynamic behaviour specifications.

In this paper we continue the work started in [SSS95] where a first, very restricted form of evolving temporal specification was proposed. The extensions we are considering form a stable basis for future work in which we aim at integrating additional aspects like normative specification (based on deontic logic). In [SCT95] we sketch a vision of a future specification language incorporating several specification concepts going beyond current object-oriented specification formalisms. The work presented here is a major step into that direction. This is due to the fact that we leave the level of first-order temporal logic by allowing the manipulation of first-order specification axioms within the specification. Thereby, we introduce some kind of reasoning capabilities into the objects.

The approach we present here do not deal with the question who is allowed to change the behaviour of objects. Of course, this is an important question which must be solved for a specification framework which is intended to be used in practice.

The remainder of this paper is organized as follows: We start with sketching the current state of object specification based on temporal logic by presenting a typical example specification for information systems and by giving a basic definition of the temporal logic we use. In Sect. 3 we extend our example in a way which cannot be captured by first-order temporal logic. In order to get a grasp of the evolving dynamic behaviour of objects on the specification level we introduce an extension of temporal logic which we call *Evolving Temporal Logic* (Sect. 4). Finally, we conclude by discussing several problems left for future work.

2 Current State of Object Specification

In this section we first present the current state of object specification for information systems by giving an example specification using an object specification language. Then, we show the corresponding description in temporal logic.

2.1 Specifying Objects in Information Systems

Object specification languages based on a temporal logic framework for specifying the dynamic behaviour of objects in an information system offer a number of modelling concepts (cf. [JSHS96]): First, there are structural concepts for modelling different kinds of relationships between objects (like is-a relationships, inheritance, aggregation, etc.). Second, there is the concept of attributes for giving an internal structure to objects. Attributes have values which determine the state of an object. The third kind of modelling concepts is used for describing the temporal evolution of objects by prescribing allowed life cycles. The state of an object can only be changed by the occurrence of local events. Enabling conditions for events, general temporal constraints as well as life cycle descriptions can be used for restricting the temporal evolution of objects.

```
object class Bank
 identification BankID: (Name, No).
 attributes      Name: string.
                 No:    nat         constant
                                    restricted No≥100000 and No≤999999.
 components  Acct: Account set.
 events          Open(BankName:string, BankNo:nat)
                      birth
                      changing  Name := BankName,
                                No := BankNo.
                 OpenNewAccount(Holder:|Customer|, AcctNo:nat)
                      calling     Account(AcctNo).Open(AcctNo, Holder)
                      changing  Acct := insert(Acct, Account(AcctNo)).
                 Transfer(AcctNo1:nat, AcctNo2:nat, M:money)
                      enabled    in(Account(AcctNo1), Acct) and
                                 in(Account(AcctNo2), Acct) and M>0.00
                      calling    Account(AcctNo1).Withdrawal(M),
                                 Account(AcctNo2).Deposit(M).
end object class Bank
```

Figure 1: A specification of bank objects.

Example. In Fig. 1 and 2 object specifications of bank objects and account objects using concepts of the specification language TROLL are depicted. A bank has attributes Name and No. The latter is marked as constant, thus it must not change its value during lifetime of the object. Furthermore, this attribute is restricted to take only values out of a given range. A bank object has a set of account objects as components. There are several events which may happen to a bank object: The Open event is the birth event for a bank object giving values to the attributes Name and No. The OpenNewAccount event calls the birth event for a new account object and inserts this account object into the component set of the bank object. The Transfer event transfers a given amount of money from one account object to another one, provided both account objects are in the component set Acct of the bank object and the requested amount is positive. In addition, the called Withdrawal event for the first account as well as the called Deposit event for the second account object must currently be enabled in order to execute the transfer.

Account objects have attributes No, Holder, Balance, and Limit. Similar to bank objects, the attribute No is marked as constant and is required to take only values out of the given range. The attribute Holder refers to the customer object representing the owner of the account. The current balance of the account is given in the attribute `Balance`. The attribute `Limit` is used for allowing only a restricted overdrawing. For `Balance` and `Limit` initial values are specified. There are four kinds of events which may occur in account objects. The birth event `Open` brings the object into life and sets the attributes `Bank`, `No`, and `Holder` to the value given by the event parameters. An account can be closed by an occurrence of the event `Close`. Furthermore, we can withdraw and deposit money. An occurrence of the event `Withdrawal` is only enabled when then `Balance` will not fall below the current `Limit`. In addition we require the amount of money to be positive for both the events `Withdrawal` and `Deposit`.

object class Account
  identification AccountID: (No) .
  attributes No: nat   **constant**
                             restricted $No \geq 100000$ **and** $No \leq 999999$.
          Holder: |Customer| .
          Balance: money   **initialized** 0.00 .
          Limit: money   **initialized** 0.00
                             restricted Limit<=0.00 .
  events   Open(BID:|Bank|, AcctNo:nat, AcctHolder:|Customer|)
                  birth
                  changing Bank := BID,
                               No := AcctNo,
                               Holder := AcctHolder .
          Withdrawal(W:money)
                  enabled $W \geq 0.00$ **and** Balance $- W \geq$ Limit
                  changing Balance := Balance $- W$.
          Deposit(D:money)
                  enabled $D \geq 0.00$
                  changing Balance := Balance $+ D$.
          Close   **death**
end object class Account

Figure 2: A specification of account objects.

In this example there is no explicit use of temporal logic formulas. Nevertheless, it is possible to state temporal constraints, for example: If the balance of an account once becomes greater than 1,000.00, then it must never fall below 0.00 from that moment.

2.2 Translation into Temporal Logic

Here, we briefly present the translation of object specifications into temporal logic. We use a first-order, discrete, future-directed linear temporal logic which can be considered as a slightly modified version of the *Object Specification Logic (OSL)* which is presented in full detail in [SSC95].
We start with some basic definitions of temporal logic:

- We assume a collection of given propositions:e.g., p, q, r, ...

- Elementary propositions are formulas as well. In addition we may build formulas using the usual boolean operator: provided f and g are formulas then $\neg f$ and $f \wedge g$ are also formulas. Other boolean operator like $\vee$, $\rightarrow$, $\leftrightarrow$, ... are defined as abbreviation in the usual way.
- We may build formulas using the future-directed temporal operator $\Box$ (always) and $\bigcirc$ (next) in the following way: if f is a formula, then $\Box f$ and $\bigcirc f$ are formulas, too. The operator $\Diamond$ (eventually) can be introduced as abbreviation: $\Diamond f \equiv \neg \Box \neg f$.
- By introducing variables and quantifiers we obtain a first-order variant of linear temporal logic: provided x is a variable and f a formula, then $\forall x : f$ and $\exists x : f$ are formulas.

For our purposes we need several different kinds of elementary propositions:

1. $o.\text{Attr} = v$ expresses that the attribute Attr of an object o has the value v (we have adopted this form from the specification language used for our example; instead we could also take a predicate expression like $\text{Attr}(o, v)$).
2. $o.\nabla e$ stands for the occurrence of event e in object o.
3. $o. \triangleright e$ represents that event e is enabled for object o.

For the rest of this paper we need at least an intuition about the semantics of temporal logic formulas:

- A life cycle λ is an infinite sequence of states: $\lambda = \langle s_0, s_1, s_2, \ldots \rangle$. We define λ^i as the life cycle which is obtained by removing the first i states from λ, i.e. $\lambda^i = \langle s_i, s_{i+1}, s_{i+2}, \ldots \rangle$. The states in a life cycle are assumed to be mappings assigning a truth value to each elementary proposition.
- The satisfaction of a formula f by a life cycle λ (written $\lambda \models f$) is defined as follows:

$\lambda \models p$ for an elementary proposition p if p is true in state s_0 of λ.

$\lambda \models \neg f$ if not $\lambda \models f$.

$\lambda \models f \wedge g$ if $\lambda \models f$ and $\lambda \models g$.

$\lambda \models \Box f$ if for all $i \geq 0 : \lambda^i \models f$.

$\lambda \models \bigcirc f$ if $\lambda^1 \models f$.

For brevity we omit the treatment of variables. This can be done in the usual straightforward way. All variables which are not explicitly bound by a quantifier are assumed to be universally quantified. Fully-fledged definitions of syntax and semantics of first-order order-sorted temporal logics for object specification can be found for instance in [SSC95] or [Con96].

Example. Here, we only present some temporal logic formulas representing properties of the objects described in Fig. 1 and 2. We start with the effect an event occurrence has on the attributes. For instance the effect of Open events for account objects is represented by the following temporal logic formula:

$$\Box(\ a.\nabla \text{Open}(B, N, H) \rightarrow \bigcirc(a.\text{Bank} = B \wedge a.\text{No} = N \wedge a.\text{Holder} = H)\ )$$

Due to the fact that Open is a birth event it may only occur once in the life of an object. This property being inherent to the object model of the specification language TROLL is expressed by:

$$\Box(\ a.\nabla \text{Open}(B, N, H) \rightarrow \bigcirc \Box \neg (\exists B', N', H' : a.\nabla \text{Open}(B', N', H'))\ )$$

The enabling condition for `Transfer` events in bank objects can be put into a simple formula as follows:

$$\Box(\ b.\,\triangleright \mathrm{Transfer}(A_1, A_2, M) \rightarrow (\ \mathrm{Account}(A_1) \in \mathrm{Acct} \land$$
$$\mathrm{Account}(A_2) \in \mathrm{Acct} \land M > 0.00\ )\ )$$

Then, we can use a general axiom scheme for describing the requirement that only enabled events may occur (for each object o and arbitrary event e):

$$\Box(\ o.\nabla e \rightarrow o.\,\triangleright e\ )$$

Event calling as it is specified for the `Transfer` events in bank objects can be expressed by temporal logic formulas as follows:

$$\Box(\ b.\nabla \mathrm{Transfer}(A_1, A_2, M) \rightarrow (\ \mathrm{Account}(A_1).\nabla \mathrm{Withdrawal}(M) \land$$
$$\mathrm{Account}(A_2).\nabla \mathrm{Deposit}(M)\qquad)\ )$$

In this way all parts of the dynamic behaviour specification can be translated into temporal logic.

3 Going Beyond First-Order Temporal Specification

As already motivated in the introduction, the dynamic behaviour can often not totally specified in advance. Usual first-order temporal specification is too restrictive because all possible behaviours have to be fixed at specification time. For systems which run for a long time, e.g. information systems, this cannot be adequate. In fact, we have to face the often occurring situation that during the lifetime of a system the dynamic behaviour must be changed to a certain degree. For instance, a new law could require a change in the managing of bank accounts by introducing a new tax. Such changes of the dynamic behaviour cannot always be foreseen, so that they cannot be respected in advance at specification time.
Because this is an unsatisfactory situation, there is need for some specification mechanism allowing a later change of the dynamic behaviour. In order to realize this, we have to go beyond first-order temporal logic. The approach we present here is based on the introduction of a special attribute having specification axioms as values. The current value of this attribute denotes the currently valid, additional behaviour specification. Thereby, the behaviour specified in advance can be restricted during lifetime of the object.

Example: In order to demonstrate our intuition of higher-order specification we have extended the specifications of bank and account objects (see Fig. 3 and 4). In these descriptions we omit the usual first-order part which we have already seen before (Fig. 1 and 2).
Here, we explicitly introduce a special attribute `Axioms` which has sets of first-order temporal logic formulas as possible values. The value of this attribute may be changed during the lifetime of an object.
In the extended specification for bank objects we allow the manipulation of this special attribute through two additional events (called **mutators**): `AddAxioms` and `ResetAxioms`. `AddAxioms` has a first-order temporal logic formula as parameter. In case `AddAxioms` occurs its parameter value is added to the current

object class Bank
  ...
  axiom attributes
        Axioms **initialized** { };
  mutators   AddAxioms(P:Formula);
             ResetAxioms;
  dynamic specification
        AddAxioms(P)
             changing Axioms := Axioms ∪{ P };
        ResetAxioms
             changing Axioms := { };
end object class Bank;

Figure 3: Extended specification for bank objects.

value of the attribute Axioms. Thus, we can more and more restrict the possible dynamic behaviour of a bank object by simply adding additional formulas to the attribute Axioms. In this way it is now possible to modify the dynamic behaviour of a bank object in accordance to the requirements of a new law, a new banking rule, etc.

object class Account
  identification
  attributes ...
  events   ...
  axiom attributes
        Axioms **initialized** { };
  mutators Warnings;
          NoWarnings;
  dynamic specification
        Warnings
             changing Axioms := {
                  ∇Withdrawal(W) $\wedge$ Balance$-$W$<$0.00
                  $\rightarrow$ Supervisor.∇Warning(No,Balance$-$W)
                 };
        NoWarnings
             changing Axioms := { };
end object class Account;

Figure 4: Modified specification for account objects.

In contrast to the extended specification for bank objects, we only allow a quite restricted form of manipulating the dynamic behaviour of account objects. In Fig. 4 we specify two mutator events Warnings and NoWarnings. After an occurrence of the mutator event **Warnings** the value of the special attribute **Axioms** includes exactly one formula. This formula says that, in case a **Withdrawal** event occurs in this account object and the balance of this account will be negative after this withdrawal, a warning message has to be sent to an object called **Supervisor** (by calling a **Warning** event of the **Supervisor** object). An occurrence of the mutator event **NoWarnings** turns off this warning mechanism by simply resetting the attribute **Axioms** to its initial value (which is an empty set of formulas). In this way we can easily switch on and off the validity of a certain specification axiom. [1]

In our example we have presented a very general form of manipulating the dynamic behaviour (for bank objects) and a very restrictive way (for account objects). Of course, there are a lot of other more or less restrictive forms in between because our specification framework can be used in a quite flexible way. As it is already possible for usual events we may impose enabling conditions to mutator events. Thereby, an arbitrary manipulation of the behaviour specification can be prevented. This seems to be reasonable because otherwise nearly everything might happen due to nonsensical changes of the behaviour specification.

A first, more restricted approach to evolving behaviour specification is given in [SSS95] where only the switching between a number of pre-given behaviour specifications is considered. Our approach sketched here is much more liberal by allowing a more fine-grained manipulation of behaviour specifications. In the next section we briefly sketch an extended temporal logic as a semantical basis.

4 Evolving Temporal Logic

In this section we present the basic ideas for formalizing the extension of temporal logic we need for capturing the properties sketched in the previous section. We will call this extension *Evolving Temporal Logic* (ETL). Afterwards, we show how the example given in the previous section is formulated in ETL.

4.1 Basic Ideas for Formalization

The formalization of ETL is based on the basic definition of temporal logic given in Sect. 2. Here, we present a rather straightforward extension of that temporal logic.

The starting point for this extension is the treatment of the special attribute having sets of first-order formulas as values. In order to represent this special property we introduce a corresponding predicate $\mathcal{V}$ into our logic. This predicate is used to express the current validity of the dynamic behaviour axioms. For simplicity, we restrict our consideration to one special predicate over first-order temporal formulas.[2]

---

[1] Obviously, we can achieve the same behaviour of account objects with a purely first-order object specification by introducing an attribute as a switch and by using its value for invoking the warning mechanism.

[2] For dealing with several objects having different sets of currently valid behaviour axioms, we could extend this view to several predicates or to introduce an additional parameter to the predicate for referring to different objects.

This predicate is used to express the state-dependent validity of first-order formulas: $\mathcal{V}(\varphi)$ holds in a state (at an instant of time) means that the specification φ is valid w.r.t. that state.

In a more formal way we can express this as follows: if $\mathcal{V}(\varphi)$ holds for a (linear) life cycle λ (i.e., $\lambda \models \mathcal{V}(\varphi)$) then φ holds for λ as well:

$$\lambda \models \mathcal{V}(\varphi) \quad \textbf{implies} \quad \lambda \models \varphi$$

In order to avoid severe problems especially caused by substitution we assume $\mathcal{V}$ to work only on syntactic representations of first-order temporal formulas instead of the formulas themselves. Here, we use the notation $\mathcal{V}(\varphi)$ only for convinience. For a correct formal treatment we have to define an abstract data type `Formula` for first-order temporal formulas as possible parameter values for $\mathcal{V}$. In addition a function translating values of this abstract data type into corresponding formulas is needed. Then, we are able to strictly separate the usual first-order level from the higher-order part.

With regard to the reflection of $\mathcal{V}(\varphi)$ on the first-order level, we may establish the following axiom for ETL: $\mathcal{V}(\varphi) \rightarrow \varphi$.

By the predicate $\mathcal{V}$ we simulate the finite set of behaviour axioms which are currently valid. Thus $\mathcal{V}(\varphi)$ can be read as "φ is in the set of currently valid behaviour axioms". Due to $\mathcal{V}(\varphi) \rightarrow \varphi$, it is sufficient that $\mathcal{V}$ holds only for a finite set of specification axioms because the theory induced by these axioms is generated on the first-order level in the usual way.

Please note that $\mathcal{V}(\varphi)$ can be considered as an elementary proposition in ETL. Therefore, we may assume that for each state s_i in a life cycle λ there is a truth assigning function denoting the validity of $\mathcal{V}(\varphi)$ for each first-order formula φ. From the definition given before and from the usual properties of the temporal operators we can now immediately conclude:

$$\lambda \models \mathcal{V}(\Box\varphi) \quad \textbf{implies} \quad \forall i \geq 0 : \lambda^i \models \varphi$$
$$\lambda \models \mathcal{V}(\Diamond\varphi) \quad \textbf{implies} \quad \exists i \geq 0 : \lambda^i \models \varphi$$

This is due to $\lambda \models \mathcal{V}(\Box\varphi)$ implies $\lambda \models \Box\varphi$ and $\lambda \models \Box\varphi$ is defined by $\forall i \geq 0 : \lambda^i \models \varphi$ (and analogously for $\Diamond\varphi$). This special property is depicted in Fig. 5: Assume $\mathcal{V}(\Box\varphi)$ holds in state s_i in a life cycle λ. Then φ holds in all the states $s_i, s_{i+1}, s_{i+2}, \ldots$ — independent of whether $\mathcal{V}(\Box\varphi)$ is true in $s_{i+1}, s_{i+2}, \ldots$ Therefore, it should be clearly noted that there is a big difference between $\mathcal{V}(\Box\varphi)$ and $\mathcal{V}(\varphi)$. Once $\mathcal{V}(\Box\varphi)$ has become true, φ remains true forever. In contrast, if $\mathcal{V}(\varphi)$ becomes true, φ needs only to remain true as long as $\mathcal{V}(\varphi)$ does.

For the events manipulating the special attribute `Axioms` (in the specification called mutators) we need counterparts in the logic. For a general manipulation of the predicate $\mathcal{V}$ we introduce two special events $axiom^+(\varphi)$ and $axiom^-(\varphi)$ for adding an axiom to $\mathcal{V}$ and for removing an axiom from $\mathcal{V}$, respectively. From the logical point of view these two events are sufficient for representing all possible ways of manipulating the attribute `Axioms`. As introduced in Sect. 2, we use the notation $\nabla axiom^+(\varphi)$ and $\triangleright axiom^+(\varphi)$ for the occurrence and enabling of the event $axiom^+$ (analogously for $axiom^-$). Enabling can be used in constraints for restricting the manipulation. For occurrences of these events the following axioms are given:

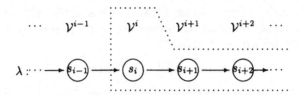

Figure 5: Interpreting Evolving Temporal Logic.

$$\nabla axiom^+(\varphi) \to \bigcirc \mathcal{V}(\varphi), \qquad \nabla axiom^-(\varphi) \to \bigcirc \neg \mathcal{V}(\varphi)$$

$\nabla axiom^+(\varphi)$ (or $\nabla axiom^-(\varphi)$) leads to $\mathcal{V}(\varphi)$ ($\neg \mathcal{V}(\varphi)$, resp.) in the subsequent state. Frame rules are assumed which restricts the evolution of $\mathcal{V}$ to changes which are caused by occurrences of the events $axiom^+(\varphi)$ and $axiom^-(\varphi)$:

$$\neg \mathcal{V}(\varphi) \wedge \bigcirc \mathcal{V}(\varphi) \to \nabla axiom^+(\varphi), \qquad \mathcal{V}(\varphi) \wedge \bigcirc \neg \mathcal{V}(\varphi) \to \nabla axiom^-(\varphi)$$

Before we show how to formulate the properties specified in Fig. 3 and 4 we want to briefly discuss the understanding of negation w.r.t. the predicate $\mathcal{V}$. The question to answer is whether $\mathcal{V}(\neg \varphi)$ is different from $\neg \mathcal{V}(\varphi)$. The answer is quite simple: From $\lambda \models \mathcal{V}(\neg \varphi)$ it follows that $\lambda \models \neg \varphi$. In contrast we cannot derive the same from $\neg \mathcal{V}(\varphi)$. Therefore, $\mathcal{V}(\neg \varphi)$ and $\neg \mathcal{V}(\varphi)$ have to be distinguished. This is of course not surprising because it corresponds to our intuition about the predicate $\mathcal{V}$.

Another important issue we do not discuss in full detail is a proof system for ETL. In fact, we think of taking a proof system for first-order linear temporal logic and modifying it a little bit in order to get a grasp of the predicate $\mathcal{V}$. As already mentioned, the main problem is substitution. We have to distinguish between variables in usual first-order formulas and variables in formulas being parameter values of $\mathcal{V}$. Although it seems that this can be done in a straightforward way, we have to work this out in detail.

4.2 Expressing the Example Using ETL

In the example given in Fig. 3 and 4 several properties are specified for the special attribute Axioms. Here, we present their formulation as formulas of ETL where the attribute Axioms is represented by the special predicate $\mathcal{V}$. Due to the fact that we have to distinguish between different objects we prefix each occurrence of $\mathcal{V}$ in a formula by a variable (or an object name) referring to the object concerned. This corresponds to the way we have prefixed predicates denoting an event occurrence or the enabling of an event for an object in Sect. 2.2.

In all the formulas given below there is an implicit universal quantification over all variables including φ. Please note that we assume φ to be a variable over an abstract data type Formula.

First, we consider the additional properties for bank objects. The way we express the initial value property for Axioms, i.e., that directly after the occurrence of the birth event Open there is no formula φ for which $\mathcal{V}(\varphi)$ holds is a little bit tricky:

$$\square(\ \bigcirc b.\mathcal{V}(\varphi) \to \neg b.\nabla \mathrm{Open}(B, N)\ )$$

The effect the so-called mutator event AddAxioms has on the value of Axioms can be described by simply reducing the occurrence of AddAxioms to an occurrence of the special pre-defined event $axiom^+$:

$$\Box(\ b.\nabla\text{addAxioms}(\varphi) \rightarrow b.\nabla axiom^+(\varphi)\ )$$

For the mutator event ResetAxioms we choose a similar way of expressing its effect:

$$\Box(\ b.\nabla\text{ResetAxioms} \wedge b.\mathcal{V}(\varphi) \rightarrow b.\nabla axiom^-(\varphi)\ )$$

Considering the property of $axiom^+$ described before we can immediately conclude:

$$\Box(\ b.\nabla\text{ResetAxioms} \wedge b.\mathcal{V}(\varphi) \rightarrow \bigcirc\neg b.\mathcal{V}(\varphi)\ )$$

Similarly we can describe the additional properties for account objects. The formula describing the initial value property of the attribute Axioms looks like that for bank objects:

$$\Box(\ \bigcirc a.\mathcal{V}(\varphi) \rightarrow \neg a.\nabla\text{Open}(B, N, H)\ )$$

However, the effect of the mutator event Warnings is rather different from the mutator event AddAxioms for bank objects. Here, only a single pre-specified formula is added to the value of Axioms:

$$\Box\left(\ a.\nabla\text{Warnings} \rightarrow a.\nabla axiom^+ \left(\begin{matrix} a.\nabla\text{Withdrawal}(W) \wedge \text{Balance} - W < 0.00 \\ \rightarrow \text{Supervisor}.\nabla\text{Warning(No, Balance} - W) \end{matrix}\right)\right)$$

Again, the effect of the mutator event NoWarnings can be expressed in the same way as we did it for the mutator event ResetAxioms for bank objects:

$$\Box(\ a.\nabla\text{NoWarnings} \wedge a.\mathcal{V}(\varphi) \rightarrow \bigcirc\neg a.\mathcal{V}(\varphi)\ )$$

In this way we have demonstrated that we are able to describe the intended properties in ETL. Of course, ETL offers additional possibilities which we did not use for our example.

Obviously, it is possible to express nearly arbitrary manipulations of the behaviour specification. From a pragmatic point of view this is not a desirable property. Therefore, we think of restricting the possibilities by means of the specification language. The specification language should only allow those ways of manipulating the dynamic behaviour specification which can be captured by the logic in a reasonable way. For instance, we should explicitly exclude any possibility to express undecidable properties.

5 Conclusions

We motivated the necessity of evolving specifications in the area of information systems and presented an approach to get a grasp of this additional requirement by integrating a new concept into an object specification language. The underlying logic is a first-order temporal logic (for objects) which is extended by a higher-order concept.

We plan to extend an existing proof system for linear temporal logic and adapt it for our logic ETL. At the time being, we are not really sure about the expressive power of ETL. Therefore, we will investigate this question by comparing ETL with different modal logics.

For using such a specification framework a methodology for developing systems based on evolving behaviour descriptions is needed. For that, larger case studies have to be considered.

References

[Con95] S. Conrad. Compositional Object Specification and Verification. In I. Rozman and M. Pivka, eds., *Proc. Int. Conf. on Software Quality (ICSQ'95), Maribor, Slovenia*, pp. 55–64, 1995.

[Con96] S. Conrad. A Basic Calculus for Verifying Properties of Interacting Objects. *IEEE Transactions on Knowledge & Data Engineering*, 18(2):119–146, 1996.

[DDP93] E. Dubois, P. Du Bois, and M. Petit. O-O Requirements Analysis: An Agent Perspective. In O. Nierstrasz, ed., *ECOOP'93 — Object-Oriented Programming, (Proceedings)*, pp. 458–481, Springer-Verlag LNCS 707, 1993.

[FM91] J. Fiadeiro and T. Maibaum. Temporal Reasoning over Deontic Specifications. *Journal of Logic and Computation*, 1(3):357–395, 1991.

[FW93] R. B. Feenstra and R. J. Wieringa. LCM 3.0: A Language for Describing Conceptual Models. Technical Report, Faculty of Mathematics and Computer Science, VU Amsterdam, 1993.

[JSHS96] R. Jungclaus, G. Saake, T. Hartmann, and C. Sernadas. TROLL – A Language for Object-Oriented Specification of Information Systems. *ACM Transactions on Information Systems*, 14(2):175–211, 1996.

[KM89] S. Khosla and T. Maibaum. The Prescription and Description of State Based Systems. In B. Banieqbal, H. Barringer, A. Pnueli, eds., *Temporal Logic in Specification*, pp. 243–294. Springer-Verlag LNCS 398, 1989.

[Mes93] J. Meseguer. A Logical Theory of Concurrent Objects and Its Realization in the Maude Language. In G. Agha, P. Wegener, A. Yonezawa, eds., *Research Directions in Object-Oriented Programming*, pp. 314–390. MIT Press, 1993.

[SCT95] G. Saake, S. Conrad, and C. Türker. From Object Specification towards Agent Design. In M. Papazoglou, ed., *OOER'95: Object-Oriented and Entity-Relationship Modeling (Proc.)*, pp. 329–340, Springer-Verlag LNCS 1021, 1995.

[SSC95] A. Sernadas, C. Sernadas, and J. Costa. Object Specification Logic. *Journal of Logic and Computation*, 5(5):603–630, 1995.

[SSE87] A. Sernadas, C. Sernadas, and H.-D. Ehrich. Object-Oriented Specification of Databases: An Algebraic Approach. In P. M. Stoecker, W. Kent, eds., *Proc. 13th Int. Conf. on Very Large Data Bases (VLDB'87)*, pp. 107–116. VLDB Endowment Press, 1987.

[SSS95] G. Saake, A. Sernadas, and C. Sernadas. Evolving Object Specifications. In R. Wieringa, R. Feenstra, eds., *Information Systems — Correctness and Reusability. Selected Papers from the IS-CORE Workshop*, pp. 84–99. World Scientific Publ., 1995.

A Description Logic Model for Querying Knowledge Bases for Structured Documents

Patrick Lambrix* and Lin Padgham +

*Department of Computer and Information Science
Linköping University, S-581 83, Linköping, Sweden
patla@ida.liu.se
+Department of Computer Science
RMIT University, Melbourne, VIC 3000, Australia
linpa@cs.rmit.edu.au

Abstract. Structure is an important characteristic of documents. In the document management community it has been realized that there is a need for querying and retrieval of documents based on the structure of the documents. In this paper we propose a knowledge-based system for representation and retrieval of documents. The model on which the system is based is an extension of the description logic model of information retrieval. We discuss the advantages of our model and we show how our model can cope with many of the desirable queries involving the structure of documents.

1 Introduction

Research in recent years shows that structure is an important characteristic of documents. Therefore we would like to be able to represent (e.g. [10]) and retrieve documents in various ways based on the structure of the document as a composite object (e.g. [4, 16, 7, 13, 5, 8, 19, 1]). There is a need for querying and retrieval restricted to parts of a document, for access to documents by their structure and for querying which combines structural data and non-structural data.

In this paper we propose a knowledge-based system based on description logics for representing and querying structured documents. Description logics are languages tailored for expressing knowledge about concepts and concept hierarchies representing the is-a relation between the concepts. We propose a system that extends the traditional description logics with constructs and specialized reasoning capabilities targeted towards the part-of relation. This provides us with a knowledge base with description and query language where we can distinguish between structural and non-structural information. Important additions

---

* Part of this work was done while the first author was visiting the Department of Computer Science of the RMIT University in Melbourne, Australia. The first author is supported by grant 95-176 from the Swedish Research Council for Engineering Sciences (TFR).

to the capabilities of the description language are that a user is able to define relations to be part-of relations, that there are constructs to treat the part-of relations in a special way, and that we allow for ordering information between the parts. The query language supports many of the needed queries based on the structure of the documents. In [15] we show that a large part of HTML can be translated into our proposed description logic. This means that we can generate description logic versions of HTML documents automatically and then use the specialized capabilities of our knowledge-based system for advanced querying of the documents.

The paper is organized as follows. In section 2 we briefly describe description logics and their use in representing documents. In section 3 we show informally which representation and query capabilities are lacking in standard description logics. Then we describe formally a description language containing constructs and reasoning facilities concerning part-of in section 4. In section 5 we show a query language based on the description logic of section 4 that can cope with a wide range of structural queries. In section 6 we discuss briefly some related work. We conclude the paper in section 7.

2 Description Logics and Structured Documents

Description logics are knowledge representation languages for expressing knowledge about concepts and concept hierarchies representing the is-a relation between the concepts. They are usually given a Tarski-style declarative semantics, which allows them to be seen as sub-languages of first-order predicate logic. The main entities in a description logic are *concepts*, that are interpreted as sets of objects over a domain, *roles* that are interpreted as binary relations over the domain and individuals that are interpreted as objects in the domain. The basic reasoning tasks are classification and subsumption checking. Subsumption represents the is-a relation. A whole family of knowledge representation systems have been built using these languages and have been used in a wide range of applications.

The language in which we can define concepts and individuals and query the knowledge base has a number of standard constructors. For instance, the **and** construct allows us to combine different properties, such as saying that *a particular document is a research-paper* **and** *appears in the ISMIS-97 proceedings*. The **atleast** and **atmost** constructs are often used in describing concepts and allow us to state such things as *a document has* **at least** *1 author*. By combining **atleast** and **atmost** we can also state an exact number of fillers for a particular relation. The **all** construct allows us to state things such as **all** *authors of a document work at a computer science department*. **Fills** allows us to state that a particular individual is in a particular relation with another individual (if it occurs in an individual description) or set of individuals (if it occurs in a concept description), or that a particular attribute has a given value for the individual (or set of individuals). For instance, we can state that *in a particular document the project name attribute is DL-project*.

In [17] a model for documents using the description logic MIRTL was presented. Documents have different orthogonal properties such as properties concerning content, structure, and graphical characteristics to which a user may refer in queries. It was shown in [17] that description logics provide languages that are rich enough to account for this multi-faceted nature of documents. The description logic presented there was used to define different types of documents, describe user information and describe thesaurus information. This means that all this information can be written in the same representation language with the same intuitive object-oriented syntax. Also the queries that a user may ask were written using the same description logic. There are some weaknesses in this model because of the fact that description logics are mainly dealing with the is-a relation, but not with other structural relations such as part-of. This means that the structural information of documents can be represented,[2] but it is not possible to use this information in a specialized way.

3 Introducing Structured Information

There are a number of ways in which the representational capability of description logics can be improved to take the structure of documents into account. First, we want to be able to distinguish between structural relations and ordinary relations. For instance, the relation between a document and its sections is a part-of relation, while the relation between a document and the person responsible for it is not. We want to be able to treat the part-of relations in a special way. For instance, when displaying the result of a query part-of relations may default to an integrated display while other relations may result in new windows. Further, it is also necessary to be able to distinguish between different kinds of part-of relations. For instance, the properties of the section parts and the title parts in a document are clearly different. These requirements can be fulfilled by introducing the notion of *part name* [18, 14] in the description logic.[3] In some situations it is useful to be able to define orthogonal part-of structures over an object, for example a document has sections, sub-sections and paragraphs as one structural breakdown of parts, with pages as an orthogonal structure. Using part names, it is possible to combine such orthogonal structures in an object description, allowing retrieval of the different parts for different purposes.

Similar to roles part names are binary relations over the domain of individuals and can actually be seen as roles with a special labeling, giving them a more specialized semantics. For the description language we need similar constructs for the part names in the language as for roles. Therefore, the constructs **allp**, **atleastp**, **atmostp** and **part-fills** are introduced as analogues of **all**, **atleast**, **atmost** and **fills**. For instance, (**allp** *title-p string*) in the definition of a document would mean that all title parts must be strings while (**atleastp** *1 section-p*)

---

[2] A structural relation such as the relation between a document and its sections would be represented in the same way as any other relation such as the relation between a document and its identification number.

[3] For a complete description of the underlying part-of model we refer to [14].

means that there should be at least one section part. In some constructs[4] we also allow to refer to the order of parts within a part name. For instance, the first section part in a document could be denoted by *section-p:1*. We say that the part name is qualified. This notion is particularly important for individuals. In a document the order of the different sections is not arbitrary. Finally, the **order-constraint** construct allows us to order different kinds of parts. For instance, to assert that the title part comes before the abstract part we write (**order-constraint** *title-p abstract-p*). The **before** construct is used to state ordering information between individuals.

In the queries we would like to be able to refer to the structure of the documents. For instance, we would like to be able to find all the direct parts of an individual (i.e. the next layer down in the hierarchy, which for a document could be title, abstract and sections). We may also wish to find all the direct and indirect parts of an individual (i.e. parts at all levels of the hierarchy, for example, including the paragraphs that are parts of the sections). To enable this kind of functionality we introduce the constructs **includes, directly-includes, included-in, directly-included-in, includes-individual, directly-includes-individual, included-in-individual,** and **directly-included-in-individual**. We illustrate their use:

(**includes** *reference*)
   gets all individuals having a part of type reference.
(**directly-includes** *reference*)
   gets all individuals having a part one level down of type reference
(**included-in-individual** *review-abstract*)
   gets all individuals that are parts of the individual review-abstract.
(**directly-included-in-individual** *review-abstract*)
   gets all individuals that are parts one level down of the individual review-abstract.

In [19] a list of different kinds of queries involving structural information is given. It is argued that these kinds of queries are all desirable in a system supporting structured documents. We show later that many of these kinds of queries can be represented in our language.

In the following two sections we introduce our framework formally. In section 4 we describe the language which we use to build a knowledge base of documents. In section 5 we extend this language to become a query language that can be used for several kinds of queries involving structural as well as non-structural information.

---

[4] Namely **allp** and **order-constraint**. See the syntax of the language.

4 A Description Logic with Part-of Reasoning

The syntax of the description language we use is defined as follows:

<*D-descr*> ::=
  ⊤ | <*concept-name*> |
  (and <*D-descr*>$^+$) |
  (test-c < *fn* > < *arg* >*) |
  (all <*role-name*> <*D-descr*>) |
  (atleast <*positive-integer*> <*role-name*>) |
  (atmost <*non-negative-integer*> <*role-name*>) |
  (fills <*role-name*> <*individual-name*>$^+$) |
  (allp <*part*> <*D-descr*>) |
  (atleastp <*positive-integer*> <*part-name*>) |
  (atmostp <*non-negative-integer*> <*part-name*>) |
  (part-fills <*part-name*> <*individual-name*>$^+$) |
  (order-constraint <*part*> <*part*>)

<*concept-name*> ::= <*symbol*>
<*role-name*> ::= <*symbol*>
<*part*> ::= <*part-name*> |
  <*part-name*>:<*positive-integer*>
<*part-name*> ::= <*symbol*>
<*individual-name*> ::= <*symbol*>
< *fn* > ::= a function in the
  host language
<*arg*> ::= expression passed to
  the test functions

Terminological axioms are used to introduce names for concepts and definitions of those concepts. Let A be a concept name (<*symbol*>) and C a concept description (<*D-descr*>). Then terminological axioms can be of the form: A ≤ C for introducing necessary conditions (primitive concepts), or A ≐ C for introducing necessary and sufficient conditions (defined concepts). This description language then allows us to make definitions such as

    document ≐ (and (atleast *1 projectnumber*) (atmost *1 projectnumber*) (atleast *1 responsible*) (atmost *1 responsible*) (atleastp *1 title-p*) (atmostp *1 title-p*) (allp *title-p string*) (atleastp *1 abstract-p*) (atmostp *1 abstract-p*) (allp *abstract-p abstract*) (atleastp *3 section-p*) (allp *section-p section*) (allp *section-p:1 introduction*) (allp *reference-p reference*) (order-constraint *title-p abstract-p*) (order-constraint *abstract-p section-p*) (order-constraint *section-p reference-p*))

In this example a document is defined as something that has exactly one project number, exactly one responsible, exactly one title part and that part has to be a string, exactly one abstract part and that part has to be an abstract, and at least three section parts and they all have to be sections. The first section part also has to be an introduction. If there are reference parts then these must be references. We also have the constraints that the title part must come before the abstract part, the abstract part before the section parts, and the section parts before the reference parts.

An interpretation for the language consists of a tuple $< \mathcal{D}, \ll_{\mathcal{D}}, \varepsilon >$, where $\mathcal{D}$ is the domain of individuals, $\ll_{\mathcal{D}}$ a set of partial orders over the domain $\mathcal{D}$ (i.e. to each object in $\mathcal{D}$ we have an associated partial order) and ε the extension function. The partial orders allow for an order between the parts of a composite object. This order between two parts is dependent on the composite object that is considered. This means that a part p_1 can come before another part p_2 in a first composite object, but that in a second composite object p_2 comes before p_1. The extension function is defined in the standard way for description logics, but extended to deal also with part names. The extension function maps part names and roles into sub-sets of $\mathcal{D} \times \mathcal{D}$, concepts into sub-sets of $\mathcal{D}$ and individuals into elements of $\mathcal{D}$ such that $\varepsilon[i_1] \neq \varepsilon[i_2]$ whenever $i_1 \neq i_2$. The semantics for the different constructs are as follows. For convenience we write $y \lhd_n x$ for $<y,x>$ $\in \varepsilon[n]$ where n is a part name which means then that y is a direct part of x with name n. We say that y is a part of x (notation $y \lhd^* x$) if there is a chain of direct parts from x to y.

$\varepsilon[\top] = \mathcal{D}$

$\varepsilon[(\textbf{and } A\ B)] = \varepsilon[A] \cap \varepsilon[B]$

$\varepsilon[(\textbf{test-c } \textit{fn args})] = \{x \in \mathcal{D} \mid \textit{fn(args)} = \text{TRUE}\}$

$\varepsilon[(\textbf{all } r\ A)] = \{x \in \mathcal{D} \mid \forall\, y \in \mathcal{D}\colon <x,y> \in \varepsilon[r] \rightarrow y \in \varepsilon[A]\}$

$\varepsilon[(\textbf{atleast } m\ r)] = \{x \in \mathcal{D} \mid \sharp \{y \in \mathcal{D} \mid <x,y> \in \varepsilon[r]\} \geq m\}$

$\varepsilon[(\textbf{atmost } m\ r)] = \{x \in \mathcal{D} \mid \sharp \{y \in \mathcal{D} \mid <x,y> \in \varepsilon[r]\} \leq m\}$

$\varepsilon[(\textbf{fills } r\ i_1\ ...\ i_m)] = \{x \in \mathcal{D} \mid <x,\varepsilon[i_1]> \in \varepsilon[r] \wedge ... \wedge <x,\varepsilon[i_m]> \in \varepsilon[r]\}$

$\varepsilon[(\textbf{allp } n\ A)] = \{x \in \mathcal{D} \mid \forall\, y \in \mathcal{D}\colon y \lhd_n x \rightarrow y \in \varepsilon[A]\}$

$\varepsilon[(\textbf{atleastp } m\ n)] = \{x \in \mathcal{D} \mid \sharp \{y \in \mathcal{D} \mid y \lhd_n x\} \geq m\}$

$\varepsilon[(\textbf{atmostp } m\ n)] = \{x \in \mathcal{D} \mid \sharp \{y \in \mathcal{D} \mid y \lhd_n x\} \leq m\}$

$\varepsilon[(\textbf{part-fills } n\ i_1\ ...\ i_m)] = \{x \in \mathcal{D} \mid \varepsilon[i_1] \lhd_n x \wedge ... \wedge \varepsilon[i_m] \lhd_n x\}$

$\varepsilon[(\textbf{order-constraint } p_1\ p_2)] =$
$$\{x \in \mathcal{D} \mid \forall\, y_1, y_2 \in \mathcal{D}\colon (y_1 \lhd_{p_1} x \wedge y_2 \lhd_{p_2} x) \rightarrow y_1 \ll_x y_2\}$$

Statements about individuals rather than about concept definitions can be asserted in the assertional language. The statement $i :: C$ for a concept description C means that $\varepsilon[i] \in \varepsilon[C]$ and the statement $i :: (\textbf{before } i_1\ ...\ i_m \textbf{ in } j)$ means that $\varepsilon[i] \ll_{\varepsilon[j]} \varepsilon[i_1]$ and ... and $\varepsilon[i] \ll_{\varepsilon[j]} \varepsilon[i_m]$. The concept and order statements can be combined with the **and** constructor that denotes the intersection operation. Below we show how a specific document *review-document* with its different parts, the title *Review*, the abstract *review-abstract*, and the sections *intro, comments* and *conclusion* is defined. *review-document* satisfies the definition of document as defined above. We note that, as description logics use an open world assumption, the definitions may contain only partial information about the individuals.

review-document :: (**and** *document* (**fills** *project-name DL-project*) (**fills** *responsible John*) (**part-fills** *title-p Review*) (**part-fills** *abstract-p review-abstract*) (**part-fills** *section-p intro comments conclusion*))

Review :: (**and** *string* (**before** *review-abstract* **in** *review-document*))

review-abstract :: (**and** *abstract* (**before** *intro* **in** *review-document*))

intro :: (**and** *section introduction* (**before** *comments* **in** *review-document*))

comments :: (**and** *section* (**before** *conclusion* **in** *review-document*))

conclusion :: *section*

Our description logic system maintains the is-a hierarchy of concepts as well as a part-of hierarchy for individuals based on $\lhd^*$ (and part names). These two hierarchies are used to find answers to queries about the documents in the knowledge base. It can be shown that the standard operations in description logics are decidable for our language and the complexity is even polynomial for the case where we have unqualified part names [14]. In the next section we define our query language and show which kinds of queries can be answered.

5 Queries

The query language is the same as the description language, but extended with constructs that allow us to have queries referring to the part-of hierarchy while not needing to specify the exact level in the part-of hierarchy or the names of the parts. This means that although it is possible to have queries that specify the complete path in the part-of hierarchy, we can have queries where this path does not have to be specified as well. For instance, the query (or concept definition) (**and** document (**allp** section-p:1 (**allp** title-p (**test-c**[5] contains-word[6] retrieval)))) is a query where the full path is given. The query retrieves the documents having a title containing the word "retrieval" in the first section. The query (**and** document (**includes** (**and** title (**test-c** contains-word retrieval)))) on the other hand represents the documents that include a part that is a title and that contains the word "retrieval". This title can occur at any level in the part-of hierarchy. For instance, it could be the document title or one of the section titles. The syntax and semantics of the language are as follows.

$< Q - descr > ::=$ $\top \mid < D - descr >$ (where Q-descriptions are used) $\mid$
       (**directly-includes** $< Q - descr >$) $\mid$
       (**includes** $< Q - descr >$) $\mid$
       (**directly-included-in** $< Q - descr >$) $\mid$
       (**included-in** $< Q - descr >$) $\mid$
       (**directly-includes-individual** $< individual - name >^+$) $\mid$
       (**includes-individual** $< individual - name >^+$) $\mid$
       (**directly-included-in-individual** $< individual - name >^+$) $\mid$
       (**included-in-individual** $< individual - name >^+$)

$\varepsilon[(\textbf{directly-includes } C)] = \{x \in \mathcal{D} \mid \exists\, y \in \mathcal{D}, n \in \mathcal{N}: y \lhd_n x \wedge y \in \varepsilon[C]\}$

$\varepsilon[(\textbf{includes } C)] = \{x \in \mathcal{D} \mid \exists\, y \in \mathcal{D}: y \lhd^* x \wedge y \in \varepsilon[C]\}$

$\varepsilon[(\textbf{directly-included-in } C)] = \{x \in \mathcal{D} \mid \exists\, y \in \mathcal{D}, n \in \mathcal{N}: x \lhd_n y \wedge y \in \varepsilon[C]\}$

$\varepsilon[(\textbf{included-in } C)] = \{x \in \mathcal{D} \mid \exists\, y \in \mathcal{D}: x \lhd^* y \wedge y \in \varepsilon[C]\}$

$\varepsilon[(\textbf{directly-includes-individual } i)] = \{x \in \mathcal{D} \mid \exists\, n \in \mathcal{N}: \varepsilon[i] \lhd_n x\}$

$\varepsilon[(\textbf{includes-individual } i)] = \{x \in \mathcal{D} \mid \varepsilon[i] \lhd^* x\}$

$\varepsilon[(\textbf{directly-included-in-individual } i)] = \{x \in \mathcal{D} \mid \exists\, n \in \mathcal{D}: x \lhd_n \varepsilon[i]\}$

$\varepsilon[(\textbf{included-in-individual } i)] = \{x \in \mathcal{D} \mid x \lhd^* \varepsilon[i]\}$

Our language allows us to perform most of the queries that are listed as being desirable in [19]. We discuss briefly each of those classes of queries and show some examples we support. We then discuss briefly the examples we are not currently able to support.

---

[5] The **test-c** functionality is a functionality available in the CLASSIC description logic [6] system that allows us to use programs that return a boolean value as test functions outside of the actual description logic. This means that we can add in the traditional information retrieval techniques in this framework (e.g. [20]).

[6] In the examples we use contains-word to find the occurrence of a particular word. However, this function may well be used to find conjunctions or disjunctions of words.

5.1 Supported Queries

1. word by word access

A typical query in this class is to find documents containing combinations of words. In our framework we can model this as in the query (**and** document (**includes** (**test-c** contains-word retrieval))). This query retrieves the documents that include a part that contains the word "retrieval". The level at which this part occurs is not important. It can be a title, a section, a paragraph, etc. The actual matching is done using a test function contains-word, which can be a traditional information retrieval function.

2. query scope restricted to sub-documents

In our language it is possible to express queries where the scope of the query is not a complete document but only a part of a document. An example of such a query is to find the documents where the word "retrieval" occurs in the title: (**and** document (**allp** title-p (**test-c** contains-word retrieval))). The following query returns the documents in which the first section contains the word "retrieval": (**and** document (**allp** section-p:1 (**test-c** contains-word retrieval))).

For multiple parts and parts at arbitrary levels we cannot use the names of the parts, but we can use the include constructs and the domains of the parts. For instance, to find a document where some paragraph contains the word "retrieval" we would perform the following query: (**and** document (**includes** (**and** paragraph (**test-c** contains-word retrieval)))). This query would look for the parts of the document which are paragraphs and contain the word "retrieval".

3. retrieval of sub-documents

In this type of query we only want to retrieve parts of the documents such as in the query to find the sections that contain a particular word: (**and** section (**test-c** contains-word retrieval) (**included-in** document)). It is also possible to use specific individuals in a query. For instance, the following query finds all paragraphs of the particular document ISMIS-97-proceedings that contain a particular word: (**and** paragraph (**test-c** contains-word retrieval) (**included-in-individual** ISMIS-97-proceedings)).

4. access by the structure of documents

These queries have to do with traversing the part-of hierarchy. For instance, we could want to find all the direct parts of a document: (**directly-included-in** document). To find all parts within a section (regardless of the level) we write the following: (**included-in** section). The documents sharing a particular paragraph par1 can be found using the following query: (**and** document (**includes-individual** par1)). Information about different branches in the part-of hierarchy can be used. For instance, the following more complex query finds the sections that together with a particular abstract and title make up a document: (**and** section (**included-in** (**and** document (**part-fills** title-p Review) (**part-fills** abstract-p review-abstract)))).

5. non-structural information

This capability was already present in [17]. For instance, one could ask for the documents for which John was responsible. This is represented by the following query: (**and** document (**fills** responsible John)).

6. combine structural and non-structural information

It is obvious that we can mix the structural and non-structural parts of our language in the queries.

5.2 Other Queries

Some queries presented in [19] are not supported by the language. They include ranked queries, disjunction queries and some queries using the ordering information of parts.

1. ranked queries

Our language does not rank documents with respect to relevance to the query. An extension to this framework would be necessary. A possibility would be to extend this description logic to deal with probabilities in a way similar to what is proposed in [22].

2. query scope restricted to sub-documents

An example in this category that we do not directly support is the query to find the documents for which the first paragraph contains a particular word. In the case where the document has paragraphs as direct parts we can use the query (**and** document (**allp** paragraph-p:1 (**test-c** contains-word retrieval))). However, when the paragraphs are contained in the document but not as direct parts we cannot express the query in the language without using other information.[7]

3. access by the structure of documents

As in the previous case we may not be able to express some queries regarding the order of the parts. For instance, we cannot write a query to find all individuals which have as first part a title. Allowing this kind of query would require that we allow in the definition of a concept to say things such as 'the first part' regardless of the part name. This would require an extension of the description language. However, in the case where we have complete information about the structure of the document in the document base (as would normally be the case in a static document base) we could just retrieve the individuals using the description logic system functionality and check whether their first part is a title.

4. access to different types of documents with one query

Our description logic does not contain an OR-construct. Consequently, to access different types of documents as in a query to find the articles, papers and books satisfying a certain requirement would require writing several different queries. However, this may be simply an interface issue.

6 Related Work

The related work can be divided into two parts. First we have the document systems that allow for querying the document base based on the structure of the

---

[7] In this particular case we could make use of the fact that the first paragraph is the first paragraph of the first section. The query would then be (**and** document (**allp** section-p:1 (**allp** paragraph-p:1 (**test-c** contains-word retrieval)))).

documents. In [16] a query language is specified for retrieving information from hierarchically structured documents. The language is influenced by SQL and Nial. Four different categories of search capabilities are considered: simple selection and navigation, simple object selection conditions, contextual conditions and object specification. In [8] the object-oriented database management system O_2 is extended to handle SGML documents. The data model was extended to include ordering information and union of types. The query language O_2SQL is extended with new constructs among which the notion of path variables. The work in [4] defines a query language to allow for querying multimedia documents based on content as well as structure. The work is part of the MULTOS project. A database system that supports retrieval operations for heterogeneous collections of structured documents is described in [7]. In [13] SQL is extended to provide access to structured text described by SGML in text-relational database management systems. The ELF data model for SGML documents and the query language SGQL are introduced in [1].

We consider the aspects that are discussed in all approaches. The traversal of the part-of hierarchy can be done in several ways. It can be done by specifying a complete path which is supported by all systems, by specifying a partial path [4, 8] or by not specifying the path at all [4, 16, 7, 13, 8, 1]. In the latter case we may want to include type information in the query. Few systems support using information about different branches in the part-of hierarchy in a query [16]. Few systems give support for the ordering of parts [8, 1]. There are some queries that we do not support, but that are available in other systems. For instance, some systems support union types [8, 1] and ranked queries [1].

An interesting observation is that none of the above systems provide the expressivity to cope with every category of queries as described in [19]. It seems that these systems, as our framework, do not handle some of the queries involving the restriction of the query scope to sub-documents and the access by the structure of documents. However, by using the description logic model we have a formal tool to study exactly which kind of queries are possible or computationally feasible and which are not.

Another kind of related work is the work on introducing part-of in description logics. A nice overview is given in [3]. Most proposals have an engineering application in mind [11, 23, 21]. The work in [9] is targeted towards a natural language application. Some other proposals concentrate on a particular aspect of the interaction between part-of and is-a [12, 2]. Our approach differs from most other approaches in that our framework is based on a formal model for part-of (see [14]), we allow for differentiating between different kinds of part-of relations and we allow for queries with respect to a part-of hierarchy. The only other approach that defines a formal model for part-of is [9]. Most of the other approaches allow for representation of one part-of relation which is usually considered as a predefined role and therefore no special constructs are introduced for part-of. In [21] six different categories of part-whole relations are supported while [23] allows full flexibility by differentiating between different kinds of part-of relations as we do. The other approaches concentrate on defining part-of on concept level and do not consider a part-of hierarchy for individuals or querying with respect to part-of for individuals.

7 Conclusion

In [17, 22] it has been shown that description logics are a useful logical framework to represent, maintain and query knowledge bases of documents. In this paper we show how a description logic for composite objects is particularly useful for knowledge bases of structured documents. We show that many of the desired queries can be performed within our language.

Currently, we are finishing the implementation of the proposed description logic using the description logic system CLASSIC [6]. Preliminary test results in another domain are promising. In [15] we show that a large part of HTML can be modeled within our proposed description logic. We have implemented a system that takes HTML documents and converts them into descriptions in our description logic. This provides us with a means for creating real-world test-beds for our system in the form of knowledge bases of structured documents.

References

1. Arnold-Moore, T., Fuller, M., Lowe, B., Thom, J., Wilkinson, R., 'The ELF data model and SGQL query language for structured document databases', *Proceedings of the Australasian Database Conference*, pp 17-26, Adelaide, Australia, 1995.
2. Artale, A., Cesarini, F., Grazzini, E., Pippolini, F., Soda, G., 'Modelling Composition in a Terminological Language Environment', *Proceedings of the ECAI Workshop on Parts and Wholes*, pp 93-101, Amsterdam, August 1994.
3. Artale, A., Franconi, E., Guarino, N., Pazzi, L., 'Part-Whole Relations in Object-Centered Systems: An Overview', *Data and Knowledge Engineering*, Vol 20(3), pp 347-383, 1996.
4. Bertino, E., Rabitti, F., Gibbs, S., 'Query Processing in a Multimedia Document System', *ACM Transactions on Office Informations Systems*, Vol 6(1), pp 1-41, 1988.
5. Blake, G., Conses, P., Kilpeläinen, P., Larson, P., Snider, T., Tompa, F., 'Text/relational Database Management Systems: Harmonizing SQL and SGML', *Proceedings of the International Conference on Applications of Databases*, LNCS 819, pp 267-280, Vadstena, Sweden, 1994.
6. Borgida, A., Brachman, R., McGuinness, D., Resnick, L., 'CLASSIC: a structural data model for objects', *Proceedings of the ACM International Conference on Management of Data - SIGMOD 89*, pp 58-67, 1989.
7. Burkowski, F., 'Retrieval Activities in a Database Consisting of Heterogeneous Collections of Structured Text', *Proceedings of the 15th ACM International Conference on Research and Development in Information Retrieval - SIGIR 92*, pp 112-125, Copenhagen, Denmark, 1992.
8. Christophides, V., Abiteboul, S., Cluet, S., Scholl, M., 'From Structured Documents to Novel Query Facilities', *Proceedings of the ACM International Conference on Management of Data - SIGMOD 94*, pp 1-22, 1994.

9. Franconi, E., 'A Treatment of Plurals and Plural Qualifications based on a Theory of Collections', *Minds and Machines: Special Issue on Knowledge Representation for Natural Language Processing*, Vol 3(4), pp 453-474, November 1993.

10. Goldfarb, C.F., *The SGML Handbook*, Clarendon Press, Oxford, 1990.

11. Hors, P., 'Description logics to specify the part-whole relation', *Proceedings of the ECAI Workshop on Parts and Wholes*, pp 103-109, Amsterdam, August 1994.

12. Jang, Y., Patil, R., 'KOLA: A Knowledge Organization Language', *Proceedings of the 13th Symposium on Computer Applications in Medical Care*, pp 71-75, 1989.

13. Kilpeläinen, P., Manilla, H., 'Retrieval from Hierarchical Texts by Partial Patterns', *Proceedings of the 16th ACM International Conference on Research and Development in Information Retrieval - SIGIR 93*, pp 214-222, Pittsburgh, PA, USA, 1993.

14. Lambrix, P., *Part-Whole Reasoning in Description Logics*, Ph.D. Thesis 448, Department of Computer and Information Science, Linköping University, 1996.

15. Lambrix, P., Shahmehri, N., Åberg, J., 'Towards Creating a Knowledge Base for World-Wide Web Documents', *Proceedings of the IASTED International Conference on Intelligent Information Systems*, Grand Bahama Island, Bahamas, 1997.

16. MacLeod, I., 'A Query Language for Retrieving Information from Hierarchic Text Structures', *The Computer Journal*, Vol 34(3), pp 254-264, 1991.

17. Meghini, C., Sebastiani, F., Straccia, U., Thanos, C., 'A Model of Information Retrieval based on a Terminological Logic', *Proceedings of the 16th ACM International Conference on Research and Development in Information Retrieval - SIGIR 93*, pp 298-307, Pittsburgh, PA, USA, 1993.

18. Padgham, L., Lambrix, P., 'A Framework for Part-of Hierarchies in Terminological Logics', *Principles of Knowledge Representation and Reasoning: Proceedings of the Fourth International Conference - KR 94*, pp 485-496, Bonn, Germany, 1994.

19. Sacks-Davis, R., Arnold-Moore, T., Zobel, J., 'Database systems for structured documents', *Proceedings of the International Symposium on Advanced Database Technologies and Their Integration*, pp 272-283, Nara, Japan, 1994.

20. Salton, G., McGill, M., *Introduction to Modern Information Retrieval*, McGraw-Hill, Tokio, 1983.

21. Sattler, U., 'A Concept Language for an Engineering Application with Part-Whole Relations', *Proceedings of the International Workshop on Description Logics*, pp 119-123, Roma, Italy, 1995.

22. Sebastiani, F., 'A Probabilistic Terminological Logic for Modelling Information Retrieval', *Proceedings of the 17th ACM International Conference on Research and Development in Information Retrieval - SIGIR 94*, pp 122-130, Dublin, Ireland, 1994.

23. Speel, P.-H., Patel-Schneider, P.F., 'CLASSIC Extended with Whole-Part Relations', *Proceedings of the International Workshop on Description Logics*, pp 45-50, Bonn, Germany, 1994.

Refining First Order Theories
with Neural Networks

M. Botta, A. Giordana, R. Piola

Dipartimento di Informatica, Università di Torino
C.so Svizzera 185, 10149 Torino, Italy
e-mail: {botta,attilio,piola}@di.unito.it

Abstract. This paper presents the experimental evaluation of a neural network architecture that can manage structured data and refine knowledge bases expressed in a first order logic language.

This new framework is well suited to classification problems in which concept descriptions depend upon numerical features of the data and data have variable size. In fact, the main goal of the neural architecture is that of refining the numerical part of the knowledge base, without changing its structure.

Several experiments are described in the paper in order to evaluate the potential benefits with respect to the more classical architectures based on the propositional framework. In a first case a classification theory has been manually handcrafted and then refined automatically. In a second case it has been automatically acquired by a symbolic relational learning system able to deal with numerical features. An extensive experimentation ha been also done with most popular propositional learners showing that the new network architecture converges quite fastly and generalizes better than all of them.

Keywords: Learning and Knowledge Discovery, Soft Computing, First Order Logic, Connectionist learning, Theory Refinement.

1   Introduction

Several papers appeared in the last decade [15, 14, 9, 1, 8] have shown that combining knowledge based methods with connectionist learning produces algorithms exhibiting excellent performances on non trivial case studies.

This paper presents a extensive experimentation made with FONNs (First Order logic Neural Networks), a hybrid learning paradigm combining symbolic learning in First Order Logics with error gradient descent in order to refine numerical terms in Horn clause classification theories [5]. With respect to previous works, FONNs bring into a neural network architecture the capability of dealing with structured data of unrestricted size, by allowing to dynamically bind the classification rules to different items occurring in the input data.

Should a neural network have this capability, two important advantages would be obtained. First, instances having a number of components greater than the ones in the learning set can be processed without loss of accuracy.

We will show how FONN learned from short sequences also perform well on long sequences, whereas knowledge bases learned in the propositional setting significantly degrade. Second, FONNs can be substantially smaller than their propositional counterpart even when data have a preassigned size so that the task can be framed in propositional logics. This happens because a single concept description in FOL can cover many different ground instances which, in the propositional setting, would require many specific rules. Smaller networks have a smaller number of weights to be tuned, and in general, require smaller learning sets because the Vapnik-Chervonenkis dimension of a neural network increases with the number of weights [4]. We will present results obtained for data of definite size showing that, also in this case, FONNs perform significantly better than C4.5, using small learning sets.

The experimentation is performed on an artificial problem inspired to the well known *train-going-east* problem proposed by Michalski [10] where cars are described using both categorical and continuous valued attributes.

2 Mapping First Order Logics to Neural Networks

Algorithms for mapping propositional Horn clauses to neural networks have been presented by several authors [15, 16, 8, 1]. All of them share the same basic idea that a propositional theory can be functionally described by an AND/OR graph having atomic expressions in the leaves. This graph can be transformed into a neural network by replacing the boolean $\wedge$ and $\vee$ operators in the nodes with continuous, derivable functions and by adding weights on the links. Here, the method will be extended to First Order theories. For the sake of simplicity we restrict ourselves to flat theories, consisting of range restricted Horn Clauses with functions, and negation on single literals.

As discussed in [1], propositional flat theories can be immediately transformed into Factorized RBFN by associating a radial function (hidden unit) to every clause body. Extending the method to First Order Logic entails to cope with two new points: the binding between variables and constants in the data, and the existential quantification. In general, a classification rule has the following format:

$$\forall_{y_1,\dots,y_r} \left[\exists_{x_1,\dots,x_k} \varphi(x_1,\dots,x_k,y_1,\dots,y_r) \right] \to \omega(y_1,\dots,y_r) \qquad (1)$$

being φ a conjunctive formula in a given representation language, and ω a concept to be recognized.

In order to verify such a rule on a given universe U, containing a set of constants, one must find all the models of φ existing in U. In other words, φ must be checked on all possible substitutions of variables $y_1,\dots,y_r$ in φ with constant names $a_1,\dots,a_r$ in U. For each substitution $\theta_y = \{y_1/a_1,\dots,y_r/a_r\}$ for variables $y_1,\dots,y_r$ in φ, there might be many possible substitutions for variables $x_1,\dots,x_k$ that should be taken into account. θ_y is a positive instance of ω if there exists at least one substitution θ_x for variables $x_1,\dots,x_k$ such that $\theta_x\theta_y$ satisfies formula φ.

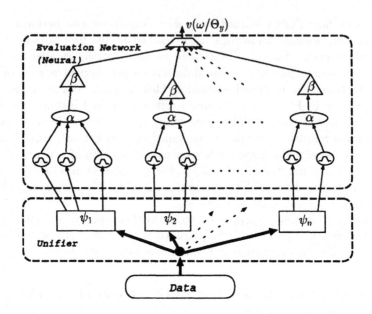

Fig. 1. FONN architecture: each branch from data up to γ represent a formula

This task can be accomplished by means of a four level architecture as described in Figure 1. The first level (Unifier) generates all possible substitutions of the variables in a logical formula with constants in the universe U represented by input data; the second level (α) evaluates the truth of the logical conditions stated by the classification rule, and the third level node (β) implements the existential quantifier semantics. For every substitution θ_y, the β operator collects the results obtained by evaluating φ on each corresponding substitution θ_x and asserts the consequent if at least one of them is "true". A fourth level (γ node) combines the assertions made by different rules.

On one hand, this architecture offers the possibility to deal with data (Universes) of unrestricted size, because the Unifier dynamically builds all the possible ground instances of a classification rule. On the other hand, the evaluation network in Figure 1 is a static structure that can be translated into a neural network in a similar way as done for the propositional case [1, 14].

In order to have a uniform mechanism for translating predicates into condition units, the concept description language has been restricted so that assertions about numeric properties can be made only by means of a special predicate having the syntactic form: $inside(f(x_1, \ldots, x_r), [a, b])$, being $f(x_1, \ldots, x_r)$ a real function defined on the input data, and $[a, b]$ a close interval in the real domain. The semantics of predicate $inside$ is defined as follows:

$$v(inside(f(x_1 \ldots, x_r), [a, b])) = \begin{cases} 1 \ if \ f(x_1, \ldots, x_n) \in [a, b] \\ 0 \ otherwise \end{cases} \quad (2)$$

Therefore, a well formed formula in a classification theory will always be of the general form:

$$\forall y_1, \ldots, y_r [\exists x_1, \ldots, x_k \psi(x_1, \ldots, x_k, y_1, \ldots, y_r) \wedge \tag{3}$$
$$\wedge \varphi(x_1, \ldots, x_k, y_1, \ldots, y_r)] \to \omega(y_1, \ldots, y_r)$$

being $\psi(x_1, \ldots, x_k, y_1, \ldots, y_r)$ a conjunctive subformula containing only *constraints* (i.e.: boolean predicates on discrete features) and $\varphi(x_1, \ldots, x_k, y_1, \ldots, y_r)$ a conjunctive subformula containing only instances of predicate *inside*.

As described in Figure 1, subformulae φ_i containing assertions about numeric features are transformed into a neural network by mapping every literal (a predicate *inside*) into a corresponding node called *detector*, and each of the connectives $\wedge$ and $\exists$ into a corresponding node α and β, provided with a continuous activation function. Finally, the output of formulae classifying a same concept ω is merged into a γ node, corresponding to the $\vee$ connective implicit in the classification theory. The constraint part ψ_i of every rule r_i is used by the Unifier in order to compute the substitutions which must be fed in the network (constraints are used to limit the number of the substitution, reducing the otherwise exponential complexity).

Detector nodes correspond to a "fuzzy" interpretation of the membership of a real value in an interval, i.e. the rectangular function (2) is transformed into a bell shape gaussian function which returns 1 only when the function f has a value falling in the center of the interval $[a, b]$ and 0 when it tends to $\pm\infty$.

More precisely, a positive literal $L_i = inside(f_i(x_1, \ldots, x_s), [a_i, b_i])$ is translated into a neuron G_i having a Gaussian activation function of center $\mu_i = (b_i + a_i)/2$ and width $\sigma_i = (b_i - a_i)/2$.

The choice of the activation function for α, β and γ nodes need a special attention. In logic, the semantics usually adopted for the $\wedge$ connective is the function which returns the minimum of the truth values (min) of the conjuncts, whereas for the $\vee$ and $\exists$ connective is the maximum (max).

A derivable approximation of the min function is provided by the arithmetic product, whereas a reasonable approximation of the max function is provided by the so called *softmax* (S_M), computed by the expression $S_M(v_1 \ldots, v_n) = \frac{\sum_{i=1}^{n} v_i e^{\lambda v_i}}{\sum_{i=1}^{n} e^{\lambda v_i}}$ The properties of S_M have been investigated in [3] where it has been applied in a fuzzy neural network. An alternative to S_M could be a simple arithmetic sum or an arithmetic sum followed by a squashing function, such as a sigmoid.

Our choice has been to use the arithmetic product as α operator ($\wedge$), S_M as β operator ($\exists$), and a weighted sum followed by a sigmoid (perceptron) as γ operator ($\vee$). Therefore:

$$\alpha(v_1, \ldots, v_n) = \prod_{i=1}^{n} v_i, \qquad \beta(v_1, \ldots, v_m) = \frac{\sum_{i=1}^{m} v_i e^{\lambda v_i}}{\sum_{i=1}^{m} e^{\lambda v_i}}, \tag{4}$$

$$\gamma(v_1, \ldots, v_s) = \frac{1}{1 + e^{-\rho \sum_{i=1}^{s} w_i v_i + \xi}}$$

The reason for this choice was due to the fact that the network obtained is a straightforward generalization of a Factorizable RBFN [11, 1], whose behavior has been widely investigated in the literature. In fact, the only difference is represented by the additional layer implementing the existential quantification.

Anyhow, it is worth noting that this choice is in some sense arbitrary and in no way pretends to be considered as an optimal one. For instance, many alternative proposals can be found in the fuzzy logic controller literature [2, 17], which have not been explored in this work and which deserve attention.

3 Network Refinement

As all activation functions in FONNs are continuous and derivable in the whole parameter space, it is straightforward to apply the classical error gradient descent technique in order to finely tune the weights w_i, the parameters μ_j and σ_j in the detector units, and the bias terms ξ.

In order to improve learning speed and classification accuracy, and to avoid overtraining, a trick implemented in the backpropagation algorithm of SNNS (Stuttgart Neural Network Simulator) was introduced: at every epoch, if the error on the current pattern is less than some threshold ε, then backpropagation on that pattern is not performed. This mechanism essentially resulted in a faster convergence, and in most cases it reached also slightly better performances.

4 The Train Check-Out Case Study

Being not aware of a standard benchmark showing the characteristics necessary to evaluate FONNs (benchmarks in the UCI repository are primarily in a form well suited for learning in *propositional* logic, while those suited for first order logic deal with symbolic values only), we decided to build a new dataset. In order to analyze the behavior of a learning algorithm, artificial datasets offer the advantage that the learning task can be made arbitrarily complex by chosing the size of the data, the distribution of the attribute values and the rule for partitioning the learning events into positive and negative ones.

Starting from the well-known *train-going-east* problem defined by Michalski [10] we extended the dataset by introducing continuous features. A car is described by a vector of four continuous and five discrete attributes. A procedure randomly generates instances of trains, each composed by 2 to MAX cars. The general problem we chose is that of deciding whether a train cannot transit on a given line. Three different instances of the problem, of increasing complexity, have been created by varying the number of cars (from 1 to 3) and the kind of attributes (numerical and discrete) involved in the decision. In order to be able to rephrase the defined problems in a propositional setting, we chose a 0-arity concept *train-cannot-go()* to be learned.

For each task, we generated a series of learning sets $\mathcal{L}_1$, $\mathcal{L}_2$ and $\mathcal{L}_3$ composed of 100, 200, 500 trains, whose length was randomly chosen between 2 and 8

Rules

learner	learning set size	task 1	task 2	task 3
handcr. KB	—	4	2	2
SMART+	100	5–8	3–9	5–7
	200	5–8	9–12	6–13
	500	2–6	16–40	8–14
C4.5	100	11–14	11–22	11–24
	200	22–29	21–28	23–32
	500	34–46	47–60	46–77
CART	100	8–12	8–12	8–10
	200	13–20	12–19	14–17
	500	25–31	36–42	31–40

Networks

learner	learning set size	task 1	task 2	task 3
handcr. KB	—	9	8	7
SMART+	100	13–24	15–36	10–34
	200	18–31	50–67	31–58
	500	5–29	108–240	26–54
CART	100	44–90	36–77	35–58
	200	101–145	65–154	74–101
	500	174–248	258–288	200–307
MLP	—	301	301	301
Cascade Correlation Network	100	259	179	259
	200	259	259	259
	500	259	259	259

Table 1. Size of the rule bases and of the neural networks built by the various learners; the ranges have been obtained by taking the minimum and the maximum complexity obtained in 5 different runs with different learning sets.

cars; a first test set (test set $\mathcal{A}$) contains 10000 trains whose number of cars was randomly chosen between 2 and 8, as for the learning sets, and a second test set contains 10000 trains (test set $\mathcal{B}$) composed by 2 to 15 cars.

Moreover, we converted the FOL version of $\mathcal{L}_i$, $\mathcal{A}$ and $\mathcal{B}$ into an equivalent propositional setting, where each train is represented by a vector of 135 features; trains with less than 15 cars were represented by filling the vector with values out of range (-1). Obviously, this is not only a waste of space: propositional learners can be unable to generalize to trains longer than those seen during learning, i.e. they cannot learn from a set of short trains such as $\mathcal{L}_i$ with only 72 significant features and then apply the acquired knowledge to the structurally more complex set $\mathcal{B}$ without loss of accuracy.

All data are available on http://www.di.unito.it/~mluser/datasets.html and are fully described in [5].

5 FONN Experimental Evaluation.

First of all, four propositional learners (C4.5 [12], CART [6], MLP [13] and Cascade Correlation [7]) have been run on the propositional definition of each problem; with each learning algorithm several experiments have been done in order to find a good setting of their own parameters. Reported results refer to the best setting we found for the three problems. Furthermore, trees generated by C4.5 and CART have been translated into a propositional theory in order to have a complexity measure allowing to compare with FONNs. Then, handcrafted sets of rules, corresponding to the ones used for classifying the instances, but with a rough approximation of the intervals, have been fed to the FONN; thirdly, the relational learner SMART+ capable of learning numeric intervals in the form

Learner	learning set size	Task 1			Task 2			Task 3		
		$\mathcal{L}$	$\mathcal{A}$	$\mathcal{B}$	$\mathcal{L}$	$\mathcal{A}$	$\mathcal{B}$	$\mathcal{L}$	$\mathcal{A}$	$\mathcal{B}$
handcrafted	100	67.0	69.4	74.7	92.0	93.7	93.7	91.6	90.8	89.6
knowledge	200	68.5	69.4	74.7	93.0	93.7	93.7	87.8	90.8	89.6
base	500	68.0	69.4	74.7	93.3	93.7	93.7	91.0	90.8	89.6
handcrafted	100	85.6	87.8	89.2	93.4	90.8	90.2	98.2	96.9	96.3
KB +	200	85.9	88.7	91.1	93.4	92.3	91.6	95.0	97.2	95.1
FONN ($\varepsilon = 0$)	500	88.8	85.8	88.4	94.4	93.7	92.9	97.5	97.4	96.7
handcrafted	100	98.0	94.3	95.9	98.4	92.6	92.1	98.4	96.9	96.3
KB +	200	96.3	96.4	97.4	96.7	94.3	93.9	98.1	97.3	96.8
FONN ($\varepsilon = 0.3$)	500	96.1	95.7	96.9	95.8	95.3	94.5	98.3	97.6	97.1

Table 2. Comparative results for the handcrafted knowledge base; all numbers refer to the percentage of correctly classified trains, averaged over five runs with learning sets generated with different seeds. All refinement runs lasted 1000 epochs.

Learner	learning set size	Task 1			Task 2			Task 3		
		$\mathcal{L}$	$\mathcal{A}$	$\mathcal{B}$	$\mathcal{L}$	$\mathcal{A}$	$\mathcal{B}$	$\mathcal{L}$	$\mathcal{A}$	$\mathcal{B}$
Crisp	100	88.6	75.1	68.5	86.2	67.3	67.8	83.4	62.2	63.2
SMART+	200	88.7	82.5	77.0	86.5	76.6	75.3	86.0	70.5	69.7
	500	90.6	89.9	89.2	85.5	76.9	74.7	86.3	79.8	78.4
fuzzified	100	80.0	71.2	66.9	80.3	69.5	69.3	79.8	65.3	65.0
SMART+	200	86.0	83.7	83.9	79.6	76.0	75.1	76.8	70.6	69.7
	500	87.1	86.5	87.9	84.3	82.6	84.1	86.5	82.5	80.4
SMART+	100	92.8	88.0	87.3	95.0	73.8	74.0	92.4	69.9	68.3
+ FONN	200	91.1	88.3	90.5	91.8	79.2	79.0	91.1	75.6	74.0
($\varepsilon = 0.3$)	500	88.6	83.6	86.6	89.5	82.8	83.0	88.9	83.2	81.8

Table 3. Comparative results for the FOL learner SMART+ The experiments with $\varepsilon = 0$ are not reported since worse in the average, confirming the data in the previous table.

(2) with reasonable approximation has been run on the three problems and the learned knowledge has been refined by the FONN; for the experiments with SMART+, we allowed the learner to produce partially inconsistent knowledge bases; in doing so, SMART+ ran faster and produced rule sets, that generalized better to the test set, when compared to the results in [5].

Table 1 reports the sizes of the rule bases produced/used in our experiments and of the neural networks produced (RBFNs or MLP in the case of propositional learners; FONNs in the case of SMART+ and handcrafted knowledge); Tables 2, 3 and 4 list the obtained accuracy. A first observation concerns the complexity of the knowledge bases: as we claimed in Section 1, a first order representation is more compact, especially with larger learning sets, and results in smaller networks.

For what concerns the accuracy results, it should be pointed out that performances of FONN do not degrade from test set $\mathcal{A}$ to test set $\mathcal{B}$, rather in some cases performances are better, whereas propositional learners cannot generalize

Learner	learning set size	Task 1			Task 2			Task 3		
		$\mathcal{L}$	$\mathcal{A}$	$\mathcal{B}$	$\mathcal{L}$	$\mathcal{A}$	$\mathcal{B}$	$\mathcal{L}$	$\mathcal{A}$	$\mathcal{B}$
	100	97.2	77.2	73.6	96.8	66.5	65.5	97.6	64.0	62.1
C4.5	200	98.5	82.9	79.7	97.4	70.7	68.4	97.8	64.6	61.4
	500	98.5	89.3	86.5	97.7	75.3	71.2	97.9	71.4	68.8
	100	93.6	75.2	73.0	89.4	67.7	64.3	90.8	65.1	62.2
CART	200	96.9	86.1	82.9	88.4	67.3	64.5	90.6	68.3	64.0
	500	98.2	93.1	90.7	92.3	71.2	68.2	92.9	73.0	66.9
Multi	100	70.2	49.5	49.6	74.0	56.0	51.8	38.0	49.5	46.9
Layer	200	68.8	50.5	50.9	76.2	61.3	63.1	41.1	52.4	57.4
Perceptron	500	58.1	50.2	50.3	60.9	58.8	53.9	48.7	55.2	55.6
Cascade	100	66.0	53.1	52.1	100.0	68.3	69.6	42.0	55.7	61.9
Correlation	200	69.0	58.9	54.6	92.5	72.1	70.7	34.3	49.4	54.2
Network	500	61.0	55.5	54.8	84.4	77.5	73.3	54.5	58.7	65.1

Table 4. Accuracy results with some propositional learners.

as well. Moreover, the translation from rules to network reduces the performances on the learning sets, but not on the test sets.

The experiments clearly indicates that the refinement step performed by FONN usually increases accuracy on both learning and test set; in some rare cases the accuracy on the learning set is worsened: this strange behavior is due to the fact that the network is aimed to minimizing the mean square error, and not the classification error; the use of a threshold ε for triggering the learning step attenuates this phenomenon.

In order to fully understand the results for propositional learners, it should be pointed out that a large part of the examples in test set $\mathcal{B}$ can be classified correctly by looking only at the initial part (all the negative trains, and all those trains where the illegal combination of cars is in the first half of the train).

The results for MLP and cascade correlation on task 3 clearly indicates that the propositional networks did not learn anything of the target concept (since the learning set was balanced, a trivial system presenting always a constant output would reach an accuracy around 50%; results under or near 50 indicate a substantially random behavior).

Finally, it is worth noting how the performance results obtained using the handcrafted knowledge base are still much better than the ones obtained from the knowledge bases learned by SMART+. This is because the structural knowledge produced by SMART+ has been obtained by pure induction from the data and only partially corresponds to the correct one since, in the present case, the possibility of guiding SMART+ using a domain theory has not been exploited.

Figure 2 shows the handcrafted knowledge base for task 3 in order to compare it with one of the rules found by SMART+ with 500 training examples.

$$\exists x_1, x_2(near(x_1, x_2, 1) \wedge x_1 \neq x_2 \wedge \neg has\_brakes(x_1) \wedge \neg has\_brakes(x_2) \wedge$$
$$inside(weight(x_1), [40; 70]) \wedge inside(weight(x_2), [40; 70])) \rightarrow train\_cannot\_go$$

$$\exists x_1, x_2(near(x_1, x_2, 1) \wedge x_1 \neq x_2 \wedge \neg has\_brakes(x_1) \wedge \neg has\_brakes(x_2) \wedge$$
$$load\_type(x_1) = 3 \wedge load\_type(x_2) = 3 \wedge$$
$$inside(weight(x_1), [30; 70]) \wedge inside(weight(x_2), [30; 70])) \rightarrow train\_cannot\_go$$

$$\exists x_1, x_2(x_1 \neq x_2 \wedge \neg has\_brakes(x_1) \wedge \neg has\_brakes(x_2) \wedge near(x_1, x_2, 1)$$
$$inside(weight(x_1), [40.0; 60.0]) \wedge inside(weight(x_2), [42.0; 58.0])) \rightarrow train\_cannot\_go$$

$$\cdots$$

$$\exists x_1, x_2, x_3(x_1 \neq x_2 \wedge x_1 \neq x_3 \wedge x_2 \neq x_3 \wedge near(x_3, x_1, 2) \wedge$$
$$near(x_3, x_2, 3) \wedge \neg has\_brakes(x_1) \wedge \neg has\_brakes(x_2) \wedge$$
$$inside(length(x_3), [11.5; 20.5]) \wedge inside(width(x_3), [2.735; 2.465]))$$
$$inside(weight(x_1), [46.0; 64.0]) \wedge inside(weight(x_2), [40.0; 60.0])) \rightarrow train\_cannot\_go$$

Fig. 2. The handcrafted knowledge base for task 3 (upper box), compared with two of the nine rules found by SMART+ (below).

6 Conclusions

This paper present a method for mapping classification theories described in a restricted form of First Order Logics, into evaluation networks (FONNs), which are an extension of Factorizable Radial Basis Function Networks. This allows to combine symbolic relational learning algorithms with connectionist algorithms in order to deal with numeric features in FOL.

The experimentation on a challenging case study designed in order to test learning programs on structured data described by means of numeric features, shows that FONNs, working in a FOL setting, generalize much better than many other propositional learners do, when working in an equivalent setting in propositional logics. This proves the claims made in Section 1.

Nevertheless, in spite of this initial successful implementation, we believe that FONNs still need much more investigation and are suitable of many improvements concerning both the learning algorithm and the operator semantics.

Moreover, extensions in order to deal with multilayer, and recursive theories might be considered.

References

1. C. Baroglio, A. Giordana, M. Kaiser, M. Nuttin, and R. Piola. Learning controllers for industrial robots. *Machine Learning*, 23:221–250, July 1996.
2. H.R. Berenji. Fuzzy logic controllers. In R.R. Yager and L.A. Zadeh, editors, *An Introduction to Fuzzy Logic Applications in Intelligent Systems*, pages 69–96. Kluwer Academic Publishers, 1992.
3. H.R. Berenji and P. Khedkar. Learning and tuning fuzzy controllers through reinforcements. *IEEE Transactions on Neural Networks*, 3(5):724–740, September 1992.

4. E.B. Blumer, A. Ehrenfeucht, D. Haussler, and M.K. Warmuth. Learnability and the Vapnik-Chervonenkis dimension. *Journal of the ACM*, 36:929–965, 1989.

5. M. Botta, A. Giordana, and R. Piola. FONN: Combining first order logic with connectionist learning. In *Proceedings of the 14th International Conference on Machine Learning ICML-97*, Nashville, TN, July 1997. Morgan Kaufmann.

6. L. Breiman, J.H. Friedman, R.A. Ohlsen, and C.J. Stone. *Classification And Regression Trees*. Wadsworth & Brooks, Pacific Grove, CA, 1984.

7. S.E. Fahlman and C. Lebiere. The cascade-correlation learning architecture. In D. S. Touretzky, editor, *Advances in Neural Information Processing Systems 2*. Morgan Kaufmann, 1990.

8. L.M. Fu. Knowledge-based connectionism for revising domain theories. *IEEE Transactions on Systems, Man and Cybernetics*, 23(1):173–182, January 1993.

9. J.J. Mahoney and R.J. Mooney. Comparing methods for refining certainity-factor rule-bases. In *Proc. of the Eleventh Internetional Workshop on Machine Learning ML-94*, Rutgers University, NJ, July 1994.

10. R. Michalski. A theory and methodology of inductive learning. In R. Michalski, J. Carbonell, and T. Mitchell, editors, *Machine Learning: An Artificial Intelligence Approach*, pages 83–134, Los Altos, CA, 1983. Morgan Kaufmann.

11. T. Poggio and F. Girosi. Networks for approximation and learning. *Proceedings of the IEEE*, 78(9):1481–1497, September 1990.

12. R.J. Quinlan. Induction of decision trees. *Machine Learning*, 1:81–106, 1986.

13. D. E. Rumelhart and J. L. McClelland. *Parallel Distributed Processing : Explorations in the Microstructure of Cognition, Parts I & II*. MIT Press, Cambridge, Massachusetts, 1986.

14. G. Towell and J.W. Shavlik. Knowledge based artificial neural networks. *Artficial Intelligence*, 70(4):119–166, 1994.

15. G.G. Towell, J.W. Shavlik, and M.O. Noordwier. Refinement of approximate domain theories by knowledge-based neural networks. In *AAAI'90*, pages 861–866, 1990.

16. V. Tresp, J. Hollatz, and S. Ahmad. Network structuring and training using rule-based knowledge. In *Advances in Neural Information Processing Systems 5 (NIPS-5)*, 1993.

17. L.A. Zadeh. Knowledge representation in fuzzy logic. In R.R. Yager and L.A. Zadeh, editors, *An Introduction to Fuzzy Logic Applications in Intelligent Systems*, pages 1–25. Kluwer Academic Publishers, 1992.

A Way of Increasing both Autonomy and Versatility of a KDD System

Ning Zhong[1], Chunnian Liu[2], and Setsuo Ohsuga[3]

[1] Dept. of Computer Science and Sys. Eng., Yamaguchi University
[2] Dept. of Computer Science, Beijing Polytechnic University
[3] Dept. of Information and Computer Science, Waseda University

Abstract. How to increase both *autonomy* and *versatility* of a knowledge discovery system is a core problem and a crucial aspect of KDD (Knowledge Discovery in Databases). Within the framework of KDD process and the GLS (Global Learning Scheme) system recently proposed by us, this paper describes a way of increasing both *autonomy* and *versatility* of a KDD system. In our approach, the KDD process is modeled as an organized society of KDD agents with multiple levels. We propose a formalism to describe KDD agents, in the style of OOER (Object Oriented Entity Relationship data model). Based on this representation of KDD agents as operators, we apply several AI planning techniques, which are implemented as a meta-agent, so that we might (1) solve the most difficult problem in a multi-strategy and cooperative KDD system: how to automatically choose appropriate KDD techniques (KDD agents) to achieve a particular discovery goal in a particular application domain; (2) tackle the complexity of KDD process; and (3) support evolution of KDD data, knowledge, and process. The GLS system, as a multi-strategy and cooperative KDD system based on the approach and using the planning mechanism, increases both autonomy and versatility.

1 Introduction

How to increase both *autonomy* and *versatility* of a knowledge discovery system is a core problem and a crucial aspect of KDD (Knowledge Discovery in Databases). Zytkow described a way of increasing cognitive autonomy in machine discovery by implementing new components of the discovery process [13], namely, greater autonomy means more discovery steps in succession performed without external intervention, and external intervention can be replaced by automated search, reasoning, and the use of background knowledge-bases. On the other hand, it has been recently recognized in the KDD community that the KDD process for real-world applications is extremely complicated [1, 2, 11, 12]. There are several levels, phases and large number of steps and alternative KDD techniques in the process, iteration can be seen in anywhere and at any time, and the process may repeat at different intervals when new/updated data comes. However, no one has begun to describe

- How to plan, organize, control, and manage the KDD process dynamically for different KDD tasks;

- How to get the system to know it knows and impart the knowledge to decide what tools are appropriate for what problems and when.

Solving of such issues needs to develop *meta levels* of the KDD process by modeling such a process. We argue that modeling of the KDD process constitutes an important and new research area of KDD, including formal specification of the process, its planning, scheduling, controlling, management, evolution, and reuse. The key issue is how to increase both *autonomy* and *versatility* of a KDD system. Our methodology is to create an organized society of KDD agents. This means

- To develop many kinds of KDD agents for different objects;
- To use the KDD agents in multiple learning phases in a distributed cooperative mode;
- To manage the society of KDD agents by multiple meta-control levels.

That is, the society of KDD agents is made of many smaller components that are called *agents*. Each agent by itself can only do some simple thing. Yet when we join these agents in an *organized* society, this leads to implement more complex KDD tasks. Based on this methodology, we also design a multi-strategy and cooperative KDD system called GLS (Global Learning Scheme). In this paper, we describe a way of increasing both autonomy and versatility of the GLS system by applying several AI planning techniques that are implemented as a meta-agent to organize dynamically the KDD process.

To be able to apply AI planning techniques, each KDD agent should be regarded as an operator, and formally described. We introduce a formalism for this purpose in the style of OOER (Object-Oriented Entity Relationship data model). For each type of KDD agents, the types of its input/output, the precondition and effect of its execution, and its functionality are explicitly specified in the data model. The most difficult problem in a multi-strategy and cooperative KDD system is that how to choose appropriate KDD techniques to achieve a particular discovery goal in a particular domain. In our method, the combination of the formal description of KDD agents and the planning mechanism gives an automatic solution to this problem (to some extent, at least). In such a KDD system, both autonomy and versatility are increased.

The basic planning mechanism is a core domain-independent non-linear planner [3, 4] plus a KDD domain specific layer. The two meta-agents (planner and controller) cooperate to decompose the overall KDD process into a KDD agents network in a hierarchical manner. That is, high-level agents are gradually decomposed into networks of sub-agents (sub-plans). To facilitate this, the type of a high-level agent has the specification listing the types of its candidate sub-agents (meanwhile a low-level agent just has the associated KDD algorithms to carry out its task). Given a (sub)goal (to build a subplan to achieve the effect of a high-level KDD agent), the planner reasons on the candidate subagent types to choose the appropriate ones and build the (sub)plan which, when executed, would achieve the (sub)goal.

In a KDD process, both the data, knowledge, and the process itself are evolving. For example, knowledge refinement on data change is an important component of the KDD process. To support the evolution, we use the techniques such as incremental replanning or integration of planning and execution, which have been successfully applied to software development process [3, 4].

2 An Architecture of KDD Process

KDD process is a multi-step process centered on data mining algorithms to identify what is deemed knowledge from databases. In [12], we model the KDD process as an organized society of autonomous knowledge discovery agents (KDD agents, for short). Based on this model we have been developing a multi-strategy and cooperative KDD system called GLS (Global Learning Scheme) which increases both autonomy and versatility. Here we give a brief summary of the architecture of the GLS system.

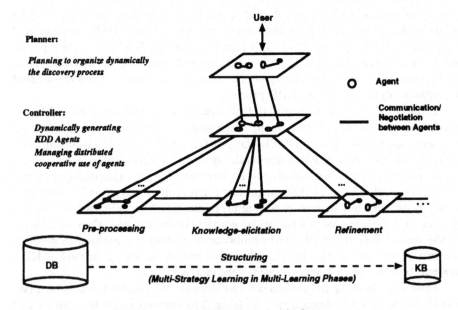

Fig. 1. The architecture of the GLS system

The system is divided into three levels: two meta-levels and one object level as shown in Figure 1. On the first meta-level, the *planning meta-agent* (planner, for short) sets the discovery process plan that will achieve the discovery goals when executed. On the second meta-level, the KDD agents are dynamically generated, executed, and controlled by the *controlling meta-agent* (controller, for short). Planning and controlling dynamically the discovery process is a key component to increase both autonomy and versatility of our system. On the object level, the KDD agents are grouped into three learning phases:

Pre-processing agents include: agents to collect information from global information sources to generate a central large database; agents to clean the data; and agents to decompose the large database into several local information sources (subdatabases), such as *CBK* (attribute oriented clustering using background knowledge), *QDR* (quantization by the division of ranges), *FSN* (forming scopes/clusters by nominal or symbolic attributes), and *SCT* (stepwise Chow test to discover structure changes in time-series data).

Knowledge-elicitation agents include: agents such as *KOSI* (knowledge oriented statistic inference for discovering structural characteristics – regression models), *DBI* (decomposition based induction for discovering concept clusters), and *GDTG* (generalization-distribution-table based generalization for discovering if-then rules).

Knowledge-refinement agents acquire more accurate knowledge (hypothesis) from coarse knowledge (hypothesis) according to data change and/or the domain knowledge. KDD agents such as *IIBR* (inheritance-inference based refinement) and *HML* (hierarchical model learning) are commonly used for this purpose.

Note that the GLS system, as a multi-strategy and cooperative KDD system, must provide alternative KDD agents for each learning phase. On the other hand, because of the complexity of databases and the diversification of discovery tasks, it is impossible to include all known/forthcoming KDD techniques. The KDD agents listed above are by no means exhaustive: they are included here because they have been developed previously by us. More agents will enter the system when the involved techniques become mature.

In terms of AI planning, no matter how many KDD agents we have, each of them is an *operator*. Each operator by itself can only do some simple thing, only when they are organized into a society, we can accomplish more complex discovery tasks. The KDD planner reasons on these operators to build KDD process plans – networks of KDD agents that will achieve the overall discovery goals when executed. But to apply AI planning techniques, we must be able to formally describe the KDD agents as operators. This is the subject of the next section.

3   Formal Description of KDD Agents

The KDD planner, as any AI planner, needs a World State Description (WSD) and a pool of Operators (Ops). We use the OOER (Object-Oriented Entity Relationship) data model to describe them. The traditional ER model has concepts of entity/relation, type/instance, instance-level attributes, and so on. The OOER model further incorporates object-oriented concepts such as subtyping, multiple inheritance, procedures, and type-level attributes/procedures, and so on. There are two kinds of types, *D&K* types and *Agent* types, for passive and active objects respectively. Figure 2 shows the (simplified) type hierarchy used in the GLS system.

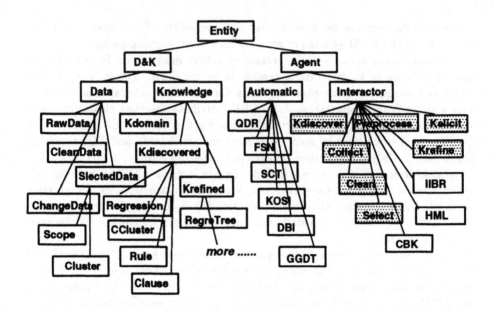

Fig. 2. The type hierarchy of the GLS system

The *D&K* types describe various data and knowledge presented in a KDD system. On the data part, we have *RawData* from the global information source, *CleanData* from the central large database, *SelectedData* (*Scope* or *Cluster*) from the subdatabases, and so on. On the knowledge part, we first distinguish among *Kdomain* (the background knowledge), *Kdiscovered* (the discovered knowledge), and *Krefined* (the refined knowledge). The type *Kdiscovered* has subtypes: *Regression* (structural characteristics), *CCluster* (conceptual clusters), *Rule* (if-then rules), *Clause* (predicate definitions), and so on. *Krefined* has subtypes *RegreTree* (family of regression models) and so on.

The *Agent* types describe various KDD techniques used in the GLS system. We distinguish Automatic (KDD algorithms) from Interactor (KDD techniques that need human assistance). *Kdiscover* means the overall KDD task, while *Preprocess, Kelicit* and *Krefine* stand for the three learning phases: preprocessing, knowledge-elicitation, and knowledge-refinement, respectively. *Collect, Clean* and *Select* are activities in *Preprocess.* Most agent types take the same technical names as mentioned in Section 2, such as *CBK, QDR, FSN, SCT, KOSI, DBI, GGDT, IIBR, HML.*

Note that in Figure 2, we show only the subtype relations among KDD objects (a subtype *is-a* special case of the supertype). For example, all of *Kdiscover, Preprocess, Kelicit, Krefine* are subtypes of Interactor. We will see below how to express the subagent relation, for example, *Preprocess, Kelicit, Krefine* are three subagents of *Kdiscover.*

Types have the ordinary instance-level attributes. For example, *D&K* has the attribute status describing the current processing status of the data/knowledge (created, cleaned, reviewed, stored, etc.), and this attribute is inherited by all subtypes of *D&K*. *Kdiscovered* has the attribute timestamps recording the time when the knowledge is discovered, and this attribute is inherited by all subtypes of *Kdiscovered (Regression, CCluster, Rule,* and *Clause*).

As for Agent types, there are additional properties defined. For example, we may have type/instance-level procedures expressing operations on the types or instances (creation, deletion, modification, etc.). However, the most interesting properties of Agent types are the following type-level attributes with information that is used by the planning meta-agent:

1. In/Out: specifying the types of the input/output of an agent type. The specified types are some subtypes of *D&K*, and the types of the actual input/output of any instance of the agent type must be subtypes of the specified types. For example, the In/Out for agent type *CBK* is:

   CleanData and *Kdomain* → $Scope$ ($ means unspecified number of)

2. Precond/Effect: specifying the preconditions for an agent (an instance of the agent type) to execute, and the effects when executed. Precond/Effect are logic formulas with the restrictions as in the classical STRIPS (see [9], for example). However, we allow more readable specifications for them. In next section we will see that the planner has a (KDD) domain-specific layer, and part of this layer will transform the high-level specifications into low-level logic formulas. As matter of the fact, a large part of the Precond/Effect, concerning constraints on input/output of the agent type, has been specified implicitly by the In/Out attribute. This is more declarative, and also because the detailed form (as conjunctions of literals) may not be able to write down at the type level. At planning time, the In/Out specification will be transformed into conjunctions of literals, then added to the Precond/Effect on which the planner reasons.

3. Action: a sequential program performing real KDD actions upon agent execution (e.g. to call the underlying KDD algorithms). It is empty for high-level agents (see below).

4. Decomp: describing possible subtasking. Instances of high-level agents (marked by shadowed boxes in Figure 2) should be decomposed into a network of subagents. Decomp specifies the candidate agent types for the subagents. For example, the Decomp for agent type *Kdiscover* is: {*Preprocess, Kelicit, Krefine*}. This specifies that a *Kdiscover* agent should be decomposed into a subplan built from *Preprocess, Kelicit* and *Krefine* agents. The exact shape of this subplan is the result of planning (in this case, the subplan happens to be a sequence of the three learning phases). As we will see in Section 4.2 about hierarchical planning, when the controller meets a high-level agent HA in the plan, it calls the planner to make a subplan to achieve the effect of HA. Then the planner searches the pool of the (sub)agent types listed in Decomp of HA, rather than Ops – the entire set of operators. Note that our

method is different from either [9] in which the subplan itself is written in Decomp, or [10] in which the decomposition is user-guided.

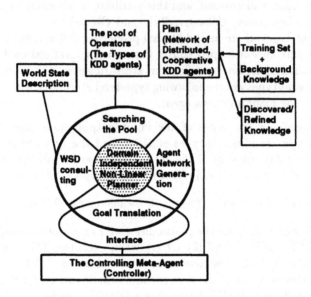

Fig. 3. The planning meta-agent coupled with the controlling meta-agent

4 KDD Process Planning

The planning meta-agent (the planner) has three layers as shown in Figure 3. The inner layer is a domain-independent non-linear planner, the middle layer deals with KDD-specific issues, and the out layer interacts with another meta-agent, the controller, to realize hierarchical planning. In the following subsections we will discuss these three layers separately, and give a scenario of KDD process planning.

4.1 Non-Linear Planning

The inner layer as shown in Figure 3 is a domain-independent non-linear planner. Given the initial world state, the discovery goal and the pool of operators (KDD agents), it starts with a dummy partial plan:

$Plan(Steps : \{s_1 : \{\}START\{initial\text{-}state\},$ % a step is denoted as {Precond}Agent{Effect}
             $s_2 : \{goal\}FINISH\{\}\},$ % a step is denoted as {Precond}Agent{Effect}
     $Ordering : \{s_1 < s_2\}$ % step s_1 is before step s_2
     $nLinks : \{\})$ % link $(s_i \rightarrow cs_j)$: s_i achieves Precond c of s_j

then expands the partial plan until finds a complete and consistent plan that solves the problem. The process can be implemented by a production system [3], or a nondeterministic algorithm:

> **while** *plan* is not a solution
> **do** pick a step *cs* from *Steps(plan)* with an unachieved precondition *c*;
> choose a step *ns* from the operator pool or *Steps(plan)* that achieves *c*;
> if there is no such step **then backtrack**;
> $Link(plan) \leftarrow Link(plan) + \{ns \rightarrow c\ cs\}$;
> $Ordering(plan) \leftarrow Ordering(plan) + \{ns < cs\}$;
> **if** *ns* is newly added to *plan*
> **then** add it to *Step(plan)* and add dummy ordering: *start* < *ns* < *finish*;
> **for** each $(s \rightarrow cs')$ in *Link(plan)* and s'' in *Step(plan)* with an effect *c*
> **do** either $Ordering(plan) \leftarrow Ordering(plan) + \{s'' < s\}$
> or $Ordering(plan) \leftarrow Ordering(plan) + \{s' < s''\}$
> if *plan* is not consistent **then backtrack**.

4.2 Hierarchical Planning

As we are dealing with real world KDD applications, a hierarchy of abstractions is essential. The process of alternatively adding detailed steps to the plan and actually executing some steps should continue until the goal is achieved. In GLS, the hierarchical planning is accomplished by the cooperation of the two meta-agents – planner and controller. The interface between them is the outer layer of Figure 3. The two meta-agents interact as follows.

At the beginning, the controller generates a high-level KDD agent HA (*Kdis-cover*, for example) with the discovery goal as its effect. This single agent HA can be regarded as the first coarse plan. When the controller tries to execute HA, it calls the planner to decompose it into a more detailed subplan. The planner works as described in the above subsection, taking the current world state as its initial-state, the effect of HA as its goal, and searching the types of subagents specified in the DECOMP attribute of HA, instead of the whole pool of operators, to achieve the goal. The produced subplan is added to the original plan, with each node linked to HA by a subagent relationship. Then the controller resumes its work (generating, executing, and controlling KDD agents according to the subplan).

Obviously this mechanism can work in multi-levels: if the controller meets another high-level agent when it executes the subplan, it will call the planner again.

4.3 KDD Specific Issues

Because the core of the planner is domain-independent, we provide a middle layer as shown in Figure 3 to deal with all KDD specific issues:

- To transform the KDD goals into STRIPS goals (logic formulas in the style of STRIPS, that is, conjunctions of literals), especially to translate the input/output constraints specified in the In/Out attribute into Pre-cond/Effect.

- To search the pool of operators (or more exactly, to search the types of subagents specified in the DECOMP attribute of a high level agent HA in the decomposition process) to introduce suitable KDD agents into the plan.
- To consult the world state description (WSD) to see if a precondition is already satisfied by the WSD, and/or help to transform the In/Out specification into conjunction of literals as part of Precond/Effect.
- To represent the resulting plan as a network of KDD agents, so the controller can dynamically generate and execute the KDD agents according to the network. The network can be also used by the user of the GLS system as a visualization tool.

4.4 A Scenario

Assume that we have a central, large space science database, each record (tuple) describing a star. The interesting attributes include CD (cluster designation), ET (effective temperature), LU (luminosity), B-V and U-B (color indexes). The facts such as we have already had a central, large database with *CleanData*, and the nominal attribute CD can be used for forming *Scopes*, etc. are explicitly stated in the initial-state (WSD). The discovery goal is to find structural characteristics hidden in the database and to refine them upon data change. Based on the specifications of WSD, goal, and KDD agent types, the planner and the controller cooperate in the manner as described in Section 4.2, and come up with a full KDD process plan as shown in Figure 4.

The process goes as follows. The initial plan consists of a single KDD agent *Kdiscover* to produce *RegreTree* that is a subtype of *Krefined*. It is decomposed into the sequential phases: *Preprocess, Kelicit,* and *Krefine* (in Figure 4, we also show the input/output types for these KDD agents). As the WSD contains the fact that we have already got *CleanData, Preprocess* can be simply done by *Select* (no need of *Collect* and *Clean*). Because the nominal attribute CD designates star clusters, and we need clustering other attributes as preparation for the next learning phase, *Select* is decomposed into *FSN* and *CBK* that can be executed in parallel and cooperatively. The result of the execution of *Select* (or its subplan) is n subdatabases.

Then the second learning phase *Kelicit* is under consideration. Here we show how to transform the In/Out of *Kelicit* into part of Precond/Effect. The original In/Out specification,

$$SelectedData \rightarrow Kdiscovered,$$

is first refined to subtypes:

$$\$Scope \rightarrow \$Regression,$$

where $ means unspecified number of. Then, by consulting the current WSD that contains n subdatabases, we have got the precondition "there are n Scopes" and

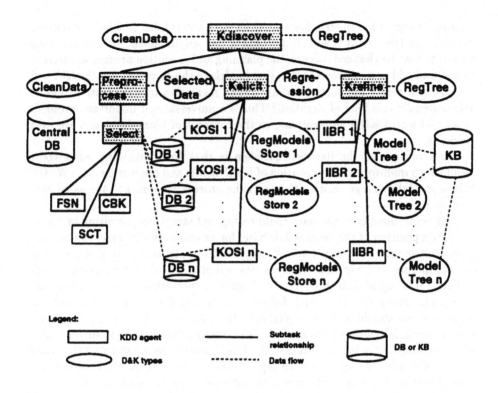

Fig. 4. A sample KDD process plan

the effect "there will be n regression model stores" (represented as conjunctions of literals). The result of decomposing *Kelicit* as shown in Figure 4 is that n *KOSIs* are needed in the subplan of *Kelicit* to learn from the n *subdatabases* separately and in parallel. (But in terms of implementation, we may install only one *KOSI* tool with multiple executions, just as in software development process, one compiler may be used simultaneously to compile several source files). In the third learning phase *Krefine,* we have a similar situation: there are n *IIBRs* to refine and manage the knowledge (regression models) discovered by the n *KOSIs* in parallel.

5   Evolution of Data, Knowledge, and KDD Process

Most of the KDD process shown in Figure 4 are automated by the cooperation of the planner and the controller, based on the formal description of WSD, goal, and KDD agents. However, there is a subtle point: the KDD process is a repetitive one involving hypotheses generation, evaluation, and refinement. When the KDD process is planned and executed first time, the original database is used and the discovered regression models are stored for each subdatabases. Later, whenever data change (new data is added, old data is deleted/modified, or even the data structure may be changed) occurs, the planning and execution process will iterate to find and add new version of regression models to the stores, and each $IIBR$ will manage and refine the corresponding tree of regression models. How to model and automate this kind of iteration? This is a universal and important problem in all real world KDD applications, as the contents of most databases are ever changing.

One solution to the iteration problem is that the controlling meta-agent should keep monitoring the execution of KDD agents and the world state (WSD). Whenever data change occurs, it restarts the process according to the same process plan.

But some changes in the data could be big and structural, resulting in different decomposition of the central database, for example. In this case, the process plan itself should be changed accordingly. For example, in Figure 4, when there are continuing and big data changes, the subplan of $Select$ may need an additional SCT agent (the bold box in Figure 4) to discover possible structure changes in time-series data. And if the reexecution of $Select$ results in more subdatabases, we should add more $KOSIs$ in the subplan of $Kelicit$. This is called $process\ evolution$. Other facts may cause process evolution as well, such as: new KDD techniques are introduced into the KDD system, the platform of the KDD system is enhanced, and so on. In [4], we have applied an incremental replanning algorithm to successfully deal with software process evolution, which is now adapted to KDD process. The main idea is to adjust the existing plan according to the changed WSD and/or KDD agents description, rather than replanning from scratch.

The full integration of planning and execution (see [9], for example) is another technique to solve the problems of execution failure, process iteration and environment change. In this method, rather than thinking of the planner and controller as separate meta-agents, we can think of them as a single meta-agent that is directly connected to an environment. The meta-agent is thought of as always being part of the way through executing a plan. Its activities include: executing some steps of the plan that are ready to be executed; refining the plan to resolve any of the standard deficiencies; refining the plan in the light of additional information obtained during execution; refining the plan in the light of data change and other unexpected changes in the environment.

6 Concluding Remarks

We presented a way of increasing both *autonomy* and *versatility* of a KDD system. Following our framework of KDD process and within the GLS system, we discussed in detail one of the meta-agents in GLS, the KDD process planning. We proposed a formalism to describe KDD agents, in the style of OOER (Object Oriented Entity Relationship data model). Based on this representation of KDD agents as operators, we apply several AI planning techniques: non-linear planning (partial-order planning) as the basic reasoning mechanism; hierarchical planning (task-decomposition) to tackle the complexity of KDD process; and replanning (or integration of planning and execution) to support data/knowledge/process evolution. The GLS system, as a multi-strategy and cooperative KDD system based on the framework and using the planning mechanism, increases both autonomy and versatility.

In comparison, GLS is mostly similar to INLEN in related systems [5]. In INLEN, a database, a knowledge-base and several existing methods of machine learning are integrated as several operators. These operators can generate diverse kinds of knowledge about the properties and regularities existing in the data. INLEN was implemented as a toolkit like GLS. However, GLS can dynamically plan and organize the KDD process performed in a distributed cooperative mode for different KDD tasks. Moreover, the refinement for knowledge is one of important capabilities of GLS that was not developed in INLEN.

GLS is implemented by KAUS. KAUS is a knowledge-based system shell developed in our group [7]. Thanks to the useful capabilities such as meta reasoning, multiple knowledge worlds/levels and the model representation in KAUS, and the recent development of distributed KAUS [8], GLS can be easily implemented and extended by KAUS. Since the GLS system to be finished by us is very large and complex, however, we have only finished several parts of the system and have undertaken to extend it for creating a more integrated, organized society of KDD agents. That is, the work that we are doing takes but one step toward a multi-strategy and distributed cooperative KDD system.

References

1. Brachman, R.J. and Anand, T. "The Process of Knowledge Discovery in Databases: A Human-Centred Approach", In *Advances in Knowledge Discovery and Data Mining*, MIT Press, (1996) 37-58.
2. Fayyad,U.M., Piatetsky-Shapiro,G, and Smyth, P. 1996. "From Data Mining to Knowledge Discovery: an Overview", In *Advances in Knowledge Discovery and Data Mining*, MIT Press, (1996) 1-36.
3. Liu, C. "Software Process Planning and Execution: Coupling vs. Integration", LNCS 498, Springer (1991) 356-374.
4. Liu, C. and Conradi, R. "Automatic Replanning of Task Networks for Process Evolution in EPOS", *Proc. ESEC'93*, LNCS 717, Springer (1993) 437-450.
5. Michalski, R.S. et al. 1992. Mining for Knowledge in Databases: The INLEN Architecture, Initial Implementation and First Results. *J. of Intell. Infor. Sys.*, KAP, 1(1):85-113.
6. Minsky,M. 1986. *The Society of Mind*, Simon and Schuster, New York.
7. Ohsuga, S. 1990. Framework of Knowledge Based Systems. *Knowl. Based Sys.*, 3(4):204-214.
8. Ohsuga, S. 1995. A Way of Designing Knowledge Based Systems. *Knowl. Based Sys.*, 8(4):211-222.
9. S.J.Russell and P.Norvig *Artificial Intelligence - A Modern Approach* Prentice Hall, Inc. (1995).
10. R. Engels "Planning Tasks for Knowledge Discovery in Databases - Performing Task-Oriented User-Guidance", *Proc. KDD-96* (1996) 170-175.
11. Zhong,N. and Ohsuga,S. "Toward A Multi-Strategy and Cooperative Discovery System", *Proc. KDD-95* (1995) 337-342.
12. Zhong,N., Kakemoto,Y., and Ohsuga,S. "An Organized Society of Autonomous Knowledge Discovery Agents", *Proc. CIA'97*, LNAI 1202, Springer (1997) 183-194.
13. Zytkow, J.M. 1993. Introduction: Cognitive Autonomy in Machine Discovery. *Machine Learning*, KAP, 12(1-3):7-16.
14. Zytkow, J.M. and Zembowicz, R., 1993. "Database Exploration in Search of Regularities", J. Intell. Infor. Sys., KAP, 2(1):39-81.

A Comparison of Attribute Selection Strategies
for Attribute-Oriented Generalization

Brock Barber
Department of Computer Science
University of Regina
Regina, Sask., Canada S4S 0A2
barber@cs.uregina.ca
(306) 585-4654

Howard J. Hamilton
Department of Computer Science
University of Regina
Regina, Sask., Canada S4S 0A2
hamilton@cs.uregina.ca
(306) 585-4079

Attribute-oriented generalization (AOG) is a knowledge discovery method that uses generalization to simplify the descriptions of patterns in database data. AOG repeatedly replaces specific values for an attribute with more general concepts according to domain-expert defined concept hierarchies. The degree of generalization is controlled by 2 user-defined thresholds. As presented by other researchers, the AOG process does not consider how interesting the results will be to the user. Given a relation retrieved from a database, many different relations can be created by generalization, some of which will be more interesting to the user than others. The attribute selection strategy, the method of choosing the next attribute for generalization, determines which of the many possible relations will be generated and thus can be used to direct the user towards the most interesting relations. We evaluate the performance of ten previously proposed and new attribute selection strategies by applying them to a 10,000 tuple public domain database and an 8,000,000 tuple commercial database. The strategies are compared using criteria that consider their ability to efficiently produce interesting results. We use measures of interestingness that consider the structure of the hierarchies that are used to guide generalization. Based on the comparison of the experimental results, a strategy that considers the complexity of the concept hierarchies was found to provide efficient and effective guidance towards interesting results.

Keywords: Learning and knowledge discovery, applications

1. Introduction

Attribute-oriented generalization summarizes and simplifies the information in a database by repeatedly replacing specific attribute values in a relation with more general concepts [5]. As related specific attribute values are grouped together into more general concepts, some tuples in the relation become redundant. By eliminating all but one of the redundant tuples, the total number of tuples in the relation is reduced. Each attribute has an associated concept hierarchy, defined by a domain expert, that guides the generalization of that attribute. A *concept hierarchy* is represented as a tree structure that has representations of all possible attribute values as leaves and a single most general concept called ANY at the root. The interior nodes of the tree represent increasing levels of generalization as the tree is ascended from the leaves to the root. Figure 1 depicts the concept hierarchies for two attributes, called Attribute A and Attribute B. A sample relation consisting of concept values for the two attributes is shown in Table 1. Table 2 shows R_A, the relation that would be obtained by generalizing values for attribute A up one level in its concept hierarchy. Table 3 shows R_B, the relation that would be obtained by generalizing attribute B.

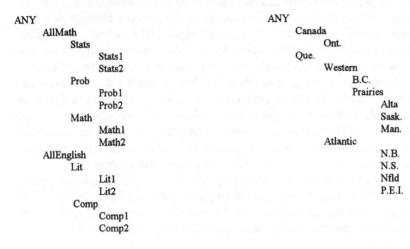

a) Concept Hierarchy for Attribute A   b) Concept Hierarchy for Attribute B

Figure 1: Concept Hierarchies for the Attributes of the Sample Relation

Att A	Att B
Stats1	B.C.
Stats2	B.C.
Prob2	B.C.
Math1	B.C.
Math2	B.C.
Stats2	N.B.
Math2	N.B.
Stats2	N.S.
Stats2	P.E.I.
Prob2	P.E.I.
Stats1	Prairies
Prob1	Prairies
Math1	Prairies
Math2	Prairies

Att A	Att B
Stats	B.C.
Prob	B.C.
Math	B.C.
Stats	N.B.
Math	N.B.
Stats	N.S.
Stats	P.E.I.
Prob	P.E.I.
Stats	Prairies
Prob	Prairies
Math	Prairies

Att A	Att B
Stats2	Atlantic
Prob2	Atlantic
Math2	Atlantic
Stats1	Western
Stats2	Western
Prob1	Western
Prob2	Western
Math1	Western
Math2	Western

Table 1: Sample Relation   Table 2: Relation R_A Table 3: Relation R_B

In AOG, the degree of generalization is governed by two user-defined thresholds. An *attribute threshold* T_a for each attribute is used to specify the maximum number of distinct attribute values for that attribute that are permitted in the final generalized relation. The *table threshold* T_t specifies the maximum number of tuples permitted in the final generalized relation. The thresholds used in AOG are non-intuitive and domain knowledge is unlikely to provide sufficient guidance about threshold values to produce useful and interesting results.

The AOG process does not consider the interestingness of the relations that can be generated during the generalization process. Given an input relation, many different relations can be created by generalization. Let GS be the *generalization space*, the set of all relations that can be produced by the generalization of zero or more attributes of the input relation according to the concept hierarchies. The generalization space is a type of version space [10] where permissible generalizations are defined by the concept hierarchies, negative examples are not considered and each hypothesis is a relation. Each relation in GS can be represented in terms of how many times each attribute has been generalized. For example, assume an input relation has three attributes a, b and c. A generalized relation $R_g(a_0b_1c_2)$ has been generated by generalizing attribute a zero times, attribute b once and attribute c twice. The relationship between relations in GS can be represented as a graph, where each node is a unique relation in GS and each link leaving a node represents a generalization of the node relation on a particular attribute.

Figure 2 shows a simple generalization graph for an input relation with three attributes. The upper left node represents the input relation and the lower-right node is the maximally generalized relation. In the *maximally generalized relation*, all attributes have been generalized to the most general concept ANY. Moving from the

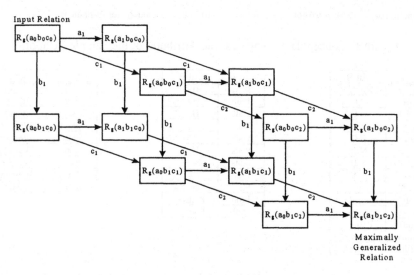

Figure 2: Graph of the Generalization Space

input relation to the maximally generalized relation can be viewed as taking a path through the graph, with each step in the path requiring the selection of an attribute to generalize. In machine learning, selection methods chose attributes to retain and others are eliminated [7]; here we select attributes to generalize one step, which may eliminate them. Applying AOG can be regarded as following a path from the input relation towards the maximally generalized relation that stops as soon as an acceptable relation is reached. If a single path is taken through the graph, some relations in the graph will not be generated. If each unique relation in the graph is assigned a value indicating its interestingness based on characteristics of the relation, it follows that the *attribute selection strategy*, the method used to select the next attribute for generalization, will affect the interestingness of the relations that can be generated. Thus, an attribute selection strategy can be used to augment or replace the attribute threshold, by guiding the user towards interesting results.

This paper describes an experimental investigation of ten different strategies for choosing the next attribute for generalization. The strategies are evaluated according to their ability to produce interesting results and their efficiency in producing these results. Other than an initial report on this research (which examined fewer strategies, with far fewer experiments on only one database) [1], no previous comparison of these strategies has appeared in the literature. The criteria used to compare the different strategies are discussed in Section 2. Section 3 describes the strategies and provides examples to illustrate their behavior. Section 4 briefly outlines the experiments, Section 5 presents and discusses the results of the experiments, and Section 6 presents our conclusions.

2. Criteria for the Evaluation of Selection Strategies

A variety of interestingness measures have been proposed (3, 6, 8, 9, 11, 14, 15) to quantify the significance of information discovered from databases. The two interestingness measures proposed in [3] are used here because they are based on the results of attribute-oriented generalization. The measures assign an interestingness value to a generalized relation based on the interestingness of the attribute values in it. An attribute value in a relation is considered to be interesting only if it corresponds to an interior concept in the appropriate concept hierarchy. An *interior* concept is defined as any non-leaf, non-ANY concept. The original values of the attributes and the ANY node of a concept tree do not provide any new information that cannot be obtained by direct database queries, so the occurrence of these values in a relation are considered to be uninteresting.

Measure I_1 is the number of attribute values in an output relation that correspond to interior concepts in the appropriate concept hierarchies. Measure I_2 considers the depths and the weighted heights of interior concepts in the appropriate concept hierarchy. The *depth* d_{cht} of a node in a concept hierarchy tree is defined so that the depth of the root node is 0 and the depth of any other node is 1 more than the depth of its parent. The *weighted height* of a node t is given by $wh_t = w(t)/n(t)$ where $n(t)$ is the number of leaf descendants of the node and $w(t) = n(t) + \Sigma\ w(c)$ where c is a child from the set of children of node t. The interestingness of the attribute value v in the concept hierarchy tree cht is $IN(v,cht) = (k)d_{cht}(v) + (1 - k)wh_{cht}(v)$. The term k has a value ranging from 0 to 1 and is used to control the relative importance assigned to the depth and weighted height factors. Since I_1 and I_2 are based on the structure of the concept hierarchies they require no additional domain knowledge and they are inexpensive to compute.

3. Attribute Selection Strategies

In Table 4, we list the attribute selection strategies considered in this study. Each strategy is classified as either lookahead (L) or predictive (P). In a *lookahead strategy*, the current relation with *m* attributes is used to generate *m* new relations. Each of the new relations is created by generalizing a different attribute in the current relation once. Properties of these new relations are used to select the best attribute to use for the actual generalization. Only one-step lookahead strategies, where a decision is made after looking ahead one generalization, are considered in this study. In a *predictive strategy*, values that exist prior to the generalization are used to make the selection. In the time complexity, *m* is the number of attributes in the input relation, n_i is the number of tuples in that relation and n_o is the number of tuples in the relation obtained by generalizing one attribute in the input relation.

Attribute Selection Strategy	S-code	Class	Complexity
Most Distinct Attribute Values	S1	P	$O(m)$
Largest Reduction in Tuples	S2	L	$O(m^2 n_o n_i)$
Smallest Reduction in Tuples	S3	L	$O(m^2 n_o n_i)$
Largest Complexity Measure M_1	S4	P	$O(m)$
Largest Complexity Measure M_2	S5	P	$O(m)$
Largest R_n/T_a	S6	P	$O(m)$
Smallest R_n/T_a	S7	P	$O(m)$
Fewest Distinct Attribute Values	S8	P	$O(m)$
Largest Interestingness Measure I_1	S9	L	$O(m^2 n_o n_i)$
Largest Interestingness Measure I_2	S10	L	$O(m^2 n_o n_i)$
Largest Interestingness Measure I_1'	S11	L	$O(m^2 n_o n_i)$
Largest Interestingness Measure I_2'	S12	L	$O(m^2 n_o n_i)$

Table 4: Attribute Selection Strategy Classification and Time-Complexity

Several of the strategies in Table 4 have been suggested in the literature (S1 in [5], S2 in (2, 5), S3 in [2], S6 in [13] and S7 in [13]). Strategies S6 and S7 were not tested because they rely on the attribute threshold.

Six new strategies based on the interestingness measures discussed in Section 2 were also examined. Strategies S9 and S10 are lookahead strategies that select the attribute for generalization which produces a generalized relation with the highest I_1 and I_2, respectively. Strategies S11 and S12 are modified versions of strategy S9 and S10 in which the generalization of an attribute to the ANY concept is not allowed, unless there are no other generalizations available.

Strategies S4 and S5 are predictive strategies that use complexity measures developed in [3] to select the attribute whose concept hierarchy has the greatest potential for interestingness. The complexity measures are closely related to the interestingness measures I_1 and I_2. The first measure of complexity, referred to as M_1, is simply the sum of the interior concepts in a concept tree t. The second measure of the complexity, referred to as M_2, is determined by the equation $M_2 = \Sigma IN(value(j,t),t)$ where t is a concept tree, j is a node in the concept tree, $value(j,t)$ is the concept value of the node and $IN(value(j,t),t)$ is the interestingness of the node.

To consider the properties of the actual attribute values in the relation being examined, only interior concepts in the concept tree with a depth less than that of the concepts in the current relation contribute to the complexity. In this way, only the concepts that may potentially be reached through further generalization are considered in the selection of the next attribute to generalize. Inactive branches are removed prior to the determination of the interestingness. An *active concept* is defined as being in the set including the leaf concepts derived from the data retrieved from the database in response to a specified learning task and any concept that can potentially be reached by tree ascension from these leaf concepts.

3.1 Examples of Attribute Selection Strategies S9, S10, S4 and S5

Lookahead strategies based on I_1 (S9 and S11) and I_2 (S10 and S12) select the attribute for generalization that would produce the most interesting relation after the generalization. As an example of how the interestingness of each concept in a relation is determined, the concept Western for attribute B in Figure 1 will be examined. The concept is an interior concept, so it is considered in the determination of the interestingness measures. There are 6 instances of the concept in relation R_B, shown in Table 3, so it adds 6 to the interestingness measure I_1. The concept hierarchy for attribute B shows that $d_{cht}(Western) = 2$ and that the concept has children B.C. and Prairies. The concept B.C. is a leaf concept so $n(B.C.) = 1$ and $w(B.C.) = 0$. The concept Prairies has 3 leaf concepts as children, each with $n = 1$ and $w = 0$. Therefore, $n(Prairies) = 1 + 1 + 1 = 3$ and $w(Prairies) = (1 + 1 + 1) + 0 = 3$. Now $n(Western) = 1 + 3 = 4$, $w(Western) = (1 + 3) + (0 + 3) = 7$ and $wh(Western) = 7/4 = 1.75$. Using $k = 0.5$, $IN(Western, cht) = 0.5(2) + 0.5(1.75) = 1.9$. Since there are 6 instance of Western in the relation, it contributes $6(1.9) = 11.4$ to the interestingness measure I_2.

The values used to determine I_1 and I_2 for R_A, shown in Table 2, and R_B are summarized in Table 5. In this table, i is the number of times a concept appears in a relation. Using the table values, $I_1(R_A) = 14$, $I_2(R_A)$ and I_2 for R_A are greater than the corresponding interestingness measures for the $= 19.5$, $I_1(R_B) = 9$ and $I_2(R_B) = 15.9$. Since both I_1 and I_2 for R_A are greater than the corresponding interestingness

Values for Relation R_A					Values for Relation R_B				
Concept	Type	i	IN	i*IN	Concept	Type	i	IN	i*IN
Stats	Interior	5	1.5	7.5	Stats1	Leaf	-	0	-
Prob	Interior	3	1.5	4.5	Stats2	Leaf	-	0	-
Math	Interior	3	1.5	4.5	Prob1	Leaf	-	0	-
B.C.	Leaf	-	0	-	Prob2	Leaf	-	0	-
N.B.	Leaf	-	0	-	Math1	Leaf	-	0	-
N.S.	Leaf	-	0	-	Math2	Leaf	-	0	-
P.E.I.	Leaf	-	0	-	Atlantic	Interior	3	1.5	4.5
Prairies	Interior	3	1	3.0	Western	Interior	6	1.9	11.4

Table 5: Values for Determination of Interestingness Measures

measures for the relation R_B, attribute A would be chosen for generalization regardless of which interestingness measure is used to make the selection.

For attribute selection strategies based on M_1 (S4) and M_2 (S5), the interestingness of all potentially active concepts is determined once for a learning task. For attribute B, we assume that each of the concepts Alta, Sask., and Man. were active and generalized to the concept Prairies in the sample relation. Since the concept Nfld is not found in the input relation, it is not active. Therefore, it is not considered in the calculation of the interestingness of the concepts Atlantic and Canada. For attribute A, the concepts Lit, Comp, English and AllEnglish are inactive.

The values used to determine the complexity measures for the sample relation attributes are summarized in Table 6. Using these values, $M_1(A) = 4$, $M_2(A) = 6.0$, $M_1(B) = 3$ and $M_2(B) = 5.1$. Since both M_1 (A) and $M_2(A)$ are greater than $M_1(B)$ and $M_2(B)$ respectively, attribute A would be chosen for generalization regardless of which complexity measure is used to make the selection.

Potentially Active for Att A			Potentially Active for Att B		
Concept	i	IN	Concept	i	IN
Stats	1	1.5	Atlantic	1	1.5
Prob	1	1.5	Western	1	1.9
Math	1	1.5	Canada	1	1.7
AllMath	1	1.5			

Table 6: Values Used for the Determination of Complexity Measures

4.0 Experimental Approach

Our experiments were performed on two databases. One database was a National Science and Engineering Research Council of Canada (NSERC) grant and award information database. It is a relatively small 10,000 tuple database. The other database was a commercial 8,000,000 tuple database provided by Saskatchewan Telecommunications (SaskTel). The strategies were tested on 475 discovery tasks on the Sasktel database and 183 discovery tasks on the NSERC database.

After the target relation was retrieved for a task, all unique relations that could be produced through one or more generalizations of the attributes in the target relation were generated, and I_1max_n and I_2max_n were determined. I_1max_n and I_2max_n are the maximum I_1 and I_2 values of relations with n tuples in the set of all possible unique relations for a task. After each generalization step $index_i$, n, m_a, I_1, I_1max_n, $\%d_1$, I_2, I_2max_n and $\%d_2$ were determined for the newly generalized relation. The value $index_i$ is the index of the attribute that was generalized to create the relation, m_a is the number of active attributes, $\%d_1$ is the percent difference between the computed I_1 of the relation and I_1max_n and $\%d_2$ is the percent difference between the computed I_2 of the relation and I_2max_n. An *active attribute* is defined as one that is not generalized to the ANY concept.

5.0 Experimental Results

The performance of a strategy for a particular task is quantified by calculating the percent difference between the actual interestingness measures of a relation with n tuples produced by the strategy and the corresponding $Imax_n$ value. The percent difference values are calculated using the equations $\%d_1 = (I_1 - I_1max_n)/I_1max_n$ and $\%d_2 = (I_2 - I_2max_n)/I_2max_n$. The relations corresponding to the I_1max_n or I_2max_n values for a task frequently lie on different paths through the attribute generalization graph. As a result, none of the strategies examined here can produce all the maxima for a task. However, these values provide an upper bound that can be used as an indication of the effectiveness of the strategies in producing interesting results.

Values for $\%d_1$ and $\%d_2$ were determined for thousands of relations with sizes ranging from 3500 tuples to 1 tuple. We consider the behavior of the strategies be more important for smaller, simpler relations that are more likely to be understandable to the user, so the discussion in this paper focuses on relations with 100 or fewer tuples. As data was collected for approximately 52,000 relations with a size within this range, it was necessary to summarize and simplify the data to facilitate analysis. This was done by calculating $\%d_{1a}$ and $\%d_{2a}$, the average $\%d_1$ and $\%d_2$ over ranges of tuples for all relations produced by each strategy in all tasks.

Table 7 presents a summary of the $\%d_{2a}$ values calculated for relations with 100 or fewer tuples for the tasks run against the SaskTel database. In this table, the strategies are ranked by $\%d_{2a}$ values for 10 tuple ranges. Similar ranked $\%d_{2a}$ data is given for the tasks run against the NSERC database in Table 8. Although both $\%d_{1a}$ and $\%d_{2a}$ were calculated for all strategies, the indicated behavior of the strategies was found to be similar regardless of whether $\%d_{1a}$ or $\%d_{2a}$ was used to examine the strategy behavior. Therefore, $\%d_{2a}$ will be used to illustrate strategy behavior in this paper.

The ranked summaries show that no single strategy provided the best performance over the entire range of interest. For the Sasktel tasks, strategy S4 yields significantly lower $\%d_{1a}$ and $\%d_{2a}$ values for relations with 1 to 10 tuples than any of the other strategies tested. Strategies 11 and 12 performed the best for relations with 11 to 100 tuples. For the NSERC tasks, strategy S4 gave the best results for relations with 1-20 tuples and either strategy S11 or strategy S12 produced the lowest $\%d_{1a}$ values and $\%d_{2a}$ for relations with 21 to 100 tuples.

Strategy S4 performs poorly in the initial stages of the generalization because the complexity measures provide a relatively inaccurate estimate of the potential for interestingness of the remaining portions of the concept hierarchies for larger relations. This is because it considers only the complexity of the remaining nodes in the hierarchies that can be reached by generalization, but not the proportioning of the concept values from the hierarchies in the relation being generalized. For example, consider a single concept value for each of two attributes in a relation, with one having many more instances in the relation than the other. The importance of the ancestor nodes of the more frequently occurring concept is not assigned any more or less weight than the ancestor nodes of the less frequently occurring value. One reason this strategy performs better near the end of the generalization process is that there are fewer multiple occurrences of the same concept values and the complexity measures provide better guidance towards interesting concepts. Additionally, since the complexity of the ANY node in a hierarchy is zero, an attribute will not be generalized to the ANY concept until there are no non-ANY generalizations to perform. This consistently seems to be an important factor in determining the ability of a strategy to produce interesting relations.

Strategies S9 and S10 perform well in initial generalizations. Near the end of the generalization process, performance is poor because these strategies eliminate attributes relatively early in the generalization process. A relation with n tuples and

Range	Rank=1 S	%d₂ₐ	Rank=2 S	%d₂ₐ	Rank=3 S	%d₂ₐ	Rank=4 S	%d₂ₐ	Rank=5 S	%d₂ₐ	Rank=6 S	%d₂ₐ	Rank=7 S	%d₂ₐ	Rank=8 S	%d₂ₐ	Rank=9 S	%d₂ₐ	Rank=10 S	%d₂ₐ
1-10	S4	-10.2	S1	-16.5	S5	-18.2	S12	-25.4	S11	-27.5	S2	-30.3	S9	-59.3	S10	-60.9	S3	-63.8	S8	-66.7
11-20	S12	-11.7	S1	-13.9	S4	-14.1	S1	-23.4	S5	-24.1	S10	-33.7	S9	-33.7	S2	-43.8	S3	-46.1	S8	-75.1
21-30	S11	-11.3	S11	-11.5	S1	-17.5	S1	-25.6	S5	-28.2	S9	-35.0	S10	-36.4	S2	-46.6	S3	-49.4	S8	-75.8
31-40	S11	5.4	S12	5.5	S4	-18.7	S1	-23.5	S9	-31.5	S5	-31.8	S10	-33.3	S2	-41.2	S3	-41.3	S8	-73.8
41-50	S11	-6.6	S12	-6.8	S4	23.5	S9	-24.0	S10	-24.8	S1	-30.1	S3	-36.4	S5	-38.0	S2	-45.1	S8	-72.2
51-60	S12	-16.4	S11	-17.5	S10	-22.4	S9	-22.8	S4	-31.5	S1	-36.7	S5	-44.6	S3	-46.6	S2	-49.2	S8	-71.8
61-70	S11	-7.2	S12	-7.4	S9	-16.7	S10	-17.0	S4	-27.3	S3	-28.2	S1	-30.8	S5	-37.7	S2	-40.8	S8	-68.9
71-80	S12	-9.4	S11	-9.5	S9	-25.1	S4	-26.4	S10	-29.4	S1	-33.3	S3	-38.7	S2	-42.0	S5	-43.7	S8	-68.3
81-90	S11	-6.1	S12	-6.6	S10	-14.1	S9	-14.2	S4	-22.5	S3	-34.9	S1	-38.0	S2	-41.8	S5	-43.6	S8	-66.0
91-100	S11	-10.3	S12	-12.0	S9	-12.1	S10	-14.4	S3	-28.5	S4	-36.8	S1	-43.3	S5	-43.6	S2	-46.2	S8	-65.8

Table 7: Strategies Ranked by $\%d_{2a}$ for SaskTel Tasks

Range	Rank=1 S	%d₂ₐ	Rank=2 S	%d₂ₐ	Rank=3 S	%d₂ₐ	Rank=4 S	%d₂ₐ	Rank=5 S	%d₂ₐ	Rank=6 S	%d₂ₐ	Rank=7 S	%d₂ₐ	Rank=8 S	%d₂ₐ	Rank=9 S	%d₂ₐ	Rank=10 S	%d₂ₐ
1-10	S4	-15.7	S5	-17.0	S1	-35.2	S12	-37.6	S11	-39.2	S2	-41.2	S9	-50.0	S10	-50.4	S3	-61.1	S8	-70.2
11-20	S4	-12.0	S5	-14.0	S12	-25.5	S12	-26.5	S11	-38.7	S10	-39.8	S1	-49.9	S3	-50.2	S2	-56.2	S8	80.6
21-30	S12	-12.9	S11	-13.6	S4	-15.0	S5	-20.2	S9	-25.8	S10	-26.2	S3	-39.4	S1	-48.3	S2	-57.4	S8	-80.4
31-40	S12	-12.9	S11	-14.4	S4	-16.4	S9	-21.6	S10	-22.0	S5	-24.2	S3	-31.6	S1	-43.8	S2	-59.8	S8	-76.9
41-50	S12	-14.7	S11	-15.5	S4	-22.9	S10	-23.4	S9	-24.0	S5	-31.5	S3	-34.8	S1	-49.2	S2	-56.7	S8	-75.1
51-60	S12	-9.7	S11	-10.8	S10	-15.6	S9	-16.3	S4	-27.6	S3	-29.3	S5	-34.1	S1	-46.6	S2	-56.3	S8	-75.4
61-70	S12	-7.7	S11	-8.3	S10	-14.6	S9	-16.4	S4	-23.1	S3	-26.3	S5	-36.5	S1	-49.2	S2	-57.2	S8	-75.1
71-80	S12	-14.7	S11	-15.5	S10	-15.5	S9	-16.4	S3	-23.0	S4	-27.7	S5	-36.3	S1	-52.4	S2	-60.3	S8	-76.1
81-90	S12	-7.8	S11	-8.8	S10	-14.7	S9	-16.9	S3	-21.6	S4	-30.4	S5	-35.7	S2	-52	S1	-52.3	S8	-76.1
91-100	S12	-10.7	S11	-11.7	S9	-17.2	S10	-17.7	S3	-18.7	S4	-19.3	S5	-26.4	S1	-49.2	S2	-55.8	S8	-77.2

Table 8: Strategies Ranked by $\%d_{2a}$ for NSERC Task

m active attributes has more potentially interesting concepts than one with n tuples and m-1 active attributes. As a result, strategies that delay the generalization of attribute values to the ANY concept until late in the generalization process are more likely to produce more interesting small relations than those, such as S9 and S10, that eliminate attributes early. For example, strategies S11 and S12, which use the same selection criteria as S9 and S10 except that the elimination of attributes is delayed as long as possible, provide significant improvement over strategies S9 and S10 for all tuple ranges. Also, with strategies S9, S10, S11 and S12, if the input relation is large, the most interesting generalizations may occur before relations are small enough to be understandable to the user. However, if the input relation is small, then generalizing to produce the most interesting relations, as with S9, S10, S11 and S12, is more appropriate.

Strategy S4 is more effective than strategies S10 and S11 for relations near the end of the generalization process because it examines the entire remaining concept hierarchies in selecting an attribute to generalize. Strategies S11 and S12 only look ahead one step in selecting an attribute. This illustrates that the short-sighted approach of one-step lookahead strategies can result in the selection of attributes that may not lead to the best results. For large relations, a poor choice of an attribute to generalize can be recovered from. A poor choice made near the end of the generalization process is harder to recover from. Since strategy S4 is the most effective for small relations and its time complexity is $O(m)$, compared to $O(m^2 n_i n_o)$ for strategies S9, S10, S11 and S12, it is the best alternative of the strategies tested.

6.0 Conclusions

The strategy based on selecting the attribute for generalization with the greatest complexity measure M_1 proved to be significantly more effective than the other strategies tested for output relations with 1 to 20 tuples. The success of this strategy can be attributed to a two factors. First, the strategy delays the generalization of attributes to the ANY concept until the end of the generalization process, ensuring that all attributes are active for as long as possible. Secondly, the strategy examines the potential for interestingness of the entire remaining hierarchies. For output relations with 21 to 100 tuples, the single step lookahead strategies based on selecting an attribute for generalization which produces the greatest I_1 or I_2 are the most effective, if they are modified to prevent the early generalization of attributes to the ANY concept. Since strategy S4, based on the complexity measure M_1, is most effective for small relations that are understandable to the user and it is more efficient than the strategies based on I_1 or I_2, it is recommended as the most suitable attribute selection strategy to replace the user-defined attribute threshold.

Our future work in evaluating attribute selection strategies for AOG will explore the use of other interestingness measures, such as those based on information theory [12][15] or variance [4] , in attribute selection strategies.

7.0 References

[1]   D.B. Barber and H.J. Hamilton, "Attribute Selection Strategies for Attribute-Oriented Generalization," *Proceedings of the Canadian AI Conference (AI '96)*, 429-441.

[2]   C. L. Carter, H. J. Hamilton and N. Cercone, *"The Software Architecture of DBLEARN,"* Technical Report CS-94-04," University of Regina, 1994.

[3]   H. J. Hamilton and D. F. Fudger, "Estimating DBLEARN's Potential for Knowledge Discovery in Databases," *Computational Intelligence,* 11(2), 1995, 1-18.

[4]   H. J. Hamilton, R.J. Hilderman and N. Cercone, "Attribute-oriented Induction Using Domain Generalization Graphs," *Proceedings of the Eighth International Conference on Tools with Artificial Intelligence,* Toulouse, France, 1996, 246-253.

[5]   J. Han, Y. Cai and N. Cercone, "Knowledge Discovery in Databases: An Attribute-Oriented Approach," *Proceedings of the 18th VLDB Conference,* Vancouver, British Columbia, 1992, 547-559.

[6]   M. Klemettinin, H. Mannila, P. Ronkainen, H. Toivonen and A. I. Verkamo, "Finding Interesting Rules from Large Sets of Discovered Association Rules," in: Adams N.R., Bhargava B.K. and Yesha Y., Eds., *Third International Conference on Information and Knowledge Management,* ACM Press, Gaitersburg, Maryland, Nov.-Dec., 1994, 401-407.

[7]   G.H. John, R. Kohavi G.H. John and L. Pfleger, "Irrelevant Features and the Subset Selection Problem," in: W.W. Cohen and H. Hirsh, Eds., *Machine Learning: Proceedings of the Eleventh International Conference,* Morgan Kaufmann, San Francisco, CA., 1994, 121-129.

[8]   J. A. Major and J. J. Mangano, "Selecting Among Rules Induced from a Hurricane Database," *Knowledge Discovery in Databases: Papers from the 1993 Workshop, Technical Report WS-93-02,* AAAI Press, Menlo Park, CA., 1993, 1-13.

[9]   C. J. Matheus, G. Piatetsky-Shapiro and D. McNeill, "Selecting and Reporting What is Interesting: The KEFIR Application to Healthcare Data," in: U. Fayyad, G. Piatetsky-Shapiro, P. Smyth and R. Uthurusamy, Eds., *Advances in Knowledge Discovery and Data Mining,* AAAI/MIT Press, Menlo Park, CA., 1995, 401-419.

[10]   T.M. Mitchell, *Version Spaces: An Approach to Concept Learning,* Ph.d thesis, Stanford University, 1978.

[11]   G. Piatetsky-Shapiro, "Discovery, Analysis and Presentation of Strong Rules," in: G. Piatetsky-Shapiro and W. J. Frawley, Eds., *Knowledge Discovery in Databases,* AAAI/MIT Press, Menlo Park, CA, 1991, 229-248.

[12]   J.R. Quinlan, *C4.5: Programs for Machine Learning,* Morgan Kaufmann, Los Altos, CA, 1993.

[13]   N. Shan, H. J. Hamilton and N. Cercone, "GRG: Knowledge Discovery Using Information Generalization, Information Reduction and Rule Generation," *7th IEEE International Conference on Tools with Artificial Intelligence,* Washington, D.C., November, 1995., 372-379.

[14]   A. Silberschatz and A. Tuzhilin, "On Subjective Measures of Interestingness in Knowledge Discovery," *Proceedings of the First International Conference on Knowledge Discovery and Data Mining (KDD-95),* Montreal, Canada, August, 1995, 275-281.

[15]   P. Smyth and R. M. Goodman, "Rule Induction using Information Theory," in: Piatetsky-Shapiro G. and Frawley W.J., Eds., *Knowledge Discovery in Databases,* AAAI/MIT Press, Menlo Park, CA, 1991, 159-176.

Boolean Reasoning for Feature Extraction Problems

Hung Son Nguyen, Andrzej Skowron

Institute of Mathematics, Warsaw University
Banacha 2, Warsaw Poland
email: son@alfa.mimuw.edu.pl; skowron@mimuw.edu.pl

Abstract. We recall several applications of Boolean reasoning for feature extraction and we propose an approach based on Boolean reasoning for new feature extraction from data tables with symbolic (nominal, qualitative) attributes. New features are of the form $a \in V$, where $V \subseteq V_a$ and V_a is the set of values of attribute a. We emphasize that Boolean reasoning is also a good framework for complexity analysis of the approximate solutions of the discussed problems.

1   Introduction

"Feature Extraction" and "Feature Selection" are important problems in Machine Learning and Data Mining (see e.g. [6, 3, 4]). In previous papers we have considered problems like: *short reduct finding problem* [16], *rule induction problem* [17], *optimal discretization problem* [12], *linear feature (hyperplane) searching problem* [13]. Our solutions of these problems are based on Boolean reasoning schema [2].

In this paper we discuss a problem of searching for new features from a data table with symbolic (qualitative) values of attributes. This problem, called *symbolic value partition problem* differs from the discretization problem. We do not assume any pre-defined order on values of attributes. Once again, we apply rough set method and Boolean reasoning to construct heuristics searching for relevant features of the form $a \in V \subset V_a$ generated by partitions of symbolic values of conditional attributes into a small number of value sets.

We also point out that Boolean reasoning can be used as a tool to measure the complexity of approximate solution of a given problem. As a complexity measure of a given problem we propose the complexity of the corresponding to that problem Boolean function (represented by the number of variables, number of clauses, etc.). It is known that for some NP-hard problems it is easier to construct efficient heuristics than for the other ones. The problem of symbolic value partition is in this sense harder than the problem of optimal discretization problem.

2   Preliminaries

We consider the Boolean algebra over $\mathbf{B} = \{0, 1\}$ and n-variable Boolean function $f : \mathbf{B}^n \to \mathbf{B}$, where $n \geq 1$.

For any sequence $a = (a\,[1],\ldots,a\,[n]) \in \mathbf{B}^n$ and any vector of Boolean variables $\mathbf{x} = (x_1,\ldots,x_n)$ we define the *minterm* m_a and *the maxterm* s_a by

$$m_a\,(\mathbf{x}) = x_1^{a[1]} \wedge x_2^{a[2]} \wedge \ldots \wedge x_n^{a[n]} \text{ and } s_a\,(\mathbf{x}) = x_1^{\neg a[1]} \vee x_2^{\neg a[2]} \vee \ldots \vee x_n^{\neg a[n]}$$

where $x^1 = x$ and $x^0 = \bar{x}$.

Theorem 1 . *(see [18])* $f\,(\mathbf{x}) = \bigvee\limits_{a \in f^{-1}(1)} m_a\,(\mathbf{x}) = \bigwedge\limits_{b \in f^{-1}(0)} s_b\,(\mathbf{x})$

These two representations are called *disjunctive (DNF)* and *conjunctive normal forms (CNF) of the function f*, respectively.

Let $\mathbf{u} = (u_1,\ldots,u_n), \mathbf{v} = (v_1,\ldots,v_n) \in \{0,1\}^n$. We use the coordinate-wise ordering, i.e. $\mathbf{u} \le \mathbf{v}$ if and only if $u_i \le v_i$ for all i. A Boolean function f is called *monotone* iff $\mathbf{u} \le \mathbf{v}$ implies $f\,(\mathbf{u}) \le f\,(\mathbf{v})$. One can show that a Boolean function is monotone if and only if it can be defined without negation [18].

Given a set of variables $S \subseteq \{x_1,\ldots,x_n\}$ we define the monomial m_S by $m_S\,(\mathbf{x}) = \bigwedge\limits_{x_i \in S} x_i$. The set S of variables is called *an implicant* of the monotone Boolean function f if and only if $m_S^{-1}\,(1) \subseteq f^{-1}\,(1)$. The set S of variables is called *a prime implicant* of a monotone Boolean function f if S is an implicant of f and any proper subset of S is not an implicant of f. We use the following properties of two problems related to monotone Boolean functions [2]:

Theorem 2. *[12] For a given monotone Boolean function f of n variables in CNF and an integer k. The decision problem for checking if there exists a prime implicant of f with at most k variables is NP-complete. The problem of searching for minimal prime implicant of f is NP-hard.*

An *information system* [15] is a pair $\mathbf{A} = (U,A)$, where U is a non-empty, finite set called the *universe* and A is a non-empty, finite set of *attributes*, i.e. $a : U \to V_a$ for $a \in A$, where V_a is called *the value set of a*. Elements of U are called *objects*.

Any information system $\mathbf{A} = (U,A)$ and a non-empty set $B \subseteq A$ define a *B-information function* by $Inf_B(x) = \{(a,a(x)) : a \in B$ for $x \in U\}$. The set $\{Inf_A(x) : x \in U\}$ is called the $A-$*information set* and denoted by $INF(\mathbf{A})$.

Any information system of the form $\mathbf{A} = (U, A \cup \{d\})$ is called *decision table* where $d \notin A$ is called *decision* and the elements of A are called *conditions*.

Let $V_d = \{1,\ldots,r(d)\}$. The decision d determines the partition $\{C_1,\ldots,C_{r(d)}\}$ of the universe U, where $C_k = \{x \in U : d(x) = k\}$ for $1 \le k \le r(d)$. The set C_k is called the $k-th$ *decision class of* $\mathbf{A}$.

With any subset of attributes $B \subseteq A$, an equivalence relation called the *B-indiscernibility relation* [15], denoted by $IND(B)$, is defined by

$$IND(B) = \{(x,y) \in U \times U : \forall_{a \in B}\,(a(x) = a(y))\}$$

Objects x,y satisfying relation $IND(B)$ are indiscernible by attributes from B. By $[x]_{IND(B)}$ we denote the equivalence class of $IND\,(B)$ defined by x. A minimal subset B of A such that $IND(A) = IND(B)$ is called a *reduct* of $\mathbf{A}$.

If $\mathbf{A} = (U, A \cup \{d\})$ is a decision table and $B \subseteq A$ then we define a function $\partial_B : U \to 2^{\{1,\ldots,r(d)\}}$, called the *generalized decision in* $\mathbf{A}$, by

$$\partial_B(x) = \{i : \exists_{x' \in U} [(x' IND(B) x) \wedge (d(x') = i)]\} = d\left([x]_{IND(B)}\right)$$

A decision table $\mathbf{A}$ is called *consistent (deterministic)* if $card(\partial_A(x)) = 1$ for any $x \in U$, otherwise $\mathbf{A}$ is *inconsistent (non-deterministic)*.

3 Some optimization problems in rough set theory

3.1 Minimal Reduct problem

Let $\mathbf{A}$ be an information system with n objects and k attributes. By $M(\mathbf{A})$ [16] we denote an $n \times n$ matrix (c_{ij}), called the *discernibility matrix* of $\mathbf{A}$ such that

$$c_{ij} = \{a \in A : a(x_i) \neq a(x_j)\} \text{ for } i, j = 1, \ldots, n.$$

A *discernibility function* $f_\mathbf{A}$ for the information system $\mathbf{A}$ is a Boolean function of k Boolean variables $a_1^*, \ldots, a_k^*$ corresponding to the attributes $a_1, \ldots, a_k$ respectively, and defined by

$$f_\mathbf{A}(a_1^*, \ldots, a_k^*) =_{df} \bigwedge_{c_{ij} \neq \emptyset} \bigvee c_{ij}^* \text{ where } c_{ij}^* = \{a^* : a \in c_{ij}\}.$$

The set of all *prime implicants* of $f_\mathbf{A}$ determines the set of all reducts of $\mathbf{A}$ [16]. In the sequel, to simplify the notation, we omit the star superscripts. Observe that the Boolean function $f_\mathbf{A}$ consists of k variables and $O(n^2)$ clauses.

A subset B of the set A of attributes of decision table $\mathbf{A} = (U, A \cup \{d\})$ is a *relative reduct of* $\mathbf{A}$ iff B is a minimal set with respect to the following property: $\partial_B = \partial_A$. The set of all relative reducts in $\mathbf{A}$ is denoted by $RED(\mathbf{A}, d)$.

Theorem 3. *[16] The decision problem for checking if there exist a (relative) reduct of length $< k$ is NP-complete. The searching problem for reduct of minimal length is NP-hard.*

3.2 Discretization making

Let $\mathbf{A} = (U, A \cup \{d\})$ be a decision table where $U = \{x_1, x_2, \ldots, x_n\}$; $A = \{a_1, \ldots, a_k\}$ and $d : U \to \{1, \ldots, r\}$. We assume $V_a = [l_a, r_a) \subset \Re$ to be a real interval for any $a \in A$ and $\mathbf{A}$ to be a consistent decision table. Any pair (a, c) where $a \in A$ and $c \in \Re$ will be called a *cut on* V_a. Let $\mathbf{P}_a$ be a partition on V_a (for $a \in A$) into subintervals i.e. $\mathbf{P}_a = \{[c_0^a, c_1^a), [c_1^a, c_2^a), \ldots, [c_{k_a}^a, c_{k_a+1}^a)\}$ for some integer k_a, where $l_a = c_0^a < c_1^a < c_2^a < \ldots < c_{k_a}^a < c_{k_a+1}^a = r_a$ and $V_a = [c_0^a, c_1^a) \cup [c_1^a, c_2^a) \cup \ldots \cup [c_{k_a}^a, c_{k_a+1}^a)$. Hence any partition $\mathbf{P}_a$ is uniquely defined and often identified as the set of cuts: $\{(a, c_1^a), (a, c_2^a), \ldots, (a, c_{k_a}^a)\} \subset A \times \Re$.

Any set of cuts $\mathbf{P} = \bigcup_{a \in A} \mathbf{P}_a$ defines from $\mathbf{A} = (U, A \cup \{d\})$ a new decision table $\mathbf{A^P} = (U, A^\mathbf{P} \cup \{d\})$ called $\mathbf{P}$-*discretization of* $\mathbf{A}$, where $A^\mathbf{P} = \{a^\mathbf{P} : a \in A\}$ and $a^\mathbf{P}(x) = i \Leftrightarrow a(x) \in [c_i^a, c_{i+1}^a)$ for $x \in U$ and $i \in \{0, \ldots, k_a\}$.

Two sets of cuts $\mathbf{P'}, \mathbf{P}$ are equivalent, i.e. $\mathbf{P'} \equiv_\mathbf{A} \mathbf{P}$, iff $\mathbf{A}^\mathbf{P} = \mathbf{A}^{\mathbf{P'}}$. The equivalence relation $\equiv_\mathbf{A}$ has a finite number of equivalence classes. In the sequel we will not discern between equivalent families of partitions.

We say that the set of cuts $\mathbf{P}$ is $\mathbf{A}$-*consistent* if $\partial_A = \partial_{A\mathbf{P}}$, where ∂_A and $\partial_{A\mathbf{P}}$ are generalized decisions of $\mathbf{A}$ and $\mathbf{A}^\mathbf{P}$, respectively. The $\mathbf{A}$-consistent set of cuts $\mathbf{P}^{irr}$ is $\mathbf{A}$-*irreducible* if $\mathbf{P}$ is not $\mathbf{A}$-consistent for any $\mathbf{P} \subset \mathbf{P}^{irr}$. The $\mathbf{A}$-consistent set of cuts $\mathbf{P}^{opt}$ is $\mathbf{A}$-*optimal* if $card\,(\mathbf{P}^{opt}) \leq card\,(\mathbf{P})$ for any $\mathbf{A}$-consistent set of cuts $\mathbf{P}$.

Theorem 4. *[12] The decision problem of checking if for a given decision table $\mathbf{A}$ and an integer k there exists an irreducible set of cuts $\mathbf{P}$ in $\mathbf{A}$ such that $card(\mathbf{P}) < k$ is NP-complete. The problem of searching for an optimal set of cuts $\mathbf{P}$ in a given decision table $\mathbf{A}$ is NP-hard.*

Let us define a new decision table $\mathbf{A}^* = (U^*, A^* \cup \{d^*\})$ where

- $U^* = \{(u,v) \in U^2 : d(u) \neq d(v)\} \cup \{\perp\}$
- $A^* = \{c : c$ is a cut on $\mathbf{A}\}$. $c\,(\perp) = 0; c\,((u,v)) = \begin{cases} 1 & \text{if } c \text{ discerns } u,v \\ 0 & \text{otherwise} \end{cases}$
- $d\,(\perp) = 0; d^*\,(u_i, u_j) = 1$ for $(u,v) \in U^*$.

It has been shown [12] that any relative reduct of $\mathbf{A}^*$ is an irreducible set of cuts for $\mathbf{A}$ and any minimal relative reduct of $\mathbf{A}^*$ is an optimal set of cuts for $\mathbf{A}$. The Boolean function corresponding to the minimal relative reduct problem $f_{\mathbf{A}^*}$ has $O\,(nk)$ variables (cuts) and $O\,(n^2)$ clauses.

3.3 Discretization defined by Hyperplanes

Let $\mathbf{A} = (U, A \cup \{d\})$ be a decision table, where $U = \{u_1, ..., u_n\}$, $A = \{f_1, ..., f_k\}$ and $d : U \rightarrow \{1, ..., m\}$ and let $C_i = \{u \in U : d(u) = i\}$ for $i = 1, ..., m$. Assuming that objects $u_i \in U$ are described by conditional attributes, we can characterize them as points: $P_i = (f_1(u_i), ..., f_k(u_i))$ in k-dimensional affine space $\Re^k$.

Any hyperplane H in $\Re^k$ is fully characterized by $(k+1)$-tuple of real numbers $(a, a_1, a_2, ..., a_k)$: $H = \{(x_1, x_2, ..., x_k) \in \Re^k : a_1 x_1 + \cdots + a_k x_k + a = 0\}$. The hyperplane H splits C_i into two subclasses defined by:

$$C_i^{U,H} = \{u \in C_i : a_1 f_1(u) + \cdots + a_k f_k(u) + a \geq 0\};$$
$$C_i^{L,H} = \{u \in C_i : a_1 f_1(u) + \cdots + a_k f_k(u) + a < 0\}.$$

We consider the discretization problems as before but instead of the cut set we take as the searching space for new features the set of characteristic functions of half-spaces defined by hyperplanes over the attribute set A. It is easy to observe that the problem of searching for an optimal set of hyperplane cuts is NP-hard. Observe that the Boolean function corresponding to this problem has $O\,(n^k)$ variables (hyperplanes) and $O\,(n^2)$ clauses. Hence the problem of searching for sub-optimal set of oblique hyperplanes is harder than the problem of searching for sub-optimal set of (parallel/orthogonal to axes) cuts.

4 Approximate Algorithms

4.1 Johnson strategy

In general, the Johnson greedy algorithm searching for shortest prime implicant of a given Boolean function of k variables $V = \{x_1, \ldots, x_k\}$ in CNF:

$$f = (x_{1,1} \vee x_{1,2} \ldots \vee x_{1,i_1}) \wedge \ldots \wedge (x_{N,1} \vee x_{N,2} \ldots \vee x_{N,i_N})$$

where $x_{i,j} \in V$, is described as follows:

Johnson strategy : Greedy algorithm
Step 1: Choose the variable $x \in V$ most frequently occurring in f.
Step 2: Remove from f all clauses containing the variable x.
Step 3: If $f \neq 0$ then go to Step 1 else go to Step 4.
Step 4: From the set of chosen variables remove superfluous variables. The obtained set of variables is returned as the result of the algorithm.

In general, the time complexity of the presented algorithm depends on the time complexity of Step 1. If there are k variables and N clauses, Step 1 takes $O(kN)$ computing steps. In some particular cases one can reduce the time complexity of this algorithm, but usually the number of variables and the number of clauses determine the complexity of the problem.

4.2 Minimal reduct finding

We apply the Johnson strategy for the discernibility function $f_{\mathbf{A}}(a_1^*, \ldots, a_k^*)$. The main task of the algorithm is to find an attribute $a \in A$ discerning the largest number of pairs of objects i.e. attribute most often occurring in entries c_{ij} of *the discernibility matrix* $M(\mathbf{A})$. The attribute a is then added to the temporary reduct and all of the cells c_{ij} containing a are replaced by the empty set $\emptyset$. The procedure is repeated until all entries of the matrix $M(\mathbf{A})$ become empty. It is easy to construct an algorithm for computing of the semi-minimal reduct in $O(kn^2)$ space and $O(kn^2 \cdot |R|)$ time, where R is a reduct constructed by the algorithm. This result can be improved. It has been shown in [14] that one can find the best attribute in $O(kn \log n)$ steps using $O(nk)$ space.

4.3 Efficient discretization algorithm

The algorithm based on Johnson's strategy described in the previous section is searching for a cut $c \in A^*$ which discerns the largest number of pairs of objects (MD-heuristic). Then we move the cut c from A^* to the resulting set of cuts $\mathbf{P}$ and remove from U^* all pairs of objects discerned by c. Our algorithm is continued until $U^* = \{new\}$. Let n be the number of objects and let k be the number of attributes of decision table $\mathbf{A}$. Then $card(A^*) \leq (n-1)k$ and $card(U^*) \leq \frac{n(n-1)}{2}$. It is easy to observe that for any cut $c \in A^*$ we need $O(n^2)$ steps to find the number of all pairs of objects discerned by c. Hence the straightforward realization of this algorithm requires $O(kn^2)$ of memory space and $O(kn^3)$ steps to determine one *cut*, so it is not feasible in practice. The MD-heuristic presented in [14] determines the best cut in $O(kn)$ steps using $O(kn)$ space only.

4.4 Searching for best hyperplanes using genetic algorithms

Let us note that the number of different partitions of a given set of objects that can be induced with a single oblique hyperplane is $O\left(n^k\right)$. This observation helps to evaluate the complexity of the *"best hyperplane"* finding.

Let H be a given hyperplane. We set $L_i = card(C_i^{L,H})$ and $R_i = card(C_i^{R,H})$ for $i = 1, \ldots, r$; $R = R_1 + \cdots + R_r$; $L = L_1 + \cdots + L_r$. It has been shown in [7] that the problem of searching for optimal oblique hyperplane using sum-minority measure is NP-complete (or NP-hard). The sum-minority measure is defined by: $SumMinor(H) = \min_{i \in \{1,\ldots,r\}} \{L_i\} + \min_{i \in \{1,\ldots,r\}} \{R_i\}$. One can apply another measure to estimate the quality of hyperplanes [12]:

$$award(H) = \sum_{i \neq j} card\left(C_i^R(H)\right) \cdot card\left(C_j^L(H)\right) = L \cdot R - \sum_{i=1}^r (L_i \cdot R_i)$$

If $award(H) > award(H')$ then the number of discernible pairs of objects from different decision classes by the hyperplane H is greater than the corresponding number defined by the hyperplane H'. This function has been applied in the MD-heuristic to measure the number of discernible pairs of objects.

Since the problems of searching for the hyperplanes are hard some heuristics are used to solve it [13]. We also use the $penalty(H)$ function:

$$penalty(H) = \sum_{i=1}^r card\left(C_i^{U,H}\right) \cdot card\left(C_i^{L,H}\right) = \sum_{i=1}^r (L_i \cdot R_i)$$

or more advanced functions to measure the quality of oblique hyperplanes:

$$power_1(H) = \frac{w_1 \cdot award(H)}{penalty(H) + w_2};$$

$$power_2(H) = w_1 \cdot award(H) - w_2 \cdot penalty(H).$$

There are numerous methods of searching for optimal hyperplanes (see e.g. [7] based on various heuristics like "simulated annealing"[7], "randomized induction"... In [13] we proposed a general method (based on genetic strategy) of searching for *optimal set of hyperplanes* by using genetic algorithm.

5 Symbolic value attribute partition problem

We have considered the real value attribute discretization problem. It is a searching problem for a partition of real values into *intervals* (the natural linear order " $<$ " in the real space $\Re$ is assumed).

In case of symbolic value attributes (i.e. without any pre-assumed order in the value sets of attributes) the problem of searching for partitions of value sets into a "small" number of subsets is, in a sense, more complicated than for continuous attributes. Once again, we apply Boolean reasoning approach to construct a partition of symbolic value sets into small number of subsets.

Let $\mathbf{A} = (U, A \cup \{d\})$ be a decision table where $A = \{a_i : U \to V_{a_i}\}$ and $V_{a_i} = \{v_1^{a_i}, v_2^{a_i}, ..., v_{n_i}^{a_i}\}$, for $i \in \{1, ..., k\}$. Any function $P_{a_i} : V_{a_i} \to \{1, \ldots, m_i\}$ (where $m_i \leq n_i$) is called *a partition of* V_{a_i}. The *rank of* P_{a_i} is the value $rank(P_i) = card(P_{a_i}(V_{a_i}))$. The function P_{a_i} defines a new *partition attribute* $b_i = P_{a_i} \circ a_i$ i.e. $b_i(u) = P_{a_i}(a_i(u))$ for any object $u \in U$.

The family of partitions $\{P_a\}_{a \in B}$ is $B - consistent$ iff

$$\forall_{u,v \in U} [d(u) \neq d(v) \wedge (u, v) \notin IND(B)] \Rightarrow \exists_{a \in B} [P_a(a(u)) \neq P_a(a(v))] \quad (1)$$

It means that if two objects u, u' are discerned by B and d, then they must be discerned by the partition attribute defined by $\{P_a\}_{a \in B}$. We consider the following optimization problem called *the symbolic value partition problem:*

SYMBOLIC VALUE PARTITION PROBLEM:

For a given decision table $\mathbf{A} = (U, A \cup \{d\})$, and a set of nominal attributes $B \subseteq A$, search for a minimal $B - consistent$ family of partitions (i.e. B-consistent family $\{P_a\}_{a \in B}$ with the minimal value of $\sum_{a \in B} rank(P_a)$).

This concept is useful when we want to reduce the attribute value sets of attributes with large cardinalities. The discretization problem can be derived from the partition problem by adding the monotonicity condition for family $\{P_a\}_{a \in A} : \forall_{v_1, v_2 \in V_a} [v_1 \leq v_2 \Rightarrow P_a(v_1) \leq P_a(v_2)]$

We propose two approaches for solving this problem, namely the *local partition method* and the *global partition method*. The former approach is based on grouping the values of each attribute independently whereas the later approach is based on grouping of attribute values simultaneously for all attributes.

5.1 Local partition

The local partition strategy is quite similar to *"Holte's 1R discretizer"[8]*. For any fixed attribute $a \in A$, we want to find such a partition P_a that keeps consistency condition (1) for the attribute a (i.e. $B = \{a\}$).

For any partition P_a the equivalence relation $\approx_{P_a}$ is defined by: $v_1 \approx_{P_a} v_2 \Leftrightarrow P_a(v_1) = P_a(v_2)$ for all $v_1, v_2 \in V_a$.

We consider the relation $\mathbf{UNI}_a$ defined on V_a as follows:

$$v_1 \mathbf{UNI}_a v_2 \Leftrightarrow \forall_{u, u' \in U} [(a(u) = v_1 \wedge a(u') = v_2) \Rightarrow d(u) = d(u')] \quad (2)$$

Theorem 5. *If P_a is a-consistent then $\approx_{P_a} \subseteq \mathbf{UNI}_a$. The equivalence relation $\mathbf{UNI}_a$ defines a minimal $a-consistent$ partition on a.*

5.2 Global partition

We consider the discernibility matrix [16] of the decision table $\mathbf{A} : \mathbf{M}(\mathbf{A}) = [m_{i,j}]_{i,j=1}^n$ where $m_{i,j}$ is the set of all attributes having different values on objects u_i, u_j i.e. $m_{i,j} = \{a \in A : a(u_i) \neq a(u_j)\}$. Observe that if we want to discern between objects u_i and u_j we have to keep one of the attributes from $m_{i,j}$. For the need of our problem we would like to have more relevant formulation: *to discern objects u_i, u_j we have to discern for some $a \in m_{i,j}$ between values of the value pair $(a(u_i), a(u_j))$.*

Hence instead of cuts used for continuous values (defined by pairs (a_i, c_j)), one can discern objects by triples $\left(a_i, v_{i_1}^{a_i}, v_{i_2}^{a_i}\right)$ called *chains*, where $a_i \in A$ for $i = 1, ..., k$ and $i_1, i_2 \in \{1, ..., n_i\}$.

One can build a new decision table $\mathbf{A}^+ = (U^+, A^+ \cup \{d^+\})$ (analogously to the table $\mathbf{A}^*$ (see Section 3.2)) assuming $U^+ = U^*; d^+ = d^*$ and $A^+ = \{(a, v_1, v_2) : (a \in A) \wedge (v_1, v_2 \in V_a)\}$. Again one can apply to A^+ e.g. the Johnson heuristic to search for a minimal set of chains discerning all pairs of objects from different decision classes.

One can see that our problem can be solved by efficient heuristics of graph coloring. The *"graph $k-colorability$"* problem is formulated as follows:

input: Graph $G = (V, E)$, positive integer $k \le |V|$
output: 1 if G is $k-$colorable, (i.e. if there exist a function $f : V \to \{1, \ldots, k\}$ such that $f(v) \ne f(v')$ whenever $(v, v') \in E$) and 0 otherwise.

This problem is solvable in polynomial time for $k = 2$, but is NP-complete for all $k \ge 3$. However, similarly to discretization, one can apply some efficient heuristic searching for optimal graph coloring determining optimal partitions of attribute value sets.

For any attribute a_i in a semi-minimal set X of chains returned from the above heuristic we construct a graph $\Gamma_{a_i} = \langle V_{a_i}, E_{a_i} \rangle$, where E_{a_i} is equal to the set of all chains in X of the attribute a_i. Any coloring of all graphs Γ_{a_i} defines an A-consistent partition of value sets. Hence heuristics searching for minimal graph coloring return also sub-optimal partitions of attribute value sets.

One can see that this time the constructed Boolean formula has $O(knl^2)$ variables and $O(n^2)$ clauses, where l is the maximal value of $card(V_a)$ for $a \in A$. Let us note also that if prime implicants have been constructed a heuristic for graph coloring should be applied to generate new features.

5.3 Example

Let us consider the decision table presented in Figure 1 and a reduced form of its discernibility matrix.

Firstly, from the Boolean function f_A with Boolean variables of the form $a_{v_1}^{v_2}$ (corresponding to the chain (a, v_1, v_2) described in Section 5.2) we find a shortest prime implicant: $[\mathbf{a}_{a_2}^{a_1} \wedge \mathbf{a}_{a_3}^{a_2} \wedge \mathbf{a}_{a_4}^{a_1} \wedge \mathbf{a}_{a_4}^{a_3} \wedge \mathbf{b}_{a_4}^{a_1} \wedge \mathbf{b}_{a_4}^{a_2} \wedge \mathbf{b}_{a_3}^{a_2} \wedge \mathbf{b}_{a_3}^{a_1} \wedge \mathbf{b}_{a_5}^{a_3}]$, which can be represented by graphs (Figure 2). Next we apply a heuristic to color vertices of those graphs as it is shown in Figure 2. The colors are corresponding to the partitions:

$$P_a(a_1) = P_a(a_3) = 1; \quad P_a(a_2) = P_a(a_4) = 2$$
$$P_b(b_1) = P_b(b_2) = P_b(b_5) = 1; \quad P_b(b_3) = P_b(b_4) = 2$$

and at the same time one can construct the new decision table (Figure 1).

A	a	b	d
u_1	a_1	b_1	0
u_2	a_1	b_2	0
u_3	a_2	b_3	0
u_4	a_3	b_1	0
u_5	a_1	b_4	1
u_6	a_2	b_2	1
u_7	a_2	b_1	1
u_8	a_4	b_2	1
u_9	a_3	b_4	1
u_{10}	a_2	b_5	1

$\rightarrow$

M(A)	u_1	u_2	u_3	u_4
u_5	$b_{b_4}^{b_1}$	$b_{b_4}^{b_2}$	$a_{a_2}^{a_1}, b_{b_4}^{b_3}$	$a_{a_3}^{a_1}, b_{b_4}^{b_1}$
u_6	$a_{a_2}^{a_1}, b_{b_2}^{b_1}$	$a_{a_2}^{a_1}$	$b_{b_3}^{b_2}$	$a_{a_3}^{a_2}, b_{b_2}^{b_1}$
u_7	$a_{a_2}^{a_1}$	$a_{a_2}^{a_1}, b_{b_2}^{b_1}$	$b_{b_3}^{b_1}$	$a_{a_3}^{a_2}$
u_8	$a_{a_4}^{a_1}, b_{b_2}^{b_1}$	$a_{a_4}^{a_1}$	$a_{a_4}^{a_2}, b_{b_3}^{b_2}$	$a_{a_4}^{a_3}, b_{b_2}^{b_1}$
u_9	$a_{a_3}^{a_1}, b_{b_4}^{b_1}$	$a_{a_3}^{a_1}, b_{b_4}^{b_2}$	$a_{a_3}^{a_2}, b_{b_4}^{b_3}$	$b_{b_4}^{b_1}$
u_{10}	$a_{a_2}^{a_1}, b_{b_5}^{b_1}$	$a_{a_2}^{a_1}, b_{b_5}^{b_2}$	$b_{b_5}^{b_3}$	$a_{a_3}^{a_2}, b_{b_5}^{b_1}$

$\rightarrow$

a^{P_a}	b^{P_b}	d
1	1	0
2	2	0
1	2	1
2	1	1

Fig. 1. The decision table and the corresponding discernibility matrix.

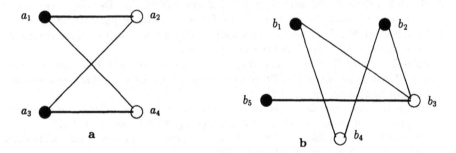

Fig. 2. Coloring of attribute value graphs.

6 Conclusions

We have presented applications of Boolean reasoning methods for different problems like: minimal reduct finding, optimal discretization making, searching for best hyperplanes, minimal partition. These examples are showing the power of this tool in searching for new features. In our system for data analysis we have implemented efficient heuristics based on those methods. The tests are showing that they are very efficient from the point of view of time complexity. They also assure high quality of recognition of new unseen cases ([13, 14]). The heuristics for symbolic value partition allow to obtain more compressed form of decision algorithm. Hence, from the minimum description length principle, one can expect that they will return decision algorithms with high quality of unseen object classification.

Acknowledgement: This work was supported by the State Committee for Scientific Research (grant KBN 8T11C01011).

References

1. Almuallim H., Dietterich T.G. (1994). Learning Boolean Concepts in The Presence of Many Irrelevant Features. *Artificial Intelligence,* **69**(1-2), pp. 279-305.
2. Brown F.M., *Boolean reasoning,* Kluwer, Dordrecht 1990.
3. Catlett J. (1991). On changing continuos attributes into ordered discrete attributes. In Y. Kodratoff, (ed.), Machine Learning-EWSL-91, *Proc. of the European Working Session on Learning,* Porto, Portugal, March 1991, LNAI, pp. 164-178.
4. Chmielewski M. R., Grzymala-Busse J. W. (1994). Global Discretization of Attributes as Preprocessing for Machine Learning. *Proc. of the III International Workshop on RSSC94* November 1994, pp. 294- 301.
5. Dougherty J., Kohavi R., Sahami M.(1995). Supervised and Unsupervised Discretization of Continuous Features, *Proceedings of the Twelfth International Conference on Machine Learning,* Morgan Kaufmann, San Francisco, CA, pp. 194-202.
6. Fayyad U. M., Irani K.B. (1992). The attribute selection problem in decision tree generation. *Proc. of AAAI-92,* July 1992, San Jose, CA.MIT Press, pp. 104-110.
7. Heath D., Kasif S., Salzberg S. (1993). Induction of Oblique Decision Trees. *Proc. 13th International Joint Conf. on AI.* Chambery, France, pp. 1002-1007.
8. Holt R.C. (1993), Very simple classification rules perform well on most commonly used datasets, *Machine Learning* 11, pp. 63-90.
9. John G., Kohavi R., Pfleger K. (1994). Irrelevant features and subset selection problem. *Proceedings of the Twelfth International Conference on Machine Learning,* Morgan Kaufmann, pp. 121-129.
10. Kerber R. (1992), Chimerge: Discretization of numeric attributes. *Proc. of the Tenth National Conference on Artificial Intelligence,* MIT Press, pp. 123-128.
11. Kodratoff Y., Michalski R.(1990): *Machine learning: An Artificial Intelligence approach,* vol.3, Morgan Kaufmann, 1990.
12. Nguyen H.S., Skowron A. (1995). Quantization of real values attributes, Rough set and Boolean Reasoning Approaches. *Proc. of the Second Joint Annual Conference on Information Sciences,* Wrightsville Beach, NC, 1995, USA, pp.34-37.
13. Nguyen H.S., Nguyen S.H., Skowron A.(1996). Searching for Features defined by Hyperplanes. in: Z. W. Raś, M. Michalewicz (eds.), *Proc. of the IX International Symposium on Methodologies for Information Systems ISMIS'96,* June 1996, Zakopane, Poland. Lecture Notes in AI **1079,** Berlin, Springer Verlag, pp.366-375.
14. Nguyen S. H., Nguyen H. S.(1996), Some Efficient Algorithms for Rough Set Methods. *Proc. of the Conference of Information Processing and Management of Uncertainty in Knowledge-Based Systems* , 1996, Granada, Spain, pp. 1451-1456.
15. Pawlak Z.(1991): *Rough sets: Theoretical aspects of reasoning about data,* Kluwer Dordrecht.
16. Skowron A., Rauszer C.(1992), The Discernibility Matrices and Functions in Information Systems. In: *Intelligent Decision Support-Handbook of Applications and Advances of the Rough Sets Theory,* Słowiński R.(ed.), Kluwer Dordrecht 1992, 331-362.
17. Skowron A., Polkowski L., Synthesis of Decision Systems from Data Tables. In T.Y Lin & N. Cercone(eds.), *Rough Sets and Data Mining, Analysis of Imprecise Data.* Kluwer, Dordrecht, pp. 259-300.
18. Wegener I. (1987). *The Complexity of Boolean Functions.* Stuttgart: John Wiley & Sons.

World Model Construction in Children during Physics Learning

Lorenza Saitta*, Filippo Neri*, Andrée Tiberghien+

* Università di Torino
Dipartimento di Informatica
Corso Svizzera 185
10149 Torino (Italy)
{saitta, neri}@di.unito.it

+Equipe COAST de l'UMR GRIC
CNRS - Université Lyon 2
Ecole Normale Supérieure de Lyon
46, Allée d'Italie
69364 LYON Cedex 07 (France)
atibergh@cri.ens-lyon.fr

Abstract

A computational approach to the simulation of cognitive modelling of children learning elementary physics is presented. Goal of the simulation is to support the cognitive scientist's investigation of learning in humans. The Machine Learning system WHY, able to handle a causal model of the domain, has been chosen as tool for the simulation. In this paper the focus will be on the knowledge representation schemes, useful to support such a simulation.

1 Introduction

To model human learning, Machine Learning (ML) methods and systems are natural candidates to provide computational tools. In recent years, they have been used so far in two contexts: either building student models in a ITS environment [Sleeman et al., 1990; Baffes & Mooney, 1996], or describing knowledge acquisition and evolution [Klahr & Siegler, 1978; Sage & Langley, 1983; Hardiman et al., 1984; Shultz et al., 1994; Schmidt & Ling, 1996]. Works in the first group try to build up a picture of what a student knows on a specific subject at a given moment, whereas works in the second group take explicitly into account conceptual change and/or human learning mechanisms. Further works that are of direct relevance concern Qualitative Physics [Forbus & Gentner, 1986].

Most models of human learning presented so far in the ML literature are based on excessively simplifying assumptions. Basically, learning is reduced to a simple classification task, performed on the basis of knowledge consisting in a set of rules or a neural net. In this paper we are interested in modelling conceptual changes in Physics learning[1]. *Conceptual Change* is a well known phenomenon in developmental psychology and educational science [Carey, 1983; Tiberghien, 1989, 1994; Vosniadou & Brewer, 1994; Smith et al., 1992; Caravita & Halldén, 1994; Chi et al., 1994; di Sessa, 1993; Vosniadou, 1994, 1995; Slotta & Chi, 1996]. Even

---

[1] This work has been performed within the project "Learning in Humans and Machines", supported by the European Science Foundation

though quite a large body of experimental findings has been collected over the years, still no single definition of conceptual change is universally accepted.

The overoall goal of our research is to model conceptual change occurring in young students, acquiring basic concept in Physics, specifically *Heat* and *Temperature* concepts. In this paper we will concetrate on the knowledge representation schemes, as details on modelling changes in the knowledge can be found elsewhere [Neri et al., 1997a; Neri et al., 1997b]. One of the main novelties, with respect to previous models, is the differentiation between the knowledge a student uses to answer questions and to interpret experimental results, and an *explanatory framework,* based on the notion of simple linear *causality.* The computational model is grounded on an epistemological framework and previous experiments by Tiberghien [1989, 1994]. The modeling tool is the ML system WHY, which acquires and revises a First Order Logic theory by exploiting a causal model of the domain and a set of examples [Saitta et al., 1993; Baroglio et al., 1994].

The specific learning context considered in this paper is the following: A group of students, at the first and second years of secondary school (12-13 years old, 6-5th grades), were exposed to a Physics course consisting of 11 sessions, once a week, including experimentation, questions, discussions and explicit teaching. Content of the course were basic concepts and qualitative relations in the domain of *heat transfer* in everyday life situations. Interviews before and after the set of teaching sessions with each student have been performed.

In the learner's theory causality plays a crucial role [White & Frederiksen, 1987; Rozier, 1988]. Taking into account the age of the learner (12-13 years), Aristotelian causalities are used as reference. In particular, *material* causality (used when students, for instance, consider that wool heats "because it is wool") and *efficient* causality (involved when there is a change, for example, when a battery lights a bulb) are considered here.

2 The Learning System WHY

WHY is a system that learns and revises a knowledge base for classification problems using domain knowledge and examples [Saitta et al., 1993; Baroglio et al., 1994; Giordana et al., 1997]. The domain knowledge consists of a *causal model* of the domain, and a body of *phenomenological theory,* describing the links between abstract concepts and their possible manifestations in the world. A complex inference engine, combining induction, deduction, abduction and prediction, is the core of the system.

The causal model C provides explanations in terms of causal chains among events, originating from "first" causes. The phenomenological theory P contains the semantics of the vocabulary terms, structural information about the objects in the domain, ontologies, taxonomies, domain-independent background knowledge, and, more importantly, a set of rules aimed at describing the manifestations of abstractly defined concepts in terms of properties, objects and events in the specific domain of application. All the knowledge structures share, in WHY, a First Order Logic based language, whose atomic predicates are partitioned into *operational* and *nonoperational.* Operational predicates are observable, whereas nonoperational predicates are only deducible.

The causal model C is represented as a directed, labelled graph, as the one reported in Figure 2. Three kinds of nodes occur in the graphs: *causal* nodes, corresponding to processes or states related by cause-effect relations, *constraint* nodes, attached to edges and representing physical or structural properties of objects, and *context* nodes, associated to causal nodes, representing contextual conditions (concomitant causes) referring to the environment. The phenomenological theory P is represented as a set of Horn clauses, and the examples are represented as ground logical formulas.

The goal of WHY is to acquire a knowledge base KB of heuristic rules, sufficient to solve a set of problems in the chosen domain. Moreover, the system gives causal explanations of its decisions. It is important to clarify the relations between the causal model C and the heuristic knowledge base KB. The causal model could be used directly to obtain answers/solutions to questions, as it is done in diagnostic systems working from first principles. However, causal reasoning is slow, and the rules in KB act as shortcuts, compiled from C. On the other hand, the fact that the rules are justified by C (being derived from it according to the method described in [Saitta et al., 1993]) guarantees their validity and correctness (obviously with respect to that of C) and also allows explanations of the given classification in terms of the deep knowledge.

3 An Example of the Modelling Methodology

In this section we will go through an example of using WHY to model the knowledge of "David", a 12 year old student of 6th grade, exposed to the teaching course on heat and temperature mentioned in Section 1.

The data available from David's history, used to build up the model, are the answers to two questionnaires and an interview both before and after teaching. Moreover, the answers to questions, the predictions of outcomes from practical manipulations, and the given explanations during each teaching session are available as well.

In order to use WHY to hypothesize David's mental models, each experiment or question is represented as an example, consisting of two parts: a description of the experimental setting and a question. The experimental setting corresponds to the descrition of the example, whereas the possible answers to the question are considered as alternative classes. Then, the process of predicting the outcome of an experiment is mapped onto the problem of predicting the correct answer. For the sake of exemplification, let us consider a question, occurring in a questionnaire, reported in Figure 1.

The first step in the modelling process is to set up the vocabulary used in teaching. By analysing the whole questionnaires and interviews, all the words relevant to the specific Physics domain have been extracted and transformed into atomic predicates of the language. Some of the predicates derived from the question in Figure 1 are reported:

$$amount(x,u,t), different(u,v), gas\text{-}stove(x),$$
$$inside(x,y), not\text{-}boiling(x,t), on(x,y),$$
$$person(z), same\text{-}features(x,y), water(x),$$
$$temp(x,T), ...$$

The complete vocabulary contains 95 words. For what concerns the semantics of the predicates, 69 of them are operational, i.e., their evaluation can be made directly on the experimental setting. For instance, person(z) and temp(x,T) are operational. Other predicates are non-operational, i.e. their truth value can be determined by deduction. For instance, the rule

$$\text{gas-stove}(x) \wedge \text{ignited}(x) \Rightarrow \text{FLAME}(x)$$

states that the predicate FLAME(x) can be asserted true on x if x is an ignited gas-stove.

Professor Tournesol makes the following experiment: He takes two saucepans A and B, pours water from a faucet into them, and he also puts a thermometer inside each of them.

The saucepans A and B are equal.
The thermometers are equal.
The two flames are equal and the saucepans are put on the gas stoves at the same time. The quantity of water in A is smaller than in B.
   After 3 minutes, the water in A and B does not boil yet. Tintin reads the indication on the thermometers inside A: it shows 50°C.

(1) Does the thermometer in B show a reading:
- Greater than 50°C
- Equal to 50°C
- Less than 50°C

(2) Why ?

Figure 1 - Example of questions occurring in the questionnaires.

Notice that for non-operational predicates, the semantics of the same term for the teacher and for David may be different according to their respective personal experience; our modelling methodology is enough expressive to account for it. For instance, the two following rules:

$\text{TEMP}(x,T) \wedge \text{greater}(T,\theta_1) \Rightarrow \text{HOT}(x)$	(Teacher)
$\text{feel-hot}(x) \Rightarrow \text{HOT}(x)$	(David)

show that the teacher evaluates the hotness of an object x according to its temperature, whereas David relies on his tactile perception.
   The second step consists in transforming all the questions in examples for WHY. For instance, the question in Figure 1 is described as follows:

<u>Example # 2 :</u> Description
person(Tournesol) $\wedge$ person(Tintin) $\wedge$ saucepan(A) $\wedge$ water(a) $\wedge$ on(A,g_a) $\wedge$
thermometer(h_a) $\wedge$ gas-stove(g_a) $\wedge$ ignited(g_a) $\wedge$ inside(h_a,A) $\wedge$
put-inside(a,A) $\wedge$ amount(a,small) $\wedge$ temp(a, 20,initial) $\wedge$
not-boiling(a, initial) $\wedge$ time-elapsed(a, short) $\wedge$ saucepan(B) $\wedge$ ... $\wedge$
time-elapsed(g_b, short) $\wedge$ same-features(h_a ,h_b) $\wedge$ ... $\wedge$
thermom-reading(h_a, 50, final)

<u>Example # 2</u> : Decisions

{GREATER-THERMOM-READING(h_b, h_a, final),
 SAME-THERMOM-READING(h_b, h_a, final),
 LOWER-THERMOM-READING(h_b,h_a, final)}

In the description of the example we may notice that the quantities have been rendered in qualitative form, such as "small" and "large" amounts of water, a "short" time period (for 3 minutes), "initial" and "final" for the beginning and ending times of the experimentation. Moreover, some background information, which David and the teacher do not need to say explicitly, are added for the system's sake, such as the fact that the room temperature is 20°C. The predicate "same-feature(x,y)" denotes functional equality between x and y without object identity.

In the decision part of the example the "classes" are defined according to the alternative possible answers.

After building up the dictionary and describing the examples, we have encoded, for reference, the teacher's phenomenological and causal theories. These bodies of knowledge are not meant to describe all the knowledge the teacher has in the field, but only the part that he/she decides is relevant for teaching. Some rules belonging to the teacher's phenomenological theory P* are the following (the complete theory contains 121 rules):

$aluminum(x) \Rightarrow METAL(x)$
$METAL(x) \Rightarrow MATERIAL(x)$
$TEMP(x,T) \wedge greater(T,\theta_1) \Rightarrow HOT(x)$
$gas\text{-}stove(x) \wedge ignited(x) \Rightarrow FLAME(x)$
$electric\text{-}plate(x) \wedge turned\text{-}on(x) \Rightarrow HEAT\text{-}SOURCE(x)$
$OBJ(x) \wedge HEAT\text{-}SOURCE(y) \wedge CONTACT(x,y) \Rightarrow TO\text{-}HEAT(x,y)$
$SAME\text{-}TEMP(x,y) \Rightarrow THERMAL\text{-}EQUILIBRIUM(x,y)$
$full\text{-}of(x,y) \Rightarrow INSIDE(y,x)$
$CONTACT(x,y) \Leftrightarrow CONTACT(y,x)$

A part of the teacher's causal model is reported in Figure 2. The graph explains that the temperature of an object increases if it is heated and its initial temperature is below its boiling threshold. As we may notice, the model may be critizised under many respects with respect to a complete theory of heat transfer. However, it represents what the teacher wants David to understand in this preliminary course.

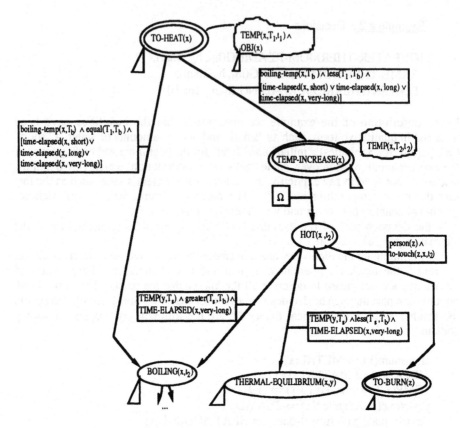

Figure 2 - Part of the teacher's causal model.

The *Matter* ontology of the teacher is reported in Figure 3. We notice that the teacher knows that an object has a temperature value associated to it, and that a material has characteristic temperatures associated to changes of state.

The teacher also uses a heuristic knowledge base KB*, containing 23 rules, one of which is the following:

$$\text{MATERIAL}(x) \wedge \text{SOLID}(x) \wedge \text{TO-HEAT}(x) \Rightarrow \text{MELTING}(x)$$

The teacher's knowledge remains the same along the whole teaching course. It is useful to model it both as a reference for representing the teaching goal, and as a mean to evaluate David's progess toward a correct understanding of the phenomena to which he is exposed.

The teacher's knowledge can be considered "correct", from his/her point of view; in fact, the teacher him/herself can validate it. On the contrary, David is unable to articulate his models of the world, and his knowledge can then be only guessed from his answer and explanations. For this reason, it needs to be validated experimentally. From the data available before teaching, an initial content can be attributed to David's C_0, P_0 and KB_0.

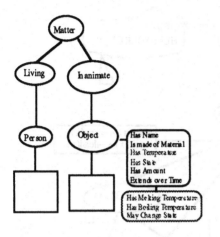

Figure 3 - Teacher's ontology for *Matter*.

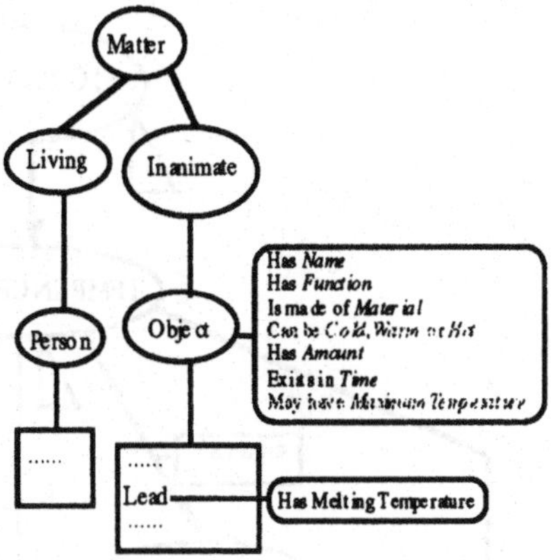

Figure 4 - David's ontology tree for *Matter*

The phenomenological theory P_0 contains 94 rules, and is not very different from the teacher's one, except for the semantics of some predicates, based on direct perception instead of an objective measurement. For the sake of comparison, in Figure 4 David's *Matter* ontology tree is reported. As we can see, David attributes to the objects the properties of being cold, warm or hot, but he does not relate them, at the beginning, with the object's temperature. Moreover, David attributes the constance of temperature during a change of state to a maximum allowed temperature for the substance.

In Figure 5, David's causal model C_0 is reported. The model is subtantially different from the teacher's one, because it is mostly oriented to deducing effects on the basis of the properties of the involved substances. Then, material causation is underlying David's explanations.

Also the heuristic knowledge base KB_0 is rather different, because David, in order to answer the questions, seems to apply rules that can be paraphrased as follows:

> "What is hot heats"
> "What is cold cools"
> "A greater cause has a greater effect"

In order to validate P_0, C_0 and KB_0, we have tried to predict the answers David would give, before teaching, to the questionnaires and interview if he actually had the hypothesized knowledge. The result is that all the answers and explanations can be correctly predicted.

4 Conclusion

We have introduced a new way of interpreting learning from the point of view of the learner's knowledge acquisition in relation with teaching, in the domain of Physics.

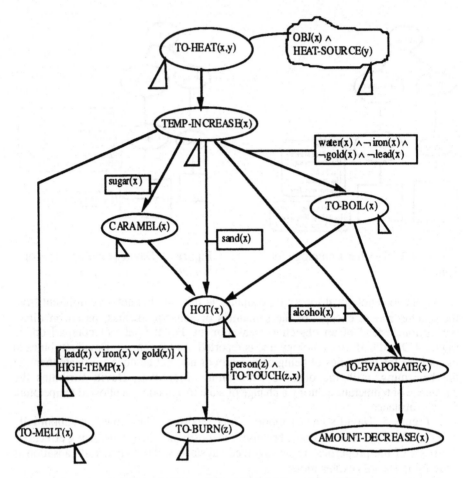

Figure 5 – Part of David's initial causal model.

The analysis of the recorded children's learning sessions allowed us to identify three basic type of conceptual change occurring during learning [Rumelhart and Norman, 1977];

Accretion

Learning by accretion *increases coverage,* in the sense that more experimental situations can be handled (independently of their correct interpretation/prediction). A rule is applicable to a situation when all the conditions specified by the rule's antecedent are defined, i.e. they have a "true" or "false" value. Accretion, then, affects both the *phenomenological theory* or the *heuristic knowledge base,* by adding to any of them a new rule. Accretion may also consists of addition of a property to an ontological node.

Tuning

Tuning *increases the number of correct predictions or explanations,* but does not modify the deep explanatory framework. It may affect the *heuristic knowledge base* or the *phenomenological theory*, by changing the preconditions in some rule or by adding new rules. Tuning may also involve the *causal model*, but only with addition/deletion in the constraint and context nodes (causal nodes and links between them cannot be changed). Tuning can be implemented by generalizing or specializing rule antecedents, or adding and deleting rules.

Restructuration

Restructuration affects the explanatory framework. It involves the *causal model*, via addition/deletion of causal nodes, or modification of causal links, and the *ontologies* of the domain, via addition/deletion of nodes or changing a node from one ontology to another.

References

Baffes P. T. and Mooney R. J. (1996). "A Novel Application of Theory Refinement to Student Modeling". *Proc. of Thirteenth National Conference on Artificial Intelligence* (Portland, OR), pp. 403-408.

Baroglio C., Botta M., Saitta L. (1994). "WHY: A System that Learns from a Causal Model and a Set of Examples". In R. Michalski & G. Tecuci (Eds.), *Machine Learning: A Multistrategy Approach, Vol IV*, Morgan Kaufmann, Los Altos, CA, pp. 319-348.

Caravita S. and Halldén O. (1994). "Re-framing the Problem of Conceptual Change". *Learning and Instruction, 4*, 89-111.

Carey S. (1983). *Conceptual Change in Childhood*. MIT Press, Cambridge, MA.

Chi M. T. H., Slotta J. D. and de Leeuw N. (1994). "From Things to Processes: A Theory of Conceptual Change for Learning Science Concepts". *Learning*

diSessa A. (1993). "Toward an Epistemology of Physics". *Cognition and Instruction, 10*, 105-225.

Forbus K.D. and Gentner D. (1986). "Learning Physical Domains: Toward a Theoretical Framework". In R. Michalski, J. Carbonell & T. Mitchell (Eds.), *Machine Learning: An Artificial Intelligence Approach, Vol. II*, Morgan Kaufmann, Los Altos, CA, pp. 311-348.

Giordana A., Neri F., Saitta L. and Botta M. (1997). "Integrating Multiple Learning Strategies in First Order Logics". *Machine Learning Journal.*. In Press.

Hardiman J., Well P. T. and Pollatsek A. D. (1984). "The Usefulness of the Balance Model in Understanding the Mean". *Journal of Educational Psychology, 76*, 792-801.

Klahr D. and Siegler R.S. (1978). "The Representation of Children's Knowledge". In H.W. Reese and L.P. Lipsitt (Eds.), *Advances in Child Development and Behavior*, Academic Press, New York, NY, pp. 61-116.

Neri F., Saitta L. and Tiberghien A. (1997a). "Modelling Physichal Knowledge Acquisition in Children with Machine Learning". Proc. of *19th Annual Conference of the Cognitive Science Society*, Stanford (CA), Morgan Kaufmann, in press.

Neri F., Saitta L. and Tiberghien A. (1997b). "Modeling Conceptual Change an Interdisciplinary Approach". Proc. of *5 Congresso dell'Associazione Italiana Intelligenza Artificiale (AI*IA97)*, Lecture Notes in Artificial Intelligence series, Springer Verlag (Roma, Italy), in press.

Rozier S. (1988). *Le Raisonnement Linéaire Causal en Thermodynamique Elémentaire*, Thèse de Physique. Université Paris 7, Paris, France.

Rumelhart D. E. and Norman D. A. (1977). "Accretion, Tuning and Restructuring: Three modes of Learning", in Cotton J. W. and Klatzky R. L. (Eds.), *Semantic Factors in Cognition* , Erlbaum (Hillsdale, NJ).

Sage S. and Langley P. (1983). "Modeling Cognitive Development on the Balance Scale Task". *Proc. 8th Int. Joint Conf. on Artificial Intelligence* (Karlsruhe, Germany), pp. 94-96.

Saitta L., Botta M., Neri F. (1993). "Multistrategy Learning and Theory Revision". *Machine Learning, 11,* 153-172.

Schmidt W.C. and Ling C.X. (1996). "A Decision-Tree Model of Balance Scale Development". *Machine Learning, 24,* 203-230.

Shultz T.R., Mareschal D. and Schmidt W. (1994). "Modeling Cognitive Developemnt on Balance Scale Phenomena". *Machine Learning, 16,* 57-86.

Sleeman D., Hirsh H., Ellery I. and Kim I. (1990). "Extending Domain Theories: two Case Studies in Student Modeling". *Machine Learning, 5,* 11-37.

Slotta J. D. and Chi M. T. H. (1996). "Understanding Constraint-Based Processes: a Precursor to Conceptual Change in Physics". *Proc. of Eighteenth Annual Conference of the Cognitive Science Society* (San Diego, CA), pp. 306-311.

Smith C., Snir J. and Grosslight L (1992). "Using Conceptual Models to Facilitate Conceptual Change: The Case of Weight-Density Differentiation". *Cognition and Instruction, 9,* 221-283.

Tiberghien A. (1989). "Learning and Teaching at Middle School Level of Concepts and Phenomena in Physics. The Case of Temperature". In H. Mandl, E. de Corte, N. Bennett and H.F. Friedrich (Eds.), *Learning and Instruction. European Research in an International Context, Volume 2.1,* Pergamon Press, Oxford, UK, pp. 631-648.

Tiberghien A. (1994). "Modelling as a Basis for Analysing Teaching-Learning Situations". *Learning and Instruction, 4,* 71-87.

Vosniadou S. (1994). "Capturing and Modeling the Process of Conceptual Change". *Learning and Instruction, 4,* 45-69.

Vosniadou S. (1995). "A Cognitive Psychological Approach to Learning". In P. Reimann and H. Spada (Eds.), *Learning in Humans and Machines: Towards an Interdisciplinary Learning Science,* Elsevier Publ. Co. , Oxford, UK, pp. 23-36.

Vosniadou S. and Brewer W.F. (1994). "Mental Models of the Day/Night Cycle". *Cognitive Science, 18,* 123-183.

White B. Y. and Frederiksen J. R. (1987). "Causal Model Progressions as a Foundation for Intelligent Learning Environments". *Techn. Report No. 6686,* BBN Laboratories, Cambridge, MA.

Document Explorer: Discovering Knowledge in Document Collections

Ronen Feldman, Willi Klösgen, Amir Zilberstein

Department of Computer Science, Bar-Ilan University, Ramat Gan, Israel, 52900
German National Research Center for Information Technology(GMD),
D-53757 St. Augustin

feldman@cs.biu.ac.il, kloesgen@gmd.de , zilbers@cs.biu.ac.il

Abstract

Document Explorer is a data mining system for document collections. Such a collection represents an application domain, and the primary goal of the system is to derive patterns that provide knowledge about this domain. Additionally, the derived patterns can be used to browse the collection. Document Explorer searches for patterns that capture relations between concepts of the domain. The patterns which have been verified as interesting are structured and presented in a visual user interface allowing the user to operate on the results to refine and redirect mining queries or to access the associated documents. The system offers preprocessing tools to construct or refine a knowledge base of domain concepts and to create an intermediate representation of the document collection that will be used by all subsequent data mining operations. The main pattern types, the system can search for, are frequent sets, associations, concept distributions, and keyword graphs. To enable the user to provide some explicit bias, the system provides a dedicated query language for searching the vast implicit spaces of pattern instances that exist in the collection.

1 Introduction

Most informal definitions (Fayyad et al. 1996) introduce *knowledge discovery in databases* (KDD) as the extraction of useful information from databases by large-scale search for interesting patterns. The vast majority of existing KDD applications and methods deal with structured databases, for example client data stored in a relational database, and thus exploits data organized in records structured by categorical, ordinal, and continuous variables. However, a tremendous amount of information is stored in documents that are nearly unstructured. The availability of document collections and especially of online information is rapidly growing, so that an analysis bottleneck often arises also in this area.

A document collection represents a special application domain and each document is related to some set of the concepts that play a role in this domain. Therefore, our knowledge discovery approach for document collections is targeted at these concepts, i.e. we seek patterns that describe (co-occurrence) relations between concepts of the domain. Data mining methods thus extract knowledge about a document domain by searching and structuring interesting concept relations and track their changes over time. Additionally, they supply new browsing capabilities using the inter-document information contained in the discovered patterns.

Following this approach, it is obvious, that knowledge discovery in the document area is a again a process that involves preprocessing, data mining, and refinement tasks. Methods of term extraction or text categorization belong to the main preprocessing tasks in this area. Data mining methods, because typically based on large-scale brute force search, produce a lot of patterns. As in KDD for structured databases, a main discovery task relates to constraining the search by operationalizing interestingness, especially to prevent the user from getting overwhelmed with too many results.

In traditional retrieval, it is assumed that the user knows in advance the concepts of documents he could be interested in, or that he selects a constructed cluster of documents. Applying KDD tools like Document Explorer means that the system takes an active role in suggesting concepts of interest to the user, as well as supply new browsing methods that rely on inter-document information. The discovery framework of Document Explorer may thus be viewed as an intermediate point between user-specified retrieval queries and unsupervised document clustering. The user typically provides some guidance to the system about the type of patterns of interest, but then the system identifies groups of pattern instances applying filtering, ordering, generalization, statistical validation and clustering techniques.

The Document Explorer System builds upon the experience that was gained from building the KDT system [Feldman and Dagan 1995], FACT [Feldman and Hirsh, 1997], and Explora [Kloesgen 1995, Kloesgen 1996].

2   Architecture of the Document Explorer System

One of the main drawbacks of the current implementation of Text Mining systems (e.g., KDT) is that they have a fixed set of KDD tools and there is no possibility to generate new tools upon demand. If the user would like to perform a task, which is not within the capability of any of the current tools, then this task just can not be done within the current systems. In order to overcome this drawback, we have developed a high level language that will be used to specify the KDD tasks that should be performed. This language called KDTL (Knowledge Discovery in Texts Language) is expressive enough to allow the specification of most KDD operations that might be requested by the user. At the same time KDTL is simple enough to be easily used by the user. This language is based on a set of primitives that are suitable for the specification of KDD tasks on text collections.

The Document Explorer system contains three main modules. The first module is the backbone of the system and it includes the KDTL query front-end where the user can enter his queries for patterns, the interpreter which parses a query and translates it into function calls in the lower levels, and the data mining and the data management layer. These two layers are responsible for the actual execution of the user's query. The data mining layer contains all the search and pruning strategies that can be applied for mining patterns. The main patterns offered in the system are frequent concept sets (Agrawal et al., 1993), associations (Agrawal et al., 1993), and distributions (Feldman and Dagan, 1995).

The embedded search algorithms control the search for specific pattern instances within the target database. This level includes also the refinement methods that filter redundant information and cluster together closely related information. The data management layer is responsible for all access to the actual data stored in the target database. This layer encapsulates the target database from the rest of the system.

The second module is the source preprocessing and categorization module. This module includes the set of source converters and the text categorization software. It is responsible for converting the information fetched from each of the available sources into a canonical format and for tagging each document with the predefined categories, and extracting all multi-word terms from the documents. In this preprocessing component, the system extracts all the information that will subsequently be used by the data mining methods.

The target database is represented as a compressed data structure, namely a Trie. The fact that we represent the documents as sets of phrases and keywords (concepts) has several implications. We have only binary attributes, and these attributes are sparse (i.e. only a fraction of the attributes appears in any given record; typically around 2-3 percent), and finally the number of records is of medium size (between 20,000-500,000 documents). The Trie is an efficient data structure that encapsulates all the information of the document collection. In this Trie, all aggregates existing in the target database are managed in a compressed format. In addition, the Trie provides an efficient approach to incrementally calculate all the aggregates, and to store and access these aggregates. Several forms of tries can be used that treat in a different way the tradeoff between space of storing the Trie and time of calculating derived results from the Trie. For more details on our Trie methods, we refer the reader to (Amir et al. 1997).

Besides the target databases, the datamining methods in Document Explorer exploit also a knowledge base on the application domain. The terms of the domain are arranged in a DAG (directed acyclical graph). The terms belong to several hierarchically arranged categories. In the application area of the Reuters newswire collection, used in this paper for application examples, the main categories correspond to countries, economic topics, persons, etc.. Each category, e.g. economic topics, has subcategories (currencies, main economic indicators, etc.). Further background knowledge is given by relations between these categories. The knowledge base for the Reuters collection includes relations between pairs of countries (e.g. countries with land boundaries), between countries and persons (nationality), countries and commodities (exports) and so on. These relations can be defined by the user or transformed by special utilities from general available sources (such as the CIA World Fact Book, or companies home pages).

Finally, the third module is the visualization module which is responsible for providing an attractive set of GUI based KDD tools (see Section 4) and graph based visualization techniques that enable the user a much easier access to the system. Keyword graphs [Feldman et al., 1997] are a special interactive visualization technique to present data mining results. Keyword Graphs extend the notion of association rules to relations between keywords and phrases occurring in different documents. A diagram of the Document Explorer System architecture is shown in Figure 1.

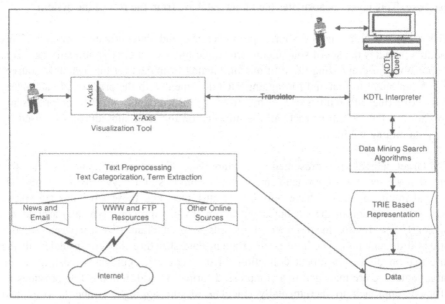

Fig. 1. Architecture of the Document Explorer system

3 Text Mining and Browsing Language

An overabundance of patterns can typically be identified in any data mining application. For a document collection, we can also validate an immense number of frequent concept sets, association rules, undirected relations between frequent concept sets, concept distributions, and relations between concept distributions. A mining and browsing language will allow to query this vast implicit set of patterns available in a given document collection. The results of a query will be presented in a graphical user interface. The user can then operate on the results to redefine the query and browse the document collection. The query language is embedded into a graphical user interface offering an easy specification to the user.

3.1 Constraint Types

Four types of constraints can be exploited to restrict the search for patterns, the number of presented patterns, and generally to deal with interestingness of results. We will describe now that nature of each constraint type.

Syntactical constraints typically refer to selections of concepts that shall be included into a query. More specifically, they refer to the components of the patterns, e.g. to the left or right hand side of a rule, the number of items in the components, etc.

Background constraints refer to the knowledge on the domain that is given in form of binary relations between concepts. Rules associating persons and countries can, for example, be constrained by the condition that an association between a person and a country excludes the nationality of the person. Associations between countries can be restricted to countries, which have no boundary, etc. We have a set of predicates that are related to entities mentioned in the document collection. Most of our predicates are binary, with one input argument and one output argument. Each of the predicates is then treated as a function that takes a keyword as input and outputs the value of the output argument. Further, whenever a function is applied to a set of keywords, the function returns all second arguments that make the predicate true for any element in the input set of keywords. The background predicates currently used in KDTL were automatically extracted from the CIA World Fact Book using a Perl script written for this purpose.

In addition to the basic quality constraints, namely support and confidence threshold, KDTL includes more advanced statistical measures provide qualities for the patterns. An association rule, for example, is additionally qualified by the significance of a statistical test (binomial test, chi-square test, etc.). A distribution of a concept group is evaluated with respect to a reference distribution. For instance, compare economic topic distribution of each EU country with overall EU economic topic distribution, or compare the topic distribution of Germany with that of France. These qualities are then used in constraints when searching for significant patterns (e.g. countries with significantly different topics distributions).

Finally, KDTL include a set of redundancy constraints. These meta-rules determine, when a pattern is suppressed by another pattern. A redundancy rule may suppress, for example, all association rules with a more special left hand side (and the same right hand side) than another association rule and a confidence that is not (significantly) higher than that of the other more general rule. Here are some meta-rules that are used as redundancy constraints by the Document Explorer system.

- Given an association $a1 = L1 \Rightarrow L2$ s/c, if we have an association $a2 = L \Rightarrow L2$ s/c, where $L \subset L1$ then $a1$ is subsumed by $a2$ and hence it is deleted.
- Given an association $a1 = L1 \Rightarrow L2$ s/c, if we have an association $a2 = L1 \Rightarrow L$ s/c, where $L2 \subset L$ then $a1$ is subsumed by $a2$ and hence it is deleted.
- Given an association $r1 = A \Rightarrow B$ s/c, if we have an association $a2 = P \Rightarrow B$ s1/c1, where $c1 \geq c$, and A is a descendant of P, then $r1$ is redundant and is deleted. A simple generalization exists for associations having more than one literal in the left-hand side.

The user can decide which of the redundancy rules he wants to be active in the current session. The system will then delete all rules that are redundant according to any of the checked rules.

3.2 The Structure of KDTL

In this section we will describe KDTL, and provide examples that show how we can isolate interesting patterns using KDTL queries. A BNF description of KDTL is shown in Figure 2. We have shown only the language statements that are related to the syntactical, background, and quality constraints. The redundancy constraints are selected by the user from a specified set of predefined constraints offered by the system.

Each query contains one algorithmic statement and several constraint statements. The constraint part of the query is structured such that the user needs to select the relevant component (i.e., the lest hand side of the association, right hand side, frequent set, or a path in a keyword graph), and then all subsequent constraint statements are applied to this component. When specifying set relations, the user can optionally specify background predicates to be applied to the given expressions. KDTL intentionally contains some redundancy in the constraints statements to enable easier specification of queries.

Algorithmic statements:

gen_rule() : *generate all matching association rules*
gen_frequent_set(): *generate all matching frequent sets*
gen_kg() : *generate a keyword graph*
gen_dkg() : *generate a directed keyword graph*
gen_dist() : *generate a distribution*

Constraint statements:

set_filter(<Set>) - *the set MUST meet the following constraints*
set_not_filter(<Set>) - *the set MUST NOT meet the following constraints*

<Set> ::= frequent_set | left | right | path

contain([<background predicate>], <Expression>) –
           the designated set must contain <expression> (or <background
           predicate>(<expression>))
subset([<background predicate>],<Expression>) –
           the designated set is a subset of <expression> (or <background
       predicate>(<expression>))
disjoint([<background predicate>],<Expression>) –
           the designated set and <expression> are disjoint (or <background
       predicate>(<expression>))
equal([<background predicate>],<Expression>) –
           the designated set is equal to <expression> (or <background
       predicate>(<expression>))

all_has(<Expression>) –

> *all members of the designated set are descendents of <expression> in the taxonomy*

```
one_has(<Expression>)  –
```

> *at least one of the members of the designated set is a descendents of <expression>*

```
property_count(<Expression>,<low>,<high>)  –
```

> *# of members that are descendents of <expression> is in the specified range.*

```
size(<Expression>,<low>,<high>)  –
```

> *size of the designated set is in the Specified range.*

```
Set_conf(real)
Set_supp(integer)


<Expression>  ::= Keyword | Category |
                  <Expression>,<Expression>  |
                  <Expression> ; <Expression>
<high>  ::= integer
<low>   ::= integer
```

Fig. 2. BNF description of KDTL

3.3 KDTL Query Examples

In this section, we show example KDTL queries executed on the reuters-22173 document collection. This is a collection of documents that appeared on the Reuters newswire in 1987. The 22173 documents were assembled, indexed with categories by personnel from Reuters Ltd. and Carnegie Group, Inc. in 1987, and further formatting and data file production was done in 1991 and 1992 by David D. Lewis and Peter Shoemaker. Each document was tagged by the Reuters personnel with a subset of 672 keywords that fell into five categories: countries, topics, people, organizations and stock exchanges.

If we are interested only in associations that correlate between a set of countries including iran, and a person, we will write the following KDTL query:

```
set_filter(left);all_has({"countries"});
contain({"iran"});
set_filter(right);all_has({"people"});
property_count("people",1,1);
set_supp(4); set_conf(0.5); gen_rule();
```

The system has found in this case four associations, in all of them Reagan was in the RHS. The interesting associations are those that include Iran and Nicaragua on the LHS. One interesting point in that example, is that when viewing the document collection we see that when Iran and Nicaragua are in the document then if there is any person in the document, Reagan will be in that document too. In other words, the association Iran, Nicaragua, <person> ⇒ Reagan has 100% confidence and is supported by 6 documents. The <person> constraint means that there must be at least one person name in the document.

```
(6,54%) Iran, Nicaragua, USA ⇒ Reagan
(6,50%) Iran, Nicaragua ⇒ Reagan
(18,19%) Iran, USA ⇒ Reagan
(19,10%) Iran ⇒ Reagan
```

In the next example we wanted to infer who are the people that were highly correlated with West Germany (the Reuters collection contain document from 1987, which is before the reunion of Germany). We then formulated a query that looked for correlation between groups of one to three people and West Germany.

```
set_filter("left");  size(1,3); all_has({"people"});
set_filter("right"); equal({"west_germany"});
set_supp(10); set_conf(0.5); gen_rule();
```

The system found five such associations, in all them the people that are on the left hand side were high official of the West Germany government. Kohl was the Chancellor, Poehl was the president of the Central Bank, Bangemann was the Economy Minister, and Stoltenberg was the Finance Minister. So if one wants to infer from a document collection who are the high officials of a given country, he can just use a similar query and get a very accurate answer. This example can be used to show how background knowledge can eliminate trivial associations. Clearly, if someone if familiar with German politics then he is not interested in getting these associations, and would like to see associations between people that are not German citizens and Germany. Adding the constraints. set_filter_not("left"); equal(nationality, "west_germany"); will eliminate all the associations shown below.

```
(8,100%) Poehl, Stoltenberg ⇒ West Germany
(6,100%) Bangemann ⇒ West Germany
(11,100%) Kohl ⇒ West Germany
(21,80%) Poehl ⇒ West Germany
(44,75%) Stoltenberg ⇒ West Germany
```

In Figure 3 and 4 we can see the GUI for defining KDTL queries. The user builds the query one constraint at a time. The tabbed dialog in Figure 4 shows how the user defines a single constraint. The results of the query are shown in Figure 5. In this query, we wanted to find all associations that connect between a set of countries and a set of economical indicator topics, if trade is not in the set. Only one association satisfied all these constraints. If we lift the last constraint and allow trade to be in the right hand side of the association we get 18 associations.

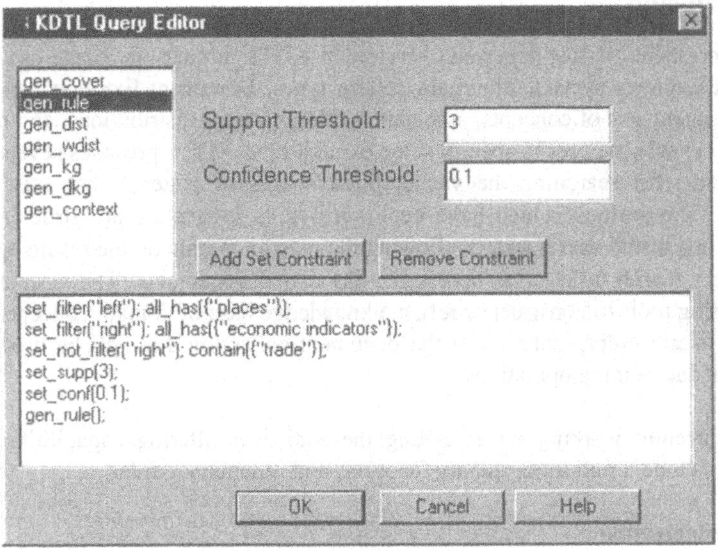

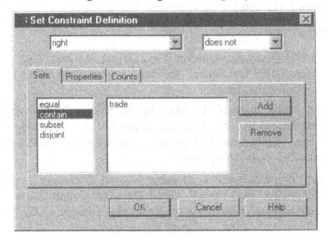

Fig. 3. Defining a KDTL Query

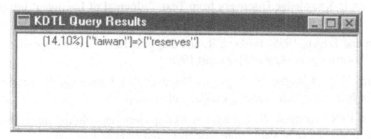

Fig. 4. Defining a Set Constraint

Fig. 5. Query Results

4 Conclusion

We have presented in this paper an overview of KDTL, a query language used in the Document Explorer system. The main pattern types, Document Explorer can search for, are frequent sets of concepts, association rules, concept distributions, and concept graphs. To enable the user to specify some explicit bias, KDTL provides several types of constraints for searching the vast implicit spaces of patterns that exist in the collection. The patterns which have been verified as interesting are structured and presented in a visual user interface allowing the user to operate on the results to refine and redirect search tasks or to access the associated documents. The system offers preprocessing tools to construct or refine a knowledge base of domain concepts and to create an internal representation of the document collection that will be used by all subsequent data mining operations.

We are currently working on extending the statistical filtering capabilities of the system to include a rich set of quality functions and redundancy rules.

Acknowledgements

This research was supported by grant # 8615 from the Israeli Ministry of Sciences, and by a GIF grant I-429-096.

5 References

[Amir et al., 1997] Amir A., Aumann Y., Feldman R., and Katz O. Efficient Algorithm for Association Generation. Technical Report, Department of Computer Science, Bar-Ilan University, Israel.

[Agrawal et al., 1995] Agrawal R., Mannila H., Srikant R., Toivonen H., and Verkamo I. Fast Discovery of Association Rules. In Advances in Knowledge Discovery and Data Mining, Eds. U. Fayyad, G. Piatetsky-Shapiro, P. Smyth, and R. Uthurusamy, pages 307-328, AAAI Press.

[Feldman et al. 1997] Feldman R., Kloesgen W. and Zilberstein A. Visualization Techniques for Exploring Data mining Results in Document Collections. In *Proceedings of the Third International Conference on Knowledge Discovery (KDD-97)*, August 1997.

[Feldman and Hirsh, 1997] Feldman R., and Hirsh H. "Exploiting Background Information in Knowledge Discovery from Text, ", Journal of Intelligent Information Systems, 1997.

[Feldman and Dagan, 1995] Feldman R. and Dagan I. KDT - knowledge discovery in texts. In *Proceedings of (KDD-95)*, August 1995.

[Kloesgen 1995] Klösgen W. Efficient Discovery of Interesting Statements. *The Journal of Intelligent Information Systems*, Vol. 4, No 1.

[Kloesgen 1996] Klösgen W. Explora: A Multipattern and Multistrategy Discovery Assistant. In *Advances in Knowledge Discovery and Data Mining*, eds.

[Fayyad et al., 1996] U. Fayyad, G. Piatetsky-Shapiro, P. Smyth, and R. Uthurusamy, Cambridge, MA: MIT Press.

Well-Behaved Evaluation Functions for Numerical Attributes

Tapio Elomaa[1] and Juho Rousu[2]

[1] Institute for Systems, Informatics and Safety, Joint Research Centre
European Commission, TP 270, I-21020 Ispra (VA), Italy
tapio.elomaa@jrc.it
[2] VTT Biotechnology and Food Research
Tietotie 2, P. O. Box 1501, FIN-02044 VTT, Finland
juho.rousu@vtt.fi

Abstract. The class of *well-behaved* evaluation functions simplifies and makes efficient the handling of numerical attributes; for them it suffices to concentrate on the *boundary points* in searching for the optimal partition. This holds always for binary partitions and also for multisplits if only the function is *cumulative* in addition to being well-behaved. A large portion of the most important attribute evaluation functions are well-behaved. This paper surveys the class of well-behaved functions. As a case study, we examine the properties of C4.5's attribute evaluation functions. Our empirical experiments show that a very simple cumulative rectification to the poor bias of *information gain* significantly outperforms gain ratio.

1 Introduction

Top-down induction of decision trees (TDIDT) works by recursively dividing a given sample into successively smaller subsets. The aim is to discover a final partition of the data in which the class distribution of the subsets reflects the classification of (future) instances. The correlation of an instance's class and its attribute values is heuristically approximated by an *evaluation function*, or a *goodness criterion*. In the most basic scheme a single attribute's value is the basis of sample partitioning: the data is greedily divided into subsets according to the value of that attribute which evaluates as the best.

If the best attribute has a small nominal domain, it is simple to continue tree construction by growing a subtree corresponding to each separate value in the domain. Handling a large nominal domain is more problematic, since the evaluation functions tend to have biases for (or against) multivalued attributes [10]. Many new evaluation functions have been developed to address this deficiency [8,11,13].

The real challenge for decision tree learning, however, is issued by *numerical attributes* with a very large, even infinite domain, which can be either discrete (integer) or continuous (real). Numerical attributes cannot be handled by the TDIDT scheme quite as naturally as nominal attributes. In real-world induction tasks numerical attribute ranges, nevertheless, regularly appear, and therefore, they also need to be taken into account [4,7–9,14–16]. Independent of the function that is used to determine the goodness of an attribute, a numerical attribute's value range needs to be categorized into two or more intervals for evaluation.

When discretizing a numerical value range we inherently meet the problem of choosing the right arity for the partitioning; i.e., into how many intervals should we split the range. This is often evaded by using *binarization* [3,14], in which the value range is split into only two intervals at a time (in one node). Further partitioning of the domain is generated by continuing the binarization of previously induced intervals further down the tree.

An alternative approach uses *greedy multisplitting* [4,8], where the value range is similarly partitioned by recursive binarization, but at once; the resulting multisplit is assigned to a single node of the evolving tree. Neither of the above-mentioned methods can guarantee the quality (as measured by the evaluation function) of the resulting partition. Algorithms for finding *optimal multisplits* have been devised by Fulton *et al.* [9] and by Elomaa and Rousu [5].

Independent of the algorithmic strategy that is used for partitioning the numerical value ranges it is important to ensure that obviously "bad" partitions are not selected by the function, i.e., that the function is *well-behaved*. A manifestation of poor behavior of an evaluation function is a partition that breaks up a sequence of successive examples of the same class, thus needlessly separating examples of a single class into different subsets.

This paper surveys the class of well-behaved evaluation functions. As a special case, we examine the evaluation functions that are used to evaluate attributes in the renowned decision tree learner C4.5 [14]. We analyze their behavior in binary and multiway partitioning. Finally, we investigate empirically the benefits of well-behavedness of an evaluation function for the predictive accuracy of a decision tree.

2 Partitioning numerical value ranges

The setting that we consider is the following. At our disposal we have preclassified data acquired from the application domain. The intent is to find a good predictor for classifying, on the basis of the given attributes, further instances from the same application domain. For that end the greedy TDIDT algorithm needs to approximate how well an attribute's values correlate with the classification of examples. The attributes respective correlations are then compared and the one that appears best is chosen to the evolving tree. For correlation comparison a fixed evaluation function is applied.

In numerical attribute discretization the underlying assumption is that we have sorted our n examples into (ascending) order by the value of a numerical attribute A. With this sorted sequence of examples in hand we try to elicit the best possible (in class prediction) binary or multiway partition along the dimension determined by attribute A.

Let $\mathrm{val}_A(s)$ denote the value of the attribute A in the example s. A *partition* $\bigcup_{i=1}^{k} S_i$ of sample S into k intervals consists of non-empty, disjoint subsets that cover the whole domain. When splitting a set S of examples on the basis of the value of an attribute A, then there is a set of thresholds $\{T_1, \ldots, T_{k-1}\} \subseteq$ Dom(A) that defines a partition $\bigcup_{i=1}^{k} S_i$ for the sample in an obvious manner:

$$
S_i = \begin{cases} \{s \in S \mid \text{val}_A(s) \leq T_1\} & \text{if } i = 1, \\ \{s \in S \mid T_{i-1} < \text{val}_A(s) \leq T_i\} & \text{if } 1 < i < k, \\ \{s \in S \mid T_{k-1} < \text{val}_A(s)\} & \text{if } i = k. \end{cases}
$$

A partition cannot be realized so that two examples with an equal value for that attribute would belong to different intervals. Therefore, a standard technique in numerical value range discretization – used also in C4.5 [14] – is to consider a categorized version of the data. That is, to put those examples that have the same value for the attribute in question into a common *bin* and consider only thresholds in between bins as potential *cut points*. Note that typically $V \ll n$, where V is the number of values in a range of a numerical attribute.

The goodness criteria that are used to evaluate candidate partitions are many (see e.g., [10]). A significant portion of them belong to the class of *impurity measures*. Perhaps the most important of them is the *average class entropy*, which is applied, e.g., in the ID3 [13] decision tree learner. Let $\bigcup_{i=1}^{k} S_i$ be a partition of S, then by $ACE(\bigcup_{i=1}^{k} S_i)$ we denote the average class entropy of the partition:

$$
ACE(\bigcup_{i=1}^{k} S_i) = \sum_{i=1}^{k} \frac{|S_i|}{|S|} H(S_i) = \frac{1}{n} \sum_{i=1}^{k} |S_i| H(S_i),
$$

where H is the entropy function, $H(S) = -\sum_{i=1}^{m} P(C_i, S) \log_2 P(C_i, S)$, in which m denotes the number of classes and $P(C, S)$ stands for the proportion of examples in S that have class C. For *cumulative* measures the impurity of a partition is obtained by (weighted) summation over the impurities of its intervals.

Definition 1. Let $\bigcup_{i=1}^{k} S_i$ be a partition of the example set S. An evaluation function F is *cumulative* if there exists a function f such that $F(\bigcup_{i=1}^{k} S_i) = c_S \cdot \sum_{i=1}^{k} f(S_i)$, where c_S is an arbitrary constant coefficient (whose value may depend on S, but not on its partitions).

In multisplitting the number of candidate partitions increases exponentially in the arity of the partition. For cumulative functions, however, dynamic programming can be used to elicit the best partition efficiently, in time quadratic in the number of bins [5].

3 The well-behavedness of evaluation functions

The aim in numerical value discretization is to obtain as pure partition as possible. Therefore, it is important for an evaluation function to favor partitions that keep examples of a same class together. In particular, a sequence of examples that belong to a single class should not be broken apart. With this behavior in mind, Fayyad and Irani [7] defined the profound concept of a *boundary point*:

Definition 2. A value T in the range of the attribute A is a *boundary point* iff in the sequence of examples sorted by the value of A, there exist two examples $s_1, s_2 \in S$, having different classes, such that $\text{val}_A(s_1) < T < \text{val}_A(s_2)$; and there exists no other example $s \in S$ such that $\text{val}_A(s_1) < \text{val}_A(s) < \text{val}_A(s_2)$.

We call the intervals separated by boundary points as *blocks*. Let B be the number of blocks in the domain. For any relevant attribute $B \ll n$, since otherwise there clearly is no correlation between the value of the attribute and the examples' classification [7]. Since boundary points are taken from among the potential cut points, it is clear that $B \leq V$ always holds.

Fayyad and Irani [7] proved that average class entropy obtains its optimal (minimal) value on a boundary point. Their proof is based on the fact that that it is *convex* (downwards) in between any two boundary points. Thus, ACE's minimum values for binary partitions can only occur at boundary points.

Convexity of a function is a property that can be detected by observing its (first and second) derivatives. However, it can be a needlessly restrictive requirement to pose to an evaluation function. Independent of the shape of the function curve, for good behavior in binarization, it suffices that the function receives its minimum value at a boundary point. Convex functions possess this property and, hence, constitute a subclass of well-behaved evaluation functions.

Shorthand notation $F(T)$ denotes the value of the evaluation function F for the binary partition that is defined by the cut point T. We consider a set of boundary points that is *augmented* by the low and high extremes of the value range as to ensure that each example set always has at least two boundary points.

Definition 3. Let S be an arbitrary example set and let $\mathcal{T} = \{T_0, \ldots, T_{B+1}\}$ be the augmented set of boundary points in S in the dimension determined by an arbitrary numerical attribute A. An evaluation function F is *well-behaved* if there exists a value T in $\mathcal{T}$ such that $F(T) \leq F(W)$ for all $W \in \text{Dom}(A)$.

Through the use of the augmented set of boundary points this definition also covers the degenerate case, where there are no natural boundary points in the example set. Definition 3 constraints search of the optimal binary partition to boundary points. If a well-behaved evaluation function is also cumulative, then it has the same desirable property in multisplitting. In order to minimize the goodness score of a partition, with respect to any such function, it suffices to examine only boundary points [5].

Theorem 4. *For any cumulative and well-behaved evaluation function F there exists a partition of an arbitrary example set such that it minimizes the value of F and the corresponding cut points are boundary points.* □

For cumulative functions the best partition of a subsample does not depend on the splitting of its complement set. Thus the required search strategy can be implemented by using dynamic programming [9,5]. The time requirement of finding the optimal partitioning into at most k intervals is $O(kB^2)$, where B is the number of blocks in the range. Hence, in practice the method is efficient enough as to recover the best partition from among all partitions (arities $2, \ldots, B$).

4 Examples of well-behaved evaluation functions

By Definition 3 an evaluation function must satisfy only very weak requirements for it to be well-behaved. It suffices that (one of) the lowest-impurity-partitions into two intervals falls on a boundary point. Clearly, convex evaluation functions fulfill this requirement. Thus, the well-behavedness of some important attribute evaluation functions is already known.

Breiman *et al.* [3,2] have studied learning regression trees using two evaluation functions: the *gini index* of diversity and the *twoing criterion*. Gini index, or the quadratic entropy, is defined as

$$GI(\bigcup_{i=1}^{k} S_i) = \sum_{i=1}^{k} \frac{|S_i|}{|S|} gini(S_i),$$

where *gini* is the function $gini(S) = -\sum_{i=1}^{m} P(C_i, S)(1 - P(C_i, S))$. Gini criterion was shown to be convex by Breiman [2] and, hence, it is also well-behaved. It is also cumulative and, therefore, would suit multisplitting if its bias of favoring high-arity partitions was balanced somehow.

Twoing criterion is based on the idea of grouping the classes into two superclasses and then finding the optimal partition for this two class problem. As twoing criterion relies on some evaluation function to actually find the best partition, its well-behavedness depends on the chosen function. Note that grouping of classes can only remove boundary points from the example sequence. Thus, using a well-behaved evaluation function ensures well-behaved functioning.

Fayyad and Irani [7] proved that the evaluation function ACE is convex (downwards) in between any two boundary points. From that result it follows that also ID3's [13] attribute evaluation function, *information gain*, is convex (upwards). Using our earlier notation it can be expressed as

$$IG(S, A) = H(S) - ACE(\bigcup_{i=1}^{k} S_i),$$

where $H(S)$ is the class entropy of the sample S prior to partitioning. The value of $H(S)$ is the same for all attributes and partitions. Hence, IG is at a maximum when ACE is at a minimum value. Thus, its well-behavedness is also clear.

Theorem 5. *The evaluation functions GI, Twoing criterion, ACE, and IG are well-behaved.* □

As to examine the extent and generality of well-behaved evaluation functions, we took two non-standard functions and proved their well-behavedness [5]: the incremental MDL exception coding scheme of Wallace and Patrick [17], denoted by *WP*, and the straightforward evaluation scheme of minimizing the training set error of a decision tree, *TSE*, which is applied, e.g., in the T2 algorithm [1]. Both of these are cumulative and were shown to be well-behaved as well.

TSE suffers from the bias of favoring high-arity partitions; the MDL measure, however, is more balanced in this respect.

Moreover, we have examined a variant of information gain function, *balanced gain*, which can be expressed as $BG(S, A) = IG(S, A)/k$, where k is the arity of the partition [5]. This simple modification to information gain attempts to balance its bias so that partitions of high arity would not be favored excessively, while keeping the function cumulative, thus ensuring its well-behavedness.

Theorem 6. *The evaluation functions WP, TSE, and BG are well-behaved.* □

All the functions above are also convex. Are there any evaluation functions that are not convex but still meet the weak requirements of a well-behaved evaluation function? For cumulative evaluation functions the definition of a well-behaved function lives up to its name. How about the ones that are not cumulative? Does the definition then discriminate between in practice well-behaving and poorly-doing evaluation functions? As a step towards answering these questions, in the following we examine the properties and behavior of evaluation functions used in the C4.5 algorithm [14].

5 Behavior of the evaluation functions of C4.5

Information gain function does not place any penalty to the increase of the arity of a partition. Therefore, it favors excessively multi-valued nominal attributes and multisplitting numerical attribute value ranges. As a rectification to this deficiency Quinlan [13] suggested dividing the *IG* score of a partition by the term $\kappa = -\sum_{i=1}^{k}(|S_i|/|S|)\log_2(|S_i|/|S|)$. The resulting evaluation function is known as the *gain ratio*

$$GR(S, A) = IG(S, A)/\kappa.$$

The renowned decision tree learner C4.5 [14] incorporates gain ratio as the default choice for attribute evaluation. It has been observed to have some difficulties in particular in connection with numerical attributes. As to overcome those problems López de Màntaras [11] has proposed to use another, but closely related evaluation function, and Quinlan [15] has recently changed the evaluation of numerical attributes in C4.5. We examine the changed evaluation strategy subsequently. Let us, however, first review the properties of the *GR* function.

Gain ratio is actually used in C4.5 in the following manner. In the first phase, the gain ratio maximizing partition is computed for each attribute. Then, instead of choosing the gain ratio maximizing partition, Quinlan [14] places an additional constraint to the partition that is determined as the best one: its *IG* score has to be at least as good as the average score among candidate partitions. This strategy tries to ensure that splits with low information gain are filtered out.

The guilty part for the risk of choosing low information gain splits is the denominator κ: it is the smaller the more uneven the partition is. The κ value can hinder a split of good information gain to be selected, if the partition induced by the split is too even. This is a bias that cannot easily be justified. In fact, one is tempted to think that the opposite strategy – that of favoring even partitions – would be just as good, if not better.

The bias induced by the denominator κ does not manifest itself yet on binarization: GR has been shown to be well-behaved [6]. It is the first known example of a well-behaved function that is not at the same time convex (c.f. [6]).

Theorem 7. *The evaluation function gain ratio is not convex, but it is well-behaved with respect to binary partitioning.* □

As gain ratio is not cumulative, its well-behavedness on binary splitting does not imply the same on multisplitting. We have given an example which shows that the gain ratio function cannot handle higher arity splitting well: from arity three onwards the partition that evaluates as best is not guaranteed to be defined on boundary points [6]. Moreover, the non-cumulativity of gain ratio means in practice that there is no efficient evaluation scheme for this function.

The same counterexample, incidentally, also applies to the *normalized distance measure* d_N proposed by López de Màntaras [11]. It too fails to select a three-way partition defined solely by boundary points. The measure can be expressed with the help of information gain as $1 - d_N(S, A) = IG(S, A)/\lambda$, where

$$\lambda = -\sum_{i=1}^{m}\sum_{j=1}^{k} \frac{N(C_i, S_j)}{|S|} \log_2 \frac{N(C_i, S_j)}{|S|},$$

in which m is the number of classes and k is the number of intervals, as usual, and $N(C, S)$ stands for the number of instances of class C in the set S. The intent is to minimize the value of distance $d_N \in [0, 1]$ or, equivalently, maximize the value of $1 - d_N$.

Once again the denominator of this evaluation function not only manages to hinder efficient evaluability, but also loses the well-behavedness that comes along with the information gain function.

Theorem 8. *The evaluation functions GR and d_N are not well-behaved with respect to multiway partitioning.* □

The latest release of C4.5 has returned to use ID3's information gain function as the evaluator of the binary splits on numerical attribute ranges [15]. However, the final selection of the attribute to be added to the evolving decision tree is left to another evaluation function. The gain ratio function has been changed with a (MDL-inspired) correction term $\mu = \log_2(V - 1)/n$, which is subtracted from the information gain in the numerator of the gain ratio formula. This modified gain ratio function gets to choose the attribute.

The correction term μ penalizes attributes with a high number of distinct values and, thus, reduces their selection likelihood. Thus the tendency to favor multivalued attributes gets reduced. However, this strategy leaves numerical attributes to be dealt differently than nominal attributes. The correction μ, incidentally, does not change the well-behavedness properties of GR, since it has a constant value for all cut point candidates.

6 Empirical experiments

The following well-behaved variant of the information gain function is contrasted to gain ratio in these empirical experiments: $BG_{\log}(S, A) = IG(S, A)/\log_2 k$. To see that it is closely related to the gain ratio, observe that the denominator κ in the formula of GR is the entropy function H applied to the sizes of the intervals, not to the class distribution. Clearly, it holds that $0 < \kappa \leq \log_2 k$. In information theoretic sense $\log_2 k$ is the entropy of the intervals when assigned equal probability regardless of their size. Thus, $BG_{\log}$ penalizes all equal arity partitions uniformly and always maximally as regards GR. Note also that $BG_{\log}$ coincides with IG in binary splitting.

$BG_{\log}$ is less heavily biased against the increase of arity of the multisplit than BG. Our earlier experiments with BG [5] convinced us that the function favors binary splits excessively, since the number of multisplits in the induced trees remains very low. Indeed, results with $BG_{\log}$ compare favorably against BG.

Our tests concern both binarization and multisplitting. We run the same set of tests for four configurations: binarization tests with C4.5 using GR and IG (i.e. $BG_{\log}$) functions and multisplitting tests using GR and $BG_{\log}$.

We implemented a dynamic programming method for finding multisplits [5] into C4.5 as well as the evaluation function $BG_{\log}$. Since no efficient optimization strategy is known for GR in multisplitting, we used the following evaluation scheme: For each attribute and for each arity, we searched for the optimal information gain partition. From a set of candidate splits generated this way the final selection was done by gain ratio. This scheme favors GR, since no "bad" splits are left for it to choose from. The differences in predictive accuracies are then explained only by the fact that gain ratio selects splits that are a little more uneven and have lower information gain than partitions selected by $BG_{\log}$.

We tested the functions on 21 real-world data sets that come mainly from the UCI repository [12]. The test strategy was 10-fold cross-validation repeated 10 times. For significance testing two-tailed Student's t-test was used. Table 1 lists the average prediction accuracies and standard deviations obtained. Symbols $++$ and $--$ denote statistically significantly better and worse performance with respect to $BG_{\log}$; $+$ and $-$ denote corresponding almost significant differences.

From Table 1 we see that in multisplitting the statistically significant differences are more often in favor of $BG_{\log}$ (5+3) than in favor of GR (3+2). Thus, it is reasonable to assume the difference of 0.8 percentage points in the average prediction accuracies over all domains to be significant as well. Even clearer edge is obtained over C4.5 using GR: $BG_{\log}$ is better than C4.5 on 7 (4+3) data sets, while C4.5 only manages to obtain 3 (1+2) "wins." As for the question whether multisplitting has anything to do with the good performance of $BG_{\log}$, observe that the multisplitting variant of $BG_{\log}$ is statistically significantly better than its binarizing counterpart on 4 domains. On the other hand, it loses statistically significantly only once and twice almost significantly.

All in all, even an almost trivial penalization added to information gain function against favoring multisplitting excessively can significantly outperform the complicated penalization attempt of gain ratio, which has led it to have

Table 1. Average prediction accuracies for C4.5 using GR and IG functions and for the multisplitting strategies using GR and BG_{log}. The symbols $++$ ($--$) denote statistically significantly better (worse) performance w.r.t. BG_{log}; $+$ and $-$ denote almost significant differences.

DATA SET	C4.5 (GR)	C4.5 (IG)	GR (multi)	BG_{log} (multi)
Annealing	$90.5 \pm 0.5^{-}$	91.6 ± 0.6	$89.4 \pm 0.5^{--}$	91.3 ± 0.4
Australian	84.7 ± 0.8	85.8 ± 0.8	$83.7 \pm 0.4^{--}$	85.3 ± 0.6
Auto insurance	$76.8 \pm 1.9^{+}$	$70.7 \pm 0.9^{--}$	$78.5 \pm 1.3^{++}$	75.2 ± 1.6
Breast W	94.7 ± 0.5	94.5 ± 0.3	$94.0 \pm 0.4^{-}$	94.7 ± 0.5
Colic	84.7 ± 0.8	84.5 ± 0.6	$85.8 \pm 0.7^{++}$	84.2 ± 0.7
Diabetes	$72.9 \pm 1.5^{-}$	74.9 ± 1.0	$73.2 \pm 1.0^{-}$	74.3 ± 1.0
Euthyroid	98.6 ± 0.1	98.8 ± 0.1	98.6 ± 0.1	98.6 ± 0.1
German	71.6 ± 0.9	$73.3 \pm 0.9^{+}$	$71.1 \pm 2.1^{-}$	72.3 ± 0.7
Glass	$68.6 \pm 2.3^{--}$	$69.8 \pm 1.4^{--}$	$68.9 \pm 1.0^{--}$	72.3 ± 1.4
Heart C	53.4 ± 1.6	53.4 ± 1.0	53.2 ± 0.7	53.7 ± 1.7
Heart H	$81.8 \pm 1.3^{+}$	$75.6 \pm 1.3^{--}$	$82.3 \pm 1.2^{+}$	79.7 ± 1.5
Hepatitis	$79.9 \pm 1.4^{--}$	81.0 ± 2.4	$79.8 \pm 1.3^{--}$	81.9 ± 1.7
Hypothyroid	99.1 ± 0.0	99.3 ± 0.0	99.2 ± 0.1	99.2 ± 0.1
Iris	93.5 ± 1.2	94.3 ± 1.3	92.5 ± 0.9	93.4 ± 0.9
Mole	$81.4 \pm 1.5^{-}$	$81.1 \pm 1.1^{--}$	81.8 ± 1.2	82.5 ± 0.9
Robot	99.3 ± 0.1	99.6 ± 0.1	99.6 ± 0.1	99.5 ± 0.1
Satellite	86.3 ± 0.5	$86.8 \pm 0.3^{++}$	$86.6 \pm 0.3^{+}$	86.0 ± 0.3
Segmentation	$86.6 \pm 1.1^{+}$	85.7 ± 1.2	$86.5 \pm 1.3^{+}$	85.4 ± 1.1
Sonar	$66.8 \pm 2.9^{--}$	75.5 ± 2.5	$65.0 \pm 3.1^{--}$	74.9 ± 2.2
Vehicle	71.8 ± 0.7	$73.0 \pm 1.3^{+}$	71.4 ± 1.2	72.0 ± 0.6
Wine	$92.5 \pm 1.1^{--}$	93.9 ± 0.9	94.2 ± 1.0	94.4 ± 1.0
AVERAGE	82.6	82.9	82.6	83.4

a poorly balanced bias. Moreover, these experiments indicate that multisplitting (on boundary points) possesses advantages over the binarization approach. However, the difference is very small if using a poorly balanced function.

7 Conclusion and future work

Well-behavedness of an evaluation function is a necessary, but not a sufficient condition for teleologically good behavior as regards numerical attributes. For cumulative evaluation functions, well-behavedness on binary splitting extends to multisplitting situations. This does not hold for evaluation functions in general; in the absence of general theory of discretization, the suitability of an evaluation function for multisplitting has to be examined per function basis.

The evaluation function gain ratio behaves well in binary splitting, but does not do the same in multisplitting. This is an indication of the fact that multisplitting is more demanding task for an evaluation function than previously believed: in addition to the well-known problem of improper biases for (or against) the increase in the arity of the partition, also the well-behavedness is hard to ensure.

Gain ratio is an example of a non-convex evaluation function that is well-behaved. All those that have been shown to behave well in multisplitting are convex and cumulative, although convexity is not necessary requirement. In order to shed more light on this matter, one should examine non-cumulative and/or non-convex evaluation functions to find out whether there exists functions that are able to guarantee for all arities that the best partition is defined solely by boundary points, or at least do that for the optimal partition over all arities.

References

1. Auer, P., Holte, R., Maass, W.: Theory and application of agnostic PAC-learning with small decision trees. In A. Prieditis, S. Russell (eds.), *Proc. Twelfth Intl. Conf. on Machine Learning* (21–29). Morgan Kaufmann, San Francisco, CA, 1995.
2. Breiman, L.: Some properties of splitting criteria. Mach. Learn. **24** (1996) 41–47.
3. Breiman, L., Friedman, J., Olshen, R., Stone, C.: *Classification and Regression Trees*. Wadsworth, Pacific Grove, CA, 1984.
4. Catlett, J.: On changing continuous attributes into ordered discrete attributes. In Y. Kodratoff (ed.), *Proc. Fifth Europ. Working Session on Learning* (164–178), Lecture Notes in Computer Science **482**. Springer-Verlag, Berlin, 1991.
5. Elomaa, T., Rousu, J.: General and efficient multisplitting of numerical attributes. Report C-1996-82. Dept. of Computer Science, University of Helsinki. 1996, 25 pp.
6. Elomaa, T., Rousu, J.: On the well-behavedness of important attribute evaluation functions. In G. Grahne (ed.), *Proc. Sixth Scand. Conf. on Artificial Intelligence* (in press). IOS Press, Amsterdam, 1997.
7. Fayyad, U., Irani, K.: On the handling of continuous-valued attributes in decision tree generation. Mach. Learn. **8** (1992) 87–102.
8. Fayyad, U., Irani, K.: Multi-interval discretization of continuous-valued attributes for classification learning. In *Proc. Thirteenth Intl. Joint Conf. on Artificial Intelligence* (1022–1027). Morgan Kaufmann, San Mateo, CA, 1993.
9. Fulton, T., Kasif, S., Salzberg, S.: Efficient algorithms for finding multi-way splits for decision trees. In A. Prieditis, S. Russell (eds.), *Proc. Twelfth Intl. Conf. on Machine Learning* (244–251). Morgan Kaufmann, San Francisco, CA, 1995.
10. Kononenko, I.: On biases in estimating multi-valued attributes. In *Proc. Fourteenth Intl. Joint Conf. on Artificial Intelligence* (1034–1040). Morgan Kaufmann, San Francisco, CA, 1995.
11. López de Màntaras, R.: A distance-based attribute selection measure for decision tree induction. Mach. Learn. **6** (1991) 81–92.
12. Merz, C., Murphy, P.: UCI repository of machine learning databases (http://www.ics.uci.edu/~mlearn/MLRepository.html). Dept. of Information and Computer Science, University of California at Irvine.
13. Quinlan, R.: Induction of decision trees. Mach. Learn. **1** (1986) 81–106.
14. Quinlan, R.: *C4.5: Programs for Machine Learning*. Morgan Kaufmann, San Mateo, CA, 1993.
15. Quinlan, R.: Improved use of continuous attributes in C4.5. J. Artif. Intell. Res. **4** (1996) 77–90.
16. Van de Merckt, T.: Decision trees in numerical attribute spaces. In *Proc. Thirteenth Intl. Joint Conf. on Artificial Intelligence* (1016–1021). Morgan Kaufmann, San Mateo, CA, 1993.
17. Wallace, C., Patrick, J.: Coding decision trees. Mach. Learn. **11** (1993) 7–22.

An Improved Inductive Learning Algorithm with a Preanalysis of Data

Janusz Kacprzyk and Grażyna Szkatuła

Systems Research Institute, Polish Academy of Sciences
ul. Newelska 6
01-447 Warsaw, Poland
E-mail: kacprzyk@ibspan.waw.pl

Abstract. We propose an improved inductive learning procedure, IP1, to derive classification rules from examples. A preanalysis of data is included which assigns higher weights to those values of the attributes which occur more often in the positive than in the negative examples. The inductive learning problem is represented as a covering problem in integer programming which is solved by a modified greedy algorithm. The results are very encouraging, and are shown for a well-known M3 (Monk's) problem.

Keywords: inductive learning, learning from examples, covering problem, 0-1 programming, greedy algorithm.

1. Introduction

By *inductive learning* (*learning from examples*) we mean the inferring of a classification rule (rule, concept description, hypothesis, ...) of a class (concept) from descriptions of individual elements of the class called (positive and negative) *examples*. Examples are described (cf. Michalski, 1983) by a set of K "attribute - value" pairs written as $e = \wedge_{j=1}^{K} \left[a_j \# v_j \right]$ where a_j denotes attribute j with value $v_j \in d_j$, and # is a relation ($=, <, >, \approx, \geq$, etc).

Inductive learning procedures should satisfy some natural requirements as, e.g.:

- *completeness*, i.e. that the classification rule must correctly describe *all* the positive examples,
- *consistency*, i.e. that the classification rule must describe *none* of the negative examples,
- *convergence*, i.e. that the classification rule must be derived in a *finite* number of steps,
- a classification rule of *minimal length* (e.g., involving the minimum number of attributes) is to be found.

We propose here a modified inductive learning procedure, IP1, based on the authors' previous work (cf. Kacprzyk and Szkatuła, 1994, 1996). A preprocessing of data (examples) is used, based on how frequently values of the particular attributes occur in the examples. These frequencies imply weights associated with those values, and the problem is represented by a Boolean (0-1) programming problem (cf. Kacprzyk and Szkatuła, 1996) solved by a modified heuristic greedy algorithm.

We test the method proposed on a standard example known as the M3 (Monk's) problem, and obtain results which are better than those reported in the literature and on Internet discussion lists.

2. Problem Formulation

Suppose that we have a set of positive, S_P, and negative, S_N, examples; $S_P, S_N \neq \varnothing$, $S_P \cap S_N = \varnothing$. Each example e is described by K attributes, $a_1, ..., a_K$, and is represented by

$$e = \bigwedge_{j=1}^{K} \left[a_j \# v_j \right] \tag{1}$$

where a_j is the j-th attribute taking on a value $v_j \in d_j = \{v_j^1, ..., v_j^{q_j}\}$, and # is a relation as, e.g., $=, <, >, \approx, \geq$, etc.; "=" will be used here, for simplicity.

An example e in (1) is composed of *selectors*, $s_j = \left[a_j \# v_j \right]$, and a conjunction of selectors is called a *complex*, i.e.

$$\bigwedge_{j \in I \subseteq \{1, ..., K\}} s_j = C \tag{2}$$

A complex C *covers* example e if all conditions on the attributes given as selectors are equal to the values of the respective attributes in the example.

We consider here the classification rules being the disjunction ("$\cup$" corresponding to "or") of complexes of type (2), i.e.

$$C^1 \cup ... \cup C^L = (s_{11} \wedge ... \wedge s_{1m}) \cup ... \cup (s_{L1} \wedge ... \wedge s_{Lm}) \rightarrow [\text{example: } \textit{positive}] \tag{3}$$

The idea of data preprocessing proposed is that for each attribute a_j, if a value occurs more frequently in the positive examples and less frequently (both relatively) in the negative examples, then it should rather appear in the rule sought.

First, we introduce the function, for each attribute $a_j, j = 1, ..., K$,

$$g_j(v) = \frac{1}{P} \sum_{m=1}^{P} \delta(e^m, v) - \frac{1}{N} \sum_{n=1}^{N} \delta(e^n, v), \quad \text{for each } v \in d_j \tag{4}$$

where $\delta(e^m, v) = \begin{cases} 1 & \text{for } v_j^m = v \\ 0 & \text{otherwise} \end{cases}$, and analogously for $\delta(e^n, v)$. Thus, (4) expresses

to what degree (from $[-1,1]$) the values $v \in d_j$ of a_j occurs more often in the positive than in the negative examples. Hence, $g_j(v) \in [-1,1]$ may be used as a *weight* of $v \in d_j$ of attribute a_j.

A complex $C = [a_{j1} = v_{j1}] \wedge \dots \wedge [a_{jm} = v_{jm}]$ corresponds to the set of indices $I = \{j1, \dots, jm\} \subseteq \{1, \dots, K\}$ equivalent to a vector $x = [x_j]^T = [x_1, \dots, x_K]^T$ such that $x_j = 1$ if selector $[a_j = v_j]$ occurs in this complex, and 0 otherwise.

An example with weight $g_j(v) \in [-1,1]$ is written as

$$e_W = \bigwedge_{j=1}^{K} \left[a_j = v_j : g_j(v) \right] \tag{5}$$

and the *weighted complex* is

$$\bigwedge_{j \in I \subseteq \{1, \dots, K\}} s_j^W = \bigwedge_{j = j1, j2, \dots, jm} s_j^W =$$

$$= [a_{j1} = v_{j1} : g_{j1}(v_{j1})] \wedge \dots \wedge [a_{jm} = v_{jm} : g_{jm}(v_{jm})] = C_W \tag{6}$$

For a weighted complex C_W its *weighted length* is

$$d_W(C_W) = \sum_{i=1}^{m} (1 - g_{ji}(v_{ji})) \cdot x_{ji} \tag{7}$$

which reflects a higher relevance of those values of attributes which occur more often in the positive than in the negative examples.

The *length of a weighted classification rule*, $R_W = (C_W^1 \cup \dots \cup C_W^L)$, is

$$d_{R_W}(C_W^1 \cup \dots \cup C_W^L) = \max_{i=1,\dots,L} d_W(C_W^i) \tag{8}$$

The problem is to find an optimal classification rule R_W^* such that

$$\min_{R_W} d_{R_W}(C_W^1 \cup \dots \cup C_W^L) \tag{9}$$

i.e. which minimizes the weighted length of the classification rule.

Since the (exact) solution of (9) is very difficult, an auxiliary problem is solved (cf. Kacprzyk and Szkatuła, 1996), seeking an R_W^* such that

$$\min_{I_1} d_W(C_W^{L_{I_1}}),\dots,\min_{I_L} d_W(C_W^{L_{I_L}}) \tag{10}$$

and the solution of (10) is in general very close to that of (9), but easier.

3. Solution by the IP1 algorithm

Problem (10) is solved by a modification of a well-known heuristic, a *greedy algorithm* (cf. Garfinkel and Nemhauser, 1978). For $e^P = [a_1 = v_1^P]\wedge\dots\wedge[a_K = v_K^P]$ we construct a 0-1 matrix $Z_{N\times K} = [z_{nj}], z_{nj} \in \{0,1\}$, $n = 1, \dots, N, j = 1, \dots, K$, which

is defined as $z_{nj} = \begin{cases} 1 & \text{for } v_j^n \neq v_j^P \\ 0 & \text{for } v_j^n = v_j^P \end{cases}$. Its rows correspond to the consecutive

negative examples, and the columns correspond to the attributes $a_1,\dots,a_K$; $z_{nj} = 1$ occurs if attribute a_j takes on different values in the positive and negative example, i.e. v_j^P in e^P and v_j^n in e^n, $v_j^P \neq v_j^n$; and $z_{nj} = 0$ otherwise. In Z there are no rows with all zero elements as, $S_p, S_N \neq \varnothing$, $S_p \cap S_N = \varnothing$, and for any positive and negative example there always exists at least one attribute taking on a different value in these examples.

Consider now the following inequality, where $\Lambda = [1,\dots,1]^T$:

$$Zx \geq \Lambda \tag{11}$$

Any vector x which satisfies (11) determines therefore uniquely some complex for which the completeness and consistence conditions hold.

The minimizations in problem (10) may be written using (11) as

$$\min_{x:\, Zx \geq \Lambda} \sum_{j=1}^{K} (1 - g_j(v_j))\cdot x_j \tag{12}$$

Therefore [cf. (9) - (10)], we obtain R_W^* such that

$$\min_{x:\, Z^1 x \geq \Lambda} d_W(C_W^{1_{I_1}}), \dots, \min_{x:\, Z^L x \geq \Lambda} d_W(C_W^{L_{I_L}}) \tag{13}$$

The minimization with respect to x in problem (13) is therefore equivalent to the determination of a 0-1 vector x^* which uniquely determines the complex with the shortest weighted length, and the satisfaction of $Zx \geq \Lambda$ guarantees that such a complex will not describe any negative example.

Problem (13) is equivalent to the covering problem in Boolean (0-1) programming which always has a feasible solution as there are no zero elements in matrix Z.

For solving (13) we apply a modification of the greedy algorithm (cf. Garfinkel and Nemhauser, 1978):

Step 1. Set the initial values: $S = S_p$, $S_N = \emptyset$, and $R_W = \emptyset$.

Step 2. Find the vector of weights G by preprocessing the examples due to (4).

Step 3. Determine a starting point (crucial for efficiency!), e.g. the so-called *centroid* (cf. Kacprzyk and Szkatuła, 1996) which is some (possibly non-existing) example in which the attributes take on values that occur most often in the positive examples and least often in the negative examples; it is a "typical" positive example [cf. a similar concept of a *typoid* proposed in Kacprzyk and Iwański (1991 - 1992)].

The positive examples $e^m \in S_P$, $m = 1, ..., P$, are written as

$$e^m = [a_1 = v_1^m] \wedge ... \wedge [a_K = v_K^m] \qquad v_j^m \in d_j, \; j = 1,...,K \qquad (14)$$

while the negative examples $e^n \in S_N$, $n = 1, ..., N$, are written as

$$e^n = [a_1 = v_1^n] \wedge ... \wedge [a_K = v_K^n] \qquad v_j^n \in d_j, \; j = 1,...,K \qquad (15)$$

For each attribute a_j, $j = 1, ..., K$, we determine such a value $v_j^* \in d_j$ which maximizes [cf. (4)]

$$\max_{v_j \in d_j} \left\{ \frac{1}{P} \sum_{m=1}^{P} \delta(e^m, v_j) - \frac{1}{N} \sum_{n=1}^{N} \delta(e^n, v_j) \right\} \qquad (16)$$

where $\delta(e^i, v_j) = \begin{cases} 1 & \text{for } v_j^i = v_j \\ 0 & \text{for } v_j^i \neq v_j \end{cases}$.

Now, we form an example, called a *centroid*

$$e^* = [a_1 = v_1^*] \wedge ... \wedge [a_K = v_K^*] \qquad (17)$$

which contains the selectors with the most typical positive values of the particular attributes. Needless to say that this example may be artificial, i.e. non existent.

We introduce a degree of similarity (with values from [0,1] between e^* and e^m [cf. (14)] as, e.g.:

$$\eta(e^m, e^*) = \frac{1}{K} \sum_{j=1}^{K} \delta(e^m, v_j^*) \qquad (18)$$

Finally, we find such a positive example $e^P \in S_P$ for which

$$\max_{m=1,...,P} \eta(e^P, e^*) \qquad (19)$$

which is the closest positive example to e^*.

The concept of a centroid is crucial for efficiency of the algorithm. For a similar concept of a *typoid*, cf. Kacprzyk and Iwański (1991 - 1992).

Then, the starting point for the next iterations is a real example, e^P, that is the closest, e.g., in the sense of (18), to the one found by (19).

Then, initially, $x^* = \left[x_1^*, ..., x_K^*\right]^T = \gamma^* = [\gamma_1^*, ..., \gamma_N^*]^T = [0, ..., 0]^T$.

Step 4. We construct $Z_{N \times K} = [z_{nj}]$, $z_{nj} \in \{0,1\}$, $n = 1,...,N$; $j = 1,...,K$, for e^P due to (16), and we assume initially that matrix $M := Z$.

Step 5. We calculate the so-called efficiency of x_j, $j = 1,...,K$ with respect to M:

$$E(x_j, M) = \sum_{i=1}^{N} m_{ij} / (1 - g_j(v_j^P)) \qquad (20)$$

and choose $x_{j^*}^*$ yielding the highest value of $E\left(x_{j^*}, M\right)$; then we set $x_{j^*}^* = 1$.

Step 6. We denote $m_{j^*} = [m_{1j^*}, m_{2j^*}, ..., m_{Nj^*}]^T$ the j^*-th column of M and calculate the new matrix M as

$$[(M)^T \times \mathrm{diag}(1 - m_{1j^*}, 1 - m_{2j^*}, ..., 1 - m_{Nj^*})]^T \qquad (21)$$

and we obtain the new vector $\gamma^* = [\gamma_1^*, ..., \gamma_N^*]^T$ given as

$$[\max(m_{1j^*}, \gamma_1^*), ..., \max(m_{Nj^*}, \gamma_N^*)]^T. \qquad (22)$$

Step 7. If $\sum_{n=1}^{N} \gamma_n^* = N$ go to Step 8, otherwise, return to Step 5.

Step 8. The 0-1 vector $x^* = \left[x_1^*, ..., x_K^*\right]^T$ found in such a way determines in the unique way the complex C_W^* sought.

Step 9. Include complex C_W^* found in Step **8** into the classification rule sought R_W^*, $R_W^* := R_W^* \cup C_W^*$, and discard from the set of positive examples S all examples covered by complex C_W^*.

Step 10. If the S remaining is empty, STOP and the rule R_W^* is the one sought; otherwise, return to Step 2.

The IP1 algorithm described above is relatively simple and efficient. We will illustrate it now on a well-known and often used standard example, the so-called Monk's (M3) problem.

4. Solving the M3 (Monk's) problem

The so-called Monk's (M3) problem concerns some creatures (robots? humanoids?) described by 7 discrete-valued attributes:

a_1 : head shape	{round, square, octagon}
a_2 : body shape	{round, square, octagon}
a_3 : is smiling	{yes, no}
a_4 : holding	{sword, flag, balloon}
a_5 : jacket colour	{red, yellow, green, blue}
a_6 : has tie	{yes, no}
a_7 : class	{class 1, class 0}

The training data set includes 122 examples (with 6 misclassifications due to noise) which represent 30% of the total number of examples, and the testing data include all the examples (432 examples). The classification is binary.

To visualise the results we use two-dimensional diagrams [cf. Wnęk, Sarma, Wahab and Michalski (1991)]. The classification accuracy of the rule derived is the percentage of testing examples correctly classified.

Basically, each part (box) of the diagram (which consists of 18 rows and 24 columns) represents the conjunction of some values of the attributes a_1, a_2, a_3 (rows), and a_4, a_5, a_6 (columns).

In Figure 1 all the training examples are shown. Those belonging to class 1 (say, the positive examples) are marked by "+", and those belonging to class 0 (say, the negative examples) are marked by "-".

The classification rules derived are shown as follows:

- misclassifications are marked by the empty boxes,
- classification into class 1 is marked by left-shaded boxes,
- classification into class 0 is marked by right-shaded boxes,

and, for instance, the classification rule for the class 0 is found to be:

[a5 = blue] ∪ [a2 = octagon] [a3 = no] ∪ [a2 = octagon] [a4 = balloon] ∪ [a2 = octagon] [a4 = flag] → [*class* = CLASS *0*]

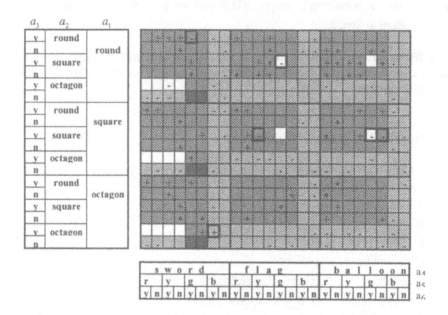

Figure 1. Training examples and the classification rules found for class 1 and class 0

In Figure 2 all testing examples are shown, with the results of the learning algorithm.

The learning phase is performed on the complete set of examples, i.e. with all the possible combinations of attributes.

We will compare the results obtained by using our IP1 procedure with the following ones from the literature:

- ID3, ID5R, AQR and CN2 - at the Department of Computer Science, University of Karlsruhe, Germany [Kreuziger, Hamann and Wenzel (1991)],
- PRISM - at the Institute of Informatics, University of Zürich, Switzerland [Keller (1991)],
- AQ17-DCI and AQ17-FCLS - at the Artificial Intelligence Centre, George Mason University [Bala, Bloedorn, Jong, Kaufman, Michalski, Pachowicz, Vafaie, Wnek and Zhang (1991)],
- IP1 - the one proposed in this paper.

165

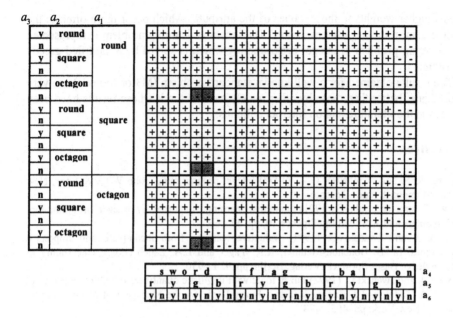

Figure 2. Testing examples and results of the IP1 algorithm (accuracy 98.6%)

The results are presented in Figure 3, and one can notice that the IP1 implementation attains the highest classification accuracy (ca. 98%) among the techniques considered.

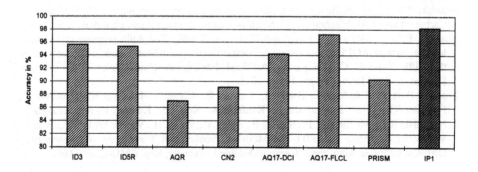

Figure 3. Classification accuracy attained by various inductive learning procedures

5. Concluding remarks

We have proposed an improved inductive learning procedure IP1 to derive classification rules from sets of examples. A preanalysis of data is included which assigns higher weights to those values of the attributes which occur more often in the positive than in the negative examples. The inductive learning problem is represented as a covering problem in integer programming which is solved by a modified greedy algorithm.

The results obtained for a well-known standard problem (M3 or Monk's) are very encouraging, better than those by other widely used methods whose results have been reported in the literature and on Internet bulletins.

References

Garfinkel R. S. and Nemhauser G. L. (1978) Integer programming. John Wiley & Sons, New York-London-Sydney-Toronto.

Iwański C. and Szkatuła G (1991) Inductive learning supported by integer programming. Computers and Artificial Intelligence 10, pp. 57 - 66.

Kacprzyk J. and Iwański C. (1991) Inductive learning from incomplete and imprecise examples. In: B. Bouchon-Meunier, R.R. Yager and L.A. Zadeh (Eds.), Uncertainty in Knowledge Bases Springer -Verlag, Berlin, pp. 424 - 430.

Kacprzyk J. and Iwański C. (1992) Fuzzy logic with linguistic quantifiers in inductive learning, In: L.A. Zadeh and J. Kacprzyk (Eds.), Fuzzy Logic for the Management of Uncertainty, Wiley, New York, pp. 465 - 478.

Kacprzyk J. and Szkatuła G. (1994) Machine learning from examples under errors in data, Proceedings of Fifth International Conference in Information Processing and Management of Uncertainty in Knowledge-Based Systems - IPMU'94 (Paris, France), Vol. 2, pp. 1047 - 1051.

Kacprzyk J. and Szkatuła G. (1996) An algorithm for learning from erroneous and incorrigible examples, International Journal of Intelligent Systems 11, 565 - 582.

Michalski R.S. (1973) Discovering classification rules using variable-valued logic system VL1. Proceedings of the Third International Joint Conference on Artificial Intelligence (IJCAI), p. 162–172.

Michalski R.S. (1983) A theory and methodology of inductive learning. In: R. Michalski, J. Carbonell and T.M. Mitchell (Eds.), Machine Learning. Tioga Press, Palo Alto, CA.

Michalski R.S., I. Mozetic, J. Hong and N. Lovrac (1986) The multi-purpose incremental learning system AQ15 and its testing application to three medical domains. Proceedings of the Fifth National Conference on Artificial Intelligence (Philadelphia, PA). Morgan Kaufmann, San Mateo, CA, pp. 1041 - 1045.

Thrun S., Bala J., Bloedorn E., Bratko I., Cestnik B., Cheng J., De Jong K., Dzeroski S., Fahlman S.E., Fisher D., Hamann R., Kaufman K., Keller S., Kononenko I., Kreuziger J., Michalski R.S., Mitchell T., Pachowicz P., Reich Y., Vafaie H., Van de Welde W., Wenzel W., Wnek J., Zhang J. (1991) The MONK's Problems. A Performance Comparison of Different Learning Algorithms. Carnegie Mellon University, Rep. CMU-CS-91-197.

Efficient Induction of Numerical Constraints

Lionel Martin, Christel Vrain

LIFO - Université d'Orléans - BP 6759
45067 Orléans Cedex 2 - France
email : {martin,cv}@lifo.univ-orleans.fr

Abstract. In this paper, we address the problem of learning an hyperplane that separates data described by numeric attributes. When data are not linearly separable, the "best" hyperplanes are those that minimize the number of misclassified examples. This topic has already been studied in many works but, as far as we know, the originality of our approach is to be based on Linear Programming technics, which appear to be very efficient. We propose two methods. In the first one, some variables are required to be integers; this enables to get one of the best solutions in terms of the number of misclassified examples, but as a counterpart, solving a Linear Programming problem which includes both real-valued and integer-valued variables is not efficient. In the second method, we relax the constraints for some variables to be integers. In that case, we get only an approximate solution to the problem, but the gain from the point of view of efficiency is so important that the process can be iterated, removing the misclassified examples that are the farthest from the learned hyperplane up to a given threshold. Experiments have been made on randomly generated examples; they show that, in average, the two methods give the same rate of noise.

1 Introduction

In this paper, we address the problem of learning an hyperplane that separates positive examples defined by numerical values from negative ones. This topic has already been studied in many works. For instance, the goal of neural networks is to learn a frontier between piecewise linear surfaces; a neural network is a composition of neurons and a neuron represents an hyperplane separating two sets of data. This problem has also been theoretically studied in the field of Statistical Learning Theory [8]. Its importance has also been noticed for learning decision trees: without linear inequalities, a linear split between data should be approximated by multidimensional rectangular regions and the induced decision tree would be larger, more complicated and also less comprehensible [1]. As far as we know, the originality of our approach is to rely on Linear Programming technics. Let us illustrate it on a toy example.

Example. Let us suppose that we have two positive and two negative examples of a concept C and let us assume that the examples are described by two attributes X_1 and X_2 as follows:
$$e_1^+ = (2,0),\ e_2^+ = (1,-1),\ e_1^- = (0,0),\ e_2^- = (1,1)$$

Let us write $P(X) = a_0 + a_1 * X_1 + a_2 * X_2$ the equation of the hyperplane we are looking for. The idea is to introduce a slack variable, $\delta(e)$, for each example e and to consider the following Linear Programming (**LP**) problem (ϵ is a fixed, small value):

$$
\begin{array}{|l}
\underline{minimize}\colon \Delta = \delta(e_1^+) + \delta(e_2^+) + \delta(e_1^-) + \delta(e_2^-) \\
\underline{subject\ to}: \\
\left\{
\begin{array}{l}
a_0 + 2 * a_1 + 0 * a_2 \geq -\delta(e_1^+) \\
a_0 + 1 * a_1 + (-1) * a_2 \geq -\delta(e_2^+) \\
a_0 + 0 * a_1 + 0 * a_2 \leq -\epsilon + \delta(e_1^-) \\
a_0 + 1 * a_1 + 1 * a_2 \leq -\epsilon + \delta(e_2^-) \\
\delta(e_1^+) \geq 0, \delta(e_2^+) \geq 0, \delta(e_1^-) \geq 0, \delta(e_2^-) \geq 0
\end{array}
\right.
\end{array}
$$

A solution to this LP problem gives a value to a_0, a_1, a_2, $\delta(e_1^+)$, $\delta(e_2^+)$, $\delta(e_1^-)$ and $\delta(e_2^-)$. Let C be the constraint $P(X) \geq 0$. A positive (respectively negative) example e is correctly classified by C if $\delta(e) = 0$. In the previous example, the solution is:

$$a_0 = -50,\ a_1 = 25,\ a_2 = -50 \text{ and } \delta(e) = 0, \text{ for all } e.$$

The equation of the hyperplane is therefore:

$$P(X) = 0 \text{ where } P(X) = +25 * X_1 - 50 * X2 - 50.$$

Let us suppose now that we have another positive example, namely $e_3^+ = (0, 1)$. Two new constraints are added to the previous LP problem:

$$a_0 + 0 * a_1 + 1 * a_2 \geq -\delta(e_3^+) \text{ and } \delta(e_3^+) \geq 0$$

The solution is:

$$a_0 = 50,\ a_1 = -25,\ a_2 = -50,\ \delta(e_1^-) = 50 \text{ and } \delta(e) = 0, \text{ for all } e,\ e \neq e_1^-.$$

This means that the equation of the learned hyperplane is:

$$P(X) \geq 0 \text{ with } P(X) = -25 * X_1 - 50 * X_2 + 50$$

and that the negative example e_1^- is misclassified, i.e. it satisfies the inequality $P(X) \leq 0$.

In our framework, a solution to the problem minimizes the expression $\Delta = \delta(e_1^+) + \delta(e_2^+) + \delta(e_3^+) + \delta(e_1^-) + \delta(e_2^-)$; Δ does not correspond to the number of misclassified examples, since $\delta(e)$ is only required to be a positive real. This explains why we call it an *approximate solution*. In order to get a better solution, we iterate the process by removing some misclassified examples, those that are the farthest from the learned hyperplane.

Comparison with other works :

First, the work we present here is far different from what is done in neural networks: in that field, the way the coefficients (or weights) of the neurons are learned is mostly based on the back-propagation method [7].

The method proposed in [1] for inducing linear inequalities relies also on an iteration of a process: at each step of the process, a linear inequality is built and the process stops when the improvement of a given criterion is less than a fixed threshold. At each iteration, the same set of data is considered, whereas we propose to remove some misclassified examples. Moreover, the way inequalities are built differs: at each iteration, we build a new inequality by solving a new

Linear Programming problem, whereas in [1], they transform the inequality built at one step by iteratively modifying the coefficients of each variable X_i.

In [8], the aim is to find an optimal hyperplane that both separates data without errors and maximizes the distance between the closest vectors. The framework is very close to our Linear Programming setting. Nevertheless, their goal is different from ours and the problem is written as the problem of minimizing $\phi(\omega) = \|w\|^2$, under the constraints $y_i * [(\omega * x_i) + b] \geq 1$, where ω denotes a vector of R^n, b denotes a real and for $1 \leq i \leq l$, $x_i \in R^n$, $y_i \in \{1, -1\}$, (x_i, y_i) denotes an example. Moreover, their methods for solving such a problem is based on the search for the saddle point of a Lagrange functional, whereas our method is based on Linear programming techniques.

The paper is organized as follows. Section 2.1 describes the mixed integer method, that was first proposed in [6]. It enables to learn the best constraint in terms of the number of misclassified examples, but it is not very efficient. Section 2.2 presents the Linear Programming method, in which no variables are required to be integers and Section 3 presents some extensions and experimental results.

2 Efficient Induction of numeric constraints

2.1 Induction of linear constraints

Formalization of the method We consider a set of positive examples, $E^+ = \{e_1^+, \ldots, e_p^+\}$, and a set of negative examples, $E^- = \{e_1^-, \ldots, e_n^-\}$. Each example e is characterized by a set of numeric values, represented by the vector $\mathbf{X}(e) = (X_1(e), \ldots, X_m(e))$. The problem is to find a constraint C that is satisfied by the largest number of positive examples and the smallest number of negative ones; in the following, such a constraint (which is not necessarily unique) is called *the best constraint*. A positive example which does not satisfy C or a negative one which satisfies C is called an *example misclassified by* C, it can be considered either as noise, or as a particular case.

Let $\mathbf{X}$ denote the vector $(X_1, \ldots, X_m)$, we propose to search for the best constraint written as a linear inequality:
$$P(\mathbf{X}) = a_0 + a_1 * X_1 + \ldots + a_m * X_m \geq 0$$
If there exists such a constraint, satisfied by each positive example and satisfied by no negative ones, then the following set of inequalities holds:

$$(*) \begin{cases} a_0 + a_1 * X_1(e_1^+) + \ldots + a_m * X_m(e_1^+) \geq 0 \\ \quad \ldots \\ a_0 + a_1 * X_1(e_p^+) + \ldots + a_m * X_m(e_p^+) \geq 0 \\ a_0 + a_1 * X_1(e_1^-) + \ldots + a_m * X_m(e_1^-) < 0 \\ \quad \ldots \\ a_0 + a_1 * X_1(e_n^-) + \ldots + a_m * X_m(e_n^-) < 0 \end{cases}$$

Let us now consider this set of inequalities as a system of inequations, where a_i, $0 \leq i \leq n$ denotes a variable and for all $e \in E^+ \cup E^-$ and for all j, $1 \leq j \leq m$,

$X_j(e)$ is a fixed value, namely the value of the example e on the variable X_j. A solution of this system gives therefore the coefficients of an hyperplane which separates positive examples from negative ones. Nevertheless, such a system can be unsolvable.

In order to handle noisy examples, we propose to introduce a new variable, denoted by $\delta(e)$, for each example. If the best constraint $C = P(\mathbf{X}) \geq 0$ is satisfied by the positive example e^+, we have $P(\mathbf{X}(e^+)) \geq 0$. Conversely, if a positive example e^+ does not satisfy C, there exists a positive value ω such that the constraint $P(\mathbf{X}(e^+)) \geq -\omega$ holds. Finally, in both cases, the constraint:

$$P(\mathbf{X}(e^+)) = a_0 + a_1 * X_1(e^+) + \ldots + a_m * X_m(e^+) \geq -\omega * \delta(e^+)$$

holds, where $\delta(e^+)$ is either 0 (when e^+ satisfies C) or 1 (when e^+ does not satisfy C). In the same way, for each negative example e^-, the following constraint holds:

$$P(\mathbf{X}(e^-)) = a_0 + a_1 * X_1(e^-) + \ldots + a_m * X_m(e^-) < \omega * \delta(e^-)$$

where $\delta(e^-)$ is either 0 (when e^- does not satisfy C, i.e. , $P(\mathbf{X}(e^-)) < 0$) or 1 (e^- satisfies C, i.e. $P(\mathbf{X}(e^-)) \geq 0$, e^- is misclassified by C).

The system (*) can then be rewritten into the system:

$$(**) \begin{cases} a_0 + a_1 * X_1(e_1^+) + \ldots + a_m * X_m(e_1^+) \geq -\omega * \delta(e_1^+) \\ \quad \ldots \\ a_0 + a_1 * X_1(e_p^+) + \ldots + a_m * X_m(e_p^+) \geq -\omega * \delta(e_p^+) \\ a_0 + a_1 * X_1(e_1^-) + \ldots + a_m * X_m(e_1^-) < \omega * \delta(e_1^-) \\ \quad \ldots \\ a_0 + a_1 * X_1(e_n^-) + \ldots + a_m * X_m(e_n^-) < \omega * \delta(e_n^-) \\ \forall e \in E^+ \cup E^-, \delta(e) = 0 \ OR \ \delta(e) = 1 \end{cases}$$

which has always a solution, as for instance the solution defined by $a_i = 0$ for all i, $\delta(e^+) = 0$ for all $e^+ \in E^+$ and $\delta(e^-) = 1$ for all $e^- \in E^-$. As mentioned above, an example e is misclassified by the constraint:

$$P(X) \geq 0, \text{ with } P(X) = a_0 + a_1 * X_1 + \ldots + a_m * X_m$$

iff $\delta(e) = 1$ (which means that e is a positive example and $P(X(e)) < 0$ or e is a negative example and $P(X(e)) \geq 0$). Therefore, a solution to the problem (**) which minimizes the number of misclassified examples must minimize the quantity:

$$\Delta = \delta(e_1^+) + \ldots + \delta(e_p^+) + \delta(e_1^-) + \ldots + \delta(e_n^+)$$

We propose to write this problem as a Linear Programming Problem, which is usually solved by the Simplex Method. In order to achieve this, we have to

- express the constraint $\forall e \in E^+ \cup E^-, \delta(e) = 0 \ OR \ \delta(e) = 1$ as a set of inequalities. This can be done by adding the constraint $0 \leq \delta(e) \leq 1$ for each example e, and by requiring the variable $\delta(e)$ to be an integer. In this case, the problem is called a mixed integer linear programming problem, since some variables are required to be integers. Nevertheless, solving a mixed system is not efficient. This explains why we relax this constraint and we only require $\delta(e)$ to be a positive real. Then the constant ω can be removed, since $\delta(e)$ can be as high as necessary.

– change the strict inequalities associated to negative examples into large inequalities; this is done by replacing each constraint

$$a_0 + a_1 * X_1(e_i^-) + \ldots + a_m * X_m(e_i^-) < \omega * \delta(e_i^-)$$

by the constraint

$$a_0 + a_1 * X_1(e_i^-) + \ldots + a_m * X_m(e_i^-) \leq -\epsilon + \omega * \delta(e_i^-)$$

where ϵ represents a fixed and small value.

Finally, the problem is specified by

Table 1. Approximate LP specification

minimize: $\Delta = \delta(e_1^+) + \ldots + \delta(e_p^+) + \delta(e_1^-) + \ldots + \delta(e_n^-)$
subject to
$\quad a_0 + a_1 * X_1(e^+) + \ldots + a_m * X_m(e^+) \geq -\delta(e^+) \quad \forall e^+ \in E^+$
$\quad a_0 + a_1 * X_1(e^-) + \ldots + a_m * X_m(e^-) \leq -\epsilon + \delta(e^-) \quad \forall e^- \in E^-$
$\quad 0 \leq \delta(e) \quad \forall e \in E^+ \cup E^-$

In the following, such a problem is called the _approximate LP specification_ and a solution to this problem is called an _approximate constraint_. On the other hand, the _exact LP specification_ is the problem obtained by adding the constraints $\delta(e) = 0$ _or_ 1, $\forall e \in E^+ \cup E^-$ to the approximate LP specification and a solution to this problem is called an _exact constraint_. The exact LP specification gives always the best solution in terms of the number of misclassified examples although this is not an efficient method. The approximate LP specification does not always give the best solution (it gives the best one at least when there exists an hyperplane separating the data), but it is a very efficient method.

Let us notice that these problems have always solutions. Many solvers for this kind of problems can be found; we get the Public Domain (free) "lp_solve" solver which is available at _ftp://ftp.es.ele.tue.nl/pub/lp_solve_. The author (Michel Berkelaar) has used the program to solve LP problems containing up to 30,000 variables and 50,000 constraints.

Let $v_\approx$ be the solution (assignment) of the approximate LP problem, given in Table 1, let $P(\mathbf{X}) = a_0 + a_1 * X_1 + \ldots + a_m * X_m$ denote the equation of the learned hyperplane and let $C = P(\mathbf{X}) \geq 0$ be the learned constraint. Each example e such that $v_\approx(\delta(e)) = 0$ is correctly classified by C; inversely, when ϵ is sufficiently small, each example e such that $v_\approx(\delta(e)) > 0$ is misclassified by C. It is important to notice that the objective function, which is equal to the sum of the $\delta(e)$, for all $e \in E^+ \cup E^-$, does not minimize the number of misclassified examples, since $\delta(e)$ is only a positive real number and therefore, the constraint C is not necessarily a good approximation of the best constraint in terms of the number of misclassified examples; this explains why we propose in next Section to iterate the process.

2.2 Approximate problem iteration

Let us consider now an approximate constraint C, i.e. , a solution to the approximate LP problem; if no example is misclassified by C, then C is also an exact constraint. Otherwise, we propose to remove some misclassified examples and to build a new approximate problem. Let us consider Figure 1.a and Figure 1.b : they are composed with the same positive examples (+) and negative examples (-) and misclassified examples are drawn in a circle.

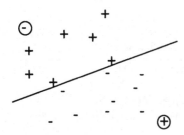 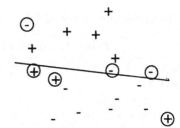

fig 1.a : best constraint   fig 1.b : approximate constraint

The underlying idea of our iteration process is that the misclassified examples that are the farthest from the hyperplane have a strong influence on the orientation of the learned hyperplane. Intuitively, the hyperplane tends to be attracted by them, as shown in Figure 1.b. If we remove them, we can smooth off their influence, as shown in Figure 1.a. This explains why we propose to remove the examples for which $v_{\approx}(\delta(e))$ is the greatest, and then to iterate the process.

First iteration Let us first recall that our method gives an approximate solution, only when there exists misclassified examples. If the best constraint that can be learned (and we can obtain it by using the exact LP specification, although it is not very efficient) misclassifies n examples, then an approximate constraint misclassifies m examples with $m \geq n$. Our goal is to obtain, with a particular approximate problem, a number p of misclassified examples, with p as near from n as possible. Before going further, let us notice that this problem depends on the set E^+ of positive examples and on the set E^- of negative ones and for this reason, it is denoted by $LP(E^+, E^-)$.

We propose to build a new approximate problem $\tilde{LP}$ as follows : Let $v_{\approx}$ be the solution of the initial approximate problem LP (Table 1); in order to reduce the number of misclassified examples w.r.t. the approximate constraint, we remove from E^+ (respectively E^-) the positive (respectively negative) examples which are far from the hyperplane, as follows. Let τ be a given rate and let

$$M = Max_{e \in E^+ \cup E^-} v_{\approx}(\delta(e))$$

we define:

$$E_1^+ = \{e \in E^+ | 0 \leq \delta(e) < \tau * M\} \text{ and } E_1^- = \{e \in E^- | 0 \leq \delta(e) < \tau * M\}$$

and we consider the approximate LP problem $LP(E_1^+, E_1^-)$. By this way, we build a series $LP(E_0^+, E_0^-) = LP(E^+, E^-)$, $LP(E_1^+, E_1^-), \ldots, LP(E_i^+, E_i^-)$ of approximate problems. Since in the worst case the best constraint misclassifies at most half of the (positive and negative) examples[1], we stop building this series when

- either no example is misclassified by $LP(E_i^+, E_i^-)$ and then the solution given by the iterated approximate algorithm is the solution obtained by $LP(E_i^+, E_i^-)$,
- or $card(E_i^+ \cup E_i^-) < card(E^+ \cup E^-)/2$ and then the algorithm fails.

This algorithm can be summarized as follows:

$$
\begin{array}{l}
E_0^+ = E^+, \quad E_0^- = E^-, \quad i = 0 \\
\text{While the solution of } LP(E_i^+, E_i^-) \text{ misclassifies some examples} \\
\quad \text{AND } card(E_i^+ \cup E_i^-) < card(E^+ \cup E^-)/2 \text{ do} \\
\qquad \text{let } v_\approx \text{ be the solution of } LP(E_i^+, E_i^-) \\
\qquad \text{let } M_i = Max_{e \in E_i^+ \cup E_i^-} v_\approx^i(\delta(e)) \\
\qquad \text{let } E_{i+1}^+ = \{e \in E_i^+ | 0 \le \delta(e) < \tau * M_i\} \\
\qquad \text{let } E_{i+1}^- = \{e \in E_i^- | 0 \le \delta(e) < \tau * M_i\} \\
\qquad i \leftarrow i + 1 \\
\quad \text{done} \\
\text{If } card(E_i^+ \cup E_i^-) \ge card(E^+ \cup E^-)/2 \\
\quad \text{then return } failure \\
\quad \text{else return the constraint obtained from } LP(E_i^+, E_i^-)
\end{array}
$$

Fig. 2: iterated approximate problem algorithm

Practically, the lower τ is, the faster this algorithm converges (i.e.: the less iterations are needed) but it might remove too many examples from the sets E_i^+ and E_i^-. The second iteration limits this problem.

Second iteration Let $LP(E_i^+, E_i^-)$ be the problem obtained at the end of the first iteration. The aim of the second iteration is to try to add some positive (respectively negative) examples to E_i^+ (respectively E_i^-), preserving the fact that $LP(E_i^+, E_i^-)$ misclassifies no examples from E_i^+ and E_i^-. This is done by adding removed examples for which $v_\approx^i(\delta(e))$ is minimal: we use here another rate τ' to determine which examples have to be considered.

The second iteration looks like the first one, except that it starts with the sets E_i^+ and E_i^-. it adds previously removed examples from E^+ and from E^- to E_i^+ and to E_i^-, while the number of examples from E^+ and from E^- that are misclassified decreases.

Experiments We have tested this algorithm on 2000 cases randomly built. For each case, we have compared the number of misclassified examples w.r.t. an exact constraint (computed with the exact LP problem) and w.r.t. an approximate

---

[1] If C is the best constraint $a_0 + a_1 * X_1 + \ldots + a_m * X_m \ge 0$ and if q is the number of misclassified examples with $q > card(E^+ \cup E^-)/2$, then the constraint $-a_0 - a_1 * X_1 - \ldots - a_m * X_m \ge 0$ is better than C.

constraint (computed with the approximate LP problem). The tests have been performed with different values for τ.

The iterative algorithm leads to a constraint as good as the best one in many cases, these cases are called *full success*. The following array gives the percentage of full success after the first iteration and after the second one. It gives also the percentage of tests for which the second iteration decreases the number of misclassified examples (improvement); this rate is given w.r.t the total number of tests, and w.r.t the number of tests for which the first iteration is not a full success.

Table 2. Results

τ	full success (1st it.)	full success (2nd it)	improvement (total tests)	improvement (non full success tests)
0.8	58.2%	64.8%	13.3%	31.9%
0.9	67.8%	71.6%	7.1%	22.0%
0.95	72.3%	74.1%	4.8%	17.3%

We can see here that in the best case, we obtain 74% of full success with the iterative algorithm. As expected, we get better results with a high value for τ, but the number of iterations is higher. Nevertheless, the efficiency of the simplex algorithm allows to choose a high value for τ (practically, the number of iterations does not exceed 10, each one requiring less than 0.2s). Concerning the second iteration, either it does not improve the solution and it requires only one iteration, or it gives a better constraint in a few number of iterations (in practice, 1 or 2 iterations).

Let us notice also that the iterative algorithm has found a solution in all the tests (more than 2000). In other words, it has never failed during the experiments.

The gain of efficiency is very significant: on a problem with 40 examples, a mixed integer LP problem requires nearly 5 mn to build the best constraint whereas the iterative algorithm executes from 1 to 6 iterations of 0.12s. Moreover, in practice, the time complexity for building an exact constraint grows exponentially w.r.t the number of examples whereas it grows linearly in the iterative algorithm.

3 Extension

Induction of non-linear constraints

In this section, we show how this method can be extended to learn non-linear constraints. In Section 2, when learning a linear constraint, we search for the most general linear constraint involving all numeric values characterizing the examples. Irrelevant attributes are those that get very low coefficients, relatively to other coefficients. It is not possible to process in the same way for learning non-linear constraints, since we do not know the expected form of the most general non-linear constraint we are looking for. For this reason, we propose to build a particular form of general non-linear constraint by considering function symbols: let Σ be a set of function symbols, we search a constraint involving each term built with the function symbols of Σ and constants characterizing the examples.

Let us notice that finding such constraints can be useful: it requires the user to give relevant functions but in many domains, an expert has an idea of functions which may be useful to characterize the examples; this is the case in the next example. In the Support Vector machine, the input vectors are also transformed in a high-dimensional feature space, which enables to introduce functions and to learn non-linear separating equations. Nevertheless, as mentioned in [8], the dimension of the new space can be too important to be really tractable. Our approach will be integrated in an Inductive Logic Programming system and only relevant terms will be used.

Numerical constraint simplifications When the previous method is used to get information understandable by a user, the simplicity of the constraint is essential. Moreover, when functional terms are added, it is important to eliminate non discriminant terms. We propose here to simplify the constraint by finding an hyperplane P satisfying $a_0 + a_1 * X_1 + \ldots + a_m * X_m = 0$ such that the number of a_i satisfying $a_i \neq 0$ is minimal.

The idea is very intuitive: let $LP(E_i^+, E_i^-)$ be the problem defining the constraint to be simplified, we propose to add the constraint $a_k = 0$ to this problem, where a_k minimizes $|a_j|, j = 1 \ldots m$. While the obtained constraint misclassifies no examples of $E_i^+ \cup E_i^-$, we iterate the process by adding new constraints $a_k = 0$.

Even if this method is simple, it is efficient since the coefficients that are required to be equal to 0 are those that have little influence on the constraint.

Example This method has been applied to the problem of characterizing the conditions under which a circle of radius r can contain a rectangle with length l and width w. From 12 positive and 12 negative examples and with the introduction of the function $square : x \mapsto x^2$, our method has built the following constraint:

$$-0.493 + 0.146 * r + 1.837 * r^2 + 0.26 * l - 0.507 * l^2 - 0.15 * w - 0.456 * w^2 \geq 0$$

Each noisy example has been detected and after simplifications, we get:

$$192.26 * r^2 - 49.00301 * l^2 - 45.7794 * w^2 \geq 0$$

which is close to the exact relation, $4 * r^2 \geq l^2 + w^2$.

4 Conclusion

We propose in this paper an iterative method for finding an hyperplane that separates positive and negative examples such that the number of misclassified examples is minimal. This method consists in successively building linear programming (LP) problems which give an approximation of this hyperplane.

The tests that have been performed show that the method gives the hyperplane minimizing the number of misclassified examples in most cases; moreover, since it is based on LP technics and on the simplex algorithm, it is very efficient, particularly for large-sized problems.

Let $P(X) = 0$ denote the equation of the learned hyperplane. We can notice that the way the LP problem is specified implies that some positive examples satisfy the equality $P(X) = 0$ and therefore the hyperplane is closer to the positive examples than to the negative ones; we could prefer an hyperplane containing no examples, for instance maximizing the distance from the closest points, as done in [8].

As another future work, we could introduce at each iteration, some of the examples removed during previous iterations: the introduced examples could be the ones which are close to the hyperplane learned at the previous iteration. In this case, the number of iterations would be higher but it would be interesting to test if, in average, this algorithm gives a better hyperplane.

Finally, we could try to update this iterative method in order to approximate the hyperplane minimizing the distances between the hyperplane and the misclassified examples, as done in [8].

References

1. Breiman, Friedman, Olshem, Stone, 1993. Classification of Regression Trees. Chapman & Hall.
2. Chvátal V., 1983. Linear Programming. Freeman.
3. Dietterich T.G., Lathrop R.H., Lozano-Perez T., 1996. Solving the Multiple-Instance Problem with Axis-Parallel Rectangles. to be published in Artificial Intelligence Journal.
4. Kijsirikul B., Numao M. et al, 1992. Discrimination-based Constructive Induction of Logic Programs, Procs. of AAAI-92, San Jose, pp.44-49, 1992.
5. Martin L., Vrain C., 1996. Induction of Constraint Logic Programs. Procs. of the Seventh International Workshop on Algorithmic Learning Theory, Lecture Notes in Artificial Intelligence 1160, Springer, pp. 169-177.
6. Martin L., Vrain C., 1997. Learning linear constraints in Inductive Logic Programming. Procs. of the European Conference on Machine Learning, ECML-97, Lecture Notes in Artificial Intelligence 1224, Springer, pp. 162-169.
7. Rumelhart D.E., Hinton G.E., Williams R.J., 1986. Learning internal representations by error propagation. Parallel distributed processing: Explorations in macrostructure of cognition, Vol. I, Bradford Books, Cambridge, MA, pp. 318-362.
8. Vapnik V.N., 1995. *The Nature of Statistical Learning Theory*. Springer.

Learning English Syllabification for Words

Jian Zhang   Howard J. Hamilton

Department of Computer Science, University of Regina

Regina, Saskatchewan, Canada, S4S 0A2

e-mail: {jian, hamilton}@cs.uregina.ca

Abstract. This paper presents the LE-SR (Learning English Syllabification Rules) learning system, which learns English syllabification rules using a symbolic pattern recognition approach. LE-SR was tested on NTC2, a 20,000 English word pronouncing dictionary. The ten-fold accuracy ranged from 94.55% to 96.05% for words and 96.81% to 97.71% for syllables.

The frequency of the rule usage indicates that most of the syllabification (86.21%) in NTC2 is covered by only 0.64% of the syllabification rules produced by LE-SR, while exceptions (2.45%) require 76.77% of the syllabification rules. This experimental result is consistent with the linguistics literature. Relatively few rules cover the vast majority of cases, but a considerable number of exceptions must be handled individually.

The learned rules can be used to divide any English word into syllables. Based on syllables, the English stress rules can be learned. Syllabification and stress greatly influence the naturalness of the output of a text-to-speech system. Existing text-to-speech systems have either obtained syllabification from a dictionary or used a few hand coded rules. Using machine learning approach to obtain these rules is a step towards producing natural speech sounding for text-to-speech systems.

1   Introduction

This paper presents the LE-SR (Learning English Syllabification Rules) learning system, which learns English syllabification rules using a symbolic pattern recognition approach. The LE-SR learning system is a part of the LEP (Learning English Pronunciation) project, which is designed to learn grapheme segmentation, syllabification, stress of syllables, and grapheme-to-phoneme translation [Zhang and Hamilton, 1996].

LE-SR is designed to learn English syllabification rules automatically. The learned rules can be used to divide any English word into syllables. Based on syllables, the English stress rules can be learned and a text-to-speech system could utter any English word (see or unseen) according to syllables instead of individual letters. Apparently, machine learning of syllabification rules has never been attempted before. Previous approaches to speech synthesis have either obtained syllabification from a dictionary or used a few hand coded rules.

In the text-to-speech literature of the last 20 years, word syllabification has been ignored. For example, [Ling and Wang, 1995] uses a grapheme-to-phoneme method to translate all graphemes into phonemes; PDtalk [Mudambi and Schimpf,

1994], DHtalk [Hochberg et al., 1991], NETtalk [Sejnowski and Rosenberg, 1987], DECtalk [Klatt, 1987], KLATtalk [Klatt, 1982], and NRLtalk [Elovitz et al., 1976] use a letter-to-phoneme method to translate all letters of a word into phonemes; MITtalk [Allen et al., 1987] translates all morphs into phonemes. That is, the words in input text are not read aloud in syllables but in single sounds, and stresses are marked on individual vowels instead of syllables. This is one reason that the word utterance of commercial speech synthesizers does not sound as natural as human speech.

The rest of this paper is organized as follows. Section 2 defines the learning problem and introduces some linguistic terminology. It also shows LE-SR's data structures and its input and output representations. Section 3 explains the LE-SR technique and presents an algorithm. An example of learning syllabification is shown in Section 4. Experimental results are presented in Section 5. Contributions of this paper are described in Section 6.

2 Statement of the Problem

For centuries, linguists of English have analyzed the syllables of English words. They discovered that an English syllable can have "zero, one, two or three consonants before the vowel and from zero to four consonants following the vowel" ([Mackay, 1987], pp. 41). This makes syllabification of English words very difficult. So far, we have not found a piece of research that presents a complete set of English syllabification rules, although partial sets of rules are often given in linguistic books [Ladeforged, 1982], [Mackay, 1987], [Kreidler, 1989], [O'Grady and Dobrovolsky, 1992].

2.1 Terminology

Following the basic principles of syllabification, a *syllable* [Ladeforged, 1982] [Kreidler, 1989] [O'Grady and Dobrovolsky, 1992] [Morris, 1991] and related linguistic terms [Zhang, 1995] are defined as follows:

Definition 1. A *grapheme* consists of one letter or a combination of letters that represents one sound unit.

Definition 2. A *sound unit* (SU) represents a phoneme (a single sound, e.g. /a/, /s/), a diphthong (complex vowel sound, e.g. /ei/), or a consonant cluster (complex consonant sound, e.g. /ks/).

Definition 3. A grapheme that corresponds to the major sound of a syllable, which is called the *peak* in linguistics, is *syllabic* (+syllabic). Otherwise, a grapheme is *non-syllabic* (–syllabic).

Definition 4. A *syllable* consists of one and only one syllabic grapheme with or without non-syllabic graphemes.

2.2 The Problem Definition

Informally, most English speakers know that a syllable must contain a vowel sound. Precisely, a syllable must contain a *syllabic grapheme*. A syllabic grapheme is the centre of a syllable [Kreidler, 1989]. Vowel graphemes are usually syllabic, but some of them can be nonsyllabic, such as silent <e> and semi-vowel <y>. Some consonant graphemes, such as <m>, <n>, and <l>, become syllabic in certain contexts. Some English speakers and dictionaries pronounce <m>, <n>, and <l> as syllabic consonants, while others treat them as ordinary consonants. Because the +/− syllabic information for graphemes can be found in any given pronouncing dictionary, LE-SR simply follows the information given.

A syllable may include one or more consonants, or it may contain none. For example, the word *a* consists of one syllable, and the syllable contains the vowel sound $/\partial/$. The word *syllabic* has three syllables, containing the $/i/$, $/æ/$, and $/i/$ sounds, which correspond to the syllabic graphemes <y>, <a>, and <i>, respectively. These examples suggest that identifying syllables for English words is not difficult because identifying vowels or syllabic consonants is fairly easy. However, determining where divisions should be placed between syllables is a nontrivial task.

Ordinary dictionaries do not divide syllables for pronunciation but for printing. When printing, if the last word in a line is too long, the word can be split across two lines according to the dictionary syllabification. According to the Gage Canadian Dictionary and the American Heritage Dictionary, the word *syllabic* is divided into *syl-lab-ic*. This syllabification is not suited to pronunciation, because *syllabic* should be pronounced with the syllables *sy-lla-bic*.

To syllabify a word for pronunciation, it must first be divided into graphemes, such as <ll> and <gh>. The task of aligning graphemes is discussed elsewhere [Zhang et al., 1997]. The goal of LE-SR is to produce a set of syllabification rules that can be applied to dividing words into syllables.

A difficulty in identifying syllables arises when words have the same letter combinations but are cut in different places. Examples are the words *uphill* and *alphabet*, where one cut is in between *ph* (*up·hill*), and the other cut is before *ph* (*al·pha·bet*). That is, the letter combination "ph" sometimes forms one grapheme <ph> and sometimes forms two graphemes <p> and <h>. Since this problem disappears after the graphemes are identified, it is not considered in this paper.

This paper also does not discuss the conflicting number of syllables in the same word due to individual usage of vocal organs (e.g., some people pronounce *sour* as one syllable and others pronounce it as two syllables). Instead, LE-SR concentrates on learning a set of consistent syllabification rules according to the NTC2 pronouncing dictionary [Zhang et al., 1997].

2.3 Data Structures and I/O Representation

Dictionary Description: The description of a word in the NTC2 pronouncing dictionary consists of six pieces of information: the word, the syllables of the word, the pronunciation symbols, the stress marks, a code (0 = regular, 1 = irregular, and 2 = foreign), and the parts of speech.

– Example: absent [[a,b],[s,e,n,t]] [[æ,b],[s,schwa,n,t]] [[p],[n]] 0 [adj,verb,tr]

The C-S-CL representation: One of the following symbols is associated with each grapheme in each input word translated by LE-SR:

```
C  = a consonant (-syllabic)
S  = a syllabic grapheme (+syllabic)
CL = consonant cluster (-syllabic)
```

Input: The input is a set of two-column learning examples transformed from the NTC2 dictionary. The first column contains words and the second column contains the syllables which comprise the words.

– Example: syllable [[s,y],[ll,a],[b,l,e]]

Output: The output is a set of syllabification rules that can be used by a text-to-speech system to syllabify words. The format of the rules is [Pattern, Cut, Nsyl], where 'Pattern' is the set of graphemes between two syllabic graphemes, 'Cut' identifies the cut between two syllables, and 'Nsyl' records the number of syllabic graphemes in the word.

– Example: [[S,C,S,CL,S], [[S,C,S],[CL,S]], 3]

– Interpretation: If the pattern 'S,C,S,CL,S' is found in a word which contains 3 syllabic graphemes, then the syllables are cut between 'S' and 'CL'.

3 Approach

The first step in syllabification is to find two syllabic graphemes and determine their pattern, and the second step is to determine where to cut. All vowels are syllabic except some of those represented by the graphemes <e> and <y>. This raises some problems. For example, in the word *eye*, the first <e> (together with <y>) is pronounced as /ai/, but the second <e> is silent. Because a silent sound cannot form a syllable alone, the last <e> belongs to the same syllable as <ey>. Another kind of problem is that the semi-vowel <y> is sometimes syllabic (in *pretty*) and sometimes non-syllabic (in *yes*). To solve these two problems, LE-SR simply uses <e> and <y> as their representations instead of the C-S-CL representation. They are then treated as special cases where they appear.

Another concern is that some syllables are formed by consonant graphemes, such as <n> in *button* and <l> in *apple*. These are problems of pronunciation rather than of syllabification. They vary according to different dictionaries. Therefore, they are treated as given in the dictionary used by LE-SR.

It is relatively easy for LE-SR to learn potential rules for dividing syllables after the pattern is found because NTC2 provides many examples. However, it is very hard to determine which rules are good because one pattern can have several types of cut. Consider the following pattern and its three possible cuts. The frequency is indicated in the third column of the examples:

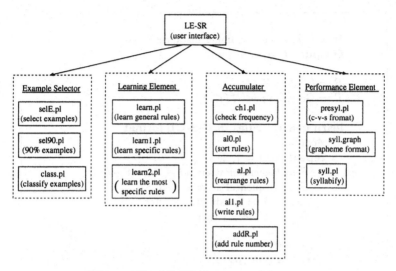

Fig. 1. The LE-SR Structure Diagram

```
[[S,C,S],[[S,C,S]],2]. 15.
[[S,C,S],[[S],[C,S]],2]. 1623.
[[S,C,S],[[S,C],[S]],2]. 45.
```

The pattern is taken from example words containing two syllabic graphemes. To determine which cut should be chosen as a candidate rule, LE-SR combines a statistical approach with the symbolic pattern recognition approach. That is, LE-SR calculates the frequency for each cut. The frequency is indicated in the third column of the above example. LE-SR chooses the cut that has the highest frequency. In our example, it is [[S,C,S], [S],[C,S]], 2] with a frequency of 1,623.

3.1 The LE-SR Structure

LE-SR consists of the 13 Prolog programs shown in Figure 1. These Prolog programs are connected to the LE-SR user interface, which is a C-shell program. As shown in Figure 1, the Prolog programs are divided into four units: the Example Selector (ES), the Learning Element (LE), the Accumulator (AC), and the Performance Element (PE).

ES provides learning examples to LE and testing examples to PE. LE obtains candidate rules for syllabification. These rules are sent to AC for filtering. AC uses statistical information to select the best rules and order them. Finally, PE uses the rules to perform syllabification. If the accuracy of syllabification is satisfactory, the process stops. Otherwise, a new loop starts with the incorrectly syllabified words as input examples.

3.2 The LE-SR Algorithm

Figure 2 shows the LE-SR algorithm which controls the learning process. This algorithm is simple and relatively efficient. It requires about 40 minutes to learn

Input: T, a set of training instances
Output: R, general rules

$R := \langle \ \rangle, I := T$
$T := \text{GetExamples}(NTC2)$

learn general rules in C-S-CL format
 $Acc_0 := 0$
 repeat for $i = 1, 2, 3, ...$
  $S := \text{GeneratePatterns}(T, I, \text{"C} - \text{S} - \text{CL"})$
  $S' := \text{SequencePatterns}(T, R, S)$
  $(Acc_i, I) := \text{Syllabify}(T, S', Acc_{i-1})$
  if $Acc_i > Acc_{i-1}$ **then**
   $R := S'$
  end if
 until $I = \phi$ or $Acc_i = Acc_{i-1}$

learn more specific rules in C-S-CL-e-y format
 repeat above with "C-S-CL-e-y" instead of "C-S-CL"

learn specific rules in grapheme format
 repeat above with grapheme instead of "C-S-CL-e-y"

Fig. 2. The LE-SR Algorithm

syllabification rules from a 20,000 word dictionary running on a Sun Sparc station. The algorithm is relatively fast because it is polynomial and does not backtrack.

4 A Descriptive Example

Consider the following instances and their C-S-CL representations:

1. abacus -- [S,C,S,C,S,C] [[S],[C,S],[C,S,C]]
2. biological -- [C,S,S,C,S,C,S,C,S,C] [[C,S],[S],[C,S],[C,S],[C,S,C]]
3. calculation -- [C,S,C,C,S,C,S,C,S,C] [[C,S,C],[C,S],[C,S],[C,S,C]]
4. physically -- [C,S,C,S,C,S,C,S] [[C,S],[C,S],[C,S],[C,S]]

From the first instance, LE-SR saves the pattern [S,C,S] and the cut [[S],[C,S]]. The second example gives the patterns [S,S] and [S,C,S]. Since the pattern [S,C,S] has been already saved for the first example, it is not saved again. The cut for the second example is [[S],[S]]. From the third example, LE-SR takes the pattern [S,C,C,S] and the cut [[S,C],[C,S]]. The last example includes two semi-vowel graphemes where patterns are [S,C,S], [S,C,S] with cuts [[S],[C,S]] and [[S],[C,S]], respectively.

After all these examples are processed, the rules are tested and evaluated before they are transferred to the knowledge base. If inconsistent rules are found, LE-SR uses statistical information to decide which rules should be retained. Then in the second stage, more specific rules based on C-S-CL-e-y representation instead of C-S-CL are created to cover exceptions with silent ¡e¿ or the semi-vowel ¡y¿. Then in the third stage, specific rules based on grapheme information instead of the C-S-CL-e-y representation are created to cover exceptions to any of the more general rules already discovered.

5 Results

5.1 The Ten-fold Test Results

LE-SR was tested on the NTC2 [Zhang et al., 1997], a 20,000 English word pronouncing dictionary derived from the NETalk Corpus [Sejnowski and Rosenberg, 1988]. LE-SR was applied to 90% of the input instances and tested on the unseen 10% of instances. In Table 1, the accuracies of syllabifying the unseen words are shown for 10 runs. For the first run, the unseen instances were selected by removing the first of every tenth input instance before learning, i.e., $X_1, X_{11}, X_{21}, \ldots$. This experiment was repeated using $X_2, X_{12}, X_{22}, \ldots$ as unseen instances for the second experiment, and so forth. The ten-fold test accuracy ranged from 94.55% to 96.05% for words and 96.81% to 97.71% for symbolic patterns of syllables. For example, if the word *syllabification* is syllabified as [[s,y,ll,a], [b,i], [f,i], [c,a], [t,io,n]] instead of [[s,y], [ll,a], [b,i], [f,i], [c,a], [t,io,n]], then 3 out of 4 patterns are syllabified correctly, but 0 words are syllabified correctly.

Run #	Examples (90%)	Learning Accuracy		Final Accuracy	
		General	Specific	Words	Patterns
1	30,763	97.80%	94.91%	95.60%	97.42%
2	30,703	97.79%	94.77%	95.15%	97.20%
3	30,710	97.81%	95.15%	95.20%	97.17%
4	30,723	97.80%	95.04%	95.30%	97.26%
5	30,099	97.84%	94.94%	94.55%	96.81%
6	30,758	97.80%	94.72%	95.80%	97.51%
7	30,010	97.82%	94.86%	95.25%	97.23%
8	30,720	97.74%	94.71%	96.05%	97.71%
9	30,801	97.80%	94.86%	95.30%	97.19%
10	30,115	97.80%	95.04%	95.00%	97.02%
Ave.	30,540	97.80%	94.90%	95.42%	97.25%
Standard Deviation		97.80%	94.90%	95.32%	97.25%

Table 1. Reports for ten-fold tests

5.2 Rule Usage

The frequency of rule usage shown in Table 5.2 indicates that 86.21% general cases (frequency > 1,000) is covered by only 0.64% of the syllabification rules produced by LE-SR, while 2.45% exception cases (frequency $= 1$), is covered by 76.77% of syllabification rules.

Although, at first glance, English appears unsystematic, it does not mean the structure of English orthography is arbitrary. Because English is a world language, it not only provides its rich vocabulary to the world but also absorbs foreign words from other languages. The above statistics for syllabification rule usage indicate that English is not only acting as the world language, but is also the most "abused" language in the world.

Frequency (F)	# of Rules	% of Rules	Usage	% Usage
F = 1	836	76.77%	836	2.47%
F = 2	57	5.23%	114	0.34%
F = 3	29	2.66%	87	0.26%
F = 4	12	1.10%	48	0.14%
F = 5	12	1.10%	60	0.18%
$5 < F \leq 15$	52	4.78%	602	1.78%
$15 < F \leq 35$	32	2.94%	772	2.28%
$35 < F \leq 95$	27	2.48%	1,669	4.93%
$95 < F \leq 1,000$	25	2.30%	7,692	22.73%
$1,000 < F \leq 10,004$	7	0.64%	21,954	64.89%
Total	1,089	100.00%	33,834	100%

Table 2. Rule Usage Summary

LE-SR found 836 unique exception patterns in 33,834 examples. Consider the following examples. The first three have the same pattern [S,C,S] with three different cuts, all from words that have two syllabic graphemes. There are 60 exceptional cases compared to the 1,623 most common cases. This is a very common situation in English syllabification.

```
[[S,C,S],[[S,C,S]],2]. 15.
[[S,C,S],[[S],[C,S]],2]. 1623.
[[S,C,S],[[S,C],[S]],2]. 45.
```

5.3 22 Most Frequently Used Rules

Table 5.2 shows the 22 most frequently used rules for syllabifying English words. These rules alone give about 90% accuracy, even though they are only 2.02% of total number of rules produced by LE-SR. This result suggests that English syllabification is not arbitrary (as many linguists thought) [Ladeforged, 1982] [Kreidler, 1989]. The rule numbered 231 is interpreted to mean that the pattern [S,C,S] is cut between [S] and [C,S] with no other conditions. The symbol '_ _ _' means no restrictions apply, while the numbers that sometimes appear after the '/' represent the number of syllabic graphemes that the word must contain for the rule to be used. For example, the rule numbered 232 has a condition that the word must have exactly 2 syllabic graphemes.

Rule #	Frequency	Syllabification Rule
231	10,004	[S,C,S] → [[S],[C,S]] /_ _ _
203	3,590	[S,C,C,S] → [[S,C],[C,S]] /_ _ _
285	2,423	[S] → [[S]] / 1
78	2,238	[e,C,S] → [[e],[C,S]] /_ _ _
241	1,388	[S,C,y] → [[S],[C,y]] /_ _ _
277	1,168	[S,S] → [[S],[S]] /_ _ _
221	1,143	[S,C,S,C,e#] → [[S],[C,S,C,e#]] /_ _ _
164	872	[S,C,e] → [[S],[C,e]] /_ _ _
57	837	[e,C,C,S] → [[e,C],[C,S]] /_ _ _
232	650	[S,C,e#] → [[S,C,e#]] / 2
108	581	[S,CL,e#] → [[S],[CL,e#]] / _ _ _
180	428	[S,CL,y] → [[S],[CL,y]] / _ _ _
139	365	[S,C,CL,S] → [[S,C],[CL,S]] / _ _ _
199	346	[S,C,C,S,C,e#] → [[S,C],[C,S,C,e#]] / _ _ _
234	324	[S,C,e#] → [[S],[C,e#]] / 4
187	322	[S,C,C,C,S] → [[S,C,C],[C,S]] / _ _ _
107	306	[S,CL,S] → [[S],[CL,S]] / _ _ _
72	284	[e,C,S,C,e#] → [[e],[C,S,C,e#]] / _ _ _
31	242	[e,C,e] → [[e],[C,e]] / _ _ _
94	241	[e,S] → [[e],[S]] / _ _ _
97	231	[e] → [[e]] / 1
233	226	[S,C,e#] → [[S],[C,e#]] / 3

Table 3. 22 Most Frequently Used Rules (F > 200)

6 Conclusions

Three original contributions of this research are the design of the LE-SR learning system, the creation of 1089 syllabification rules from the NTC2 pronouncing dictionary, and the discovery that 86.21% of the syllabification in NTC2 (frequency > 1,000) is covered by only 0.64% of the syllabification rules produced by LE-SR, while 2.45% exception cases (frequency = 1), is covered by 76.77% of syllabification rules.

In the future, we would like to reduce the number of specific rules, especially for word exceptions, by using an automatic self-learning method that can find different information other than simple patterns. Additional information about silent graphemes such as words ending with <ed> or <e> will help the learning. Because <e> in this case is not syllabic, it should not be separated from the previous part of the pattern. By adding one more attribute to the rule format, such cases could then be included in a more general rule.

Linguists also found that some syllables are "strong" and some are "weak". A *strong syllable* is always stressed while a *weak syllable* is not always stressed. This information my help identify syllables. Also, LE-SR can be extended to learn syllabification for other alphabetical languages, such as French, German, Italian, or Spanish.

References

[Allen et al., 1987] Allen, J., Hunnicutt, S., and Klatt, D., editors (1987). *From Text to Speech: The MITalk System*. Cambridge University Press, London.

[Elovitz et al., 1976] Elovitz, H., Johnson, R., Mchugh, A., and Shore, J. (1976). Automatic translation of English text to phonetics by means of letter-to-sound rules. Technical Report NRL 7948, Naval Research Laboratory, Washington, D.C.

[Hochberg et al., 1991] Hochberg, J., Mniszewski, S., Calleja, T., and Papcun, G. (1991). A default hierarchy for pronouncing English. *IEEE Transactions on Pattern Analysis and Machine Intellegence*, 13(9):957–964.

[Klatt, 1982] Klatt, D. (1982). The Klattalk text-to-speech system. In *Proc. Int. Conf. Acoustics Speech Signal Processing*, pages 1589–1592.

[Klatt, 1987] Klatt, D. (1987). How KLATTalk became DECtalk: An academic's experience in the business world. In *Official Proceedings Speech Tech'87: Voice Input/Output Applications Show and Conference*, pages 293–294.

[Kreidler, 1989] Kreidler, C. W. (1989). *Pronunciation of English*. Basil Blackwell, Oxford, UK.

[Ladeforged, 1982] Ladeforged, P. (1982). *A Course in Phonetics*. Harcourt Brace Jovanovich, New York.

[Ling and Wang, 1995] Ling, C. and Wang, H. (1995). A decision-tree model for reading aloud. Internet server: ftp.csd.uwo.ca/pub/ling/papers/mlj-bs.ps.Z.

[Mackay, 1987] Mackay, I. R. (1987). *Phonetics: The Science of Speech Production*. Pro.Ed, Austin, Texas.

[Morris, 1991] Morris, I., editor (1991). *The American Heritage Dictionary*. Houghton Mifflin, Boston, MA.

[Mudambi and Schimpf, 1994] Mudambi, S. and Schimpf, J. (1994). Parallel CLP on heterogeneous networks. Technical Report ECRC-94-17, European Computer-Industry Research Centre GmbH, Munich, Germany.

[O'Grady and Dobrovolsky, 1992] O'Grady, W. and Dobrovolsky, M. (1992). *Contemporary Linguistic Analysis*. Copp Clark Pitman, Toronto.

[Sejnowski and Rosenberg, 1987] Sejnowski, T. and Rosenberg, C. (1987). Parallel networks that learn to pronounce English text. *Complex Systems*, 1:145–168.

[Sejnowski and Rosenberg, 1988] Sejnowski, T. and Rosenberg, C. (1988). NETtalk corpus, (am6.tar.z). ftp.cognet.ucla.edu in pub/alexis.

[Zhang, 1995] Zhang, J. (1995). Automatic learning of English pronunciation rules. Master's thesis, University of Regina, Regina, Canada.

[Zhang and Hamilton, 1996] Zhang, J. and Hamilton, H. J. (1996). The LEP learning system. In *International Conference on Natural Language Processing and Industrial Applications*, pages 293–297, Moncton, New Brunswick, Canada.

[Zhang et al., 1997] Zhang, J., Hamilton, H. J., and Galloway, B. (1997). English graphemes and their pronunciations. In *Proceedings of Pacific Association for Computational Linguistics*. Accepted.

Towards Conceptual Query Answering

S. C. Yoon
Dept. of Computer Science
Widener University
Chester, PA 19013

Abstract

With the increase in the volume and complexity of databases, we need much more sophisticated query-processing schemes in databases to satisfy the needs of truly intelligent user-machine interfaces required by new generation database applications. In this paper, we introduce a partially automated method for conceptual query answering which is a mechanism to answer queries specified with general and abstract terms rather than primitive data stored in databases. Conceptual query answering consists of two phases: preprocessing and execution. In the preprocessing phase, we discover useful and interesting abstract terms by building a set of concept hierarchies constructed by generalization of primitive data stored in a database into appropriate higher level concepts. Then, we construct an abstracted database by generalizing and preprocessing primitive data in frequently referenced relations. Specifically, we find frequent conjuncts of the attributes which have meaningful correlations and replace the values of those attributes with the abstract terms defined in their concept hierarchies or results of aggregation functions on the values. In the execution phase, we receive a user's conceptual query and process the query with the concept hierarchies and the abstracted database. The contribution of this paper is that we develop a framework for processing conceptual queries. In addtion, we suggest strategies to reduce the computational complexity of the conceptual query answer generation process.

Keywords: Conceptual Query, Concept Hierarchy, Abstracted Database

1 Introduction

Traditionally, database systems have accepted queries specified with precise search expression directly based on primitive data stored in databases, which requires users to fully understand information related to the databases. For example, "who is the manager of the *research* department located in *Philadelphia* ?" or "list the courses which Prof. *Johnson* in the dept. of *Computer Science* is teaching". As the size and complexity of databases with the advance in storage technologies have been increased, users may prefer to express queries with more general and abstract information instead of primitive terms directly based on the data stored in a database. Often, users may not formulate precise query conditions because they may not be familiar with contents stored in the database. In those cases, the users need to ask general queries involving meaningful abstract terms that do not directly come from information stored in a database. This kind of queries is referred as *conceptual queries*. For example, a user may wish to query "what are *expensive* restaurants in the *Delaware Valley* area which are visited by *senior* people ?". The query uses abstract terms, "*expensive*", "*Delaware Valley*", and "*senior*" which are not stored explicitly in the database.

A conceptual query can be expressed in terms of predefined abstract terms such as *expensive*, *Delaware Valley*, and *senior* that can be derived from primitive information in a database.

We believe conceptual queries provide users with the flexibility of expressing query conditions at a relatively high-level concept, which relaxes the requirement of the preciseness of query conditions, and allow them to ask more general questions to a database. However, the current database systems do not support conceptual queries. We believe there will be more database applications where it is important to be able to pose queries in terms of abstract terms, rather than expression directly based on primitive data. There is a need for much more sophisticated query-processing schemes such as conceptual query answering to enhance the usefulness and flexibility of databases to satisfy the needs of truly intelligent user-machine interfaces required by new generation database applications. This motivates the development of mechanisms for processing conceptual queries.

In this paper, we introduce a partially automated method for conceptual query answering which is a mechanism to answer queries specified with general and abstract terms quickly and intelligently. The contribution of this paper is that we develop a framework for processing conceptual queries. In addition, we suggest strategies to reduce the computational complexity of the conceptual query answer generation process.

This paper is structured as follows. Section 2 introduces motivating examples to show the advantages of conceptual queries. Section 3 surveys related works. Section 4 presents our approach to handle a conceptual query. Section 5 explains our approach with examples. Section 6 discusses our conclusions and possible extensions of our work for future research.

2 Motivating Examples

The following examples illustrate the advantages of conceptual query answering.

Example 1   Suppose we have a database of car sales transactions. For example, a marketing manager at the company who is interested in the sale patterns of various types of customers may formulate a query asking "what kinds of cars are preferred by *young* single people with a *high* income who live in *suburb* areas ?", which contains abstract terms such as *"young"*, *"high income"*, and *"suburb"*. Even though the answer can provide very meaningful information to the manager, current databases can not answer the query because those terms are not actual values stored in the database. That is, there is no place in the database where those terms are explicitly mentioned. If a database system can process conceptual queries involving abstract terms, the system helps nonexpert users make ad-hoc queries easily and find useful and meaningful answers.

Example 2   Suppose there is a database of flight schedules. For example, a user wants to plan a travel from Philadelphia to Orlando but is unfamiliar with the flight schedules. Then, the user may ask a general question such as "What *late morning* flights are available from Philadelphia to Orlando at a *reasonable* fare ?" Current databases can not process the query which will assist the user to refine the original query or pose more restriction on the query because *late morning* and *reasonable fare*

are not the primitive values stored in the database. That is, knowledge such that *late morning* typically means between 10:30 A.M. and noon is not stored in the database. In this case, conceptual query answering helps users form their queries with more accurate expressions.

Example 3 Suppose that there is a database of a university environment. Let us assume that the *student* relation is a frequently referenced relation and that there have been many query patterns related to major in the relation. We can construct generalized student relations to include general and abstract information related to major from the student relation. Now, we have a query asking "What is the number of *science* majors whose GPA is *excellent* ?". If we can answer the query with the generalized student relation which includes the general major *science*, it will be efficient and effective because we do not need to access the actual database.

As the above examples show, the capability of conceptual query answering enhances the usefulness and flexibility of a database and provides an interface for users to specify their interested set of data easily. Furthermore, answers for conceptual queries may be a valuable resource used for a competitive advantage in promotion and marketing. If we can answer such queries with preprocessed information such as generalized relations, it is expected to be faster and less costly because we don't have to access databases. We believe that many new applications are well served by conceptual queries. In this paper, we show how to process a conceptual query with the help of the concept hierarchies and the generalized relations.

3 Related Works

In this section, we survey related works to our approach in the area of conceptual query answering. Recently, there have been several research works aimed at improving conventional query answering in various data models, including relational and deductive models. Two major areas are intensional query answering and cooperative query answering.

Intensional query answering generates intensional answers which are conditions and characteristics that justify or explain extensional answers. An overview of the various intensional query answering techniques is given in [9]. These works share a common goal to generate answers in a more abstract form. Their works consider integrity constraints, and/or deduction rules, and/or extensional answers to generate intensional answers. Even though intensional query answering and conceptual query answering use some kind of generalization, there is a difference between those two approaches. The latter approach deals with queries expressed with predefined abstract terms to generate answers at the ground levels whereas the former approach deals with integrity constraints, and/or deductive rules, and/or extensional answers to generate more abstract answers. In that sense, the latter approach is top-down whereas the former approach is bottom-up.

Cooperative query answering answers queries cooperatively by analyzing the intent of queries. Cuppens and Demolombe [3] have shown methods to provide cooperative answers by rewriting queries with additional variables or additional entities satisfying less restrictive conditions, which carry relevant information for users. Chu et al. [2] have explored a method for generalizing queries in order to provide generalized and associated information which is relevant to the queries. In Chu et al. [2], they start with a query, generalize the conditions in the query, and then generate a cooperative answer. The major difference between cooperative answering and conceptual answering is that the former approach provides additional information that is not explicitly requested by queries while the latter approach starts with queries specified with abstract terms and refines the terms in the queries to more specific conditions to find answers. Conceptual query answering is a process to provide answers to imprecisely specified queries with some general terms. In that sense, the latter approach is top-down whereas the former approach is bottom-up.

Our approach uses concept hierarchy that is introduced by Han et al.[5]. In [5], the attribute domains were defined in the given concept hierarchies and, in turn used to generalize the attribute values in a table. They used the hierarchies as a method for mining characteristics and discriminant rules in relational databases. However, our approach uses the hierarchies as background knowledge for formulating and answering conceptual queries. We apply and extend their approach to the process of conceptual query answering.

4 Our Approach

In this section, we present our approach to process conceptual queries. We divide our approach into two phases: preprocessing and execution. The preprocessing phase is done statically once while the execution phase has to be performed at run time. The preprocessing phase is independent of queries posed to a database and hence is computed once prior to the processing of any conceptual query. We now consider each phase in detail.

4.1 Preprocessing Phase

In this phase, we discover useful and interesting abstract terms by building a set of concept hierarchies constructed by generalization of data stored in a database. A concept hierarchy provides an organized structure representing the values of an attribute domain at different abstraction levels. Concept hierarchies may be constructed with knowledge provided by domain experts. A concept hierarchy consists of nodes labeled by concepts. The nodes in the hierarchy contain different levels of concepts. That is, a concept hierarchy may form a taxonomy of concepts. A higher level concept is more general and covers more cases than a lower level concept. The concept in a node is subsumed by the concept of its parent node. The bottom levels of the hierarchy are the distinct specific values or ranges of numerical values for an attribute. The other levels are database views or summaries of data in the attribute. Databases can only represent the bottom level in the concept hierarchy and the higher levels are not explicitly present in databases. In our approach, concept hierarchies have necessary background knowledge which directs conceptual query processing. That is, the concepts in concept hierarchies can be used to formulate complicated expressions quickly in conceptual queries.

When we build concept hierarchies, we need to control the number of concept hierarchies. So, we choose only attributes that have occurred frequently in past queries as candidate attributes. For each candidate attribute, we build a concept hierarchy if the attribute satisfies one of the following two cases:

Case 1: If the attribute has a large set of distinct nonnumeric values, high-level concepts for those values are existed.

Case 2: If the attribute has a large set of distinct numerical values, finite number of meaningful intervals(a range of values) based on the distribution of the attribute values are existed.

When we build a concept hierarchy, we may use a threshold value to control the number of levels in the hierarchy. The threshold value can be specified by a user or a domain expert to provide the upper bound on the number of levels.

In this phase, we also construct an abstracted database by preprocessing and generalizing primitive data in frequently referenced relations. Specifically, we remove some attributes and replace the values of attributes by abstract terms defined in concept hierarchies or results of aggregation functions on the values. During this process, we merge identical tuples in the relation and store the total count of such merged tuples. The challenge is how to perform generalization selectively because a large number of combinations of different sets of attributes is possible. It is unrealistic to store all of the possible generalized relations because a large number of combinations of different sets of attributes is possible. So, we need to perform generalization selectively. We apply the following heuristic guideline when we construct an abstracted database.

Step 1: select frequently referenced relations from previous database usage patterns. For each selected relation,

Step 2: remove rarely used attributes but retain frequently referenced ones by considering past query patterns.

Step 3: select a frequently referenced attribute as a generalization criterion.

Let us assume that the relation *student*(name, major, GPA, address, sex) is a frequently referenced relation in a university database and that there have been many query patterns related to major. In this case, the generalization criterion is the attribute major.

Step 4: keep the attributes that have meaningful correlations with the generalized criterion and remove attributes that do not have any correlations.

For example, the attributes, student's major and GPA, may be correlated, while there is little chance that attributes, student's name and address, are related. Knowledge relating major and GPA is more useful than knowledge relating name and address.

Step 5: cluster data retained in the relation according to the generalization criterion, generalize the values in the criterion in multiple layers, and create a generalized relation for each layer.

For example, the relation student is partitioned according to their majors. That is, all the computer science majors are stored in one partition, all the math majors are stored in a second partition, and so on. During this process, different majors can be merged into a general major. For example, math, chemistry, and physics can be merged into a general major, science. Different general majors can be merged into a more general major. For example, science, social science, and humanity can be merged into a more general major, arts and sciences. That is, the major can be generalized into several layers. We may construct a generalized student relation for each layer. A user or an expert may specify explicitly a designated concept as the starting concept or a desirable concept. We create generalized relations with the designated concept.

The group by operation may be used to cluster data.

Step 6: generalize the values of the retained attributes except the attribute used as the criterion in each generalized relation with the concept hierarchies of those attributes and store the generalized information in the relation.

For example, assume that there is meaningful relationship between major and GPA in the relation student. Then, we generalize the values of the attribute GPA in each generalized student relation and store general characteristic information for each generalized major in terms of GPA in each generalized student relation.

Our database consists of two major components defined as follows:

1. Extensional database, which consists of all the relations.

2. Abstracted database, which consists of all generalized relations which include more general and abstract information extracted from their corresponding original relations stored in the extensional database. The relations in the abstracted database are also much smaller than their original relations in the extensional database and provide a global view of their original relations in the extensional database.

When we generalize relations, we use a technique similar to attribute-oriented generalization in knowledge discovery in databases [5]. The relation R can be generalized to the relation R', then R'', and so on. For efficiency of access, we can create an index for general terms and the names of the generalized relations including those terms.

4.2 Execution Phase

Upon receiving a conceptual query, we need to figure out what constitues a query. Conceptual queries can be divided into three types according to the types of conditions in the queries: complex conceptual query, simple conceptual query, and mixed conceptual query. Each type has its appropriate query processing scheme.

In the complex conceptual query type, queries can not be answered directly by searching only the abstracted database. Our main goal in this type of query is to find an equivalent rewriting Q', which can be processed by current database systems, for a given conceptual query Q. Q' is expressed with the set of precise conditions on data in a database. In this case, we perform specialization process which finds the set of precise conditions directly based on primitive data. After identifying abstract terms contained in the query, appropriate mappings are performed to transform the abstract terms into the set of the conditions based on the primitive data. That is, we specialize each abstract term by descending its concept hierarchy one level at a time from the level including the abstract term until we reach the bottom level of the hierarchy in order to find all precise conditions for the abstract term. Often, the abstract term includes more than one less generalized concept. That is, a higher level concept corresponds to multiple lower level concepts. In this case, we need to find a set of conditions from each less generalized concept path in the hierarchy. If an abstract term has more than one descendant at lower level, we perform specialization process for each descendant. Then, we need to combine the conditions from each less generalized concept path into a set of all conditions for the abstract term. We repeat the specialization process until we find all the conditions which the abstract term subsumes. That is, we repeatedly substitute each abstract term with its corresponding lower-level concept(s) until we find specific conditions based on data stored in the database. This step transforms a more generalized concept into a less generalized concept. To reduce searching time for an appropriate level in a concept hierarchy, a user or an expert may specify explicitly a concept level as the desirable starting level. After transforming the conceptual query into its equivalent query that is expressed in terms of conditions on primitive data, we process the query to collect answers by using available query optimization techniques. To process this type of query, main steps are to map the abstract terms referred to in a query into appropriate levels in concept hierarchies and to move downward along the concept hierarchies to transform the abstract terms into the set of precise conditions.

In the simple conceptual query type, a query can be processed directly by accessing only the abstracted database. In this case, we map the query conditions into appropriate generalized relations in the abstracted database and process the conditions in those relations without accessing the extensional database. A query in this type inquires about general characteristics or summary information of a particular portion of data in a database. Since the abstracted database is usually much smaller than the original database, the query processing is expected to be more efficient if done in the abstracted database. If we use the index on abstract terms, we can avoid retrieving any generalized relations but the required one. A certain query may involve a join operation of two or more generalized relations in the abstracted database. In this case, we can perform the operation if they can be joined with equality conditions on attributes that are either keys or foreign keys in a way that guarantees that no spurious tuples are generated. If a user needs a less general answer, we may perform back substitution, which is a process of replacing high-level concepts in the answer by their corresponding specific conditions that define those concepts.

In the mixed conceptual query type, the conditions in queries are combination of complex conceptual query type conditions and simple conceptual query type conditions. We divide the conditions referred to in queries into two groups, conditions which should be transformed into a set of conditions based on primitive data with concept hierarchies and conditions which can be answered with the abstracted databases. For the conditions in the first group, we apply the techniques which are used in complex conceptual query processing. For the conditions in the second group, we apply the techniques which are used in simple conceptual query processing.

5 Examples

In this section, we explain the implementation of conceptual query answering mechanisms with some examples in details.

In the example 1, a marketing manager may formulate a query asking "what kinds of cars are preferred by *young* people with a *high* income who live in *suburb* areas ?", which contains abstract terms such as "young", "high income", and "suburb". The schema of the relation Customer is shown as follows.

Customer(Name, Age, Income, Address, Zipcode, Type-of-car)

The original SQL query can be formulated as follows.

Select   Type-of-car
From   Customer
Where   Age=*young* and Income=*high* and Zipcode=*surburb*

After each abstract term is mapped into its appropriate level in the existing concept hierarchy and the specialization process is performed, the query can be automatically refined to the following query.

Select   Type-of-car
From   Customer
Where   (Age>20 and Age<35) and (Income>55000) and
           (Zipcode>19071 and Zipcode<19081)

Young is refined to age between 20 and 35, high income corresponds to an income greater than 55000, and suburb is substituted with zipcode between 19072 and 19080.

In the example 3, we partitioned students into clustered groups according to their majors, such as math, chemistry, and physics. Different majors can be merged into a general major. For example, math, chemistry, and physics can be merged into a general major, science. We find a set of attributes from past query patterns which show meaningful correlations with major. Assume that the attribute GPA is one of them. Then, find abstract terms in the GPA conceptual hierarchy. There are three categories: poor, average, and excellent. For each major in each generalized relation, we have those categories. We may have the following generalized relation Student[1].

Generalized Relation Student[1]

Major	GPA	Count
Science	Excellent	20
Science	Average	100
Science	Poor	25
⋮	⋮	⋮
Engineering	Poor	28

Now, we have a query asking "What is the number of science majors whose GPA is excellent ?". The original SQL query can be formulated as follows.

Select   Count
From   Student
Where   Major=Science and GPA=excellent

The query can be answered using the generalized relation Student[1] efficiently.

The first two queries in section 2 belong to the complex conceptual query type while the last query belongs to the simple conceptual query type. Now, let's consider a query which belongs to the mixed conceptual query type. Assume that a user may ask a query "What are expensive restaurants in the Delaware Valley area which are visited by senior people ?". The schemas of the two relations are shown as follows.

Restaurant(Price-range, Location, Name, Accepted-card-type, Specialty)
Person(Name, Age, Favorite-restaurant, Address, Income, Profession)

Suppose that we have the following generalized relation Restaurant[1] in the abstracted database.

Price-range	Location	Name
Expensive	Delaware Valley	Res A
Average	South New Jersy	Res B
Cheap	Lehigh Valley	Res C
⋮	⋮	⋮
Expensive	Delaware Valley	Res W

The original SQL query can be formulated as follows.

Select   Restaurant.Name
From   Restaurant, Person
Where   Price-range=*Expensive* and Location=*Delaware Valley* and
          Restaurant.Name=Favorite-restaurant and Age=*Senior*

To process the query, we first find the names of the restaurants whose price-range is expensive and whose location is Delaware Valley with the generalized relation *Restaurant*[1]. Then, find the names of the restuarnts which are visited by people whose age is grater than 65. The first two conditions do not need to be refined, whereas the last condition is refined to age greater than or eqaul to 65. That is, for the first two conditions, we apply the techniques used in the simple conceptual query type, whereas we apply the techniques used in the complex conceptual query type for the last condition. In this example, those two relations, *Restaurant*[1] and Person can be joined because they are joined on key attributes.

6   Conclusion

When a user needs to retrieve information in current databases, the user provides a precise search expression that identifies the information to be retrieved. Conventional queries, expressed with precise conditions directly based on data stored in databases, are not always the best means of efficient and effective communications between users and database systems. We often need to express queries involving concepts at different levels of abstraction. Current databases can not answer queries involving concepts at any level higher than the level of the actual values.

In this paper, we have presented a method for conceptual query answering which is a mechanism to answer queries specified with abstract terms. We have applied and extended the method [5] to our task that processes conceptual queries. Conceptual queries may allow users to ask more useful and meaningful questions than current queries could ever do. In addition, users can outline requests that may be hard or impossible to describe with a standard SQL query, which enhances the man-machine interface to databases. We believe many new applications, such as market databases which do require ad-hoc querying, are well served by conceptual queries that can use more high-level concepts, which relax the requirements of queries in current databases.

Our approach provides a simple and reasonable way of processing conceptual queries, involving abstract terms at different levels of abstraction, in database systems. We have implemented a prototype system to validate the proposed concept. Our preliminary experimental results reveal that this approach provides a systematic and efficient way to achieve conceptual query answering.

It may be interesting to use different computational methodologies to process conceptual queries. Our approach can be applied with some modifications to other data models, including object-oriented and deductive ones.

References

[1] L. Cholvy and R. Demolombe, "Querying a rule base", *Proceedings of the First International Conference on Expert Database Systems*, pp. 365-371, 1986

[2] W. Chu and Q. Chen, "Neighborhood and associative query answering", *J. of intelligent information systems*, vol. 1, pp. 355-382, 1992

[3] F. Cuppens and R. Demolombe, "Extending answers to neighbour entities in a cooperative answering context", *Decision Support Systems*, pp. 1-11, 1991

[4] V. Dhar and A. Tuzhilin, "Abstract-driven pattern discovery in databases", *IEEE Transactions on Knowledge and Data Engineering*, vol. 5, no. 6, pp. 926-938, 1993

[5] J. Han, et.al., "Data-driven discovery of quantitative rules in relational datbases", *IEEE Transactions on Knowledge and Data Engineering*, vol. 5, no. 1, pp. 29-40, 1993

[6] T. Imielinski, "Intelligent query answering in rule based systems", *Journal of Logic Programming*, Vol. 4, No. 3, pp.229-258, 1987

[7] A. Motro, "Using integrity constraints to provide intensional answers to relational queries", *Proceedings of 15th VLDB Conference*, pp. 237-246, 1989

[8] A. Motro and Q. Yuan, "Querying database knowledge", *Proceedings of the International Conference on Management of Data*, pp. 173-183, 1990

[9] A. Motro, "Intensional answers to database queries", *IEEE Transactions on Knowledge and Data Engineering*, Vol.6. No. 3, pp. 444-454, 1994

[10] G. Piatetsky-Shapiro, and W.J. Frawley, eds., *Knowledge discovery in databases*, AAAI/MIT Press, 1991

[11] A. Pirotte, et.al., "Controlled generation of intensional snswers", *IEEE Transactions on Knowledge and Data Engineering*, Vol.3, No. 2, pp. 221-236, 1991

[12] S. C. Yoon, et.al., "Intelligent query answering in deductive and object-oriented databases", *Proceedings of 3rd ACM International Conferenece on Information and Knowledge Management*, pp.244-251, 1994

[13] S.C. Yoon, et.al., "Semantic query processing in object-oriented frameworks", *Proceedings of 4th ACM International Conferenece on Information and Knowledge Management*, pp.150-157, 1995

[14] S.C. Yoon and L.J. Henschen, "Mining knowledge in object-oriented frameworks for semantic query optimization", *SIGMOD Workshop on Data Mining and Knowledge Discovery*, pp.109-116, 1996

An Implementation Platform for Query-Answering in Default Logics: Theoretical Underpinnings

Torsten Schaub[1,2] and Pascal Nicolas[1]

[1] LERIA, Faculté de Sciences, Université d'Angers, 2 Boulevard Lavoisier, F-49045 Angers
[2] Institut für Informatik, Universität Potsdam, Postfach 60 15 53, D-14415 Potsdam

Abstract: We present a uniform framework for implementing the variety of consistency checks needed for an implementation platform for query-answering in default logics. Our approach is centered around the concept of local proof procedures that allow for validating each inference step when it is performed. The resulting system is unique in offering simultaneously the expressiveness of multiple default logics.

1 Introduction

We propose a general approach to consistency checking in *default logics* [11]: A default logic augments classical logic by *default rules* that differ from standard inference rules in sanctioning inferences that rely upon given as well as absent information. A default rule $\frac{\alpha\,:\,\beta}{\gamma}$ has two types of antecedents: A *prerequisite* α, established if α is derivable, and a *justification* β, established if β is consistent in a certain way. If both conditions hold, the *consequent* γ is concluded by default. A set of such conclusions (sanctioned by default rules and classical logic) is called an *extension* of an initial set of facts.

We are interested in query-answering in default logics and hence we elaborate on proof procedures that allow for determining whether a formula is in some extension of a default theory. This question was first addressed in [11]. A common difficulty encountered is the integration of deduction and consistency checking. Unlike other approaches like [11, 14], putting forward more or less global consistency checks, we envisage guarenteeing consistency each time a default rule is considered. Such a consistency-driven search for a default proof prunes "inconsistent" applications of default rules in advance. Yet, such successive checks can be very expensive. The question is thus whether we can prune "inconsistent subproofs" while restricting our attention to ultimately necessary consistency checks: We observe that a formula is consistent (or satisfiable) iff it has a model. In fact, checking whether a model satisfies a formula can be done in linear time in propositional logic. This leads us to the following approach: We start with a model of the initial set of facts. Each time, we apply a default rule, we check whether the actual model satisfies the underlying default assumptions. If this is the case, we continue proving. If not, we try to generate a new model of the initial set of facts satisfying the current as well as all default assumptions underlying the partial default proof at hand. If we succeed, we simply continue proving under the new model. Otherwise, we know that the considered default assumption cannot be assumed in a consistent way.

This work builds on [4], where the aforementioned idea was applied to the restricted setting of normal default theories, as a somewhat greatest common fragment of default logics. In fact, full-fledged default logics, like classical [11], justified [8], constrained [5], or rational default logic [9], differ only in the way they address consistency. For implementing these systems, we can thus restrict our attention to the treatment of consistency, while relying for the implementation of further default logic specific techniques like deduction and groundedness on those developed for normal default theories (cf.

[12]). Concretely, we thus presuppose in the sequel an arbitrary yet fixed default theorem proving module interacting with the consistency handling module specified in this paper. A further particularity of our approach stems from the desire to center it around local proof procedures that allow for validating each inference when it is performed. As already put forward in [11], this is feasible in the presence of the property of *semi-monotonicity*. As detailed in Section 2, this property allows us to consider a relevant subset of default rules while answering a query. Note that in the absence of such a property a proof procedure must necessarily consider all default rules in the given theory. For addressing the above spectrum of default logics, we found our approach on the context-based framework for default logics proposed in [1]. In this approach, each variant of default logic corresponds to a fragment of a more general and uniform default reasoning system, called *contextual default logic*. This has also the advantage that we may mix multiple conceptions of default logics in the same setting.

2 The general setting: Contextual default logic

Default logics differ in the way they address consistency: While classical and justified default logic employ a rather local notion of consistency by separately verifying the consistency of each justification, constrained and rational default logic take a global approach by stipulating that all justifications have to be jointly consistent.

Let us first look at two examples reflecting different notions of consistency. Consider first the so-called "broken-arms" example [10]: We have defaults saying that a robot's arm is usable, unless it is broken. Now, suppose we are told that one of the robot's arms, the left one or the right one, is broken. This gives the following formalization: [3]

$$(D_1, W_1) = \left(\left\{ \frac{:\neg Bl}{Ul}, \frac{:\neg Br}{Ur} \right\}, \{Bl \vee Br\} \right) . \tag{1}$$

The facts assert that the left arm, Bl, or the right arm, Br, is broken, while the defaults express that an arm is usable, Ul or Ur, if we can consistently assume that it is not broken, ¬Bl or ¬Br, respectively. We note that the facts and the defaults' justifications are jointly inconsistent. In classical and justified default logic, theory (1) has one extension with Ul and Ur. This is so because each justification, ¬Bl and ¬Br, is (only) required to be separately consistent with the extension; thus tolerating incompatible justifications. In this way, these default logics direct us to conclude that both arms are usable even though one of them is known to be broken. A different solution is offered by constrained and rational default logic, from which we obtain one extension with Ul and another one with Ur. According to [10], this is the preferred solution in this example.

There are however other classes of commonsense reasoning patterns that require the treatment of justifications found in classical and justified default logic: For repairing, the mechanic relies on the following rules of thumb: if it is possible that the arm's failure is caused by hardware, Ha, then take the tool-box, To; if it is possible that it is due to a software problem, So, then take the laptop, La. In our setting, hard- and software errors cannot appear simultaneously (¬Ha ∨ ¬So). We give the following formalization:

$$(D_2, W_2) = \left(\left\{ \frac{:Ha}{To}, \frac{:So}{La} \right\}, \{\neg Ha \vee \neg So\} \right) . \tag{2}$$

As in the "broken-arms" example, we obtain in classical and justified default logic a single extension containing To ∧ La, while constrained and rational default logic yield

---

[3] The formulation in [10] uses semi-normal rules; this leaves the example unaffected.

two extensions, one containing To and another one containing La. Now, however, the intuitively more appealing result is obtained in classical and justified default logic since they direct us to take toolbox and laptop. Observe that even though the "repair" example relies on intuitions different from the ones behind the "broken-arms" example, both formalizations are equivalent modulo renaming.

For brevity, we refrain from commenting this any further and refer the reader to the literature for a detailed discussion [10, 3, 5]. In summary, this literature shows that there is not only a formal need for distinct notions of consistency in order to capture different default logics, but moreover a need stemming from knowledge engineering due to numerous commonsense examples that demand one or the other conception to be handled in the intuitively more appealing way.[4]

2.1 The general setting: Contextual default logic

In order to combine variants of default logic, one has to compromise different notions of consistency. [1] capture this by means of the notion of *pointwise closure* $Th_S(T)$:

Definition 1. Let T and S be formula sets. For non-empty T, the pointwise closure of T under S is defined as $Th_S(T) = \bigcup_{\phi \in T} Th(S \cup \{\phi\})$, otherwise, $Th_S(\emptyset) = Th(S)$.

Given two sets of formulas T and S, we say that T is *pointwisely closed under* S iff $T = Th_S(T)$. For illustration, consider how we can express the "context" witnessing the derivation of To $\wedge$ La from Theory (2) in classical default logic:

$$Th_{\{\neg Ha \vee \neg So, To, La\}}(\{Ha, So\}) \tag{3}$$

This set comprises two consistent, deductively closed sets of formulas, one containing Ha and another one containing So; taken together, these two sets are inconsistent and would thus yield any formula by applying deductive closure.

In this approach, one considers three sets of formulas: A set of facts W, an extension E, and a certain *context* C such that $W \subseteq E \subseteq C$. The set of formulas C is somehow established from the facts, the default conclusions, as well as from all underlying consistency assumptions, given by the justifications of all applied default rules. For those familiar with the aforementioned default logics, this approach trivially captures the application conditions found in existing default logics: For $\frac{\alpha : \beta}{\gamma}$, eg. $\alpha \in E$ and $\neg \beta \notin E$ in classical default logic, and $\alpha \in E$ and $\neg(\beta \wedge \gamma) \notin C$ in constrained default logic.

This variety of application conditions motivates an extended notion of a default rule [1]: A contextual default rule δ is an expression of the form

$$\frac{\alpha_W \mid \alpha_E \mid \alpha_C : \beta_C \mid \beta_E \mid \beta_W}{\gamma}$$

where for $x \in \{W, E, C\}$, formula α_x is called x-prerequisite, also $pre_x(\delta)$, β_x is called x-justification, also $jus_x(\delta)$, and γ is the consequent, also $con(\delta)$.[5] For convenience, we omit tautological components; a non-existing component must thus be identified with a tautology.

---

[4] Interestingly, Reiter already anticipated in [11, p. 83] that *"providing an appropriate formal definition of this consistency requirement is perhaps the thorniest issue in defining a logic for default reasoning"*.

[5] This extends to sets of rules in the obvious way (eg. $jus_E(D) = \bigcup_{\delta \in D} \{jus_E(\delta)\}$).

A contextual default theory is a pair (D, W), where D is a set of contextual default rules and W is a consistent[6] set of formulas. A contextual extension is a pair (E, C), where E is a deductively closed set of formulas and C is a pointwisely closed set of formulas [1]:

Definition 2. Let (D, W) be a contextual default theory and let E and C be sets of formulas. Define $E_0 = W$, $\quad C_0 = W$ and for $i \geq 0$

$$\Delta_i = \left\{ \frac{\alpha_W \mid \alpha_E \mid \alpha_C : \beta_C \mid \beta_E \mid \beta_W}{\gamma} \in D \;\middle|\; \begin{array}{ll} \alpha_W \in Th(W), & \alpha_E \in E_i, \quad \alpha_C \in C_i, \\ \neg\beta_C \notin C, & \neg\beta_E \notin E, \neg\beta_W \notin Th(W) \end{array} \right\}$$

$$E_{i+1} = Th(W \cup con(\Delta_i)) \quad C_{i+1} = Th_{W \cup con(\Delta_i) \cup jus_C(\Delta_i)}(jus_E(\Delta_i))$$

Then, (E, C) is a contextual extension of (D, W) if $(E, C) = (\bigcup_{i=0}^{\infty} E_i, \bigcup_{i=0}^{\infty} C_i)$.

The extension E is built by successively introducing the consequents of all applying contextual default rules. For each partial context C_{i+1}, the partial extension E_{i+1} is united with the C-justifications of all applying contextual default rules.[7] This set is united in turn with each E-justification of all applying contextual default rules.

[1] shows that classical, justified, and constrained default logic are embedded in contextual default logic. [7] extends these embeddings to rational default logic. For brevity, we exemplarily give the resulting mappings and refer the reader to [1, 7] for the corresponding equivalence results:

Definition 3. Let (D, W) be a default theory. We define

$$\Phi_{DL}(D, W) = \left(\left\{ \frac{|\alpha| : |\beta|}{\gamma} \;\middle|\; \frac{\alpha : \beta}{\gamma} \in D \right\}, W \right) \qquad \text{(Classical default logic)}$$

$$\Phi_{JDL}(D, W) = \left(\left\{ \frac{|\alpha| : \gamma|\beta \wedge \gamma|}{\gamma} \;\middle|\; \frac{\alpha : \beta}{\gamma} \in D \right\}, W \right) \qquad \text{(Justified default logic)}$$

$$\Phi_{CDL}(D, W) = \left(\left\{ \frac{|\alpha| : \beta \wedge \gamma||}{\gamma} \;\middle|\; \frac{\alpha : \beta}{\gamma} \in D \right\}, W \right) \qquad \text{(Constrained default logic)}$$

$$\Phi_{RDL}(D, W) = \left(\left\{ \frac{|\alpha| : \beta||}{\gamma} \;\middle|\; \frac{\alpha : \beta}{\gamma} \in D \right\}, W \right) \qquad \text{(Rational default logic)}$$

These embeddings extend to variants of default logic relying on labeled formulas (or *assertions* [3]): [5] shows that constrained and cumulative default logic [3] are equivalent modulo representation. The same is shown by [6] for classical and Q-default logic [6], and by [7] for rational and CA-default logic [6], respectively.

For example, we obtain for the two theories given in (1) and (2), the following contextual counterparts:

$$\Phi_{CDL}(D_1, W_1) = \left(\left\{ \frac{|| : \neg Bl \wedge Ul ||}{Ul}, \; \frac{|| : \neg Br \wedge Ur ||}{Ur} \right\}, \{Bl \vee Br\} \right) \qquad (4)$$

$$\Phi_{JDL}(D_2, W_2) = \left(\left\{ \frac{|| : To | Ha \wedge To |}{To}, \; \frac{|| : La | So \wedge La |}{La} \right\}, \{\neg Ha \vee \neg So\} \right) \qquad (5)$$

It is instructive to verify that $\Phi_{JDL}(D_2, W_2)$ has a single contextual extension containing $To \wedge La$, while $\Phi_{CDL}(D_1, W_1)$ yields two distinct extensions, one containing Ul and another with Ur. This is due to the different consistency requirements used in each theory. While the C-justification of $\frac{|| : \neg Br \wedge Ur ||}{Ur}$ must not only be consistent with the

---

[6] This is no real restriction, but it simplifies matters.

[7] Observe that $Th_{W \cup con(\Delta_i) \cup jus_C(\Delta_i)}(jus_E(\Delta_i)) = Th_{E_{i+1} \cup jus_C(\Delta_i)}(jus_E(\Delta_i))$.

extension at hand but moreover with all justifications of other applying default rules, the E-justification of $\frac{\parallel:\, \text{To}\,\mid\, \text{Ha}\wedge\text{To}\mid}{\text{To}}$ requires consistency with the extension only. This is why both default rules of $\Phi_{\text{JDL}}(D_2, W_2)$ contribute to its single extension, whereas each rule of $\Phi_{\text{CDL}}(D_1, W_1)$ engenders a distinct extension.

In order to capture the family of default logics described in Definition 3, we may restrict ourselves to contextual default rules of the following form:

$$D^\star = \left\{ \frac{\mid \alpha \mid \,:\, \beta_C \mid \beta_E \mid}{\gamma} \right\} \tag{6}$$

As motivated in the introductory sections, our approach relies on the ability of forming default proofs in a *local* fashion: We call a contextual default theory (D, W) *semi-monotonic* if we have for any two subsets D' and D'' of D with $D'' \subseteq D' \subseteq D$ that if (E'', C'') is a contextual extension of (D'', W), then there is a contextual extension (E', C') of (D', W) such that $E'' \subseteq E'$ and $C'' \subseteq C'$. For example, theories (5) and (4) are semi-monotonic. Actually, justified and constrained default logic enjoy semi-monotonicity in full generality. Clearly, this carries over to the corresponding fragments of contextual default logic, so that our approach applies immediately to these default logics. Notably, this extends to the union of the respective default theories; thus allowing for treating some default rules according to justified default logic and others according to constrained default logic. As a consequence, this may handle mixed theories such as "$\Phi_{\text{CDL}}(D_1, W_1) \cup \Phi_{\text{JDL}}(D_2, W_2)$". For classical and rational default logic, on the other hand, we must restrict ourselves to semi-monotonic fragments. (Such fragments should be determinable by appropriate stratification techniques; a concrete adaptation of such techniques remains however future work.)

For furnishing an appropriate proof theory, we provide next a more proof-theoretic characterization of contextual extensions in the presence of semi-monotonicity:

Theorem 4. *Let (D, W) be a semi-monotonic contextual default theory such that $D \subseteq D^\star$ and let E and C be sets of formulas. Then, (E, C) is a contextual extension of (D, W) iff there is some maximal $D' \subseteq D$ that has an enumeration $\langle \delta_i \rangle_{i \in I}$ such that for $i \in I$, we have:*

$$\left\{ \begin{array}{l} E = Th(W \cup con(D')) \\ C = Th_{E \cup jus_C(D')}(jus_E(D')) \end{array} \right\} \tag{7}$$

$$W \cup con(\{\delta_0, \ldots, \delta_{i-1}\}) \vdash pre_E(\delta_i) \tag{8}$$

$$\left\{ \begin{array}{r} W \cup con(\{\delta_0, \ldots, \delta_i\}) \cup jus_C(\{\delta_0, \ldots, \delta_i\}) \nvdash \neg jus_E(\delta_k) \\ \text{for } k \in \{0, \ldots, i\} \end{array} \right\} \tag{9}$$

It is instructive to verify that this specification makes E and C coincide when dealing with normal default theories, no matter which translation is used for turning them into a contextual theory. Also, Condition (9) reduces to $W \cup con(\{\delta_0, \ldots, \delta_{i-1}\}) \nvdash \neg con(\delta_i)$.

As another example, consider the instantiation of this definition for constrained default logic: While Condition (8) as well as the specification of E in (7) remain the same, the definition of C reduces to $C = Th(E \cup jus_C(D'))$ thus dealing with deductively closed sets. Another simplification is observed when regarding Condition (9) due to the absence of E-justifications: [8]

$$W \cup con(\{\delta_0, \ldots, \delta_{i-1}\}) \cup jus_C(\{\delta_0, \ldots, \delta_{i-1}\}) \nvdash \neg con(\delta_i) \vee \neg jus_C(\delta_i)$$

---

[8] To be precise, all E-justifications are tautological rather than non-existent.

Now, a default proof for a formula φ from a contextual default theory (D, W) is a finite sequence of contextual default rules $\langle \delta_i \rangle_{i \in I}$ with $\delta_i \in D$ for all $i \in I$ such that $W \cup \{con(\delta_i) \mid i \in I\} \vdash \varphi$ and Condition (8) and (9) are satisfied for all $i \in I$. By semi-monotonicity and compactness, φ is then in some extension of (D, W) iff there is a default proof for φ from (D, W). Clearly, the derivation of φ from W and $\langle \delta_i \rangle_{i \in I}$ and Condition (8), that is groundedness of $\langle \delta_i \rangle_{i \in I}$, are treated as with standard normal default theories. So that we can concentrate on the implementation of Condition (9).

3   Model-based consistency checking

In the sequel, we formalize the model-based approach sketched in the introductory section. For normal default theories, it is actually sufficient to furnish a single model of the premises in W satisfying all default conclusions in a proof at hand. In the presence of putatively contradictory E-justifications, however, we need more complex model structures for guaranteeing compatibility. In fact, we need now several models of W, all of which must entail the consequents and the C-justifications of the default rules involved in the current derivation, while there must be at least one model of each E-justification among them. Observe that the models covering E-justifications are not necessarily distinct; distinctness is only necessary in the presence of contradictory E-justifications.

Let us make this precise in the sequel. For a formula ϕ and a set of models M, we write $M \models \phi$ if $m \models \phi$ for all $m \in M$; and $M \not\models \phi$ if $m \models \neg\phi$ for some $m \in M$. For a set of formulas S, we define its set of models as $Mod(S)$. First, we account for the semantic counterpart of the notion of pointwise closure (cf. Definition 1): For sets of formulas S and T, we define[9]

$$Mod_S(T) = \begin{cases} \bigcup_{\phi \in T} Mod(S \cup \{\phi\}) & \text{if } T \neq \emptyset \\ Mod(S) & \text{otherwise} \end{cases}$$

For a set of formulas W and a sequence of contextual default rules $\langle \delta_i \rangle_{i \in I}$ of form (6), we are then interested in the set of models $Mod_S(T)$ obtained by taking

$$S = W \cup con(\{\delta_i \mid i \in I\}) \cup jus_C(\{\delta_i \mid i \in I\}) \quad \text{and} \quad T = jus_E(\{\delta_i \mid i \in I\}).$$

For readability, we abbreviate this set of models by $M_W(I)$; in analogy, we denote its subset $\{m \in M_W(I) \mid m \models jus_E(\delta_i)\}$ by $M_W^i(I)$ for $i \in I$. In fact, for non-empty I, $M_W(I)$ equals $\bigcup_{i \in I} M_W^i(I)$, each of which covers a different E-justification $jus_E(\delta_i)$ in $jus_E(\{\delta_i \mid i \in I\})$.

Consider the semantic counterpart of the pointwisely closed set given in (3):

$$Mod_{\{\neg Ha \vee \neg So, To, La\}}(\{Ha, So\}) = Mod(\{Ha, \neg So, To, La\}) \cup Mod(\{\neg Ha, So, To, La\})$$

The latter model sets actually comply with $M_W^1(\{1, 2\})$ and $M_W^2(\{1, 2\})$, where $\{1, 2\}$ is the index set corresponding to the default rules in $\Phi_{DL}(D_2, W_2)$. Such sets of models furnish solely the domain from which we select individual models witnessing the compatible application of default rules.

In order to characterize compatible default proofs $\langle \delta_i \rangle_{i \in I}$ from a set of premises W, we consider non-empty subsets M of $M_W(I)$ such that $M \cap M_W^i(I) \neq \emptyset$ for all $i \in I$; and we use $\sqsubseteq_I$ to indicate by writing $M \sqsubseteq_I M_W(I)$ that this structural set inclusion property holds. Observe that for non-empty I the existence of such a set M implies that

---

[9] For finite T, this is actually equivalent to $Mod(S \cup \{\vee_{\varphi \in T} \varphi\})$.

all underlying sets $M_W^i(I)$ are non-empty. This guarantees that M contains at least one model for each E-justification $jus_E(\delta_i)$. In case I is empty, we also deal with a non-empty subset M of $M_W(\emptyset) = Mod(W)$; we write $M \sqsubseteq_\emptyset M_W(\emptyset)$. The non-emptiness of M is guaranteed, since W is assumed to be consistent.

For contextual default rule $\delta_i = \frac{|\alpha| : \beta_C | \beta_E |}{\gamma}$ and some index set $I = K \cup \{i\}$, Function ∇ addresses Condition (9) in Theorem 4 by mapping triples of form $\langle M, W, \langle \delta_k \rangle_{k \in K} \rangle$ with $M \sqsubseteq_K M_W(K)$ onto triples of the same format if Condition (9) is true; it yields $\bot$ if Condition (9) is false: $\nabla(\delta_i, \langle M, W, \langle \delta_k \rangle_{k \in K} \rangle) =$

$$
= \begin{cases}
\langle M, W, \langle \delta_i \rangle_{i \in I} \rangle & \text{if } M \models \gamma \wedge \beta_C \text{ and } m \models \beta_E \text{ for some } m \in M \\
\langle M', W, \langle \delta_i \rangle_{i \in I} \rangle & \text{if } M \not\models \gamma \wedge \beta_C \text{ or } m \not\models \beta_E \text{ for all } m \in M \\
& \quad \text{and for } M' \sqsubseteq_K M_W(K), \\
& \quad \quad M' \models \gamma \wedge \beta_C \text{ and } m' \models \beta_E \text{ for some } m' \in M' \\
\bot & \quad \text{if there is no } M'' \sqsubseteq_K M_W(K), \\
& \quad \quad M'' \models \gamma \wedge \beta_C \text{ and } m'' \models \beta_E \text{ for some } m'' \in M''
\end{cases}
$$

Note that $M' \sqsubseteq_K M_W(K)$ implies $M' \neq \emptyset$ even though $K = \emptyset$ due to the consistency of W. As anticipated in the discussion of Theorem 4, we may restrict our attention to singleton sets M' in the absence of E-justifications. M' must contain multiple models when dealing with inconsistent E-justifications. In the worst case, that is when dealing with n pairwisely inconsistent E-justifications, M' includes at most n distinct models.

The following result shows that this approach is in accord with the conception of consistency expressed in Definition 4.

Theorem 5. *Let W be a set of formulas and $\langle \delta_i \rangle_{i \in I}$ a sequence of contextual default rules such that $\delta_i \in D^\star$ for all $i \in I$. Then, we have for all $i \in I$ and $K = \{0, \ldots, i-1\}$ and $L = \{0, \ldots, i\}$ that if there is a set of models $M \sqsubseteq_K M_W(K)$, then there is either a non-empty set of models $M' \sqsubseteq_L M_W(L)$ such that*

$$\nabla(\delta_i, \langle M, W, \langle \delta_k \rangle_{k \in K} \rangle) = \langle M', W, \langle \delta_l \rangle_{l \in L} \rangle \text{ iff Condition (9) is true}$$
$$\text{or} \quad \quad \nabla(\delta_i, \langle M, W, \langle \delta_k \rangle_{k \in K} \rangle) = \bot \text{ iff Condition (9) is false.}$$

Observe that M and M' need not be distinct; thus covering the first two cases of ∇.

Function ∇ gives a general description of our approach while making precise the intuition given above. We refine this specification in the sequel for the propositional case. As before, we presuppose a proof procedure caring about deduction and groundedness, as given in (7) and (8), along with a mechanism for finding models of formulas in conjunctive normal form (CNF). The usage of formulas in CNF as opposed to arbitrary ones is motivated by the need for continuous modifications (like additions and subsequent reductions) to the formulas handed over to the consistency check. These operations can be implemented more effectively for formulas in CNF. For illustration, we display CNF formulas in matrix-notation, as done in the connection method [2]. That is, a *matrix* is simply a set of sets of literals; it is often displayed two-dimensionally, as in Figure 1 and 2. Each set (or column) in a matrix represents a *clause* of a CNF formula. A *path* through a matrix is a set of literals, one from each clause. We are actually interested in paths that do not contain complementary literals, since they constitute partial models of the underlying formula. As opposed to complete propositional models, such partial models fix only the truth-values of certain literals; hence, they are refineable along their degrees of freedom.

For implementation, we must provide efficient means for supporting model searching. For this purpose, we use *extended model matrices* of form $\langle M, \{M_i\}_{i \in I} \rangle$, where M is a (compact) matrix representation of $W \cup con(\{\delta_i \mid i \in I\}) \cup jus_C(\{\delta_i \mid i \in I\})$ and the M_i are additional (compact) matrices representing $jus_E(\delta_i)$, respectively, for some default proof fragment $\langle \delta_i \rangle_{i \in I}$ from (D, W). We start with an extended model matrix of form $\langle C_W, \emptyset \rangle$ comprising the clausal form C_W of W and a singular set of models $M = \{m\}$ for some $m \models W$. Coexisting model sets and extended model matrices are invariantly coupled via satisfiability. That is, for a model set M and an extended model matrix $\langle M, \{M_i\}_{i \in I} \rangle$, we have $\forall i \in I. \exists m \in M. m \models M \cup M_i$. (This is trivially true for tautological E-justifications yielding $M_i = \emptyset$.) It is important to observe that a model like m may cover multiple matrices of form M_i whenever they are jointly consistent with M. That is, the number of involved E-justifications, $|I|$, is only an upper bound for the number of models in M.

As detailed in [4] for normal default theories, an important reduction of the search space for models is obtained (i) by appeal to continued model-preserving reductions of the model matrices and (ii) by information supported by the underlying theorem prover by means of lemmas. For (i), we consider UNIT-reductions and subsumptions. In the former case, we replace a clause $\{L_1, \ldots, L_n\}$ by $\{L_1, \ldots, L_{i-1}, L_{i+1}, \ldots, L_n\}$ in the presence of some unit-clause $\{\neg L_i\}$, while in the latter, we delete clause $\{L_1, \ldots, L_n\}$ in the presence of one of its proper subsets (cf. [2]). Actually, these techniques apply also in the general case, although we must pay some more attention to their scope of applicability. This is due to the fact that we share M with all matrices of form M_i. In fact, a separate treatment of all instances of form $M \cup M_i$ would allow for applying all techniques in an unrestricted way, yet at the cost of more redundancy. As a consequence, we allow for applying freely UNIT-reductions and subsumptions on M, while modifications resulting from the same reductions on $M \cup M_i$ are restricted to M_i. For (ii), we restrict lemma usage to those depending on default rules involved in the current default derivation only. This is reasonable and actually highly efficient since these lemmas are trivially compatible with the derivation at hand. They are addable to M which allows for reductions in the entire extended model matrix, including matrices like M_i. See [4] for details.

Let us illustrate this by verifying compatibility of default proof

$$\left\langle \frac{\|: \text{To} \mid \text{Ha} \wedge \text{To} \mid}{\text{To}}, \frac{\|: \text{La} \mid \text{So} \wedge \text{La} \mid}{\text{La}} \right\rangle$$

($\langle \delta_1, \delta_2 \rangle$ for short) for $\text{To} \wedge \text{La}$ from $\Phi_{\text{JDL}}(D_2, W_2)$. We start by putting an arbitrary model of C_{W_2} into our model set, M_0. The extended model matrix $\langle C_{W_2}, \emptyset \rangle$ is given in the first line of Figure 1. Applying one of the above rules after the other, yields:

$$\nabla(\delta_1, \langle M_0, W_2, \langle \rangle \rangle) = M_1 \qquad \nabla(\delta_2, \langle M_1, W_2, \langle \delta_1 \rangle \rangle) = M_2$$

where model sets M_0, M_1 and M_2 are given in Figure 1. M_1 is obtained from M_0 simply by extending the only model; this model ensures the compatible application of δ_1. M_2 necessitates the generation of another model satisfying the E-justification of δ_2.

Let us take a closer look at the underlying extended model matrices. Applying δ_1 makes us add its C-justification To_{δ_1} to C_{W_2}, resulting in M', whereas its E-justification $\text{Ha}_{\delta_1} \wedge \text{To}_{\delta_1}$ engenders the creation of M'_1. Observe that M' itself is not

$$\begin{bmatrix} \neg\text{Ha} \\ \neg\text{So} \end{bmatrix} \quad \emptyset$$

$\langle C_{W_2}, \emptyset \rangle$ $\qquad\qquad\qquad\qquad\qquad M_0 = \{ \{\neg\text{So}\} \}$

$$\begin{bmatrix} \neg\text{Ha} & \text{To}_{\delta_1} \\ \neg\text{So} & \end{bmatrix}\begin{bmatrix} \text{Ha}_{\delta_1} & \text{To}_{\delta_1} \end{bmatrix} \quad\rightsquigarrow\quad \begin{bmatrix} \neg\text{Ha} & \text{To}_{\delta_1} \\ \neg\text{So} & \end{bmatrix}\begin{bmatrix} \text{Ha}_{\delta_1} & \end{bmatrix}$$

$\langle M', \{M_1'\} \rangle$ $\qquad\qquad\qquad\qquad M_1 = \{ \{\neg\text{So}, \text{To}_{\delta_1}, \text{Ha}_{\delta_1}\} \}$

$$\begin{bmatrix} \neg\text{Ha} & \text{To}_{\delta_1} & \text{La}_{\delta_2} \\ \neg\text{So} & & \end{bmatrix}\begin{bmatrix} \text{Ha}_{\delta_1} \\ \text{So}_{\delta_2} & \text{La}_{\delta_2} \end{bmatrix} \quad\rightsquigarrow\quad \begin{bmatrix} \neg\text{Ha} & \text{To}_{\delta_1} & \text{La}_{\delta_2} \\ \neg\text{So} & & \end{bmatrix}\begin{bmatrix} \text{Ha}_{\delta_1} \\ \text{So}_{\delta_2} & \end{bmatrix}$$

$\langle M'', \{M_1'', M_2''\} \rangle$ $\qquad\qquad M_2 = \left\{ \begin{matrix} \{\neg\text{So}, \text{To}_{\delta_1}, \text{La}_{\delta_2}, \text{Ha}_{\delta_1}\} \\ \{\neg\text{Ha}, \text{To}_{\delta_1}, \text{La}_{\delta_2}, \text{So}_{\delta_2}\} \end{matrix} \right\}$

Fig. 1. Governing compatibility while deriving To $\wedge$ La from $\Phi_{\text{JDL}}(D_2, W_2)$.

reducible. However, we may reduce $M' \cup M_1'$ by subsumption. But even though there are two alternatives for deletion, such a reduction must only affect clauses in M_1'. This is why $\{\text{To}_{\delta_1}\}$ is deleted in M_1' and not in M'. The same type of reduction is applied in the following step. Actually, when applying δ_2, we are forced to generate an alternative model since the E-justifications of δ_1 and δ_2 are contradictory. This does however not prevent their joint application, as explained above. Finally, M_2 contains a model for $M'' \cup M_1''$ and another for $M'' \cup M_2''$.

For a complement, let us see why

$$\left\langle \frac{\|: \neg\text{Bl}\wedge\text{Ul}\|}{\text{Ul}}, \frac{\|: \neg\text{Br}\wedge\text{Ur}\|}{\text{Ur}} \right\rangle$$

($\langle \delta_1', \delta_2' \rangle$ for short) is no compatible default proof for Ul $\wedge$ Ur from $\Phi_{\text{CDL}}(D_1, W_1)$. The proceeding is illustrated by Figure 2. First of all, we observe that this example

$$\begin{bmatrix} \text{Bl} \\ \text{Br} \end{bmatrix} \quad \emptyset$$

$\langle C_{W_1}, \emptyset \rangle$ $\qquad\qquad\qquad\qquad\qquad M_0 = \{ \{\text{Br}\} \}$

$$\begin{bmatrix} \text{Bl} & \neg\text{Bl}_{\delta_1'} & \text{Ul}_{\delta_1'} \\ \text{Br} & & \end{bmatrix} \quad \emptyset \quad\rightsquigarrow\quad \begin{bmatrix} & \neg\text{Bl}_{\delta_1'} & \text{Ul}_{\delta_1'} \\ \text{Br} & & \end{bmatrix} \quad \emptyset$$

$\langle M', \emptyset \rangle$ $\qquad\qquad\qquad\qquad M_1 = \{ \{\text{Br}, \text{Ul}_{\delta_1'}, \neg\text{Bl}_{\delta_1'}\} \}$

$$\begin{bmatrix} \text{Br} & \neg\text{Bl}_{\delta_1'} & \text{Ul}_{\delta_1'} & \neg\text{Br}_{\delta_2'} & \text{Ur}_{\delta_2'} \end{bmatrix} \quad \emptyset \quad\rightsquigarrow\quad \begin{bmatrix} \emptyset & \neg\text{Bl}_{\delta_1'} & \text{Ul}_{\delta_1'} & \neg\text{Br}_{\delta_2'} & \text{Ur}_{\delta_2'} \end{bmatrix} \quad \emptyset$$

$\langle M'', \emptyset \rangle$ $\qquad\qquad\qquad\qquad M_2 = \emptyset$

Fig. 2. Denial of compatibility while deriving Ul $\wedge$ Ur from $\Phi_{\text{CDL}}(D_1, W_1)$.

does not comprise any (non-tautological) E-justifications; hence there are no secondary matrices in the extended model matrix. Applying δ_1' makes us add its C-justification $\neg\text{Bl}_{\delta_1'} \wedge \text{Ul}_{\delta_1'}$ to C_{W_1}, resulting in M', from which we obtain a singular model set $M_1 = \{ \{\text{Br}, \text{Ul}_{\delta_1'}, \neg\text{Bl}_{\delta_1'}\} \}$. M' is then reduced by UNIT-reduction. Next, our inference engine makes us check compatibility for δ_2'. The model in M_1 does not satisfy the

C-justification of δ_2', that is, $\{\mathsf{Br}, \mathsf{UI}_{\delta_1'}, \neg\mathsf{BI}_{\delta_1'}\} \not\models \neg\mathsf{Br}_{\delta_2'} \wedge \mathsf{Ur}_{\delta_2'}$. Thus, we look for a new model testifying joint compatibility of δ_1' and δ_2'. For this purpose, we extend the last model matrix by δ_2''s C-justification, resulting in $\boldsymbol{M''}$. Applying immediate reductions yields a matrix with an empty clause, which indicates inconsistency. In this case, we were thus able to detect inconsistency without performing an actual consistency check. In terms of function ∇, we have

$$\nabla(\delta_1', \langle M_0, W_1, \langle\rangle\rangle) = M_1 \qquad \nabla(\delta_2', \langle M_1, W_1, \langle\delta_1'\rangle\rangle) = \perp$$

where M_0 and M_1 are given in Figure 2.

4 Conclusion

We have presented a uniform framework for implementing query-answering in diverse default logics. We addressed this by proposing a model-based approach to consistency checking that encompasses the variety of consistency checks found in existing default logics. Our approach is centered around the concept of local proof procedures that allow for verifying the validity of each inference step when it is performed. The resulting system is unique in offering simultaneously the expressiveness of multiple default logics. An experimental analysis with test series is given in [13].

References

1. P. Besnard & T. Schaub. An approach to context-based default reasoning. *Fundamenta Informaticae*, 23(2-4):175-223, 1995.
2. W. Bibel. *Automated Theorem Proving*. Vieweg, 1987.
3. G. Brewka. Cumulative default logic: In defense of nonmonotonic inference rules. *Artificial Intelligence*, 50(2):183-205, 1991.
4. S. Brüning & T. Schaub. A model-based approach to consistency-checking. In Z. Ras & M. Michalewicz, *Int'l Symp. on Methodologies for Intell. Systems*, 315-324. Springer, 1996.
5. J. Delgrande, T. Schaub & W. Jackson. Alternative approaches to default logic. *Artificial Intelligence*, 70(1-2):167-237, 1994.
6. L. Giordano & A. Martinelli. On cumulative default logics. *Artificial Intelligence*, 66(1):161-179, 1994.
7. T. Linke & T. Schaub. Towards a classification of default logics. *Journal of Applied Non-Classical Logics*, 1997. To appear.
8. W. Łukaszewicz. Considerations on default logic – an alternative approach. *Computational Intelligence*, 4:1-16, 1988.
9. A. Mikitiuk & M. Truszczyński. Rational default logic and disjunctive logic programming. In A. Nerode & L. Pereira, *Int'l Workshop on logic Programming and Non-monotonic Reasoning.*, 283-299. MIT Press, 1993.
10. D. Poole. What the lottery paradox tells us about default reasoning. In R. Brachman et al., *Int'l Conf. on the Principles of Knowledge Representation and Reasoning*, 333-340, 1989. Morgan Kaufmann.
11. R. Reiter. A logic for default reasoning. *Artificial Intelligence*, 13(1-2):81-132, 1980.
12. T. Schaub & S. Brüning. Prolog technology for default reasoning. In W. Wahlster, *Europ. Conf. on Artificial Intelligence*, 105-109. Wiley, 1996.
13. T. Schaub & P. Nicolas. The XRay system, its implementation and evaluation. In J. Dix & U. Furbach, *Int'l Conf. on Logic Programming and Non-Monotonic Reasoning*, Springer, 1997. To appear.
14. C. Schwind. A tableaux-based theorem prover for a decidable subset of default logic. In M. Stickel, *Conf. on Automated Deduction*. Springer, 1990.

Automating Spoken Dialogue Systems

Mona Singh,[1,2*] James Barnett,[2] Munindar P. Singh[1**]

[1] Department of Computer Science
North Carolina State University
Raleigh, NC 27695-8206, USA

[2] Dragon Systems Inc.
320 Nevada Street
Newton, MA 02160, USA

mona_singh@ncsu.edu

Abstract. Spoken dialogue interfaces apply in a number of applications. Engaging in meaningful conversation presupposes the ability to recognize and generate different conversational moves, and to adaptively carry on a dialogue. Although the portability of dialogue interfaces is highly desirable, few current approaches address it seriously.

We describe a portable toolkit for constructing spoken dialogue interfaces. We present the representations and techniques used to customize an interface to a particular domain and application. Our approach relies on shallow knowledge of the domain, and interprets a rule-based model of the dialogue.

1 Introduction

Spoken dialogue interfaces have been widely recognized as being highly desirable for a number of applications [1, 6]. There are two important dimensions of a user interface: user-friendliness and developer-friendliness. The former is improved through *mixed-initiative* dialogue, and the latter through *portability*. Mixed-initiative dialogue means that the system dynamically shares control of the dialogue with the user. Portability refers to ease of applying the interface to a new domain or application (portability across languages has to do with lower-level aspects, and we ignore it here).

Current systems tend to be limited along both of the above dimensions. They are frequently system-centric in requiring rigid control of the dialogue, and frequently tied to a specific application [7], such as air travel information or train schedules [1]. Although components of these systems might be portable, there is clear need for *toolkits* to facilitate system construction [6].

* Mona Singh and James Barnett are supported by the National Institute of Standards and Technology under grant NIST-70NANB5H1181.
** Munindar Singh is supported by the NCSU College of Engineering, the National Science Foundation under grants IRI-9529179 and IRI-9624425, and IBM corporation.

Before we come to the technical details, we outline our major design criteria. Our work is being performed in the research division of a speech recognition products vendor. The applicability of our research to products is an essential factor. Our goal is to market a commercial toolkit that can be used by programmers to build applications of interest to end-users (some of these applications are built in-house). These programmers would customize the toolkit as appropriate by acquiring knowledge, and developing application programs. Importantly, as a commercial reality, the programmers using the product are not expected to be specialists in AI or linguistics (Fraser & Dalsgaard make a similar observation [6]). Thus, the complex models used in classical knowledge-based systems are not feasible. This echoes a sentiment from recent work in information retrieval and text extraction [4]. Consequently, we have been forced to make particular design trade-offs in attempting to maximize user-friendliness (e.g., as reflected in mixed-initiative dialogue) without compromising developer-friendliness (e.g., as reflected in portability). We believe, however, that our considerations are not far different from toolkit approaches in general.

The design of a portable toolkit poses special challenges. We must ensure that the toolkit is generic, and can be readily customized to a wide variety of applications. On the other hand, full automation is not required—wizards that suggest good defaults to developers can help increase their productivity. Lastly, there is an incentive to use the most robust, rather than the fanciest, techniques in the toolkit.

This paper focuses on the adaptive management of conversational moves. Our contribution is in an approach that facilitates the developer's task

- without rigid control of the user's actions, and
- using a not-very-complex knowledge representation.

Section 2 describes our system architecture, and the models necessary to customize it. Section 3 presents the generic parts of our toolkit. It describes the conversational moves and dialogue controller, as well as an algorithm for proposing utterances for the conversational moves. Section 4 presents a sample dialogue. Section 5 presents the key features of our toolkit.

2 Architecture and Key Models

Our system is customized to a specific application and domain through the following main models. For concreteness, we consider the application of giving healthcare advice.

2.1 Domain Model

Since a dialogue system must support a conversation between a human and an information system, it is important to model the structure of the latter. The Domain Model (DM) does just that. It provides a static *conceptual* model of the domain, which includes the key concepts and their interrelationships.

A conceptual model of the data is easy to understand, and is a key step in developing an information system [3].

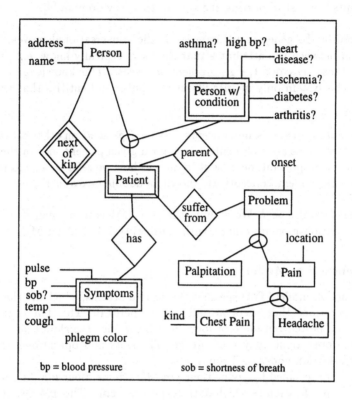

Fig. 1. Simplified Domain Model for Healthcare

The DM is expressed using a variant of the Entity-Relationship (ER) approach [3]. The ER approach diagrammatically captures a high-level view of the data, independent of its physical storage. Figure 1, which is loosely based on a very small part of a healthcare advisory model [2, pp. 70–232], illustrates the key ideas. The basic concepts of ER diagrams are *entities, attributes,* and *relationships*. An entity describes a class of real or abstract objects that are worth talking about—e.g., *patient*. An attribute gives some simple, direct properties of entities—e.g., *name*. A relationship defines a specific relation among entities— e.g., *suffer from*. We include information on the cardinality of a relationship, and whether participation in it is required or optional.

Entities can be subclasses of other entities; they inherit the attributes and relationships of their superclasses. Importantly, we attach *action* descriptions to the ER model. The actions describe what operations a user may carry out in the given application—e.g., *assess risk*.

Thus, the DM gives the main concepts of interest to an application, but does not supply any of the background common-sense knowledge. Indeed, ER models are small—typically, proportional to the number of tables or columns in a relational database, for instance. Thus, we only require shallow knowledge, which limits the cost of porting the system to a new domain [4].

Identifiability. To generate utterances for the conversational moves, we must distinguish between the attributes that the users typically know, e.g., *temperature*, and those they don't, e.g., *problem or disease*. This knowledge is given in the DM. The system only queries about attributes and entities that are known to the user.

Independent existence. Some concepts may be *dependent* on other concepts. For example, *symptoms* are well-defined only for a given patient, not in themselves. Dependence is important, because it influences how we refer to a concept during a dialogue. Dependent concepts are shown as double boxes in Figure 1.

Relational logical model. We assume that the DM is in a cleaned up form in which all relationships are binary, with cardinality 1-1, 1-M, or M-1.

2.2 Transaction Model

The transaction model (TM) specifies the desired actions, which are the domain-specific operations that users are allowed to perform. The TM is essentially specified as a nested template or form, which specifies the slots that users may fill and the operations they may invoke. The slots and operations are jointly termed transaction nodes or Tnodes.

Actions are specified by giving their *procedure name*, their *input* slots, *outputs* slots, and a specification of which of the inputs are *vital*. The TM also includes a specification of the likelihood of (a) different slots being filled, and (b) different operations being invoked. These likelihoods are used in disambiguating the users' utterances when necessary. The TM representation maximizes the flexibility with which the slots are filled, which is crucial in enabling mixed-initiative dialogue.

In order to carry out an effective dialogue, it is also important to model the dynamic properties of the different actions. For this reason, we incorporate the abstractions of commit, rollback, and checkpoint as conversational moves in the toolkit. The TM specifies where and how to incorporate them, based on the application and the view being presented to the users.

2.3 Dialogue Model

The dialogue model describes the desired properties of the conversation with the user. These are given in terms of user and system rule-sets that specify the *dialogue control strategy*, which encodes when and how the different conversational moves are exercised in the dialogue. Confusable slots may be set up for paraphrasing instead of verification, since paraphrasing is likelier to resolve ambiguity more reliably [11]. Factors such as the level of confidence in the speech input and the anticipated confusability of the subslots can influence the selection of moves [9].

The dialogue model carries the functionality to determine the meanings of the users utterances, and to deal appropriately with the user. Some of this functionality is simply derived from the specifications provided by the developer in terms of the DM, TM, and the grammars for the various slots. However, a significant component of the dialogue is conducted based on more flexible specifications of dialogue control strategies, and of the allowed conversational moves. These specifications are given as rule-sets.

3 Generic Components of the Toolkit

The above models are interpreted by the *dialogue controller*, which is the core of the toolkit. At run-time, the system constructs internal representations that involve dialogue nodes (Dnodes) linked to appropriate Tnodes—operations and slots. The Dnodes are automatically generated as needed for each Tnode in the TM. The system maintains a history of the ongoing conversation in terms of the Dnodes that are instantiated. The history is used to determine the appropriate rules to apply at a given stage in the conversation.

3.1 Conversational Moves

A variety of conversational moves and coherence relations have been proposed to explain the structure of discourse [10, 12]. While useful, these moves are not sufficient for transaction-oriented applications, especially with spoken interfaces [8]. While researchers acknowledge this fact, traditional moves may not even cover simple database access applications.

The moves should be powerful enough to represent the dynamic properties of the underlying actions. For example, making an appointment requires that the user commit to the agreed upon time; if the user is a no show, she may be liable for charges. Similarly, the interface should be able to guarantee that the appointment is in fact made. This limits the flexibility in other respects. For example, if a patient want to schedule two separate appointments in the same time-frame, she must be able to hold a spot without committing to it, or be able to cancel her commitment (so as to reschedule). Similarly, the user might want to checkpoint (or bookmark) a state of the dialogue to be able to return to it in case of error or confusion. The toolkit provides the above abstractions as conversational moves; the dialogue model specifies where and how to incorporate them, based on restrictions imposed by the TM.

We propose seven classes of conversational moves. For reasons of space, we do not describe all the moves in detail, but give examples of each class below.

Transactional. These moves deal with the backend system, and are inherently asymmetric between the user and system. For example, a user's request for information is treated as invoking an operation—a query. Transactional moves include *request for information, information, offer to perform an operation, invoke an operation, undo an operation,* and *further development.*

Authorizational and Commissive. Many applications require the user to explicitly authorize the system to take some action on his behalf. This authorization might involve the user committing some transactions, with social or economic effects beyond the dialogue. Authorizational moves include *offer to commit* and *commit.*

Error Detection and Correction. These are moves through which the system and the user find and remove miscommunications and misunderstandings. Error detection and correction moves include *request for verification, paraphrasing, request for confirmation, verification, confirmation, correction,* and *restatement.* In principle, these could all be performed by the system or the user. Some of these, e.g., *paraphrasing,* if attempted by a user, might be difficult for the system to understand.

Interactional. These moves enable the system and user to maintain their conversation history. Interactional moves include *request for location, location, topicalization, request for options, options, return to prior context space, offer to checkpoint, checkpoint, rollback, interruption,* and *silence.*

Presentational. These are moves through which the system gives information to the user. The realization of presentational moves depends on the media available for interaction. In general, we assume that either the presentation can be of (a) some atomic entity, possibly large like a picture, or (b) some structured entity, such as a set of documents. Atomic entities can be viewed based on their physical components; structured entities can also be viewed based on their logical structure. A generic toolkit can only include a means to present the results serially (temporally or spatially), and a means to identify components. Presentational moves include *request a component, present logical component, request scrolling, present physical component, serialize, request attention,* and *grant attention.*

Assistance. These are moves through which the system helps the user in understanding the meaning of the different steps in the given dialogue. Assistance moves include *request for explanation, explanation,* and *feedback.*

Sessional. These are moves through which the user and system initiate, resume, and close their conversations. Sessional moves include *initiate, authenticate, request preferences, set preferences, close,* and *resume.*

3.2 Dialogue Controller

The dialogue controller is the heart of our system. This is the module that interprets the application-specific models, and orchestrates the conversation with the user in a way that respects those models.

To ensure mixed-initiative dialogue, the controller gives the user an opportunity to speak (and allows interruptions where possible). This is processed during the *user phase*. When the user relinquishes control of the dialogue, the *system phase* is initiated.

User phase. The user phase invokes the recognizer with a list of possible grammars for the nodes (slots or actions) in the TM. The recognizer produces a list of interpretations along with the matching grammar and (depending on the recognizer) the confidence in the match. The controller picks out the node yielding the best interpretation. The best interpretation is determined by a metric that prefers the best confidence and highest probability of occurrence—the latter is based on the probability of a particular node being the next node. From the selected slot, the controller applies the rules describing the user interactions (these are as encoded in the user-rules rule-set).

System phase. In this phase, the controller selects the best target action based on the current probabilities. Unlike in the user phase, no slot can be selected. Once the target action is determined, the controller checks if enough is known to execute it. Specifically, if the vital inputs for the action are not known (at a high enough confidence level), the controller attempts to obtain those values from the user. When the values are obtained, the system executes the appropriate procedure and presents the results. The execution can involve checkpointing and committing, which as explained in section 3.1, gives the user an opportunity to cause backend system actions in a controlled manner.

History matching. The apply-strategy module takes a node, a history, and a rule-set to determine what to do. The rule-set declaratively captures the intended behavior of the system. The rules are if-then rules with a pattern in the antecedent and an action in the consequent. We allow rules with antecedents that have a predicate-variable structure, and provide restricted constructs for the temporal aspects.

The rule-set is matched against the history to find the best (i.e., most specific) match. The action of this rule is executed on the given node. We allow actions for each of the conversational moves. The details of matching are beyond the scope of this paper, but we present a partial set of rules for verification, simplified and sanitized for ease of exposition.

If you are at a node and the confidence level is <0.5 and the node is verifiable, then verify the node. This rule can match any node whose name is bound to ?node. ?value is its likeliest value and ?conf is the corresponding confidence in the recognized speech. This is the most basic rule for verifiable Tnodes.

```
if (Tnode ?node (?value ?conf))
    AND (?conf < 0.5)
    AND (verifiable? ?node)
then VERIFY ?node
```

Thus rules that match the dialogue history are executed and determine what the next conversational move should be.

3.3 Move Generation

Based on the action desired by the user, the dialogue control strategy determines a specific system move. This invokes the move generation module to produce the appropriate utterance. The generation module uses knowledge encoded in the DM and TM. In practice, a developer would design—and fine tune—the DM and TM concurrently with testing the generation. We discuss certain aspects of the DM that are especially important to generation, following which we describe our strategic and tactical algorithms.

Handle. An effective dialogue requires that there be something that the system and the user can both refer to, and assume the other party will know. We call this default starting point the *handle* of a dialogue model. As a last resort, the handle can be taken to be the user himself—the meaning of *you*. We should then be able to ask who are you and what do you want. Good DMs would have an entity for the user, or for something equally salient, such as the *patient*. In selecting pronouns, it matters whether the conversant and the *patient* are the same person.

Relative significance. Knowledge of the relative significance of entities is used in choosing utterances appropriately. In principle, this knowledge is part of the dialogue model, although it is more practical to put in the DM, where the entities are defined. In general, identifiable entities are more significant, as are entities that exist independently (as explained in section 2.1).

3.3.1 Strategic Algorithm
The strategic algorithm attempts to generate utterances necessary to have the dialogue proceed in a manner that respects the TM, while allowing the user to share control with the system. This algorithm is essentially heuristic graph search. For informational prompts, we assume we know a relevant action. If all its vital inputs are known, we can proceed with it. Otherwise, we make a list of all missing inputs (even the nonvital ones). We find the entities these attributes occur in. These entities become the terminal points. We use a number of heuristics to identify likely starting points, and to search for a set of paths from the starting points to the terminal points. We lack the space to include these heuristics here.

Given a path, we proceed along it by querying for entities along it. To move from an entity to the next, we use the intervening relationship to generate the relationship prompts, e.g., *What is the patient's nurse's name?* When we arrive at a terminal entity, we query the user for the necessary attributes of that entity. For this purpose, we use the tactical algorithm.

3.3.2 Tactical Algorithm The new entity's identifier is first introduced by referring to it by a linguistic construction that relates both the known with the unknown entity. When the new entity has been identified, the tactical algorithm is invoked to query the remaining attributes.

Consider informational prompts. Such prompts need to be generated for all slots. In order to generate natural language utterances from the DM, we need heuristics to generate queries to obtain information about specific attributes and whole entities via their identifiers. Assuming our DM states that patients take medications, we can generate utterances such as *What medication is the patient taking?* The other moves are similar.

The tactical rules apply when the entity's identifier slot has been filled and the entity is the active referent. For entities that are not current, but were previously identified, we use the strategic algorithm to "revive" them in the dialogue.

Our algorithm essentially derives simple templates from the DM. It proposes a set of utterances that the developer can choose from. Further, we use heuristics to choose among the various templates during a dialogue. The idea is to use varying templates even for successive instances of the same conversational move. This helps reduce the monotony of the dialogue.

4 An Example Dialogue

We present a brief example of a dialogue. Here **U** refers to the user and **S** to the system. Comments are in the typewriter font.

`User calls in.`
U: *I have a problem and I was wondering if I could get some help.*
S: *What kind of a problem do you have?*
U: *Well, I have pain in the chest.*
S: *Do you have chest pain?* `verifying a vital slot.`
U: *Yes.*
S: *What kind of pain is it? Is it dull and persistent?* `Enumerating the possible values of the attribute kind. All possible values are prompted for till the first positive response.`
U: *No.*
S: *Is it stabbing?*
U: *No.*
S: *Is it crushing?*
U: *Yes, it's sort of crushing.*
S: *When did the crushing pain begin?* `Confirmation of the kind of pain`
U: *Yesterday afternoon.*

. . .

5 Conclusions

Our toolkit can conduct mixed-initiative dialogue and is portable with relatively little effort. Our approach has the following distinct features. It

- models the dialogue control strategy as rules instead of finite state automata, which is typical, e.g., [5].
- incorporates reasoning about the confidence levels of the recognizer, if such information is available.
- dynamically determines desired actions based on user input.
- incorporates the ability to commit and rollback.
- helps generate utterances for moves.

Well-designed information systems almost always have ER models associated with them already. Several commercial products exist to help construct good ER models for database applications. We are considering enhancements to a product to include actions, TMs, as well as features to display the possible utterances for different moves. We are presently experimenting with $ERWin^{TM}$, which is a leading product. However, our approach is independent of any such tool.

References

1. James Allen, Bradford Miller, Eric Ringger, and Teresa Sikorski. A robust system for natural spoken dialogue. In *Proc. 34th Meeting of the ACL*, 1996.
2. AMA. *The American Medical Association Family Medical Guide*. Random House, 1987.
3. Carlo Batini, Stefano Ceri, and Sham Navathe. *Conceptual Database Design: An Entity-Relationship Approach*. Benjamin Cummings, 1992.
4. Jim Cowie and Wendy Lehnert. Information extraction. *Communications of the ACM*, 39(1):80–91, January 1996.
5. N. Dählback and A. Jönsson. An empirically based computationally tractable dialogue model. In *Proc. 14th Conference of the Cognitive Science Society*, 1992.
6. Norman Fraser and Paul Dalsgaard. Spoken dialogue systems: A European perspective. In *Proc. International Symp. Spoken Dialogue*, 25–37, 1996.
7. Masato Ishizaki, Yasuharu Den, Syun Tutiya, Masafumi Tamota, and Shu Nakazato. Classifying dialogue tasks: Task oriented dialogue reconsidered. In *Proc. International Symp. Spoken Dialogue*, 37–40, 1996.
8. Arne Jönsson. Dialogue actions for natural language interfaces. In *Proc. 14th International Joint Conference on Artificial Intelligence*, 1405–1411, 1995.
9. C. Proctor and S. Young. Dialogue control in conversational speech interfaces. In M. Taylor, F. Neel, and D. Bouwhuis, editors, *The Structure of Multimodal Dialogue*, 385–399. Elsevier, 1991.
10. R. Reichman. *Getting Computers to Talk Like You and Me*. MIT Press, 1986.
11. S. Tanaka, S. Nakazato, K. Hoashi, and K. Shirai. Spoken dialogue interface in dual task situation. In *Proc. International Symp. Spoken Dialogue*, 153–156, 1996.
12. David Traum and Elizabeth Hinkelman. Conversation acts in task-oriented spoken dialogue. *Computational Intelligence*, 8:575–599, 1992.

Handwritten Digit Recognition by Local Principal Components Analysis

Władysław Skarbek[12] and Krystian Ignasiak[3]

[1] Polish-Japanese Institute of Computer Techniques
Koszykowa 86, 02-008 Warsaw, Poland, email: skarbek@ipipan.waw.pl
[2] Institute of Computer Science, Polish Academy of Sciences
[3] Electronics and Information Technology Department, Warsaw Univ. of Technology

Abstract. A neural algorithm for Local Principal Components Analysis (LPCA), i.e. Principal Component Analysis (PCA) performed in data clusters, is presented. It is applied to find local linear models for compact representation of experimental data. The local models are used for pattern recognition what gives a new recognition procedure called local subspace method. For handwritten numerals from NIST database, the technique reaches the recognition rate of about 99.4%.

1 Introduction

Principal Components Analysis (PCA) is a classical statistical modelling method which fits a linear model to experimental data (Hotelling [1]). In the technique an object of interest ω from a class Ω is represented by a data item $\mathbf{x}$ (so called feature vector or measurement vector) from the Euclidean space R^N while the population Ω of objects is modelled by a random, zero mean variable $\mathbf{X}$. A K-dimensional $(1 \leq K \leq N)$ linear model is specified by K normalized and mutually orthogonal vectors $\mathbf{w}_1, \ldots, \mathbf{w}_K$ from R^N which span K-dimensional subspace (KLT subspace) of the largest variance for $\mathbf{X}$. It is easy to show that K eigenvectors of the covariance matrix $\mathbf{R}_{xx} = E\left(\mathbf{X}\mathbf{X}^T\right)$, corresponding to K largest eigenvalues, define such a linear model. Further, we identify the linear model with the matrix $\mathbf{W} = [\mathbf{w}_1, \ldots, \mathbf{w}_K]$ with $\mathbf{w}_i$ placed into i-th column.

Despite the optimality of a linear model obtained by PCA, the error of such modelling depends on data distribution and it can be large. Especially, multimodal random variables are not suitable for linear modelling. Moreover, it is known that at the given N, K, and the covariance matrix $\mathbf{R}_{xx}$, the least PCA error is achieved by the Gaussian distribution.

In order to reduce the modelling error, nonlinear models must be considered. One of possible approaches is the approximation of nonlinear stochastic manifolds by linear subspaces defined locally in different areas of the data space.

In brief: Local Principal Components Analysis (LPCA) performs Principal Component Analysis in data clusters created in a vector data space. However, we should be aware that clustering process could be affected by PCA, and obviously PCA could depend on current clusters.

In section 2 a generic algorithm is described and next it is specialized to the neural algorithm for LPCA. The neural network approach is based on Oja/RLS learning rule recently introduced by Kung [9].

Essentially, PCA was used in pattern recognition for two goals:

- data compression: reducing the dimensionality from N of data vector $\mathbf{x}$ to K of data vector $\mathbf{y} = \mathbf{W}^T(\mathbf{x} - \bar{\mathbf{x}})$ in order to accelerate the classification task;
- subspace method (Watanabe [12], Oja [8]): defining a new proximity function for pattern matching which measures the distance from the principal subspace of the i-th class, i.e. replacing $(\mathbf{x} - \bar{\mathbf{x}}_i)^T(\mathbf{x} - \bar{\mathbf{x}}_i)$ by:

$$\rho_i(\mathbf{x}) \doteq (\mathbf{x} - \bar{\mathbf{x}}_i)^T \left(\mathbf{I} - \mathbf{W}_i \mathbf{W}_i^T \right) (\mathbf{x} - \bar{\mathbf{x}}_i) \tag{1}$$

where $\bar{\mathbf{x}}_i$ is the centroid of the i-th class and $\mathbf{W}_i$ is the linear model of the i-th class.

We should emphasize that in our approach we use local analysis LPCA which splits original classes into subclasses corresponding to determined data clusters. Therefore the index i in the above rule goes over all subclasses of all classes.

2 Algorithm for LPCA

Local Principal Components Analysis can be implemented as the result of mutual interaction of two processes: a clustering process and a PCA process. Processes based on neural network computations have several natural execution points where a cooperation between processes can be arranged:

- after updating of a single weight (*weight level*);
- after updating of a group of weights, for instance weights of the given neural element or weights of the given network layer (*group of weights level*);
- after reading a single data item and updating the whole neural network (*data item level*);
- after one epoch, i.e. after reading the whole training data set (*epoch level*);
- after all epochs (*task level*).

The above possible modes of cooperation are listed in decreasing order of computational complexity. Here, the clustering process is leading, i.e. the epoch is meant as the epoch in clustering.

Separation of clustering process from PCA process (task level) appears a wrong idea as in some clusters the data items still create highly nonlinear data manifolds. In order to get approximate linearity in clusters we have to increase significantly their number which in turn deteriorates representation efficiency. Task level was used in the algorithm proposed for nonlinear dimension reduction by Kambhatla and Leen in [3].

Though it is relatively easy to modify both, Kohonen's learning scheme [4] for data clustering and Oja's learning rule [7] for PCA to get an "on line algorithm" of data item level, the resulting computational scheme is not only of higher complexity, but also less stable than epoch level algorithms (see Joutsensalo and Miettinen [2]).

Therefore we advocate LPCA which performs PCA in clusters after each clustering epoch (epoch level communication).

Let N be the dimensionality of the data space, K - the dimensionality of local linear models, and L - the number of data clusters.

LPCA algorithm can be conveniently described using a collection U of L *computational units* $(L = |U|)$. The unit $i \in U$ in a discrete moment has a state $q_i = (Z_i, c_i, W_i, N_i)$ where:

- Z_i - current list of data items from training set $X \subset R^N$, assigned to the unit i;
- c_i - reference vector for Z_i (at the end of the epoch it is the centroid of the list Z_i);
- $W_i \in R^{N \times K}$ - $N \times K$ matrix (at the end of the epoch K principal vectors of i-th linear model are in its columns);
- $N_i \subset U$ - units which are currently recognized as *neighbors* of the unit i; we assume that $i \in N_i$.

In design of any clustering method we have to choose a *proximity measure* $\rho_i(x)$, $i \in U$, $x \in R^N$ which is used when x is to be joined to a cluster. We consider here two proximity measures based on Euclidean norm $\| \cdot \|$:

- *proximity to centroid* ρ_i^c:

$$\rho_i^c(x) \doteq \|x - c_i\|^2 \qquad (2)$$

- *proximity to subspace* ρ_i^s:

$$\rho_i^s(x) \doteq \|Q_i(x - c_i)\|^2 \qquad (3)$$

- where $Q_i = I - W_i W_i^T$.

As Q_i is symmetrical and idempotent $(Q_i^2 = Q_i)$ then we obtain an equivalent form for ρ_i^s :

$$\rho_i^s(x) \doteq (x - c_i)^T Q_i (x - c_i) \qquad (4)$$

Note that

$$\rho_i^c(x) = \rho_i^s(x) + \left\| W_i W_i^T (x - c_i) \right\|^2 \qquad (5)$$

Therefore if for some reasons W_i is the zero matrix then $\rho_i^s = \rho_i^c$.

Further, it will be convenient to assume that if either c_i or W_i is not defined then $\rho_i(x) = \infty$.

We should emphasize that the direct computation of ρ_i^s from the definition (3) requires $O(N^2)$ time what can be quite expensive for large N. Therefore we recommend the following simple computational scheme with $O(NK)$ of time complexity:

$$x' = x - c_i;$$
$$y = W^T x';$$
$$\text{return } x' - W_i y;$$

Generic LPCA Algorithm

Input: $N, K, L, X \subset R^N$
Output: $(\mathbf{c}_i, \mathbf{W}_i), i = 1, \ldots, L$ – linear local models
Method:
  for each $i \in U$:
    $Z_i := \emptyset$; Init $\mathbf{c}_i$, $\mathbf{W}_i$, and N_i;
  loop
    for each $\mathbf{x} \in X$:
      $i(\mathbf{x}) := \texttt{Argmin}(\mathbf{x}, L, \rho)$;
      for each $i \in U$:
        if $i \in N_{i(\mathbf{x})}$ **then** $Z_i := Z_i \cup \{\mathbf{x}\}$;
    for each $i \in U$:
      $\mathbf{c}_i := \overline{Z_i}$;
      $\mathbf{W}_i := \texttt{PCA}(N, K, Z_i)$;
    if $\texttt{Stop}(\mathbf{c}, \mathbf{W}, X)$ **then return**;
    for each $i \in U : Z_i := \emptyset$; Update N_i;

The bar denotes here the mean operator which actually calculates the centroid of elements in the given list. Note also that $\cup$ operation joins elements to a list, so duplicates of elements in Z_i are possible.

Observe that the above algorithm contains as the special case the PCA algorithm (for $L = 1$) and the LBG clustering algorithm (for $K = 0$).

A concrete LPCA algorithm is obtained from the above generic algorithm by the specification of the following meta variables: ρ, Init, Argmin, PCA, Stop, and Update. Several such specifications with references to the literature are described by the first author in [10]. Here only one possible way is presented.

Our algorithm is not "true SOM" type algorithm as neighborhoods are fixed to $N_i = \{i\}$. Reference vectors $\mathbf{c}_i$ are initially chosen randomly from the training data set X and the proximity measure $\rho = \rho^s$.

Initially the matrix $\mathbf{W}_i$ is set to zero, so for the first epoch the proximity measure $\rho_i = \rho_i^s = \rho_i^c$. In our LPCA results of Argmin depend not only on currently computed proximity values ρ_i^s but on the distance to the closest reference vector in the previous epoch, too. In this way we avoid possible cases when a data item $\mathbf{x}$ is close to a subspace centered on a quite distant reference vector. Let $i'(\mathbf{x})$ be the index of the closest reference vector computed in the previous epoch (say $= 1$ if no previous epoch). Then $i(\mathbf{x})$ in the current epoch is computed conditionally:

$$i(\mathbf{x}) \doteq \begin{cases} \arg\min_{i \in U} \rho_i^s(\mathbf{x}) & \text{if } \rho_{i(\mathbf{x})}^c(\mathbf{x}) < \alpha \rho_{i'(\mathbf{x})}^c(\mathbf{x}) \\ i'(\mathbf{x}) & \text{otherwise,} \end{cases}$$

where typically $\alpha = 1.5$.

For PCA in the given cluster Oja/RLS learning scheme [9] is used which gives a good approximation of the principal component:

$$y = \mathbf{w}^T \mathbf{x}$$
$$\Delta \eta = y^2 \tag{6}$$
$$\Delta \mathbf{w} = (y/\eta)(\mathbf{x} - y\mathbf{w})$$

The above updating scheme is applied for each $\mathbf{x} \in X$. Initially $\mathbf{w}$ is set to arbitrary non zero vector from data set X. The learning rate η is initially set to zero. We assume that X is mean shifted, i.e. $E(X) = 0$.

The next principal eigenvector is obtained recursively by applying the scheme (6) to a data set X' which is a deflated (by $\mathbf{w}$) version of the previous data set X:

$$X' \doteq \{\mathbf{x} - (\mathbf{x}^T \mathbf{w})\mathbf{w} \mid \mathbf{x} \in X\} .$$

3 LPCA Based Pattern Recognition

For the given data set X, LPCA finds local models for existing data clusters in X. Such a model is defined by two elements: the centroid of the cluster $\overline{\mathbf{x}}$ and the matrix of the principal components $\mathbf{W} \in R^{N \times K}$. In recognition we deal with classes of objects and separate data sets for each class. Therefore we have as many local models as the number of all data clusters found in all data sets. We can number all of them from one to say L, and identify the result of LPCA stage by L local models $(\overline{\mathbf{x}}_i, \mathbf{W}_i)$, $i = 1, \ldots, L$. As a result, the classifier is designed for L new classes Ω_i which are subclasses of original ones. In practice, original random variable representing measurements for the original class is multimodal while in subclasses found by LPCA it tends to be unimodal.

The recognition is based on identifying of a subclass j for which the minimum of the decision function $\rho_i(\mathbf{x})$, defined by the formula (3), is achieved:

$$j = \arg \min_i \rho_i^s(\mathbf{x}) \tag{7}$$

In a sense the above decision rule leads to a distance classifier. Distance based classifiers were strongly criticised. When as a distance the Euclidean norm is chosen, recognition results are poor indeed (cf. experimental results below). However, in LPCA approach the distance from the local subspace changes the situation dramatically. We get extremely high recognition rates with moderate increase of time by the factor of K, i.e. about one order of magnitude.

4 Experimental results

We have applied LPCA method for handwritten digits stored in NIST database (see sample input data in Fig. 1) which were collected from zip codes handwritten on envelopes. The database includes about 200 thousands of pictures for already segmented digits.

Looking on correlation of principal vectors computed for different symbols (Table 1), the subspace method seems a suitable tool for such data.

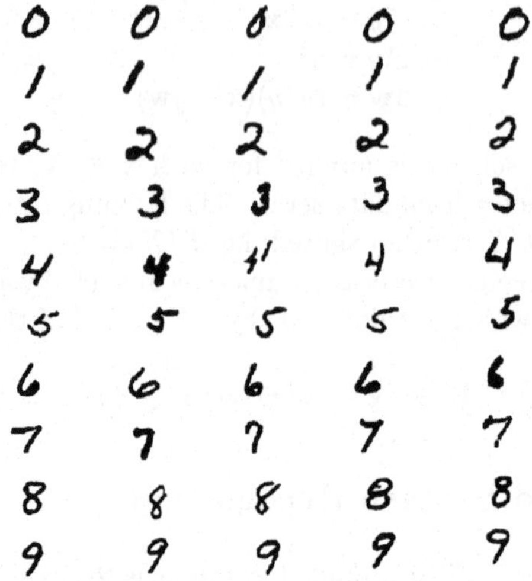

Fig. 1. Sample input data.

4.1 Vector data extraction from image data

Each picture in NIST database has the binary for with the fixed resolution of 128 rows and 128 columns. However, the digit itself occupies a small part of the picture. For convenience of file handling on PC for experiments about 20 thousands pictures were chosen randomly from the original database. Each experimental session of our recognition program begins from a random choice of about seven thousands pictures for local model learning and from the remaining set, the same number of random testing pictures. The results of recognition at such circumstances appear to be stable, i.e. they change a little from one experimental session to another.

	0	1	2	3	4	5	6	7	8	9
0	1.00	-0.41	0.47	0.42	0.27	-0.02	0.66	-0.36	0.36	0.32
1	-0.41	1.00	-0.20	-0.47	-0.37	0.21	-0.53	0.39	-0.50	-0.46
2	0.47	-0.20	1.00	0.69	-0.10	0.19	0.47	0.18	-0.01	-0.05
3	0.42	-0.47	0.69	1.00	0.07	0.17	0.50	-0.01	0.33	0.13
4	0.27	-0.37	-0.10	0.07	1.00	-0.42	0.21	-0.75	0.66	0.84
5	-0.02	0.21	0.19	0.17	-0.42	1.00	0.02	0.40	-0.53	-0.45
6	0.66	-0.53	0.47	0.50	0.21	0.02	1.00	-0.25	0.23	0.19
7	-0.36	0.39	0.18	-0.01	-0.75	0.40	-0.25	1.00	-0.58	-0.87
8	0.36	-0.50	-0.01	0.33	0.66	-0.53	0.23	-0.58	1.00	0.67
9	0.32	-0.46	-0.05	0.13	0.84	-0.45	0.19	-0.87	0.67	1.00

Table 1. Correlation between principal vectors for different symbols.

The vector data extraction is implemented in two steps (cf. Figure 2). Firstly, the conversion from binary image to gray scale image is performed by counting the percentage of black pixels in the neighborhood of the current pixel. Secondly, the background is cropped out and the remaining foreground part is resized to the resolution $n \times n$ where typically $n = 10-20$. The resizing operation is actually a decimation filter implemented by simple averaging of those pixel values which enter into the given superpixel.

Fig. 2. Preprocessing step: original binary image, its gray scale version, and reducing to 10 by 10 pixel grid.

4.2 Results for distance to class centroids

Our program can be specialized to a distance classifier by setting the subspace dimension to zero and the number of clusters in each class to one. The results of classification for a random sample of about seven thousands testing examples is shown in the Table 2. The entry n_{ij} of i-th row and j-th column contains the number of data samples which belong to the class i and are recognized as digits from the class j. We obtain for this classical method about 87% of recognition rate what is rather a poor result.

	0	1	2	3	4	5	6	7	8	9	[%]
0	532	2	6	4	1	7	5	0	1	0	95.3
1	0	489	10	6	12	1	11	0	55	2	83.5
2	8	3	478	3	3	1	18	3	9	2	90.5
3	5	4	10	540	1	4	0	8	16	3	91.4
4	0	23	2	0	469	0	4	0	6	35	87.0
5	3	4	1	55	2	445	1	0	3	5	85.7
6	2	21	2	2	3	9	496	0	1	0	92.5
7	5	63	0	0	7	1	0	483	0	22	83.1
8	0	40	10	27	5	10	2	1	414	32	76.5
9	0	22	0	1	22	0	0	18	13	480	86.3

Table 2. Classification results for the distance method: $N = 20 \times 20$, $k_{PCA} = 0$, $k_{VQ} = 1$, global rate=87.20%.

4.3 Results for distance to class subspaces

In these experiments we test the subspace method which is obtained in our program by setting the number of clusters in each class to one. The dimension K of the subspace for each class is set to the same value. From the table 3, we see that increasing K from one to 16, results in increase of the global recognition rate. However, further increase of K up to maximum possible value N results in worse performance.

	0	1	2	3	4	5	6	7	8	9	all
1	95.5	95.9	92.8	94.9	88.5	91.9	96.5	92.4	81.3	89.8	91.95
2	97.1	98.1	92.8	94.9	89.4	95.6	98.0	94.0	84.7	91.4	93.59
3	99.3	100	93.0	95.9	93.0	95.2	98.1	95.5	86.9	96.2	95.31
4	99.3	99.8	93.2	94.4	93.5	95.6	98.5	94.3	89.5	96.4	95.45
5	99.1	99.8	92.2	94.3	94.6	97.5	98.5	94.3	89.8	97.3	95.75
6	98.9	99.8	95.2	96.8	95.2	96.0	98.3	94.3	90.6	97.3	96.25
7	99.3	99.7	96.4	96.5	95.9	96.3	98.3	95.0	92.4	97.5	96.73
8	99.3	99.8	96.2	96.6	95.9	95.6	98.3	96.7	93.0	98.0	96.95
9	99.3	99.8	97.0	96.8	97.2	94.4	98.1	97.6	93.3	98.9	97.25
10	99.5	100	95.8	97.5	97.2	94.6	98.7	99.0	93.5	98.4	97.42
11	99.6	99.7	95.6	98.1	97.8	95.0	98.7	98.6	93.5	98.6	97.53
12	99.6	99.7	95.8	98.3	98.0	95.0	98.9	99.5	93.4	98.4	97.65
13	99.6	99.8	96.0	98.3	97.4	96.3	98.7	99.3	93.4	98.2	97.71
14	99.8	99.8	96.2	98.1	97.8	95.8	98.5	99.3	93.9	98.2	97.75
15	100	99.7	97.0	97.6	97.6	96.0	98.3	99.3	94.0	98.2	97.77
16	99.8	99.8	96.8	97.3	97.6	97.3	98.7	99.7	93.9	97.8	97.87

Table 3. Recognition rates for the subspace method: $N = 20 \times 20$, $k_{PCA} = 1-16$, $k_{VQ} = 1$.

The recognition rate in individual classes can achieve its maximum for its individual K but for the design simplicity we have decided in this research not to incorporate this fact into the program.

4.4 Results for distance to class local subspaces

The local subspace method was tested for different dimensionality K of local subspaces and different number L of clusters in classes. Results are presented in Table 4. Similarly to the subspace method further increase of K deteriorates algorithm's performance too. The increase of L to values more than three makes results less confident as the number of samples per cluster decreases to the level at which learning of the local model by the neural approach is not possible.

	0	1	2	3	4	5	6	7	8	9	all
1	97.9	99.8	94.5	94.6	93.9	96.3	97.2	90.9	87.3	96.0	94.84
2	98.9	100	94.7	96.5	93.5	97.1	98.3	96.0	89.3	95.7	96.00
4	99.3	100	96.6	97.0	97.2	98.3	99.1	96.4	90.6	97.7	97.20
8	99.6	100	97.5	98.3	97.8	98.1	98.9	99.3	94.6	98.9	98.31
16	99.5	100	99.3	99.6	99.3	98.9	99.3	99.8	98.7	99.6	99.41

Table 4. Recognition rates for the local subspace method: $N = 20 \times 20$, $k_{PCA} = 1, 2, 4, 8, 16$, $k_{VQ} = 3$.

In order to compare the performance of the subspace method versus the local subspace method on the basis of two previous tables (row $k_{PCA} = 16$), we arrange the table 5.

digit	0	1	2	3	4	5	6	7	8	9	all
PCA	99.8	99.8	96.8	97.3	97.6	97.3	98.7	99.7	93.9	97.8	97.87
LPCA	99.5	100	99.3	99.6	99.3	98.9	99.3	99.8	98.7	99.6	99.41

Table 5. Recognition rates at $K = 16, N = 20 \times 20, L = 3$ for the standard subspace method and the local subspace method.

4.5 Results for maximum Gaussian likelihood method

From the statistical point of view the least error of recognition is achieved by the maximum likelihood method. However, this theory requires the knowledge of probability distributions in clusters. For multidimensional data with big N there is no effective general method to estimate such distributions. The only exception is the case when the probability distributions in clusters are Gaussians. Then the estimation can be made by the projection of data onto the subspace of K principal components and the optimal estimation of the truncated tail using Kulback-Leibler distortion measure. We have implemented this estimation and the results of such classifier are presented in Table 6. We see that the results are worse even from the subspace method. This fact means that the assumption about Gaussianity in clusters is wrong.

	0	1	2	3	4	5	6	7	8	9	all
1	97.1	99.1	94.1	93.6	93.4	95.3	96.2	90.3	86.5	95.6	94.12
2	97.5	99.3	94.3	94.7	93.4	96.5	97.7	93.3	88.8	95.5	95.10
4	98.2	99.3	95.4	95.2	94.4	96.8	98.2	94.7	89.9	96.4	95.85
8	98.7	99.3	96.7	96.5	95.6	97.0	98.5	96.1	90.0	97.2	96.56
16	98.9	99.4	97.4	97.7	97.7	98.1	98.4	97.5	94.6	97.8	97.75

Table 6. Maximum likelihood method: dimension of principal subspace used for Gaussian estimation $K = 1, 2, 4, 8, 16$, $k_{VQ} = 3$.

5 Conclusions

Local Principal Components Analysis, i.e. Principal Component Analysis performed in data clusters, when applied for pattern recognition problem, appears to be a better tool than classical subspace method. The reason is in ability of discrimination for existing subclasses in the given pattern class. For handwritten numerals the technique reaches the recognition rate of about 99.4%. Results for maximum likelihood method assuming Gaussian distribution of data in clusters are worse than subspace method what means that the assumption about the probability distributions is wrong for NIST database of handwritten numerals.

References

1. Hotelling, H.: Analysis of a complex of statistical variables into principal components. Journal of Educational Psychology, **24** 1933 417-441
2. Joutsensalo, J., Miettinen, A.: Self-organizing operator map for nonlinear dimension reduction. ICNN'95, 1995 IEEE International Conference on Neural Networks. **1(1)** 1995 111-114
3. Kambhatla, N., Leen, T.K.: Fast nonlinear dimension reduction. ICNN'93, 1993 International Conference on Neural Networks. **3** 1993 1213-1218
4. Kohonen, T.: The self-organizing map. Proc. of IEEE **78** 1990 1464-1480
5. Kohonen, T.: Self-Organizing Maps. Springer, Berlin, 1995
6. Linde, Y., Buzo, A., Gray, R.M.: An algorithm for vector quantizer design. IEEE Trans. Comm. COM-**28** 1980 28-45
7. Oja E.: Principal components, minor components, and linear neural networks. Neural Networks **5** 1992 927-935
8. Oja E.: Subspace methods of pattern recognition. Research Studies Press, England, 1983
9. Diamantaras, K.I., Kung, S.Y.: Principal component neural networks. John Wiley & Sons, New York, 1996
10. Skarbek, W.: Local Principal Components Analysis for Transform Coding. 1996 Int. Symposium on Nonlinear Theory and its Applications, NOLTA'96 Proceedings, Research Society NTA, IEICE, Japan, Oct. 1996 381-384
11. Suen, C.Y., Legault, R., Nadal, C., Cheriet, M., Lam, L.: Building a new generation of handwriting recognition systems. Pattern Recognition Letters, **14** 1993 303-315
12. Watanabe, S., Pakvasa, N.: Subspace method of pattern recognition. Proc. of 1st Int. Joint Conf. on Pattern Recognition, 1973

From Conceptual Model to Internal Model

John Debenham

Key Centre for Advanced Computing Sciences, University of Technology, Sydney,
PO Box 123, NSW 2007, Australia
debenham@socs.uts.edu.au

Abstract. A uniform formalism is used to model all stages of knowledge-based systems design. In this approach data, information and knowledge are all represented in this single uniform formalism. This formalism incorporates two classes of constraints which are applied to data, information and to knowledge. A conceptual model is a representation of the system expertise using this formalism. An internal model is derived from the conceptual model and from a specification of the system transactions and the performance constraints. The internal model is a complete system specification. The internal model is derived in two steps. First, the conceptual model and a specification of the system transactions are used to derive the functional model. The functional model shows how the knowledge in the conceptual model should be employed to deliver the transactions. Second, the internal model is derived from the functional model and from the performance constraints. Using a broad definition of 'best', the problem of deriving the best functional model, and the problem of deriving an internal model are both NP-complete.

1. Introduction

The construction and simplification of a conceptual model for knowledge-based systems is described in [1]. The development of that conceptual model into a complete system specification is discussed here. In that conceptual model, the data, information and knowledge in an application are all represented using a single uniform formalism as "items". The terms 'data', 'information' and 'knowledge' are used in a rather idiosyncratic sense. The *data* in an application are those things which could be represented naturally as simple variables, the *information* is those things which could be represented naturally in relations, and the *knowledge* is those things which could be represented naturally in some rule language. Each item incorporates two classes of constraints. Constraints for knowledge are thus included in the conceptual model [2].

The representation of a knowledge item in the conceptual model does not presume a particular "if-then" interpretation of that item. In general, a single knowledge item will represent a number of different "if-then" rules. The conceptual model [1] represents only the system expertise; it does *not* represent the transactions that the system will be required to deliver. The conceptual model does *not* identify those "if-then" interpretations of the knowledge items that are necessary to deliver the required system functionality. Further the conceptual model does *not* identify those data and information items that are to be stored, those items that are to be deduced and those items that are not required in the final system. The internal model contains more detail than the conceptual model. The internal model is a complete system specification. The "internal model" represents only the knowledge that is necessary to deliver the required functionality of the knowledge-based system, and identifies those items which are to be actually stored and those items which are to be deduced.

The problem of deriving the "best" internal model from the conceptual model is discussed here. This problem is divided into two sub-problems. Using a broad definition of "best" these two sub-problems are NP-complete.

The first step in a design methodology [3] for knowledge-based systems is the construction of a *requirements model* which specifies *what* the system should be able to do [4]. The requirements model will not be described here. The second step in that design methodology is the construction of a *conceptual model* [1]. The conceptual model inherits the specification of *what* the system should be able to do by links from the requirements model. In general the conceptual model may be redundant. To derive the "best" internal model from the conceptual model first a "functional model" is constructed and second an "internal model" is constructed. The *functional model* is "functional" in the sense that it shows how rules derived from the knowledge in the conceptual model may be employed to deliver the transactions specified in the requirements model. This functional model is *not* redundant. The functional model is derived from the conceptual model and from a specification of the system transactions. The *internal model* is a complete system specification [5] [6]. The internal model specifies which items in the functional model should be stored and which should be deduced. The internal model is derived from the functional model and from the performance constraints. Using broad definitions of "best", the problem of deriving the best functional model, and the problem of deriving an internal model are both NP-complete.

2. Conceptual model

Items are a uniform formalism for representing the data, information and knowledge things in a conceptual model; each item incorporates two powerful classes of constraints. The key to this uniform representation is the way in which the "meaning" of an item, called its *semantics*, is specified. Items may be viewed either formally as λ-calculus expressions or informally as schema [1]. The λ-calculus view provides a sound theoretical basis for the work; it is *not* intended for practical use.

Items have a *name* which by convention is written in italics. The *semantics* of an item is a function which *recognises* the members of the *value set* of that item. The value set of a data item at a certain time τ is the set of labels which are associated with a population that implements that item at that time. The value set of an information item at a certain time τ is the set of tuples which are associated with a relational implementation of that item at that time. Knowledge items have value sets too. Consider the rule "the sale price of parts is the cost price marked up by a universal mark-up factor"; suppose that this rule is represented by the item named *[part/sale-price, part/cost-price, mark-up]*, then the value set of this item is the set of quintuples associated with [part, sale-price, part, cost-price, mark-up] at that time. This approach to semantics extends to complex, recursive knowledge items too.

Items are named triples; they consist of the item's semantics, value constraints and set constraints. A *value constraint* is an expression which must be satisfied by any member of the item's value set. A *set constraint* is a structural constraint on an item's value set; for example, a constraint on the size of the value set. Some items have "components". Items which do not have components are called "basis items";

basis items represent simple data things. Given a value set D_A, a *basis item A* will have the form:

$$A[\ \lambda x \bullet [J_A(x)] \bullet,\ \lambda x \bullet [K_A(x)] \bullet,\ (L)_A\ ]$$

where $J_A(x) = $ is-a$[x{:}D_A]$, K_A is an expression which is satisfied by the members of the value set and L is a set constraint on the value set such as the cardinality constraint "< 100" meaning that the value set has less than 100 members. A non-basis item A is defined as follows. Given a set of n items $\{A_1,..., A_n\}$ the *components* of A, given an n-tuple $(m_1, m_2,..., m_n)$, $M = \displaystyle\sum_{i=1}^{n} m_i$, if:

- S_A is an M-argument expression of the form:

$$\lambda y_1^1...y_{m_1}^1...y_{m_n}^n \bullet [S_{A_1}(y_1^1,...,y_{m_1}^1)\ \wedge\ ......\ \wedge\ S_{A_n}(y_1^n,...,y_{m_n}^n)\ \wedge$$
$$J_A(y_1^1,...,y_{m_1}^1,...,y_{m_n}^n)] \bullet$$

- V_A is an M-argument expression of the form:

$$\lambda y_1^1...y_{m_1}^1...y_{m_n}^n \bullet [V_{A_1}(y_1^1,...,y_{m_1}^1)\ \wedge\ ......\ \wedge\ V_{A_n}(y_1^n,...,y_{m_n}^n)\ \wedge$$
$$K_A(y_1^1,...,y_{m_1}^1,...,y_{m_n}^n)] \bullet$$

- C_A is an expression of the form:

$$C_{A_1} \wedge C_{A_2} \wedge...\wedge C_{A_n} \wedge (L)_A$$

where L is a logical combination of:
- a *cardinality constraint*;
- "Uni(A_i)" for some i, $1 \leq i \leq n$, a *universal constraint* which means that "all members of the value set of item A_i must be in this association", and
- "Can(A_i, X)" for some i, $1 \leq i \leq n$, where X is a non-empty subset of $\{A_1,..., A_n\} - \{A_i\}$, a *candidate constraint* which means that "the value set of the set of items X functionally determines the value set of item A_i".

then the named triple $A[\ S_A, V_A, C_A]$ is an n-adic *item* with *item name A*, S_A is called the *semantics* of A, V_A is called the *value constraints* of A and C_A is called the *set constraints* of A. For example, the information item named *part/cost-price*; could be defined as:

$$part/cost\text{-}price[\ \lambda xy \bullet [\ S_{part}(x) \wedge S_{cost\text{-}price}(y) \wedge costs(x,\ y)\ ] \bullet,$$
$$\lambda xy \bullet [\ V_{part}(x) \wedge V_{cost\text{-}price}(y) \wedge ((x < 1999) \rightarrow (y \leq 300))\ ] \bullet,$$
$$C_{part} \wedge C_{cost\text{-}price} \wedge$$
$$(Uni(part) \wedge Can(cost\text{-}price, \{part\}))_{part/cost\text{-}price}\ ]$$

The knowledge item *[part/sale-price, part/cost-price, mark-up]* could be defined as:

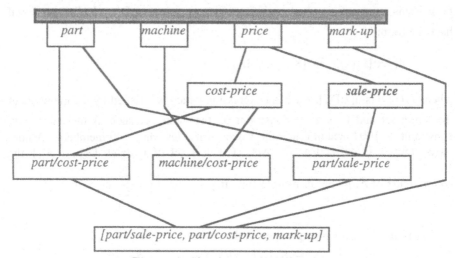

Figure 1 Simple conceptual map

$[part/sale\text{-}price, part/cost\text{-}price, mark\text{-}up][$
$\quad \lambda x_1 x_2 y_1 y_2 z \cdot [\ S_{part/sale\text{-}price}(x_1, x_2)$
$\quad\quad \wedge \ S_{part/cost\text{-}price}(y_1, y_2) \wedge S_{mark\text{-}up}(z)$
$\quad\quad \wedge \ ((\ x_1 = y_1 \ ) \rightarrow \ (x_2 = z \times y_2))] \cdot,$
$\quad \lambda x_1 x_2 y_1 y_2 z \cdot [\ V_{part/sale\text{-}price}(x_1, x_2)$
$\quad\quad \wedge \ V_{part/cost\text{-}price}(y_1, y_2) \wedge V_{mark\text{-}up}(z)$
$\quad\quad \wedge \ ((\ x_1 = y_1 \ ) \rightarrow \ (\ x_2 > y_2 \ ))] \cdot,$
$\quad C_{part/sale\text{-}price} \wedge \ C_{part/cost\text{-}price} \wedge C_{mark\text{-}up} \wedge$
$\quad\quad (\text{Uni}(part/sale\text{-}price) \wedge \text{Uni}(part/cost\text{-}price)$
$\quad\quad \wedge \text{Can}(part/sale\text{-}price, \{part/cost\text{-}price, mark\text{-}up\})$
$\quad\quad \wedge \text{Can}(part/cost\text{-}price, \{part/sale\text{-}price, mark\text{-}up\})$
$\quad\quad \wedge \text{Can}(mark\text{-}up, \{part/sale\text{-}price, part/cost\text{-}price\})$
$\quad\quad)_{[part/sale\text{-}price, part/cost\text{-}price, mark\text{-}up]} \ ]$

which appears rather clumsy, but this item represents the knowledge of three different rules, and it contains two types of constraint. These constraints are not included in most other knowledge representation formalisms.

The *conceptual model* is a collection of items and a *conceptual map* which shows the name if each item in the conceptual model and the relationship of each item to its components. A simple conceptual map is shown in Figure 1.

3. Functional model

The functional model is derived from the conceptual model and from a specification of the system transactions. The conceptual map shown in Figure 1 contains only one knowledge item, namely *[part/sale-price, part/cost-price, mark-up]*. That single

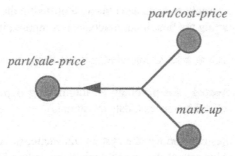

Figure 2 One interpretation of *[part/sale-price, part/cost-price, mark-up]*

knowledge item represents three "if-then" rules. Suppose that three system transactions are to derive *part/sale-price*, to accept input for *part/cost-price* and to accept input for *mark-up* then the knowledge required to support these three transactions is the rule represented on a "dependency diagram" shown in Figure 2. Each knowledge item in the conceptual model will contribute at most one "if-then" interpretation to support the transactions in the functional model.

We assume that the conceptual model is complete in the sense that it contains sufficient knowledge to deliver the required functionality. In other words, we assume that the specification of what the system is required to do leads naturally to the identification of items in the conceptual model that can accommodate directly the system transactions. The *input items* are those items which can accommodate the system inputs and whose value set is actually stored [7] [8]; the input information items may be stored in a relational database. The *output items* are those items which are used directly to service the identified queries. The input items and the output items together are called the *transaction items*. A *sufficient* set of rules is one which enables a complete value set for each output item to be deduced from the value sets of the input items, and which is minimal in the sense that no rules can be removed without violating this property. A *functional model* is a collection of rules and a functional diagram that shows, on one diagram, the dependency diagrams for all of the rules so that each rule is shown just once. For example, Figure 3 shows a functional diagram for a functional model with eight rules; three output items are shown on the left, and four input items are shown on the right. The transaction items are identified in the functional diagram using arrows.

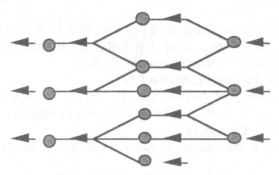

Figure 3 Functional diagram

Suppose that the transaction items have been identified in the conceptual model. The problem of constructing the functional model is decomposed into:

- the problem of selecting a set of knowledge items from the conceptual diagram, and
- for each item selected, the problem of identifying a particular "if-then" interpretation (as defined by the candidate constraints)

so that the resulting rules can support the system transactions. A *selection* is set of rules that enables the value sets of the output items to be deduced from the value sets of the input items. The problem of constructing the functional model is "to choose the selection of least complexity". The *complexity of a selection* is the sum of the complexities of the items in that selection. It is assumed that an item cannot have negative complexity. This additive definition of complexity of items in a selection is quite reasonable because any least complex selection will contain at most one item with any specified item as its head component. Head components are identified by the candidate constraints. Three complexity measures for items are:

- The *trivial measure*, by which the complexity of any item is unity.
- The *domain measure*, by which the complexity of any item is its number of components.
- The *relation measure*, by which the complexity of any item is an estimate of the time to retrieve a tuple from that item's value set if it were stored as a relation.

These simple measures make no attempt to capture the structure of the item. They make no attempt to measure the complexity of an item's semantics.

A solution to the functional model construction problem is a selection of least complexity. Each item in a solution will be represented on the *functional diagram*.

RESULT
The functional model construction problem is NP-complete. The functional model construction problem remains NP-complete if this problem is restricted to circuitless sets of items with non-recursive semantics.

Proof
The proof is by reduction to the "Optimum solution to AND/OR graphs" problem [9].

An AND/OR graph can be transformed into a set of items so that the problem of finding the optimum solution to the AND/OR graph is thus transformed into a restriction of the functional model construction problem.

Given an AND/OR graph, proceed as follows.

Each AND construct of the form $A \leftarrow (B_1 \wedge B_2 \wedge ... \wedge B_n)$, with n arcs, is replaced by an item $[A, B_1, B_2, ..., B_n]$ with n components with set constraint:

$$Can(A, \{B_1, B_2, .., B_n\})$$

and the complexity of this item is the sum of the weights of the arcs flowing from the AND node "A".

Each OR construct of the form $A \leftarrow (B_1 \vee B_2 \vee ... \vee B_n)$, with n arcs, is replaced with n items $[A, B_1], [A, B_2],..., [A, B_n]$ with set constraints:

$Can(A, \{B_1\})$

$Can(A, \{B_2\})$

. . . .

$Can(A, \{B_n\})$

respectively, and the complexities of these n items are the weights of the corresponding arcs flowing from the OR node "A".

The semantics of the items which have been constructed in the proof above are required to functionally determine the component A in terms of the other components. Subject to this requirement the item semantics can have any form. The set of items which has been constructed does not contain a circuit.

The (unique) item which is not in the body of a candidate constraint in any other item is the (single) output item. The set of items which are not the subject of a candidate constraint are the set of input items. Thus an optimal solution to the given AND/OR graph will transform to a solution of the functional model construction problem for this set of items. The functional model construction problem remains NP-complete for circuitless sets of items with arbitrarily simple semantics.

4. Internal model

The internal model is constructed from the functional model and from a specification of the system constraints. The problem of constructing the internal model is:

- to decide which of the items in the functional model should actually be stored in addition to the input items so that:
- the "system constraints" are satisfied and
- the overall "system performance" is optimal.

A set of items whose value sets are stored, excluding the input items, is called a *storage allocation*. The *system constraints* are the maximum permissible cost of response for each transaction and the maximum amount of available storage. The *system performance* of an internal model is:

$$\sum_{q \in Q} \tau(q) \times f(q)$$

where Q is the set of transaction items. τ is a "cost function": $\tau(q)$ is the "cost to service the transaction q"; and f is the "expected frequency function": $f(q)$ is the "expected frequency of presentation of the transaction q".

For each transaction q, T(q) denotes the maximum permissible cost of response. For each item r, $\gamma(r)$ is the cost of storing the value set of r as a relation, and C is the total cost of the available storage. The internal model construction problem is:

Given a functional model, given Q the set of transactions, given T(q) for each $q \in Q$, and given C, to choose a set of items R in the functional model to be actually stored such that:

$$(\forall q \in Q) \ \tau(q) \leq T(q) \text{ and } \sum_{r \in R} \gamma(r) \leq C$$

are satisfied and

$$\sum_{q \in Q} \tau(q) \times f(q)$$

is minimised.

This discussion is restricted to "primary recursion" only. Denoting items by letters from the set $\{A,B,C,D,E\}$, a rule containing a clause of the form:

$$A \leftarrow A, B, C$$

ie. where an item name appears both as the head of the rule and within the body of the rule is called *primary recursive*. The restriction to primary recursion means that exotic forms of recursion such as:

$$A \leftarrow B, C, D \qquad A \leftarrow B$$
$$C \leftarrow A, E, F \qquad C \leftarrow E$$

where the rule with head A has C in its body and vice versa, would be excluded. This does not impose a significant restriction in practice.

The operational constraints and optimality criterion noted in the definition of the internal model construction problem together comprise a complex set of conflicting constraints.

RESULT

The internal model construction problem is NP-complete.

Proof.

In the proof, the internal model construction problem will be restricted and transformed; this restriction and transformation is equivalent to the "Minimum Cut Into Bounded Sets" problem which is known to be NP-complete [10].

First assume that there is only one output item, o, and one input item, i. Then the internal model construction problem now reads:- Given a functional model, given constants $T(o)$, $T(i)$ and C, to choose a set of items R to be the storage allocation such that:

$$\tau(o) \leq T(o), \quad \tau(i) \leq T(i) \text{ and } \sum_{r \in R} \gamma(r) \leq C$$

are satisfied and

$$(\tau(o) \times f(o)) + (\tau(i) \times f(i))$$

is minimised.

Second, adopt the following trivial measure for τ, this measure defines $\tau(q)$ to be the number of rules involved in servicing the transaction q. In addition restrict the problem to the special case when $T(o) = T(i) = T$. Then the internal model construction problem may be stated as: Given a functional diagram, given constants T and C, to choose a set of items R to be the storage allocation such that:

the number of rules needed to deduce the value set of output item o from the value sets in R is less than or equal to T;

the number of rules needed to deduce the value sets in R from the value set of i is less than or equal to T, and

$$\sum_{r \in R} \gamma(r) \leq C$$

are satisfied, and

$$(\tau(o) \times f(o)) + (\tau(i) \times f(i))$$

is minimised.

Represent this restriction of the internal model construction problem on a functional diagram, and transform that diagram into its graph theoretic dual. On this dual representation, items are denoted by arcs and rules are denoted by nodes. Ignore the expression to be minimised, that is, just consider the operational constraints. The internal model construction problem as restricted so far now reads: Given a dual representation, constants T and C, to choose a partition of the set of nodes in the graph, V, into two disjoint sets V_1 and V_2 such that the single transaction item q is directly connected to a node in V_1 and the single input item u is directly connected to a node in V_2 such that:

$$|V_1| \leq T, \quad |V_2| \leq T \quad \text{and} \quad \sum_{r \in R} \gamma(r) \leq C$$

where |V| means "the number of elements in the set V", and R is the set of arcs with one node in V_1 and the other in V_2.

This final restriction and transformation of the internal model construction problem is precisely the "Minimum Cut into Bounded Sets" problem. This completes the proof. This proof shows that the problem of finding *a* solution to the internal model construction problem is NP-complete, never mind the problem of finding an *optimal* solution.

Corollary.

Given a functional model, the problem of finding a solution which satisfies the operational constraints, but which is not necessarily optimal, to the internal model construction problem is NP-complete.

The "Minimum Cut into Bounded Sets" problem remains NP-complete even if $\gamma(r) = 1$ $(\forall r \in R)$, and if $T = |V| \div 2$. Thus the following restriction of the internal model construction problem is also NP-complete: Given a dual diagram and constant C, to choose a partition of the nodes of the diagram into two disjoint sets V_1 and V_2 such that the single output node q is connected to a node in V_1 and the single input node u is connected to a node in V_2 such that:

$$|V_1| = |V| \div 2, \quad |V_2| = |V| \div 2 \quad \text{and} \quad |R| \leq C$$

In the special case when $T = |V|$ the problem of finding an admissible, but not necessarily optimal, solution to the internal model construction problem reduces to satisfying the single constraint:

$$\sum_{r \in R} \gamma(r) \leq C$$

which can be solved in polynomial time by the minimum cut algorithm [11].

5. Conclusion

The problem of deriving the internal model from the conceptual model in a uniform knowledge representation has been decomposed into the functional model construction sub-problem and the internal model construction sub-problem. These two sub-problems have been shown to be NP-complete. The complexity of the functional model construction problem is derived on the basis of a broad definition of a "best" selection of rules. The complexity of the internal model construction problem is derived on the basis of simple constraints on the performance of the system transactions.

References

1.   J.K. Debenham, "Knowledge Simplification", in proceedings 9th International Symposium on Methodologies for Intelligent Systems ISMIS'96, Zakopane, Poland, June 1996, pp305-314.
2.   J.K. Debenham, "Knowledge Constraints", in proceedings Eighth International Conference on Industrial and Engineering Applications of Artificial Intelligence and Expert Systems IEA/AIE'95, Melbourne, June 1995, pp553-562.
3.   J.K. Debenham, "Integrating Knowledge Base and Database", in proceedings 10th ACM Annual Symposium on Applied Computing SAC'96, Philadelphia, February 1996, pp28-32.
4.   J.K. Debenham, "Unification of Knowledge Acquisition and Knowledge Representation", in proceedings International Conference on Information Processing and Management of Uncertainty in Knowledge Based Systems IPMU'96, Granada, Spain, July 1996, pp897-902.
5.   R. Capobianchi, M. Mautref, M. van Keulen and H. Balsters, "An Architecture and Methodology for the Design and Development of Technical Information Systems", in proceedings 9th International Symposium on Methodologies for Intelligent Systems ISMIS'96, Zakopane, Poland, June 1996, pp511-520.
6.   F. Lehner, H.F. Hofman, R. Setzer, and R. Maier, "Maintenance of Knowledge Bases", in proceedings Fourth International Conference DEXA93, Prague, September 1993, pp436-447.
7.   H. Katsuno and A.O. Mendelzon, "On the Difference between Updating a Knowledge Base and Revising It", in proceedings Second International Conference on Principles of Knowledge Representation and Reasoning, KR'91, Morgan Kaufmann, 1991.
8.   J.K. Debenham, "Understanding Expert Systems Maintenance", in proceedings Sixth International Conference on Database and Expert Systems Applications DEXA'95, London, September, 1995.
9.   S. Sahni, "Computationally Related Problems", SIAM Computing, Vol 3, No 4, (1974), pp 262-279.
10.   M.R. Garey, D.S. Johnson, and L. Stockmeyer, "Some simplified NP-complete graph problems.", Theoretical Computer Science, Vol 1, No 3, 1976, pp 237-267.
11.   S. Even, "Graph Algorithms", Computer Science Press, 1979.

Speeding GA-Based Attribute Selection for Image Interpretation

Qi Zhang

Machine Learning and Inference Laboratory
George Mason University
Fairfax, VA 22030, USA
qzhang@aic.gmu.edu

Abstract

This paper addresses the problem of GA-based attribute selection. Previous work in this direction has mainly focused on problem representation so that a genetic algorithm could work on it searching for a satisfactory attribute subset. Even though good experimental results were reported, they were usually acquired at the cost of time. This paper presents a novel approach to this problem. In particular, it introduces attribute quality measure during genetic evolution in order to make some promising attributes more likely to appear in a new generation. In this way, the evolution process is faster, and satisfactory results can be achieved in less time. Preliminary experimental results in image interpretation show that this approach is promising.

KEYWORDS: evolutionary computation, attribute selection, image interpretation.

1 Introduction

Image interpretation has important military and civil applications such as detecting military targets in images taken from airplanes or finding tumors in medical images. A set of attributes of high quality for describing objects is crucial to the recognition or interpretation performance of such systems.

Defining good attributes is problem-dependent and is beyond the scope of this paper. Of particular interest here is how to select a satisfactory subset from candidate attributes because it is known that (1) there is nonlinear interaction among attributes such that no two attribute subsets have the same discriminating power and (2) simply adding an attribute can possibly degrade system performance (e.g., Kreithen, 1993). In addition to possible better results, another benefit from attribute selection is that it can make a system work faster due to fewer attributes.

Many researchers contributed to the area of attribute selection (e.g., Forsburg, 1976; John et al., 1993; Koller and Sahami, 1996; Vafaie and De Jong, 1993; Bala et al., 1995). Recently, the GA-based approach to this problem has attracted some researchers (e.g., Vafaie and DeJong, 1993; Bala et al., 1995). This approach seems promising and good results were reported (e.g., Bala et al., 1995). However, these results were usually acquired at the expense of time spent in genetic evolution. In this paper, we propose a novel way of using genetic algorithms to address attribute selection, which achieves good results without consuming much time. We introduce easily available attribute quality measure into GA evolution to speed the process of searching for a satisfactory subset from candidate attributes. This idea is demonstrated in a multistrategy learning system which combines a genetic algorithm (De Jong, 1996) and the inductive learning program AQ15c (Michalski et al., 1986, Wnek et al., 1995). Specifically, it starts with a statistical analysis of candidate attributes and selects some potentially promising ones and makes them more likely to appear in the first generation of genetic evolution. As for an evolved attribute subset, AQ15c is called to perform learning and testing upon actual image data. The testing accuracy is taken as the fitness value of this given subset and is also assigned, in a statistical way, to those attributes appearing in the subset. Statistically good attributes have a better chance of being selected into an attribute subset of the next generation. This process ends when a satisfactory subset is found or the maximal number of generations is reached. Preliminary experiments done in attribute selection for interpretation of natural scene images (Michalski et al., 1996) show a pronounced speeding of GA-based search for a good attribute subset.

2 Background

Attributes are the basis for man or machine to interpret, classify or recognize scenes or objects from images. However, it is known that due to possible nonlinear interaction among attributes, not any set of attributes can produce the same good results. Thus, attribute selection is needed whose goal is selecting the best subset or a satisfactory one according to some criterion. Image interpretation is a good application domain for attribute selection as there usually exist many numerical attributes and the amount of data is huge, and it is hard to find out, at a glance or by a simple computation, which attribute subset could lead to better results.

A question arises: what is the meaning of a "good" attribute? We observe that there are two kinds of "good" attributes: individually good and collectively good. An attribute is *individually* good if it itself satisfies some requirements based on analysis of its properties and given data. For example, orthogonality is such a requirement which indicates an attribute's property of measuring different aspects of data. Another example of such requirements is separability which indicates an attribute's ability to separate different object classes. However, there is one problem with selecting attributes directly according to these requirements: though such a set of attributes could lead to satisfactory results, it is not guaranteed because of the nonlinear interaction among attributes. The other problem is that requirements such as orthogonality are rarely operational even by a human being, and requirements such as separability seem to be operational but cannot be determined in reality because of the large number of object classes, and the huge amount of data and noise within the data. An attribute is *collectively* good if the set of attributes in which this attribute appears brings good results to a system. This concept of "good" captures the cooperation and nonlinear interaction among attributes and is exactly the goal of so-called attribute selection.

The relationship between this two kinds of good attributes is: a satisfactory attribute subset usually contains some individually good attributes; in other words, individually good attributes can be collectively good; a collectively good attribute is not necessarily individually good. The reason for us to introduce the concepts of individually good and collectively good is that their relationship has not drawn enough attention and been utilized for attribute selection.

A naive method for attribute selection is to generate each possible subset of attributes and then test the system performance. However, this method is almost never used in reality because its time cost is exponential with regard to the number of attributes. Another method is ranking candidate attributes based on some criterion followed by deleting some attributes with lower ranks (e.g., Baim, 1982). This method can quickly determine an attribute subset, but it ignores the possible nonlinear interactions among attributes. Some researchers (e.g., Imam and Vafaie, 1994) use heuristic search in attribute selection. This method usually runs fast; however, it could end up with a locally optimal attribute subset. Like the ranking method, this approach is unable to capture nonlinear interaction among attributes and moreover when the number of attributes is large, it is hard or impossible to find effective heuristics that can be used to guide a search process. Forsburg (1976) used an adaptive random search method which increased the probabilities of being selected of those attributes which appeared in generated knowledge descriptions (i.e., they are *relevant* attributes) to make them more likely be selected in the next subset.

Researchers also use genetic algorithms to address the issue of attribute selection (e.g., Vafaie and DeJong, 1993; Bala et al., 1995). This approach utilizes the explorative power of genetic algorithms and searches for a satisfactory attribute subset which captures nonlinear attribute interaction in some degree without exhaustive search. This method can produce good results, especially in the case of a large number of attributes. The work by Bala et al. (1995) is a good example. However, previous work adopting this approach has mainly focused on how to represent a problem so that a genetic algorithm could run on it. It should be pointed out that such a GA-based approach normally consumes much time in genetic evolution, and it becomes even worse when the number of attributes is large, the amount of data is huge and determining a fitness value needs some time. This is often the case in image interpretation. This paper addresses this problem by introducing attribute quality measure into genetic evolution.

3. Methodology

3.1 Attribute Quality Measure

The above observation of two kinds of attribute goodness and their relationship is the basis of this paper. The best or a satisfactory attribute subset usually cannot exist without containing individually good attributes. So during genetic evolution, it may be better to let individually good attributes be more likely to appear in generations. Based on this idea, we try to determine individually good attributes by introducing attribute quality measure and increase their probabilities of appearing in an individual of a generation. In contrast, previous work treated each attribute in an equally fair way. Though in this way the explorative power could be strong, many individuals (i.e., attribute subsets) in a generation contain few or no individually good attributes, and so the whole evolution is likely to consume much time before generating a subset meeting some acceptability criterion.

There are two situations in which attribute quality measure can be introduced into GA evolution: forming the first generation and mutating within one individual of a generation during evolution. We refer to these two sorts of quality measure as *static* and *dynamic* respectively in this paper.

Static quality measure is acquired from analysis of attributes based on given data before evolution. Separability is one property which can be evaluated to some degree from given data and we therefore use it for static quality measure. Other properties such as orthogonality cannot be computed directly from data and therefore must be determined by the designer; thus, they are not considered here. For each attribute, we try to evaluate its separability and assign a value to it. Attributes with high values are considered to be individually good. We increase their probabilities of appearing in the individuals (attribute subset) of the first generation. Notice that these attributes are not guaranteed to appear in the individuals of the first generation.

Static quality measure: C is a set of numbers representing classes. For an attribute A_k ($1 <= k <= N$, where N is the number of candidate attributes), calculate the mean and standard deviation of each class i ($i \in C$) in this attribute from given data (or sampled data), say $\overline{x_{ik}}$ and σ_{ik}. Then A_k's static quality measure is defined as

$$\sum_{\{i,j\} \subseteq C; i < j} \frac{2}{\pi} \tan^{-1} \left[\frac{(\overline{x_{ik}} - \overline{x_{jk}})^2}{1000\sigma_{ik} * \sigma_{jk} + \varepsilon} \right].$$

In the above, ε is a very small number preventing the denominator from being zero. Note that this formula is designed for numerical attributes (in our experiments, all attributes are numerical). For nominal attributes, the methods such as PROMISE (Baim, 1982) are suitable.

Dynamic quality measure is calculated during the evolution process. If an attribute subset, i.e., an individual in a generation, results in good results, then every attribute in this subset will get some credit. If on the average one attribute has a high credit value, then its probability of surviving the mutation so as to appear in a new individual in the next generation is increased. This credit information is used as dynamic quality measure and tries to capture largely the concept of *individually good* and to some degree the concept of *collectively good*.

Dynamic quality measure: For an attribute A_k, add the credit values of all the previous individuals (i.e., attribute subsets) since the first generation in which A_k appeared and divide this sum by the number of such individuals. The result is defined as the dynamic quality measure of attribute A_k.

In the above, the credit value is problem-dependent. In this paper, we use classification accuracy on testing data as an individual's fitness value and also as its attributes' credit value.

In fact, there are many possible ways of defining static or dynamic quality measure for attributes, if reasonable. For example, PROMISE [Baim, 1982] can be used for evaluating static quality measure. The key is to let promising attributes have higher probabilitiy of appearing in individuals in upcoming generations.

3.2 GA-Based Attribute Selection

An individual in a generation could be considered as a string of 1s and 0s, in which 1 indicates the attribute is used in this individual and 0 not. The genetic evolution proceeds according to the following steps:

Step 1: Select the top t_1 attributes according to static quality measure.

Step 2: Increase their probabilities of appearing in individuals of the first generation by δ_1.

Step 3: Randomly select attributes to generate individuals of the first generation.

Step 4: For each individual in a generation, determine its fitness value and the credit value of each attribute used in this individual.

Step 5: If some termination criterion is satisfied, then output the satisfactory attribute subset and stop.

Step 6: Determine each attribute's dynamic quality measure.

Step 7: Do fitness proportional selection and uniform crossover to generate new individuals for the next generation.

Step 8: Mutate within each new individual. Two ways: (1) standard mutation, i.e., every attribute has $1/N$ probability of being mutated (N is the number of candidate attributes); (2) dynamic quality measure enhanced mutation: select the top t_2 attributes according to dynamic quality measure and increase their survival probabilities by δ_2.

Step 9: Go to Step 4 to continue the evolution.

In step 3, each attribute can be assigned a value between 0.0 and 1.0 according to a uniform distribution over [0.0, 1.0]. The threshold of selecting an attribute for an individual can be 0.5 and so each attribute is selected with probability 0.5. However, the probabilities of those selected top t_1 attributes should be increased (our experiments used a probability of 0.75) in order that they can more likely appear in the first generation. In step 8, an attribute usually has a probability of 0.5 being mutated. In this work, for each of the selected top t_2 attributes, its probability of being mutated is decreased (0.3 in our experiments) if it already appears in the individual and is increased (0.7 in our experiments) if it does not appear in this individual. The evolution stops when a predefined number of generations are produced, or a termination criterion is satisfied.

4 Example

4.1 Natural Scene Interpretation

We applied a combination of a genetic algorithm and the inductive learning program AQ15c to attribute selection in natural scene interpretation (Michalski et al., 1996), in which the system is asked to label the class of each area in a natural scene image (see Fig. 1).

4.2 Attribute Definitions

Each pixel in a image is taken as the pixel of interest and a set of attributes are extracted for it. A total of 17 attributes were used in experiments. The first nine are computed according to properties of the pixel itself: (1) red value; (2) green value; (3) blue value; (4) intensity; (5) saturation; (6) hue; (7) relative red value = red - min(red, green, blue); (8) relative green value = green - min(red, green, blue); (9) relative blue value = blue - min(red, green, blue).

Fig. 1. A natural scene image.

-1	-4	-6	-4	-1
0	0	0	0	0
2	8	12	8	2
0	0	0	0	0
-1	-4	-6	-4	-1

(10) horizontal line operator

-1	0	2	0	-1
-4	0	8	0	-4
-6	0	12	0	-6
-4	0	8	0	-4
-1	0	2	0	-1

(11) vertical line operator

-1	-4	-6	-4	-1
-2	-8	-12	-8	-2
0	0	0	0	0
2	8	12	8	2
1	4	6	4	1

(12) horizontal edge operator

-1	-2	0	2	1
-4	-8	0	8	4
-6	-12	0	12	6
-4	-8	0	8	4
-1	-2	0	2	1

(13) vertical edge operator

-1	0	2	0	-1
-2	0	4	0	-2
0	0	0	0	0
2	0	-4	0	2
1	0	-2	0	1

(14) horizontal V-shape operator

-1	-2	0	2	1
0	0	0	0	0
2	4	0	-4	2
0	0	0	0	0
-1	-2	0	2	1

(15) vertical V-shape operator

1	-4	6	-4	1
-4	16	-24	16	-4
6	-24	36	-24	6
-4	16	-24	16	-4
1	-4	6	-4	1

(16) frequency spot operator

1	-2	1
-2	4	-2
1	-2	1

(17) Laplacian operator

Fig. 2, Laws' energy filters for generating attributes.

The other eight attributes are computed according to Laws' energy filters in Fig. 2, which detect information such as directionality and roughness around the pixel of interest (Laws, 1980). The usage of each matrix is such: let the center of a matrix positioned at the pixel of interest, multiply each value in the matrix by the gray value of the pixel in the corresponding position, sum all the products to get the attribute value.

4.3 Data and Discretization

A 20 x 20 area of each class within the natural scene is selected from Fig. 1 (boxes) and 17 attributes are computed for each pixel in the area. Fig. 3 gives some examples. 60% of all the selected data are randomly taken for learning and the other 40% for testing (Weiss and Kulikowski, 1992). Note that before learning rules to describe pixels by using AQ15c, the value of each attribute is uniformly discretized to one of fifteen levels for the experiments in this paper. Actually any discretization scheme is applicable here. A pixel description (i.e. rule) learned by AQ15c is exemplified in Fig. 4.

A1	A2	A3	A4	A5	A6	A7	A8	A9	A10	A11	A12	A13	A14	A15	A16	A17
6	6	5	6	2	6	1	0	0	5	5	5	3	2	9	1	5
8	7	6	7	2	6	2	1	0	6	6	5	5	7	9	2	6

Fig. 3. 17 attribute values of 2 selected rock pixels.

Rock <:: [A1=5..14] [A5=0..4] [A13=3..10] [A14=1..7] [A15=9..12]

Fig. 4. One of the learned rules of rock pixels.

4.4 Static Attribute Quality Measure

Static quality measure is calculated for every attribute based on randomly selected training data. See Fig. 5.

A1	A2	A3	A4	A5	A6	A7	A8	A9
8.390	5.324	8.328	4.769	5.116	11.122	9.591	12.456	5.000

A10	A11	A12	A13	A14	A15	A16	A17
6.661	8.912	8.199	7.536	8.075	6.582	8.967	3.957

Fig. 5 Static attribute information

From our experience, static quality measure for attributes like hue, and relative red and green values (A6, A7, A8 respectively) should be high, and the above values reflect this.

5 Experiments and Discussion

5.1 Experimental Results

The genetic algorithm in De Jong (1996) was adopted. The population size was 20 and the experiments were done on a Sparc 2 workstation.

Three kinds of experiments were done: "traditional" refers to the way described in (Bala et. al., 1995); "static" means only static quality measure is introduced into genetic evolution; "static+dynamic" means both static and dynamic quality measure are used. 10 runs were performed for each kind of experiment. The average testing accuracy is plotted as best-so-far in the Y axis against the number of births in the X axis (Fig. 6).

5.2 Discussion

Fig. 6 shows a significant speeding effect due to introduced attribute quality measure. Dynamic quality measure did not result in much improvement at the early phase of evolution, because a few generations are not able to capture the statistical goodness of each attribute. When there were enough generations created, dynamic quality measure worked to some degree. Note that both static and dynamic quality measures had a strong positive effect on evolution speed. It is possible to gain better performance if we do not give credit to each attribute in an individual during evolution but rather only these attributes which were actually used in obtained knowledge descriptions because only they contributed to acquired testing accuracy (Forsburg, 1976).

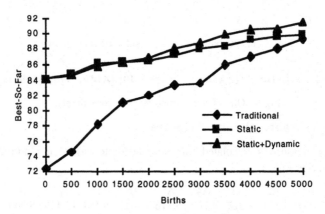

Fig. 6. The comparison of evolution speeds. Best-So-Far is testing accuracy.

For the success of attribute quality measure, the design of formulas of quality measure seems crucial. We tried another formula for static quality measure (not shown in this paper) but the speeding effect was not good. We set parameters t_1 and t_2 in the above methodology to 5. We also tried selection of the top 3, 4, 6 attributes for probabilities to be increased. The results showed that the top 5 were the best for this given problem. We consider this issue to be problem-dependent and very important. If a system itself knows too much about the properties of candidate attributes, it could simply select them, and this way would clearly produce very good results quickly. Obviously, this is not always true. It is the case that only some of them may be selected. If too many attributes' probabilities are increased without well-founded understanding of them, then the evolution process is subject to going to and staying at some local optimum or spending more time in finding a satisfactory subset than without attribute quality measure. On the other hand, selecting too few attributes may not produce the desired speeding effect. Thus selection of a appropriate number of attributes for probability increase is important.

Note that our methodology is similar to the work by Forsburg (1976) but different in many aspects. Attribute quality measure is like *information content value* mentioned there; nonetheless the latter did not touch upon the concept of *static* quality measure. Even though Forsburg adopted a random search, its theoretical properties were unclear. To some degree, the work there can be considered as a special case of our methodology with population size being one (no crossover, no mutation) and thus its search is not so powerful and systematic as genetic algorithms are. Further, we cannot evaluate its performance in terms of accuracy and speeding effect since they were not reported there.

6 Conclusion

This paper describes a promising way of speeding GA-based attribute selection by introducing attribute quality measure. It combines a genetic algorithm and the inductive learning program AQ15c into a multistrategy learning system. Quality measure of each attribute is introduced to determine whether to increase its survival probability. Experimental results are presented to show the feasibility of this methodology. The preliminary results indicate an improvement in time in comparison with previous GA-based work in which the main focus was on representing a problem so that a genetic algorithm could work on it.

There are some aspects which require further work. Among them, selection of an appropriate number of attributes whose probabilities of survival are going to be increased is of special interest. It is desirable to find an adaptive way of determining this number so that the system could run more independently of the system designers and domain experts. Another future experiment is to take as testbed more attributes and more application domains, especially in the case of large number of attributes (only 17 attributes were tested in this paper to show the methodology). Further, it is worthwhile to design other effective formulas to calculate attributes' quality levels, so as to capture more attribute properties.

We believe that in application domains with large quantities of numerical data such as image interpretation, introduction of attribute quality measure is a promising way to speed up GA-based attribute selection.

Acknowledgments

The author would like to thank Dr. Michalski and Dr. Kaufman for their criticism and suggestions to the earlier draft of this paper. This research was conducted in the Machine Learning and Inference Laboratory at George Mason University. The Laboratory's activities are supported in part by the Defense Advanced Research Projects Agency under grant F49620-95-1-0462 administered by the Air Force Office of Scientific Research, in part by the National Science Foundation under grants DMI-9496192 and IRI-9020266, and in part by the Office of Naval Research under grant N00014-91-J-1351.

References

Baim, P.W., 1982. The PROMISE Method for Selecting Most Relevant Attributes for Inductive Learning Systems. *Reports of the Intelligent Systems Group*, Department of Computer Science, University of Illinois at Urbana-Champaign, ISG 82-5.

Bala, J., Huang, J., Vafaie, H., DeJong, K. and Wechsler, H, 1995. Hybrid Learning Using Genetic Algorithms and Decision Trees for Pattern Classification. *Proceedings of the Fourteenth International Joint Conference on Artificial Intelligence*, August, Motreal, Quebec, Canada.

De Jong, K., 1996. *Evolutionary Computation: Theory and Practice*. MIT Press.

Forsburg, S., 1976. AQPLUS: An adaptive random search method for selecting a best set of attribute from a large collection of candidates. Internal Report, Department of Computer Science, University of Illinois, Urbana, Illinois.

Imam, I.F., and Vafaie, H., 1994. An Empirical Comparison Between Global and Greedy-like Search for Attribute selection. *Proceedings of the Seventh Florida Artificial Intelligence Research Symposium*, May, Pensacola Beach, FL., pp. 66-70.

John, G., Kohavi, R., and Pfleger, K., 1994. Irrelevant Features and the Subset Selection Problem. *Proceedings of the Eleventh International Conference on Machine Learning*, July, Rutgers University in New Brunswick, New Jersey, pp. 121-129.

Koller, D., and Sahami, M., 1996. Toward Optimal Feature Selection. *Proceedings of the Thirteenth International Conference on Machine Learning*, July, Bari, Italy, pp. 284-292.

Kreithen, D.E., Halversen, S.D. and Owirka, F.J., 1993. Discriminating Targets from Clutter. *Journal of MIT Lincoln Lab.*, pp. 25-52.

Laws, K., 1980. Textured Image Segmentation. Ph.D. Thesis, University of Southern California, Department of Electrical Engineering.

Michalski, R.S., Mozetic, I., Hong, J., and Lavrac, N., 1986. The Multipurpose Incremental Learning System AQ15 and its Testing Application to Three Medical Domains. *Proceedings of the Fifth National Conference on Artificial Intelligence*, August, Philadelphia, PA., pp. 1041-1045.

Michalski, R.S., Zhang, Q., Maloof, M.A., and Bloedorn, E., 1996. The MIST Methodology and Its Application to Natural Scene Interpretation. *Proceedings of Image Understanding Workshop*, Palms Spring, CA., pp. 1473-1479.

Vafaie, H. and De Jong, K., 1993. Robust Feature Selection Algorithms. *Proceedings of the International Conference on Tools with AI*, Boston, MA., pp. 356-364.

Weiss, S.M., & Kulikowski, C.A., 1992. *Computer systems that learn: classification and prediction methods from statistics, neural nets, machine learning and expert systems*, Morgan Kaufmann, San Mateo, CA.

Wnek, J., Kaufman, K., Bloedorn, E., and Michalski, R.S., 1995. Selective Induction and Learning System AQ15c: the Method and User's Guide. *Reports of the Machine Learning and Inference Lab.*, MLI 95-4, Machine Learning and Inference Lab., George Mason University, Fairfax, VA.

Using Recurrent Selection to Improve GA Performance

Ben S. Hadad and Christoph F. Eick
hadad@swbell.net, ceick@cs.uh.edu
Department of Computer Science
University of Houston
Houston, TX 77204-3475

Abstract

Genetic algorithms (GA's) are based on the idea that solutions to otherwise intractable problems can be derived by mimicking natural evolution. With a few exceptions, however, GA's are limited to haploid implementations with random breeding among a single population, failing to exploit a number of strategies that are found in nature. Plant breeders recognize that too-strict selection among the progeny in a given generation results in reduced diversity, which can, in turn, cause inbreeding depression, a decline in the average fitness of the population. *Recurrent selection* is a multistep breeding method designed to solve this problem, improving a plant population's fitness without excessive loss of diversity. This paper explored the use of recurrent selection for Genetic Algorithms. We see major advantages in this approach in oscillating environments which cycle among several different states as well as in stationary environments. The main advantage of recurrent selection is the maintenance of genetic diversity in even relatively small populations. We demonstrated the benefits of using recurrent selection for the 0/1 knapsack problem with changing weights and with the Schwefel function. Further research on harder dynamic and stationary problems is called clearly called for, as is further application of models based on a horticultural model.

1. Introduction

Plant breeders recognize that too-strict selection among the progeny in a given generation results in a reduced population, which can, in turn, cause inbreeding depression, a decline in the average fitness of the population. *Recurrent selection* is a multistep breeding method designed to solve this problem, improving a plant population's fitness without excessive loss of diversity. Allard [1] describes several variations on this theme, but the basic process proceeds as follows.

1. Plants from a heterozygous source are self-fertilized, or *selfed*
2. Selection takes place among the F1 (first generation) progeny.
3. Intercrossing is performed among a superior subset of the progeny. All possible crossing combinations are made between these superior progeny, resulting in generation F2.
4. The resulting F2 generation serves as a feed stock for a repetition of step one [1].

In the example in Figure 1, the two organisms in the F0 generation are each selfed three times to produce a total of six progeny in the F1 generation. Selection is imposed on this generation, and four of the F1 generation, A, B, C, and D, are chosen. These four are intercrossed in all possible combinations, yielding an F2 generation. This F2 generation is used as the new F0 generation in the next cycle.

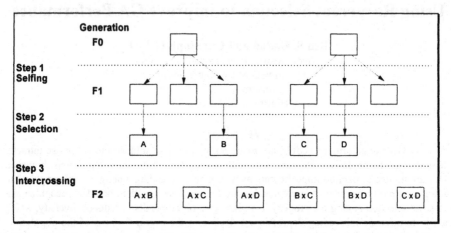

Figure 1 Recurrent selection, a multigenerational strategy used by plant breeders to improve stock while maintaining diversity.

Adapting this method to GA's required a few decisions. In the first step, how many organisms should there be in the F1 generation? How should competition be arranged? We chose, in these tests, to generate five progeny for each member of the F0 (original) population, and to arrange for competition among those six (five progeny and one progenitor) for a single place in the F1 generation. In the third step, the idea of *all possible* crossing combinations was weakened somewhat to enable a larger proportion of each generation to breed to generate F2 without generating an intractable number of combinations. The F0 population was 150 in all trials. With five progeny generated by each of the F0 organisms, F1 was allowed to expand to a size of 900. This constituted step one. F1 was then selected down to a size of 150 using stochastic selection without replacement. Intercrosses were limited in step three to generating an F2 population of 150 to create a population size usable for F0 without imposing further selection.

2 Polyploidy

Brindel [2], as a part of her doctoral dissertation, considered several methods for simulating dominance in Genetic Algorithms, involving either global or local control. In one of these, a haploid evolving chromosome controls diploid dominance; each organism carries an extra chromosome, which is used to record dominance. These dominance vectors evolve via mutation and crossover. Goldberg [4] has objections to this method for its lack of correspondence with natural systems and for the lack of linkage between the two chromosomes and the haploid dominance vector. Additionally, he notes that Brindel used only stationary cases in her test bed.

In these experiments, we use a structure similar to Brindle's, using an extra dominance determining chromosome, referred to here as a *dominance vector*, along with a crossover control vector, used to increase the linkage between the dominance vector and the chromosomes. Section two of this paper describes our approach in detail. Section three presents empirical data comparing conventional and recurrent

Haploid Organism																	
Chromosome 1	1	0	1	1	0	1	0	1	0	1	1	1	1	0	0	1	0
Dominance Control	1	1	0	0	1	0	1	0	1	0	0	1	0	1	0	0	1
Crossover Control	1	0	0	1	0	0	0	1	0	0	0	1	0	1	0	0	1
Phenotype	1	0	1	1	0	1	0	1	0	1	1	1	1	0	0	1	0
Diploid Organism																	
Chromosome 1	1	0	1	1	0	1	0	1	0	1	1	1	1	0	0	1	0
Chromosome 2	0	0	0	1	0	0	1	1	1	0	1	0	1	1	0	1	1
Dominance Control	1	1	0	0	1	0	1	0	1	0	0	1	0	1	0	0	1
Crossover Control	1	0	0	1	0	0	0	1	0	0	0	1	0	1	0	0	1
Phenotype	1	0	0	1	0	0	1	1	1	0	1	1	1	1	0	1	1
Tetraploid Organism																	
Chromosome 1	0	0	1	1	0	1	0	1	0	1	1	1	1	0	0	1	0
Chromosome 2	0	0	0	1	0	0	1	1	1	0	1	0	1	1	0	1	1
Chromosome 3	0	1	0	0	0	1	1	1	0	1	0	1	1	0	1	0	1
Chromosome 4	0	1	0	0	1	1	1	0	1	0	1	1	0	1	0	1	1
Dominance Control	1	1	0	0	1	0	1	0	1	0	0	1	0	1	0	0	1
Crossover Control	1	0	0	1	0	0	0	1	0	0	0	1	0	1	0	0	1
Phenotype	0	1	0	0	1	0	1	0	1	0	0	1	0	1	0	0	1

Figure 2: Three organisms: haploid, diploid, and tetraploid. Each organism carries one dominance vector one crossover vector, and one phenotype vector.

methods, benchmarked with a 0/1 knapsack problem with oscillating weight constraints and with the Schwefel function.

2.1 Data Structures and the Reproductive Algorithm

The algorithm for reproduction follows closely that observed in natural systems, with modifications to accommodate the structure of the organisms:

- *Selection*: Polyploid 'parents' are chosen using stochastic selection with replacement, i.e., roulette wheel.
- *Gametogenesis*: The diploid organisms each form two haploid gametes via meiosis. Meiosis involves crossing over at some number of points on the two chromosomes. The two gametes formed each contain a haploid resultant of crossing over between the organism's two chromosomes. At this stage in the algorithm, mutation is applied to both chromosomes and control vectors.
- *Fusion of Gametes*: Haploid gametes are picked at random, and are fused to form a diploid organism.

2.1.1 Chromosomal Structure of the Organisms

The organisms used in these experiments have, in addition to a full haploid or polyploid complement of chromosomes, three extra chromosome-like structures, the first controlling dominance, the second controlling crossover, and the third as a convenience for recording the current phenotype of the organism. Three examples of such organisms are given in Figure 2. The function of each of these structures is explained in the sections following.

2.1.2 Diploidy and Dominance

Each organism has a dominance vector having the same form as the organism's chromosomes. This structure is key in the translation from the organism's genotype to its phenotype. The dominance vector evolves with the organism. Consider the partial representation of an organism in Figure 3.

The cases labeled A, which are heterozygous, have a phenotype determined by the value of the dominance control vector. In the first case labeled A, 0 is said to dominate, and of the two bits, 0 is the one expressed. In the second, 1 dominates and is the bit expressed in this heterozygous instance. In both of the instances labeled B, the two loci are homozygous, and the phenotype is therefor not influenced by the dominance control vector.

	A							B	B						A
Chromosome 1	0 1 1 1 1 1 0 1	1 1	0 1 0 0 1 1	0
Chromosome 2	1 1 1 0 1 0 0 0	1 1	0 0 1 1 1 0	1
Dominance Control	0 0 1 1 1 1 1 0	0 1	1 1 0 0 0 1	1
Resultant Phenotype	0 1 1 1 1 1 0 0	1 1	0 1 0 0 1 1	1

Figure 3: The effect of a dominance control vector on the phenotype of a diploid organism. In case A, The dominance control vector determines the phenotype. In case B, the dominance control vector has no effect on the phenotype.

2.1.3 Crossover Control in Gametogenesis

In an effort to maintain a link between dominance control vectors and chromosomes, a crossover control vector is used to dictate where crossover may occur in

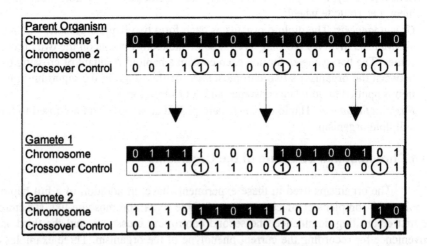

Figure 4: The crossover control vector dictates where a chromosome can split during gametogenesis. Crossover occurs at only some of the possible locations. The dominance and phenotype vectors have been omitted for clarity's sake.

gametogenesis, as illustrated in Figure 3. Gametogenesis, by default, copies Chromosome 1 into Gamete 1 and Chromosome 2 into Gamete 2. Before each bit is copied, the bit in the corresponding position of the crossover control vector is checked. If the crossover control bit is 1, there is a chance (50% in these trials) that crossover will begin taking place (or cease taking place) at that locus. If the bit is 0, crossover does not start or stop at this point. This method of crossover, with a varying number of crossover points, is referred to as segmented crossover and is investigated more thoroughly elsewhere [5][3]. Special cases of this sort of crossover include uniform crossover, where every other bit is crossed over, and copying, where no crossover occurs. The circled 1's in Figure 3 indicate those spots where crossover was either initiated or terminated in this example.

2.1.4 Crossover Control in Fusion

Each gamete contains, in addition to its chromosome(s), a copy of the dominance and control vectors from its parent. When two zygotes fuse, then, they bring together a greater than whole set of genetic information. The problem of two extra control vectors is reconciled by using crossover at the time of fusion between these control vectors. The crossover control vector, at this time, controls not only the crossover of data in the dominance vector, but in the crossover control vector itself. This not only brings to the correct sum the complement of chromosomes, but allows for the evolution of these vectors as well. Further, it provides some linkage, albeit loose, between chromosomes and their control vectors since these vectors only cross over at points at which both crossover control vectors allow, although, once not necessarily at every point at which they allow. Figure 5 provides an example of the fusion of two such gametes.

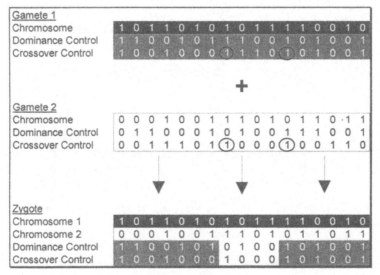

Figure 5: Each gamete has its own version of dominance and crossover vectors. When the gametes fuse, the two vectors cross over with their counterparts. The same crosssover points are used for both the dominance and crossover vectors.

3 Experimental Evaluation

This section reports on experiments that compare standard and recurrent approaches for a 0/1 knapsack problem with time varying weight constraints and with the stationary Schewfel function. All runs of the program were conducted on a population of 150 at a mutation rate of 0.01 per bit and a base crossover (or switching) rate of 50%, attenuated by the contents of the crossover control vector. Selection was made via stochastic selection with replacement using a generational GA written in C++, compiled using GCC and run under Linux on a Pentium PC.

3.1 The Test Bed

As did Smith and Goldberg [7] and Ng and Wong [6], we used as a test function a 17 object 0/1 knapsack problem with oscillating weight constraints for comparing performance. Figure 6 (from [7]) is a table of the weights and values of the seventeen objects, along with two optimal packings for weight constrains of 60 and 104.

Weight constraints were enforced by subtracting from the sum of the values included in the knapsack a penalty function, $P = C(\Delta W)^2$, where ΔW represents the amount by which the organism's solution exceeds the weight constraint and C is 20. This yields an overall fitness function of $\sum_{i=1}^{17} (x_i v_i) - P$, where x_i is either one

Number	Value	Weight	W = 60 Optimal	W = 104 Optimal
i	v_i	w_i	x_i	x_i
1	2	12	0	0
2	3	5	1	1
3	9	20	0	1
4	2	1	1	1
5	4	5	1	1
6	4	3	1	1
7	2	10	0	0
8	7	6	1	1
9	8	8	1	1
10	10	7	1	1
11	3	4	1	1
12	6	12	1	1
13	5	3	1	1
14	5	3	1	1
15	7	20	0	1
16	8	1	1	1
17	6	2	1	1
Total:	91	122	13	15

Optimum V: $\sum_{i=1}^{17} x_i v_i = 71$ Optimum V: $\sum_{i=1}^{17} x_i v_i = 87$

W at Optimum V: $\sum_{i=1}^{17} x_i w_i = 60$ W at Optimum V: $\sum_{i=1}^{17} x_i w_i = 100$

Figure 6: The 17 object 0/1 knapsack problem with two different weight constraints. The last two columns show the two optima, given the weight constraints. The optima differ in bits 3 and 15.

or zero, indicating inclusion or exclusion of the ith object, and v_i is the value of the ith object. Negative fitness values are adjusted to zero.

We also tested a stationary function, proposed by Schwefel:

$$F = \sum_{i=1}^{N} - x_i \sin(\sqrt{|x_i|})$$

For this set of tests, N was set to 1. Test runs were limited to 100 generations, with $x \in [-512, 511]$. As was the case with the knapsack trials, each of these trials was, in turn, run 20 times, and these 20 runs were averaged for an end result for each set of parameters. Unlike those used in the knapsack function, bitstrings are used here to represent floating point values. Thirty bit precision was maintained throughout these experiments. Since this function presents the problem of finding a minimum, we solved for $1/F(x)$. A graph of $1/F(x)$, with a granularity of 1 (i.e., ten bit precision) in the ordinate, and with the value of $F(0)$ excluded, is given in Figure 7.

In each of the trials, we began with a weight constraint of 104. After half the cycle length, the constraint was switched to 60. At the end of the cycle, the constraint was again reset to 104. Each trial was allowed to run for 10 cycles, with cycle lengths of 30, 80, and 300 generations (i.e., for 300, 800, and 3000 generations altogether). Each of these trials was run 20 times, and these 20 runs were averaged for an end result for each set of parameters.

3.1.1 Recurrent Selection Used to Solve the 0/1 Knapsack Problem

The first function considered was the nonstationary. Each trial was allowed to run for 10 cycles, with cycle lengths of 14, 30, 80, and 300 generations. Each set of parameters was then run 20 times and averaged for a final result.

As shown graphically in the illustrations following (Figure 7), the primary concern in each case was to measure the difference between the output of the algorithm and the true optimum for each constraint. To compare the results of runs made on one set of parameters with those made on another, we required some sort of numerical measure of error. We calculated the second moment about the true optimum,

$$M_2 = \frac{\sum_{i=1}^{G} (T_i - X_i)^2}{G}$$, for each case, where T_i is the true optimum for generation I; X_i

is the output from the GA at generation i; and G is the number of generations in the trial. The magnitude of this figure reflects the accumulated error, and like the statistical variance (or second moment about the *mean* value), magnifies the import of the worst of the errors made by the GA during the run. Note that the shorter cycles, with lengths of 14 and 30 generations, yield to the newer technique, with ordinary diploid reproduction performing more successfully in experiments with longer cycles. This method, recurrent selection, sacrifices some diversity and memory of old solutions in order to allow for faster, more accurate responses to environmental change.

In the graphs presented in Figure 7, the weakness at longer cycle lengths of the recurrent selection routine becomes more evident. The recurrent selection examples for 80 and 300 generation cycle lengths exhibit the typical drop-off at the transition from the higher weight constraint to the lower weight constraint, indicating that the loss of diversity was such that the population no longer had a "memory" of the old solution, and was therefore harshly penalized by the overweight penalty function discussed earlier.

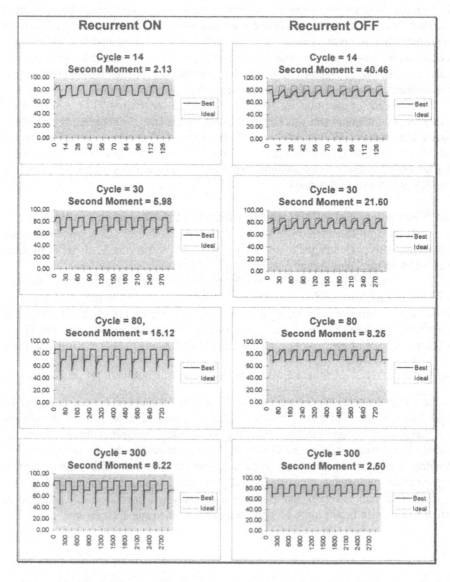

Figure 7: Graphical data comparing solutions for the 0/1 non-stationary knapsack problem with, and without, recurrent selection.

3.1.2 Recurrent Selection Used to Solve the Schwefel Function

As a second benchmark function, we also tested a stationary function proposed by Schwefel. Test runs were limited to 100 generations, with $x \in [-512,511]$. As was previously the case, each of these trials was run 20 times, and these 20 runs were averaged for an end result for each set of parameters.

In both the diploid and tetraploid cases, the use of recurrent selection improved the performance of the algorithm during its 100 generation run. In the diploid case, however, the algorithm took nearly twice as many generations to arrive at its solution as the non-recurrent version. Yet it is evident, on reference to the graphs in Figure 8, that by the time the non-recurrent solution had reached its optimum at generation 13, the recurrent algorithm had already exceeded that value. Reference to the figures used to create the graphs reveals a value of 1.37E+09 for the diploid recurrent version in generation 13.

The recurrent method, then, is well adapted for use with stationary functions. Table 1 reflects the results for a traditional GA applied to the Schwefel function. Peak values for the haploid case were higher than those for the diploid case. By using a technique that fosters slightly less diversity than ordinary diploidy, i.e., diploidy with recurrent selection, a result better than either of those from Table 1 was obtained.

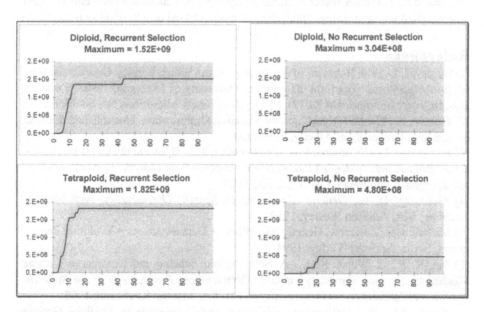

Figure 8: Graphical results of the solution for the Schwefel function using recurrent and non-recurrent algorithms.

4 Conclusions

This paper explored the use of recurrent selection for Genetic Algorithms. We see major advantages in this approach in oscillating environments which cycle among several different states as well as in stationary environments. The main advan-

Sckwefel Statistics			
Type of Run	Visible (gen)	Peak (gen)	Peak (value)
Haploid	5	12	4.56E+08
Diploid	10	13	3.04E+08
Tetraploid	12	20	4.80E+08

Table 1: Outcomes of the trials using an unaugmented GA on the Schwefel function.

tage of recurrent selection is the maintenance of genetic diversity in even relatively small populations. The exact mechanism for this advantage is not yet clear, though the alternating reduction in size of the search space that takes place in the selfing stage may be the driving force for the performance enhancement.

We demonstrated the benefits of using recurrent selection for the 0/1 knapsack problem with changing weights and with the Schwefel function. In shorter cycle tests using the knapsack benchmark, and in each test using the Schwefel benchmark, the recurrent approach significantly outperformed the conventional implementation. Additionally, the tetraploid implementation held, in it least one case, advantages over the diploid case. Further research on harder dynamic and stationary problems is called clearly called for, as is further application of models based on a horticultural model.

References

[1] Bagley, J. D., The Behavior of Adaptive Systems Which Employ Genetic and Correlation Algorithms. (Doctoral dissertation, University of Michigan). 1967, *Dissertation Abstracts International* 28(12), 5106B. (University Microfilms No. 68-7556).

[2] Brindle, A., Genetic Algorithms for Function Optimization. Unpublished doctoral dissertation, University of Alberta, Edmonton.

[3] Eschelman, L. J., Caruana, R.A., and Schaffer, J.D., Biases in the Crossover Landscape, *Proceedings of the 3rd International Conference on Genetic Algorithms*, Morgan Kaufmann Publishers, Los Altos, CA, 1989.

[4] Goldberg, D. E., *Genetic Algorithms in Search, Optimization, and Machine Learning*, MA, Addison Wesley, 1989.

[5] Michalewicz, Zbigniew, Genetic Algorithms + Data Structures = Evolution Programs, Berlin, Springer-Verlag, 1994.

[6] Ng, K. P., & Wong, K. C., A New Diploid Scheme and Dominance Change Mechanism for Non-Stationary Function Optimization, *Proceedings of the Sixth International Conference. on Genetic Algorithms*, CA, Morgan Kaufmann, 1995.

[7] Smith, R.E., & Goldberg, D.E., Diploidy and Dominance in Artificial Genetic Search, *Complex Systems 6(1992)*, 251-285.

A Coevolutionary Approach to Concept Learning

A. Giordana, L. Saitta and G. Lo Bello

Dipartimento di Informatica, Università di Torino, Italy
e-mail:{attilio,saitta,lobello}@di.unito.it

Abstract. This paper presents a highly parallel genetic algorithm, designed for concept induction in propositional and First Order logics. The parallel architecture is an adaptation to set covering problems of the diffusion model developed for optimization problems.

Moreover, the algorithm exhibits other two important methodological novelties related to the Evolutional Computation field. First, it combines niches and species formation with co-evolution in order to learn multimodal concepts. This is done by integrating the Universal Suffrage selection operator with the co-evolution model recently proposed in the literature. Second, it makes use of a new set of genetic operators, which maintain diversity in the population.

The experimental comparison with previous systems, not using coevolution and based on traditional genetic operators, shows a substantial improvement in the effectiveness of the genetic search.

1 Introduction

In the recent literature, Genetic Algorithms (GAs) emerged as valuable search tools in the field of concept induction [2, 8, 6, 3]. The feature that looks particularly attractive for this task is their exploration power, potentially greater than that of traditional search methods.

This paper describes a GA-based inductive learner, oriented to acquire concepts described in First Order Logic. Its architecture relies on a computational model characterized by the absence of global memory, which extends the diffusion model previously developed for GAs. The underlying distributed architecture allows a natural introduction of coevolution. Coevolution has been defined by [7, 10] and refers to the possibility of guiding evolving populations through a global feed-back.

Our starting point is the theory of niches and species formation, which already proved to be effective in learning disjunctive concept definitions. A disjunctive concept definition consists of a set of conjunctive logical formulas, each one capturing a different modality of the target concept. As niches and species formation is a way of addressing multi-modal search problems, disjunctive concept induction naturally fits in this framework. Several recent algorithms, such as COGIN [6] and REGAL [3], exploit this idea, even though they adopt different methods for promoting species formation.

As discussed in [3], methods based on species formation only can require very large populations when small species are required to survive in the presence of very large one. For this reason REGAL, adopts a long term control strategy resembling to co-evolution, in order to reduce the pressure among the species. Here, we propose a new method which combines the Universal Suffrage selection operator with an explicit co-evolutionary strategy similar to the one proposed by [10].

Moreover, this paper presents another substantial novelty, with respect to REGAL and other GA designed for concept induction tasks, which consists in a new set of genetic operators which explicitly aims at preserving the diversity in the population. Preserving diversity reduces premature convergency and increases the effectiveness of the genetic search.

As it will be shown in section 6, the new algorithm, while preserving the accuracy of REGAL shows a substantial reduction in the complexity of the genetic search.

2   Learning Concepts with Genetic Algorithms

The task of learning concept definitions from examples can be stated as follows. Given a learning set $E = E^+ \cup E^-$, consisting of positive and negative examples of a target concept ω, and a logical language L, the task consists in finding a logical formula $\Phi \in L$, which is true of all the positive examples E^+ and false of all the negative ones E^-. If such a Φ is found, the definition $\Phi \to \omega$ holds. Depending on the case, the logical language L can be a propositional or a First Order one. Independently of the order of L, the general structure of a concept definition Φ is a disjunction $\Phi = \phi_1 \vee \phi_2 \vee \ldots \vee \phi_n$ of conjunctive definitions $\phi_1, \phi_2, \ldots, \phi_n$, each one representing a different modality of the concept ω. In the following we will assume that L is a VL_{21} language like the one used by Induce [9] and by REGAL [3].

As previously mentioned, an appealing method to exploit GAs in Machine Learning consists in combining species and niches formation [5] with co-evolution [10]. Several examples can be found in [10] for learning behavioral strategies. In the following we will consider a two-level architecture whose lower level is a distributed GA, which searches for conjunctive descriptions by promoting the formation of species in the populations. The upper level applies a coevolutive strategy that performs two tasks: on one hand, it continuously updates a disjunctive description, combining together individuals chosen from the different species evolved at the lower level; on the other hand, it interacts with the lower level with the aim of favoring the evolution of those species that better go together in the current disjunctive description. The system REGAL [3] is a first example of how such an architecture can be implemented.

However, the way niching and coevolution are integrated in REGAL and in other systems like Samuel [10] is not very suitable to exploit large network computers. In fact, these systems are still based on the network (or island) model described by Goldberg [4], where niches tend to be identified with single computational nodes. Therefore, the available parallelism is limited by the number of emerging species. In order to overcome this limitation, we designed a different computational model, where the notion of global mating pool has been abandoned. As described in Figure 1, the architecture of the resulting system, G-NET, encompasses three kind of nodes: 1) Genetic nodes (*G-nodes*), where individuals mate and reproduce, 2) Evaluation nodes (*E-nodes*), where individuals are evaluated, and 3) a Supervisor node, which coordinates the computation of the G-nodes according to the coevolutive strategy.

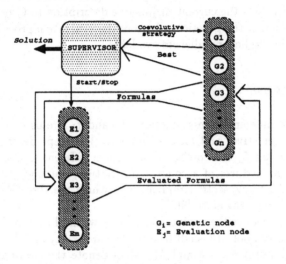

Fig. 1. Parallel Architecture

In G-NET, positive concept instances are considered elementary niches, and each G-node computes an elitist GA, which evolves a micro-population settled on a specific niche. In other words, each G-node searches for the "best" formula covering the positive learning instance associated with it. The same elementary niche can be assigned to many G-nodes at the same time, so that the number of actually active G-nodes depends only upon the available resources and not on the problem. The Supervisor decides when and how many active copies of a niche must exist.

Upon receiving an individual, an E-node evaluates it on the learning set, computes a fitness value and sends it back (together with the computed information) to the set of G-nodes (broadcast communication), activating thus new genetic cycles. When a G-node finds a solution which is better than the ones it already has, according to a local fitness function f_L, it sends it to the Supervisor as a candidate for assembling the global disjunctive description. Periodically, the Supervisor resumes and actuates the co-evolutive strategy: first, it assembles a global disjunctive solution, out of the locally best solutions it received from the G-nodes, trying to optimize a global fitness function f_G. Afterwards, it gives a feed-back to the G-nodes, in order to guide the genetic search towards solutions that better integrate each other in a global disjunctive description. This co-evolutive strategy consists of two components which act independently. The first component controls the amount of search that has to be done on different niches and determines the number of G-nodes assigned to each niche. Those niches, which developed solutions "weak", in a global context, are given more processors in order to increase the chance of improving their local solutions. The second component supplies a corrective term to the local fitness function, which allows the genetic search to be explicitly guided towards local solutions which contribute to increase the quality of the global solution. To this aim, the Supervisor broadcasts the current disjunctive description to G-nodes.

The separation of the genetic cycle from the evaluation process simply aims at increasing the explicit parallelism available.

3 The Fitness

In G-NET, two different fitness functions f_G and f_L are used in order to evaluate global (disjunctive) and local (conjunctive) concept descriptions, respectively. The function f_G is a combination of three different terms, corresponding to three different features of a concept description, namely: completeness (v), consistency (w) and syntactic simplicity (z), which are three standard criteria used in machine learning since [9].

In order to introduce the analytic form of f_G we need to introduce some basic definitions. The symbol M^+ shall denote the cardinality of E^+, i.e the number of positive training instances, and M^- shall denote the cardinality of E^-, i.e the number of negative training instances. Let φ be a inductive (disjunctive or conjunctive) hypothesis; $m^+(\varphi)$ and $m^-(\varphi)$ shall denote the number of positive and negative instances covered by φ, respectively. For the sake of simplicity we will write m^+, m^-, and so on, the argument φ is evident from the context.

Therefore, the completeness is evaluated as $v = m^+/M^+$ whereas the consistency is evaluated as an exponential function $w = e^{-m^-}$ of the covered negative examples. The syntactic simplicity is evaluated as the ratio $z = m^+/(N_a + m^+)$, being N_a the number of conditions occurring in a formula. In practice z tries to capture the information compression represented by the syntactic form with respect to its extension on the learning set. As long as N_a decreases z increases approaching to 1.

The analytic form for the global fitness f_G is then defined by the expression:

$$f_G(\Phi) = (1 + Av(\Phi) + Bz(\Phi))\, w(\Phi)^C \tag{1}$$

where A, B and C are user tunable constants which allow to weight the different components.

The local fitness f_L for an hypothesis ϕ adds a corrective term to expression (1) in order to account for how much ϕ contributes to improve (worsen) the current global concept description. Let Φ be the disjunctive concept description currently elaborated by the Supervisor and broadcasted to the G-nodes.

Let, moreover, ϕ be a conjunctive hypothesis in a G-node. The fitness $f_L(\phi)$ is evaluated as:

$$f_L(\phi) = (1 + Av(\phi) + Bz(\phi))w(\phi)^C + (f_G(\Phi') - f_G(\Phi)) \qquad (2)$$

being Φ' the formula obtained by adding ϕ to Φ and eliminating all redundant disjuncts but ϕ.

4 The Genetic Nodes

Conjunctive solutions (individuals) are represented as bitstrings of fixed length as in REGAL [3]. In the bitstring every bit represents a logical condition; if the bit is "1" the condition occurs in the formula, if it is "0" it does not. This correspondence can always be established, provided that a limit is imposed on the maximum complexity of a conjunctive formula.

Every G-node executes a genetic algorithm aimed at finding the formula that better covers the concept instance it has been assigned to. The architecture (see Figure 2) comprises the program encoding the genetic cycle, a small memory containing the local population, an input port receiving the individuals sent from the E-nodes, and an output port sending the new individuals to the E-nodes. As the local population is kept small (from 5 to 40 individuals) a non-standard replacement policy is used, in order to enforce diversity: all the individuals in the same node are required to be different, so that a richer genetic information is present in the population.

The individuals arriving at the input gate of a G-node are all those evaluated by the E-nodes; then, they may or may not cover the specific instance e assigned to it. Even though the goal of the G-node is to find formulas covering e, individuals not covering e can nevertheless carry information useful to find better generalizations for the individuals which actually cover e. Therefore, individuals both covering and not covering e are allowed to enter in the population, but a policy is adopted which does not allow the individuals not covering e take over the other ones.

A G-node repeats the following cyclic procedure, until stopped by the supervisor:

Cellular Genetic Algorithm

1. Select two individuals from the local population with probability proportional to their fitness
2. Generate two new individuals φ_1 and φ_2 by applying the genetic operators
3. Broadcast copies of φ_1 and φ_2
4. **While** the network is ready **do**
   (a) Receive some individuals ψ from the network according to rule (3) (see below)
   (b) Replace ψ in the local population by playing a tournament step for each one of them
5. Go to step 1

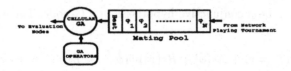

Fig. 2. G-node architecture.

Proportionate selection is used, whereas replacement is made using the tournament policy, adapted to the local need, as it will be explained in the following. First of all, every individual arriving from the network is subject to a probabilistic filter which can accept or refuse it.

$$\textbf{if } \varphi \textit{ belongs to the local population } \textbf{then } \textit{reject } \varphi \qquad (3)$$
$$\textbf{else if } \varphi \textit{ matches the learning event } e$$
$$\textbf{then } \textit{accept } \varphi \textit{ with probability } \textbf{pcv}$$
$$\textbf{else } \textit{accept } \varphi \textit{ with probability } \textbf{puc}$$

In (3), $p_{cv} \in [0, 1]$ is a user defined parameter, whereas, p_{uc} is computed as $p_{cv}(1 - \nu)^6$ being ν the proportion of individuals non covering e in the population. In this way the pressure of the individuals not covering e is automatically limited. Each individual that goes through the filter competes for entering in the population: an opponent is randomly selected and the victory is assigned with probability proportional to the respective fitness.

In each G-node the currently best solution cannot be replaced by a worse individual. Periodically, all G-nodes send a copy of the best found individuals to the supervisor, which reacts reassigning the examples to the G-nodes.

The reproduction operators are a task specific crossover and a task specific mutation. All operators are implemented in such a way that they always produce offsprings different from the parents. The *crossover* is a combination of the *two point crossover* with a variant of the *uniform crossover* [11], modified in order to perform either generalization or specialization of the hypotheses. A detailed description can be found in [1].

5 The Co-evolutive Control Strategy

The medium-term control strategy actuated by the Supervisor node is based on a co-evolutive approach. It basically goes through a cycle in which it receives the best solution found by each one of the G-nodes, elaborates the current disjunctive concept description Φ, and then gives a feedback to the G-nodes according to a coevolutionary strategy.

At the moment, the algorithm used for working out a disjunctive description is based on a hill climbing optimization strategy. At first, all conjunctive solutions collected from the G-nodes are included into a redundant disjunctive description Φ'. Then, Φ' is optimized, by eliminating the disjuncts which are not necessary.

This is done by repeating the following cycle until Φ' reaches a final form Φ which cannot be optimized further:

1. Search the disjunct ϕ such that $f_G(\Phi' - \phi)$ shows the greatest improvement.
2. Set $\Phi' = \Phi' - \phi$

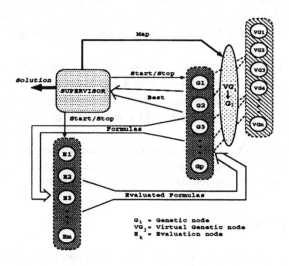

Fig. 3. The medium term coevolutive strategy

The first component of the co-evolutive control strategy on the G-nodes' activity is reminiscent of the techniques used in operating systems for multiplexing the CPU among the processes in execution. According to the model in Section 2, every positive example in the learning set is associated to a local learning task performed by one or more processes executed by the G-nodes. For distinguishing G-nodes from the elementary learning tasks, we will denote the latter as VG-nodes (Virtual Genetic nodes); more specifically, VG_i ($1 \leq i \leq |E_i^+|$) will denote the learning task associated to the example $e_i \in E^+$.

The Supervisor keeps track of the solution state of every VG-node VG_i, i.e. the best solution found for it, a selection (possibly empty) of the individuals found in the populations evolved by the G-nodes associated to it and other information, such as the number c_i of computational events, related to task VG_i, occurred during the past computation. The kernel of the co-evolutive control strategy is the algorithm used for accounting the events related to every task. As soon as formulas covering many examples will begin to develop, we will find spontaneously born clusters of G-nodes which elect the same formula as current best individual in their population. This can be interpreted as a form of implicit cooperation which led to the generation of a formula representative of the work of all of them. Therefore, the Supervisor attributes to a VG-node VG_i all the events produced by the G-nodes sharing the best formula attributed to VG_i.

When, at the end of a cycle, the control strategy is actuated, the VG-nodes are reassigned to G-nodes. The criterion for the reassignment is that of balancing the work spent for every task VG_i on the basis of the number c_i of computational events. Let C be the maximum value for c_i ($1 \leq i \leq |E^+|$), the Supervisor computes for every VG_i the amount $g_i = C - c_i$ of computational events necessary to balance the computational cost for it. Afterwards, the VG-nodes are stochastically assigned to G-nodes with probability proportional to g_i divided by the fitness $f_{L_i}^{(best)}$ of the currently best formula covering VG_i. Then the G-nodes are initialized with the information saved in the corresponding VG-nodes and restart.

The effect of this strategy is that of focusing the computational resources on the VG-nodes covered by formulas having a low fitness or a low ratio m^+/M^+. In fact, the VG-nodes falling in these cases will have either a low value for $f_i^{(best)}$ or a high value for g_i, because they will accumulate the computational events with few other VG-nodes.

The second component of the co-evolutive strategy reduces to broadcasting the current disjunctive description Φ to all G-nodes, so that they can update the local fitness f_L for the individuals in the local populations.

6 Experimental Evaluation

In order to have a comparison with REGAL, which can be considered the source of inspiration of the current system, we will report a benchmark on the *Mushrooms* dataset and on *Thousand Trains* dataset, used in [3].

A first comparison shows the benefits of using the co-evolutive control strategy illustrated in Section 5. A second comparison is with REGAL and shows how our system can obtain solutions of at least the same quality as REGAL with a smaller computational cost.

For the Mushrooms dataset the task consists in discriminating between *edible* and *poisonous* mushrooms. The dataset consists of 8124 instances, 4928 of edible mushrooms and 3196 of poisonous ones. Each instance is described by a vector of 22 discrete, multi-valued attributes. By defining a condition for each one of the attribute values, a global set of 126 constraints is obtained, which leads to bitstrings of 126 bits for encoding the individuals. Randomly selected sets of 4000 instances (2000 edible + 2000 poisonous) have been used as learning sets, while the remaining 4124 instances have been used for testing. The system can always found a perfect definition for both classes, covering all the examples and no counterexamples on the test set, as also REGAL and other induction algorithms can do.

The Thousand Trains dataset represents an artificial learning problem in First Order Logic obtained by extending the well known *Trains Going East or Going West* problem proposed by Michalski in order to illustrate Induce' learning capabilities [9]. In this case 500 examples of trains going east and 500 trains going west have been generated using a stochastic generator. A detailed description can be found in [3].

The parameter, which has been used by the previous Genetic Algorithms to evaluate the quality of the found solution, has been the complexity of the final disjunctive solution, measured as the total number of conditions present in it. In the machine learning literature, simple solutions are considered preferable among a set with the same performances.

In Figure 4(a) we report the evolution of the complexity for the Mushrooms dataset, in terms of the number of genetic cycles executed by all the G-nodes, globally. Here it is possible to appreciate the effect of the co-evolution and of the

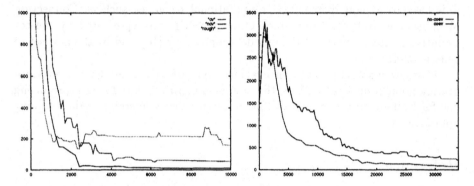

Fig. 4. (a) Evolution of the complexity of the solution vs the genetic cycles: Using the complete operator set and the coevolutive strategy (cv); disactivating the co-evolutive strategy (ncv); using random assignment and REGAL' reproduction operators (rough). (b) Using the co-evolution strategy (coev); disactivating the co-evolution strategy (no-coev).

new reproduction operators, separately. When the co-evolution was disactivated, the G-nodes were assigned to VG-nodes using an equal probability.

An analogous comparison which illustrates the benefit of co-evolution on the Thousand Trains dataset is reported in Figure 4(b). A comparison between RE-

Table 1. Comparison between G-Net and REGAL

System	G–Net		REGAL	
	avg	min	avg	min
Complexity	11	11	21.40	13
Cost	13218	12560	31130	23900

GAL and G-NET on the task of finding a definition for the concept of *poisonous mushroom* is reported in Table 1. We notice that G-NET can reach a complexity smaller than REGAL with a smaller computational cost. We believe that this improvement is substantially due to the use of the mutation operator.

7 Conclusion

A new distributed model for a Genetic Algorithm designed for concept induction from examples has been presented. The algorithm presents several important novelties. A first novelty is represented by the fine-grained distributed mating pool, which eliminates every notion of common memory in the system so that it is easy to exploit distributed computational resources such as Connection Machines and Network Computers. Other novelties are represented by the co-evolutive strategy inspired to the model proposed by [10], and by the new set of genetic operators.

The new algorithm has been evaluated on non trivial induction tasks obtaining good results. Therefore, the new architecture seems to be a promising one for facing computing intensive induction problems emerging in data mining applications.

References

1. C. Anglano, A. giordana, G. Lo Bello, and L. Saitta. A network genetic algorithm for concept learning. In *Seventh Int. Conference on Genetic Algorithms*, East Lansing, MI, 1997. To appear.
2. K.A. De Jong, W.M. Spears, and F.D. Gordon. Using genetic algorithms for concept learning. *Machine Learning*, 13:161–188, 1993.
3. A. Giordana and F. Neri. Search-intensive concept induction. *Evolutionary Computation*, 1996. Winter Issue.
4. D.E. Goldberg. *Genetic Algorithms*. Addison-Wesley, Readings, MA, 1989.
5. D.E. Goldberg and J. Richardson. Genetic algorithms with sharing for multimodal function optimization. In *Int. Conf. on Genetic Algorithms*, pages 41–49, Cambridge, MA, 1987. Morgan Kaufmann.
6. D.P. Greene and S.F. Smith. Competition-based induction of decision models from examples. *Machine Learning*, 13:229–258, 1993.
7. P. Husbands and F. Mill. Co-evolving parasites improve simulated evolution as an optimization procedure. In *4th Int. Conf. on Genetic Algorithms*, pages 264–270, Fairfax, VA, 1991. Morgan Kaufmann.
8. C.Z. Janikow. A knowledge intensive genetic algorithm for supervised learning. *Machine Learning*, 13:198–228, 1993.
9. R. Michalski. A theory and methodology of inductive learning. In J. Carbonell R. Michalski and T. Mitchell, editors, *Machine Learning: An AI Approach*, pages 83–134, Los Altos, CA, 1983. Morgan Kaufmann.
10. M.A. Potter, K.A. De Jong, and J.J. Grefenstette. A coevolutionary approach to learning sequential decision rules. In *6th Int. Conf. on Genetic Algorithms*, pages 366–372, Pittsburgh, PA, 1995. Morgan Kaufmann.
11. G. Syswerda. Uniform crossover in genetic algorithms. In *3th Int. Conf. on Genetic Algorithms*, pages 2–9, Fairfax, VA, 1989. Morgan Kaufmann.

Representation of Music in a Learning Classifier System

Francine Federman and Susan Fife Dorchak

Computer Science / Management Engineering Dept.
C.W. Post Campus of Long Island University
Northern Blvd., Brookville, NY 11548
email: <federman@hornet.liunet.edu>, <dorchak@hornet.liunet.edu>

Abstract. NEXTPITCH, a learning classifier system using genetic algorithms, inductively learns to predict the next note in a nursery melody. This paper presents an analysis of different representations of specific features of Western tonal music. The rationale for the specific note representations merges ideas from learning classifier systems and genetic algorithms with concepts espoused by the music cognition community. Our results are correlated by analyses of variance statistical routines.

1   Introduction

The focal point of this paper is to compare and analyze different representations of specific features of Western tonal music within the construct of a learning classifier system (LCS). Inspired by the work on "classifier systems" of John Holland (Holland, et al., 1986; Goldberg, 1989), we have been working on a program to model human learning of music. Our program, NEXTPITCH, models the inductive learning of Western tonal melodies by an LCS using a genetic algorithm (GA) as the optimization mechanism. NEXTPITCH adapts Goldberg's Simple Classifier System (SCS), a subset of an LCS, to the domain of music.

Our hypothesis is that the way in which notes are represented will effect the performance of the system. Each musical note has multiple features; among them are dynamics, timbre, duration, and pitch, which consists of note name, octave, and accidental. Since notes are grouped into phrases and motives, the relationship between notes is important. The issue becomes which features to represent, how to represent them, and how they affect the performance of the system. To this end, we tested the model with several note representations.

2   Overview

2.1 Music Learning

Previous work in the area of LCS has involved the learning of sequential patterns. Riolo (1988), for example, used a classifier system to predict letter sequences. One example of sequential patterns which is not often studied in relation to classifier systems is music. Simon & Sumner (1993) examined the theory that music consists of patterns and is multidimensional by extending the work of Simon & Kotovsky (1963), which involved a pattern induction program using a sequence of letters as input. Music differs from other sequential learning because it consists of several related attributes (e.g., pitch and duration) and it has a hierarchical structure (e.g., it is divided into phrases which combine to form larger phrases). Thus, music presents a complex example of sequential learning.

This study is a logical extension of the previous work in LCS applied to the task of music learning. The specific task to be modeled is how a listener learns to develop expectations of future musical events based on what has been heard so far. A listener has expectations, at any point in a piece, about what is to follow. That is, based on the notes just heard, a limited set of notes can follow (Dowling, 1993). Our model, NEXTPITCH, predicts each note in a sequence of notes (after the first) and maintains a set of rules that represent the melody that is being learned.

2.2 Basics of a Learning Classifier System

An LCS consists of three distinguishable components: the *performance system*, the *credit assignment system*, and the *rule discovery system*. The performance system interacts directly with the environment and has parallel rule activation. The credit assignment system or *apportionment of credit* (AOC) allows the system to evaluate and learn the relative value of different rules. The *bucket brigade algorithm* (BBA) is one common AOC algorithm used. Finally, the rule discovery system is where the system "learns" new rules. It is here the GA is used to generate rules and replace less useful rules.

The principal processing of an LCS follows the general operational cycle of a genetics-based machine learning system, stated by Smith and Goldberg (1990) as follows:

1. Use the input interface to code the current environmental signal and place the resulting messages on the message list.
2. Determine the set of classifiers that are matched by the current messages.
3. Resolve conflicts between matched classifiers to determine the set of active classifiers.
4. Purge the message list.
5. Add the active classifiers' messages to the message list.
6. Generate action signals to the environment.
7. If a reward is present, allocate credit.

One execution of this sequence is called an "iteration." The GA is activated periodically after a specified number of operational cycles. The actions of the AOC subsystem are implemented in steps 3, 4, 5, and 7.

2.3 Genetic Algorithms and LCS

Genetic algorithms (Holland, et al., 1986) are search procedures based on natural genetics. The GA is theoretically proven to be robust through a search space. In any GA problem, the first step is to encode the parameters as a fixed-length string. The GA searches for strings that are similar; therefore the encoding selected is vital.

The basic execution cycle of a GA (Goldberg, 1989) is:

1. Select pairs of highly fit schemata.
2. Apply genetic operators to produce new strings.
3. Replace the weakest of the population with the new strings.

In each cycle, the GA is working with a population that is closer to optimum. Thus, the GA is guided towards areas of the search space that will lead to the improvement of those strings that are represented. The classifier system in our research uses this GA with some enhancements as suggested in Goldberg (1989).

In Step 1, the GA applies its procedure to classifiers randomly selected from those classifiers that have the highest strength and are thus highly fit. In our research, "stochastic sampling with replacement," also known as "roulette wheel selection," is the method used.

The three fundamental operators used in Step 2 of the execution cycle of a GA are *reproduction, crossover*, and *mutation*. The most highly fit classifiers get to reproduce. Reproduction duplicates copies of classifiers in proportion to their fitness. Simple crossover is applied by first selecting two highly fit parent classifiers and then choosing a random position on which to split. All positions after the split point are swapped between parents and the strings are reunited to create new offspring. Mutation is applied bit by bit to all classifiers at random.

The purpose of Step 3 of the execution cycle of a GA, is to replace the weakest portion of the population, focusing on the size of the population to be replaced. The conditions for replacement of classifiers by the GA are low performance and similarity to the new classifiers created. Similarity is computed by counting those positions that match. Those classifiers with low performance which are more similar to the classifiers being inserted into the population are replaced.

2.4 Note Representation

The number of ways to represent music is limitless. We organized the problem of music representation using our experiences with our earlier models (Federman, 1996), the LCS literature, and music research. Our research incorporates representations of pitch and representations of relational properties that have been carefully selected based on concepts from LCS and music psychology. Primarily, all representations encode the features of pitch name along with octave and accidental information. Then, all representations are supplemented by encoding the relational properties between two notes: contour, duration and interval.

This research attempts to determine whether a simple numerical representation or a cognitively-based representation yields better performance. We classify the note representations into two categories based on the encoding of pitch information: *whole-pitch* and *pitch-plus*. The whole-pitch category represents all pitch information as a single number that is a direct encoding of the chromatic steps of the Western tonal scale. The pitch-plus representations are formulated through a subdivision of the pitch information before encoding in a effort to depict how people perceive pitch.

2.5 Rationale for Note Representations

2.5.1 Ideas from Music Cognition

There are two theories of music perception that comprise the backbone of our note representations. The first, based on Sheppard (1982), emphasizes the way people perceive the similarity of pairs of pitches. Sheppard theorizes that there is a multidimensional representation of pitch using pitch height and the chroma circle. Pitch height refers to how pitches differ by octave and the chroma circle refers to ordering pitches that are a tonal half-step apart in the scale. This study incorporates two of the ideas presented by Sheppard: (1) pitch-plus representations allow for the pitch height dimension and (2) the whole-pitch representations reflect the chroma circle concept.

The second theory refers to Dowling's (1993) observation of the way people perceive and come to learn the music of their culture. He suggests that pitch categories (classes) are programmed into the brain just by listening to music. There are twelve pitch classes: C, C#, D, D#, E, F, F#, G, G#, A, A#, and B. In his studies, Dowling uses melodies spanning only those classes in the C major scale (C, D, E, F, G, A, and B). The two pitch-plus representations use these pitch classes.

Music theorists say it is the relationship between successive notes that permits music learning. Both adults and children use contour and intervals to recognize familiar melodies (Dowling and Harwood, 1986; Trehub, et al., 1985). Other researchers present the ideas that the duration of notes and the rhythmic contours are important to music acquisition (Davidson, et al., 1981). The representations in this study include the relational qualities of contour, duration and interval between two notes.

2.5.2 Ideas from LCS and GA

The literature states that the most representative encoding for LCS and GA consists of a binary alphabet (Goldberg, 1989). The binary alphabet has more schemata (similarity templates that describe strings having similarities at certain positions) resulting in a greater probability of matching one schema to another (Holland, 1992). This is of importance when the GA performs replacement in the SCS model incorporated in the NEXTPITCH program. This replacement of similar population members involves the substitution of the least fit classifiers (those less relevant to the task) by the more fit classifiers (those more relevant) most similar to them. The increased probability of matching a least fit classifier to one more fit results in a greater chance of replacement by a more meaningful classifier. Consequently, of the available possibilities for encoding, the binary alphabet is most often selected for use in LCS and GA.

In this study, we use two examples of a binary alphabet: binary coding and Gray coding. The binary code method uses Base 2 to assign numbers to each value and then encodes those numbers using the binary alphabet. The Gray code representation also uses a binary system with the binary alphabet; however, when going from one coded group to the next, only one bit in the group changes.

2.6 Note Representations Defined

There are two categories of encodings for the note representations used in this research: those that represent pitch information and those that represent relational information. This research tests four different encodings for pitch information and one encoding for the relational information.

2.6.1 Pitch Information Representations

The music features included in all representations are pitch name, accidental and octave. All pitch information representations encode notes in a number of octaves around middle C; the octave starting with middle C is called the third octave. Both the whole-pitch and pitch-plus representations use five bits to encode pitch; however, the way these five bits are broken up differs in the various representations.

Table 1: Whole-pitch Codes

Pitch	Decimal Value	Binary Code	Gray Code
G#2	0	00000	00000
A 2	1	00001	00001
A#2	2	00010	00011
B 2	3	00011	00010
C 3	4	00100	00110
C#3	5	00101	00111
D 3	6	00110	00101
D#3	7	00111	00100

Whole-pitch Representations: The whole-pitch representations use all five bits as a group to encode the pitch information (pitch name, accidental, and octave) as a single number. This code allows for the representation of a range of 30 pitches and two encodings for rests. All notes of the chromatic scale are sequentially numbered, starting with G# below middle C as zero, A as one, and continuing up for 30 notes to C# in the fifth octave of the 88-key piano. This numbering labels middle C as 4 and C# in the fifth octave as 29, with rests as 30 and 31. Examples of the differences in whole-pitch representation between Binary Code Whole-pitch and Gray Code Whole-pitch are illustrated in Table 1.

Table 2: Pitch Class Codes

Pitch	Decimal Value	Binary Code	Gray Code
C	0	000	000
D	1	001	001
E	2	010	011
F	3	011	010
G	4	100	110
A	5	101	111
B	6	110	101
Rest	7	111	100

Pitch-plus Representations: The five bit pitch-plus representation uses the first three bits to represent pitch name and the last two more bits to represent the accidental and the octave respectively. The accidental bit represents a natural as "0" and a sharp as "1" (scales are selected so there are no flats). The octave bit represents a pitch in the third octave as "0," and a pitch in the fourth octave as "1." The melodies tested here only span one octave; therefore a representation that allows only two octaves is sufficient. Table 2 shows the two pitch-plus representations based on pitch class: Binary Code Pitch-plus and Gray Code Pitch-plus. In these two representations, the seven pitches of the C major scale are used to assign decimal numbers to each pitch class.

Table 3: Sample Representations of Pitch Information

	C 3	C# 3	F 3	F# 3	C 4	C# 4
Whole-pitch						
Binary Code	00100	00101	01001	01010	10000	10001
Gray Code	00110	00111	01101	01111	11000	11001
Pitch-plus						
Binary Code	00000	00010	01100	01110	00001	00011
Gray Code	00000	00010	01000	01010	00001	00011

Table 3 contrasts the four pitch information representations for the notes C and $C^{#}$ in the third octave, F and $F^{#}$ in the third octave, and C and $C^{#}$ in the fourth octave.

2.6.2 Relational Information

Music is not just a series of isolated notes; instead the patterns are formed by adjacent notes. The encoding of appropriate relational information supplements each of the pitch representations in additional bits to yield a more descriptive representation of Western tonal music. This relational information of *contour*, *duration*, and *interval* is expressed in Gray code.

Contour is defined as the pattern of ups and downs of pitch from note to note in a melody. This feature is represented by a two bit Gray code where "00" means no change; "01" means up; "10" means down; and "11" means that there was no prior note information.

Duration is defined as the correlation of time between two notes. This feature is represented by a two-bit Gray code where "00" means they are the same length; "01" means the current note is longer, "10" means the current note is shorter, and "11" means there is no prior note information.

Interval is defined as the pitch distance between two notes and is represented by a three-bit Gray code. A major 2nd becomes "000," unison "001," major 3rd "011," perfect 5th "010," perfect 4th "110," minor 3rd "111," major 6th "101," and a minor 2nd becomes "100."

3   NEXTPITCH

3.1 The Model

NEXTPITCH organizes the problem of learning by forming rules based on what has been heard. Like people, the model induces the rules of music by "listening" and "observing" the repetition of the melody. As the number of repetitions of a melody increases, the rules become more directed and the ability "to know" the melody is heightened.

In NEXTPITCH, the classifiers represent possible three-note transitions in a piece of music where the condition of a classifier represents a possible two-note input sequence and the action of a classifier represents a predicted next pitch. This allows NEXTPITCH to "learn" the consecutive note transitions within each three-note sequence. The LCS environment is a piece of music, and the input interface encodes the notes into our desired representation of pitch and relational informational properties. The message list contains the encoded representation of the input notes. The output interface picks the best match and predicts the next note. A reward is given for the correct prediction.

We run NEXTPITCH through one complete test execution of 300,000 iterations for the four representations. This processing encompasses 1440 runs of the program.

3.2 The Results

Fig. 1 organizes the results by note representation. It should be noted that in all histograms, the y-axis represents the number of runs. The bins on the x-axis labeled "percent correct" each include tests whose best performance (the percentage of correct predictions during the last three times through the input melody) is within a range of values (i.e. the 50% bin includes values from 49.5% to 59.5% inclusive). All note representations have results ranging from 30% to 90% correct. By inspecting the results we cannot confirm which is the superior note representation; therefore, further analysis is necessary.

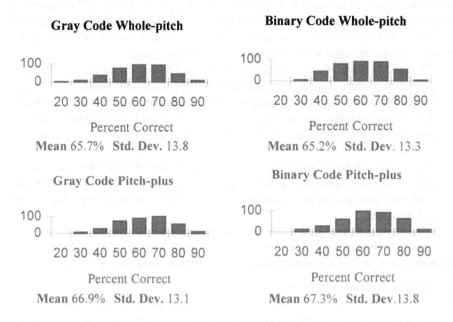

Figure 1: Best Performance Results

4 Analysis of Results

The LCS with a GA is a stochastic system whose performance depends on chance. For example, two factors that may affect performance are the particular set of randomly generated classifiers initially chosen and the particular random number seeds used. Thus, in order to evaluate whether one execution of an LCS is better than another, we must evaluate whether the differences in the observed performances are due to chance. We run various instantiations of our model many times and use the tools of statistics to evaluate whether observed differences are statistically reliable.

4.1 Analysis of Variance (ANOVA) Methodology

For the previously stated reasons, we performed the ANOVA discussed in this section. The objective of our analysis is to evaluate the relative performance of note representation rather than the absolute performance.

To use an ANOVA, the data must follow a normal distribution. Although the individual data values are not normally distributed (Fig. 1), the Central Limit Theorem asserts that distributions of means of samples tend to conform to the normal distribution, even if the distributions from which the samples were drawn are not normal. ANOVA analyzes the means of the data, which are normally distributed.

We use a trimmed data set as input to the ANOVA. This is performed by grouping the tests (i.e. note representation). The minimum and maximum values for each group are dropped and the middle three values retained. Trimming the results reduces the number of data values from 1,440 (each representing the best performance of one run) to 864 data values. The literature supports this idea of selecting a subset of results for an ANOVA (Schaffer, et al., 1989). The reason for comparing only the middle values is that the "F test" in an ANOVA is sensitive to differences in the whole range of values. Thus, we interest ourselves less with the endmost values and more with the mean results within a group.

The ANOVA will identify those effects found to be significant ($p < 0.05$, where p is probability) while also leading to meaningful insights. Furthermore, according to established practices, when the F test has $p < 0.05$, one may reject the null hypothesis. For this investigation the two null hypotheses state: (1) there is no difference between whole-pitch and pitch-plus and (2) there is no difference between binary code and Gray code.

To examine these issues we perform one independent ANOVA on the trimmed data set. To help us continue our note representation evaluation, we subdivide our data into two variables that represent two characteristics: whole-pitch/pitch-plus and binary/Gray code.

The denominator of the F ratio, the within groups mean square, is an estimate of the average variability in the groups (i.e. note representation). The value for the denominator is 48.1. We adopt the conventional format for reporting the results.

4.2 Whole-pitch and Pitch-plus

One of the issues of this paper was whether a cognitively motivated representation, pitch-plus (PP) would do better than a simple numeric representation, whole-pitch (WP). The means supported our hypothesis and are statistically significant. The value for the F ratio is: WP/PP $F(2,863) = 13.7$, $p < 0.05$, showing that there is a difference between whole-pitch and pitch-plus. The mean for whole-pitch is 65.3% and the mean for pitch-plus is 67.0%, thus showing that pitch-plus outperforms whole-pitch. A further breakdown of Table 4 shows the means by binary and Gray Code.

Table 4: Means by Gray Code / Binary Code vs. Whole-pitch / Pitch-plus

	Whole-pitch	Pitch-plus
Gray Code	65.6%	66.8%
Binary Code	65.0%	67.3%

These statistics show that our more cognitively motivated representations pitch-plus, outperform the non-psychologically motivated representations, whole-pitch. This supports the literature which states that representations which are correlated to the domain knowledge perform better (Caruana and Schaffer, 1988).

Why does pitch-plus outperform whole-pitch? It is our contention that pitch-plus outperforms whole-pitch because the whole-pitch representations are harder to learn than the pitch-plus representation. Recall that whole-pitch represents a note by five bits, incorporating all information, while pitch-plus separates three bits of note, one bit octave, and one bit accidental. The purpose of the GA is to apply its operators with the goal of yielding more meaningful classifiers. The crossover operator breaks up classifiers and reforms them. When this operator is applied to pitch-plus representations, there is less chance of disruption because the three bits for note name will more likely stay together during crossover and keep a meaningful classifier. In contrast, in the five bits used by whole-pitch, there is a higher chance of disruption of the note representation.

In addition, the mutation operator changes a bit in a classifier at random. When it is applied to the pitch-plus representation, it has a higher likelihood of yielding a more fit classifier than when applied to the whole-pitch representation. If the three bits for note name are correct, a mutation on either bit 4 (accidental) or bit 5 (octave) may yield a better classifier, or (if the two bits are correct) then a mutation on bits 1-3 may lead to a better classifier.

However, in whole-pitch, a mutation on a bit may create a classifier that is completely different, because the five bits represent a single value. If the mutation is on either one of the high order bits (bits 1-3) or one of the low order bits (bits 4-5), then there is a major change in the note representation. For example, a mutation on bit 2 of pitch representation "00001" leads to "01001." In Binary Code Whole-pitch, this would be a change from A in the second octave to F in the third octave producing an octave change and an unrelated note, therefore a less meaningful classifier. In contrast, using the previous example, in Binary Code Pitch-plus this would be a change from C in the fourth octave to E in the fourth octave, producing no octave change, therefore a more relevant classifier. As a second example, a mutation on bit 4 of "10001" leads to "10011." In Binary Code Whole-pitch, this would be a change from $C^{\#}$ in the fourth octave to $D^{\#}$ in the fourth octave, a completely different note; however, in Binary Code Pitch-plus this would be a change from G in the fourth octave to $G^{\#}$ in the fourth octave, only a change in accidental, therefore producing a more meaningful classifier.

4.3 Binary Code and Gray Code

We investigate whether binary code or Gray code is superior by comparing the categories of binary code to Gray code, collapsing the note representations within the ANOVA. The F value for the ANOVA was large, indicating that the means of the two groups, binary code and Gray code, are not statistically different. The value for the F ratio is: binary/Gray code $F(2, 863) = 0.02$, $p > 0.05$. The means for Binary Code is 66.1% and the means for Gray Code is 66.2%; reflecting a difference between the means of less than .2%.

These findings agree with Caruana and Schaffer (1988) who state that Gray code is not statistically different from binary code although Gray code may sometimes actually be superior. Existing literature prefers Gray code to binary code, but there is little experimental evidence to support this. In our research, Gray code performed slightly better. For statistical analysis, our population is considered small; therefore, we conclude there is insufficient empirical evidence for us to state categorically whether Gray coding or binary is superior for this purpose.

5   Conclusion

We found that cognitively motivated representations of note information perform better.   The representation chosen for a learning system plays a role in the performance of that system. The contribution from this paper is how to represent the many characteristics of music. We suggest that researchers intending to represent music should use a representation which separates pitch from accidental and octave and additionally includes the relational information between notes.

References

1. Caruana, R. A., and J. D. Schaffer. 1988. Representation and Hidden Bias: Gray vs. Binary Coding for Genetic Algorithms. In *Proc. of the Fifth International Conference on Machine Learning*. San Mateo, Ca.: Morgan Kaufman, Inc.

2. Davidson, L., P. McKernon, and H. Gardner. 1981. The Acquisition of Song: A Developmental Approach. In *Documentary Report of the Ann Arbor Symposium: Applications of Psychology to the Teaching and Learning of Music*. Reston, Va.: Music Educators National Conference.

3. Dowling, W. J. 1993. Procedural and Declarative Knowledge in Music Cognition and Education. In T. J. Tighe, and W. J. Dowling, eds., *Psychology and Music*. Hillsdale, N. J.: Lawrence Erlbaum.

4. Dowling, W. J., and D. L. Harwood. 1986. *Music Cognition*. Orlando, Fla.: Academic Press, Inc.

5. Federman, F. H. 1996. *A Study of Various Representations Using NEXTPITCH: A Learning Classifier System*. Ph.D. Dissertation, Department of Computer Science, Graduate Center of C.U.N.Y., New York.

6. Goldberg, D. E. 1989. *Genetic Algorithms in Search, Optimization, and Machine Learning*. Reading, Ma.: Addison-Wesley.

7. Holland, J. H. 1992. *Adaptation in Natural and Artificial Systems*. Cambridge, Ma.: The MIT Press.

8. Holland, J. H., K. J. Holyoak, R. E. Nisbett, and P. R. Thagard. 1986. *Induction*. Cambridge, Ma.: The MIT Press.

9. Riolo, R. L. 1988. LETSEQ: An Implementation of the CFS-C Classifier System in a Task-domain that Involves Learning to Predict Letter Sequences. *Logic of Computers Group, Division of Computer Science and Engineering*. University of Michigan, Ann Arbor.

10. Schaffer, J. D., Caruana, R. A., L. J. Eshelman, and R. Das. 1989. A Study of Control Parameters Affecting Online Performance of Genetic Algorithms for Function Optimization. In J. D. Schaffer, ed., *Proc. of the Third International Conference on Genetic Algorithms*. San Mateo, Ca.: Morgan Kaufman, Inc.

11. Sheppard, R. N. 1982. Structural Representations of Musical Pitch. In D. Deutsch, ed., *The Psychology of Music*. Orlando, Fla.: Academic Press, Inc.

12. Simon, H. A., and K. Kotovsky. 1963. Human Acquisition of Concepts for Sequential Patterns. *Psychological Review*. Vol. 70, No. 6, pp. 534-546.

13. Simon, H. A., and R. K. Sumner. 1993. Pattern in Music. In S. M. Schwanauer and D. A. Levitt, eds., *Machine Models of Music*. Cambridge, Ma.: The MIT Press.

14. Smith, R. E., and D. E. Goldberg. 1990. Reinforcement Learning With Classifier Systems. In Zeigler and Rozenblit, eds., *Proc.: AI, Simulation and Planning in High Autonomy Systems*. Alamitos, Ca.: IEEE Computer Society Press.

15. Trehub, S. E., B. A. Morongiello, and L. A. Thorpe. 1985. Children's Perception of Familiar Melodies: The Role of Intervals, Contour, and Key. *Psychomusicology*, Vol. 5, pp. 39-48.

On Multi-class Problems and Discretization in Inductive Logic Programming

Wim Van Laer[1], Luc De Raedt[1], Sašo Džeroski[2]

[1] Department of Computer Science, Katholieke Universiteit Leuven
Celestijnenlaan 200A, B-3001 Heverlee, Belgium
[2] Department of Intelligent Systems, Jožef Stefan Institute
Jamova 39, 1111 Ljubljana, Slovenia
Email:{WimV,LucDR}@cs.kuleuven.ac.be, saso.dzeroski@ijs.si

Abstract. In practical applications of machine learning and knowledge discovery, handling multi-class problems and real numbers are important issues. While attribute-value learners address these problems as a rule, very few ILP systems do so. The few ILP systems that handle real numbers mostly do so by trying out all real values applicable, thus running into efficiency or overfitting problems.

The ILP learner ICL (Inductive Constraint Logic), learns first order logic formulae from positive and negative examples. The main characteristic of ICL is its view on examples, which are seen as interpretations which are true or false for the target theory. The paper reports on the extensions of ICL to tackle multi-class problems and real numbers. We also discuss some issues on learning CNF formulae versus DNF formulae related to these extensions. Finally, we present experiments in the practical domains of predicting mutagenesis, finite element mesh design and predicting biodegradability of chemical compounds.

Keywords: Learning, Knowledge Discovery, Inductive Logic Programming, Classification, Discretization.

1 Introduction

The ILP system ICL (Inductive Constraint Logic, see [7]) does not employ the traditional ILP semantics in which examples are clauses that are (resp. are not) entailed by the target theory. It rather takes the view that examples are logical interpretations that are a model (resp. not a model) of the unknown target theory. This view originates from computational learning theory where it was originally applied to boolean concept-learning [18], but recently upgraded towards 1st order logic [6] where it is known as learning from interpretations [4].

The ICL system can be considered an upgrade of the attribute value learning system CN2 [3]. However, whereas CN2 learns boolean concepts in DNF form, ICL learns first order theories in CNF form.

In this paper, we import further features of attribute value learning into the ILP system ICL. First, it is shown that ICL can also learn DNF concepts. This is realized using a (logically sound) transformation on inputs and outputs. Secondly, CN2's way of handling multi-class problems (i.e. problems where examples can belong to more than 2 classes) is also incorporated within ICL. Thirdly, and most importantly, (as many other ILP systems) ICL has problems with handling real numbers. In attribute value learning, discretization has recently received a lot of attention (cf. [2, 9]) and proven to be a valuable technique. We show how Fayyad and Irani's discretization technique ([11, 9]) can be modified for use in ILP and more specifically in ICL.

The paper is structured as follows. In Section 2, some logical background is given and the framework in which ICL works is described. Section 3 discusses some issues on the CNF and DNF representations used in ICL. In Sections 4 and 5, we show how we can handle problems with more than two classes and data with real numbers. Section 6 describes some experiments that indicate the usefulness of the newly incorporated features in ICL. Section 7 concludes.

2 The Learning System ICL

An overview of ICL can be found in [7]. Here, we will describe the framework of ICL in an informal way and discuss some practical aspects.

But first we will introduce some concepts from logic (for an introduction to first order logic and model theory, we refer to [14, 12]).

A first order alphabet is a set of predicate symbols, constant symbols and functor symbols. An atom $p(t_1, ..., t_n)$ is a predicate symbol p followed by a bracketed n-tuple of terms t_i. A term t is a variable V or a function symbol f immediately followed by a bracketed n-tuple of terms t_i. Constants are function symbols of arity 0. A literal l is an atom or the negation of an atom. Atoms are positive literals, negated atoms are negative literals.

A **CNF** (Conjunctive Normal Form) expression is of the form
$$(\forall V_{1,1}, ..., V_{1,v_1} : l_{1,1} \vee ... \vee l_{1,n_1}) \wedge ... \wedge (\forall V_{k,1}, ..., V_{k,v_k} : l_{k,1} \vee ... \vee l_{k,n_k})$$
where $l_{i,j}$ are literals and $V_{i,1}, ..., V_{i,v_i}$ are variables occurring in $l_{i,1} \vee ... \vee l_{i,n_i}$.

A **DNF** (Disjunctive Normal Form) expression is of the form
$$(\exists V_{1,1}, ..., V_{1,v_1} : l_{1,1} \wedge ... \wedge l_{1,n_1}) \vee ... \vee (\exists V_{k,1}, ..., V_{k,v_k} : l_{k,1} \wedge ... \wedge l_{k,n_k})$$
where $l_{i,j}$ are literals and $V_{i,1}, ..., V_{i,v_i}$ are variables occurring in $l_{i,1} \wedge ... \wedge l_{i,n_i}$.
The symbol $\forall$ reads 'for all' and stands for universal quantification, and $\exists$ reads 'there exists' and stands for existential quantification. For instance, the formula $\exists C, T : triangle(T) \wedge circle(C) \wedge in(C, T)$ states that there exist a triangle and a circle such that the circle is inside the triangle.

A *Herbrand interpretation* over a first order alphabet is a set of ground atoms constructed with the predicate, constant and functor symbols in the alphabet. A Herbrand interpretation corresponds in the boolean or propositional case to a variable assignment. The meaning of a Herbrand interpretation is that all atoms in the interpretation are true, and all other atoms are false.

A *substitution* $\theta = \{V_1 \leftarrow t_1, ..., V_n \leftarrow t_n\}$ is an assignment of terms $t_1, ..., t_n$ to variables $V_1, ..., V_n$.

By now, we can define the *truth and falsity* of an *expression* in a Herbrand interpretation (if an expression is true in an interpretation we also say that the interpretation is a model for the expression):

A **ground literal** l is true in an interpretation I if and only if l is a positive literal and $l \in I$, or l is a negative literal and $l \notin I$.

A **CNF** expression (defined as above) is true in an interpretation if and only if for all i and for all substitutions θ such that $(l_{i,1} \lor ... \lor l_{i,n_i})\theta$ is ground, at least one of the $l_{i,j}\theta$ is true in I.

A **DNF** expression (defined as above) is true in an interpretation I if and only if there exists an i and a substitution θ such that $(l_{i,1} \land ... \land l_{i,n_i})\theta$ is ground, and all $l_{i,j}$ are true in I.

Let us illustrate this rather complicated definition. It states that e.g. *flies* $\lor$ ¬*bird* $\lor$ ¬*abnormal* is true in the interpretations $\{flies\}, \{abnormal\}$ but false in $\{bird, abnormal\}$. Similarly, it allows us to say that $\exists C, T : triangle(T) \land circle(C) \land in(C,T)$ is true in $\{triangle(t), circle(c), in(c,t), large(c), small(t)\}$ and false in $\{triangle(t), circle(c)\}$. Furthermore, $\forall X : polygon(X) \lor ¬square(X)$ is true in $\{square(s), polygon(s)\}$ and in $\{circle(c)\}$ but false in $\{square(s)\}$.

2.1 The Framework of ICL

ICL is a classification system within the framework of *learning from interpretations*. In this framework, the following choices are made: examples are (Herbrand) interpretations and a hypothesis covers an example if the hypothesis is true in the interpretation. ICL can thus be described as follows:

Given a set of positive and negative examples, and a language $\mathcal{L}_{\mathcal{H}}$, find a first order theory $\mathcal{H} \subset \mathcal{L}_{\mathcal{H}}$ that is complete (covers all positive examples) and consistent (covers no negative examples).

At the moment, ICL can learn first order theories in Conjunctive Normal Form (CNF) and Disjunctive Normal Form (DNF) (see also section 3).

To illustrate the *learning from interpretations* paradigm and our ICL setting, we take one of the Bongard problems. These are general problems developed by the Russian scientist M. Bongard in his book *Pattern recognition*. Each problem consists of 12 figures, six of class $\oplus$ and six of class $\ominus$. One example problem can be found in Fig. 1. The goal is to discriminate between the two classes.

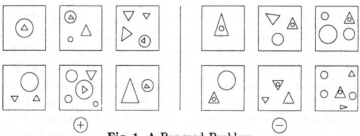

Fig. 1. A Bongard Problem

Each of these figures can be described by a set of facts. Take for instance the upper left example in Fig. 1. It consists of a small triangle, pointing up, which is in a large circle. This figure can be described as: $I = \{triangle(f1), small(f1), up(f1), circle(f2), large(f2), in(f1,f2)\}$. The following DNF theory is consistent and complete: $\exists X \exists Y : triangle(Y) \wedge in(Y, X)$. This theory says that for each figure of class $\oplus$ there exists a triangle that is inside another object.

2.2 Practice

Currently, ICL is implemented in ProLog by BIM. Several heuristics (based on CN2) are incorporated to handle noise. This means that the learned theory need not be strictly complete and consistent with the training set: a theory might not cover all positives, and not all negatives need to be excluded by the theory. ICL has several user-tunable parameters, such as the significance level for significance tests, the maximum number of literals in disjuncts/conjuncts in CNF/DNF, the beam size, and the search heuristic. More details on the algorithm (based on the covering approach of CN2 with unordered rules) and the heuristics can be found in [7].

To specify the hypothesis language, ICL uses the same declarative bias as CLAUDIEN, i.e. DLAB (declarative language bias, see [5]). DLAB is a formalism for specifying an intensional syntactic definition of the language $\mathcal{L}_{\mathcal{H}}$. For CNF, the hypothesis is a conjunction of clauses, and DLAB specifies the allowed syntax for the head and the body. For DNF, the hypothesis is a disjunction of rules (each rule being a conjunction of literals), and DLAB specifies the allowed syntax for the positive and negative literals. This is automatically translated into a refinement operator (under θ-subsumption) for the specified language which is used by ICL to traverse the search space. A small example:

```
{false <-- 0-len:[len-len:[lumo(Lumo), lt(Lumo, 1-1:[-1, -2])],
              len-len:[atom(A1, Elem1, Type1, Charge1),
                   lt(Charge1, 1-1:[-0.2, -0.1, 0, 0.1])]]}
```

Min-Max:List means that at least Min and at most Max literals of List are allowed (len is the length of List). Note that lt(Lumo, 1-1:[-1,-2]) is a shorthand for 1-1:[lt(Lumo, -1), lt(Lumo, -2)].

3 CNF and DNF Representation

Originally, ICL learned a hypothesis in conjunctive normal form (CNF). This is inherited from its older twin system CLAUDIEN (see [5]).

In [15], R. Mooney presents 2 dual algorithms, one for learning CNF and one for learning DNF. However, it turns out that the CNF algorithm can be used to learn DNF formulae provided that the role of the positives and the negatives is swapped, the negation of the tests is used and the result is negated (this property was not mentioned in Mooney's paper). Thus, the CNF version of ICL can be used to learn DNF. For convenience, we have adapted the output procedure of ICL-CNF so that it can produce a DNF output.

Experiments indicate there is a difference in classification accuracy when learning CNF or DNF. In the mutagenesis case this is very clear. Table 1 shows the theory accuracy for the learned DNF and CNF theory. Theory complexity also differs. This is important in the light of Mooney's [15] experiments. He argued that the reason for the differences in accuracy and complexity can be explained by the difference in CNF and DNF. From the property above, it follows that there is an alternative explanation. The differences can be explained as well by the differences in learning the negative concept instead of the positive one.

4 Multi-class Problems

In the previous sections, ICL has been described as a learning system that can be applied to problems with 2 classes of examples. Given a set of positive and negative examples for a class c, ICL learns a theory T^c (in CNF $=(D_1 \wedge ... \wedge D_n)$, in DNF $= (C_1 \vee ... \vee C_n)$) that discriminates between the positive and negative examples. An unseen example is then classified as class c if the example is a model for the theory T^c (i.e. in CNF: all clauses/disjuncts D_i of the theory cover the example; in DNF: at least one conjunct C_i of the theory covers the example). Otherwise the example is assumed not to be of class c.

In many applications with two classes, this is sufficient. But if we have m classes, it's not sufficient to learn just one theory (one would only be able to discriminate between one class and all the others). We should learn m theories, one for each class. The question then is, how to apply this set of theories to an unseen example in order to predict its class? (This is also useful for problems with two classes, as errors in one theory can be undone by the other theory).

In ICL, we use a similar strategy as in CN2 (see [3]). Given a problem with m classes $(m \geq 2)$, we first learn m separate DNF theories for the m different classes. When merging these theories $T_1...T_m$ into $T_{multi}=(C_{1,1} \vee ... \vee C_{1,n_1} \vee ... \vee C_{m,1}...\vee C_{m,n_m})$, we store with each rule/conjunct $C_{i,j}$ in T_{multi}, the distribution of covered (training) examples among the classes (this is a vector $V_{i,j}$ of length m, where the kth element of $V_{i,j}$ is the number of examples of class c_k covered by $C_{i,j}$). In addition, a default class (the majority class in the training data) is stored with T_{multi}. Then, given an (unseen) example e and a multi-class theory T_{multi}, we use the following algorithm to decide on the class of e:

- initialise the vector V of length m with each $V_k=0$
- for each conjunct $C_{i,j}$ in T_{multi}, if $C_{i,j}$ covers e, add $V_{i,j}$ to V.
- if no $C_{i,j}$ covers e (thus all V_k are 0), return the default class
  else, let V_k be the maximum in V, and return class k

5 Discretization

The motivation for discretizing numeric data is two-fold and based on findings from attribute value learning. On the one hand, there is an efficiency concern, and on the other hand, one may sometimes obtain higher accuracy rates.

Procedures currently used to handle numbers in ILP and those used in older versions of CLAUDIEN[5], are quite expensive. The reason is that for each candidate clause, all values for a given numeric variable have to be generated and considered in tests. In large databases, the number of such values can be huge, resulting in a high branching factor of the search. Furthermore, discretization is done at runtime, i.e. it is repeated for every candidate clause. If one clause is a refinement of another one, a lot of redundant work may be done.

What we propose is to generate beforehand some interesting thresholds to test upon. Thresholds are thus computed only once (instead of once for each candidate clause considered). The number of interesting thresholds (to be considered when refining clauses) is also kept to a minimum, yielding a smaller branching factor. This has also yielded positive results in attribute value learning, cf. [2].

Though we present the procedure as applied in the ICL system, it also generalizes to other ILP systems The discretization procedure is tied with the DLAB parameter of ICL, which defines the syntax of the clauses that may be part of a hypothesis. In the template of section 2.2, the user has specified some possible thresholds for ICL. But where do they come from? Up to now, the user had to specify them. In most applications, this is not straightforward. We extend ICL with the capability to produce the possible thresholds itself.

When looking at the DLAB-templates it is often possible to identify a number of meaningful sub-clauses. We will call such sub-clauses *queries*. One could consider each such query that involves a numeric argument as a kind of numeric attribute. There is one important difference with regard to attribute value learning: one example may have multiple values for such a numeric query or attribute.

In our approach to discretization, the user has to identify the relevant queries and the variables for which the values are to be discretized. In DLAB:

```
dlab_template(
  'false <-- 0-len:[len-len:[lumo(Lumo), lt(Lumo, c_lumo)],
                    len-len:[atom(A1, Elem1, Type1, Charge1),
                             lt(Charge1, c_charge) ]]').
dlab_query(c_lumo, 1-1, discretize(lumo(Lumo), Lumo)).
dlab_query(c_charge, 1-1,
            discretize(atom(A1, Elem1, Type1, Charge1), Charge1)).
```

The resulting numeric attributes are then discretized using a simple modification of Fayyad and Irani's method, and the result is fed back into the DLAB template. The details of the Fayyad and Irani's method can be found in [11] and [9].

Fayyad and Irani's stopping criterion, which is based on the minimal description length principle, is very strict, in the sense that the method generates very few subintervals. When applying this criterion in ICL almost no subintervals would be generated. Therefore, we have chosen to let the method take as a parameter the desired number of thresholds to be generated (default 20). A second adaptation made to Fayyad and Irani's method specifically concerns nondeterminacy. Due to the fact that an example may have multiple or no values for a numeric attribute, we use a sum of weights instead of the number of examples in the appropriate places of Fayyad and Irani's formulae (i.e. when we count the real values that are less than a threshold, we sum their weights). The sum of the weights of all values for one numeric attribute or query in one example always equals one, or zero when no values are given.

6 Experiments

We have done experiments in three domains.

The data in the mutagenesis domain (see [17]) consists of 188 molecules, of which 125 are active (thus mutagenic) and 63 are inactive. A molecule is described by listing its atoms atom(AtomID,Element,Type,Charge) (the number of atoms differs between molecules, ranging from 15 to 35) and the bonds bond(Atom1,Atom2,BondType) between atoms. For the experiments, we have used the same four sets of background knowledge as in [17].

The data set for finite element mesh design [8], consists of 5 structures and has 13 classes (= 13 possible number of partitions for an edge in a structure). In total, the 5 structures consist of 278 edges (each edge is taken as an example). The background knowledge is relatively large and contains information on edge types, boundary conditions, loadings and the geometry of the structure.

The task in the biodegradability domain [10] is to predict the half-time of aqueous biodegradation of a compound from its chemical structure. The biodegradation time has been discretized into 4 classes: fast, moderate, slow and resistant. The structure of a compound is represented by facts about atoms and bonds, much like in the mutagenesis domain. An additional background predicate calculates the molecular weight (a real number) for each compound.

We have performed all the experiments with version 3 of ICL for Solaris2.5. The timings we give have been measured on a SUN Ultra 2 (168Mhz). The accuracies have been estimated using a n-fold cross-validation (mostly 10-fold). In some experiments, we used four different settings: for S_1 and S_2 the heuristic is set to laplace, for S_3 and S_4 to m_estimate (with parameter m set to 2). The significance level is set to 0.99 for S_1 and S_3 and to 0.90 for S_2 and S_4.

The mutagenesis domain requires the use of discretization, as it has real numbers. The mesh design domain requires the multi-class extension of ICL, as 13 classes are present. The biodegradability domain requires the use of both.

6.1 The Mutagenesis Experiments

Despite the fact that the multi-class feature of ICL is not needed for the mutagenesis domain, it turns out to be helpful. In table 1 we see that the multi-class theory always has a higher predictive accuracy than the CNF/DNF theory.

Muta	Accuracies (%)						Timings (s)			
	DNF	CNF	multi-DNF	Progol	Foil	TILDE	ICL	Progol	Foil	TILDE
BG1	79.3	69.7	81.4	76	61	75	276	117039	4950	93
BG2	80.3	72.3	81.9	81	61	79	423	64256	9138	355
BG3	85.6	82.4	86.2	83	83	85	440	41788	0.5	221
BG4	85.1	86.2	88.8	88	82	86	673	40570	0.5	651

Table 1. Accuracies and timings for the four different backgrounds of the mutagenesis data, with setting S_2 (the other three settings give similar results), using manual discretization. (The results for PROGOL, FOIL and TILDE have been taken from [1].)

The results in table 1 are obtained by supplying ICL with the possible boundaries for real-valued variables manually (the language looks like the dlab in section 2.2, but is more complex). Herefore, we needed some insight in the data. But what if we do not have this knowledge? We can then use the discretization feature of ICL. Table 2 shows the results of using the same language bias as in table 1, but using the discretization feature of ICL on the numerical variables. The results are comparable to the ones in table 1. We also tried to use all values appearing in the data (a very naive approach) for background 2. Learning one multi-theory then takes about 10 hours, which is about 30 times slower as compared to the other experiments! The accuracy is more or less the same.

Muta	Accuracies (%)			Timings (s)
with discretization	DNF	CNF	multi	multi
BG2	79.8	78.2	83.0	835
BG3	85.6	84.0	86.2	840
BG4	84.6	84.6	86.2	947

Table 2. Accuracies and timings of ICL for three different backgrounds of the mutagenesis data, with setting S_2 and using the **discretization** feature.

6.2 The Mesh Design Experiments

In this domain, the use of the multi-class extension is necessary as there are 13 classes. We performed tow experiments for each of the four settings, the results of which can be found in table 3:

- Exp_1: 5 runs have been done, each time using the edges of one structure for testing, and the edges from the other four structures for learning;
- Exp_2: a 10-fold cross-validation.

Mesh	Accuracies (%)				Timings (s)			
	S_1	S_2	S_3	S_4	S_1	S_2	S_3	S_4
Exp_1	46.8	49.3	50.0	49.3	206	211	315	332
Exp_2	65.1	64.7	66.5	70.1	192	190	223	307

Table 3. Results of ICL on the Mesh data (learning a multi-class).

When comparing the performance of ICL on Exp_1 with other learning systems (results taken from [1]), ICL has the highest predictive accuracy: ICL (50%), TILDE (36%), FOIL (21%), INDIGO (38%), FFOIL (44%) and FORS (31%).

6.3 The Biodegradability Experiments

While extensive experimentation has been conducted in the other two domains, the biodegradability domain is a relatively new one. It requires both the multiclass and the discretization facilities of ICL. Discretization is performed on the molecular weight and the charge values for individual atoms. The maximum number of thresholds is set to 20 (the current default).

The best result in this domain was achieved with setting S_4: an accuracy of 58.1% as measured by the leave-one-out procedure. These are the best results achieved so far in this domain (at the time of writing this paper). The problem is difficult because of the small number of very diverse examples.

7 Conclusion

We have indicated how several well-established attribute value learning techniques can be upgraded for use in the ILP system ICL. This includes the relation between CNF and DNF, discretization and multi-class problems.

We also showed with some experiments in 3 domains (mutagenesis, biodegradability and mesh) that ICL performs very good in these three domains.

In the future, we intend to do more experiments in other domains. Also, we might try other techniques for learning multi-classes, and look further into the possibilities of discretization.

We have proposed several extensions of the ICL ILP system, based on techniques developed for attribute-value approaches. These include the possibility to learn constraints on either CNF or DNF, handle multiple classes, and handle real numbers by using discretization.

These extensions are important for the use of ICL in practical domains, as demonstrated by our experimental evaluation of the extended ICL on three practical domains. Multi-class learning can help even when there are only two classes. Discretization increases efficiency at no cost to accuracy. Finally, learning DNF may sometimes be advantageous to learning CNF, due to the differences between learning the positive and learning the negative concept.

Regarding directions for further work, we note that multiple rules/theories are currently combined using the same approach as in CN2. It might be useful to look into different possibilities to merge several theories in one multi-class theory. We might look, for example, into the Bayesian approach used in [16].

Acknowledgements

Wim Van Laer and Luc De Raedt are supported by the Fund for Scientific Research, Flanders. Sašo Džeroski is supported by the Slovenian Ministry of Science and Technology. This research is also part of the ESPRIT project no. 20237 on Inductive Logic Programming II.

The Mutagenesis and Mesh datasets are made public by King and Srinivasan [17] resp. Dolšak [8], and are available at the ILP data repository [13].

More info on ICL: http://www.cs.kuleuven.ac.be/~wimv/ICL/main.html.

References

1. H. Blockeel and L. De Raedt. Experiments with top-down induction of logical decision trees. Technical Report CW 247, Dept. of Computer Science, K.U.Leuven, January 1997.
2. J. Catlett. On changing continuous attributes into ordered discrete attributes. In Yves Kodratoff, editor, *Proceedings of the 5th European Working Session on Learning*, volume 482 of *Lecture Notes in Artificial Intelligence*, pages 164–178. Springer-Verlag, 1991.
3. P. Clark and R. Boswell. Rule induction with CN2: Some recent improvements. In Yves Kodratoff, editor, *Proceedings of the 5th European Working Session on Learning*, volume 482 of *Lecture Notes in Artificial Intelligence*, pages 151–163. Springer-Verlag, 1991.
4. L. De Raedt. Induction in logic. In R.S. Michalski and Wnek J., editors, *Proceedings of the 3rd International Workshop on Multistrategy Learning*, pages 29–38, 1996.
5. L. De Raedt and L. Dehaspe. Clausal discovery. *Machine Learning*, 26:99–146, 1997.
6. L. De Raedt and S. Džeroski. First order jk-clausal theories are PAC-learnable. *Artificial Intelligence*, 70:375–392, 1994.
7. L. De Raedt and W. Van Laer. Inductive constraint logic. In *Proceedings of the 5th Workshop on Algorithmic Learning Theory*, volume 997 of *Lecture Notes in Artificial Intelligence*. Springer-Verlag, 1995.
8. B. Dolšak and S. Muggleton. The application of Inductive Logic Programming to finite element mesh design. In S. Muggleton, editor, *Inductive logic programming*, pages 453–472. Academic Press, 1992.
9. J. Dougherty, R. Kohavi, and M. Sahami. Supervised and unsupervised discretization of continuous features. In A. Prieditis and S. Russell, editors, *Proc. Twelfth International Conference on Machine Learning*. Morgan Kaufmann, 1995.
10. S. Džeroski, B. Kompare, and W. Van Laer. Predicting biodegradability from chemical structure using ILP. Submitted.
11. U.M. Fayyad and K.B. Irani. Multi-interval discretization of continuous-valued attributes for classification learning. In *Proceedings of the 13th International Joint Conference on Artificial Intelligence*, pages 1022–1027, San Mateo, CA, 1993. Morgan Kaufmann.
12. M. Genesereth and N. Nilsson. *Logical foundations of artificial intelligence*. Morgan Kaufmann, 1987.
13. D. Kazakov, L. Popelinsky, and O. Stepankova. ILP datasets page [http://www.gmd.de/ml-archive/datasets/ilp-res.html], 1996.
14. J.W. Lloyd. *Foundations of logic programming*. Springer-Verlag, 2nd edition, 1987.
15. R.J. Mooney. Encouraging experimental results on learning cnf. *Machine Learning*, 19:79–92, 1995.
16. U. Pompe and I. Kononenko. Probabilistic first-order classification, 1997. Submitted.
17. A. Srinivasan, S.H. Muggleton, M.J.E. Sternberg, and R.D. King. Theories for mutagenicity: A study in first-order and feature-based induction. *Artificial Intelligence*, 85, 1996.
18. L. Valiant. A theory of the learnable. *Communications of the ACM*, 27:1134–1142, 1984.

Discovering Empirical Equations
from Robot-Collected Data

Kuang-Ming Huang & Jan M. Żytkow[†]

[†] Dept. of Computer Science, University of North Carolina, Charlotte, NC 28223
and Institute of Computer Science, Polish Academy of Sciences
zytkow@uncc.edu

Abstract. Discovery of multidimensional empirical equations has been
a task of systems such as BACON and FAHRENHEIT. When confronted
with data collected in a robotic experiment, BACON-like generalization mechanism of FAHRENHEIT reached an impasse because it found
many acceptable equations for some datasets while none for others. We
describe an improved generalization mechanism that handles both problems. We apply that mechanism to a robot arm experiment similar to
Galileo's experiments with the inclined plane. The system collected data,
determined empirical error and eventually found empirical equations acceptable within error. By confronting empirical equations developed by
FAHRENHEIT with theoretical models based on classical mechanics, we
have shown that empirical equations provide superior fit to data. Systematic deviations between data and a theoretical model hint at processes
not captured by the model but accounted for in empirical equations.

1 Robotic experiment and challenges of real data

We describe a discovery mechanism that makes several improvements over the
BACON-like search for multidimensional empirical equations. It has been mo-
tivated by an impasse reached by the existing systems, such as BACON and
FAHRENHEIT, applied to data produced automatically in robotic experiments.

1.1 Challenges to BACON-like search for equations

BACON-like search for multidimensional equations proceeds step by step, adding
one independent variable at a time. Suppose the experimenter collects data by
setting the values of three variables x_1, x_2, and x_3, and measuring y. The final
goal is an equation that combines y, x_1, x_2, x_3. It can often be expressed in a
form convenient for predictions: $y = f(x_1, x_2, x_3)$. At any step of BACON's
generalization from data to equations, independent variables can be divided
in three categories: (1) those that have already been used in an equation (for
example, x_1), (2) one variable that is being added (for example, x_2), and (3)
those variables which have been kept constant in all experiments (x_3).

Generalization to x_2 is triggered when an equation has been found for y and
x_1. The generalization process starts from data collection: for each value of x_2

an equation is sought for y and x_1. Data collection is successful when BACON reaches an externally selected number n of equations of the same algebraic form $f(y, x_1, A_1, \ldots A_k) = 0$, which may have different values of parameters $A_1, \ldots A_k$. Each equation corresponds to one value of x_2. The following table summarizes the "higher level" data used for generalization. Each a_{ij} represents a j-th value of parameter A_i:

x_2	$A_1 \ \ldots \ A_k$
v_1	$a_{11} \ \ldots \ a_{k1}$
v_2	$a_{12} \ \ldots \ a_{k2}$
$\ldots$	$\ldots \quad \ldots \ \ldots$
$\ldots$	$\ldots \quad \ldots \ \ldots$
v_n	$a_{1n} \ \ldots \ a_{kn}$

Now the task is to find k equations of the form $A_i = g_i(x_2)$, $i = 1, \ldots, k$ that link x_2 with each of $A_1, \ldots A_k$, one at a time. Those equations can be used to eliminate $A_1, \ldots A_k$ in the original equation $y = f(x_1, A_1, \ldots A_k)$. As a result, the equation for y uses two independent variables x_1 and x_2 plus several new parameters $B_1, \ldots B_m$, which can be used to generalize the equation to the next independent variable.

BACON works fine when it discovers a single equation per dataset, the same for all data. Langley et al. (1987) offer many examples of successful search, but pay little attention to the many ways in which the BACON search may fail. Even a simple failure at one of many steps causes the whole system to fail and halt. In this paper we describe solutions to the following problems:

1. Search results in multiple alternative equations, that offer acceptable fit to data. If equations of different form are best for different datasets, which equation should be selected for generalization?

2. No equation of common form is acceptable for each dataset. This prevents a meaningful generalization, as all values of any given parameter A_i such as the slope of linear equation, must have the same meaning, so the induction over different values makes sense.

3. Equations can be evaluated when the measurement error is known. In BACON, the value of error is provided from the outside, but it should be determined by experiments since it is specific to a given experiment setup. Evaluation may be overly demanding or too permissive if the system uses wrong values of error. A discovery method should use data to infer the error and then propagate the error so that it applies at all stages of the discovery process.

1.2 Experiment setup

Let us distinguish between two meanings of experiment. In the first meaning, an experiment includes the investigated empirical system S, the manipulating and measuring equipment and the strategy of using them. We shall call it a setup experiment. In the second meaning, an experiment is a single cycle of interaction between the experimenter and empirical system S. The cycle consists of creating a particular state of S, determined by the values of some variables, and in measuring the response of S in terms of other variables. In this paper we consider a discovery system that performs many experiments in the second sense, by varying objects and their properties within the fixed setup.

1.3 Empirical space

BACON and FAHRENHEIT operate within a fixed empirical setup. The scope of their experiments can be represented by a simple formal space. Consider M control variables $x^1, \cdots, x^M$ and N dependent variables $y^1, \cdots, y^N$. Each $x^i, i = 1, ..., M$, is limited to a set of values X^i, that is to the scope of manipulations. Each $y^i, i = 1, ..., N$ can be measured within a set of values Y^i. The values of all variables form a Cartesian product $\mathcal{E}$ of $M + N$ dimensions. Each dimension is a segment of values between a minimum and a maximum.

Experiments are the only way for obtaining information about $\mathcal{E}$. Each experiment consists of enforcing a value for each independent variable $x^i, i = 1, \cdots, M$, and of measuring afterwards the values of $y^j, j = 1, \cdots, N$.

The values of each variable carry empirical error. In this paper we will only consider error of dependent variables. The values of error, ε^i, can vary across Y^i. They can be determined by FAHRENHEIT in the course of experimentation, as we shall see later. Because of the finite size and the minimum grain level determined by the error of each variable, the space $\mathcal{E}$ is finite from the perspective of possible manipulations and measurements.

1.4 Relation to other systems

Although the new methods described in this paper actually expand FAHRENHEIT (Żytkow, 1996), in this paper we only consider a subset of FAHRENHEIT similar to BACON-3 (Langley et al. 1987). In consequence, for the sake of simplicity, we describe the new methods as additions to BACON-3.

Just as BACON-3 uses BACON-1, FAHRENHEIT uses Equation Finder (EF; Zembowicz & Żytkow, 1991) to generate bi-variate equation. Bi-variate equation finding has been the most popular area of automated discovery (e.g. Nordhausen & Langley, 1990; Moulet, 1992; Dzeroski & Todorovski, 1993). EF can be distinguished by its broader space of equations and systematic use of error.

Experiments conducted by FAHRENHEIT and simulated experiments of BACON occur within a given setup. Kekada (Kulkarni & Simon, 1987) offers a broader perspective on experiments, designing them within a number of setups and providing links between experiments in different setups.

Nordhausen and Langley's IDS (1990), although capable of deriving multidimensional equations and placing them in sophisticated theories, does not control experiments and neither deals with the choices among many alternative equations nor consistently handles empirical error.

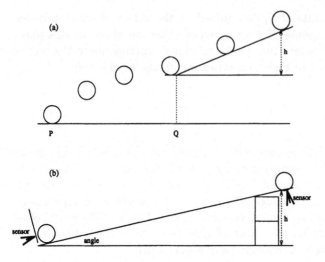

Fig. 1. (a) Galileo's experiment. A ball is rolling down the inclined plane. The experimenter controls height h. When the ball reaches the bottom of the ramp it assumes horizontal direction and falls to the floor at point P. The distance PQ is proportional to velocity. (b) Our experiment. A cylinder moves a fixed distance between a sensor at the top of the ramp and the sensor installed in the buffer at the bottom.

2 Experiment description

In distinction to our previous automated experiments (eg. Zytkow, Zhu & Hussam, 1990) in the domain of chemistry, this time we used a robot arm and the measurement of mechanical motion. We also wanted to evaluate our robotic discovery system on a well-known experiment that influenced the foundation of mechanics.

2.1 Galileo's discovery

Galileo investigated the motion of objects rolling down an inclined plane. A ball, released from the top of the inclined plane depicted in Figure 1a, rolled down and finally hit the bottom. Galileo was not able to measure the accurate time at which the ball reached the bottom, but he could indirectly measure the final velocity. He attached a "jumping board" to the bottom of the inclined plane, so that reaching the bottom the ball assumed horizontal velocity and fell through the air to hit the floor at point P. Galileo used the distance PQ between the jumping board and point P to calculate the velocity of the ball at the bottom of the slope. After a sequence of experiments in which he varied the height h from which the ball started to roll, he derived a theory of velocity v,

$$v = \sqrt{ah}, \qquad a = constant. \tag{1}$$

Fig. 2. The experiment setup. The robot arm is reaching for the first cylinder. Four cylinders have been placed in the cylinder container, while the other five can be seen at the lower right corner of the picture. Holes of different diameter are readily visible. The inclined board has been set at the lowest angle. The board has a bumper attached at the lower end on the left to hold the bottom touch sensor and stop the cylinders.

Galileo's theory influenced the foundations of modern mechanics. It was empirically inaccurate, however, partly because he did not consider momentum of inertia of the rolling body.

2.2 Experiment setup

In our experiment we used the inclined plane, but a precise time measurement has been easier for us than the measurement of velocity. Two touch sensors, to signal the beginning and the end of the process, have been placed at fixed points at the top and bottom of the inclined plane at distance D (50.2cm) and attached to the computer (cf. Figure 1b, 2). The equivalent of Galileo's equation (1) expressed in terms of time t, angle α and Earth acceleration g is,

$$t = \sqrt{\frac{2D}{g sin(\alpha)}}. \tag{2}$$

In our experiments we also wanted to capture the influence of angular momentum on motion. Instead of a ball, we used nine cylinders of the same length (5.9cm) and equal external diameter (4.5cm), with holes of different radius drilled symmetrically through the ax of each cylinder. Their internal diameters differ from 0cm to 4cm by 0.5 cm increments (cf. Figure 2).

Since the fixed locations of touch sensors determined the scope of motion, instead of various locations on the fixed board that Galileo used as his initial states, we varied the angle of the inclined plane. Altogether we used five angles.

Thus, the empirical space consisted of two independent variables (angle and mass) and one dependent variable (time difference between the final and the initial state). The robot arm placed a cylinder of mass m_i at the location of the top sensor (initial state) and then picked it up at the final state, at the location of the bottom sensor.

3 Discovery process

We linked the operational procedures that transport the cylinders and measure time to the FAHRENHEIT discovery mechanism (Żytkow, 1996). For the purpose of this experiment, a subset of FAHRENHEIT has been used, essentially equivalent to BACON-3 (Langley et.al., 1987). Since BACON-3 mechanism is widely known, we will remind it only briefly and concentrate on the new elements.

3.1 Experimentation

The experiments can be summarized as a 3D nested loop:

```
FOR angle FROM angle-1 TO angle-5
  FOR mass FROM mass-1 TO mass-9
    FOR repeat FROM 1 TO 50
      move mass on top of board at angle
      release gripper
      start timer at interrupt from top sensor
      time(angle, mass, repeat) = read timer at interrupt from bottom sensor
```

Nine objects, five angles and fifty repetitions for each pair led to 2250 experiments. At about 30 seconds per experiment, data collection took about 20 hours.

3.2 Error detection

For each cylinder and each angle, the mean value of 50 repetitions has been used as the value of time, while the doubled value of the estimated standard deviation has been used as time measurement error.

3.3 The use of empirical error

The vast majority of discovery systems have been simplistic in handling empirical error. Although many systems include error parameters, they disregard the variety of ways in which error should be used throughout the discovery process.

Consider the data in the form $D = \{(x_i, y_i, e_i) : i = 1, ..., N\}$ and the search for equations of the form $y = f(x)$ that fit (x_i, y_i) within the limits of error e_i. For the same data $\{(x_i, y_i) : i = 1, ..., N\}$, the smaller is the error e_i, the closer fit is required between data and equations. Among the equations that fit the data at error e_i, only some will be acceptable at a smaller error, so that a smaller error may reduce the ambiguity of search for equations.

Knowledge of error, prior to the search for equations, is used in several ways by Equation Finder (EF: Zembowicz & Żytkow, 1991):

1. When the error varies for different data, $\chi^2 = \sum_{i=1}^{N} \left(\frac{y_i - f(x_i, A_1, \ldots, A_q)}{\sigma_i} \right)^2$ (the weighted chi-square value) is used to compute the best values $a_1, \ldots, a_q$ for model f, enforcing better fit to the more precise datapoints. $\sigma = e_i / 2$.

2. Error is used in the evaluation of equations. Error of each datum can be interpreted as the standard deviation of the normal distribution of y's for the value of x. For each equation E, knowledge of that distribution permits the computation od the probability that the data have been generated by adding the value of y obtained from E and the value drawn randomly from the normal distribution defined by the error of each datum. This is a plausible null hypothesis for testing, as normal distributions are often a good approximation of error.

3. As many other equation-finding systems, EF generates new terms by transforming the initial variables x and y. Error values are propagated to the new terms and used in search for equations that use those terms.

4. Error is propagated to the values of $A_1, \ldots, A_q$ in the fitted equations.

5. If the error of a parameter is larger than the absolute value of that parameter, EF assumes that the parameter value is zero. If this happens to the parameter at the highest degree polynomial term, the equation is eliminated. This tool can eliminate the overfitting polynomial solutions.

3.4 Multiple alternative equations

Consider the search for empirical equations. The space of algebraic equations can be built by repeated combination of three spaces determined by (1) the set of models that are directly fitted to data, (2) the set of transformations that generate new terms, and (3) the choice of tuples of terms to be used in the equations. BACON-1 uses (1) constant or linear fit, (2) transformations * and /, (3) pairs of terms, at least one of them derived from the dependent variable. EF uses (1) polynomial equations up to a degree determined by data, (2) transformations *, /, exp. log, sqrt, (3) pairs of terms such that one is derived solely from x, while the other uses occurrences of y.

As a general principle, in automated discovery the search control should follow the simple-first strategy. If two solutions enjoy comparable support by data, the simpler of the two should be preferred. It has less parameters that require empirical interpretation. Simplicity is determined by factors such as the number of parameters in the equation and the number of term transformations used. When the simplicity criteria cannot be reduced to a single scale, solutions can be only arranged into partially ordered simplicity classes.

Since the order of search in each simplicity class is arbitrary, the search driven by simple-first control should stop after examining all solutions in the simplicity class C in which it found the first acceptable solution, or in the case of partially ordered simplicity classes should examine all classes not more complex than class C. EF conducts the search with a fixed acceptance threshold normally set at Q=0.001 and a fixed polynomial degree determined by data. To avoid explosive search, the depth in the number of transformations has been also limited (to one transformation for each of x and y).

3.5 Equations for time as a function of angle, at fixed mass

Following BACON-3 method, Equation Finder (EF) has been applied for each mass from mass-1 to mass-9, to data in the format (angle, time, error of time). Because of the small number of 5 datapoints and their monotonicity, EF limits the search to linear fit. Repeated application of EF led to nine sets of equations, one for each data set. The same five equations out of 46 considered by EF have been consistently the best in each data set. We shall call them eq_1 – eq_5:

$$eq_1: y = (A + B\sqrt{x})/x \qquad eq_2 \quad y = \exp(A + B\log x) \qquad eq_3 \quad y = 1/(A + B\sqrt{x})$$
$$eq_4 \quad y = \log(A + B/x) \qquad eq_5 \quad y = \sqrt{A + B/x}$$

These five equations have been accepted at least in six data sets each, but unaccepted in some data sets. The best five equations generated by EF for mass-2 are reproduced below in a slightly edited lisp form:

```
Y = (/ 1 (+ A (* B (SQRT X))))      (A B) = (-0.083 0.370) +- (0.016 0.004)    Chi2 = 8.77    Q = 0.033

Y = (/ (+ A (* B (SQRT X))) X)      (A B) = (0.732 2.680) +- (0.104 0.038)     Chi2 = 9.19    Q = 0.027

Y = (EXP (+ A (* B (LOG X))))       (A B) = (1.176 -0.545) +- (0.015 0.006)    Chi2 = 11.46   Q = 0.010

Y = (SQRT (+ A (/ B X)))            (A B) = (-0.0710 9.403) +- (0.0118 0.153)   Chi2 = 21.41   Q = 8.63d-5

Y = (LOG (+ A (/ B X)))             (A B) = (1.216 13.260) +- (0.018 0.232)    Chi2 = 30.10   Q = 1.31d-6
```

EF returns error for the value of each parameter. For instance, in the last equation, the value 1.216 of A has error 0.018, while the value 13.260 of parameter B has error 0.232. The first three have been accepted, since their probability Q has been higher than the threshold value $Q_a = 0.001$.

3.6 Generalization to mass

Different equations have been the winners for different masses and none has been acceptable for all masses. This motivated us to expand FAHRENHEIT by a module which prioritizes the equations and redefines their acceptability.

Even if no single form of equation is acceptable for all datasets, generalization should be attempted. The situation is similar to the evaluation of a single equation. Even if an occasional data point is at a distance greater than error from the value predicted by equation, the probability of fit can be still high and the fit can be accepted.

FAHRENHEIT has been expanded to consider each form of equation accepted in at least two thirds of datasets by EF, generalizes all such equations and computes the probability measure Q in the same way as for 2-D equations. For comparison, we also compute several other evaluation metrics. Consider the equations for mass 1–9, summarized below by three measures:

1. The total of ranks of a given equation type in nine sets of equations. For instance, equation-1 was the first twice (2pts), second three times (6pts), third twice (6pts), and fourth twice (8pts), for the total of 22pts.

2. Total χ^2 for all nine equations. The best measure of fit.

3. The ratio of datasets in which the equation was accepted to all datasets.

MEASURE: 1. RANK   2. CHI-2 TOTAL   3. ACCEPTANCE RATIO

eq_1	22	68.8	8/9
eq_2	24	65.3	8/9
eq_3	26	71.0	8/9
eq_4	31	104.4	6/9
eq_5	32	101.4	6/9

The results show that three equation types are distinctly better. Each of the three equations has been accepted at the probability threshold 0.001 for eight out of nine masses.

The following postulates follow from our analysis: (1) a few unacceptable fits, unless very bad (big value of χ^2) do not disqualify a given type of equation; (2) not accepted equations must be remembered at the first level, since some of them will be used at the next level if accepted in the majority of datasets.

The first three equations have been admitted to the next level of search, but for comparison we also used eq_4. Each equation has two parameters, A and B.

For each equation type, FAHRENHEIT creates two datasets, one for parameter A and one for B: $(m_i, A_i, \varepsilon_{A_i})$ and $(m_i, B_i, \varepsilon_{B_i})$. The value of error for each parameter value has been generated by EF at the first level. Now EF is applied to both datasets. The best fits are shown below for the best two equations. Notice, that the majority of searches have been successful without any term transformations.

```
eq'1:  time = (A + B * SQRT(angle)) / angle
For A:  A = (+ Aa (* Ab mass)) ,      (Aa Ab) = (0.248 0.0018) +- (0.1020 0.0005)   Chi2 = 15.0   Q = 0.036
For B:  B = (+ Ba (* Bb mass)) ,      (Ba Bb) = (3.016 -0.0026) +- (0.035 0.0002)   Chi2 = 7.7    Q = 0.361

eq'2:  time = EXP(A + B * LOG(angle))
For A:  A = (LOG (+ Aa (* Ab mass mass))) , (Aa Ab) = (3.09  -2.9e-6) +- (0.03 6.4e-7)   Chi2 = 23.9   Q = 0.001
For B:  B = (+ Ba (* Bb mass)) ,      (Ba Bb) = (-0.509 -1.65e-4) +-(0.006 3.24e-5)  Chi2 = 16.5   Q = 0.021
```

To produce equations of the form $t = g(angle, mass)$, the equations for A and B can be substituted into the original equation $t = f(angle)$.

4   Evaluation of the results

We shall now investigate the quality of the equations proposed by FAHRENHEIT.

4.1   Empirical equations vs. data

Total χ^2 ($\sum_{i=1}^{N}[(y_i - f(x_i))/\sigma_i]^2$) and the corresponding probability Q summarize the fit of equation $y = f(x)$ to data (x_i, y_i, σ_i). Residua $f(x_i) - y_i$ provide detailed information about local areas of fit and misfit. The analysis of residua demonstrates no substantial areas of misfit between data and predicted values, leading to the conclusion that empirical equations provide a joint description of all phenomena that contributed to the data.

The total χ^2 for each type of equation is shown below. We computed χ^2 for each of the four final equations, and we also show the number obtained by totaling χ^2 for each of the nine equations at the first level (for mass). For each equation, both numbers offer answers to an important question: how much fit is lost in generalization from bi-variate equations derived on the first level to the equation derived at the second level. The χ^2 for the final equation must be bigger that the total of χ^2's for the first level equations because the values of A and B derived from equations at the second level cannot be as good as the best one, while the best fit has been assured for each equation on the first level.

Equation:	eq1	eq2	eq3	eq4	mechanics
chi-2 level1:	69	65	71	104	
chi-2 level2:	109	113	115	154	711

The total χ^2 values of the best equations show that the global fit of the theoretical equation (5) (see last column at level2, above) was far worse than that of the best empirical equations.

4.2 Galileo's theory vs. data

After the cylinder is released by the gripper and starts rolling down, the top touch sensor changes its state from engaged to released and the timer is turned on. When that happens, however, the cylinder has already rolled a short distance of about 0.7cm, and its initial velocity $V1$ is greater than zero. We haven't reduced this distance to zero as we wanted to keep a safety margin, so that the top sensor is always successfully engaged. Galileo's theory from section 2.1, applied to our setup, leads to the equation:

$$t = \sqrt{\frac{2D}{gsin(\alpha)}} - \sqrt{\frac{2d}{gsin(\alpha)}} \tag{3}$$

We used this equation to predict time for each of the nine cylinders at each angle. Since Galileo's theory does not capture rotational energy and momentum of inertia, the predicted values offer a very poor fit to data. The residua are at the level of about 25 percent of the empirical values, compared to about 1% of the prediction error of our best empirical equations. The original equation of Galileo, however, could do better, since the constant was determined from his data, eliminating the systematic underfit.

4.3 Theoretical equation vs. data

The following theoretical equation on time t of descent of a hollow cylinder of mass m, derived from classical physics, combines loss of potential energy, gain in kinetic energy of translation, and gain in the kinetic energy of rotation:

$$t = \sqrt{\frac{D(4M - m)}{sin(\alpha)gM}} \tag{4}$$

where D is the distance rolled by the cylinder, M is mass of a solid cylinder of the same diameter as the given cylinder (mass m), and g is Earth acceleration. From equation 4 we derive the theoretical equation that takes into account distance d that the cylinder covered before the top sensor was released

$$time = \sqrt{\frac{D(4M - m)}{sin(\alpha)gM}} - \sqrt{\frac{d(4M - m)}{sin(\alpha)gM}} \tag{5}$$

$D = 50.2cm$, $d = 0.7cm$. We used $g = 980.03cm/s^2$ received from physicists in our building.

The analysis of residua for the theoretical equation (5) suggests that additional factors, not accounted for in the theoretical model, systematically alter results in two areas. For the smallest angle the time predicted from (5) is systematically shorter than the time measured, while for larger angles, the time predicted from (5) is systematically longer. Cylinder sliding is a likely factor at higher angles. Energy dissipation by static friction is likely at the lowest angle.

5 Conclusions

Robotic systems that interact with the real world, gathering empirical data and developing theories, make an attractive long-term goal for machine discovery. Automation of discovery meets a demanding test when applied on robots.

Our reconstruction of Galileo's experiment shows that a simple discovery system linked to a simple robot arm can generate empirical equations that fit the data better than equations derived from a well-established theory. The influence of processes that are hard to represent in a theoretical model can be captured by empirical equations.

It may be futile to expect a robot discoverer to deliver a distinctly superior single solution, typically sought in machine discovery. For automated systems, single solutions are a desired but unlikely borderline between no solutions and many solutions. Automated discoverer may require plenty of further knowledge to gain the perspective necessary to make choices between competing equations and to move from empirical equations to basic theories.

References

Dzeroski, S. & Todorovski, L. 1993. Discovering Dynamics, *Proc. of 10th International Conference on Machine Learning*, 97-103.

Kulkarni, D., & Simon, H.A. 1987. The Process of Scientific Discovery: The Strategy of Experimentation, *Cognitive Science, 12*, 139-175.

Langley, P.W., Simon, H.A., Bradshaw, G., & Zytkow J.M. 1987. *Scientific Discovery; Computational Explorations of the Creative Processes*. Boston, MA: MIT Press.

Moulet, M. 1992. A symbolic algorithm for computing coefficients' accuracy in regression, in: Sleeman D. & Edwards P. eds. *Proc. 9th Int. Conference on Machine Learning*.

Nordhausen, B., & Langley, P. 1990. An Integrated Approach to Empirical Discovery. in: J.Shrager & P. Langley eds. *Computational Models of Scientific Discovery and Theory Formation*, Morgan Kaufmann Publishers, San Mateo, CA, 97-128.

Zembowicz, R. & Żytkow, J.M. 1991. Automated Discovery of Empirical Equations from Data. In Ras. Z. & Zemankova M. eds. *Methodologies for Intelligent Systems*, Springer-Verlag, 1991, 429-440.

Żytkow, J.M., Zhu, J. & Hussam, A. 1990. Automated Discovery in a Chemistry Laboratory, *Proceedings of the AAAI-90*, AAAI Press, 889-894.

Żytkow, J.M. 1996. Automated Discovery of Empirical Laws, *Fundamenta Informaticae, 27*, p.299-318.

Induction of Positive and Negative Deterministic Rules based on Rough Set Model

Shusaku Tsumoto

Department of Information Medicine, Medical Research Institute,
Tokyo Medical and Dental University
1-5-45 Yushima, Bunkyo-ku Tokyo 113 Japan
E-mail: tsumoto.com@mri.tmd.ac.jp

Abstract. *One of the most important problems on rule induction methods is that they cannot extract rules which plausibly represent negative information on experts' decision processes. This paper first discusses the characteristics of two measures, classification accuracy and coverage and shows that accuracy and coverage are measures of both positive and negative rules, respectively. Then, an algorithm for induction of positive and negative rules is introduced. The proposed method is evaluated on medical databases, the experimental results of which show that induced rules correctly represent experts' knowledge.*

1 Introduction

Rule induction methods are classified into two categories, induction of deterministic rules and probabilistic ones[1, 2, 3, 4, 6, 8]. While deterministic rules is supported by positive examples, probabilistic ones is supported by large positive examples and small negative samples. That is, both kinds of rules select positively one decision if a case satisfies their conditional parts.

However, domain experts do not use only positive reasoning but also negative reasoning, since a domain is not always deterministic. For example, when a patient does not have a headache, migraine should not be suspected: negative reasoning plays an important role in cutting the search space of differential diagnosis[7]. Therefore, negative rules should be induced from databases in order to achieve plausible decision processes.

In this paper, the characteristics of two measures, classification accuracy and coverage is discussed, which shows that both measures are dual and that accuracy and coverage are measures of both positive and negative rules, respectively. Then, an algorithm for induction of positive and negative rules is introduced. The proposed method is evaluated on medical databases, the experimental results of which show that induced rules correctly represent experts' knowledge. The paper is organized as follows: in Section 2, a brief description of rough set theory is made and characteristics of accuracy and coverage are discussed. Section 3 presents an induction algorithm for positive reasoning. Section 4 gives experimental results. Section 5 discusses the problem of our work and finally, Section 6 concludes our paper.

2 Rough Set Theory and Probabilistic Rules

2.1 Rough Set Theory

Rough set theory clarifies set-theoretic characteristics of the classes over combinatorial patterns of the attributes, which are precisely discussed by Pawlak [3, 9].
This theory can be used to acquire some sets of attributes for classification and
can also evaluate how precisely the attributes of database are able to classify
data.

Table 1. An Example of Database

	age	loc	nat	prod	nau	M1	class
1	50-59	occ	per	0	0	1	m.c.h.
2	40-49	who	per	0	0	1	m.c.h.
3	40-49	lat	thr	1	1	0	migra
4	40-49	who	thr	1	1	0	migra
5	40-49	who	rad	0	0	1	m.c.h.
6	50-59	who	per	0	1	1	psycho

DEFINITIONS: loc: location, nat: nature, prod:
prodrome, nau: nausea, M1: tenderness of M1,
who: whole, occ: occular, lat: lateral, per:
persistent, thr: throbbing, rad: radiating,
m.c.h.: muscle contraction headache,
migra: migraine, psycho: psychological pain,
1: Yes, 0: No.

Let us illustrate the main concepts of rough sets which are needed for our
formulation. Table 1 is a small example of database which collects the patients
who complained of headache. First, let us consider how an attribute "loc" classify the headache patients' set of the table. The set whose value of the attribute
"loc" is equal to "who" is $\{2,4,5,6\}$, which shows that the second, fourth, fifth
and sixth case (In the following, the numbers in a set are used to represent
each record number). This set means that we cannot classify $\{2,4,5,6\}$ further
solely by using the constraint $R = [loc = who]$. This set is defined as the indiscernible set over the relation R and described as follows: $[x]_R = \{2,4,5,6\}$.
In this set, $\{2,5\}$ suffer from muscle contraction headache("m.c.h."), $\{4\}$ from
classical migraine("migraine"), and $\{6\}$ from psycho("psycho"). Hence we need
other additional attributes to discriminate between "m.c.h.", "migraine", and
"psycho". Using this concept, we can evaluate the classification power of each
attribute. For example, "nat=thr" is specific to the case of classic migraine ("migraine"). We can also extend this indiscernible relation to multivariate cases, such
as $[x]_{[loc=who]\wedge[nau=0]} = \{2,5\}$ and $[x]_{[loc=who]\vee[nat=no]} = \{1,2,4,5,6\}$, where $\wedge$
and $\vee$ denote "and" and "or" respectively. In the framework of rough set theory,

the set $\{2,5\}$ is called *strictly definable* by the former conjunction, and also called *roughly definable* by the latter disjunctive formula. Therefore, the classification of training samples D can be viewed as a search for the best set $[x]_R$ which is supported by the relation R. In this way, we can define the characteristics of classification in the set-theoretic framework.

For further information on rough set theory, readers could refer to [3, 9, 10].

2.2 Classification Accuracy and Coverage

Definition of Accuracy and Coverage Classification accuracy and coverage (true positive rate) is defined as:

$$\alpha_R(D) = \frac{|[x]_R \cap D|}{|[x]_R|}, \text{ and } \kappa_R(D) = \frac{|[x]_R \cap D|}{|D|},$$

where $|A|$ denotes the cardinality of a set A, $\alpha_R(D)$ denotes a classification accuracy of R as to classification of D, and $\kappa_R(D)$ denotes a coverage, or a true positive rate of R to D, respectively. In the above example, when R and D are set to $[nau = 1]$ and $[class = migraine]$, $\alpha_R(D) = 2/3 = 0.67$ and $\kappa_R(D) = 2/2 = 1.0$.

It is notable that $\alpha_R(D)$ measures the degree of the sufficiency of a proposition, $R \rightarrow D$, and that $\kappa_R(D)$ measures the degree of its necessity. For example, if $\alpha_R(D)$ is equal to 1.0, then $R \rightarrow D$ is true. On the other hand, if $\kappa_R(D)$ is equal to 1.0, then $D \rightarrow R$ is true. Thus, if both measures are 1.0, then $R \leftrightarrow D$.

MDL principle of Accuracy and Coverage One of the important characteristics of the relation between classification accuracy and coverage is a trade-off relation on description length, called MDL principle[5] which is easy to be proved from the definitions of these measures.

Let us define the description length of a rule as:

$$\mathcal{L} = -\log_\in \alpha_\mathcal{R}(\mathcal{D}) - \log_\in \kappa_\mathcal{R}(\mathcal{D}),$$

which represents the length of a bit strings to describe all the information about classification of accuracy and coverage. In this definition, the length of coverage corresponds to the cost of "theory" in MDL principle because of the following theorem on coverage.

Proposition 1 Monotonicity of Coverage. *Let*
R_j *denote an attribute-value pair, which is a conjunction of R_i and $[a_{i+1} = v_j]$.*
Then,

$$\kappa_{R_j}(D) \le \kappa_{R_i}(D).$$

Proof.
Since $[x]_{R_j} \subseteq [x]_{R_i}$ holds, $\kappa_{R_j}(D) = \frac{|[x]_{R_j} \cap D|}{|D|} \le \frac{|[x]_{R_i} \cap D|}{|D|} = \kappa_{R_i}(D)$. $\qquad\square$

Then, from their definitions, the following relation will hold unless $\alpha_R(D)$ or $\kappa_R(D)$ is equal to 1.0: [1]

$$\mathcal{L} = -\log_2 \alpha_R(D) - \log_2 \kappa_R(D)$$
$$= -\log_2 \frac{P(R \cap D)}{P(R)} - \log_2 \frac{P(R \cap D)}{P(D)}$$
$$= -\log_2 \frac{(P(R \cap D)P(R \cap D)}{P(D)P(R)}$$
$$\geq -\log_2 \frac{P(R)}{P(D)}.$$

$P(R)$ and $P(D)$ are defined as:

$$P(R) = \frac{|[x]_R|}{|U|} \quad and \quad P(D) = \frac{|D|}{|U|},$$

where U denotes the total samples.

When we add an attribute-value pair to the conditional part of a rule, the cardinality of $[x]_R$ will decrease and equivalently, the value of $P(R)$ will be smaller. Thus, $\log_2 P(R)$ will approach to $-\infty$ as a result.

Thus, if we want to get a rule of high accuracy, the coverage of this rule will be very small, which causes the high cost of the description of rules. On the other hand, if we want to get a rule of high coverage, the accuracy of this rule will be very small, which also causes the high cost of the description of rules.

It also means that a rule of high accuracy should be described with additional information about positive examples which do not support the rule, or that a rule of high coverage should be described with additional information about negative examples which support the rule.

The main objective of this paper is to point out that we should use negative rules as additional information for positive rules, as shown in the next subsection. [2]

2.3 Positive Rules

A positive rule can be defined as a rule supported by only positive examples, which means that the classification accuracy of a rule is equal to 1.0. Thus, a positive rule is represented as:

$$R \rightarrow d \quad s.t. \quad R = \wedge_j[a_j = v_k], \quad \alpha_R(D) = 1.0$$

---

[1] Since MDL principle do not consider the concept of coverage, it is difficult to incorporate the meaning of coverage in an explicit way. However, as discussed in the section on negative rules, the situation when the coverage is equal to 1.0 has a special meaning to express the information about negative reasoning. It will be our future work to study the meaning when the coverage is equal to 1.0. in the context of the description length of "theory".

[2] Negative rules are not equivalent to information about positive examples which do not support the positive rules, but they include it implicitly.

In the above example, one positive rule of "m.c.h." is:

$$[nau = 0] \rightarrow m.c.h. \quad \alpha = 3/3 = 1.0.$$

This positive rule is often called deterministic rules. However, in this paper, we use a term, positive (deterministic) rules, because deterministic rules which is supported only by negative examples, called negative rules, is introduced as in the next subsection.

2.4 Negative Rules

Before defining a negative rule, let us first introduce an exclusive rule, the contrapositive of a negative rule[8]. An exclusive rule can be defined as a rule supported by all the positive examples, which means that the coverage of a rule is equal to $1.0.$[3] Thus, an exclusive rule is represented as:

$$R \rightarrow d \quad s.t. \quad R = \vee_j[a_j = v_k], \quad \kappa_R(D) = 1.0.$$

In the above example, exclusive rule of "m.c.h." is:

$$[M1 = 1] \vee [nau = 0] \rightarrow m.c.h. \quad \kappa = 1.0,$$

From the viewpoint of propositional logic, an exclusive rule should be represented as:

$$d \rightarrow \vee_j[a_j = v_k],$$

because the condition of an exclusive rule correspond to the necessity condition of conclusion d. Thus, it is easy to see that a negative rule is defined as the contrapositive of an exclusive rule:

$$\wedge_j \neg[a_j = v_k] \rightarrow \neg d,$$

which means that if a case does not satisfy any attribute value pairs in the condition of a negative rules, then we can exclude a decision d from candidates. For example, the negative rule of m.c.h. is:

$$\neg[M1 = 1] \wedge \neg[nau = 0] \rightarrow \neg m.c.h.$$

In summary, a negative rule is defined as:

$$\wedge_j \neg[a_j = v_k] \rightarrow \neg d \quad s.t. \quad \forall[a_j = v_k] \ \kappa_{[a_j = v_k]}(D) = 1.0,$$

where D denotes a set of samples which belong to a class d.

It can be also called a deterministic rule, since a measure of negative concept, coverage is equal to 1.0.

---

[3] Exclusive rules represent the necessity condition of a decision.

procedure *Exclusive and Negative Rules*;
  var
    L : *List*; /* A list of elementary attribute-value pairs */
  begin
    $L := P_0$; /* P_0: A list of elementary attribute-value pairs given in a database */
    while $(L \neq \{\})$ **do**
      begin
        Select one pair $[a_i = v_j]$ from L;
        if $([x]_{[a_i=v_j]} \cap D \neq \phi)$ **then do** /* D: positive examples of a target class d */
          begin
            $L_{ir} := L_{ir} + [a_i = v_j]$; /* Candidates for Positive Rules */
            if $(\kappa_{[a_i=v_j]}(D) = 1.0)$ **then** $R_{er} := R_{er} \wedge [a_i = v_j]$;
            /* Include $[a_i = v_j]$ in the Exclusive Rule */
          end
        $L := L - [a_i = v_j]$;
      end
    Construct Negative Rules: take the contrapositive of R_{er}.
end {*Exclusive and Negative Rules*};

Fig. 1. Induction of Exclusive and Negative Rules

3 Algorithms for Rule Induction

3.1 Induction of Negative Rules

The contrapositive of a negative rule, an exclusive rule is induced as an exclusive rule by the modification of the algorithm introduced in PRIMEROSE-REX[8], as shown in Figure 1. Negative rules are derived as the contrapositive of induced exclusive rules.

3.2 Induction of Positive Rules

Positive rules are induced as inclusive rules by the algorithm introduced in PRIMEROSE-REX[8], as shown in Figure 2. For induction of positive rules, the threshold of accuracy and coverage is set to 1.0 and 0.0, respectively.

3.3 Example

Let us consider the example shown in Table 1. First, applying the algorithm for induction of negative rules, we obtain the following exclusive rules:

$m.c.h. \rightarrow [prod = 0] \vee [M1 = 1]$
$migra \rightarrow [age = 40 - 49] \vee [nat = thr] \vee [prod = 1] \vee [nau = 1] \vee [M1 = 0]$
$psycho \rightarrow [age = 50 - 59] \vee [loc = who] \vee [nat = per] \vee [prod = 0] \vee [nau = 1]$
$\qquad\qquad \vee [M1 = 1]$

Thus, induced negative rules are:

procedure *Positive Rules*;
  var
    i : *integer*;
    M, L_i : *List*;
  begin
    $L_1 := L_{ir}$; /* L_{ir}: A list of candidates generated by induction of exclusive rules */
    $i := 1$; $M := \{\}$;
    for $i := 1$ **to** n **do** /* n: Total number of attributes given in a database */
      begin
        while ($L_i \neq \{\}$) **do**
          begin
            Select one pair $R = \wedge[a_i = v_j]$ from L_i;
            $L_i := L_i - \{R\}$;
            if $(\alpha_R(D) > \delta_\alpha)$ **then do** $S_{ir} := S_{ir} + \{R\}$;
            /* Include R in a list of the Positive Rules */
            else $M := M + \{R\}$;
          end
        $L_{i+1} :=$ (A list of the whole combination of the conjunction formulae in M);
      end
end {*Positive Rules*};

Fig. 2. Induction of Positive Rules

$\neg[prod = 0] \wedge \neg[M1 = 1]$ $\rightarrow \neg\ m.c.h.$
$\neg[age = 40 - 49] \wedge \neg[nat = thr] \wedge \neg[prod = 1] \wedge \neg[nau = 1] \wedge \neg[M1 = 0] \rightarrow \neg\ migra$
$\neg[age = 50 - 59] \wedge \neg[loc = who] \wedge \neg[nat = per] \wedge \neg[prod = 0]$
$\wedge\neg[nau = 1] \wedge \neg[M1 = 1]$ $\rightarrow \neg\ psycho$

Then, applying the algorithm for induction of positive rules, we obtain the
following positive rules:

$$[loc = occ] \rightarrow m.c.h.$$
$$[nau = 0] \rightarrow m.c.h.$$
$$[nat = thr] \rightarrow migra$$
$$[prod = 1] \rightarrow migra$$
$$[M1 = 0] \rightarrow migra$$

It is notable that we cannot obtain any positive rule for "psycho", but that
we have one negative rule for it.

4 Experimental Results

For experimental evaluation, we introduce a new system, called PRIMEROSE-
REX2, which implements the algorithm discussed in Section 3. PRIMEROSE-
REX2 is applied to the following three medical domains: headache(RHINOS
domain), whose training samples consist of 1477 samples, 10 classes, and 20 attributes, cerebulovasular diseases, whose training samples consist of 620 samples,

Table 2. Experimental Results (Accuracy: Averaged)

Method	Headache	CVD	Meningitis
PR-REX2(Positive and Negative)	91.3%	89.3%	92.5%
PR-REX2(Positive)	68.3%	71.3%	74.5%
Experts	95.0%	92.9%	93.2%
PR-REX	88.3%	84.3%	82.5%
CART	85.8%	79.7%	81.4%
AQ15	86.2%	78.9%	82.5%

DEFINITIONS: CVD:Cerebrovascular Disease,
PR-REX2: PRIMEROSE-REX2.

15 classes, and 25 attributes, and meningitis, whose training samples consists of 213 samples, 3 classes, and 27 attributes.

The experiments are performed by the following three procedures. First, these samples are randomly splits into new training samples and new test samples. Second, using the new training samples, PRIMEROSE-REX2 induces positive and negative rules. Third, the induced results are tested by the new test samples. These procedures are repeated for 100 times and average all the estimators over 100 trials.

Experimental results are shown in Table 2. The first and second row show the results obtained by using PRIMROSE-REX2: the results in the first row is derived by using both positive and negative rules and those in the second row is derived by only positive rules. The third row shows the results derived from medical experts. For comparison, we compare the classification accuracy of inclusive rules with that of PRIMEROSE-REX (induction of exclusive rules and probabilistic rules), CART and AQ-15, which is shown in the fourth and the fifth row. These results shows that the combination of positive and negative rules outperforms not only positive rules, but also probabilistic rules (PRIMEROSE-REX) and other rule induction methods.

5 Discussion

As discussed in Section 3, positive and negative rules are:

$PositiveRule:$ $\quad \wedge_j[a_j = v_k] \rightarrow d \quad s.t \quad \alpha_{\wedge_j[a_j=v_k]}(D) = 1.0$

$NegativeRule:$ $\wedge_j \neg[a_j = v_k] \rightarrow \neg d \quad s.t. \quad \forall[a_j = v_k] \; \kappa_{[a_j=v_k]}(D) = 1.0.$

Positive rules are exactly equivalent to deterministic rules, which is defined in [3]. So, the disjunction of positive rules corresponds to the positive region of a target concept (decision attribute). On the other hand, negative rules corresponds to the negative region of a target concept. From this viewpoint, probabilistic rules correspond to the combination of the boundary region and the positive region (mainly the boundary region).

Thus our approach, the combination of positive and negative deterministic rules captures the target concept as the combination of positive and negative information. Interestingly, our experiment shows that the combination outperforms the usage of only positive rules, which suggest that we need also negative information to achieve higher accuracy. So, although our method is very simple, it captures the important aspect of experts' reasoning and points out that we should examine the role of negative information in experts' decision more closely.

Another aspect of experts' reasoning is fuzzy or probabilistic: in the rough set community, the problems of deterministic rules are pointed by Ziarko[9], who introduces Variable Precision Rough Set Model (VPRS model). VPRS model extends the positive concept with the precision of classification accuracy: the relation, the classification accuracy of which is larger than the precision (threshold), will be regarded as positive. Thus, in this model, rules of high accuracy are included in an extended positive region.

Analogously, we can also extend the negative concept with the precision of coverage, which will make an extended negative region. The combination of those positive and negative rules will extend the approach introduced in this paper, which is expected to gain the performance or to extract knowledge about experts' decision more correctly. It will be a future work to check whether the combination of extended positive and negative rules will outperform that of positive and negative deterministic rules.

Another interest is a measure of boundary region: a measure of positive information is accuracy and one of negative information is coverage. Probabilistic rules can be measured by the combination of accuracy and coverage[8], but the combination of two measures is difficult to compare each rule: to measure the quality of boundary. It will also be one of the imporant future research directions.

6 Conclusion

In this paper, the characteristics of two measures, classification accuracy and coverage is discussed, which shows that both measures are dual and that accuracy and coverage are measures of both positive and negative rules, respectively. Then, an algorithm for induction of positive and negative rules is introduced. The proposed method is evaluated on medical databases, the experimental results of which show that induced rules correctly represent experts' knowledge, compared with previous approaches.

References

1. Clark, P., Niblett, T. (1989). The CN2 Induction Algorithm. *Machine Learning*, **3**, 261-283.
2. Michalski, R. S., Mozetic, I., Hong, J., and Lavrac, N. (1986). The Multi-Purpose Incremental Learning System AQ15 and its Testing Application to Three Medical Domains. *Proceedings of the fifth National Conference on Artificial Intelligence*, 1041-1045, AAAI Press, Palo Alto, CA.

3. Pawlak, Z. (1991). *Rough Sets*. Kluwer Academic Publishers, Dordrecht.
4. Quinlan, J.R. (1993). *C4.5 - Programs for Machine Learning*, Morgan Kaufmann, CA.
5. Rissanen, J. (1989). *Stochastic Complexity in Statistical Inquiry*, World Scientific, Singapore.
6. Tsumoto, S. and Tanaka, H. (1995). PRIMEROSE: Probabilistic Rule Induction Method based on Rough Sets and Resampling Methods. *Computational Intelligence*, **11**, 389-405.
7. Tsumoto, S. (1997). Empirical Induction of Medical Expert System Rules based on Rough Set Model. PhD dissertation(in Japanese).
8. Tsumoto, S. and Tanaka, H. (1996). Automated Discovery of Medical Expert System Rules from Clinical Databases based on Rough Sets. Proceedings of the Second International Conference on Knowledge Discovery and Data Mining 96, pp.63-69, AAAI Press.
9. Ziarko, W. (1991). The Discovery, Analysis, and Representation of Data Dependencies in Databases. in: Shapiro, G. P. and Frawley, W. J. (eds), *Knowledge Discovery in Databases*, AAAI press, Palo Alto, CA, pp.195-209.
10. Ziarko, W (1993). Variable Precision Rough Set Model. *Journal of Computer and System Sciences*, **46**, 39-59.

Autonomous Database Mining and Disorder Measures

Lawrence J. Mazlack[*]

Computer Science
University of Cincinnati
Cincinnati, Ohio 45221-0030

Abstract

The essential question of database mining is how to computationally identify the most useful information. The discussed approach is to sift out non-useful data until useful information is discovered. This approach contrasts to existing approaches that assume they can select and rank order the most useful data when confronted by all the data, useful and non-useful. The problem with this is that it is computationally infeasible to look at all the data; so, heuristic choices are made. These choices strongly constrain what might be discovered.

OVERVIEW

Databases have significant amounts of stored data. This data continues to grow exponentially. The data is known to be valuable because it was collected to explicitly support particular enterprise activities. There could well be valuable, undiscovered relationships in the data. The issue is how best to recognize them.

Database mining seeks to discover noteworthy, unrecognized associations between data items in an existing database. The potential of discovery comes from the realization that alternate contexts may reveal additional valuable information. A metaphor for database discovery is mining. The metaphor is to somehow 'sift' through the 'ore' of a database to discover information 'nuggets'. Data mining elicits knowledge that is implicit in the databases. In a sense, we could say that database mining may make implicit knowledge available for use.

A number of different things may be the subject of mining. Most often, the goal has been recognizing inter-item relationships. However, it is also possible to seek to recognize the equivalent of human concepts. Concepts reflect items. A measure of the success of a concept boundary is reduced internal cognitive dissonance.

One way to try to discover new information is to try to consider the relationship between every item. This may work when there are relatively few things to consider. However, in a large collection of data, the problem is too computationally complex. For this reason, two dominant paradigms have evolved. In one, before analysis starts, humans define what attributes might be of interest. Sometimes the structure of the relationship(s) is defined. In some efforts, human guidance may continue during mining.

The other dominant paradigm computationally develops a metric to identify attributes of greatest interest. Most often, the metric is based on Shannon's information theory. In large data sets, because of computational complexity, a training set is used. This approach has the disadvantages that it necessarily imposes sequence dependencies on the results. Also, the quality of the results depends on the quality of the training set. A

---

[*]Significant portions of this work was done while visiting with

BISC, Computer Science
University of California
Berkeley, California

more subtle concern is that Shannon was interested in minimum length decision coding and a metric so based may not be appropriate for all types of mining.

A third paradigm is suggested here. A goal is autonomous or unsupervised mining. Given that, predefining items of interest is counter-intuitive. However, considering everything is too computationally expensive. The paradigm is that information can be discovered through eliminating the uninteresting. Informally, this third paradigm addresses complexity difficulties by sifting out attributes that provide the least information to form cohesive, comprehensible information groups. A metric and methodology to sift out the less interesting is considered. The methodology concentrates what is discovered. (Metaphorically, the data is concentrated into 'nuggets' of information.) The metric suggested is the dissonance within a data partition. This is contrasted to the more common approaches that attempt best to discriminate between individual data items. How to measure and control disorder dissonance is the focus of this work.

Approaching the problem using a cohesion enhancement paradigm has the benefit of avoiding the intractability of combinatorial complexity that arises in attempting to discover relationships between all the elements. Cohesive information is also more easily understood. Data can be formed into information nuggets by discarding non-useful data while partitioning the remaining data into the equivalent of human concepts.

Partitioning may be supported by forming granules within an attribute. Attributes containing granularized data can be more easily partitioned. Normally, granules are formed on scalar data. Difficulties with unsupervised recognition of granules in ordered data lie with (a) the number of granules to be used and (b) the range of values to be included in a particular granule. There are known ways of clustering data when the number of clusters is known and/or the initial cluster seeds are known. However, in autonomous mining, this information is usually not available. The approach suggested by this work is to use a variation of the 'mountain method'.

DETAILED DISCUSSION

1 Introduction

A number of different database mining techniques may be used. There are two basic approaches: unsupervised or supervised search. Much of the existing work has used some form of supervised search. However, supervised search limits the results because it is necessary to determine in advance the subjects that are of interest. This is contra-intuitive to the broadest goals of finding unexpected, interesting things. In keeping with more ambitious goals, this work considers autonomous mining.

One problem with autonomous mining is that of combinatoric explosion. In a typical database, there may be hundreds of attributes. To consider fully the interrelationships between all the attributes is computationally prohibitive. Possible heuristic help comes from the realization that many of the combinatoric combinations do not appear to have much information. This leads to this work's controlling heuristic that focusing on reducing disorder to increase coherence and decreasing dissonance.

The heuristic assumption is that reducing cognitive dissonance increases useful information. The speculation is that database exploration can be accomplished through a progressive reduction of cognitive dissonance. This will be done by progressively discarding attributes that have limited information value and by partitioning the data to increase information within the resulting partitions.

2 Background

2.1 Induction

Database mining has its roots in the fields of inductive inference. Database mining techniques often incrementally consider database records with the goal of building a classification tree. This is in keeping with much of classical machine learning. Much of the research on database mining has been done using top-down inductive methods.

2.2 Approaches

There are several ways to classify database mining work. One way is by the amount of semantic domain knowledge used. *Guided* or *supervised* methods may use domain knowledge to direct the search. When no semantic domain knowledge is involved, the method is generally *autonomous, unguided* or *unsupervised*. On a different axis, work can also be classified as: *incremental* or *non-incremental*. Incremental methods discover information by processing individual records one at a time. What may be discovered and the decision basis for the algorithms depends on the choices between supervised/autonomous and incremental/non-incremental.

2.2.1 Incrementalization

A database is characterized by growth. Transactions and updates are everyday occurrences that result in changes to the database. Consequently, the validity of mined information may degrade when the data within the database changes.

Incremental methods take what has already been learned from previous data mining efforts and modify the discovered knowledge to adapt to new data. Incremental algorithms can process each new record as a separate instance. New instances may result in altering the results. Cobweb [Fisher, 1987] is an early incremental work. This was later extended with Arachne [Gennari, Langley, Fisher, 1989]. In practice, many of the incremental methods are limited. While they can handle new records, they cannot handle changes other than record additions (i.e., changes may require reconsidering the entire database).

Incremental methods may be either supervised or autonomous. For example, Sprouter [Hayes-Roth, McDermott, 1987] induced supervised abstractions. Smyth and Goodman [1991] used supervised discovery and incremental processing.

2.2.2 Domain Knowledge

Domain knowledge is information about the semantics of the database as opposed to information about syntax of the data (e.g., data types or attribute values). Domain knowledge is commonly used to improve efficiency, guide mining, and recognize when interesting things. Domain knowledge may be encoded as well as come directly from the user. The utility of domain knowledge helps in making choices on a basis using a criterion other than goodness of fit [Quinlan, 1992].

Fully recognizing authentically interesting information out of what is discovered requires domain knowledge [Ayel, Laurent, 1991]. However, embedding domain knowledge in a context sensitive structure is a difficult task in itself [Lenat, Guha, 1990].

Some supervised systems encode domain knowledge directly. Generally, when knowledge is encoded, the programs usually are relatively efficient, but are limited to being used within that domain. Domain knowledge coming from user interaction can be used to guide mining [Piatetsky-Shapiro, Matheus, 1991] [Anwar, Beck, 1992] [Hayes-Roth, McDermott, 1987] [Zytkow, Baker, 1992] [Zhong, Oshuga, 1993].

Unsupervised methods use non-semantic heuristics rather than domain knowledge. The knowledge supplied to these systems only includes the syntactic characteristics of the database. Therefore, these systems can be applied to more than one semantic domain. Heuristics are often from the following areas: information theory [Agrawal, Imielinski, Swami, 1993] [Smyth, Goodman, 1991], fuzzy sets, rough sets [Ziarko, 1991, 1995], and statistics [Shen, 1991] [Langley, Iba, Thompson, 1992].

2.2.3 Reducing Search

Supervised methods use some form of external problem guidance while unsupervised methods are more purely reactive to their problem world. Supervised search typically has some well-defined goal or objective. The selection of the concerned attributes constrains the results [Langley, 1994]. Unsupervised mining, on the other hand, does not have a predefined goal beyond 'finding interesting and useful patterns'.

Unsupervised mining has design implications. The first is that since there is no clearly defined objective, it is difficult to tell when something worthwhile has been found. Without a goal, how does the mechanism decide which of many possible alternatives is the best (or at least a good) way to go? Also, how does the mechanism know when to stop? In other words, without a way of telling what you are looking for, how do you know when you have found it?

Autonomous mining requires that some heuristic metric must be used to provide a working definition of what is interesting or useful. This metric can then guide the search. The metric can also be used to evaluate the degree of interestingness of different results. An unsupervised search strategy has potentially high complexity because of combinatorial explosion between attributes; as well as, the effects of noisy and incomplete data. There are techniques that attempt to eliminate noisy data and predict missing data [Langley, 1981]. The main difficulty is combinatorial explosion. Supervised search can use domain knowledge to reduce the search space; however, only heuristics are available for unsupervised search.

The suggested approach is the converse of most unsupervised database mining approaches. Instead of seeking to recognize the desirable; the undesirable is eliminated. The final and/or intermediate results are not necessarily symmetric to approaches that attempt first to identify the most interesting. While the idea of screening out the less desirable goes back to early man's minineral mining efforts, it is not a widely used technique in database mining. Instead, mining has followed the lead of classical machine learning with a focus on attribute selection [Baim, 1988].

2.3 Crispness

Crispness is a concern. Most mining techniques implicitly assume that the data is clean and that the data can eventually be effectively clustered on a precise metric. However, the reality is that the data is often imperfect, that some values are inherently imprecise. Also, partitioning based on a heuristic is implicitly imprecise. Another consideration is that the boundaries between groups of data are not necessarily crisp. Similarly, the assignment of records to a particular group is likewise not necessarily crisp.

Imperfect data may arise because of variability in measurement; for example, the same measurement device, reading the same condition, may return values differing over a tolerance range. Data may also be imperfect in that it may be noisy (due to error) or incomplete. Various techniques have been exploited to learn from non-crisp data.

One class of solutions implicitly considers impreciseness to be an impediment to correctness and uses a variety of techniques to reduce the data variability. Techniques included are filtering, thresholds, statistics, and partial matching [Chan, 1989] [Chen, 1985] [Dzeroski, 1991] [Mathews, 1993].

The other approach is to consider much data to be inherently non-crisp and seeks to work with the data while retaining its non-crispness. Of the approaches to handling non-crisp data, fuzzy methods are the most mature. There is a considerable history in using fuzzy techniques to form clusters [Zadeh, 1976] [Bezdek, 1992]. Other complementary approaches focus on the overlapping between sets. They include Dempster-Shafer Theory [Shafer, 1976] and Rough Sets [Pawlak, 1991]. While these techniques are different, they are also some connections [Skowron, 1990]. Much of the existing work using approximate techniques on databases is on allowing non-crisp (i.e., partial match) queries of databases. For example, Vassiliadis [1994] uses fuzzy queries while Schocken [1993] considers Dempster-Shafer.

2.4 Measuring Cohesion

Approaching the problem using a cohesion enhancement paradigm has the benefit of avoiding the intractability of combinatorial complexity that arises in attempting to discover relationships between all the elements. Cohesive information is also more easily understood. Cohesive data groups can be thought of as information 'nuggets'.

Reducing disorder in a database or in its parts may increase comprehension through increasing cohesion. Before you can computationally decrease something, it is necessary to measure what is being decreased. Given a disorder metric, it may be possible to measure the disorder and then reduce the disorder to profitably mine data. But, before computationally decreasing something, it is necessary to measure what is decreased. Because disorder metrics measure a heuristic, they are by their nature, implicitly imprecise. They are often explicitly imprecise as well.

Many different disorder measures have been suggested. Many of these have focused on a particular attribute's fit with a classification scheme. Possibly the most common database mining disorder metric is entropy [Quinlan, 1986] that in turn is based on Shannon's information theory. Quinlan induced efficient decision trees from a database of cases using a disorder metric called *entropy*. This work's approach and objective are somewhat different from Quinlan. Quinlan sought to determine the attribute *sequence* that most efficiently discriminates among the database partitions when viewed from the perspective of the target attribute. The proposed work is not particularly interested in capturing the partitioning sequence, although it may be an artifact of the process. However, several other disorder measures have been proposed with a variety of nomenclatures and purposes. Perhaps, the broadest term is 'uncertainty'. Some of these metrics are *total uncertainty* [Pal, 1993], *dissonance* or *conflict* [Yager, 1983], *confusion* [Hohle, 1981], *non-specifity* [Higashi, 1983] [Dubois, 1985], *discord* [Klir, 1990], *global uncertainty* [Lamata, 1987], *total uncertainty* [Klir, 1990].

Lastly, it should be noted that mining based on cohesion means that singularities are not considered something interesting to discover; undoubtedly, sometimes it may be of interest to find singularities (or anomalies). It is a matter of selecting a heuristic. If the strategy is to increase cohesion, singularities will be necessarily discarded. Contrariwise, if singularities are of interest, dissonance is valued and cohesion is down played. This work increases cohesion and consequently does not seek singularities.

3 Approach Overview

3.1 Rationale

There are a number of different techniques that can be used to mine a database. Many of them use some form of supervised search; i.e., before and/or during mining, they receive direction as to the target. For example, in a medical database, the goal could be identifying anomalous services by physician. However, supervised search limits the results because it is necessary to determine in advance the subjects that are of interest. This is almost contra-intuitive to the general goal of conducting database mining of finding unexpected, interesting things.

On the other hand, unsupervised search has a problem with combinatorial explosion. In a typical database, there may be hundreds of attributes. To consider fully the interrelationships between all of them is prohibitive. Possible heuristic help comes from the realization that many of the combinatoric combinations do not appear to have much information theoretic value. This leads to a heuristic focusing on increasing coherence.

This work considers autonomous search based on identifying groups of data that have the most information value. The research speculation is that database mining can be accomplished through a progressive reduction of cognitive dissonance. The heuristic assumption is that reducing cognitive dissonance increases information. Another way of saying this is: finding groups of records having a high degree of internal coherence is likely to produce interesting results. This is done by progressively discarding attributes that have limited information value and by partitioning the data to increase information. This research is interested in using humanly intelligible metrics.

3.2 Disorder Metrics

There are many possible ways of measuring disorder. Most of the disorder metrics that have been used have used the idea that categorizing data by placing the data into a graph structure will reduce the total disorder in a vector space. This is certainly true in the original message encoding domain that this work was done in.

However, while there is recent doubt [Webb, 1996] if this always is the most efficient and effective strategy, there are broader questions. One is the problem of applying the technique in a large data set. (Generally, large data sets are sampled and the results are assumed to be general.)

Another is whether the results are necessarily too fine grained to be humanly useful. (Generally, fine grained rules are captured from the generated graph.) Also, there is the presumption that mined results can be readily understood and used by humans when represented as a hierarchical graph. Human decision makers generally rely on tabular, summary data.

This work suggests that database partitioning is a more meaningful way to discover interesting results. A database is already primarily organized into records and secondarily into attributes containing domain values. It arguably is more meaningful to retain the structure of records and attributes while mining.

The purest disorder partitions might occur if it was computationally possible to separate data sub-tables as if they were clouds of spectral data. However, spectral data is usually of small dimensionality (dimension = 1 to 3). In contrast, a database's dimensionality is the count of database attributes. As this well may run to the hundreds, it is not possible to consider all the data as a cloud to be separated by some measure of all the values in combination.

The most humanly comprehensible, and computationally attainable is to use the distinctiveness of the values within attributes. Attributes are drawn from domains. Generally, the enumeration of values in non-scalar domains is not great. Thus, partitioning a given domain based on similarity is usually possible.

Most databases use a relational form that can be described as a constrained table. A table of data T is made up of elements $t_{i,j}$ where i represents the row of the data table; and, j represents an attribute of the database. The data table row is usually called a tuple or record. The values of a particular attribute, j, are drawn from a closely defined domain. Domains may be defined either as an enumerated list or as a bounded scalar.

There are many possible ways of measuring database table disorder. Focusing on a single attribute may be satisfactory. Or, it might be better to explore combinations of attributes, each attribute treated separately. Alternatively, it might be best to develop a single disorder metric by functionally combining all items of a table as a whole.

Partitioning will be on combinations of individual attribute's distinctiveness. Distinctiveness is simply how many distinct, or identifiably different, values there are in an attribute within a partition. For example, if one attribute has three different values and another has two different values, the one with fewest values has the least disorder.

A good heuristic would seem to be choosing to create partitions with attributes having the least disorder. But, there are at least two ways of doing this. One, minimizing the total disorder over all the attributes by partitioning to have the minimum over all Σ $d_{j,p}$ where d represents the disorder of an attribute, j represents an attribute, and p represents a candidate partition. This would entail putting boundaries between all possible partitions, p. This is infeasible in any significantly large database.

Another approach is to partition on attributes that are already have the least disorder. That is, if one attribute has two distinct values and the other has three distinct values, partition on the one with the fewest values. This approach is simplest and most computationally obtainable.

There are other variations that sit in various places in between these approaches.

As it is both more understandable and achievable, the simpler approach to metric construction will be used. Consequently, combinations of attributes will be considered with disorder computed within each attribute separately.

3.3 Partitioning

Cohesion is enhanced, in part, by progressively partitioning the data to reduce intra-item dissonance within the resulting partitions. The partitioning produces progressively more coherent sub-tables of data. Each step in the partitioning sequence affects later results as partitions are recursively formed on existing partitions. Competing taxonomies must be retained until it is possible to identify interesting results. A speculation is that it will be possible to select computationally, using artifacts from the mining process, results having the greatest potential interestingness.

If a table of data T is made up of elements $t_{i,j}$ where i represents the row (or tuple) of data and j represents an attribute of the database, T is partitioned by placing the rows into different partitions. The partitions are constructed so that the coherence of the resulting partitions is greater than the coherence of the initial data table.

In some cases, a non-crisp partitioning might be more desirable. Partitioning may be imprecise either because non-crisp data are involved or because the partition boundaries are imprecise. Both crisp and non-crisp cases are of interest. To do non-crisp partitioning, fuzzy or rough set methodologies might be useful.

3.3.1 Partitioning On Crisp Data

Partitions can be formed using the distinctness of attributes with crisp data attributes. T can be partitioned on the distinctiveness of attributes so that each partition only contains only a single value for a particular attribute. For example, the table in *Figure 3.1* is split into two sub-partitions on $t_{i,2}$. T could also have been partitioned into two different sub-partitions on $t_{i,6}$. However, partitioning on $t_{i,2}$ also partitions on $t_{i,7}$; thus, the partitioning is accomplished on two attributes as opposed to one. This presents a possibly useful partitioning heuristic of partitioning on the maximum count of attributes. Notice there could also have been a partitioning into three partitions.using $t_{i,1}$. The preferable count of partitions (i.e., more, less, some count) is a research question that is to be addressed experimentally.

original

$t_{i,1}$	$t_{i,2}$	$t_{i,3}$	$t_{i,4}$	$t_{i,5}$	$t_{i,6}$	$t_{i,7}$
a	b	c	d	z	w	g
t	b	c	h	e	p	g
k	b	c	r	f	w	g
k	m	n	s	h	p	j
t	m	t	s	x	w	j
a	m	v	s	d	p	j

partitioned

$t_{i,1}$	$t_{i,2}$	$t_{i,3}$	$t_{i,4}$	$t_{i,5}$	$t_{i,6}$	$t_{i,7}$
a	b	c	d	z	w	g
t	b	c	h	e	p	g
k	b	c	r	f	w	g
k	m	n	s	h	p	j
t	m	t	s	x	w	j
a	m	v	s	d	p	j

Figure 3.1 Partitions formed on crisp data attributes. Partitions formed on $t_{i,2}$ and $t_{i,7}$

Attributes with fully distinct values cannot be partitioned except into the pathological full enumeration case. Also, completely distinct domains do not provide conceptual abstraction possibilities. Consequently, attributes with completely distinct values can be removed. This is illustrated in *Figure 3.2*. However, if the domain of the attribute is ordered, granularization may be desirable before removing an attribute with distinct values. In this case, an attribute with distinct values might be carried forward with an eye to eventual granularization.

Name	Variety	Type	Brand	Manufacturer	Birth Place	Citizen	Units Monthly
Anderson	corn	vegetable	Tasty	General Foods	Berkeley	USA	3.5
Bach	cherries	fruit	Bounty	Archer Daniels	Cleveland	USA	3.7
Carey	cherries	fruit	Yummy	General Foods	New York	USA	2.6
Fraser	beans	vegetable	Harvest	Archer Daniels	Chicago	USA	3.9
Gupta	carrots	vegetable	Bounty	Archer Daniels	Bombay	foreign	3.3
Hart	strawberries	fruit	Plenty	Archer Daniels	Columbus	USA	2.7
Jackson	plums	fruit	Savory	General Foods	Cincinnati	USA	3.5
Liu	carrots	vegetable	Prize	Archer Daniels	Shanghai	foreign	3.4
Meyer	strawberries	fruit	Appeal	General Foods	Cincinnati	USA	2.9
Monk	carrots	vegetable	Savory	General Foods	Cincinnati	USA	3.8
Wang	beans	vegetable	Reward	Archer Daniels	Nanjing	foreign	3.2
Wise	mangos	fruit	Yummy	General Foods	Pacifica	USA	3.9

remove

Figure 3.2 Removing an attribute that has completely distinct values

After a partition has been formed, again remove attributes within a partition that have completely distinct values. The table constituting the rest of the partition is then labeled by the removed attribute. (This is shown in *Figure 3.3*.) This generates *abstraction sets*. Abstraction sets capture discovered hierarchies in the data. Abstraction sets can be drawn from partitions where a uniform attribute can be removed from a partition. Abstraction sets from *Figure 3.3* would be: Type/Variety, Type/Brand, Type/Manufacturer, Type/Birth Place, Type/Citizen, Type/Units. For example, for Type/Brand: vegetable ∈ corn, beans, carrots; and, for Type/Variety: fruit ∈ cherries, strawberries, plums.

Variety	Type	Brand	Manufacturer	Birth Place	Citizen	Units
corn	vegetable	Tasty	General Foods	Berkeley	USA	3.5
beans	vegetable	Harvest	Archer Daniels	Chicago	USA	3.9
carrots	vegetable	Bounty	Archer Daniels	Bombay	foreign	3.3
carrots	vegetable	Prize	Archer Daniels	Shanghai	foreign	3.4
carrots	vegetable	Savory	General Foods	Cincinnati	USA	3.8
beans	vegetable	Reward	Archer Daniels	Nanjing	foreign	3.2
cherries	fruit	Bounty	Archer Daniels	Cleveland	USA	3.7
cherries	fruit	Yummy	General Foods	New York	USA	2.6
strawberries	fruit	Plenty	Archer Daniels	Columbus	USA	2.7
plums	fruit	Savory	General Foods	Cincinnati	USA	3.5
strawberries	fruit	Appeal	General Foods	Cincinnati	USA	2.9
mangos	fruit	Yummy	General Foods	Pacifica	USA	3.9

remove

Figure 3.3   Removing an attribute that has uniform values within a sub-partition, capturing resulting abstraction sets.

It is speculated that the hierarchies captured in an abstraction set may, under some conditions, be useful to refine further a partition. If they can be used, the speculation is that these abstraction sets may be of particular interest as discovered information.

3.3.2 Non-Crisp Partitioning And Granularization

Partitioning may be extended to include non-crisp values by using linguistic values to represent imprecise data. One possible formation of linguistic variables is on granularized, ordered values. While it is more common to form linguistic variables on scalar data; it may also be useful to form linguistic variables on non-scalar, ordered values. However, it is unclear how to measure the closeness of non-scalar ordered values. While there is unsupervised learning experience in forming scalar data clusters and granules, there is little experience in unsupervised formation of non-scalar data clusters.

Granularization has two advantages:

- Attributes containing granularized data can be more easily partitioned into large partitions.
- Partitioning may proceed by placing the same granule of an attribute value granule into neighboring partitions for different records.

Placing the same attribute value into alternative partitions may potentially be accomplished either by fuzzy or rough sets. Arguably, test score semantics [Zadeh, 1981] could be used for a limited amount of data. However, when faced with large amounts of data, other techniques need to be used. One possible fuzzy technique is to define membership functions that can be placed into either of two neighboring partitions.

Forming the partition boundaries on multiple attributes in a large database is not computationally simple. When adding granularized semantic values to the mix, the problem becomes even more complex. Potentially, the tools of operations research might be brought to bear on what is essentially a fuzzy multi-objective linear programming problem. Sakawa [1987] suggests that satisficing methods for fuzzy problems are possible.

Increasing cohesion may be supported by forming granules on ordered data. Granule size is an important issue, both for human cognitive understanding and for unsupervised partitioning that is to take advantage of fuzzy granules. The finer the grains, the greater is the partitioning difficulty. Alternatively, if the grains are too large, useful information may be lost. Zadeh has informally observed (in 1996 seminars) that experience in control design indicates that the appropriate count of membership functions is generally between 5 and 7. While database mining experience may eventually dictate otherwise, in the absence of other information, this would appear to be a good starting point.

It is an open question whether granules for data mining should be the same size (i.e., either scalar dimensionality or member count). It may be more convenient to arbitrarily divide a domain into equal scalar segments; but, it may not be the most satisfactory. For example, if ages are recorded in tenths; i.e., 0.0, 0.1, 0.2, ... ; a reasonable, useful human granularization might be [infant, adolescent, adult, senior] or [infant, adolescent, young-adult, adult, senior, aged]. In both cases, the granules overlap and the range of values is differentially sized. This case is different from the upward hierarchy granule recognition from data already implicitly placed into linear groups. For example, granularizing student Grade Point Averages (GPAs) of [0.0, 0.1, ... , 3.9, 4.0] into A $\in$ [3.0, ... , 4.0], B $\in$ [2.0, ... , 3.0), etc.

Difficulties with unsupervised recognition of granules in ordered data lie with the number of granules to be used; and, the range of values to be included in a particular granule. There are known ways of clustering data when the number of clusters is known [Bezdek, 1981] and the initial cluster seeds are known. However, in unsupervised search, this information is usually not available.

One possible approach is to use a variation of the 'mountain method' to estimate cluster centers [Yager, 1993] [Chiu, 1991, 1994]. Then, use these results as the starting point to another method (such as fuzzy c-means clustering) to further refine the results. The 'mountain method' procedure uses a metric to identify where there is the greatest density of values. This is the initial cluster center. Then, reduce the density metric for other points in the neighborhood and find the next point with the highest (adjusted) density and consider this to be the next cluster center. The process is recursively repeated.

SUMMARY

Autonomous database mining is being examined. Various combinations of discovering interesting information through successively partitioning a database using dissonance reduction are considered. Approximate reasoning techniques to address inherently non-crisp numbers and imprecise partitions will be used. This is being done to determine which, if any dissonance reduction techniques hold promise in discovering interesting information as a product of database mining.

BIBLIOGRAPHY

Bibliographic references have been omitted due to space limitations. They may be obtained from the author.

KOMET – A System for the Integration of Heterogeneous Information Sources

J. Calmet, S. Jekutsch, P. Kullmann, J. Schü

Institut für Algorithmen und Kognitive Systeme (IAKS)
Fakultät für Informatik, Universität Karlsruhe
Am Fasanengarten 5, 76131 Karlsruhe, Germany
{calmet,jekutsch,kullmann,schue}@ira.uka.de

Abstract. We present KOMET, an architecture for the intelligent integration of heterogeneous information sources. It is based on the idea of a mediator, which is an independent software layer between an application and various knowledge sources which need to be accessed. We present an especially suitable logic-based language for encoding typical mediation tasks like conditional preference strategies, schema integration or data inconsistency resolution. Using annotated logic, KOMET is able to perform various common types of reasoning, such as probabilistic, fuzzy, paraconsistent and certain types of temporal and spatial reasoning. In combination with an extensible type system and the embedding of external knowledge sources as constraint domains, our mediation language offers a rich framework, which not only facilitates access to structured information, but as well supports unstructured and semi-structured information. A number of examples show the practical application of our approach.

Keywords: Intelligent Information Systems, Knowledge Integration, Mediator

1 Introduction

The evolution of technology in the last couple of decades has led to a vast increase of information that is easily accessible with computers. But using all this information in connection is nearly impossible due to this very process yielding a broad variety of hardware platforms, operating systems, data management systems and data formats. Many information retrieval tasks are based on a multitude of information which is highly scattered among different information systems and services. To do a forecast on stock quotes one needs data on current and previous quotes, both normally available on completely different information systems.

The idea of such a so-called mediator system was first introduced by Wiederhold [Wie92]. His architecture makes use of a central component which facilitates the access to different knowledge sources without impairing the autonomy and heterogeneity of the involved sources. This approach has much in common with the federated database approach. But in contrast to federated database systems, the mediator approach uses a broader concept of *information source*. Not only traditional databases with different data models are considered as sources, but also unstructured information like world wide web pages, software packages like computer algebra systems, spreadsheet calculators or pattern recognition software and knowledge-based sources like expert systems or neural nets. Information sources are coupled to the mediator using *wrapper* or *translator* modules which map queries in the mediator format to queries in the source- specific query language (Figure 1). Another major task of these components is the transformation of the retrieved data from the source-specific representation into the mediator data model.

In this paper we present KOMET, a shell for developing dedicated mediators by means of a declarative language. There are few projects which deal with information integration in a comparable generality. Closely related projects in this field of research are HERMES [AE95] and TSIMMIS [PGMU96]. HERMES also uses annotated logic for the mediatory knowledge base, but uses a different approach for the query translation. Its rule-rewriting approach requires much more a priori anticipation of the kind of queries that might occur. Only queries for which corresponding templates have been established can be send to a data source. The language of HERMES does not support negation and is not as flexible in its type system. To the best of our knowledge, KOMET is the first system that implements the evaluation of the well-founded semantics for annotated logic programs. TSIMMIS emphasizes the integration of semi-structured information sources. It makes use of a special data model for representing this information. In our opinion, this approach has the major drawback that even though structured information can be represented, its processing is far less efficient than would be possible by retaining the structure. We have deliberately chosen a structured approach, since it adequately supports structured data sources in terms of efficiency. At the same time our framework facilitates the integration of unstructured and semi-structured information due to its extensible type system.

In the sequel, first the architecture and language of the KOMET system are described. The third section gives some examples that show the practical use of the KOMET language. Section four describes how unstructured and semi-structured information can be represented and processed in our framework. Finally, the conclusions section discusses future directions of our work.

2 KOMET – A Mediator System Based on Annotated Logic

The KOMET (Karlsruhe Open MEdiator Technology) system[1] is a knowledge-based mediator shell for intelligent information integration. From the user's perspective, the system provides a set of views on the underlying data. On the basis of these views, the user can pose queries to the system in a uniform way without having to consider the location and format of the underlying knowledge. The basic KOMET architecture is depicted in figure 1.

---

[1] http://iaks-www.ira.uka.de/iaks-calmet/research/kamel-komet/

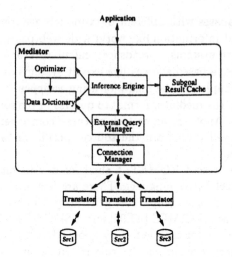

Fig. 1. Mediator Architecture.

The heart of our system is an efficient engine for evaluating annotated logic programs under the well-founded semantics, enhanced with constraints for integrating external knowledge sources. The engine uses SLG resolution [CW93] which has following advantages over other evaluation procedures:

- SLG resolution is a partial deduction procedure, consisting of several fundamental transformations. A query is transformed step by step into a set of answers. The use of transformations seperates logical issues of query evaluation from procedural ones.
- SLG resolution is sound and complete with respect to the well-founded partial model for all non-floundering queries.
- The computation rule for selecting a literal from a rule body as well as the control strategy for selecting transformations to apply are arbitrary.
- It avoids both positive and negative loops and always terminates for programs with the bounded-term-size property [CW93].
- For function-free programs, it has polynomial time data complexity for well-founded negation.

Similar to OLDT resolution[2], tabulation is used to avoid redundant computations. It is additionally needed to guarantee termination. We have extended SLG resolution for processing of annotated logic programs with a many-sorted type system.

Besides the inference engine, the KOMET system core comprises the *Subgoal Result Cache*, the *External Query Manager* with a *Connection Manager*, the *Optimizer* and the *Data Dictionary*. The *Subgoal Result Cache* is used for tabulation during the resolution process. A buffering strategy keeps query results

---

[2] Ordered Linear resolution for Definite clauses with Tabulation

across queries if suitable. The *External Query Manager* appears as a constraint solver in the mediator. It decomposes constraint parts of clauses with the help of the *Optimizer* and sends partial conjunctive constraints to the *Translators* which correspond to individual information sources. The *Connection Manager* coordinates and monitors network access. The *Data Dictionary* contains meta data about all registered information sources, relations, functions and data types. Systems predicates allow the access of this information and thus facilitate meta reasoning.

The integration of arbitrary information sources into a mediator system requires transformations on different levels. On the semantic level the source-specific schema needs to be transformed into a schema useful for the mediation task. In our framework, this is done by the inference engine using schema integration rules. On the data representation level information needs to be transformed from the source-specific data model into the common data model and vice versa. Figure 2 illustrates the levels of integration.

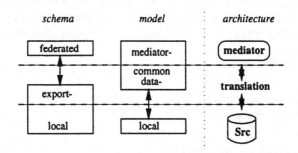

Fig. 2. Translation of model and schema

In our architecture translation connotes transformation of queries posed by the inference engine into the source-specific query language (e.g. SQL) as well as the involved data model transformations. We have developed an environment for rapid implementation of query translators for arbitrary types of information sources [CJS97]. Based on compiler techniques, it uses rules which describe how the constructs of the mediator language are mapped to the native language constructs of a specific source. This approach can be used to build translator hierarchies and allows the reuse of certain translator functionality. In the remainder of this paper, we will focus on how the KOMET language can be used to handle typical mediation tasks.

3 The KOMET Language

The KOMET language is a declarative language which implements a many-sorted annotated logic [KS92] with a high degree of flexibility. It provides a set of basic data types and truth value sets which can be extended using a programming interface. The KOMET language defines the common data model.

In annotated logic, each fact has a truth value appended to it. Annotated logic only imposes some restrictions on the algebraic structure wihich the set of truth values has to form. This property allows to choose among a number of common logics, which range from two-valued logic to fuzzy logic and certain types of temporal and spatial logic. In this sense, annotated logic is generic.

A KOMET program is made up of a set of constant symbols, variable symbols, function symbols and predicate symbols. Since KOMET is based on annotated logic, each predicate declaration requires the assignment of a truth value type.

STRING and FOUR are predefined data and truth value types, respectively. FOUR comprises t (true), f (false), u (unknown) and c (contradiction). For simplicity we will use this truth value type for the following examples. Example 1 shows how recursive clauses allow us to calculate the *transitive closure* of a predicate which is not possible with plain SQL. Due to the use of well- founded semantics, recursive clauses which contain negation are also allowed. For the program in the following example, the query isAncestor(X,Y):[t] would return the three results (X=Paul,Y=Ann),(X=Ann,Y=Mary) and (X=Paul,Y=Mary).

Example 1. Clauses

```
#predicates
isChild(STRING,STRING):[FOUR]
isAncestor(STRING,STRING):[FOUR]

#clauses
isAncestor(X,Y):[t] <- isChild(Y,X):[t]
isAncestor(X,Y):[t] <- isAncestor(X,Z):[t] & isChild(Y,Z):[t]
isChild('Ann','Paul'):[t]
isChild('Mary','Ann'):[t]
```

To be able to limit the data which defines a derived predicate, KOMET allows the use of constraints which can be constructed form constraint relations and functions. In our system, constraint relations have the general form *domain::function(argumentlist)* and can be used in the conjunction of a clause body. Naturally, each data type such as ULONG provides a number of predefined domain functions and relations for the basic boolean and mathematical operators. Each data type and each truth value type therefore represents a constraint domain in the KOMET system.

The KOMET system looks at an *external knowledge source* also as a constraint domain which supplies a set of functions and relations which represent the knowledge that is available from the knowledge source. Following example shows how databases can be introduced.

Example 2. Mediator program

```
#domains
DB1 = ODBC(MyDb.CFG)
```

```
DB2 = DDBC(HisDb.CFG)

#predicates
Address1(STRING,STRING,STRING):[REAL01]
Address2(STRING,STRING,STRING):[FOUR]
Names_DB1(STRING,STRING):[FOUR]

#clauses
Address1(X,Y,Z):[1.0] <- DB1::ADDRESS(X,Y,Z)
Address1(X,Y,Z):[0.5] <- DB2::ADDRESS(X,Y,Z)

Names_DB1(X,Y):[t] <- DB1::ADDRESS(X,Y,Z)
Address2(X,Y,Z):[t] <- DB1::ADDRESS(X,Y,Z)
Address2(X,Y,Z):[t] <- DB2::ADDRESS(X,Y,Z) &
                       not Names_DB1(X,Y):[t]
```

MyDb.CFG refers to a configuration file which lists the available functions and predicates. The information in this file is called *export schema* (see figure 2) of an information source, expressed in the common data model of KOMET. Dependent on the knowledge source, this file may also contain information on how these functions are mapped onto the functionality of the knowledge source.

Example 2 shows how to build a mediator for two telephone databases which contain conflicting data. DB1 is assumed to be reliable whereas we are not confident in DB2. The mediator program shows two possibilities for resolving possible conflicts. The definition of Address1 does not suppress any data, it just appends a truth value to each data set, depending on its origin. The predicate Address2 will prefer the telephone number from DB1 if there is an entry in both databases for one person. This way, incorrect entries will not be visible at all.

4 Mediation Examples Using the KOMET Approach

In the following we will show how typical mediation tasks can be expressed in the KOMET framework using clauses and annotations. For the sake of a shorter and clearer presentation, we use a slightly simplified syntax and avoid obvious declarations in this section.

Knowledge Inconsistencies

In a mediatory environment, it may be necessary to distinct knowledge from different sources. It is useful to rename the predicates so that objects from different knowledge sources are disjoint. Any identities between predicates must then be reestablished explicitly. The annotation lattice $\mathcal{P}(\{Src_1, \ldots, Src_n\})$ with the usual subset ordering is introduced for this purpose, where Src_i is an identifier for an external domain.

In the following we provide two examples how annotated logic may help:

– Conflict solving: Using lattices like $\mathcal{FOUR}$[3] it is possible to represent clauses

---

[3] consisting of $\perp$ = *unknown*, t = *true*, f = *false* and $\top$ = *inconsistent*

which explicitly state how to deal with conflicting knowledge, e.g.

$$buy\_stock(IBM) : [\{m\}, f] \leftarrow buy\_stock(IBM) : [\{Src_1, Src_2\}, \top]$$

If the knowledge sources Src_1 and Src_2 disagree ($\top$) on whether to buy IBM, the mediator (m) rather should be careful about it.

- Preference of sources: The following clauses express a preference of a source with respect to a particular single proposition. It is a somewhat complicated case: Src_1's value is more reliable in the case that it differs by no more than 10 from the value of Src_2. In the other case, Src_2's value needs to be stored as the mediators opinion about the salary.

$$Salary(Name, Sal) : [\{Src_1\}, t] \leftarrow DB1 :: Salary(Name, Sal)$$
$$Salary(Name, Sal) : [\{Src_2\}, t] \leftarrow DB2 :: Salary(Name, Sal)$$
$$Salary(Name, Sal) : [\{m\}, t] \leftarrow Abs(Sal - Sal2) \leq 10 \ \& $$
$$Salary(Name, Sal) : [\{Src_1\}, t] \ \& $$
$$Salary(Name, Sal2) : [\{Src_2\}, t]$$
$$Salary(Name, Sal2) : [\{m\}, t] \leftarrow Abs(Sal - Sal2) > 10 \ \& $$
$$Salary(Name, Sal) : [\{Src_1\}, t] \ \& $$
$$Salary(Name, Sal2) : [\{Src_2\}, t]$$

Semantic Similarities

A relation $Professor(Id, Name)$ in the domain DB1 and $Secretary(Id, Name)$ in the domain DB2 may be *generalized* in the context of the university administration office:

$$Staff(Id, Name) : [\{m\}, t] \leftarrow DB1 :: Professor(Id, Name)$$
$$Staff(Id, Name) : [\{m\}, t] \leftarrow DB2 :: Secretary(Id, Name)$$

There is also the possibility to express semantic proximity by means of fuzzy values [SK93].

Domain Incompatibilities

- Synonyms: In two different knowledge sources the identity between attributes may be established by the following clauses:

$$Employee(Id) : [\{m\}, t] \leftarrow DB1 :: Employee(Id, Name)$$
$$Employee(Id) : [\{m\}, t] \leftarrow DB2 :: Personnel(Id, Name)$$

- Data Representation Conflicts: Suppose that in the above example in the DB1 database the Id is defined as a 9 digit integer whereas the Id in DB2 may be defined as a String. Thus, data conversion is required by means of a constraint function $Convert\_Str\_to\_Int$ which is provided by the domain SYS:

$$Employee(Id) : [\{m\}, t] \leftarrow DB2 :: Personnel(Name, SId) \ \& $$
$$Id = SYS :: Convert\_Str\_to\_Int(SId).$$

Schema Conflicts

- Schema Isomorphism Conflicts: In this conflict, semantically similar entities have a different number of attributes.

$$Instructor(No, Phone) : [t] \leftarrow DB1 :: Instructor(SS, Phone)$$
$$Instructor(No, Phone1) : [t] \leftarrow DB2 :: Instructor(SS, Phone1, Phone2)$$

- Missing Data Item Conflict: Analogously default values can be defined, or values might be calculated if they are missing in one source.

5 Unstructured and Semi-structured Information

One goal in the development of KOMET was to support different types of information sources in the most efficient manner. This can be achieved by exploiting a source's characteristics and abilities as far as possible. A structured approach has the advantage that it can efficiently support well-structured information which is the case for a large part of the available information. At the same time, our structured approach allows the support of unstructured and semi-structured information as it is flexible enough for representing and processing these types of information. The key feature for this capability is the extensible type system of KOMET.

5.1 Unstructured Information

A basic KOMET type can be regarded as an abstract data type for which functions and relations have to be defined according to a certain minimal programming interface. Additional functions and relations can be incorporated into the KOMET type and used in the constraint part of clauses. However, KOMET has no knowledge of the internal structure of a data type[4]. This property is the basis for incorporation of unstructured information. Consider a text archive where each text is stored in an individual file. Additionally, assume we have a text analysis software package which scans texts for a number of keywords. For use in KOMET, we would create a new data type TEXT, which can e.g. be constructed from an existing C++-class. For the implementation of this type we have the choice of storing the text *itself* in a data item or using some kind of handle like a file name. Next, we must construct a constraint domain which allows us to access the texts files of the archive. Finally, we can add a relation CONTAINS to this domain, which takes a list of keywords and a text as arguments and determines whether the text contains all of them or not.

---

[4] A special case are types which have been defined in a mediator program with the KOMET language

Example 3. Unstructured information

```
#sorts
KEYLIST = LIST(STRING)

#predicates
Search(TEXT,KEYLIST):[FOUR]

#clauses
Search(X,Y):[t] <- ARCH::FETCH(X) & ARCH::CONTAINS(Y,X)
```

The above example shows a mediator program that retrieves all texts that contain a list of keywords. Note, that the internal representation has no influence on the coding of the mediator program. It does influence the implementations of the involved relations though. It is up to the calling application to interpret data items of type TEXT appropriately.

5.2 Semi-structured Information

The KOMET type system can as well be used for representing semi-structured information. Together with some functions and relations for access, processing and aggregation we are able to process this kind of information in our framework in a similar manner as described in related projects [PGMU96]. The following simple example shows how this could be achieved. FLEXTYPE denotes a data type which can hold different data types and corresponds to the pair *(type, value)*.

Example 4. Semi-structured information

```
#sorts
OBJECT = STRUCT(OID:STRING,LABEL:STRING,DATA:FLEXTYPE)

#predicates
Address(OBJECT):[FOUR]

#clauses
Address(OBJECT::MERGE(A1,A2)):[t] <-
        SRC1::FETCH(A1) & SRC2::FETCH(A2)
        OBJECT::EQ(A1,'LastName',A2,'LastName')
```

The MERGE function merges two objects of type *set* into one new object of type *set* and assigns a new unique object identifier to it. Relation EQ takes two objects of type *set* and checks two of its elements which are referenced by their label for equality. The given program demonstrates how semi-structured objects from different sources may be merged in the mediator. Clearly, many other operations necessary for integration can be realized in our framework.

6 Conclusions

In this paper we presented the KOMET environment for building mediators. Its language and architecture is well suited to serve typical mediation tasks in a heterogeneous environment. The language has formal semantics and is declarative, which supports easy construction of the mediatory knowledge base. The extensible type system together with the felxible concept for accessing external knowledge also facilitates processing of unstructured and semi-structured information.

KOMET will be applied in the project STEM[5] which aims at developing a software system to assist land managers in environmentally sensitive areas with long term sustainable decisions.

The core functionality described in this paper has been realized in a prototypical system. It is coded in C++ and runs under the Solaris and Windows operating systems. A graphical front end for debugging mediator clauses [CDJS96] and for semi-automatic construction of schema integration clauses have also been realized. Theoretical work has been done on view maintenance in a mediator architecture [Sch95].

Future work will focus on different aspects of query optimization and security in mediator systems. On the knowledge level we will investigate knowledge acquisition and use of common ontologies in the mediator context.

References

[AE95]   S. Adalı and R. Emery. A uniform framework for integrating knowledge in heterogenous knowledge systems. In *Proc. 11th IEEE International Conference on Data Engineering*, pages 513–521, Taipei, Taiwan, March 1995.

[CDJS96] J. Calmet, D. Debertin, S. Jekutsch, and J. Schü. An executable graphical representation of mediatory information systems. In *Proc. 12th IEEE International Conference on Data Engineering*, pages 124–131, New Orleans, March 1996.

[CJS97]   J. Calmet, S. Jekutsch, and J. Schü. A generic query-translation framework for a mediator architecture. In *Proc. 13th International Conference on Data Engineering, Birmingham, U.K.*, pages 434–443, April 1997.

[CW93]   W. Chen and D. S. Warren. Query evaluation under the well-founded semantics. In *Proceedings of the 12th Annual ACM Symposium on Principles of Database Systems*, pages 168–179. ACM, ACM Press, 1993.

[KS92]   M. Kifer and V. S. Subrahmanian. Theory of generalized annotated logic programming. *Journal of Logic Programming*, 12(1):335–367, 1992.

[PGMU96] Y. Papakonstantinou, H. Garcia-Molina, and J. Ullman. Medmaker: A mediation system based on declarative specifications. In *Proc. 12th International Conference on Data Engineering*, pages 132–141. IEEE Computer Society, February 1996.

[Sch95]   J. Schü. *Updates and Query-Processing in a Mediator Architecture*. PhD thesis, Universität Karlsruhe, 1995.

[SK93]   A. Sheth and V. Kashyap. So far (schematically) yet so near (semantically). In D. K. Hsiao, E. J. Neuhold, and R. Sacks-Davis, editors, *Interoperable Database Systems*, pages 283–312. IFIP, Elsevier Science Pubslihers, 1993.

[Wie92]   G. Wiederhold. Mediators in the architecture of future information systems. *IEEE Computer*, 25(3):38–49, March 1992.

---

[5] http://www.cogsci.ed.ac.uk/ stem/

Towards AI Formalisms for Legal Evidence

Ephraim Nissan[1] and Daniel Rousseau[2]

[1] CMS, Univ. of Greenwich, Wellington St., Woolwich, London SE18 6PF, UK.
[2] Knowledge Systems Lab., Comp. Sci. Dept., Stanford Univ., CA 94305, USA.

The discipline of *artificial intelligence for law* [36, 7], for all its accomplishments, e.g., in modeling argumentation [62, 54, 34, 15, 30, 51], has generally not dealt with legal evidence. For the latter domain [55, 63, 39, 29] formalization was developed, instead, in *forensic statistics* [65, 64, 60, 66, 61, 55, 2], as well as in *jury modeling* [20, 21, 17]. Recent developments in the respective research communities [38] are bringing closer these domains. We claim that the time is ripe for endeavors aiming at constructing *integrated evidence support systems* for investigative and legal purposes, combining several paradigms. We introduce our own *dramatis personae* approach, within AI models of agents and planning. In the narrative approach we are currently investigating, *self-exculpatory explanation* in the tradition of Nissan's *ALIBI* [32, 13, 46] is extended to account for multi-agent action. Management of the narrative's cast of characters can benefit from a multi-agent scenario simulation environment inspired by the Stanford *Cybercafe* [57], along with explicit modeling of the dialectic of actors' mental states and linguistic exchanges (in line with Rousseau's *PSICO* [56, 58, 42]).

1 Escaping Liability With ALIBI

The task of an agent trying to prove his/her/its innocence is *self-exculpation.* Self-exculpation does not necessarily take place in a legal setting. It applies as well to a toddler denying wrongdoing (cf. [4]). To our knowledge, *ALIBI*, developed by Nissan's team, has been the first program ever whose task was the generation of self-exculpation [32, 13, 46]. Basically, ALIBI is a planner trying to detect alternative courses of action, with different conditions or weights applying. The input fed into ALIBI is a charge against the defendant, who is impersonated by the program. The charge —a rudimentary "police report"— is composed of a list of actions. Even though the program itself does not have a strong model of episodes, to humans faced with ALIBI's input and output, reasoning is definitely concerned with a coherent episode. The optimization side of ALIBI more clearly entered the picture with the version named *ALIBI 3*. Like ALIBI 1 and ALIBI 2 (the latter enhanced with a simple NLP interface), ALIBI 3 proposes several alternative accounts of the actions appearing in the charge, with an effort being made to exclude from the explanation such admissions that involve liability. ALIBI 3 is also able, short of an innocent explanation, to admit to some lesser offense than as emerging from the input "police report".

Processing has the program recursively decompose the actions in the input, into a tree of actions, down to elementary, atomic actions. Moreover, actions are stripped of their *deontic* (i.e., moral or legal) connotation. For example, "stealing" is stripped down to "taking", and it's up to the system to concoct such a plan where that act of taking fits in a way that is legitimate for the defendant. Generating the justification corresponds to a reconstitution of actions into a different tree. Then the terminal actions in the decomposition tree are differently reconstituted into alternative explanations that eliminate or minimize liability.

A man is accused of having shot and wounded a jeweller, while robbing him. One effect of "wounding" is that the wounded jeweller was unable to take care of his property. This is exploited by an excuse ALIBI makes. It states that, having shot the jeweller incidentally, the defendant did take away property, but it was in order to look after it and then return it. (ALIBI has no model of contrary-to-duty obligations [67, 52, 53], cf. [25, p. 385].) Another effect of "wounding" is that the wounded jeweller needed medical aid. The defendant may supplement his excuse by claiming he *ran* away, in order to get such help for the jeweller.

"Armed threat" is an interpretation involving the effect of holding and possibly pointing some weapon, but ALIBI may try to admit to physically holding the object (which happens to be a weapon), while denying the intentions ascribed (of threatening an interlocutor who is therefore a victim), possibly implying an inadequacy of the defendant at realizing the interlocutor's interpretation of the situation. Actually, one excuse ALIBI tries, is that the defendant was carrying the weapon for an innocent purpose, and, possibly forgetting about its presence, was innocently talking to the victim, and was unaware the latter acted by feeling threatened. (See in [43] a pragmatic perspective on threats.)

2 Limitations and Desiderata

In ALIBI's knowledge-base, information is stored in logic form about standard actions, effects, and situations. Distinguish between *typical* situations (cf. [45]) and *clear* cases in the legal sense (and these, from *landmark* cases). The court has to determine whether the extremes of certain sets of conditions apply to the case at hand. There is a debate, in jurisprudence, as to whether a demarcation can be found between *clear cases*, i.e., cases for which agreement between competent lawyers can be expected, and *hard cases*, that lead to expert disagreement. In the 1980s, Anne von der Lieth Gardner developed a celebrated program [18] that tries to distinguish easy from hard cases. ALIBI, instead, is not concerned with a legal setting. Explanations are at the lay commonsense, not technically legal level [13]. quote In ALIBI, excuse-finding exploits degrees of freedom within the non-observable part of the process whose ascertained part is interpreted in the given accusation: as an early phase of performing its task, ALIBI identifies mischievous elements ascribed in this accusation. Classificatory reasoning concerning this phase was the issue in a system developed by Meldman [[41], cf. [18, Sec. 4.4.1]] which tries to identify, in an input set of facts, intentional torts in cases of assault and battery; examples match exactly, or by replacement in an abstraction hierarchy of objects or kinds of events. ALIBI does not try to figure out whether there is going to be disagreement in court on *judicial* grounds. Instead, more preliminarily, it tries to deny the broader, non-observed context implied by accusers, and it is that way that torts are denied or diminished.

Moreover, ALIBI is weak on the story coherence side. In handling the stories, we feel it is important to be able to combine the lessons learnt from the conceptual-dependency school of narrative processing (e.g., [11]), and semiotician of law Bernard Jackson's insights on "anchored narratives" [26] —the anchors being such constraints as, in a sense, the undeniable elements of ALIBI's input. This is just one of the desiderata. ALIBI does not have a multi-agent model of reasoning and action. Also, unlike *PSICO* (see below), it does not have an actual capability for dialog.

Besides, to the extent that the narrative to be reasoned about embeds linguistic expression, ALIBI cannot handle it. This way, assessing verbal threats (as opposed to armed threat) is outside ALIBI's capabilities. See e.g. [1] on computational approaches to intentionality and ascription based on the analysis of natural-language utterances. In psychology, the ascription of intentions is just a facet of *attribution,* i.e., "the ways in which ordinary people, acting as 'intuitive scientists', explain human actions and events to themselves" [12, p. 87]. Distinguish requested circumscribed explanations as in a defense situation, from, in general, a narration about the Self, where an account is conceptualized and proposed possibly of long spans out of one's biography. Like in defense, such a task also requires coherent reorganization of events and mental states [33].

ALIBI does not consider testimony and acceptability in court. Instead, the *HRA* automated legal advisor is used to determine whether user's statements come within the definition of hearsay (and thus can be expected to be rejected in court). In HRA, an attempt was made tries to incorporate a story model, with criteria of narrative coherence to match "the way lawyers, judges, jurors organize story information" [35]. (As opposed to a legal perspective, see [40, 16] on testimony in the perspective of the philosophy of knowledge.)

To augment a model such as ALIBI's with the ability to handle mental states and dialog, consider Rousseau's *PSICO* [56, 58, 42], a prototype that simulates interactions between software agents which interpret, plan, and perform communicative acts and reason on mental states such as goals and beliefs. PSICO accounts for phenomena from human conversations: turn-taking, stereotyped sequences (openings, closings, etc.), and interconnected speech acts.

For legal narratives as in ALIBI, we wish to enable reasoning about a story to apply to a cast of characters, instead of just one individual, the defendant as in ALIBI. We draw upon Rousseau and B. Hayes-Roth's *Cybercafe* [57], an application of the *Virtual Theater* project [22]. In a Virtual Theater application, where synthetic actors (portraying characters) —either autonomous and fully improvising, or "avatars" directed in the main by users and only partly improvising— can interact with each other and with users to create interactive stories resorting to text, animation and possibly speech. The current version of the *Cybercafe* features an autonomous actor playing the role of a waiter, and an avatar portraying a customer. The user-interface contains two windows: one presenting the actions that a user can select for his or her avatar, and one textually describing how the story unfolds in the current context. A user can direct his or her avatar by selecting buttons corresponding to actions that can be performed by the customer in the current context. Actions performed by any actor are displayed by a text animator in a window containing the description of the interaction. The Cybercafe is based on local improvisation, which means that all characters decide their behavior relying on the current state of the world and the actions that they can perform. Reasoning on mental states is quite simplified in the system. Possible states of the world, that can be considered as potential goals, and transitions between those states are modeled using state machines. Actions that an actor can perform to realize the (possibly multi-agent) transitions correspond to its abilities. A synthetic actor knows a list of irrelevant actions for each potential state (e.g., a character who is seated cannot sit neither walk). *Cybercafe* accounts for personality, but characters enact a (flexible) scenario.

Other relevant capabilities are related to those of Jameson's *IMP* [27], a dialog system (impersonating a realtor) that may try to mislead on purpose, without actually lying. It would not volunteer damaging information, unless a direct, specific relevant question is made. IMP has a goal of maintaining a neutral image of itself and an impression of completeness for its own answers. It even simulates insulted surprise if an intervening question by the customer seems to imply (by detailed questioning) that IMP is concealing information.

3 A Few Considerations on Representation

Our combined efforts aim at deriving —from ALIBI, PSICO, and the *CyberCafe*— a unified vision of how to formalize multi-agent actions and the associated mental states (cf. also the *SEPPHORIS* representation for conditions, events, legal stipulations, and procedural prescriptions involving these [44]). Augmenting an ALIBI remake with such a (possibly syncretistic) formalism would enable the artificial defendant (or, possibly, any character from the investigative or legal narrative) to reason on the mental states and the actions to discover self-alibis that could be used to exculpate or incriminate someone accused of a crime. Such an attempt could at best supplement professional tools from forensic statistics for organizing the evidence, in an investigative or legal context. The merit of the approach is in trying to endow such integrated tools with capabilities beyond a probabilistic procedure, by adding a meta-level of automated or machine-assisted reasoning with social or physical commonsense.

Here is a possible action schema for stealing:*

```
ACTION-SCHEMA:    Steal(AGT(v-agent),OBJ(v-object),PAT(v-agent2))
PRECONDITIONS:    Own(AGT(v-agent2),OBJ(v-object))
~Int.to(v-agent2,Give(AGT(v-agent2), RCPT(v-agent),OBJ(v-object)))
EFFECTS:          + Own(AGT(v-agent),OBJ(v-object))
        - Own(AGT(v-agent2),OBJ(v-object))
     + ~Int.to(v-agent, Give(AGT(v-agent),
                              RCPT(v-agent2),OBJ(v-object)))
CONSTRAINT:       NON-EQUAL(v-agent,v-agent2)
ALTERNATIVES:     Take(AGT(v-agent),OBJ(v-object))
        Borrow(AGT(v-agent),OBJ(v-object),FROM(v-agent2))
TRAIT: Honesty(-5)
```

The preconditions specify the conditions that must be present before the action is applied. They can be physical or mental states. *Int.To* is an example of modal operator for a mental state like intention. It is based on [19], except we just use

---

* On *temporal* representations customized for in AI & Law, see [50, 68, 24, 37]. One important aspect is *derogation*, i.e., the dynamics of the normative corpus, where laws are added or abrogated. Qualitative *spatial* reasoning [3] exhibits similarities to temporal reasoning [10], but the legal domain involves special problems [47].

the first two parameters in an action schema, without considering time. This way, *Int. To(x,y)* means that x has the intention to perform the action y. (Let us defer the discussion of mental states.)

The effects specify the new states after the performance of the action (preceded by a + sign) and the states that are no longer effective at that stage (preceded by a − sign). Constraints apply to the parameters of the action description. An alternative can be used to exculpate the agent performing the action by attenuating his or her action. The set of preconditions and effects is slightly different for those alternatives to be less incriminating for the agent performing the action. In the example, stealing could be considered as a kind of taking if the agent did not know that the object belonged to somebody else *(moral luck* [69] is a broader issue). It could be considered as a kind of borrowing if the agent had the intention to give back the object to its owner later. (On agents' beliefs about their own or others' obligations, cf. [48].)

Finally the traits specify how the action is evaluated with respect to some personality traits. For this purpose, use is made of a numeric scale going from −10 to 10. Provisionally, let us assume this kind of representation of traits, is acceptable for the domain of application we are envisioning in this paper. In the example considered, −5 would correspond to the dishonesty (or legal unacceptability) of the act of stealing, the negative value standing for it being an offense. Clearly, in a legal context it may be questionable that a judgment that belongs in court be already attached to a core description of action. In this paper, we are provisionally adopting such scoring nevertheless. The scoring in ALIBI 3 is somewhat more sophisticated —in respect to the action (characters' traits are ignored)— but the same remark applies to it as well. The representation of the scores of honesty, as shown here, is very simple; it is akin to the way the scoring of characters' traits works in the *Cybercafe* [57]. Considerations have to be made, more in general, about the mechanics behind such a rating. Personality traits can be very complex, they are in some relation to experienced and displayed emotions and attitudes toward others; e.g., a character can be very friendly in general (say, a value of 8), except when most angry at someone (value of −8), which restricts opportunities for violent behavior. Rating an action in terms of personality traits is just an indicator of its selection likelihood by the given character. Mental states such as beliefs, mutual beliefs, intentions, commitments, and abilities are very important to determine the responsibility of an agent in any legally significant situations possibly involving complicity. In relation to agents' abilities, *incentive contracting* is possibly involved in complicitous action. In incentive contracting [31, 59], an agent may contract to another agent (that does not necessarily shares the same goals) a task that the former cannot perform (either at all, or as effectively). We can adopt a formalism based on [19] to model the modalities necessary to reason on mental states with respect to the action schemas:

$Bel(G, p, T_p, C_p)$: agent G believes that the proposition p is true at time T_p in the context C_p (a proposition may be a state or any of the modalities described here);

$MB(G_1, G_2, p, T_p, C_p)$: agents G_1 and G_2 mutually believe that the proposition p is true at time T_p in context C_p ;

$Int.To(G, a, T_i, T_a, C_a)$: agent G has the intention, at time T_i , of performing action a at time T_a in context C_a ;

$Int.Th(G, p, T_i, T_p, C_p)$: agent G has the intention, at time T_i , that proposition p be true at time T_p in context C_p ;

$Pot.Int.To(G, a, T_i, T_a, C_a)$:   at time T_i , agent G considers the possibility of performing action a at time T_a in context C_a ;

$Pot.Int.Th(G, p, T_i, T_p, C_p)$:   at time T_i , agent G considers the possibility of wanting that proposition p be true at time T_p in context C_p ;

$Exec(G, a, T_a, C_T)$:   agent G has the ability to perform action a at time T_a under the constraints C_T ;

$Commit(G, a, T_a, T_i, C_a)$:   agent G commits him/her/itself at time T_i regarding the performance of action a at time T_a in context C_a ;

$Do(G, a, T_a, C_T)$:   agent G performs action a at time T_a under constraints C_T .

Actions and propositions are described using conceptual graphs, as we do in action schemas. We can use those modalities in several ways with respect to the action schemas. Consider the following example:

> John and George wanted money. They went to a bank. John pointed a revolver to a cashier and asked for money. George pointed a revolver to other people over there. After John got the money from the cashier, they ran away.

John and George clearly stole the money from the bank. We can likely establish their responsibility because of the following mental states:

- John and George both believed that the cashier, for the bank, had money;
- John and George shared the belief they could get the money by force;
- John showed his intentions of robbery, by pointing a gun on the cashier;
- George showed his intention to steal the money by pointing a revolver to people at the bank while John was with the cashier;
- Once they had the money, they ran away, and there is no reason to believe they went into that trouble harboring any intention to bring it back (an intention they didn't state, and of which they made no display).

Contrast the latter to another situation, in which somebody sharing your place (possibly a relative) takes a banknote from the table and rushes away before the post office closes down. You see, there is a bill to pay, and the person also blurted out something about the bill, the timetable, or the post office. You have no reason to entertain the hypothesis s/he is about to elope (moreover leaving in place far more valuable property). We could eventually have different possible types of mental states associated with an action; e.g., pointing a revolver on someone for joke, or, instead, to get something from that person or another person (or a group of persons including the one threatened: who on the other hand, could even be an accomplice), or, then, to kill that particular person. Some probability or other likelihood factor could be associated with the preconditions or effects. Such factors could be used to interpret events when some facts are missing to understand clearly what happened. Which leads us to forensic statistics.

4   Modeling Approaches for Legal Evidence

From the 1970s, research into computing for the law has eventually come to be published in several conference series, and several journals as well. For historical reasons, the scope of these journals encompasses also computer law, an altogether different domain. The early 1990s have seen the emergence of a journal with a more focused scope, *Artificial Intelligence and Law* [7]. From acquaintance with the research community, and an attentive search through the literature, emerged that *legal evidence* [55, 63, 39, 29] is a conspicuous absentee from the discipline (but cf. [5]). The main reason for that is historic. Law yields such a potential for computing and AI applications, that concentrated efforts across researchers have results to show especially in those areas which offered the least resistance to formalization. Another reason is biographic and demographic. For example, entering computer science was part of the curriculum of many a logician from the philosophy of law, just as it was for other logicists; among modal logics, especially *deontic logics* [28, 70, 6] have been pursued among the theorists of legal computing. As to the cohorts of empiricists, first of computing and then of AI, they either approached the domain in terms of maximal feasibility projects, or, then, they invested originally not very formal approaches from AI. Research in difficult areas such as argumentation —of much interest for AI basic research as well as for the legal application domain— was pursued (and has been booming in the last few years: e.g., [62, 54, 34, 15, 30, 51]), because the given competent researchers were there, and eventually came to be emulated.

The pool of AI researchers at the intersection of the AI research community and legal scholarship is demographically limited, and whereas important AI subdisciplines are well represented, such other paradigms are in the main absent, that potentially, together, would enable more global and thorough processing of legal narratives (before and during litigation, or, in the penal realm, offense, investigation, and legal proceedings). One factor in the absence of legal evidence from AI & Law research, is that legal evidence encompasses the investigative stage, upstream of going to court. Some of the forensic sciences (whose specialists are expert witnesses in court) use mathematics or computing [9, 8] in specialistic niches, whereas general criteria of assessment of the evidence, when getting mathematical, have done so especially within a probabilistic paradigm [55]. Forensic statistics has its expert witnesses, just as medicine, psychology, ballistics, civil engineering, even stylistics and entomology do. Formal models of argumentation have not been concerned with the expect witnesses, with one glaring exception from outside the AI & Law mainstream community: G. Holmström-Hintikka [23] has shown the value of J. Hintikka's interrogative model of inquiry for developing a formal account of expert witnesses.

Arguably, the research of Tillers and Schum (the latter, a computer scientist) has led the way from forensic statistics in a direction that becomes definitely relevant for artificial intelligence research [65, 64, 60, 66, 61], and that already provides an operational decision-support system. It combines Wigmore graphs (these are a domain-oriented formalism), and Bayesian computations, and is a landmark along the path towards what we term an *integrated evidence support system*. Another direction of research aims at formalized models of jurors' and the jury's decision-making: several approaches exist [20, 21], with some work being done within the paradigmatic cluster we term intelligent technologies [17].

To promote a synthese across the disciplines, [38] brings together contributions on probabilistic models (from either forensic statistics, or AI), and complementary approaches other than probabilistic. Research into agents, agents' beliefs and their ascription, and narrative structure fit in this broad, if heterogeneous compartment. Apart from the role of particular paradigms within AI, it's the test of integration that is paramount. Cross-fertilization, however, cannot be entirely successful unless AI scholarship in general becomes aware of the challenge of AI & Law in general, and of legal evidence in particular, for the development of significant AI basic research that could not as naturally develop otherwise.

References

1. Allen, J.F. 1983. "Recognizing Intentions from Natural Language Utterances". In M. Bradie and R.C. Berwick (ed), *Computational Models of Discourse.* MIT Press.
2. Allen, R.J. 1997. "Rationality, algorithms and juridical proof: a preliminary inquiry". Lead article, special issue, *Int. J. of Evidence and Proof.*
3. Asher, N. and Sablayrolles, P. 1995. "A typology and discourse semantics for motion verbs and spatial PPs in French". *Journal of Semantics* 12(2): 163–209.
4. Barrett, K.C., Zahn-Waxler, C. and Cole, P.M. 1993. "Avoiders vs. amenders: implications for the investigation of guilt and shame during toddlerhood?". *Cognition & Emotion* 7(6): 481–506.
5. Bennun, M.E. 1996. "Computerizing criminal law: problems of evidence, liability and *mens rea*". *Information & Communications Technology Law* 5(1): 29–44.
6. Brown, M.A. and Carmo, J. (eds) 1996. *Deontic Logic, Agency and Normative Systems.* Berlin: Springer-Verlag.
7. Berman, D.H., Hafner, C.D. and Sartor, G. (eds) 1992–. *Artificial Intelligence and Law* (journal). Dordrecht: Kluwer.
8. Bohan, T.L. 1991. "Computer-aided accident reconstruction: its role in court". SAE Technical Paper Series (12 p.).
9. Caldwell, C., V.S. Johnston 1989. "Tracking a criminal suspect through 'face-space' with a genetic algorithm". *Proc. 3rd Int. Conf. Genetic Algorithms,* 416–421.
10. Cohn, A.G., Gooday, J.M. and Bennett, B. 1994. "A comparison of structures in spatial and temporal logics". In R. Casati and G. White (eds), *Philosophy in the Cognitive Sciences.* Vienna: Hölder-Pichler-Tempsky.
11. Dyer, M.G. 1983. *In-Depth Understanding: A Computer Model of Integrated Processing of Narrative Comprehension.* Cambridge, MA: The MIT Press.
12. Edwards, D. and Potter, J. 1995. "Attribution". Ch. 4 in R. Harré and P. Stearns (eds), *Discursive Psychology in Practice.* London: SAGE, 87–119.
13. Fakher-Eldeen, F., Kuflik, Ts., Nissan, E., Puni, G., Salfati, R., Shaul, Y. and Spanioli, A. 1993. "Interpretation of imputed behavior in ALIBI (1 to 3) and SKILL". *Informatica e Diritto,* Year XIX, 2nd Series, Vol. II, No. 1/2: 213–242.
14. Fikes, R.E. and Nilsson, N.J. 1971. "STRIPS: A new approach to the application of theorem proving to problem solving". *Artificial Intelligence* 2: 89–205.
15. Freeman, K. and Farley, A.M. 1996. "A model of argumentation and its application to legal reasoning". *Artificial Intelligence and Law* 4(3/4): 157–161.
16. Fricker, E. 1987. "The epistemology of testimony". *Aristotelian Society Supplementary Volume* 61: 57–83.
17. Gaines, D.M., Brown, D.C. and Doyle, J.K. 1996. "A computer simulation model of juror decision making". *Expert Systems With Applications* 11(1): 13–28.
18. Gardner, A. v.d.L. 1987. *An Artificial Intelligence Approach to Legal Reasoning.* Cambridge, MA: The MIT Press.
19. Grosz, B., Kraus, S. 1996. "Collaborative plans for complex group action". *AIJ* 86.
20. Hastie, R. (ed) 1993. *Inside the Juror: The Psychology of Juror Decision Making.* Cambridge, U.K.: Cambridge University Press.
21. Hastie, R., Penrod, S.D. and Pennington, N. 1993. *Inside the Jury.* Cambridge, MA: Harvard University Press.

22. Hayes-Roth B. and van Gent, R. 1996. "Story-making with improvisational puppets and actors". Tech. Rep. KSL-96-05, Knowl. Sys. Lab., Stanford.

23. Holmström-Hintikka, G. 1995. "Expert witnesses in legal argumentation". *Argumentation* 9(3): 489–502.

24. Holt, A.W., Meldman, J.A. 1971. "Petri nets and legal systems". *Jurimetrics* 12(2).

25. Holyoak, K.J. and Cheng, P.W. 1995. "Pragmatic reasoning from multiple points of view: a response". *Thinking & Reasoning* 1(4): 373–389.

26. Jackson, B.S. 1996. " 'Anchored narratives' and the interface of law, psychology and semiotics". *Legal and Criminological Psychology* 1(1): 17-45.

27. Jameson, A. 1983. "Impression monitoring in evaluation-oriented dialog: the role of the listener's assumed expectations and values in the generation of informative statements". *Proc. 8th IJCAI,* Karlsruhe, Vol. 2, pp. 616–620.

28. Jones, A.J.I. and Sergot, M. 1992. "Deontic logic in the representation of law: towards a methodology". *Artificial Intelligence and Law* 1(1): 45–64.

29. Keane, A. 1994. *The Modern Law of Evidence,* 3rd edn. London: Butterworth.

30. Kowalski, R.A., Toni, F. 1996 "Abstract argumentation" *AI&Law* 4(3/4):275–296.

31. Kraus, S. 1996. "An overview of incentive contracting". *AIJ* 83(2): 297–346.

32. Kuflik, Ts., Nissan, E. and Puni, G. 1991. "Finding excuses with ALIBI: alternative plans that are deontically more defensible". *Computers and Artificial Intelligence* 10(4): 297-325 (1991). Also in J. Lopes Alves (ed), *Information Technology & Society: Theory, Uses, Impacts.* Lisbon: Associação Portuguesa para o Desenvolvimento das Comunicações, & Sociedade Portuguesa de Filosofia: 484-510 (1992).

33. Linde, C. 1993. *Life Stories: The Creation of Coherence.* New York: Oxford UP.

34. Loui, R.P. and Norman, J. 1995. "Rationales and Argument Moves" *Artificial Intelligence and Law* 3(3): 159–190.

35. MacCrimmon, M.T. 1989. "Facts, stories and the hearsay rule". In A.A. Martino (ed), *Logica, Informatica, Diritto: Legal Expert Systems (Pre-proceedings of the Third International Conference,* Florence. 2 vols. + Appendix). Florence: Istituto per la Documentazione Giuridica, Vol. 1, pp. 461–475.

36. Martino, A.A. 1994. "Artificial intelligence and law". *International Journal of Law and Information Technology* 2(2): 154–193.

37. Martino, A.A. and Nissan, E. (eds) 1997. *Models of Time, Action, and Situations.* Special issue in preparation for *Artificial Intelligence and Law.*

38. Martino, A.A. and Nissan, E. (eds) 1997. *Formal Approaches to Legal Evidence. Part 1: Probabilistic Models. Part 2: Belief & Agency, Relevancy, and Argumentation.* Special issue in preparation for *Artificial Intelligence and Law.*

39. May, R. 1995. "Criminal practice". In *Criminal Evidence,* 3rd edn. London: Sweet & Maxwell.

40. McDowell, J. 1994. "Knowledge by hearsay". In B.K. Matilal and A. Chakrabarti (eds), *Knowing from Words.* Dordrecht: Kluwer.

41. Meldman, J.A. 1975. "A preliminary study in computer-aided legal analysis". Dissertation. Technical Report MAC-TR-157. Cambridge, MA: MIT.

42. Moulin, B. and Rousseau, D. 1994. "A multi-agent approach for modelling conversations". In *Proceedings of the International Avignon Conference AI 94, Natural Language Processing Sub-Conference,* Paris, France, June 1994, pp. 35–50.

43. Nicoloff, F. 1989. "Threats and illocutions". *Journal of Pragmatics* 13(4): 501–522.

44. Nissan, E. 1995. "SEPPHORIS: an augmented hypergraph-grammar representation for events, stipulations, and legal prescriptions". *Law, Computers, and Artificial Intelligence* 4(1): 33–77.

45. Nissan, E. 1995. "Meanings, expression, and prototypes". *Pragmatics and Cognition* 3(2): 317–364.

46. Nissan, E. 1996. "From ALIBI to COLUMBUS: the long march to self-aware computational models of humor". In J. Hulstijn and A. Nijholt (eds), *Automatic Interpretation and Generation of Verbal Humor*. Univ. Twente, pp. 69–85.

47. Nissan, E. (in press). "Notions of place" (2 parts, 104 p.). In A.A. Martino (ed), *Norms: Logic & Computation. In Memoriam Carlos E. Alchourrón*. Pisa: SEU.

48. Nissan, E. and Shimony, S.E. 1997. "VEGEDOG: formalism, vegetarian dogs, and partonomies in transition". *Computers and Artificial Intelligence* 16(1): 79–104.

49. Parry, A. 1991. "A universe of stories". *Family Process* 30(1): 37–54.

50. Poulin, D., Mackaay, E., Bratley, P., Frémont, J. 1992. "Time Server: a legal time specialist". In A. Martino (ed), *Expert Systems in Law*. North-Holland, 295–312.

51. Prakken, H. and Sartor, G. 1996. "A dialectical model of assessing conflicting arguments in legal reasoning". *Artificial Intelligence and Law* 4(3/4): 331–368.

52. Prakken, H. and Sergot, M.J. 1996. "Contrary-to-duty obligations". *Studia Logica* 57: 91–115.

53. Prakken, H. and Sergot, M.J. 1996. "Dyadic deontic logic and contrary-to-duty obligations". In D.N. Nute (ed), *Defeasible Deontic Logic: Essays in Nonmonotonic Normative Reasoning*. (Synthese Library.) Dordrecht: Kluwer.

54. Rissland, E.L., Skalak, D.B. and Friedman, M.T. 1996. "BankXX: supporting legal arguments through heuristic retrieval". *Artificial Intelligence and Law* 4(1): 1–71.

55. Robertson, B. and Vignaux, G.A. 1995. *Interpreting Evidence: Evaluating Forensic Science in the Courtroom*. Chichester, West Sussex: Wiley.

56. Rousseau, D. 1995. "Modelisation et simulation de conversations dans un univers multi-agent". Ph.D. Dissertation. Technical Report 993, Department of Computer Science and Operational Research, University of Montreal.

57. Rousseau, D. 1996. "Personality in synthetic agents". Technical Report KSL-96-21, Knowledge Systems Laboratory, Stanford University.

58. Rousseau, D., Moulin, B. and Lapalme, G. 1997. "Interpreting communicative acts and building a conversational model". *Journal of Natural Language Engineering*.

59. Sappington, D. 1984. "Incentive contracting with asymmetric and imperfect precontractual knowledge". *Journal of Economic Theory* 34: 52–70.

60. Schum, D. 1993. "Argument structuring and evidence evaluation". [20]: 175–191.

61. Schum, D. and Tillers, P. 1991. "Marshalling evidence for adversary litigation". *Cardozo Law Review* 13(2/3): 657–704.

62. Skalak, D.B. and Rissland, E.L. 1992. "Arguments and cases: an inevitable intertwining". *Artificial Intelligence and Law* 1(1): 3–44.

63. Tillers, P. 1983. "Modern theories of relevancy". Section 37 in *Wigmore on Evidence* (i.e., *'Evidence in Trials at Common Law' by John Henry Wigmore)*, in Ten Volumes; *Volume IA, Tillers Revision*, P. Tillers (revision). Boston: Little, Brown & Co., pp. 1004–1095.

64. Tillers, P. 1989. "Webs of things in the mind: a new science of evidence". Review of D. Schum, *Evidence and Inference for the Intelligence Analyst* (2 vols). Lanham, MD: Univ. Press of America, 1987. *Michigan Law Review 87(6):* 1225–1258.

65. Tillers, P. and Green, E.D. (eds) 1988. *Probability and Inference in the Law of Evidence*. Dordrecht: Kluwer.

66. Tillers, P. and Schum, D. 1991. "A theory of preliminary fact investigation". *U.C. Davis Law Review* 24(4): 931–1012.

67. Tomberlin, J. 1981. "Contrary-to-duty imperatives and conditional obligation". *Nous* 16.

68. Vila, L. and Yoshino, H. 1995. "Temporal representation for legal reasoning". *Proceedings of the Third International Workshop on Legal Expert Systems for the CISG*.

69. Williams, B. 1981. "Moral luck". In his *Moral Luck*. Cambridge UP, pp. 20–39.

70. Wright, von, G.H. 1951. "Deontic logic". In his *Logical Studies*. London: Routledge.

Type Extensibility of a Knowledge Representation System with Powersets

Cécile Capponi

Projet SHERPA, INRIA Rhône-Alpes
655 ave. de l'Europe — 38330 Montbonnot — France

Abstract. This paper deals with KRSs (knowledge representation systems) close to frame systems including description logic and object-based systems. The main relation that leads to inferences is *subsumption* which is usually computed over knowledge descriptions that refer to data types. Although subsumption between knowledge terms is well-defined, its implementation on external data types depends upon the host language which is used for the actual implementation of data types. As a consequence, no KRS is able to integrate a new (external) data type such that its values can be safely involved in subsumption and further inferences. This is the problem addressed in this paper. The solution we propose relies on the design of a polymorphic type system connected to both the KRS and the host language. It is designed so that it can extend the KRS with any type implementation available in the host language (standard atomic types, library, package, etc.). Meanwhile, the values of the new type get safely involved in the KRS reasoning processes. The presented type system prevents the incompleteness of subsumption due to its incomplete processing on external data.

1 Introduction

Knowledge representation systems (KRSs) aim at helping people in an application domain to both organize and describe the knowledge related to this domain. Most of all, these KRSs require the development of expressive representation languages. Description logic systems (DLSs, also called terminological languages, or KL-ONE family [3]) are close to object-based languages, because they allow one to identify and describe knowledge as either groups or individuals.

The problem we address is to provide an object-based KRS (OBKRS) with an extensible collection of computable data types which can be used as parts of knowledge descriptions, while ensuring the type consistency of knowledge bases. In a KRS, knowledge terms are dynamically typed by subsets of values — namely powersets — built from the whole set of values a data type captures. Faced with these powersets, the extensibility of a OBKRS type collection gets different of what classical extensible type systems use to consider.

The paper is organized as follows: in section 2 we introduce the main features of OBKRSs, which are used further on in section 3 to identify the ways data types are processed within knowledge bases. The presented results are important to sketch the type system satisfying our purpose. In the section 4, we present the main organization of the METEO type system we designed for OBKRSs. We then present how METEO may be easily and dynamically used to extend the type collection of the KRS. Finally, in section 5, we compare our study with previous results in the area of DLSs.

2   Basics of Object-Based KRSs

Object-based knowledge representation systems (OBKRSs) stem from frame-based systems, except that they distinguish between frames that denote individuals (instances) and frames that denote sets (class).

Individual elements of the application domain are represented in the knowledge base by *instances*. Individual elements of the application domain can be classified into meaningful groups of somehow similar elements. That widespread organization principle is translated in an object-based knowledge base through the classification of instances into *classes*. Thus a class represents a set of individual elements it describes by means of *attributes*. These attributes are then valued in the description of instances. Attributes basically represent relevant characteristics of individuals. The description of an attribute in a class is the association of a domain (set of values or objects) with the attribute name. Such a domain is specified through *descriptors*.

Class *today-play-6/49*
   Attributes:
     numbers: set integer; card [6;9];
            among [1;49];
     player: in *Person*;
     outlay: in integer; interval [1;+∞];
     date: in Date; value (12,03,1996);

Instance *Pl#2A1* is-a *today-play-6/49*
   Attributes:
     numbers =   {1 4 9 23 24 41 45}
     player =   *Person#621AA4*
     outlay =   5
     date =   (12,03,1996)

The description on the top is this of a class that is intended to group all the plays of a 6/49 lottery draw of a given day. The description on the bottom is this of an instance of the class (is-a relationship). *Person* is a class of the knowledge base intended to represent human individuals, *Person#621AA4* is an instance of *Person*, Date is a data type; interval, in, value, card and among are descriptors. The descriptors associated to *numbers* in the class description together define all sets of a cardinality ranging from 6 to 9, whose elements are integer values ranging from 1 to 49.

Terms of the KRL are given a denotational semantics. The interpretation domain is $\mathcal{U}$; it contains all type values and instances, which are unit elements, as well as lists or sets constructed from unit elements. Let us consider a class attribute $\langle a : d \rangle$, where a is the identifier of the attribute and d is its domain: $d = \delta_1; \cdots; \delta_n$; (each δ_i is a descriptor). The denotation of the attribute in $\mathcal{U}$ is: $\|\langle a : d \rangle\| = \cap_{i \in [1;n]} \|\delta_i\|$ (see [4] for descriptor syntax and semantics). The description of an instance is a conjunction of valued attributes: it is written $I = \{\langle a_i = v_i \rangle\}_{i \in [1;m]}$. Similarly, the description of a class is written $C = \{\langle a_j : d_j \rangle\}_{j \in [1;n]}$. The denotation of the class C in $\mathcal{U}$ is: $\|C\| = \{I = \{\langle a_i = v_i \rangle\}_{i \in [1;m]} \in$

$\mathcal{U} \mid n \leq m$ and $\forall j \in [1; n], v_j \in \|d_j\|\}$.

Two general and fundamental relations exist among terms. They deal with a specific way of organizing knowledge that is usual in many application domains.

First, *attachment* is a binary relation, written $\in_\alpha$, defined between an instance and a class. It signifies that the individual the instance represents belongs to the group which the class denotes in the application domain. Attachment is partly defined on descriptions of involved terms. The restrictions on descriptions are necessary conditions for a whole attachment relationship to be agreed upon in the knowledge base. Let $I = \{\langle a_i; v_i \rangle\}_{i \in [1;m]}$ be an instance and $C = \{\langle a_i; d_i \rangle\}_{i \in [1;n]}$ be a class. Then the attachment between two term descriptions satisfies: $i \in_\alpha C \implies m \leq n$ and $\forall i \in [1; m] : v_i \in d_i$. For example, this condition is satisfied conjointly by the instance *Pl#2A1* and the class *today-play-6/49*. Thus the instance *Pl#2A1* can safely be attached to the class *today-play-6/49* according to both descriptions.

Second, *specialization* is a binary relation, written $\leq_\sigma$, defined between two classes. It signifies the inclusion of the group represented by the most specialized class in the group represented by the less specialized class. As for attachment, specialization leads to necessary restrictions on involved term descriptions. Let $C_j = \{\langle a_i : d_{ji} \rangle\}_{i \in [1;n_j]}$, $j = 1, 2$, be two classes. Then specialization between class descriptions satisfies: $C_1 \leq_\sigma C_2 \implies n_2 \leq n_1$ and $\forall i \in [1; n_2] : d_{1i} \subseteq d_{2i}$.

In DLSs, both specialization and attachment are merged towards a unique relation, namely subsumption [14]. In the following, we may refer to subsumption in order to denote both specialization and attachment.

Any OBKRS is provided with pre-defined inference mechanisms. They are activated either by the knowledge base user or by another process, in order to deduce new knowledge according to already represented knowledge. Most of these mechanisms stem from frame language inference mechanisms, such as filters or default values. Yet the main inference mechanism is the so-called *classification*, also defined by DLSs [10]. Type checking and type inferences are actually essential during the execution of any of those mechanisms.

3 Characterization of Types in KRSs

Types as dealt in KRSs are attribute descriptions, and further class descriptions as records of attribute descriptions.. They are subsets of values built over the set captured by the initial data type associated with each attribute. Those powersets are incrementally — by inheritance — constructed through descriptors applied on a same attribute.

Whatever the initial type of an attribute is (`int`, `list`, etc.), the powersets are always used on the same way during type checking and inferences, according to a set-based semantics. Given the definitions of necessary conditions for both attachment and specialization and the way attribute types are used, we define an algebra which any data type of the KRS collection should implement.

Each data type $T = \langle V; O \rangle$, where V is a set of values and O is a set of operations on these values, is associated with an algebraic structure over the powerset of V. This algebraic structure specifies the way the KRS operates in a common way on all subsets of any data type. We write this algebra $\mathcal{A}_T = \langle 2^V ; E \rangle_T$ where E contains set operations.

On one hand, data types are implemented in the host language. On the other hand, in order to perform type checking, the KRS relies on the implementation of $\mathcal{A}_T$. Yet a new data type is generally introduced in the KRS through a membership predicate while its actual implementation is a black box. As a consequence, the KRS is no longer able to generate $\mathcal{A}_T$. Then no type checking nor type inference is processed over those powersets.

For example, assuming that e-int (even integer) is a data type implemented in the host language, let us then consider the four attribute domains below:

$$a_1 \text{ in integer; interval } [0;+\infty]; \qquad a_2 \text{ in e-int; interval } [4;+\infty];$$
$$a_3 \text{ in e-int; interval } [0;+\infty]; \text{ except } 4\ 6\ 8;$$
$$a_4 \text{ in e-int; interval } [0;2]\ [10;+\infty];$$

The KRS can infer neither $\|a_3\| = \|a_4\|$ nor $\|a_2\| \subset \|a_1\|$, unless e-int has been defined as a sub-type of integer. Yet in this last case, there is no way for the KRS to check the consistency of such a subsumption relationship as long as the system cannot interpret host language predicates.

The KRS cannot guarantee the safety and the completeness of specialization over powersets built over new data types. Thus, subsumption tests which involve classes containing these attribute descriptions are incomplete.

Avoiding the above incompleteness requires the KRS to be able to access the properties and relevant features of any new data type. The way the new data type is related to existing data types must also be known by the KRS. In other word, the solution is to connect any data type $T = \langle V ; O \rangle$ to the KRS while extracting from O the operations and properties that are essential for the managing of 2^V. For example, when a data type is characterized as a total order (property defined in O), any of its powersets may be uniquely expressed by an ordered list of intervals. There is the idea underlying the design of the type system sketched in the next section; the type system gives several implementations of $\mathcal{A}_T$ according to several characterized and important properties. Then, adding a new data type is partly carried out through its attachement to predefined properties. Such an attachment leads to the inheritance of the implementation of $\mathcal{A}_T$ according to the specified generic properties.

4   The METEO Type System

As pointed out in the previous section, a solution to type collection extensibility in an OBKRS is the design of a type system where both host data types and knowledge term types are to be handled. The type system METEO (Module of Extensible Types for Expressive Objects) resulting from our study is presented in this section. It is made up of two type levels:

- *C-types*: encapsulated and formated implementations of host data types
- *δ-types*: canonical expressions for powersets.

4.1 C-types as Implementations of Data Types

METEO contains a whole set of C-types. A C-type is defined, in a minimal fashion, by two operations. Let $\mathcal{U}$ be the set of universal values.

- $\in_T: \mathcal{U} \mapsto$ Bool, is the membership predicate, from any value, to the type T
- $=_T: T \times T \mapsto$ Bool, is the equality predicate between two values of T

A C-type is a data type, that is a double $\langle V; O \rangle$ where V is a set of values and O is a set of operations applying to values. O must include the two above operations, especially since the membership predicate actually characterizes V. In addition to the minimal operations above, many others which are useful in a knowledge base may be implemented in the definition of a C-type. For example, the C-type **list** of METEO contains all the usual operations applying to lists, such as **map**, **catenate**, etc.

C-types are ordered according to C-sub-typing. It is a set-based partial order. $T_1 = \langle V_1; O_1 \rangle$ may be a C-sub-type of $T_2 = \langle V_2; O_2 \rangle$, written $T_1 \preceq T_2$, if $V_1 \subseteq V_2$. A rich tree of C-types, named $\mathcal{T}$, is provided by METEO, as shown on figure 1.

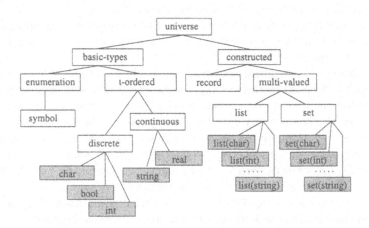

Fig. 1. METEO C-type tree $\mathcal{T}$. Only white C-types actually do exist in the minimal setting of METEO. Although grey tint C-types do not exist in the minimal setting, they can be easily integrated by the designer as addressed further on.

In $\mathcal{T}$, middle C-types are mainly used to factor out generic properties about lower C-types. $\mathcal{T}$ is actually built with object-oriented principles, namely inheritance of properties and methods. Hence, operations that are based on generic properties are defined within middle types as second order functions and are inherited along the C-sub-typing order. For example, the C-type **t-ordered** factors out all kinds of totally ordered types. It implements general algorithms, such as sorting. Then, whatever the total order relation may be, all its C-sub-types (**discrete**, **int**, etc.) inherit those general algorithms.

In addition to its usual definition, each C-type $T = \langle V; O \rangle$ is associated with an algebraic structure $\mathcal{A}_T = \langle 2^V; E \rangle$ where E contains the usual set operations. METEO defines, for each C-type, the implementation of this structure, according to the explicited generic properties of the C-type. Hence, the management of powersets is implemented in C-types, through several operations of E, mainly membership ($\in_{\delta,T}$), inclusion ($\leq_{\delta,T}$), GLB and LUB (resp. $\sqcap_{\delta,T}$ and $\sqcup_{\delta,T}$), and set difference ($\setminus_{\delta,T}$). In METEO, the powersets are named δ-types.

4.2 Internal Language for Powersets

The second level of types in METEO deals with the management of normal forms that express subsets of C-type values, called δ-types.

δ-types are intended to express powersets of C-types. It is a double $\delta t = \langle T; e(T) \rangle$ where T is the C-type the δ-type is attached to and $e(T)$ is a syntactic expression representing the set denoted by δt. The expression $e(T)$ is a normal form, *i.e.* that two different δ-types from the same C-type never denote the same set of values.

The syntax of δ-types is distributed among C-types. It takes into account the specific properties of C-types that are useful in order to make the syntax optimal. For this purpose, C-types are grouped into algebraic classes of C-types, according to the useful properties they share. For instance, powersets of **discrete** are expressed by lists of closed-bound intervals, which specializes the way its C-super-type **t-ordered** expresses δ-types, by lists of open-bound intervals.

Normalization of δ-types in METEO has the same purpose as normalization described in [1]. It is an operation that computes the normal form δt^N associated with any newly created δ-type δt. A normal form is itself a δ-type. METEO deals only with normal forms. The normalization operation is used to guarantee the following property: $\forall \delta t_1^N = \langle T; e_1(T) \rangle, \delta t_2^N = \langle T; e_2(T) \rangle : e_1(T) \neq e_2(T) \iff \|\delta t_1^N\| \neq \|\delta t_2^N\|$.

Since the δ-type syntax is distributed among C-types, the normalization operation is defined for each class of C-types, according to each syntax. Normalization is achieved through a syntactic rewritting system which is fully presented, as well as proven sound, complete, and confluent in [4].

δ-sub-typing and Other Set-Based Operations. δ-types from the same C-type $T = \langle V; O \rangle$ are partially ordered according to δ-sub-typing. δ-sub-typing is directly issued from set inclusion available in $\mathcal{A}_T$ (section 4.1). Like normalization, δ-sub-typing is implemented according to the distributed syntax, *i.e.* for each class of C-types. For example, δ-sub-typing between two **discrete** δ-types leads to the computation of inclusion between two ordered sets of closed-bound intervals. Following the same sketch, the others set-based operations of E are distributed among classes of C-types.

γ-Sub-Typing. In order to be able to check set inclusion between two δ-types from different C-types which are related by C-sub-typing (*e.g.* **integer** and **e-int**), δ-sub-typing is extended as γ-sub-typing.

γ-sub-typing is a relation that links two δ-types from different C-types. It is computed by the combination of both C-sub-typing and δ-sub-typing. Let $t_1 = \langle T_1; e_1(T_1) \rangle$ and $t_2 = \langle T_2; e_2(T_2) \rangle$ be two δ-types, and $T_2 \preceq T_1$. γ-sub-typing between t_2 and t_1 is written $t_2 \preceq_\gamma t_1$ and is defined as follows: $t_2 \preceq_\gamma t_1 \iff (T_1 = T_2 = T$ and $t_2 \leq_{\delta,T} t_1)$ or $(T_2 \prec T_1$ and $t_2 \leq_{\delta,T_2} h(t_1))$, where h is a non-strict inclusion-preserving mapping between δ-types from two different but related C-types [4]. Basically, h maps a δ-type of the upper C-type to a δ-type of the lower C-type, such that inclusion is preserved through h.

4.3 Connecting METEO to the OBKRS Through δ-types

The design of METEO is independent of the KRS, yet δ-types are the results of the typing of knowledge terms; *i.e.* METEO can be instantiated by the typing of a knowledge base. The typing of a knowledge base is thus the core of the interfacing between the KRS and METEO.

The typing of a knowledge term is made up of two main steps. First, attribute descriptions are translated towards δ-types according to the initial data type of each attribute. Then resulting δ-types are normalized. Only the first step takes part in the interface between the KRS and METEO, while the other one, unlike it is carried out in [1], is an internal process of METEO.

Due to the typing of the whole knowledge base, each knowledge term is associated with a δ-type. The set-based operations applying to δ-types are equivalent to the type checking operations of the KRS. Consequently, each operation that was used to manipulate knowledge term descriptions is now associated with a semantically equivalent operation in METEO that manipulates δ-types. For example, δ-sub-typing between record δ-types is equivalent to specialization between class descriptions.

4.4 Extensibility of METEO

The extensibility of METEO is independent of the KRS it is intended to be dedicated to. This section addresses the way METEO fully deals with type collection extensibility while preserving knowledge base type consistency.

Adding a New Data Type. Due to the C-type hierarchy, METEO is both a polymorphic and an extensible type system. Adding a C-type may be achieved dynamically by the designer. First, the designer selects a C-super-type. Second, (s)he declares links towards required operations which are implemented in the host language. Let us recall that these operations are mainly the membership and equality predicates, plus possibly some specific operations that represent properties required by the C-super-type. Once the previous two steps are achieved, the new C-type is fully and immediately integrated into METEO, as any other predefined C-type. Indeed, the formated implementation of the new C-type is generated by METEO by setting up dynamic links between METEO predefined modules and the actual implementation of the new data type. The function used to link a host language data type to METEO is named `create-adt`. For example, adding the C-type `date` $\preceq$ `discrete` is performed by executing the following code:

```
(create-adt 'date
    supertype: 'discrete
    equal: 'dateq
    member: 'datep
    order: 'ldate
    succ: '+day
    pred: '-day )
```

where the quoted symbols are names of functions implemented in the host language. The designer must define the order function on `date` values, as well as `pred` and `succ`, because they are required by the given C-super-types `t-ordered` and then `discrete`. These three functions are mandatory for they allow δ-types of `Date` to be represented by lists of closed-bound intervals. In addition, the designer may define any other function applying to `date` values that would be used in the knowledge base.

Extensibility and δ-type Management. The extensibility of METEO is actually protected along δ-type management. Indeed, whenever a designer adds a new data type, (s)he does not have to define the sub-language associated to the new type; the syntax of δ-types is inherited from the C-super-type, as well as all the set-based operations applying to them. This possibility is due to the fact that for any new implemented data type T, the powerset algebra $\mathcal{A}_T$ is automatically generated. Therefore, the designer does not have to deal with δ-type management and further attribute domain management.

As previously said, no KRS is able to deal with the example section 3 in a sound manner. With the connection of METEO to the KRS, not only the new data type `e-int` can be added, but this addition goes with the automatic generation of all set-based operations that manage subsets of even values, such as normalization or subsumption through inclusion. Hence, METEO computes the type of all four attributes:

$$\text{type}(a_1) = \langle\ \text{integer}\ ;\ [0;+\infty_{\text{int}}]\ \rangle \qquad \text{type}(a_2) = \langle\ \text{e-int}\ ;\ [4;+\infty_{\text{e-int}}]\ \rangle$$
$$\text{type}(a_3) = \text{type}(a_4) = \langle\ \text{e-int}\ ;\ [0;2] + [10;+\infty_{\text{e-int}}]\ \rangle$$

Then METEO is syntactically able to infer that $\|a_3\| = \|a_4\|$, thanks to the normalization process which ensures a syntactic equality over δ-types whenever (and only when) there is a semantic equality. Moreover, γ-sub-typing is used to check whether or not $\|a_2\| \subseteq \|a_1\|$, where h is the homormorphism that translates δ-types of `integer` towards δ-types of `e-int`: $h(\ \text{type}(a_1)\ ) = \langle\ \text{e-int}\ ;\ [0;+\infty_{\text{e-int}}]\ \rangle$. Then, using δ-sub-typing among δ-types of `e-int`, it is straightforward for METEO to conclude that $h(\text{type}(a_2)) \leq_{\delta,\text{e-int}} \text{type}(a_1)$, *i.e.* according to the definition of γ-sub-typing, $\text{type}(a_2) \leq_\gamma \text{type}(a_1)$.

4.5 About the Implementation of METEO

METEO has been implemented for TROPES [12] with the programming language ILOG-TALK [9]. Since METEO carries out the descriptional operations of TROPES, it cooperates with all inference and checking processes of TROPES, such as classification [5] and categorization [13] among others, as well as with error handling or knowledge revision [6]. At last, METEO weakly cooperates with the constraint management system of TROPES [8] during the computation and storage of attribute domain reductions for arc-consistency.

5 Related Works

5.1 METEO vs. Other Type Systems

No type system has been designed so far to deal with the specificities of a KRS that stem from frames: powersets of any data type are to be dynamically handled in order to ensure the type consistency of knowledge bases. Although some programming languages permit constructions of powersets (*e.g.* **range** over numeric types in Ada), those constructions remain poor and no dynamic management over subsets is allowed. Actually, no type system do handle the dimension corresponding to powersets (δ-types) of usual data types (C-types), whereas it is one of the specificities of METEO.

5.2 METEO vs. KRS Similar Abilities to Manage Types

Type collection extensibility is still a problem in most KRSs in the area of description logic systems, for example. Despite some incomplete solutions, such as TEST-H in CLASSIC, only two systems provide the designer with type collection facilities in such a way that type checking remains sound. The TEST-H predicate of CLASSIC is currently studied in order to deal with concept subsumption [2]. The system K-REP [11] provides the designer with an API in order to facilitate the integration of a new data type T, although (s)he still has to program the set-based functions of $\mathcal{A}_T$. The design of METEO has been achieved according to formal observations close to those B. Gaines reported in [7] regarding data type extensibility and KRSs. As a consequence, the underlying mainframe of METEO is close to the open system of Gaines, especially on the way both deal with class types as constrained record types [4].

6 Conclusion

The usual data types available in a knowledge representation system (KRS), namely the type collection of the KRS, are not always sufficient for the development of knowledge bases that require complex data structures (*e.g.* molecular biology). This problem relies partly on type checking and completeness of inference processes within the knowledge bases.

This paper presented the type system METEO which has been designed to maintain the type consistency of knowledge bases in presence of external data types. METEO is a polymorphic type system due to the hierarchical and generic organization of data types. This means that new data types may be added through dynamic predefined links that METEO sets up between the implementation of the types in the host language and the knowledge representation system. When a new data type is added, the handling of its powersets (which are the types of knowledge term descriptions) is fully and automatically generated by METEO. There is the main originality of METEO, because no existing KRS is able to warrant the completeness of set-based reasoning processes as soon as a new external data type is used in the knowledge base. The main organization of METEO can be safely of use to any description logic system.

References

1. A. Borgida and R.J. Brachman. Protodl : a customizable knowledge base management system. In *1st CIKM*, pages 482–490, Baltimore (MA, US), 1992.
2. A. Borgida, C.L. Isbell, and D.L. McGuinness. Reasoning with black boxes: handling test concepts in CLASSIC. In *International Description Logics Workshop*, Cambridge (MA, US), November 1996.
3. R.J. Brachman and J.G. Schmoltze. An overview of the KL-ONE knowledge representation language. *Cognitive Science*, 9:171–216, 1985.
4. C. Capponi. Design and implementation of a type system for a knowledge representation system. Rapport de Recherche 3096, INRIA Rhône-Alpes, France, January 1997.
5. C. Capponi, J. Euzenat, and J. Gensel. Objects, types and constraints as classification schemes. In *Knowledge Retrieval, Use and Storage for Efficiency*, Santa Cruz (CA, US), August 1995.
6. Y. Crampé. A characterisation of revision in object-based knowledge representation. ISMIS'97, poster Session, Oak Ridge National Laboratory, October 1997.
7. B.G. Gaines. A class library implementation of a principled open architecture knowledge representation server with plug-in data types. In Ruzena Bajcsy, editor, *13th International Joint Conference on Artificial Intelligence*, volume 1, pages 504–509, Chambéry (France), September 1993. Morgan Kaufmann.
8. J. Gensel. Contraintes et représentation de connaissances par objets. application au modèle TROPES. thèse de 3ème cycle, Université Joseph Fourier, Grenoble, France, October 1995.
9. ILOG, Gentilly (France). *ILOG TALK, version 3.1 (Beta 1)*, 1994.
10. R. MacGregor. Inside the LOOM classifier. *SIGART Bulletin, Special issue on implemented knowledge representation and reasoning systems*, 2(3):88–92, June 1991.
11. F.J. Oles, E.K. Mays, and R.A. Weida. The algebraic essence of K-REP. In *International Description Logics Workshop*, Cambridge (MA, US), November 1996.
12. Projet SHERPA, INRIA Rhône-Alpes, Grenoble (France). *TROPES, version 1.0 reference manual*, June 1995.
13. P. Valtchev and J. Euzenat. Classification of concepts through products of concepts and abstract data types. In *1st International Conference on Data Analysis and Ordered Structures*, pages 131–134, Paris (France), June 1995.
14. W.A. Woods. Understanding subsumption and taxonomy: a framework for progress. In J.F. Sowa, editor, *Principles of Semantic Networks*, chapter 1, pages 45–94. Morgan Kaufmann, 1991.

Planning Based on View Updating in Deductive Databases

Dolors Costal and Antoni Olivé

Universitat Politècnica de Catalunya
Departament LSI,
Jordi Girona Salgado, 1-3. E-08034 Barcelona -- Catalonia
e-mail: [dolors I olive]@lsi.upc.es

Abstract. This paper describes an approach to planning based on viewing the planning problem description as a deductive database and on extending techniques for the view update problem in deductive databases to solve planning problems. We provide a formal and expressive model to represent a planning problem and a sound and complete plan generation method to solve it. From this work it becomes clear that a planning problem and a view update problem have strong similarities.

1 Introduction

A classical planning problem [FiN71] can be stated as follows:
- given a description of the world or domain of the problem
- given an initial state of that world
- given a goal to accomplish
- obtain one or several plans (sets of actions) able to perform the transition between the initial state and a final state in which the desired goal holds.

A planning method has to provide both a way to *represent* a planning problem and its solutions and a way to *generate* plans for the problems it is able to represent.

The representation used by a planning method is important because it characterizes the planning problems the method is able to solve. Therefore, the kind of representation used defines the capabilities and limitations of the method. In this paper we show that deductive databases (DDBs) can be used to represent planning problems. A DDB able to represent a planning problem must have some specific features. We define temporal DDBs that provide a formal and expressive environment for planning problem representation.

This representation permits us to extend techniques developed in the area of deductive databases for view updating to perform plan generation. View updating has attracted much research in the DDB area. Several methods do exist. In this paper we present a method for generating plans which uses an extension of the Events Method [TeO95]. The Events Method gives a complete set of correct solutions to a view update request. A similar approach of borrowing ideas from DDB technology for planning has been followed by Moerkotte et al. in their CDP planner [DMM+91] and by Denecker et al. [DMM92].

The work presented in this paper pretends to foster the cross-fertilization between the planning and the deductive database areas. From it, it will become clear that solving a planning problem has strong similarities with solving a view update problem in a DDB. Then, new solutions or strategies for one of the areas may be useful to the other area as well.

Furthermore, in previous works [CoO92,CTU+96] we have shown that our planning method, due to the expressivity of the representation used, can be applied to the validation of conceptual models of information systems. One of the approaches to help the designer during the validation task is to provide reasoning capabilities about the conceptual model. A planning method can provide this reasoning capabilities if the representation used is able to express the conceptual model. In [CoO92,CTU+96] it can be seen that the representation used by our planning method is able to express a wide range of conceptual models and that it helps to perform their validation.

The rest of the paper is organized as follows. In section 2, we define DDBs which represent a planning problem and its solutions, and we explain the contributions of that representation. In section 3, we formulate plan generation in the context of our DDBs as a view update problem, we present our extension of the Events Method to generate plans and we compare our plan generation method to others also based on DDB technology [DMM+91, DMM92]. Finally, section 4 gives the conclusions.

2 Representing Planning Problems and their Solutions by Temporal Deductive Databases

In this section, we introduce the main components of a DDB and then we will define DDBs able to represent a planning problem and its solutions.

2.1 Deductive Databases

A DDB consists of three finite sets: a set F of facts, a set R of deductive rules and a set I of integrity constraints. The set of facts is called the *extensional database* (EDB) and the set of deductive rules is called the *intensional database* (IDB). Database predicates are partitioned into derived predicates and base predicates. A base predicate appears only in the EDB and (possibly) in the body of deductive rules. A derived predicate appears only in the intensional part. Every DDB can be defined in this form [BaR86].

A deductive rule is a formula of the form $p(X_1,...,X_n) \leftarrow L_1 \wedge ... \wedge L_m$ with $m \geq 1$, where $p(X_1,...,X_n)$ is an atom denoting the conclusion and $L_1,...,L_m$ are literals (that is, atoms or negated atoms) representing conditions. All variables that appear in the formula are assumed to be universally quantified. The terms in the conclusion must be distinct variables, and the terms in the conditions must be variables or constants. Condition predicates may be ordinary or evaluable ("built-in"). The former are base or derived predicates, while the latter are predicates, such as the comparison or arithmetic predicates, that can be evaluated without accessing a database.

Integrity constraints are closed first-order formulas that base and/or derived facts are required to satisfy. We deal with constraints that have the form of a denial $\leftarrow L_1 \wedge ... \wedge L_m$, with $m \geq 1$, where the L_j are literals and variables are assumed to be universally quantified over the whole formula. More general constraints can be transformed into this form as described in [LlT84]. For the sake of uniformity, we associate to each integrity constraint an inconsistency predicate icn, and thus they have the same form as deductive rules. We call them inconsistency rules.

We assume every rule to be allowed [Llo87], i.e. any variable that occurs in the rule has an occurrence in a positive condition of an ordinary predicate. We also assume the set of rules is stratified as defined in [ABW88].

2.2 Temporal Deductive Databases to Represent a Planning Problem and its Solutions

The possibility of describing derived information and integrity constraints provided by deductive databases is very useful to represent planning problems and their solutions (as will be illustrated in section 2.3). Nevertheless, for representing these planning problems we need deductive databases with some additional specific features in order to be able to specify not only the static knowledge but also the dynamic knowledge about the domain. We have defined a kind of temporal deductive database in order to express that dynamic knowledge.

Our temporal deductive databases are related with those that can be found in the literature [BCW93] in the sense that they are able to describe temporal information. The difference is that they are oriented to the representation of all the elements that appear in a planning problem and to permit the adaptation of a view update method to perform plan generation. They incorporate a model of time: database facts have an associated time point which indicates the time in which the fact holds and some temporal properties are satisfied by database states. They also store all events (or operators) that occur in the planning world as base facts. In the following we describe the features of these temporal DDBs in more detail.

Base predicates in our temporal DDBs represent event types (or operator schemata). Each fact of a base predicate, called base fact represents an occurrence of an event (or operator instance) in the planning domain. By convention, the last term of a base fact gives the time when the event occurred. If $p(a_1,..., a_n,t_i)$ is a base fact we say that $p(a_1,..., a_n)$ is true or holds at t_i.

All times are expressed in a unique time unit small enough to avoid ambiguities. A planning world has a life span L defined as a set of consecutive time points, expressed in the given time unit, $L=\{t_\alpha,...,t_\omega\}$, where t_α and t_ω are the first and last time points of the life span, respectively. There is a standard base predicate time(Time). A fact time(t) holds if t belongs to the life span.

In the example of figure 2.1, that will be used throughout the paper, there are four base predicates (apart from standard predicate time): offer, enrol, transfer and cancel. A base fact offer(c,t) indicates that course c has been offered as a new course at time t. A base fact enrol(s,c,t) denotes that student s enrols in course c at time t. A base fact transfer(s,fc,tc,t) means that, at time t, student s is transferred from course fc to course tc. A base fact cancel(c,t) indicates that course c is cancelled at time t.

Derived predicates in our temporal DDBs correspond to the relevant types of knowledge about the planning domain. Each fact of a derived predicate, called derived fact, represents an information about the state of the world at a particular time point. Derived predicates also have a last term that gives the time when the information holds.

Integrity constraints in our temporal DDBs represent conditions that base and/or derived facts are required to satisfy at any time point. Their associated inconsistency predicates also have a last time term which indicates when the integrity constraint would be violated.

Rules for derived and inconsistency predicates are required to be time-restricted. This means that, if we have a rule $p(X_1,...,X_n,T) \leftarrow L_1 \wedge ... \wedge L_m$, for every positive literal $q(...,T1)$ of a base or derived predicate q occurring in the body, the condition $L_1 \wedge ... \wedge L_m \rightarrow T1 \leq T$ must hold. This ensures that $p(X_1,...,X_n,T)$ is defined in terms of q-facts holding at time T or before.

In figure 2.1 there are six derived predicates with their corresponding (and hopefully self-explanatory) rules. For example, a derived fact offered(c,t) indicates that course c is being offered at time t and a derived fact cancelled(c,t1,t) means that course c has been cancelled sometime between $t1$ and t.

There are also seven inconsistency predicates in figure 2.1. For example, ic1 would be violated at time t and a fact ic1(t) would hold if course c was offered as a new course at time t and it was already offered at the previous time point $t-1$.

Base predicates
time(Time)
offer(Course,Time)
cancel(Course,Time)
enrol(Student,Course,Time)
transfer(Student,Course,Course,Time)

Derived predicates
offered(C,T)← offer(C,T1) $\wedge$ T1≤T $\wedge$ time(T) $\wedge \neg$ cancelled(C,T1,T)
cancelled(C,T1,T)← cancel(C,T2) $\wedge$ time(T1) $\wedge$ T2>T1 $\wedge$ time(T) $\wedge$ T2≤T
takes(S,C,T)← enrolled(S,C,T1) $\wedge$ T1≤T $\wedge$ time(T) $\wedge \neg$ transferred(S,C,T1,T)
enrolled(S,C,T)← enrol(S,C,T)
enrolled(S,C,T)← transfer(S,Fc,C,T)
transferred(S,C,T1,T)← transfer(S,C,Tc,T2) $\wedge$ time(T1) $\wedge$ T2>T1 $\wedge$ time(T) $\wedge$ T2≤T
fellows(S1,S2,T)← takes(S1,C,T) $\wedge$ takes(S2,C,T) $\wedge$ S1≠S2

Integrity constraints
ic1(T)← offer(C,T) $\wedge$ time(T1) $\wedge$ T1=T−1 $\wedge$ offered(C,T1)
ic2(T)← cancel(C,T) $\wedge$ time(T1) $\wedge$ T1=T−1 $\wedge \neg$ offered(C,T1)
ic3(T)← takes(S,C,T) $\wedge \neg$ offered(C,T)
ic4(T)← enrol(S,C,T) $\wedge$ transfer(S,Fc,C,T)
ic5(T)← enrol(S,C,T) $\wedge$ time(T1) $\wedge$ T1=T−1 $\wedge$ takes(S,C,T1)
ic6(T)← transfer(S,Fc,Tc,T) $\wedge$ time(T1) $\wedge$ T1=T−1 $\wedge$ takes(S,Tc,T1)
ic7(T)← transfer(S,Fc,Tc,T) $\wedge$ time(T1) $\wedge$ T1=T−1 $\wedge \neg$ takes(S,Fc,T1)

Fig. 2.1. Example of temporal DDB

Each state of our temporal DDBs has an associated time point t. A state corresponding to time point t consists of all base facts with time $\leq$ t. In particular, there is a fact time(t_i) for all t_i that belongs to the interval $[t_\alpha,t]$ where t_α is the first time point of the life of the planning world.

Let D be a state of our temporal DDB corresponding to a time point t. When we update D we obtain an updated database D' corresponding to a time point t' such that t'>t. We call *temporal interval of the transition* the interval [t+1,t']. Note that we consider updates that, in general, reflect the passing of several time points.

Let p be a derived predicate in database D. We denote by p' the same predicate evaluated in the updated database D'. Database states satisfy some temporal properties:

1- Facts hold at existing times

$$\forall X,T \ (p(X,T) \to time(T))$$

where X is a vector of variables. From the extension of the time predicate this property states that only facts that hold at a time $t_i \in [t_\alpha,t]$ are allowed at a state corresponding to a time t. Then, this must also be accomplished in the updated database D': $\forall X,T \ (p'(X,T) \to time'(T))$.

2- Old facts remain in the updated database

$$\forall X,T \ (p(X,T) \to p'(X,T))$$

This ensures that past information is not deleted.

3- The time of the new facts belongs to the temporal interval of the transition

$$\forall X,T \ (p'(X,T) \wedge \neg p(X,T) \to time'(T) \wedge \neg time(T))$$

This property states that a fact added to the database (that is, a fact that did not hold in D but does hold in D') has a time term that belongs to the temporal interval of the transition.

Note that, as a consequence of the previous properties and the definition of the extension of predicate time, an update will only have the insertions of base facts with a time term belonging to the temporal interval of the transition ($[t+1,t']$) and the insertions of base facts time(t+1),...., time(t'), have to be in the update. There will be no deletions nor modifications. We call this type of updates, *temporal updates*.

We have described a kind of temporal DDB that represents knowledge about a planning domain and the behaviour of its states. Now, we are able to describe how the *initial state*, the *goal* and the solution *plans* of the planning problem can be represented in the context of those temporal DDBs.

An *initial state* for a planning problem that corresponds to a time t_0 in which the planning problem is established is represented by the database state at time point t_0. Only the extensional part of the database state (base facts) must be included in the initial state description because the rest can be deduced. For example, the following set of base facts: {time(1), offer(db,1), time(2), time(3), enrol(john,db,3)} specifies an initial state at time 3 in which course *db* is offered and *john* is enrolled in it.

A *goal* to accomplish at a final state is described by a closed first-order formula that has to be satisfied at the final state. We deal with goals that have the form of a denial $\leftarrow L_1 \wedge ... \wedge L_m$, with m≥1, where the L_j are literals and variables are assumed to be universally quantified over the whole formula. More general goals can be transformed into this form as explained in [LlT84]. For the sake of uniformity, we associate to it a new derived predicate g(T) and thus it has the same form as the deductive rules. In general, it is not necessary to define the specific time point corresponding to the final state in which the goal must be satisfied. However, for presentation purposes, we assume that such state corresponds to a time t_f. For example: g(T) $\leftarrow$ takes(john,ai,T) $\wedge$ takes(peter,ai,T) $\wedge$ ¬takes(john,db,T) at time t_f represents the goal that *john* takes *ai*, *peter* takes *ai* and *john* does not take *db* at that time.

A *plan* can be defined as a set of base facts. These base facts represent the events that have to occur in the planning domain to obtain a final state that satisfies the desired goal departing from the initial state. For example, the following set of base facts: P={time(4), offer(ai,4), time(5), transfer(john,ai,db,5), enrol(peter,ai,5)} represents the plan of offering *ai* at time 4, transferring *john* from *ai* to *db* at time 5 and enrolling *peter* in *ai* also at time 5.

2.3 Contributions of the Representation

Most representations used by planning methods are based on that of STRIPS [FiN71] which at the same time is strongly related to the situation calculus [Gre69,Rei92].

Our representation is able to express all the concepts used in the representation of STRIPS or situation calculus. We illustrate this for the case of STRIPS using the example of figure 2.2. In STRIPS, the knowledge about the planning problem world is expressed by means of operators. Each operator has a precondition, i.e. a wff which states the conditions under which the operator is applicable. Each operator has also a delete list and an add list, i.e., the list of facts that are deleted and added, respectively, when the operator is applied. The STRIPS example of figure 2.2 includes the subset that is expressible in STRIPS of the figure 2.1 example. Note that all kind of elements that appear in the STRIPS example have a correspondence to elements of our representation.

operator: offer(c)	**operator: cancel(c)**
precondition: ¬ offered(c)	precondition: offered(c)∧¬ ∃S takes(S,c)
delete list: ∅	delete list: offered(c)
add list: offered(c)	add list: ∅
operator: enrol(s,c)	**operator: transfer(s,fc,tc)**
precondition: offered(c)∧¬takes(s,c)	precondition: offered(c)∧takes(s,fc)∧¬takes(s,tc)
delete list: ∅	delete list: takes(s,fc)
add list: takes(s,c)	add list: takes(s,tc)

Fig. 2.2. STRIPS example

Some authors have introduced representations that permit to specify derived informations, context-dependent actions and/or integrity constraints: SIPE [Wil84], Pednault's approach [Ped91], Weld's UCPOP [Wel94], CDP [DMM+91], Abductive Event Calculus [DMM92], GEM [Lan87]. Our representation also provides these capabilities: deductive rules permit to specify derived information and context-dependent actions while inconsistency rules permit to specify integrity constraints.

To illustrate the usefulness of derived information or context-dependent actions, consider predicate *fellows* of figure 2.1. It is a predicate that can not be represented without the possibility of defining derived information or context-dependent actions. Consider the STRIPS example, in order to specify predicate *fellows*, operators *enrol* and *transfer* would have to add facts of that predicate under certain conditions but these conditional additions are not expressible in STRIPS.

Integrity constraints, in some cases, permit to express in a synthetic way several different preconditions of operators. For example, integrity constraint *ic3* of figure 2.1

(which specifies that it is not possible to have students taking a course that is not being offered) synthesizes part of three different preconditions of the STRIPS example: for operator *cancel*, that no students are taking the cancelled course; for *transfer*, that the course to which the student is transferred is being offered; and for *enrol*, that the course to which the student is enrolled is being offered.

Although plans are executed along time, planning methods which use a representation based on that of STRIPS or situation calculus do not represent time explicitly. Time advances implicitly with state changes. A state change is induced by the execution of an action. These representations do not allow to express temporal concepts such as: duration of actions, simultaneity of actions, goals referring to several different time points and changes caused by the simple passing of time. Some works propose temporal logics with an explicit representation of time in order to express the previous concepts: McDermott [Der82], Allen [AlK83], Lansky [Lan87]. These works use specific temporal operators or reified-style predicates which complicate the logical formalism. A contribution of our work is to provide those concepts in a more simple way by using a temporal explicit representation based on time points which does not need the addition of new kinds of components to the formalism.

Actions with duration are specified as derived predicates. For example, an action with a duration of D time points may be:

action-with-duration(X,D,T) ← begin-action(X,T1) ∧ time(T) ∧T1≤T∧T1>T-D∧D>0,

where *begin-action* is a base predicate. Another example of action with duration is the case of an action which holds between two base events that begin and end it:

action-between-events(X,T) ← begin-action(X,T1) ∧ time(T)∧T1≤T∧ ¬ended(X,T1,T)
ended(X,T1,T) ← end-action(X,T2) ∧ time(T1) ∧ T2>T1 ∧ time(T) ∧ T2≤T

where *begin-action* and *end-action* are base predicates.

Our representation permits to express simultaneous actions. For example, the plan: P={time(4), offer(ai,4), time(5), transfer(john,ai,db,5), enrol(peter,ai,5)} describes that *john* will be transferred and *peter* will be enrolled simultaneously. It also permits to express knowledge about the possibility and the effects of simultaneous actions. For example, the integrity constraint: ic4(T)← enrol(S,C,T) ∧ transfer(S,Fc,C,T) forbids to enrol and transfer the same student to the same course simultaneously. Note that this integrity constraint has not a correspondent in the STRIPS example of figure 2.2.

Goals may refer to several different time points in our representation. For example, the goal: g(T) ← takes(john,ai,T) ∧ time(T1) ∧ T1=T-3 ∧ ¬takes(peter,ai,T1) ∧ enrol(peter,C,T1) indicates that at the time of the final state t_f *john* must take the *ai* course and three time points before *peter* must not take the *ai* course and there must be an action of enrolling *peter* to a course. Note that our goal representation may specify explicit actions that must be included in the plan.

We may describe information that changes by the simple passing of time. For example: beginner(S,C,T) ← enrolled(S,C,T1) ∧ T1≤T ∧ time(T) ∧ ¬transferred(S,C,T1,T) ∧ T1≥T-100. A student ceases to be a beginner in a course after 100 time points of his enrolment in it without the occurrence of any action.

Our temporal DDBs provide an expressive and at the same time simple formalization for planning problem representation.

3 Generating Plans by View Updating

In this section we describe the view update problem and show that the problem of plan generation can be formulated as a view update problem in the context of our temporal DDBs.

3.1 The View Update Problem

View updating is concerned with determining how a request to update a view (derived fact) can be appropriately translated into correct updates of the underlying base facts.

View updates may be insertions or deletions of derived facts. A translation T of an insertion of a derived fact $p(c)$ (resp. deletion of $p(c)$) in a database state D, is a set of insertions and/or deletions of base facts such that $p'(c)$ is (resp. is not) a logical consequence of the completion [Llo87] of the database state D' obtained by updating D according to T $(D'=D \cup T)$.

In general, several translations may exist. A translation is minimal when there is not a subset of it which is also a translation.

3.2 Plan Generation as View Updating

Plan generation can be formulated as a view update in the context of our temporal DDBs.

Consider a planning problem described in terms of a temporal DDB. Let D be a state of the temporal DDB at a time t_0 that corresponds to the initial state of the planning problem, that is, its extensional part are the base facts of the initial state description. Let $g(T)$ be the derived predicate that describes the goal and t_f the time point at which the goal must hold.

Plan generation for the planning problem is equivalent to obtaining the translation for the view update request of inserting the derived fact $g(t_f)$ in D.

From the definition of translation given above it follows that $g'(t_f)$ is a logical consequence of the completion of the database state D' obtained by updating D according to the translation. Database state D' represents the final state at time t_f of the planning domain and, thus, the final state satisfies the goal. The translation represents the solution plan because it performs the transition from the initial state of the planning problem to a final state that satisfies the goal.

Observe that the translation or solution plan, as an update on a temporal DDB, must be a temporal update. This means that the solution plan consists of a set of base facts to be inserted (there are no deletions). Furthermore, the time term of the inserted base facts belongs to the temporal interval of the transition $[t_0+1, t_f]$ and contains the insertion of facts $time(t_i)$ for all t_i such that $t_0+1 \le t_i$ and $t_i \le t_f$.

Several solution plans may exist. A plan is minimal when there is not a subset of it which is also a plan.

A solution plan has to satisfy the integrity constraints of the planning problem. Consistent plan generation can also be formulated in terms of view updating. We define a new derived predicate $cg(T)$ with the following rule: $cg(T) \leftarrow g(T) \wedge \neg ic$ and we define ic with the rules: ic←ic1(T),..., ic←icn(T) where ic1(T), ..., icn(T) are the inconsistency predicates of the database.

Now, consistent plan generation is equivalent to obtaining the translation for the view update request of inserting the derived fact $cg(t_f)$ in D. Note that this guarantees that integrity constraints are satisfied for all time points of the plan.

As an example, consider the planning domain described by the temporal DDB of figure 2.1. Consider also an initial state at time 3 described by a state D of the database with the following set of base facts: {time(1), offer(db,1), time(2), time(3), enrol(john,db,3)}, and consider a goal described by: g(T)← takes(john,ai,T) ∧ ¬offered(db,T) to accomplish at a final state corresponding to time t_f. One of the translations for the view update request of inserting the derived fact $cg(t_f)$ in D is the following set of base facts to be inserted: P={time(4), offer(ai,4), time(5), transfer(john,db,ai,5), time(6), cancel(db,6)}. In effect, the database D' obtained by updating D according to P has the following base facts: {time'(1), offer'(db,1), time'(2), time'(3), enrol'(john,db,3), time'(4), offer'(ai,4), time'(5), transfer'(john,db,ai,5), time'(6), cancel'(db,6)}, and thus the derived fact cg'(6) holds in D'.

At the same time, P is a solution for the planning problem we have represented with that temporal DDB. It corresponds to the solution of offering course *ai* at time 4, transferring *john* from *db* to *ai* at time 5 and cancelling *db* at time 6. It reaches a final state at time 6 that satisfies the goal.

3.3 Soundness and Completeness

Previous formulation of plan generation as a view update in our temporal DDBs facilitates the definition of soundness and completeness of a plan generation method for the planning problems represented by them.

Soundness: Let D be a state of a temporal DDB that corresponds to the initial state of a planning problem and let g(T) be the goal to satisfy at time point t_f. If P is a solution plan obtained by the plan generation method, then P is a temporal update and $cg(t_f)$ is a logical consequence of the completion of D ∪ P (i.e. the database state obtained by updating D according to P).

Completeness: Let D be a state of a temporal DDB that corresponds to the initial state of a planning problem and let g(T) be the goal to satisfy at time point t_f. If P is a minimal plan corresponding to a temporal update and $cg(t_f)$ is a logical consequence of the completion of D ∪ P then P is a solution plan obtained by the plan generation method.

3.4 Extension of the Events Method to Plan Generation

Any sound and complete view update method for the class of databases described in section 2.1 and providing solutions which are temporal updates may be used for plan generation.

The Events Method [TeO95] is a sound and complete method for view updating for the class of databases considered in section 2.1 (not temporal). In [Cos95] we have introduced a plan generation method based on extending the Events Method to deal with view updating in the context of our temporal DDBs. This extension obtains solutions which are temporal updates, that is, they satisfy our temporal properties and maintain a correct extension of predicate time. We have proved that this extension is sound and complete [Cos95].

We have studied some techniques to improve the efficiency of the application of the method for a subset of the considered planning problems [Cos95].

We do not include the description of our plan generation method and of the techniques to improve its efficiency for space reasons. The method and the efficiency improvement techniques have been implemented in Quintus-prolog language.

3.5 Related Plan Generation Methods

There are some other plan generation methods which are also based on deductive database techniques.

CDP [DMM+91] uses a sound and complete planning algorithm which is based on techniques for detecting and resolving inconsistencies from DDB technology for a part of the search. The problem of restoring DDB consistency is strongly related to the view update problem. Because of this, that part of the search in CDP is similar to our plan generation method. The difference is that in our method the whole plan generation process is uniformly based on DDB techniques.

Another main difference between CDP and our plan generation method is the kind of planning problems considered. CDP provides a formal characterization of a planning problem in which the static knowledge is represented by a DDB. The dynamic knowledge is described by operator specifications. Operators perform transitions between database states. An operator has some preconditions and performs additions and/or deletions of base facts to the database. Therefore, the dynamic knowledge is not embedded in the DDB and it is described apart from it. In contrast, our method uses a DDB to represent both the static and dynamic part of a planning problem. In CDP a DDB state is atemporal. Operators are external to the representation of the world. As a consequence this representation can only be used for planning problems where some assumptions on its dynamic behaviour are satisfied: actions cannot have duration, simultaneous actions are not permitted, goals cannot refer to several different time points and changes caused by the passing of time are not allowed. These assumptions are not required in our method.

In [DMM92] the SLDNFA abductive proof procedure is introduced. It extends SLDNF and is able to generate plans for planning problems described in Abductive Event Calculus. A similar abductive proof procedure has been used for view updating in DDBs [KaM90]. SLDNFA is sound and complete.

The main difference between SLDNFA and our plan generation method lies, as in the case of CDP, on the kind of planning problems considered. Abductive Event Calculus uses a discrete, point-based theory of time, it allows the specification of derived properties, context-dependent actions and integrity constraints. Although the Abductive Event Calculus provides a time model it imposes some restrictions that make necessary to establish the same dynamic assumptions on the planning problems also needed in CDP.

4 Conclusions

We have presented an approach to planning that is based on representing the planning problem as a kind of temporal DDB and on extending techniques for the view update problem in DDBs to generate plans. From this work, it is clear that a planning problem and a view update problem have strong similarities.

We have joined concepts of two different areas of research. This fosters the cross-fertilization of ideas between them and facilitates the application of new solutions or strategies for one of the areas to the other one. It also allows us to make contributions to both areas. We contribute to the planning area with a formal, expressive and at the same time simple formalism to represent planning problems. This formal representation permits us to give a definition of soundness and completeness of a plan generation method for the represented planning problems. Finally, we are able to define a plan generation method sound and complete for the wide range of our represented planning problems. We contribute to the DDB area because our plan generation method can be seen as a view update method for our temporal DDBs. Some of the efficiency improvement techniques we have developed for plan generation in [Cos95] are applicable to improve the efficiency of the Events Method for view updating.

Acknowledgements

We would like to thank the members of the IS group and the anonymous referees for their helpful comments. This work has been partially supported by PRONTIC CICYT program project TIC95-0735.

References

[ABW88]   K.R.Apt, H.A.Blair, A.Walker, 'Towards a Theory of Declarative Knowledge', *Foundations of Deductive Databases and Logic Programming (J. Minker Ed.)*, 89-148, Morgan-Kaufman, 1988.

[AlK83]   J.F.Allen, J.A.Koomen, 'Planning Using a Temporal World Model', *Proc. IJCAI'83*, 741-747, 1983.

[BaR86]   F.Bancilhon, R.Ramakrishnan, 'An Amateur's Introduction to Recursive Query Processing', *Proc. ACM SIGMOD*, 16-52, 1986.

[BCW93]   M.Baudinet, J.Chomicki, P.Wolper, 'Temporal deductive databases", in [TCG93], 294-320, 1993.

[Cos95]   D. Costal, *Un mètode de planificació basat en l'actualització de vistes en bases de dades deductives*, PhD Thesis, Dept. of LSI, Universitat Politècnica de Catalunya, Barcelona, 1995.

[CoO92]   D.Costal, A.Olivé, 'A method for reasoning about Deductive Conceptual Models', *Proc. of the CAiSE-92*, 612-631, 1992.

[CTU+96]   D.Costal, E.Teniente, T.Urpí, C.Farré, 'Handling Conceptual Model Validation by Planning', *Proc. of the CAiSE-96*, 255-271, 1996.

[Der82]   D. McDermott, 'A Temporal Logic for Reasoning About Processes and Plans', *Cognitive Science*, 6, 101-105, 1982.

[DMM92]   M.Denecker, L. Missiaen, M.Bruynooghe, 'Temporal reasoning with Abductive Event Calculus', *Proc. 10th ECAI*, 384-388, 1992.

[DMM+91]   M.Decker, G.Moerkotte, H.Müller, J.Possega, 'Consistency Driven Planning', *Proc. 5th EPIA*, 195-209, 1991.

[FiN71]   R.E.Fikes, N.J. Nilsson, 'STRIPS: A new approach to the application of theorem proving to problem solving', *Artificial Intelligence*, **2**, 189-208, 1971.

[Gre69]   C.Green, 'Application of theorem proving to problem solving', *Proc. IJCAI-69*, 741-747, 1969.

[KaM90]   A.Kakas, P.Mancarella, 'Database Updates through Abduction', *Proc. 16th VLDB*, 1990.

[Lan87]   A.Lansky, 'A Representation of Parallel Activity based on Events, Structure and Causality', *Reasoning about Actions and Plans: Proc. of the 1986 Workshop*, 123-159, Morgan Kaufmann, 1987.

[Llo87]   J.W.Lloyd, *Foundations of Logic Programming*, 2nd edn., Springer, 1987.

[LlT84]   J.W.Lloyd, R.W.Topor, 'Making Prolog more expressive', *J. Logic Programming*, **3**, 225-240, 1984.

[Ped91]   E.P.D.Pednault, 'Generalizing Nonlinear Planning to Handle Complex Goals and Actions with Context-Dependent Effects', *Proc. IJCAI'91*, 240-245, 1991.

[Rei92]   R. Reiter, 'Formalizing database evolution in the situation calculus', *Proc. Fifth Generation Computer Systems*, 600-609, 1992.

[TCG+93]   A.U.Tansel, J.Clifford, S.Gadia, S.Jajodia, A.Segev, R.Snodgrass, *Temporal databases. Theory, Design and Implementation*, The Benjamin/Cummings Publishing Company, 1993.

[TeO95]   E.Teniente, A.Olivé, 'Updating Knowledge Bases while Maintaining their Consistency', *The VLDB Journal*, **4**, 1995.

[Wel94]   D.Weld, 'An Introduction to Least Commitment Planning', *AI Magazine*, **15**, 26-61 1994.

[Wil84]   D.E.Wilkins, 'Domain-independent Planning: Representation and Plan Generation', *Artificial Intelligence*, **22**, 269-301, 1984.

Generic and Fully Automatic Content Based Image Retrieval Architecture

Suresh K Choubey[1] and Vijay V. Raghavan[2]

[1] Magnetic Resonance Center, General Electric Medical Systems, Waukesha, WI 53188, USA
[2] Center for Advanced Computer Studies, University of Southwestern Louisiana, Lafayette, LA 70504, USA

Abstract. Content-based retrieval requires the choice of distance functions for determining inter-image distances. Distance functions considered to be desirable for computing inter-image distances are often too expensive, computationally, to be used for on-line retrieval from large image databases. In this paper, we propose a generic and efficient content-based image retrieval architecture where the original images are mapped on to an abstract feature space such that the desired (or real) inter-image distances correspond to the distances between the vector representations of the images in the feature space. It is shown that it is more efficient to compute distances between these feature vectors and use them as estimates of the real distances. We have conducted experiments using color as the low-level feature. The results show a substantial reduction in the size of the feature space. The experimental results also indicate that high accuracy is achieved for the set of queries tested.

1 Introduction

An Enormous amount of image data is being generated at an ever-increasing rate. It is accumulated from satellites, finger printing and mug-shot devices in law-enforcement agencies, medical applications and entertainment industry. Image databases are becoming common in medicine, law-enforcement agencies, art galleries and museum management, geographic information systems, weather forecasting (meteorological science), trademark and copyright database management, picture archiving and communication systems and multimedia encyclopedias. This leads to the necessity of large image databases. Image databases (IDB) are large collection of images. Image Retrieval (IR) problem is concerned with retrieving images that are relevant to user's requests from an image database.

A *content-based image retrieval* (CBIR) uses information from the content of images for retrieval and helps the user retrieve images relevant to the contents of a query image. By content, we mean computable low-level features such as color, shape, texture, object centroids and boundaries. A CBIR system is required to manage the image data efficiently. For a given query the image content of the query is directly compared with that of the images in the image database and a desired number of images close to the query image is retrieved. However, CBIR remains a very difficult problem as the technology for doing retrieval is still in the process of getting mature. It is very difficult to extract semantics associated with a given image [1].

Approaches to CBIR can be classified into two broad classes of *attribute-based* and *feature-based*. In attribute-based approach, the image contents are modeled as a set of attributes extracted manually or semi-automatically and managed within the framework of conventional database management system. In a feature-based CBIR, images are represented by their contents and the comparison is made between the contents of the query and the images in the image database [1]. They have been discussed in detail in [2].

The *feature-based* approach can be further classified based on the dependence of retrieval process on how generic the approach is and the degree of automation. In our context, a generic system is defined as the one, where the processing steps remain largely the same for different choices of image content. Approaches to feature-based CBIR can be *semi-automatic non-generic*, *semi-automatic generic*, *automatic non-generic*, or *automatic generic*. The most desired *feature-based* approach is a *generic and fully automatic* approach.

An IR system should be automatic and efficient to give an acceptable response time. The use of low-level features in the feature-based image retrieval systems makes the approach automatic but not necessarily efficient. The use of "real" distance in the retrieval process can be computationally very expensive. For example, in the case of retrieval by color, accounting for the effect of color correlations is time consuming. For this, most of the processing that can be done *a priori*, should be done off-line and as little computation as possible should be done on-line. The IR system should also be generic enough to be transparent when different low-level features are used with almost no or very little changes.

We propose a generic and efficient feature-based CBIR architecture. This is based on the work done by Goldfarb [3] to bridge the gap between syntactic and statistical pattern recognition for classification problems. We have reported image retrieval specific to color only in [4] and image retrieval by texture in [5]. In this paper, we discuss the general architecture of our approach and provide preliminary experimental results for retrieval by color to show the effectiveness of the proposed approach.

In this approach, a "real" inter-image distance is used to compute high-level (composite) features for images in the database and to generate a training set. The real inter-image distance is defined by specifying a distance function according to which a user wants to perform the retrieval. The training set is used to compute the feature vector for a query image. In this case, the real distances of the query image to only the images in the training set (and not the whole image database) needs to be computed. This makes this approach efficient as the training set has fewer images compared to the number of images in the database and the computation of real distance is expensive. The image retrieval is done by using estimated distance between the query and the images of the image database. It may be noted that in our approach a query is expected to be in the form of either an image or an intermediate representation specifying certain low-level image properties.

This paper is organized into six sections. Sect. 2 briefly discusses the current approaches to solutions of IR problems by other researchers and our motivation. In Sect. 3, we define the problem formally. In Sect. 4, we propose our generic approach for an efficient CBIR. Sect. 5 describes the experiments and the results. Sect. 6 provides the conclusion and future work.

2 Related Work and Motivation

Literature shows that the low-level features have been used extensively as a discriminating feature in automatic IR. The use of low-level features may make the information and storage retrieval system automatic but not necessarily efficient.

Chang et al. [6] have used color as a discriminating feature for image retrieval. They use real distance between images to index the images in the image database. For a given query, the images in the image database are ranked on the basis of real distance between the query image and the images in the image database. Hence the on-line retrieval is very computation intensive. Faloutsos et al. [7], while using low-level features such as color, have tried to make it more efficient by using estimated distance instead of real distance. They reduce the search space by eliminating many images from consideration by using an estimated distance in such a way that a lower bound lemma is satisfied. This lemma does not allow the elimination of relevant images, but may retain many non-relevant images. Then they perform the search on the basis of real distance in the search space with fewer images. The use of estimated distance does not usually preserve the order induced by the real distance among the images. Thus, they can not use a nearest neighbor type search. Also the distance estimation is non-generic. This approach may end up computing real distance for a large proportion of original images. In [8], the authors have tried to make the retrieval efficient at the cost of accuracy by reducing the image resolution (the process is called quantization). However, when images are quantized to such a low resolution, there is a very strong possibility of loosing important color information relevant to differentiating one image from other.

We therefore see the need for an efficient and effective on-line image retrieval technique where the expensive real distance computation is performed with respect to only a few images and the images are represented by means of low-dimensional feature vectors. When mapping the original images to a feature space, it is desirable that the real inter-image distances are preserved in order to facilitate nearest neighbor type searches.

3 Problem Definition

Let us assume that an image database is populated with a set (or a collection) of images $O_0, O_1, O_2, ...O_{n-2}, O_{n-1}$. Let this collection be denoted by U. Let Q be a query image.

Let the real inter-image distance Π between any two images O_i and O_j be denoted by $\Pi(O_i, O_j)$.

The user can specify a query to retrieve a number of relevant images. Let h be the number of images, closest to the query image Q, that the user wants to retrieve, assuming that $h < n$.

This image retrieval problem can be defined as the *efficient* retrieval of the best h images according to Π from a database of n images.

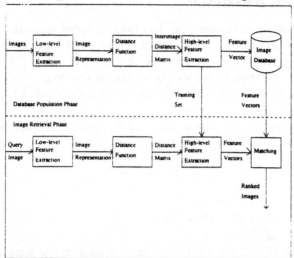

Figure 1: An Architecture of the Proposed System

4 Proposed Method

The whole image database is divided into *initial* and *incremental* image sets. The complete image storage and retrieval process is done in two phases of database population and image retrieval. The database population phase uses low-level image properties such as color to compute the real inter-image distance for images of initial image set. The initial image set is expected to be much smaller than the image database itself. The high-level image feature vectors for these images are computed very efficiently in addition to the generation of training set. These feature vectors have considerably fewer features compared to the intermediate image representation and the extent to which they preserve the real inter-image distances among the images, can be controlled. The training set has even fewer images compared to the initial image set. Images from the incremental image set are added using their real distances to only the images in this training set. In the image retrieval phase, we obtain a low-level (or intermediate) representation of a query image, compute its inter-image distance from the images in the training set, compute the query feature vector by using the training set generated in the database population phase, and use the Euclidean distance of this query feature vector from the feature vectors of the images in the image database. The architecture is given in Fig. 1. Our architecture is unique with respect to the generation of the training set during the database population stage. All the possible low-level image processing work of feature extraction is performed *a priori* at data population time. Only the query processing is done on-line when the query image becomes available. This leads to an effective, efficient, and flexible image retrieval system.

4.1 Theoretical Background

Let P be the subset of images that has been sampled from the set U to be representative of all possible image classes. This set of images is also referred as the *initial image set*. Let $|P| = k, where \ k \leq n$. The value of k should be as small as possible, in order to achieve faster training period.

According to Goldfarb [3], the dissimilarity measure between two objects can be defined as follows:

Let a pseudometric space be a pair (P, Π), where P is a set of images and Π is a non negative real-valued mapping: ·

$$\Pi : P \times P \to R^+ \tag{1}$$

satisfying following two conditions:

(a) $\forall O_1 \in P, \forall O_2 \in P \quad \Pi(O_1, O_2) = \Pi(O_2, O_1)$

(b) $\forall O \in P \quad \Pi(O, O) = 0$

The mapping Π is called a pseudometric (or inter-image distance) function. This inter-image distance will be used from this point on and is the only information about images that will be required in the rest of the image retrieval process.

From the inter-image distances computed between each pair of images in the initial set, a $k \times k$ interdistance matrix is constructed. This matrix is symmetric about the diagonal and the diagonal elements are zero, based on the two properties of the distance measure, defined earlier.

If the number of images in the initial image set is $k \quad (i.e., |P| = k)$, then the interdistance matrix D is defined as:

$$D = (\Pi_{ij})_{0 \leq i, j \leq k-1}, \tag{2}$$

Π_{ij} in the above equation is equal to $\Pi(\beta(O_i), \beta(O_j))$. Here β, which is an intermediate representation of low-level image features, is defined as

$$\beta : P \to \varphi, \tag{3}$$

where φ is the space of possible representations of low-level image features.

Following discussions lead to a theorem [3] that lays the condition for preserving the inter-image distance of an interdistance matrix into the derived feature space.

Definition 1: A pair of non-negative numbers (p, q) will be called the *vector signature* of a finite pseudometric space (P, Π), if there exists an isometric embedding

$$\alpha : (P, \Pi) \to R^{(p,q)} \tag{4}$$

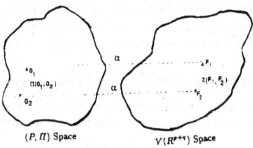

Fig. 2. Mapping of (P, Π) to V Space

where $\Pi(\beta(O_1), \beta(O_2)) = \| \alpha(O_1) - \alpha(O_2) \|_2 \quad \forall O_1, O_2 \in P$, such that for any other similar isometric embedding of (P, Π) into $R^{(n_1, n_2)}$, we have $n_1 \geq p, n_2 \geq q$. The α is called a *vector representation* of (P, Π).

In other words, (p, q) is the vector signature of a finite pseudometric space (P, Π), if $R^{(p,q)}$ is a minimal pseudo-Euclidean vector space, within which (P, Π) can be isometrically represented. This idea is illustrated in Fig. 2. Isometric embedding ensures that there exists a distance preserving mapping [3]:

Definition 2: Let (P, Π) be the pseudometric space defined earlier and let V be a vector space over R of dimension $k - 1$, and let $\{a_i\}_{1 \leq i \leq k-1}$ be a basis of such a vector space. A quadratic form on this vector space is given by:

$$\Psi(x) = \sum_{i,j=0}^{k-1} \frac{1}{2}(\Pi_{0i}^2 + \Pi_{0j}^2 - \Pi_{ij}^2)x^i x^j, \tag{5}$$

for $x = (x^1, \ldots, x^{k-1})$. Here x^i and x^j are the coordinates of x with respect to the standard basis $\{a_i\}$.

Theorem 1: A finite pseudometric space (P, Π) has the vector signature (p, q), iff the quadratic form given in definition 2 has the signature (p, q).

Determining whether a quadratic form has a desired signature requires the use of results on symmetric bilinear forms on (P, Π) and their connection to quadratic forms. The proof of Theorem 1 is given in [9].

A corollary of the theorm is as follows: A finite pseudometric space (P, Π) can be isometrically represented in the Euclidean $m(m = p + q)$–dimensional space iff the quadratic form given in Definition 2 is positive and of rank less than m.

4.2 Database Population Phase

A procedure called "ComputeFeatureVector()" to compute the feature vectors of images is given in [2, 4, 5]. This procedure also generates the training sample by calling "GenerateTrainingSet()". This training sample is used to compute query feature vector and feature vectors for images in the incremental image set. This procedure is executed during database population phase only and is also not given here due to space consideration. This algorithm can also be found in [2, 4, 5].

The execution of the ComputeFeatureVector() gives feature vectors of all the images in the initial set. Let these feature vectors be denoted by $F_0, F_1, \ldots, F_{k-1}$. Images in incremental image set $(F_k, F_{k+1}, \ldots, F_{n-2}, F_{n-1})$ are added on-line.

4.3 Estimated Interimage Distance and Image Retrieval

Let F_i, and F_j be the feature vectors for images O_i and O_j. Then the estimated inter-image distance between two images O_i and O_j can be determined as:

$$Z(O_i, O_j) = E(F_i, F_j) \qquad (6)$$

where E is the Euclidean distance between the feature vectors of images O_i and O_j.

Note that the estimated inter-image distance is computed from the feature vectors of images and not the image representations. Also, the computation is very inexpensive, as the feature vectors have much reduced number of elements. The estimated inter-image distance *does* preserve the real inter-image distance between two images. It can be used instead of real inter-image distance for image retrieval very efficiently.

Given the query image Q, one can readily determine the orthogonal projection (w) of Q onto the vector representation space $R^{(p,q)}$. An algorithm called "ComputeQueryVector()" to compute the feature vector of the query image is also given in [2, 4, 5].

Let the query feature vector be given by F_q. Since the matrix T [2, 4, 5] can easily be computed during the database population phase, the only on-line computations are those of $b_j, 1 \leq j \leq m$. This is perfectly feasible since one has control over the dimension m of the representation space.

Once the query feature vector is computed, we compute the estimated inter-image distance between the query feature vector and all the images of U by using the Euclidean distance between the query feature vector and the feature vectors of database images. The estimated distance is given by:

$$Z(O_i, Q) = E(F_i, F_q), \quad for \quad i = 0, 1, \ldots, n-1 \qquad (7)$$

Where E is the Euclidean distance between feature vectors F_i and F_q respectively of images O_i and query image Q.

4.4 Discussion of Proposed Mapping Scheme

Following are the advantages and motivation of using the proposed mapping scheme:

- Compared to multidimensional scaling (where the mapping is to and from vector representations) [10] this approach transforms original images into an intermediate representation to create inter-image distance matrix. Thus, the intermediate representation does not have to be a vector representation; it may be a string representation (in the case of shape representation) or involve other syntactic or structural representations.

- Interimage distance does not have to a metric. It may be pseudometric. This allows us to apply the mapping technique to a wider range of application areas.
- In neural networks (e.g., Kohonen's feature map [11, 12]), the mapped feature space is restricted to be low (1 to 3) dimensional. In our mapping, there is no such restriction.
- In Kohonen map [11, 12]), distances between all image pairs should be available at the start to construct the map. Hence, that technique can not support incremental addition of new images.

5 Experiments and Results

A set of experiments using color was designed to test the retrieval effectiveness of the proposed method. Color images from the Department of Water Resources (DWR) repository, maintained at University of California, Berkeley have been used.

We have used RGB color space and uniform quantization method to quantize the images. Most of the display devices use RGB display. Uniform quantization is a simple method and a good choice in the absence of information regarding the color distribution of the images. Color histograms can be used to describe characteristics of the unique color distributions of the physical objects, if they are well defined. For example, sunset can be described with the right percentage of the constituent colors of red, green, and blue.

We have used an inter-image distance function for retrieval by image color content, also used by Faloutsos et al., Chang el al., and other researchers [6, 7, 13]. The *real inter-image distance* function $\Pi(X, Y)$ between two images O_X and O_Y, can be computed as follows:

$$\Pi(X, Y) = (X - Y)^t A(X - Y) = \sum_{i,j}(x_i - y_i)a_{ij}(x_j - y_j), \tag{8}$$

where elements a_{ij} represent the cross correlation between color i and color j, *for* $0 \le i, j \le L - 1$, and $X = \beta(O_X), Y = \beta(O_Y)$. This compensation takes into account the fact that colors are usually not orthogonal. The commonly used value of L is 64 or 256.

Images numbered 0 through 31 from four distinctive color groups with predominant green, red, yellow, and blue colors were used in this experiment. These images were quantized to 64 colors and quantized images were used to compute the color histograms for every image in the image set. From the histograms, the color correlation matrix and then real inter-image distance between each images were computed. From these inter-image distances (inter-image matrix), the high-level image feature vectors were computed. For ease of presentation, we have randomly picked 8 images to be used as query images and have ranked other images in the image set with closest image next to the query image, based on real and estimated inter-image distances. We have used R_{norm} performance measure, which was first introduced in LIVE-Project [14] and is discussed in detail in [2].

	R1	R2	R3	R4	R5	R6	R7	R8	R9	R10	R11	R12	R13	R14	R15
Z(10(0645.0010))	10	24	2	3	15	0	26	9	18	14	31	27	13	11	19
Π(10(0645.0010))	10	24	0	15	2	14	26	8	9	13	18	27	31	1	3
Z(12(0812.0020))	12	13	14	15	9	8	11	3	23	22	24	10	16	2	20
Π(12(0812.0020))	12	13	14	15	22	8	9	3	2	20	11	10	28	16	17
Z(14(0812.0040))	14	13	15	12	8	9	10	11	24	2	3	22	28	31	26
Π(14(0812.0040))	14	13	15	12	10	9	8	2	22	11	24	28	3	16	0
Z(22(1202.0082))	22	28	30	21	16	11	31	29	23	25	26	1	2	8	18
Π(22(1202.0082))	22	30	21	16	28	29	1	25	2	11	23	18	12	13	31
Z(24(1202.0084))	24	10	26	2	31	18	8	0	9	1	19	11	27	15	3
Π(24(1202.0084))	24	10	26	31	2	8	9	0	1	18	15	14	11	25	30
Z(25(1202.0085))	25	29	26	30	28	21	22	31	24	19	1	23	2	16	11
Π(25(1202.0085))	25	30	21	22	28	29	26	10	24	19	1	2	31	27	0
Z(29(1624.0044))	29	25	21	28	30	22	26	16	23	31	11	1	24	4	2
Π(29(1624.0044))	29	30	21	16	22	26	25	31	28	23	1	24	11	2	17
Z(30(1625.0004))	30	25	22	31	29	28	26	1	21	2	24	23	16	0	18
Π(30(1625.0004))	30	25	22	29	31	21	2	28	1	26	0	16	18	23	8

Table 1: Comparison of Ranking (Z = Estimated Distance, Π = Real Distance)

Query Image	R_{norm}
10(0645.0010)	.915323
12(0812.0020)	.875000
14(0812.0040)	.883065
22(1202.0082)	.860887
24(1202.0084)	.870968
25(1202.0085)	.862903
29(1624.0044)	.877016
30(1625.0004)	.907258

Table 2: R_{norm} Values for Query Images.

5.1 Results

The result is tabulated in Table 1. Due to the limited space, only top fifteen retrieved images are shown in this table. For every query image, the first row in the table gives the ranking based on estimated inter-image distance and the second row gives the ranking based on the real inter-image distance. In essence, this table illustrates the correspondence between the rankings based on estimated and real inter-image distances.

After quantization, every image had 64 low-level features. However, after high level features were computed, every image were represented by only five high-level features. Hence, we were able to reduce the feature space dimensions from 64 to 5 to make on-line computation very efficient.

Also as we see in Table 1 that almost all top 15 images are also in top 15 when estimated distance is used to rank the images instead of real distance. For example, in Table 1, top 13 images by real distance are also in top 13 positions by estimated distance for query image 10. For query image 12, top 14 images by real distance are in top 15 images by estimated distance. In fact for this image, top 4 images were exactly at the same ranks. We notice the same for image no. 14. The degree of accuracy in the match can further be improved by adjusting the threshold value that we use to decide the number of high level image features.

Another significant result that contributes to efficiency is that during the computation of query feature vector, we did not have to compute its distance to every image in the database. Instead, we used the training set generated during the initial database population stage.

The R_{norm} for the above query images is given in Table 2. They are computed based on rankings of all 32 images. The average R_{norm} for all these query images is 0.88. The values for R_{norm} also suggest that the rankings of images for a given query image according to estimated distances is in agreement to large extent with the rankings based on real distances.

6 Conclusion

We have proposed a generic and efficient automatic CBIR architecture. Except for the computation of inter-image distances, our method is generic relative to image properties such as shape, or texture instead of color. Our experimental results for retrieval by color show that the dimension of the feature space can be substantially reduced (64 to 5), while preserving real inter-image distances. R_{norm} of estimated inter-image distance with respect to the real inter-image distance for all the query images is 0.88. Our on-line computation for a given query image is substantially reduced as it needs to compute the real distances only between the query image and the images in the training sample generated during the image database population.

It will be useful to study the indexing of database images using an effective spatial indexing mechanism such as R^*-tree, after image feature vectors have been computed. Also the rankings obtained by using proposed method should be evaluated against rankings provided by an expert.

References

1. V. Gudivada and V. Raghavan, "Content-Based Image Retrieval Systems," *IEEE Computer*, vol. 28, no. 9, pp. 18–22, 1995.
2. S. K. Choubey, *Generic and Fully Automatic Content-Based Image Retrieval Using Color Shape and Texture*. PhD thesis, University of Southwestern Louisiana Lafayette LA 70504, 1997.
3. L. Goldfarb, "A Unified Approach to Pattern Recognition," *Pattern Recognition*, vol. 17, no. 5, pp. 575–582, 1984.
4. S. K. Choubey and V. V. Raghavan, "Generic and fully automatic content-based image retrieval using color," in *Pattern Recognition in Practive V*, (Vlieland, Netherland), June 1997.
5. S. K. Choubey and V. V. Raghavan, "Generic and fully automatic content-based image retrieval using texture," in *International Conference on Imaging Science, Systems, and Applications (CISST'97)*, (Las Vegas, Nevada), pp. 228–237, June-July 1997.
6. S. F. Chang, A. Eleftheriadis, and D. Anastassiou, "Development of Columbia's Video on Demand Testbed," *International Journal of Image Communication- Signal Processing*, vol. 8, no. 3, pp. 191-207, 1996.
7. C. Faloutsos *et al.*, "Efficient and Effective Querying by Image Content," *Journal of Intelligent Information Systems*, vol. 3, no. 3, pp. 231–262, 1994.
8. X. Wan and C. C. J. Kuo, "Color Distribution Analysis and Quantization for Image Retrieval," in *Storage and Retrieval for Still Image and Video Database* (I. K. Sethi and R. C. Jain, eds.), San Jose, CA, pp. 8–16, January 1996.
9. L. Goldfarb, "A New Approach to Pattern Recognition," in *Progress in Machine Intelligence and Pattern Recognition*, (L.N. Kanal and A. Rosenfeldi, eds., vol. 2, North Holland Publishing Company, 1985.
10. J. D. Carroll and P. Arabie, "*Multidimensional scaling*," in *M. R. Rosenzweig and L. W. Porter, (eds.) Annual Preview of Psychology*, vol. 31, pp. 607–649, 1980.
11. T. Kohonen, "Self-Organized Formation of Topologically Correct Feature Maps," *Biological Cybernetics*, vol. 43, pp. 59–69, 1982.
12. T. Kohonen, *Self-Organization and Associative Memory*. Berlin, Germany: Springer-Verlag, 1984.
13. A. K. Jain and A. Vailaya, "Image Retrieval Using Color and Shape," *Pattern Recognition*, vol. 29, no. 8, pp. 1233–44, 1996.
14. P. Bollmann *et al.*, "The LIVE-Project—Retrieval Experiments Based on Evaluation Viewpoints," in *ACM/SIGIR Conference on Research & Development in Information Retrieval*, (Montreal, Canada), pp. 213–214, June 1985.

Program Synthesis from Examples by Theory Formation

Jutta Eusterbrock

Computing Science Department, University of Aberdeen
Aberdeen AB24 3UE, Scotland, UK
email: jeusterbrock@csd.abdn.ac.uk

Abstract. This paper presents a logic-based framework which integrates an incremental generic method for learning from examples into program synthesis with generic theories. It allows to incorporate constraints, strategic and domain specific knowledge in an additive way. We derive a knowledge-based synthesis method which is based on the computational paradigm of "divide-and-conquer" as a meta-level proof method. The generic method provides a basis to construct case solutions of more general requirement specifications with efficiency constraints. Based on the abstracted results of example computations an automatic extension of problem descriptions may be performed. The emphasis is elucidating that learning techniques may support construction of definitions required for the derivation of efficient programs. The system has been used to synthesize a previously unknown mathematical algorithm.

1 Introduction

The formal approaches to synthesis consist almost exclusively of specifications of the form (cf. [2, 10, 13, 14, 19, 20, 22])

$$\forall X[\exists Y : prop_{in}(X) \Rightarrow prop_{out}(X,Y)].$$

where $prop_{in}$ denotes some condition on the *input* X and $prop_{out}$ denotes a description of the desired relation between X and *output* Y. But functional correctness of programs is only one development objective. Other relevant properties could concern time and space complexity or structural criteria. Hence, we allow requirement specifications to include additional constraints, especially cost constraints. This results in generic requirements $Spec_{constraint}$

$$\forall U[\exists Z : prop_{in}(U) \Rightarrow prop_{out}(U,Z) \wedge c(U,Z) \leq |U|].$$

To tackle the inherent exponential search complexities and the deficiencies of pure deductive methods, our approach assumes synthesis to be an incremental and experimental theory formation process. The essential parts of this methodology will be outlined. Declarative domain theories are transformed into efficient target programs satisfying $Spec_{constraint}$. The process is divided into the following phases, which could be performed in a non-linear, eg. cyclic way.

- Specification: Interactive elaboration of formal domain models and strategic knowledge from some informal intentions;
- Experimentation: Constructive meta-level proving of examples/cases of the intended requirement specification, experimenting with several heuristics and evaluating search processes;
- Abstraction from automatically derived detailed knowledge;
- Maintenance: Refinement and simplification of sets of requirements and derived formulas into consistent, complete and non-redundant sets;
- Logical Validation and Learning: Proving the correctness of discovered knowledge and storing it permanently;
- Extraction of target code or systems from meta-level proofs;
- Application of the Synthesised System.

Another SEAMLESS feature concerns re-usability, easy extensibility and correctness. A knowledge-based synthesis system is considered to be build up from reusable distributed knowledge sources which capture various facets of domain and synthesis knowledge. SEAMLESS provides a logic-based framework, based on a domain-independent multi-layer architecture (cf. [7]), distinguishing the layers *domain knowledge, generic domain abstractions* and *distributed dynamic knowledge sources*, each layer divided into the levels *data types, declarative theories, derived knowledge/methods*. The seamless connection of heterogenous knowledge sources on various abstraction layers is realized by viewpoints. *Viewpoints* (cf. [7]) provide instantiations of generic theories which lift object level expressions to the metalevel. Arbitrary pieces of strategic knowledge which satisfy the soundness axioms associated with a generic method can be *added* without effecting the correctness of methods. However, adding strategic knowledge may improve search complexities. The viewpoint approach is far more flexible than the specialisation of theories by translation of function and predicate symbols (cf. [21]). Within SEAMLESS, methods denote verified theorems which are derived from generic theories (cf. [14]). We will refer to this methodological framework, as well as to the implemented toolkit, as "SEAMLESS" in the remainder of this paper. It is organized around the basic development phases. Section 2 declaratively specifies the domain theory of a challenging mathematical problem and operationalises the domain theory for generic synthesis based on the "divide-and-conquer" principle. Section 3 shows how to construct example solutions. Section 4 introduces various new abstraction techniques which will be applied to derive sound and hypothetical knowledge from cases. Some examples in section 5 illustrate the techniques to maintain dynamically created knowledge sources. In Section 6 empirical results are summarized. The paper concludes with a discussion.

2 Domain Modeling

We use Horn clause logic enriched with abstract data types as specification language. As a mathematical challenging problem, we analyze the synthesis of efficient and optimal selection algorithms. The selection problem is to find the

$i - th$ largest element of a totally ordered set, initially knowing a partial ordering and using a minimum number of pairwise comparisons. The selection problem is a classical problem in computer science (cf. [1, 2]). It is estimated (cf. [11]) that a brute-force search takes more than a century to compute the optimal bound for selecting the $5 - th$ largest element. Hence, the same authors developed a heuristic domain specific program which computes the optimal bounds for small values of $i, n, n \leq 10$.

Domain Declaration   *Selection_Problem*
Uses   *Poset*

Sorts   *poset, domain, bool,* $\mathbb{N}$

Predicates
selection : $\mathbb{N} \times poset \times poset \rightarrow bool$
new_rel : $poset \times (domain \times domain) \rightarrow bool$
add_rel : $poset \times (domain \times domain) \times poset \rightarrow bool$
succ : $poset \times domain \rightarrow \mathbb{N}$

Axioms
$selection(1, \lambda(P), S)$ $\Leftarrow P = ..[S, \_].$
$selection(I, [D, Rel], S)$ $\Leftarrow \exists X \in D : succ([D, Rel], X) \geq |D| - I + 2$
        $\land PNew = P \setminus X \land selection(I - 1, PNew, S).$
$selection(I, P, S)$ $\Leftarrow new\_rel(P, [X, Y]) \land compare(C, X, Y)$
        $\land add\_rel(P, C, PNew)$
        $\land selection(I, PNew, S).$
$new\_rel([Dom, Rel], [X, Y])$ $\Leftarrow X \in Dom \land Y \in Dom \land X \neq Y$
        $\land (X < Y) \notin Rel \land (X > Y) \notin Rel.$
$add\_rel([Dom, Rel], C, New]$ $\Leftarrow New = Rel \cup C.$

Fig. 1. Specification of Selection Problems

A formal specification of the selection problem is given Figure 1. It is based on the abstract data type *Poset*, introduced in [8]. Posets are represented one-to-one by ground terms. A canonical representative of the isomorphism can be constructed by substituting constants by variables. Eg. $\lambda(a(b(c), d), e(b(c)), f)$ implements the poset $[\{a > b, b > c, a > d, e > b\}, \{a, b, c, d, e, f\}]^1$. Operations are implemented by term rewriting. Eg. *add_rel* implements adding of relations, *new_rel* enumerates comparison pairs. *succ* computes the number of successors. The SEAMLESS approach is based on the "divide-and-conquer" principle and has this in common with many schema-guided approaches for algorithm synthesis [20, 13]. The essence of the "divide-and-conquer" principle is to be described as follows: to solve any problem, first select a split-element, then decompose the problem into subproblems and compute the solutions of these subproblems, and finally construct the solution of the whole problem by composing subsolutions.

---

[1] λ is a dummy node, denoting an artificial maximum of all elements.

Smith[21] proposed to capture design knowledge by algebraic specifications. Theory morphism translate the predicate and function symbols of domain theories into the design theories such that soundness axioms are preserved. However, search complexities are in general untractable. In solving mathematical problems, humans make use of already proven theorems and relationships between formulas, eg. in order to select the next subgoal to be proven. In order to be able to deal with strategic knowledge in an additive way, we introduce a more general and flexible approach. Generic design knowledge is captured by meta-level theories, which model abstract properties of domain theories by soundness axioms. Domain theories and meta-level theories are connected by viewpoints which lift object-level expressions into meta-level expressions. Generic theories are divided into an essential part and additional metapredicates to classify strategic knowledge. Figure 2 shows the viewpoint which lifts the selection theory into a generic decomposition theory. The choice of the decomposition and composition predicates and the well-founded ordering is data-type dependent.

Viewpoint Θ_{VpSel}
Uses $Selection\_Problem$
$Data\_Type\_Formula$

Sortinterpretation
$def\_type(goal, \Leftarrow \exists S : selection(I, P, S))$.

Basic Axioms
$minimal\_goal(selection(1, \lambda(P), P)) \qquad \Leftarrow P = ..[S, \_]$.
$<_{goal} (\exists S' : selection(1, P', S'),$
$\qquad\qquad \exists S'' : selection(I, P'', S'')) \qquad \Leftarrow P' < P''$.
$split\_goal(\exists S : selection(I, P, S), X) \qquad \Leftarrow new\_rel(P, X)$.
$decompose\_goal(G, [X, Y], G', G'') \qquad \Leftarrow G = \exists S : selection(I, P, S)$
$\qquad\qquad\qquad \land add\_relation(P, Y < X, P')$
$\qquad\qquad\qquad \land add\_relation(P, X < Y, P'')$
$\qquad\qquad\qquad \land G' = \exists S' : selection(I, P', S')$
$\qquad\qquad\qquad \land G'' = \exists S'' : selection(I, P'', S'')$.

Fig. 2. Lifting of the Selection Theory into a Decomposition Theory

Extensions of this decomposition theory comprise the strategic relations: *behavioural equivalence, reduction, generalization* and generic predicates for modeling *control knowledge*. Most important, the algorithm design knowledge, eg. lower bounds, which is mandatory for automated synthesis of efficient and optimal algorithms (cf. [17]) can be captured by metalevel knowledge.

3 Efficient Synthesis of Case Solutions

The formula $\Leftarrow \exists Z : U = \lambda(a(b), c(d), e) \land select(3, U, Z) \land c(3, U, Z) \leq 4$ specifies a program to select the third largest element of $\{a, b, c, d, e\}$ with at most 4 comparisons, initially known $\{a > d, b > c\}$. A generic synthesis method *know_div_conquer*, realizing the "divide-and-conquer" principle and enabling the incorporation of strategic knowledge, is derived as metatheorem from a decomposition theory. Constructive solutions are returned from the meta-level proof

$$\Gamma \cup \Theta_{VpSel} \vdash know\_div\_conquer(Spec, Proof, Bool)$$

when Γ comprises the definition of the generic "knowledge-based divide-and-conquer method", the viewpoint Θ_{VpSel} connects the divide-and-conquer theory with the domain theory of the selection problem. *Proof* collects successful branches as a proof tree, if a goal is provable (i. e. *Bool* = *true*) and all the failure branches, If a goal fails (*Bool* = *false*). Figure 3 sketches a succesful proof of the initially given specification which is decomposed in a way that a lemma applies which was proven by Kislitsyn. Based on the substitutions of the *split* predicate, specifications can be transformed into efficient programs.

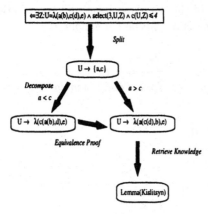

Fig. 3. Constructive Meta-level Proof

Metainterpretation allows the system to keep track of the search process which led to the resulting proof. The information obtained this way will be evaluated yielding positive and negative substitutions of the desired split function, factual knowledge about the (non-)provability of subgoals and optimal selection functions for subproblems to be solved. However, this specific derived knowledge is of little value for re-use in further proof searches and its addition would result in an exponential growth of the data base. In accordance with [16] we will regard sets of objects as *behaviourally equivalent* ($\simeq$), if they react "similar" with respect to a given input/output relation. This means that a problem is solvable for an object A, if, and only if it can be solved for a behaviourally equivalent object B. Considering the complexity of selection problems, isomorphism induces behavioural equivalence on posets. Hence, more comprehensive assertions stating knowledge about congruence classes - rather than single cases - can then be included in the knowledge base and re-used furtheron as valid knowledge. Taking the results in [8], the abstraction from a single object to a congruence class is efficiently implemented by syntactic generalization. Knowledge is efficiently retrieved by matching and unification.

4   Formula and Function Generation by Abstraction

Rather than perform the search processes each time, we are led to ask if we could automatically synthesize strategic knowledge and programs from specific case solutions and equivalence classes that would compute the solutions of more general requirement specifications. Most approaches to inductive inference and machine learning employ the same syntactic procedure for constructing more general formulas from cases. This inductive inference is realized in two steps: first, certain constants occurring in the formula are replaced by variables. The latter are bound by universal quantifiers added in a second step. However, this technique fails to provide an explicit description of properties of the original formula and it fails to provide function definitions. Thus, we employ more sophisticated abstraction methods instead of the common technique outlined above. Our notion of abstraction is closely related to natural concepts of abstraction and concept formation which are discussed for example in [18] and can be used for proof discovery [4]. Abstraction is the computation of a set of semantical properties which characterizes a given object, i. e. assigns it to a certain class of objects. Properties are relevant if they are shared by all members of the class. For syntax-guided abstraction, we introduce *types* . Types shall describe semantical properties, which are "easy" to verify by syntactically defined term properties. They are unary predicates together with sets of defining axioms and subtype axioms. Subtype relations describe logical entailment. An expression of the form $p \sqsupset q$ will be used to abbreviate the formula $\forall X : p(X) \Leftarrow q(X)$. In the following, the symbols $\top, \bot$ denote *true* and *false*, respectively. $t_{|N}$ denotes the subterm s of t at occurrence N. $degree(t)$ denotes the arity of t. $|occ(s,t)|$ is the number of occurrences of s in t. Type systems are exemplified in Figure 4.

$\Phi_1 : \{\forall T : typ_1'(T) \Leftarrow |occ(T_{|1,1}, T)| \geq 2, \forall T : typ_2'(T) \Leftarrow |occ(T_{|1,1}, T)| \geq 3,$
$\quad typ_2' \sqsupset typ_1'\}$

$\Phi_2 : \{\forall T : typ_1''(T) \Leftarrow degree(T_{|1}) \geq 0, \ \forall T : typ_2''(T) \Leftarrow degree(T_{|1}) \geq 1,$
$\quad \forall T : typ_3''(T) \Leftarrow degree(T_{|1}) \geq 2, \ \forall T : typ_4''(T) \Leftarrow degree(T_{|1}) \geq 3,$
$\quad typ_1'' \sqsupset typ_0'', typ_2'' \sqsupset typ_1'', typ_3'' \sqsupset typ_2'', typ_4'' \sqsupset typ_3''\}$

Fig. 4. Definition of Type Systems

Having introduced types, we can define the abstraction rule, which serves to construct hypotheses from case-based knowledge.[2] Let $p(t)$ denote any atom.

$$\frac{p(t)}{\forall U : p(U) \overset{hyp}{\Leftarrow} typ_1(U) \wedge \ldots \wedge typ_i(U) \wedge \ldots typ_r(U)}$$

provided that $\Phi \vdash typ_1(t) \wedge \ldots \wedge typ_i(t) \wedge \ldots \wedge typ_r(t)$ for any type system Φ.

---

[2] We employ a three-valued logic. Formulas with the value *maybe* will be indexed by the symbol *hyp*.

While the abstraction method introduced above can be used to synthesize predicate definitions from instances, it fails to provide a means for the construction of non-boolean functions. A general approach to the construction of functions from examples consists in searching for the right combination of selector and constructor functions which describe finite sequences of input/output pairs of functions in a uniform way. This approach was studied mainly for the LISP selectors and constructors $cons, car, cdr$. Summer [22] constructs from the input-output pair $f([[a, b], [c, d], [e, f]]) = [b, d, f]$ the general description

$$\forall X : f(X) = cons(cadar(X),$$
$$cons(cadadr(X),$$
$$cons(cadddr(X), nil))) \Leftarrow atom(cdddr(X)).$$

Many important applications lend themselves to more general structures other than linear lists. We therefore have extended this technique to arbitrary term structures, using the binary selector $root : term \times path\_expression \rightarrow f\_symbol$ to construct function definitions from input-output examples. Moreover, to prevent overgeneralization, we allow to restrict the domain of variables by preconditions. For example, consider the input-output relation

$$f\_split(3, \lambda(a(b(c), d), e(b(c)), f)) = [b, e].$$

$b = root(\lambda(a(b(c), d), e(b(c)), f)|_{11}), e = root(\lambda(a(b(c), d), e(b(c)), f)|_2)$. Preconditions are synthesized by type abstraction with respect to the type system Φ_1. The minimal types which abstract from the given term are computed. This yields the most specialized formula which describes the ground formula:

$$\forall T : f\_split(3, T) = [X, Y] \overset{hyp}{\Leftarrow} |occ(T_{|1,1}, T)| \geq 2 \wedge$$
$$X = root(T_{|1,1}) \wedge Y = root(T_{|2}).$$

5 Maintenance

Knowledge acquisition by abstraction from sets of positive and negative cases one-to-one may cause redundancy and inconsistencies. So the generic task to be solved can be stated as follows: Given a set of atoms - labelled as positive or negative - $ex_1, ex_2, \ldots = \Pi^+ \cup \Pi^-$ and a type system Φ. which may be empty, construct a minimal set of formulas named Δ, such that

$$\forall Ex \in \Pi^+ : \Delta \cup \Phi \vdash Ex; \quad \forall Ex \in \Pi^- : consistent(\Delta \cup Ex).$$

The set of formulas Δ_i is obtained by assigning the i-th example a formula π_i by abstraction. At each iteration, the program Δ_{i-1} is tested as to whether it satisfies the given examples and is modified accordingly into the program Δ_i according to the following generic case divisions:

- Δ_{i-1} subsumes π_i. Then $\Delta_i = \Delta_{i-1}$.

- $\pi_i \cup \Delta_{i-1}$ is inconsistent. Then $\Pi^+ \cup \Pi^-$ has to be abstracted again with respect to an extended type system, which provides discriminating properties.
- In all other cases, Δ_i is constructed from Δ_{i-1} by adding π_i and eliminating the formulas which are subsumed by π_i.

These generic procedures can be specialised to yield useful techniques for the simplification of synthesis knowledge.

Supsumption and elimination of redundant formulas Taxonomic theories are taken into account of by "theory subsumption".

$$\forall T : f\_split(3, T) = [X, Y] \overset{hyp}{\Leftarrow} |occ(T_{|1,1}, T)| \geq 2 \wedge degree(T_{|1}) \geq 2 \wedge$$
$$X = root(T_{|1,1}) \wedge Y = root(T_{|2}). \tag{1}$$

$$\forall T : f\_split(3, T) \qquad = [X, Y] \overset{hyp}{\Leftarrow} degree(T_{|1}) \geq 2 \wedge$$
$$X = root(T_{|1,1})) \wedge Y = root(T_{|2}). \tag{2}$$

Hence, (1) is subsumed by (2) ((1) $\sqsubseteq$ (2)) and can be eliminated.

Removal of inconsistencies Sets of formulas which are inconsistent are modified such that the resulting set subsumes all positive examples and none of the negative formulas may be subsumed. Abstracting from
$\{f\_split(3, \lambda(a(b(c), d), e(b(c)), f) = [b, e], f\_split(3, \lambda(a(b(c)), e(b(c))) \neq [b, e]\}$
with respect to the type system Φ_1 yields

$$\forall T : f\_split(3, T) = [X, Y] \overset{hyp}{\Leftarrow} |occ(T_{|1,1}, T)| \geq 2 \wedge$$
$$X = root(T_{|1,1}), Y = root(T_{|2}).$$

$$\exists T : f\_split(3, T) \neq [X, Y] \wedge 3 > |occ(T_{|1,1}, T)| \geq 2 \wedge$$
$$X = root(T_{|1,1}), Y = root(T_{|2}).$$

The resulting inconsistency is removed by enriching the type system $\Phi_1 \to \Phi_1 \cup \Phi_2$ (cf. Figure 4) and starting the abstraction process again. This yields

$$\forall T : f\_split(3, T) \quad = [X, Y] \overset{hyp}{\Leftarrow} |occ(T_{|1,1}, T)| \geq 2 \wedge degree(T_{|1}) \geq 2 \wedge$$
$$X = root(T_{|1,1}) \wedge Y = root(T_{|2}). \tag{3}$$
$$\exists T : f\_split(3, T) \neq [X, Y] \wedge 3 > |occ(T_{|1,1}, T)| \geq 2 \wedge 2 > degree(T_{|1}) \geq 1$$
$$X = root(T_{|1,1}) \wedge Y = root(T_{|2}). \tag{4}$$

Generalization In order to keep the set's magnitude reasonable, we apply compression procedures to decrease the amount of hypotheses. First, formulas are generalized. Second, formulas which are subsumed by the generalized formulas are eliminated. Two sorts of generalization rules are employed: Omission of preconditions, and ascension in the hierarchy which is induced by subsumption. Generalization are to be chosen in a way that avoids inconsistencies. For example, (3) can be generalized into (2), which is consistent with (4).

6 Experimental Synthesis of Optimal Correct Algorithms

The newly developed techniques and methods are incorporated in the SEAM-LESS synthesis system. SEAMLESS communicates with a composite graphlay-out component which is used for the visualization of constructive metalevel proofs (cf. [9]). Some features have been made accessible through a World-Wide Web user-interface. Various experiments have been carried out to synthesize optimal algorithms for the selection problem.

Combinatorial Cases

- To comment on the importance of the knowledge-based approach, we just observe that our implemented prototype exhibited "reasonable" times, ie. seconds, minutes, hours, days and not years or centuries, once numerous theorems encoding strategic knowledge had been implemented.
- A substantial reduction of search complexities can be achieved by re-use of learned knowledge:
  - Reasoning by analogy using the lemmata constructed by behavioral equivalence speeds the search time by a factor of approximately 2.
  - Derived hypotheses (cf. sections 4, 5) represent the complete factual know-ledge about the optimality of splitting in a condensed form. Re-using these learned strategies, further queries can be proven more efficiently up to a factor of 10.
- The experiments yielded a **mathematically relevant result**: Using SEAM-LESS interactively, we were able to construct an algorithm for the selection of the third-largest of a set of 22 elements. The algorithm improves in terms of worst-case comparison operations all the algorithms published so far. More-over, it corrects the lower bound, given in [1] for a single value [6, 5].

Mathematical induction and recursion Until yet, no formal means for proving the correctness of programs synthesised from examples are provided, assuming inductively constructed domains. The synthesis theorem, proven in [6] identifies the following major steps sufficient for constructive synthesis of efficient recursive programs.

- Generalize a given requirement specification by exchanging the input condition $prop_{in}$ by a more general one, $prop_{gen} \sqsupset prop_{in}$.
- Define a well-founded ordering on the generalized domain.
- Define an appropriate $split - function$ which induces decompositions which reduce the generalized problem to one which leaves the input condition in-variant with decreasing order.
- Verify the minimal cases.

Although the design principle is well-understood, its application to the solution of complex problems requires creativity: Solving elementary problems like the generation of a maximum algorithm using the SEAMLESS system is straightfor-ward. Abstracting from the results of one example computation, an executable correct algorithm is constructed. However, when we attempted to attack the more ambitious problem of generating efficient recursive programs for selecting the 3-rd element from examples, we ran into severe problems.

- Some examples failed to provide any information that could be used to describe the corresponding class of input values.
- Case solutions are not determined uniquely. Not all solutions are characteristic for a class.
- Abstract descriptions of solutions are not determined uniquely. Not every description of a characteristic example describes its class.

Finding an efficient recursive algorithm involves a lot of user interaction, incorporation of domain specific knowledge and tuning of abstraction mechanism by weight functions.

7 Concluding Remarks

We presented a generic framework and experimental results for synthesis as theory formation process. Contrary to pure deductive methods, this approach avoids to force software designers to pinpoint requirements, their strategy and the domain theory completely before starting the synthesis process. The framework integrates and generalizes techniques which stem from different areas and contexts. It incorporates seminal work on program synthesis from examples with program schemas [10, 22], on debugging of logic programs [19], and on deductive program synthesis applying formalized design tactics (cf. [13, 15, 20]). For the first time, we showed how to perform syntax-guided reasoning from examples, given the abstract data type *poset* instead of lists. The experiments with the prototypical implementation illustrate that solutions to complex mathematical problems can be synthesized. The system delivers constructive meta-level proofs, close to the mathematical notation, which will be visualized or transformed into programs. Having abstract proofs distinguishes SEAMLESS from pure deductive and heuristic domain specific problem solving programs (cf. [11]). The architecture allows to organize synthesis knowledge into re-usable encapsulated pieces. Heterogenous knowledge sources can be seamless integrated by viewpoints. Any kind of synthesis knowledge can be easily added. Within the KRAFT project (cf. [12]), we want to adopt this architecture and the synthesis methods to build a new kind of system distributed over the net which combines, re-uses and transforms knowledge from various sources to synthesize customized programs.

References

1. M. Aigner. Selecting the top three elements. *Discrete Applied Mathematics*, 4:247–267, 1982.
2. W. Bibel. Syntax-directed, semantics supported program synthesis. *Artificial Intelligence*, 14:243–261, 1980.

3. W. Biermann. Fundamental mechanisms in machine learning and inductive inference. In W. Bibel and Ph. Jorrand, editors, *Fundamentals of Artificial Intelligence*, pages 171–220. Springer Verlag (LNCS 232), 1987.

4. S.L. Epstein and N.S. Sridharan. Knowledge representation for mathematical discovery: Three experiments in graph theory. *J. of Applied Intelligence*, 1(1):7–32, 1991.

5. J. Eusterbrock. Errata to "Selecting the top three elements" by M. Aigner: A Result of a computer assisted proof search. *Discrete Applied Mathematics*, 41:131–137, 1992.

6. J. Eusterbrock. *Wissensbasierte Verfahren zur Synthese mathematischer Beweise: Eine kombinatorische Anwendung*, volume 10 of *DISKI*. INFIX, 1992.

7. J. Eusterbrock. A multi-layer architecture for knowledge-based system synthesis. In *Proc. ISMIS*, pages 582–592. Springer Verlag, 1996.

8. J. Eusterbrock. Canonical term representations of isomorphic transitive dags for efficient knowledge-based reasoning. To appear in Proc. KRUSE'97, 1997.

9. J. Eusterbrock and M. Nicolaides. The visualization of constructive proofs by compositional graph layout: A world-wide web interface. *Proc. CADE Visual Reasoning Workshop, Rutgers University*, 1996.

10. Pierre Flener. *Logic Program Synthesis from Incomplete Information*. Kluwer Academic Publishers, 1995.

11. W. Gasarch, W. Kelly, and W. Pugh. Finding the i-th largest of n for small i,n. *Sigact News*, 27(2):88–96, 1996.

12. P. Gray and et al. KRAFT: Knowledge fusion from distributed databases and knowledge bases. In R. Wagner, editor, *Proc. Int'l Workshop on Databases and Expert Systems*, page to appear, 1997.

13. M. Heissel, T. Santen, and D. Zimmermann. A generic system architecture for strategy-based software development. Technical report, Technische Universität Berlin, 8 1995.

14. Chr. Kreitz. The representation of program synthesis in higher order logic. In H. Marburger, editor, *GWAI-90, 14th German Workshop on Artificial Intelligence*, pages 171–180. Springer Verlag, 1990.

15. M. Lowry and J. Van Baalen. Meta-Amphion: Synthesis of efficient domain-specific program synthesis systems. *Automated Software Engineering*, 4(2):199–242, 1997.

16. M.R. Lowry. *Algorithm Synthesis through Problem Reformulation*. PhD thesis, Stanford University, 1989.

17. McCartney. Synthesizing algorithms with performance constraints. In *Proc. AAAI-87, Sixth Nat. Conf. on Artificial Intelligence*, volume 2, pages 149–154. Am. Ass. for Art. Int., 1987.

18. B. Meltzer. Proof, abstraction and semantics in mathematics and artificial intelligence. In A. Marzollo, editor, *Topics in Artificial Intelligence*, pages 2–9. Springer Verlag, Wien New York, 1979.

19. E.Y. Shapiro. *Algorithmic Program Debugging*. ACM Distinguished Dissertations, The MIT Press, 1982.

20. D.R. Smith. Top-down synthesis of divide-and-conquer algorithms. *Artificial Intelligence*, 27:43–96, 1985.

21. D.R. Smith. Constructing specification morphisms. *Journal Symbolic Computation*, 15:571–606, 1993.

22. P.D. Summers. A methodology for lisp program construction from examples. *Journal of the Association for Computing Machinery*, 24(1):161–175, 1977.

Interval Approaches for Uncertain Reasoning

Y.Y. Yao[1] and S.K.M. Wong[2]

[1] Department of Computer Science, Lakehead University
Thunder Bay, Ontario, Canada P7B 5E1
E-mail: yyao@flash.lakeheadu.ca

[2] Department of Computer Science, University of Regina
Regina, Saskatchewan, Canada S4S 0A2
E-mail: wong@cs.uregina.ca

Abstract. This paper presents a framework for reasoning using *intervals*. Two interpretations of intervals are examined, one treats intervals as bounds of a truth evaluation function, and the other treats end points of intervals as two truth evaluation functions. They lead to two different reasoning approaches, one is based on interval computations, and the other is based on interval structures. A number of interval based reasoning methods are reviewed and compared within the proposed framework.

1 Introduction

Traditionally, inference is performed using a single-valued truth evaluation function. A proposition takes a single element from a set of truth values as its truth value. For example, in classical logic, a proposition is either true or false. In many-valued logic systems such as fuzzy logic, a proposition takes a number between 0 and 1 as its truth value. In probabilistic logic, the truth value of a proposition is also a number between 0 and 1, but is associated with a probabilistic interpretation. These approaches have many practical problems [11]. It may be unrealistic to expect an expert to provide a precise and reliable truth evaluation function. The maintenance of consistency using single-valued functions may be a difficult task. To resolve some of these problems, various proposals have been suggested using intervals as truth values [2,3,10–12,15,17–19]. These studies have resulted in many interval based tools for uncertain reasoning, such as incidence calculus [3,20], interval structures [14], belief and plausibility functions [12], necessity and possibility functions [4], and interval fuzzy reasoning [19].

There are at least two interpretations regarding the physical meanings of interval-valued truth. Intervals may be interpreted as bounds of an unknown single-valued truth evaluation function. Alternatively, the end points of intervals can be interpreted as two truth evaluation functions, each is a single-valued evaluation function. The main objective of this paper is to outline a framework for interval based reasoning and to study some basic issues. With respect to the two interpretations of interval-valued truth, we introduce the corresponding reasoning methods, one is based on interval computations, and the other is based on interval structures.

2   Interval based Reasoning

We consider three basic notions, propositional formulas, truth values, and evaluation functions, in a reasoning system. Given a particular situation, typically we have a finite and non-empty set of primitive propositions Φ, which can be regarded as a set of basic events [5]. The set $L(\Phi)$ of propositional formulas generated by Φ is the closure of Φ under negation ($\neg$) and conjunction ($\wedge$). For convenience, we define two special formulas $\top$ and $\bot$. Other connectives such as the disjunction ($\vee$), implication ($\rightarrow$), and equivalence ($\leftrightarrow$) can be defined in terms of negation and conjunction. Let V denote a set of truth values. A truth evaluation function $v : L(\Phi) \longrightarrow V$ is a mapping from the set of propositional formulas to the set of truth values. It provides interpretations of elements of $L(\Phi)$ in terms of elements of V. For this reason, an evaluation function is also referred to as a *meaning* function. Usually, certain operations are defined on the set of truth values in order to interpret the logical connectives in $L(\Phi)$. An evaluation function must also satisfy a set of axioms. The following examples are special reasoning systems.

Example 1. Two-valued propositional logic. In the classical two-valued propositional logic, the set of truth values is the two-element Boolean algebra $B_2 = \{T, F\}$. An evaluation function v from $L(\Phi)$ to B_2 should satisfy the axioms:

$$
\begin{array}{ll}
\text{(c1)} & v(\bot) = F, \quad v(\top) = T, \\
\text{(c2)} & v(\neg\phi) = \neg v(\phi), \\
\text{(c3)} & v(\phi \wedge \psi) = v(\phi) \wedge v(\psi), \\
\text{(c4)} & v(\phi \vee \psi) = v(\phi) \vee v(\psi).
\end{array}
$$

Note that the same set of symbols is used for both operations on $L(\Phi)$ and B_2. These axioms are not a minimal set.

Example 2. Min-max fuzzy logic. In the min-max fuzzy system $([0,1], 1-(), \min, \max)$ proposed by Zadeh [21], the set of truth values is the unit interval $[0,1]$ with lattice operations min and max. In this system, an evaluation function fv satisfies the axioms:

$$
\begin{array}{ll}
\text{(f1)} & fv(\bot) = 0, \quad fv(\top) = 1, \\
\text{(f2)} & fv(\neg\phi) = 1 - fv(\phi), \\
\text{(f3)} & fv(\phi \wedge \psi) = \min(fv(\phi), fv(\psi)), \\
\text{(f4)} & fv(\phi \vee \psi) = \max(fv(\phi), fv(\psi)).
\end{array}
$$

In general, one may interpret fuzzy logic connectives using triangular norms (t-norms) and conorms (t-conorms) [7].

Example 3. Probabilistic logic. In probabilistic logic, the set of truth values is the unit interval $[0,1]$ with arithmetic operations, such as addition and multiplication. An evaluation function P in this system must satisfy the axioms:

$$
\begin{array}{ll}
\text{(p1)} & P(\bot) = 0, \quad P(\top) = 1,
\end{array}
$$

(p2) $P(\neg\phi) = 1 - P(\phi),$

(p3) $P(\phi \wedge \psi) = P(\phi) + P(\psi) - P(\phi \vee \psi),$

(p4) $P(\phi \vee \psi) = P(\phi) + P(\psi) - P(\phi \wedge \psi).$

Axiom (p3) is equivalent to (p4), and (p2) can be derived from other axioms.

Example 4. Incidence calculus – possible worlds semantics of logic. Let W denote a set of *possible worlds*. The power set 2^W, equipped with set-theoretic operations $\sim$, $\cap$, and $\cup$, is used as the set of truth values [3,17,20]. An evaluation function i associates a proposition in $L(\Phi)$ with a subset of W, and must satisfy the axioms:

(i1) $i(\bot) = \emptyset, \quad i(\top) = W,$

(i2) $i(\neg\phi) = \ \sim i(\phi),$

(i3) $i(\phi \wedge \psi) = i(\phi) \cap i(\psi),$

(i4) $i(\phi \vee \psi) = i(\phi) \cup i(\psi).$

The set $i(\phi)$ may be interpreted as the subset of possible worlds in which ϕ is true. The evaluation function i is referred to as an *incidence mapping* [3].

The above examples cover both numeric and non-numeric evaluation functions. A common feature of these systems is that the set of truth values V is equipped with an order relation. Suppose $\preceq$ is an order relation on V, for two elements $a, b \in V$ such that $a \preceq b$, we define a *closed* interval:

$$[a,b] = \{x \mid a \preceq x \preceq b\}. \tag{1}$$

That is, the interval $[a, b]$ consists of all elements between two end points a and b. Typically, the system $(V, \preceq)$ is a lattice. Let $I(V)$ denote the set of all closed intervals on V. We assume that V has a universal maximum element, denoted by 1, and a universal minimum element, denoted by 0. Clearly, $[0, 1]$ belongs to $I(V)$. With the notion of intervals, one may consider an evaluation from $L(\Phi)$ to $I(V)$. This provides an interval extension of the proposed framework.

The introduction of the interval extension is motivated by practical needs. In many situations, it may be difficult to specify precisely and consistently an evaluation function from $L(\Phi)$ to V satisfying certain axioms. To resolve this problem, one may use a pair of lower and upper bounds which define the range of the actual evaluation function. In this case, intervals are interpreted as bounds of an unknown evaluation function. Formally, we can introduce a pair of evaluations $v_*, v^* : L(\Phi) \longrightarrow V$ such that $v_*(\phi) \preceq v(\phi) \preceq v^*(\phi)$ for all $\phi \in L(\Phi)$, where v denotes the actual evaluation function. In general, the lower and upper evaluations v_* and v^* belong to a class of evaluations that are different from those of the class containing v, denoted by C_v. The evaluations v_* and v^* may be interpreted as *constraints* that characterize the following subset of evaluations in C_v:

$$IC(v_*, v^*) = \{u \in C_v \mid v_*(\phi) \preceq u(\phi) \preceq v^*(\phi) \text{ for all } \phi \in L(\Phi)\}. \tag{2}$$

In the absence of any information for a particular proposition, the trivial interval $[0, 1]$ may be used. One important feature of this interpretation is that we assume the existence of an evaluation function. The notion of intervals represents our ignorance regarding the actual evaluation function.

It may also happen that one cannot determine the exact class of evaluation functions because of a lack of knowledge. That is, we may not assume the existence of a single-valued evaluation function. One may use a pair of evaluation functions that produce interval evaluations. Each of the evaluation functions may satisfy different axioms. For example, the lower evaluation is a belief function, while the upper evaluation is a plausibility function. Although intervals, in this case, can be regarded as constraints representing available information and knowledge, we may not explicitly express such constraints similar to equation (2).

The two interpretations of intervals can be related to different views of the theory of belief functions [12]. A pair of belief and plausibility functions produces an interval representation of uncertainty. There are at least two views for the interpretation of belief and plausibility functions. One view treats them as a pair of bounds that defines a family of probability functions [6], in a way similar to equation (2). Smets [13] referred to this interpretation as type-1 probabilistic reasoning, which is an upper and lower probability model. Our first interpretation of intervals corresponds to this view. In the type-2 model referred to by Smets, no probability function is postulated to exist. Belief and plausibility functions are not considered as being bounds of a probability function, but as degrees of belief. Our second interpretation of intervals conforms to this view.

A key notion in interval based inference is the interval-valued truth. The inference process depends very much on the interpretation of such intervals. In order to deal with operations and interpretations of interval-valued truth, we present two methods in the subsequent sections, namely, interval computations and interval structures.

3 Power Algebras and Interval Computations

This section examines the notion of power algebras [1] and two special power algebras, one for numeric interval-valued truth and the other for non-numeric interval-valued truth.

3.1 Power algebras

Let U be a set and $\circ$ a binary operation on U. One can define a binary operation $\circ^+$ on subsets of U as follows [1,18]:

$$X \circ^+ Y = \{x \circ y \mid x \in X, y \in Y\}, \tag{3}$$

for any $X, Y \subseteq U$. In general, one may lift any operation f on elements of U to an operation f^+ on subsets of U, called the power operation of f. Suppose

$f : U^n \longrightarrow U$ $(n \geq 1)$ is an n-ary operation on U. The power operation $f^+ :$ $(2^U)^n \longrightarrow 2^U$ is defined by [1]:

$$f^+(X_0, \ldots, X_{n-1}) = \{f(x_0, \ldots, x_{n-1}) \mid x_i \in X_i \text{ for } i = 0, \ldots, n-1\}, \quad (4)$$

for any $X_0, \ldots, X_{n-1} \subseteq U$. This provides a universal-algebraic construction approach. For any algebra $(U, f_1, \ldots, f_k)$ with base set U and operations $f_1, \ldots, f_k$, its power algebra is given by $(2^U, f_1^+, \ldots, f_k^+)$.

The power operation f^+ may carry some properties of f. For example, for a binary operation $f : U^2 \longrightarrow U$, if f is commutative and associative, f^+ is commutative and associative, respectively. If e is an identity for some operation f, the set $\{e\}$ is an identity for f^+. If an unary operation $f : U \longrightarrow U$ is an involution, i.e., $f(f(x)) = f(x)$, f^+ is also an involution. On the other hand, many properties of f are not carried over by f^+. For instance, if a binary operation f is idempotent, i.e., $f(x, x) = x$, f^+ may not be idempotent. If a binary operation g is distributive over f, g^+ may not be distributive over f^+.

A special type of power algebra is called interval algebra, in which operations on elements of U are lifted to intervals of U, instead of arbitrary subsets of U. In doing so, the power operation f^+ may carry additional properties of f. The notion of interval algebras forms a basis of uncertain reasoning with intervals. Two such interval algebras are examined in the following subsections.

3.2 Interval number algebra

An *interval number* $[\underline{a}, \overline{a}]$ with $\underline{a} \leq \overline{a}$ is the set of real numbers defined by:

$$[\underline{a}, \overline{a}] = \{x \mid \underline{a} \leq x \leq \overline{a}\}. \quad (5)$$

The set of all interval numbers is denoted by $I(\Re)$. Degenerate intervals of the form $[a, a]$ are equivalent to real numbers.

One can perform arithmetic operations on interval numbers by lifting arithmetic operations on real numbers [8]. Let A and B be two interval numbers, and let $*$ denote an arithmetic operation $+, -, \cdot$ or $/$ on pairs of real numbers. An arithmetic operation $*$ may be extended to pairs of interval numbers A, B:

$$A * B = \{x * y \mid x \in A, y \in B\}. \quad (6)$$

The result $A * B$ is again a closed and bounded interval unless $0 \in B$ and the operation $*$ is division (in which case, $A * B$ is undefined). They can be computed by using formulas: for $A = [\underline{a}, \overline{a}]$ and $B = [\underline{b}, \overline{b}]$,

$$\begin{aligned}
A + B &= [\underline{a} + \underline{b}, \overline{a} + \overline{b}], \\
A - B &= [\underline{a} - \overline{b}, \overline{a} - \underline{b}], \\
A \cdot B &= [\min(\underline{a}\,\underline{b}, \underline{a}\,\overline{b}, \overline{a}\,\underline{b}, \overline{a}\,\overline{b}), \max(\underline{a}\,\underline{b}, \underline{a}\,\overline{b}, \overline{a}\,\underline{b}, \overline{a}\,\overline{b})], \\
A / B &= [\underline{a}, \overline{a}] \cdot [1/\overline{b}, 1/\underline{b}], \quad 0 \notin [\underline{b}, \overline{b}].
\end{aligned} \quad (7)$$

In the special case where both A and B are positive intervals, the multiplication can be simplified to:

$$A \cdot B = [\underline{a}\,\underline{b}, \overline{a}\,\overline{b}], \quad 0 \leq \underline{a} \leq \overline{a}, \ 0 \leq \underline{b} \leq \overline{b}. \tag{8}$$

One may lift any operations on real numbers, such as min and max, to power operations on intervals of real numbers [19]. Interval number algebra may serve as a basis for interval reasoning with numeric truth values, such as interval fuzzy reasoning [19], and interval probabilistic reasoning [11,16].

Example 5. Interval min-max fuzzy reasoning. Using the results from interval number algebra, we obtain the following inference rules for interval fuzzy reasoning [19]:

(if2) $\quad [fv_*(\neg\phi), fv^*(\neg\phi)] = [1 - fv^*(\phi), 1 - fv_*(\phi)],$

(if3) $\quad [fv_*(\phi \wedge \psi), fv^*(\phi \wedge \psi)] = [\min(fv_*(\phi), fv_*(\psi)), \min(fv^*(\phi), fv^*(\psi))],$

(if4) $\quad [fv_*(\phi \vee \psi), fv^*(\phi \vee \psi)] = [\max(fv_*(\phi), fv_*(\psi)), \max(fv^*(\phi), fv^*(\psi))].$

This is an interval extension of the system given in Example 2.

Example 6. Interval probabilistic reasoning. According to the laws of probability and interval number algebra, we have the following rules for interval probabilistic reasoning [16]:

(ip2) $\quad [P_*(\neg\phi), P^*(\neg\phi)] = [1 - P^*(\phi), 1 - P_*(\phi)],$

(ip3) $\quad P_*(\phi \wedge \psi) \geq \max(0, P_*(\phi) + P_*(\psi) - P^*(\phi \vee \psi)),$

$\quad\quad\ \ P^*(\phi \wedge \psi) \leq \min(P^*(\phi), P^*(\psi), P^*(\phi) + P^*(\psi) - P_*(\phi \vee \psi)),$

(ip4) $\quad P_*(\phi \vee \psi) \geq \max(P_*(\phi), P_*(\psi), P_*(\phi) + P_*(\psi) - P^*(\phi \wedge \psi)),$

$\quad\quad\ \ P^*(\phi \vee \psi) \leq \min(1, P^*(\phi) + P^*(\psi) - P_*(\phi \vee \psi)).$

It is an interval extension of the system given in Example 3. Inference rules (ip3) and (ip4) cannot be expressed using equality as that of (if3) and (if4) in interval fuzzy reasoning. This stems from the fact that probabilistic logic is not truth-functional.

3.3 Interval set algebra

Given two sets $A_1, A_2 \in 2^U$ with $A_1 \subseteq A_2$, the subset of 2^U,

$$\mathcal{A} = [A_1, A_2] = \{X \in 2^U \mid A_1 \subseteq X \subseteq A_2\}, \tag{9}$$

is called a closed *interval set* [15]. The set A_1 is called the lower bound of the interval set and A_2 the upper bound. An interval set is a set of subsets bounded by two elements of the Boolean algebra $(2^U, \cap, \cup, \sim)$. Let $I(2^U)$ denote the set of all closed interval sets.

Let $\cap, \cup$ and $-$ be set intersection, union and difference defined on 2^U. We define the following binary operations on interval sets by lifting set-theoretic operations. For two interval sets $A = [A_1, A_2]$ and $B = [B_1, B_2]$, the interval set intersection, union and difference are respectively defined as:

$$A \sqcap B = \{X \cap Y \mid X \in A, Y \in B\},$$
$$A \sqcup B = \{X \cup Y \mid X \in A, Y \in B\},$$
$$A \setminus B = \{X - Y \mid X \in A, Y \in B\}. \tag{10}$$

The above defined operators are closed on $I(2^U)$, namely, $A \sqcap B$, $A \sqcup B$ and $A \setminus B$ are interval sets. In fact, these interval sets can be explicitly computed by:

$$A \sqcap B = [A_1 \cap B_1, A_2 \cap B_2],$$
$$A \sqcup B = [A_1 \cup B_1, A_2 \cup B_2],$$
$$A \setminus B = [A_1 - B_2, A_2 - B_1]. \tag{11}$$

The interval set complement $\neg[A_1, A_2]$ of $[A_1, A_2]$ is defined by $[U, U] \setminus [A_1, A_2]$. This is equivalent to $[U - A_2, U - A_1] = [\sim A_2, \sim A_1]$. Obviously, we have $\neg[\emptyset, \emptyset] = [U, U]$ and $\neg[U, U] = [\emptyset, \emptyset]$. The system $(I(2^U), \sqcap, \sqcup)$ is a completely distributive lattice [9].

The set algebra $(2^U, \cap, \cup, \sim)$ is a special Boolean algebra. By using the same argument, one can lift operations in a Boolean algebra or a lattice [19]. Such interval algebras may be used for reasoning with interval extension of classical logic [17], and interval incidence calculus [20].

Example 7. A three-valued propositional logic. For the two-element Boolean algebra $B_2 = \overline{\{T, F\}}$, the set of all intervals is $I(B_2) = \{[F, F], [F, T], [T, T]\}$. It may be regarded as the truth values of a three-valued logic [19]. In this case, interval truth evaluation function v_*, v^* from $L(\Phi)$ to $I(B_2)$ should satisfy the axioms:

(ic2) $[v_*(\neg\phi), v^*(\neg\phi)] = [\neg v^*(\phi), \neg v_*(\phi)],$

(ic3) $[v_*(\phi \wedge \psi), v^*(\phi \wedge \psi)] = [v_*(\phi) \wedge v_*(\psi), v^*(\phi) \wedge v^*(\psi)],$

(ic3) $[v_*(\phi \vee \psi), v^*(\phi \vee \psi)] = [v_*(\phi) \vee v_*(\psi), v^*(\phi) \vee v^*(\psi)].$

We therefore obtain a three-valued logic from the two-valued logic given in Example 1.

Example 8. Interval incidence calculus. The incidence calculus given in Example 4 can be extended to an interval version. In this case, the following axioms are used [17]:

(ii2) $[i_*(\neg\phi), i^*(\neg\phi)] = [\sim i^*(\phi), \sim i_*(\phi)],$

(ii3) $[i_*(\phi \wedge \psi), i^*(\phi \wedge \psi)] = [i_*(\phi) \cap i_*(\psi), i^*(\phi) \cap i^*(\psi)],$

(ii4) $[i_*(\phi \vee \psi), i^*(\phi \vee \psi)] = [i_*(\phi) \cup i_*(\psi), i^*(\phi) \cup i^*(\psi)].$

Interval incidence calculus may be interpreted in term of the three-valued logic in Example 7. The set $i_*(\phi)$ may be interpreted as the subset of possible worlds in which the truth value of ϕ is $[T, T]$, while $i^*(\phi)$ is the subset of possible worlds in which the truth value of ϕ is $[T, T]$ or $[F, T]$.

4 Interval Structures

The notion of interval structure was introduced by Wong, Wang and Yao [14] as a non-numeric representation of uncertainty. It may be considered as another interval extension of incidence calculus [3]. Let W denote a set called possible worlds. An interval structure is a pair of mappings $\underline{i}, \overline{i} : L(\Phi) \longrightarrow 2^W$ satisfying the following axioms: for $\phi, \psi \in L(\Phi)$,

(lp) $\underline{i}(\phi) = \sim\overline{i}(\neg\phi), \qquad \overline{i}(\phi) = \sim\underline{i}(\neg\phi),$

(l1) $\underline{i}(\bot) = \emptyset,$

(l2) $\underline{i}(\top) = W,$

(l3) $\underline{i}(\phi \wedge \psi) = \underline{i}(\phi) \cap \underline{i}(\psi),$

(u1) $\overline{i}(\bot) = \emptyset,$

(u2) $\overline{i}(\top) = W,$

(u3) $\overline{i}(\phi \vee \psi) = \overline{i}(\phi) \cup \overline{i}(\psi).$

The set $\underline{i}(\phi)$ may be interpreted as the subset of possible worlds in which ϕ is known or can be proved to be true, and $\sim \overline{i}(\phi)$ the subset of possible worlds in which ϕ is known or can be proved to be false. Interval structures may be regarded as an interval extension of incidence mappings. When $\underline{i} = \overline{i}$, the interval structure reduces to an incidence mapping.

For an interval structure $(\underline{i}, \overline{i})$, we have the property:

$$\underline{i}(\phi) \subseteq \overline{i}(\phi), \tag{12}$$

for any $\phi \in L(\Phi)$. They may be considered as the end points of the interval set:

$$[\underline{i}(\phi), \overline{i}(\phi)] = \{X \mid \underline{i}(\phi) \subseteq X \subseteq \overline{i}(\phi)\}. \tag{13}$$

The interval set corresponding to $(\underline{i}(\neg\phi), \overline{i}(\neg\phi))$ is:

$$[\sim\overline{i}(\phi), \sim\underline{i}(\phi)] = \neg[\underline{i}(\phi), \overline{i}(\phi)]. \tag{14}$$

Interval sets corresponding to $(\underline{i}(\phi \wedge \psi), \overline{i}(\phi \wedge \psi))$ and $(\underline{i}(\phi \vee \psi), \overline{i}(\phi \vee \psi))$ are:

$$[\underline{i}(\phi \wedge \psi), \overline{i}(\phi \wedge \psi)] = [\underline{i}(\phi) \cap \underline{i}(\psi), \overline{i}(\phi \wedge \psi)],$$
$$[\underline{i}(\phi \vee \psi), \overline{i}(\phi \vee \psi)] = [\underline{i}(\phi \vee \psi), \overline{i}(\phi) \cup \overline{i}(\psi)]. \tag{15}$$

In general, they cannot be obtained from the interval set operations. Therefore, interval set algebra and interval structures offer two different approaches for interval reasoning.

Consider a special class of interval structures satisfying the axioms [20]:

(l4) $\underline{i}(\phi) \subseteq \underline{i}(\psi)$ or $\underline{i}(\psi) \subseteq \underline{i}(\phi),$

(u4) $\overline{i}(\phi) \subseteq \overline{i}(\psi)$ or $\overline{i}(\psi) \subseteq \overline{i}(\phi),$

for any $\phi, \psi \in L(\Phi)$. We call such a class *consonant* interval structures. Axioms (I4) and (u4) can be equivalently expressed as:

(I5) $\underline{i}(\phi \wedge \psi) = \underline{i}(\phi)$ or $\underline{i}(\phi \wedge \psi) = \underline{i}(\psi)$,

(u5) $\overline{i}(\phi \vee \psi) = \overline{i}(\phi)$ or $\overline{i}(\phi \vee \psi) = \overline{i}(\psi)$.

In general, an interval structure does not have such properties.

The concept of incidence mappings is related to probabilistic reasoning. Let P_W denote a probability function defined on 2^W, and i an incidence mapping from $L(\Phi)$ to 2^W. The truth evaluation function defined by:

$$P(\phi) = P_W(i(\phi)), \tag{16}$$

is a probability function defined on $L(\Phi)$. For an interval structure $(\underline{i}, \overline{i})$, a pair of truth evaluation functions defined by:

$$\underline{P}(\phi) = P_W(\underline{i}(\phi)),$$
$$\overline{P}(\phi) = P_W(\overline{i}(\phi)), \tag{17}$$

is a pair of belief and plausibility functions [14]. Furthermore, if $(\underline{i}, \overline{i})$ is a consonant interval structure, $\underline{P}$ and $\overline{P}$ are a pair of necessity and possibility functions [20].

Reasoning with interval-valued truth obtained from interval structures should follow the axioms of interval structures. It provides an approach different from and complementary to inference based on interval computations.

5 Conclusion

Interval based reasoning is a practical solution to problems in inference with incomplete, insufficient, or inconsistent information. Instead of using a single-valued truth evaluation functions, one assigns each proposition with an interval-valued truth. At least two views can be adopted for the interpretation of such intervals. Intervals may be interpreted as bounds of an unknown single-valued truth evaluation function. Alternatively, the end points of intervals can be interpreted as defining two truth evaluation functions, each is a single-valued evaluation function. With respect to such interpretations, we have presented a framework of interval reasoning. Two classes of interval reasoning approaches are introduced based on interval computations and interval structures. They are different from and complementary to each other.

References

1. C. Brink, Power structures, *Algebra Universalis*, **30**, 177-216, 1993.
2. P.P. Bonissone, Summarizing and propagating uncertain information with triangular norms, *International Journal of Approximate Reasoning*, **1**, 71-101, 1987.

3. A. Bundy, Incidence calculus: a mechanism for probabilistic reasoning, *Journal of Automated Reasoning*, **1**, 263-283, 1985.

4. D. Dubois, and P. Prade, *Possibility Theory: an Approach to Computerized Processing of Uncertainty*, Plenum Press, New York, 1988.

5. R. Fagin, and J.Y. Halpern, Uncertainty, belief, and probability, *Computational Intelligence*, **7**, 160-173, 1991.

6. J.Y. Halpern, and R. Fagin, Two views of belief: belief as generalized probability and belief as evidence, Artificial Intelligence, **54**: 275-317, 1992.

7. G.J. Klir, and B. Yuan, *Fuzzy Sets and Fuzzy Logic: Theory and Applications*, Prentice Hall, New Jersey, 1995.

8. R.E. Moore, *Interval Analysis*, Englewood Cliffs, New Jersey, Prentice-Hall, 1966.

9. C.V. Negoiţă, and D.A. Ralescu, *Applications of Fuzzy Sets to Systems Analysis*, Basel, Birkhäuser Verlag, 1975.

10. Z. Pawlak, Rough sets, *International Journal of Computer and Information Sciences*, **11**, 341-356, 1982.

11. J.R. Quinlan, Inferno: a cautious approach to uncertain inference, *The Computer Journal*, **26**, 255-269, 1983.

12. G. Shafer, *A Mathematical Theory of Evidence*, Princeton University Press, Princeton, 1976.

13. P. Smets, Resolving misunderstandings about belief functions, *International Journal of Approximate Reasoning*, **6**, 321-344.

14. S.K.M. Wong, L.S. Wang, and Y.Y. Yao, On modeling uncertainty with interval structures, *Computational Intelligence*, **11**, 406-426, 1995.

15. Y.Y. Yao, Interval-set algebra for qualitative knowledge representation, *Proceedings of the Fifth International Conference on Computing and Information*, 370-374, 1993.

16. Y.Y. Yao, A comparison of two interval-valued probabilistic reasoning methods, *Proceedings of the 6th International Conference on Computing and Information*, May 26-28, 1994, Peterborough, Ontario, Canada. Special issue of *Journal of Computing and Information*, **1**, 1090-1105 (paper number D6), 1995.

17. Y.Y. Yao, and X. Li, Comparison of rough-set and interval-set models for uncertain reasoning, *Fundamenta Informaticae*, **27**, 289-298, 1996.

18. Y.Y. Yao, and N. Noroozi, A unified framework for set-based computations, *Proceedings of the 3rd International Workshop on Rough Sets and Soft Computing*, Lin, T.Y. (Ed.), San Jose State University, 236-243, 1994.

19. Y.Y. Yao, and J. Wang, Interval based uncertain reasoning using fuzzy and rough sets, *Advances in Machine Intelligence & Soft-Computing*, Volume IV, Wang, P.P. (Ed.), Department of Electrical Engineering, Duke University, Durham, North Carolina, USA, 196-215, 1997

20. Y.Y. Yao, S.K.M. Wong, and L.S. Wang, A non-numeric approach to uncertain reasoning, *International Journal of General Systems*, **23**, 343-359, 1995.

21. L.A. Zadeh, Fuzzy sets, *Information & Control*, **8**, 338-353, 1965.

Qualitative Versus Quantitative Interpretation of the Mathematical Theory of Evidence

M.A. Kłopotek, S.T.Wierzchoń

Institute of Computer Science
Polish Academy of Sciences
Warszawa, Poland
e-mail: klopotek,stw@ipipan.waw.pl

Abstract. The paper presents a novel view of the Dempster-Shafer belief function as a measure of diversity in relational data bases. The Dempster rule of evidence combination corresponds to the join operator of the relational database theory. This rough-set based interpretation is qualitative in nature and can represent a number of belief function operators.
Keywords: Soft Computing, Knowledge Representation and Integration, Dempster-Shafer theory, rough set theory, relational databases, qualitative interpretation of Dempster rule.

1 Introduction

The Dempster-Shafer Theory or the Mathematical Theory of Evidence (MTE) [11, 3] shows one of possible ways of application of mathematical probability for subjective evaluation and is intended to be a generalization of bayesian theory of subjective probability [14, 20]. In spite of its numerous interesting formal properties, many attempts to provide a case-based interpretation of MTE failed [17]. Though a tendency to consider belief functions as subjective uncertainty measures is visible [14], the need for case-based interpretation as a pre-condition for practical applicability has been explicitly stressed [18]. Still this interpretation should be qualitative rather than quantitative in nature [17]. However, these requirements seem not to be met so far.

In our search for non-quantitative interpretation of MTE, our attention was attracted by the nature of the join operator of relational databases [1] or in general the multivalued dependency [2] the study of which led to invention of local computation method for uncertainty propagation of Shenoy and Shafer [15] for MTE. This in turn made the rough-set theoretic interpretation of MTE belief functions of Skowron and Busse [16] best choice for further investigation, as it was purely-case based and relational, though it is frequency based. The rough-set interpretation sheds some light onto what the concept of "evidence" may mean in experimental terms. The "evidence" there is the information part of a database record and it "supports" the decision part of a record. The complexity of combination of evidence according to the Dempster rule in [16] gave an impulse for search of a simpler way to accomplish it. It turns out that with frequency approach updating of decision parts of cases is needed (Dempster's combination is destructive). Out of this experience we decided to abandon the frequencies and concentrated on purely relational operations.

The paper is organized as follows: Section 2 briefly introduces basic MTE concepts. Section 3 recalls traditional rough set theoretic frequency interpretation of MTE from [16] and explains our insights of destructive nature of Dempster's combination with respect to frequencies. Section 4 presents our new qualitative interpretation. The paper ends with some concluding remarks.

Throughout the paper, as relational data tables are subject of rough set theory, SQL [19] query language is used to express semantics of MTE measures and operators in terms of decision tables, both with respect to traditional and our rough sets based interpretation of MTE, as SQL has the capability of expressing purely relational and frequentistic data processing.

2 Basics of the Dempster-Shafer Theory

We understand MTE measures in a very traditional way (see [8]). Let Ξ be a finite set of elements called elementary events. Any subset of Ξ be a composite event. Ξ be called also the frame of discernment. A basic probability (or belief) assignment (bpa) function is any function $m{:}2^{\Xi} \to [0,1]$ such that

$$\sum_{A \in 2^{\Xi}} m(A) = 1 \qquad m(\emptyset) = 0, \qquad \forall_{A \in 2^{\Xi}} \;\; 0 \leq m(A)$$

We say that a bpa is vacuous iff $m(\Xi) = 1$ and $m(A) = 0$ for every $A \neq \Xi$. A belief function is defined as $\mathrm{Bel}{:}2^{\Xi} \to [0,1]$ so that $Bel(A) = \sum_{B \subseteq A} m(B)$. A plausibility function is $\mathrm{Pl}{:}2^{\Xi} \to [0,1]$ with $\forall_{A \in 2^{\Xi}} Pl(A) = 1 - Bel(\Xi - A)$. A commonality function is $\mathrm{Q}{:}2^{\Xi} - \{\emptyset\} \to [0,1]$ with $\forall_{A \in 2^{\Xi} - \{\emptyset\}} \;\; Q(A) = \sum_{A \subseteq B} m(B)$.

The Rule-of-Combination of two Independent Belief Functions Bel_{E_1}, Bel_{E_2} Over-the-Same-Frame-of-Discernment (the so-called Dempster-Rule), denoted $Bel_{E_1,E_2} = Bel_{E_1} \oplus Bel_{E_2}$ is defined interms of bpa's as follows: $m_{E_1,E_2}(A) = c \cdot \sum_{B,C;A=B \cap C} m_{E_1}(B) \cdot m_{E_2}(C)$ (c - constant normalizing the sum of m to 1).

Under multivariate settings Ξ is a set of vectors in n-dimensional space spanned by the set of variables $\mathbf{X} = \{X_1, X_2, \ldots X_n\}$. If $A \subseteq \Xi$, then by projection of the set A onto a subspace spanned by the set of variables $\mathbf{Y} \subseteq \mathbf{X}$ ($A^{\downarrow \mathbf{Y}}$ we understand the set B of vectors from A projected onto $\mathbf{Y}$. Then marginalization operator of MTE is defined as follows: $m^{\downarrow \mathbf{Y}}(B) = \sum_{A;B=A^{\downarrow}\mathbf{X}} m(A)$.

Definition 1. (See [13]) Let B be a subset of Ξ, called evidence, m_B be a basic probability assignment such that $m_B(B) = 1$ and $m_B(A) = 0$ for any A different from B. Then the conditional belief function $Bel(.\|B)$ representing the belief function Bel conditioned on evidence B is defined as: $Bel(.\|B) = Bel \oplus Bel_B$.

3 Rough Set Theory. The Traditional Interpretation of Belief Functions

Skowron and Grzymala-Busse[16] and others studying rough sets developed more specifically the proposal of Shafer with respect to frequency interpretation of MTE. Let us assume that a decision table TAB of decisions D (atomic values) under conditions (information) $\mathbf{I}$ (atomic value vectors) is collected. However, $\mathbf{I}$ may not contain the complete information to make decision D. This gives rise in a natural way to the Γ mapping assigning different values of D to the same value of I. Under these circumstances the belief in a set A (subset of the domain of D) Bel(A) may be derived from a case database as follows: (in the notation of the SQL query language [19])

create view Total (Counted) as select count(*) from TAB;
*select count(*)/Counted from TAB, Total where not (**I** in (select **I** from TAB*
where not (D in A)));

Skowron and Grzymała-Busse[16] elaborated also a notion of conditioning under rough set interpretation [16, p.219 ff.] as respective measures for subtables (that is tables consisting of cases selected by a criterion). Let us condition on D belonging to the set B:

*create view SubtableTAB(D,**I**) as select X,**I** from TAB where not (**I** in (select **I** from TAB where not (D in B)));*

The belief distribution for the subtable can be calculated form the view SubtableTAB in the same way as for the TAB database. However, it is a matter of a calculation exercise to show that their notion of conditionality does not agree with that of Shafer.

Therefore, to achieve consistency with Shafer's conditioning from Def.1 we propose the following interpretation: (derivable from our approach described in the paper [5]) Let $v \in B$.

*update TAB set D=v where not (D in B) and **I** in (select **I** from TAB where D in B);*
delete TAB where not (D in B);

Let c_1,c_2 be two cases from the database TAB such that $\mathbf{I}(c_1) = \mathbf{I}(c_2)$ but $D(c_1) \neq D(c_2)$ Let be $D(c_1) \in B$ and $D(c_2) \notin B$ Then after the above update and delete operations both cases c_1, c_2 are retained in the database TAB. c_1 has retained its value $D(c_1)$. But the case c_2 was subject to a metamorphose: its $D(c_2)$ has been changed (to v). This means that the Dempster rule of combination is "destructive". Preservation of frequency interpretation under conditioning enforces ignoring the intrinsic (observed) value of an attribute and replacement of it with some other value.

A still more complex task is the interpretation of combination of two independent pieces of evidence. Skowron and Grzymała-Busse[16] elaborated a procedure consisting in transforming the combined decision tables into a kind of summary with multivalued decision columns (since non-relational) and then applying complex rational arithmetics to get finally a decision table (derived by so-called Ψ-independent combination) implementing Dempster combination of independent belief functions (consult [16] for details).

4 New Interpretation

Below we present a slight modification of the rough set interpretation of belief functions that surprisingly turns out to be both simple, elegant and straight forward and at the same time fulfills the requirement that was not matched by any known interpretations: it is qualitative and not quantitative in nature and still case-based. Furthermore we demonstrate that our new interpretation corresponds strictly to the notion of multivalued dependency, that is combination of belief functions parallels the relational join operator from database theory.

Let us define the plausibility $Pl_{TAB}(SET)$ derived from a decision table TAB with decision variable D and the set $\mathbf{I}$ of information variables as:

*create view tmpTAB(No) as select count(distinct **I**) from TAB;*
*create view plTAB as select count(distinct **I**)/No from TAB,tmpTAB where TAB.D in SET;*

Theorem 2. *The function $Pl_{TAB}(SET)$ derived from a decision table TAB with decision variable D and the set $\mathbf{I}$ of information variables is plausibility function $Pl(SET)$ in the sense of Dempster-Shafer theory.*

Proof. In MTE, the plausibility of a set SET is just the sum of basic probability assignments $m(A)$ such that $SET \cap A \neq \emptyset$. Let r be a record, $I(r)$ its information part and $D(r)$ its decision part. For the set SET, let us consider a subset R of all records from the decision table TAB such that: if $r \in R$ then $D(r) \in SET$ and for every $d \in SET$ there exists $r' \in R$ such that $D(r) = D(r')$ and there exists no record $r'' \notin R$ such that $I(r'') = I(r)$. Obviously, for two distinct sets SET' and SET'' their respective sets R' and R'' will share no records. Furthermore, $\bigcup_{SET \subseteq domain(D)} R(SET)$ will be the (relationally) identical with TAB. Hence we can consider the ratio number of records with distinct information part in $R(SET)$ divided by the number of records with distinct information parts in DT as the bpa function $m(SET)$ in the sense of MTE. But the function $Pl_{TAB}(SET)$ counts (the relative share of) the records with distinct information part such that the decision part belongs to SET. Hence in practice it is just the sum of basic probability assignments $m(A)$ such that $SET \cap A \neq \emptyset$. Therefore it is a plausibility function.

Let us first look at the following relational table DT1 (tab. 1). The column D is the decision column, A1, A2, A3 and A4 are information part of the table. The domain of the decision variable D is $\{a, b, c\}$.

Table 1. Dataset DT1 (to the left) and dataset DT2 (center), and dataset DT1 conditioned on D=$\{b,c\}$ (to the right)

Decision table DT1

Record	A1	A2	A3	A4	D
1	a	a	a	a	a
2	b	a	b	a	a
3	b	a	b	a	b
4	b	b	b	b	b
5	c	a	a	a	a
6	c	a	a	a	a
7	c	b	b	b	b
8	c	b	b	b	c
9	a	b	c	c	a
10	a	b	c	c	b
11	a	b	c	c	c
12	a	a	b	b	b
13	a	a	a	b	a
14	b	b	b	a	b
15	a	a	b	b	a
16	a	a	b	b	b
17	a	a	b	a	a
18	c	a	c	a	c

Decision table DT2

Record	B1	B2	B3	D
1	a	a	a	a
2	a	b	c	a
3	a	b	c	b
4	b	b	b	b
5	a	b	a	b
6	c	c	c	c
7	c	a	c	a
8	c	b	c	b
9	a	b	c	c
10	c	a	c	c
11	c	b	c	c
12	b	b	a	a
13	b	b	a	b
14	c	a	b	c
15	c	b	a	c
16	c	b	b	c
17	c	a	a	c
18	c	b	b	b

Decision table DT1 conditioned on D=$\{b,c\}$

Record	A1	A2	A3	A4	D
3	b	a	b	a	b
4	b	b	b	b	b
7	c	b	b	b	b
8	c	b	b	b	c
10	a	b	c	c	b
11	a	b	c	c	c
12	a	a	b	b	b
14	b	b	b	a	b
16	a	a	b	b	b
18	c	a	c	a	c

Let us calculate now plausibility $Pl_{DT1}(\{a, b\})$ from this table. There are 18 cases in the dataset. But there are only 11 cases with distinct information part I=A1+A2+A3+A4. And there are only 10 cases with decision either a or b with distinct information part I=A1+A2+A3+A4. So the plausibility is equal to 10/11. Notice that under Skowron/Busse interpretation we get $Pl = 17/18$ which is obviously a different value. The difference stems from the fundamental difference between frequency (Skowron/Busse) and relational(ours) view of the world.

Table 2. Dataset DT12' - the subset of DT12 with strongest relationship between I1 and I2

Record	A1	A2	A3	A4	B1	B2	B3	D
1	a	a	a	a	a	a	a	a
2	b	a	b	a	a	a	a	a
11	c	a	a	a	a	b	c	a
12	c	a	a	a	a	b	c	a
45	a	b	c	c	c	a	c	a
46	a	a	a	b	c	a	c	a
71	a	a	b	b	b	b	a	a
72	a	a	b	a	b	b	a	a
17	b	a	b	a	a	b	c	b
25	b	b	b	b	b	b	b	b
33	c	b	b	b	a	b	a	b

Record	A1	A2	A3	A4	B1	B2	B3	D
52	a	b	c	c	c	b	c	b
77	a	a	b	b	b	b	a	b
97	b	b	b	a	c	b	b	b
98	a	a	b	b	c	b	b	b
56	c	b	b	b	a	b	c	c
90	a	b	c	c	c	a	a	c
82	c	a	c	a	c	a	b	c
59	c	b	b	b	c	a	c	c
85	c	a	c	a	c	b	a	c
87	a	b	c	c	c	b	b	c
64	c	a	c	a	c	b	c	c
38	c	b	b	b	c	c	c	c

Notice that from the calculational rules for Dempster-Shafer theory we can derive also relational views calculating other measures: Belief $Bel_{TAB}(SET)$,

*create view belTAB as select 1-count(distinct **I**)/No from TAB,tmpTAB where not (TAB.D in SET);*

Commonality $Q_{TAB}(SET)$,

*create view tmp1TAB(CN) as select count(distinct D) from TAB where TAB.D in SET group by **I** ;*
create view qTAB as select count(*)/No from tmpTAB,tmp1TAB where CN=card(set); (card() is a function counting the elements of the set passed as its argument)

Basic belief assignment $m_{TAB}(SET)$,

*create view tmp11TAB(**I**,D) as select TAB.**I**, TAB.D+XX.D from TAB, TAB XX where TAB.D in SET and XX.**I**=TAB.**I**;*
*create view tmp12TAB(**I**,CN) as select **I**,count(distinct D) from tmp11TAB group by **I**;*
create view m as count(*)/No from tmpTAB, tmp12TAB where CN=card(SET)*card(SET);

Theorem 3. *The functions $Bel_{TAB}(SET)$, $Q_{TAB}(SET)$, $m_{TAB}(SET)$ derived from a decision table TAB with decision variable D and the set **I** of information variables are belief, commonality, basic probability/belief assignment functions resp. $Bel(SET), Q(SET), m(SET)$ in the sense of Dempster-Shafer theory.*

4.1 Conditioning as Selection of a Subtable

Let us define now the conditional belief function $Bel_{TAB}(.||B)$ representing the belief function Bel conditioned on evidence B as the belief function $Bel_{TAB\_B}(.)$ define over the view table

*create view TAB_B(**I**,D) as select **I**,D from TAB where TAB.D in B;*

In our example, $Bel_{DT1}(.||\{b,c\})$ is just Bel calculated from the table 1. Our conditional belief function matches perfectly the Shafer's definition of $Bel(.||B)$ cited above (Def.1).Notice that under Skowron/Busse interpretation, the matching of Shafer's conditionality definition had to be paid for with creating a physical copy and updating it, whereas our notion works perfectly without any updates - only selection is used just as in probabilistic conditioning.

4.2 Combination as Relational Join

Now let us discuss the most impressive property of the new interpretation. Let us consider the decision table DT2 (table 1).

Let us calculate the table DT12 as a join of DT1 and DT2 (over the common column D) so that the new decision table has as its decision column D and as its information part A1,A2,A3,A4,B1,B2,B3.

create table DT12 (A1,A2,A3,A4,B1,B2,B3,D);
insert into table DT12 from
select A1,A2,A3,A4,B1,B2,B3,DT1.D from DT1,DT2 where DT1.D=DT2.D;

Notice that in DT1, there were 11 cases with distinct information part, in DT2 - 12, and in DT12 there are only 75. You can easily check that $Bel_{DT12} = Bel_{DT1} \oplus Bel_{DT2}$. For example: $Q_{DT1}(\{a,b\}) = 3/11$, $Q_{DT2}(\{a,b\}) = 2/12$ and $Q_{DT12}(\{a,b\}) = 6/75$.

Theorem 4. *If the decision table DT1(I1,D) and DT2(I2,D) with non-overlapping information parts I1,I2 are combined by relational join operation*

select I1,I2,DT1.D from DT1,DT2 where DT1.D=DT2.D;

to form the decision table DT12(I,D) where I=I1∪I2, then $Bel_{DT12} = Bel_{DT1} \oplus Bel_{DT2}$.

Proof. This can be demonstrated by considering the "fate" of records counted on calculation of m_i. If R_1 is the set of records counted when calculating $m_1(A)$ in DT1, and if R_2 is the set of records counted when calculating $m_2(B)$ in DT2, then upon join only records $r = (I(r_1), I(r_2), D(r_1))$ with $r_1 \in R_1$, $r_2 \in R_2$, $D(r_1) = D(r_2) \in A \cap B$ will be created, hence they will be counted in support of $m(A \cap B)$. Furthermore, their number will be exactly equal to the product of the number of distinct records in R_1 times the number of distinct records in R_2, so that the Dempster formula will be matched perfectly upon normalization.

4.3 Relational Marginalization and Decombination

Notice that DT1 and DT2 in our example are both in first normal form and the domain of the attribute D is identical in both tables. Therefore we know from elementary properties of relational data tables that marginalization of DT12 over A1,A2,A3,A4,D

select distinct A1,A2,A3,A4,D from DT12;

is exactly identical with DT1. In general:

Theorem 5. *If the information part I of the decision table DT(I,D) can be split into two such parts I1,I2 that $I1 \cup I2 = I$ and $I1 \cap I2 = \emptyset$ and the relation DT is identical with* *select I1,I2,DT1.D from DT1,DT2 where DT1.D=DT2.D;*

where DT1 and DT2 are

create view DT1 as select distinct I1,D from DT;
create view DT2 as select distinct I2,D from DT;

that is there is a multivariate dependency between I1 and I2 given D, then
$Bel_{DT} = Bel_{DT\downarrow I1,D} \oplus Bel_{DT\downarrow I2,D}$.

Proof. Follows directly from theorem 4.

Let consider the unnormalized MTE measures of decision tables m'_{TAB}, Bel'_{TAB}, Pl''_{TAB}, Q'_{TAB}, such that $f'_{TAB} = f_{TAB} \cdot card(TAB^{\downarrow I})$ (card - number of distinct rows, f - m or Bel or Pl or Q) and the unnormalized combination operator $\oplus'$ such that $Bel'_{E_1,E_2} = Bel'_{E_1} \oplus' Bel'_{E_2}$ is defined as follows: $m'_{E_1,E_2}(A) = \sum_{B,C;A=B\cap C} m'_{E_1}(B) \cdot m'_{E_2}(C)$.

What may be more surprising, a kind of a reverse theorem holds:

Theorem 6. *The information part I of the decision table DT(I,D) can be split into two such parts I1,I2 that $I1 \cup I2 = I$ and $I1 \cap I2 = \emptyset$ and $Bel'_{DT} = Bel'_{DT\downarrow I1,D} \oplus' Bel'_{DT\downarrow I2,D}$ if and only if the relation DT is identical with*

select I1,I2,DT1.D from DT1,DT2 where DT1.D=DT2.D;

where DT1 and DT2 are

create view DT1 as select distinct I1,D from DT;
create view DT2 as select distinct I2,D from DT;

that is there is a multivariate dependency between I1 and I2 given D,

Proof. (An outline.) The if-part parallels exactly theorem 5. We need only pay attention to the fact that we never normalize.
The only-if-part follows from numerical calculations for Q-values of all the tables considered. If a record is counted in DT when calculating $Q'_{DT}(SET)$, then it is also counted when calculating both $Q'_{DT1}(SET)$ and $Q'_{DT2}(SET)$. If we form a join $DT1 \cdot DT2$ then $Q'_{DT1 \cdot DT2}(SET) = Q'_{DT1}(SET) \cdot Q'_{DT2}(SET)$. And this is the maximum value Q' can take in DT12. If there is ANY deviation from multivariate dependency concerning records with decision part in SET, then value of $Q'_{DT22}(SET)$ is smaller than $Q'_{DT1}(SET) \cdot Q'_{DT2}(SET)$. This proves our claim.

Remark. We can conclude that Dempster's rule of combination is equivalent with relational join and the Dempster-Shafer independence of evidence means multivalued dependence of evidence. We can also simulate other rules of combination of evidence. In the above, we assumed that given the decision, we cannot conclude from the information part I1 the value of the information part I2 in DT. This meant qualitative independence. Now let us assume the contrary in another decision table DT': given the decision d, we can totally predict I2 from I1 for all records with D(r)=d in DT' or we can totally predict I1 from I2 for all records with D(r)=d in DT'. It is immediately clear that in this case for any set of decisions the unnormalized plausibility is calculated as $Pl'_{DT'}(A) = max(Pl'_{DT'\downarrow I1,D}(A), Pl'_{DT'\downarrow I2,D}(A))$. We can conclude for normalized plausibility that we deal here with the know rule of combination of dependent evidence: $Pl'_{DT'}(A) = max(\alpha \cdot Pl'_{DT'\downarrow I1,D}(A), (1-\alpha) \cdot Pl'_{DT'\downarrow I2,D}(A))$ where α ranges from 0 to 1 (depending on proportions between the numbers of distinct information parts I1 and I2). An example of DT' resulting from maximally dependent combination of DT1 and DT2 is visible in table 2.

4.4 Multivariate Beliefs and Multidecision Tables

We can extend our consideration to tables with multiple decision variables. In a straight forward way we can extend our definition of MTE measures to such tables and consider multivariate belief distributions (in all the decision variables). It is trivial to see that dropping a decision variables does not diminish the diversity of the information part. Hence dropping a decision variable Di from the set of decision variables **D** has the same effect as dropping a variable in the belief function. That is for any set B of decision vectors in variables **D**-{Di}: $m_{T_{AB \downarrow} \mathbf{D}_{-\{Di\}}}(B) = m_{TAB}^{\downarrow \mathbf{D} - \{Di\}}(B) = c \cdot \sum_{A;B=A \downarrow \mathbf{D}_{-\{Di\}}} m(A)_{TAB}$ (c - normalizing factor)

The operator of projection $\downarrow$ should be understood as the MTE projection operator applied to a belief function.

Let DTM be a decision table with decision variables D1 and D2. Let the information part consist of two disjoint parts I1 and I2. Let us consider the following views:

create view DTM1 (I1,D1) as select distinct I1,D1 from DTM;
create view DTM2 (I2,D2) as select distinct I2,D2 from DTM;
create view DTM12 as select distinct I1,I2,D1,D2 from DTM1,DTM2;

If now the table DTM12 is relationally identical with DTM, then we shall say that the decision variables D1 and D2 are independent in the decision table DTM. It is not surprising that: $Bel_{DTM} = Bel_{DTM}^{\downarrow D1} \oplus Bel_{DTM}^{\downarrow D2}$. This means that independence of decision variables in a decision table implies independence of variables in the corresponding belief function.

Let DTX be a decision table with decision variables D1, D2 and D3. Let the information part consist of two disjoint parts I1 and I2. Let us consider the following views:

create view DTX1 (I1,D1,D3) as select distinct I1,D1,D3 from DTX;
create view DTX2 (I2,D2,D3) as select distinct I2,D2,D3 from DTX;
create view DTX12 as select distinct I1,I2,D1,D2,D3 from DTX1,DTX2 where DTX1.D3=DTX2.D3;

If now the table DTX12 is relationally identical with DTX, then we shall say that the decision variables D1 and D2 are independent given D3 in the decision table DTX. It is not surprising that: $Bel_{DTX} = Bel_{DTX}^{\downarrow D1,D3} \oplus Bel_{DTX}^{\downarrow D2,D3}$. But this means that the variables D1 and D2 are independent given D3 in the belief function Bel_{DTX} in the sense of Shenoy's VBS.

These results mean that analysis of independence and conditional independence of variables in a belief function corresponding to a decision table may serve as an indicator of presence or absence of independence or multivalued dependence in the decision table.

5 Concluding Remarks

A novel case-based interpretation of MTE belief functions which is qualitative in nature and has the potential to represent a number of MTE operations has been presented. The interpretation is based on rough sets (in connection with decision tables), but differs from previous interpretations of this type e.g. [16] in that it counts the diversity rather than frequencies in the decision table. Given a definition of the MTE measure of objects in the interpretation domain (decision table) we can perform operations in the interpretation domain (e.g.

combining decision tables) and the measure of the resulting object is derivable from measures of component objects via MTE operator (e.g. combination). We demonstrated this property for Dempster rule of combination, marginalization, Shafer's conditioning, independent variables, Shenoy's notion of conditional independence of variables. Other known case-based (frequency or probabilistic) interpretations fall short of this property. E.g. in [16] complex rational number arithmetics, unnatural for decision tables, is needed to achieve compatibility of the final decision table with Dempster rule of combination. In [6] (probabilistic interpretation) only lower and upper bounds are found for Dempster rule. In [4] (probability structures interpretation) the belief function obtained from the Dempster rule is a potential, but not necessary result of the corresponding probabilistic structure combination operation. See also [17] for discussion of other interpretations.

The paper presents SQL statements performing the calculations of the MTE measures and the MTE related operations on the decision tables.

The new interpretation may be directly applied in the domain of multiple decision decision tables: independence of decision variables or Shenoy's conditional independence in the sense of MTE may serve as an indication of possibility of decomposition of the decision table into smaller but equivalent tables. Furthermore it may be applied in the area of Cooperative Query Answering [9]. The problem there is that a query posed to a local relational database system may contain an unknown attribute. But possibly other cooperating db systems know it and may explain it to the queried system in terms of known attributes, shared by the various systems. The uncertainties studied in the decision tables arise here in a natural way and our interpretation may be used to measure these uncertainties in terms of MTE (as diversity of support). Furthermore, if several cooperating systems respond, then the queried system may calculate the overall uncertainty measure using MTE combination of measures of individual responses.

Now we can ask how to understand then a MTE belief function in the light of our experience. One possibility is to consider the belief function as a measure of diversity of support. This is an obvious departure from frequency interpretations proposed by Shafer and others. No mater how frequently the same piece of evidence is presented, it is counted once. This insight may encourage to revise other known interpretations of MTE. In the "legal" interpretations e.g. [14], the witnesses in favor of a hypotheses should be counted separately, if their statements differ in unimportant details permitting to deduce that their statements are personal and not studied in. In the "probability of provability" approach [7] not a probability of correctness, but rather the number of distinct valid proofs of a statement should be counted. In the "possible world semantics" [10] the worlds should not be assigned a probability, but rather distinct possible worlds should be counted that differ in non-essential details. Then the operation of combination of independent evidence in the "legal" interpretation is just mixing compatible statements of two sets of witnesses (which saw the same event from different perspective) and counting different possible combinations.

Please notice also that the rough-set interpretation sheds some light onto what the concept of "evidence" may mean. The "evidence" are just different sets of information attributes and the "independence" means (deterministic) unpredictability of attribute values of the one set from the other set. This should not be confused with predictability of the decision variable. Nor with stochastic predictability which may be present. In the "legal" interpretation, independence would be measured with non-predictability of insignificant details.

Further studies on interpreting other known MTE operators in the spirit of qualitative interpretation presented in this paper are needed and may reveal new potential applications of MTE to real world problems.

References

1. Beeri C., Fagin R., Maier D., Yannakakis Y.: On the desirability of acyclic database schemes, *Journal of the Association for Computing Machinery*, vol. 30, no 3, 1983, 479-513.
2. Delobel C.: Normalization and hierarchical dependencies in the relational data model, *ACM Transactions on Database Systems*, vol. 3, no 3, 1978, 201-222.
3. Dempster A.P.: Upper and lower probabilities induced by a multi-valued mapping. *Ann. Math. Stat..* **38**(1967), 325-339.
4. Fagin R., Halpern J.Y.: Uncertainty, belief, and probability. *Comput. Intell.* **7**(1991), 160-173.
5. Kłopotek M.A.: Interpretation of belief function in Dempster-Shafer Theory *Foundations of Computing & Decision Sciences*, Vol. 20 No 4, 1995, pp.287-306
6. Kyburg Jr H.E.: Bayesian and non-Bayesian evidential updating. *Artificial Intelligence* **31**(1987), 271-293.
7. Pearl J.: *Probabilistic Reasoning in Intelligent Systems: Networks of Plausible Influence.* Morgan and Kaufmann, 1988
8. Provan G.M.: A logic-based analysis of Dempster-Shafer Theory, *International Journal of Approximate Reasoning* **4**(1990), 451-495.
9. Ras, Z.W.: Query processing in distributed information systems, *Fundamenta Informaticae Journal*, Special Issue on Logics for Artificial Intelligence, IOS Press, Vol. XV, No. 3/4, 1991, 381-397
10. Ruspini E.H.: The logical foundation of evidential reasoning, Tech. Note 408, SRI International, Menlo Park, Calif. USA, 1986.
11. Shafer G.: *A Mathematical Theory of Evidence.* Princeton University Press, Princeton, 1976.
12. Shafer G.: Belief functions: An introduction. In: Shafer G., Pearl J.,eds, *Readings in Uncertain Reasoning.* Morgan Kaufmann Pub.Inc., San Mateo CA, (1990), 473-482.
13. Shafer G., Srivastava R.: The Bayesian and Belief-Function Formalisms. A General Prospective for Auditing. In: Shafer G., Pearl J.,eds, *Readings in Uncertain Reasoning.* Morgan Kaufmann Pub.Inc., San Mateo CA, (1990), 482-521.
14. Shafer G.: Perspectives on the theory and practice of belief functions. *International Journal of Approximate Reasoning* **4**(1990), 323-362.
15. Shenoy P.P.: Conditional independence in valuation based systems. *International Journal of Approximate Reasoning* **109**(1994),
16. Skowron A., Grzymała-Busse J.W.: From rough set theory to evidence theory. In:Yager R.R., Kasprzyk J. and Fedrizzi M., eds, *Advances in the Dempster-Shafer Theory of Evidence.* J. Wiley, New York (1994), 193-236.
17. Smets Ph.: Resolving misunderstandings about belief functions. *International Journal of Approximate Reasoning* **6**(1992), 321-344.
18. Wasserman L.: Comments on Shafer's "Perspectives on the theory and practice of belief functions". *International Journal of Approximate Reasoning* **6**(1992),367-375.
19. Vang A.: *SQL and Relational Databases.* Microtrend Books, Slawson Communications Inc., 1991
20. Wierzchoń S.T.: On plausible reasoning, in: M.M.Gupta, T.Yamakawa eds.: *Fuzzy Logic in Knowledge Based Systems, Decision and Control* , North-Holland Amsterdam, 1988, 133-152.

Knowledge Discovery from Databases with the Guidance of a Causal Network

Qiuming Zhu and Zhengxin Chen
Department of Computer Science, University of Nebraska, Omaha, NE 68182

Abstract

The advancement of knowledge discovery from databases (KDD) has been hampered by the problems such as the lack of statistical rigor, overabundance of patterns, and poor integration. This paper describes a new model for KDD that applies a causal network to guide the discovery processes. The new model not only allows the user to express what kind of knowledge to be discovered, but also uses the user intention to alleviate the overabundance problem. In this new model, the causal network is applied to represent the relevant variables and their relationships in the problem domain, and in due course updated according to the extracted knowledge. An interactive data mining process based on this model is described. The approach allows a knowledge discovery process to be conducted in a more controllable manner. Fundamental features of the new model are discussed, and an example is provided to illustrate the discovery processes using this model.

Keywords: Knowledge discovery from databases, Causal networks, Goal-driven.

I. Introduction

In recent years knowledge discovery from databases (KDD) has made great progress (Cercone *et al.* 1993). According to Piatetsky-Shapiro (1991), knowledge discovery is the nontrivial extraction of implicit, previously unknown, and potentially useful information from data. Therefore KDD is the overall process of discovering useful knowledge from databases, such as incorporating appropriate prior knowledge and proper interpretation of the results. Knowledge discovery differs from machine learning in that the task is more general and is concerned with issues more specific to databases. The process is typically interactive and iterative. However, as noted by Piatetsky-Shapiro *et al* (1994), the progress of KDD has been slowed by problems such as lack of statistical rigor in knowledge extraction processes, overabundance of knowledge patterns generated in the intermediate and final stages of the discovery, and poor integration of the KDD systems with the databases and decision support systems.

When looked at the above problems, we found that most existing approaches of KDD is data-driven in nature. In Han et al. (1993) several data-driven strategies have been identified for learning characteristic rules from databases. These strategies include generalization, attribute removal, concept tree ascension, threshold control, rule transformation, and vote propagation. Even though the overabundance problem can be controlled at certain level by some additional effort, it is generally costly and disadvantageous to tackle this problem in data-driven approaches. It is therefore worthwhile to investigate alternatives to the solutions of this problem.

As noted by Wong and Lingras (1993), many intelligent systems employ numeric degrees of belief supplied by the users to make decisions. The problem of using domain knowledge to construct a causal network that is tailored to particular instances has been studied by several authors (Blum, 1982; Cooper, 1987; Herskovits, 1991, Cooper, 1994). Techniques have been developed to construct causal networks using variously available information. Cowell et al. used a method for generating belief functions from symbolic information such as qualitative preference relationships (Cowell *et al.* 1993). Provan and Clarke (1993) used a database of prior cases to specialize the model of their causal network construction and to update the network parameters. Many of these have shed light to our work to be described below.

In this paper, we explore the use of a goal-driven technique to control a knowledge discovery process. In this approach, causal networks (also called belief networks or Bayesian networks, Pearl 1991) are used as a tool to guide the generation of database queries and hypothetical knowledge patterns. The approach is intended to step at the intermediate and final stages of knowledge discovery and serves as one solution to the overabundance problem.

II. Fundamental Features of our New Model

In a conventional data-driven approach, it is easy to find many statistically significant patterns that are possibly obvious, redundant, or useless. To illustrate the problem, consider the task of retrieving a knowledge pattern from a database consisting of personal information such as those included in resumes. Suppose there is a need to find a set of guidelines that properly describes the necessary qualifications (as specified by a set of propositions, such as "experienced" and "responsible") for a certain kind of employee (e.g., software engineer). Notice that although the database consists of personal information, there are no attributes as specific as the propositions. One way (data-driven approach) to accomplish the task is to retrieve all information about people who are related to the title "software engineer." The next step is then considering among these people who satisfy those propositions. For example, a careful study of the retrieved data (which could be of a large number) may reveal (with certain criteria) that if a person has stayed in the same company for many years and has been promoted, then this is an indication that he or she is "responsible." However, the user may also have retrieved data that shows 30% of them living in New York city. Since 30% is a significant figure, a conclusion may look like: "New Yorkers are experienced software engineer." This obviously makes no sense.

To remedy these problems, people tried to incorporate certain rule-refining methods in data mining. However, as shown in the existing literature, to avoid the generation of too many pointless rules, a simple but useful technique is to start the knowledge-discovery process by specifying *what kind of knowledge is wanted*. In other words, users should be allowed to provide criteria (or some kind of task-oriented bias) as the original goal to guide the direction of discovery from databases. In addition, the system should be able to develop various sub-goals, and revise or refine these sub-goals dynamically with respect to the databases query results and the underlying goal. Approaches to KDD with this consideration are referred to as *goal-driven*.

One of the main concerns for the goal-driven knowledge extraction is the control and attention of the goal and sub-goals. Many researchers have noticed that the target set of extracted knowledge pattern changes when more data are obtained. For example, the case occurs when a current hypothesis is refuted by evidence and alternative explanations must be posited. There are reasons to temporarily change the focus of attention. One approach to do that is to posit a set of sub-goals that, if realized, will help determine whether the current set is still viable. The difficulty with such a scheme is the need to integrate three diverse sources of knowledge. They are: 1) causal knowledge about how events influence each other in the domain; 2) knowledge about what action sequences are feasible in any given set of circumstances; and 3) normative knowledge about how desirable the consequences are. Looking at possible solutions on these issues, we found that causal networks can be used as an effective and robust tool to implement goal-driven knowledge discovery.

A causal network is commonly modeled as a directed acyclic graph (DAG) whose nodes represent random variables and whose edges represent probabilistic dependencies. Under a causal interpretation, the edges represent direct causal influences. These influences are quantified by the conditional probability distribution values associated with each node. To derive the probability of a node, probabilities of their parent nodes, as well as the conditional probability distribution functions on their connecting edges are referenced. In the following we will describe how the causal network is used in our work to form and represent the goal and sub-goals for knowledge discovery.

III. A Causal Net Model for Goal-driven KDD

We define a model for goal-driven KDD with the use of a causal network by a 5-tuple (DB, CN, GL, UI, KP), where

DB is the database(s) based on which a knowledge discovery is conducted,
CN is a causal network used for guiding the knowledge discovery process,
GL is the goal indicating users' intention for knowledge discovery,
UI is the user interface,
KP is the knowledge patterns discovered.

The relationship among the components of this model is depicted in Fig. 1.

We assume that the user goal takes the form of a simple (probably vague) statement indicating the properties of some variables. Formally, we define a *goal in a KDD process*, $g_i \in$ GL as a proposition:

$$g_i = q_i(x, p),$$

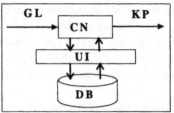

Fig. 1 Diagram of the goal-driven KDD model.

where **x** is a set of object and **p** is a set of qualifiers that applies to **x**. In a typical goal-driven KDD process, a set of such goals are to be explored and evaluated, such as

$$G_k = \{ g_{k1}, g_{k2}, g_{k3}, \dots \}, \quad G_k \subseteq G.$$

A dependency **r** is defined between any two goals g_{ki} and g_{kj} in G_k such that

$$r_{ij} = \Upsilon(g_{ki}, g_{kj});$$

where, $\Upsilon(g_{ki}, g_{kj})$ represents a dependent relation between the goals g_{ki} and g_{kj} in the way that the satisfaction of goal g_{ki} must first go through the satisfaction of goal g_{kj}. In general, a dependency **r** can be defined between two subsets of G_k, such that

$$r_{IJ} = \Upsilon(G_{kI}, G_{kJ}), \quad \text{where } G_{kI} \subset G_k, G_{kJ} \subset G_k, \text{ and } G_{kI} \cap G_{kJ} = \varnothing.$$

A quantitative function can be applied to a goal, or a set of goals, such that

$$\pi[g_i] = \pi[q_i(\mathbf{x}, \mathbf{p})] \quad \text{or}$$
$$\pi[G_{kI}] = \pi[q_{k1}(\mathbf{x}, \mathbf{p}), q_{k2}(\mathbf{x}, \mathbf{p}), \dots];$$

where $g_{k1}, g_{k2}, \dots$ are goals having certain dependency relations. The function $\pi[g_i]$ can represent the strength, uncertainty, or belief of the goals, for instance the probability value for $\mathbf{g}_i$ being true.

A *knowledge pattern* (**KP**) to be discovered in a KDD process is defined as a construct consisting of the goals, the relations among the goals, and the functions defined on them. That is, a knowledge pattern can be described as

$$\mathbf{KP}_i = (G_i, R_i, \Pi_i)$$

Where G_i is a set of goals $G_i = \{ g_{i1}, g_{i2}, g_{i3}, \dots \}$, R_i is a set of dependencies defined on G_i such that $R_i = \{ r_{i1}, r_{i2}, r_{i3}, \dots \}$. Π_I is a set of π functions defined on G_i and R_i.

Let $\mathbf{g}_i$ and $\mathbf{g}_j$ be two goals. We say that $\mathbf{g}_j$ is a sub-goal of $\mathbf{g}_i$ iff $\exists r_{ij} \in R$. Let $\mathbf{g}_i$ be a goal and G_J be a set of goals, $\mathbf{g}_i \notin G_J$. G_J is a sub-goal set of $\mathbf{g}_i$ iff

$$\forall \mathbf{g}_j \exists r_{ij} [(g_j \in G_J) \Rightarrow \Upsilon(g_i, g_j)].$$

This expression may be used to indicate a probability dependency function defined on the goal - sub-goal pairs, denoted as

$$P(g_i \mid g_j) = \pi[\ g_i \mid g_j] = \pi[q_i(\mathbf{x}, \mathbf{p}) \mid q_j(\mathbf{x}, \mathbf{p})].$$

IV. KDD Process with Causal Net Model

The process of knowledge discovery defined in the above model starts from the construction of an initial causal network. An *initial causal network* is constructed to form and represent the initial set of goal and sub-goals. These goal and sub-goals are to be expanded in the database exploration process so that the knowledge discovery will be conducted in a more content-controllable manner. The initial CN consists of
  (1) an ultimate goal which is the objective of KDD and serves as the starting point of the CN construction (the root if the CN has a tree-like structure);
  (2) a set of variables (will be regarded as sub-goals) having certain probabilistically or logic dependencies (directly or indirectly) with the ultimate goal; and
  (3) a set of inference rules (maybe hypothetical) that may be defined by some probability dependence functions (pdf) or logical relations between the ultimate goal and sub-goals.

An initial causal network could indicate possible relationships among some concepts, with or without probabilities assigned on the links. For example, Fig. 2 depicts a possible initial Causal network, where Q(x, P) represents a relationship of Q defined on x and P.

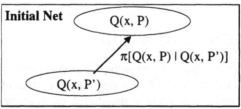

Fig. 2 An example of initial Causal Network built for data mining

Given an initial coarse causal network containing some background knowledge, variables of relevant objects and their probabilities obtained from the database are propagated in the network and are used to refine the causal network. After goal-oriented manipulation on the coarse network, a portion of the network will be updated. The resulting causal network may either be reported to the user or manipulated again for further knowledge discovery processes. These processes work together to result the generation of useful knowledge patterns..

To properly generate database queries from the causal network, a network decomposition process is invoked in the KDD process. One purpose of this process is to reduce the complexity involved in the dependency representations for the goal and sub-goals. In the decomposition process, the node connections in causal network relevant to the database attributes are identified. A structural analysis subsequently traces the connections and influences of the probabilities in the network. The decomposition process will extract a goal-related sub-network from the causal network. This sub-net is then converted to a goal-related tree by a net-to-tree conversion procedure. The constructed goal-tree is in a format suitable for converting back to the causal networks so that the causal network will be updated using the extracted knowledge from the database explorations. The sub-network is then combined with the original causal network by applying certain logic operations. The entire process can be represented by the following procedure:

1. Identify an ultimate goal GL for a KDD
2. Generate initial CN, mark the ultimate goal as the current goal and put it into a goal stack.
3. Until no goals in the goal stack
3.1 Identify a Sub-CN from the current goal
3.2 Convert the current Sub-CN to a goal-tree
3.3 Generate a conceptual query from the goal-tree
3.4 Convert conceptual query to actual query using database schema of the DB
3.5 Retrieve information from DB via a UI
3.6 Revise goal-tree according to data retrieved by actual query
3.7 Extract propositions from the retrieved information
3.8 Map the propositions back to the Sub-CN via goal-tree reverse-conversion
3.9 Incorporate the Sub-CN to CN to form a KP
3.10 Put the new nodes of CN to the goal stack.

Some details of the computational module are illustrated by an example in the next section.

V. AN EXAMPLE ILLUSTRATION

As an example, consider a database consisting of employment information including the employee educational background. The proposition *Qualifications*(**x, P**) means to find a knowledge pattern that gives a qualitative or quantitative definition of a "software engineer" as "experienced". Fig.3 shows an initial Causal network.

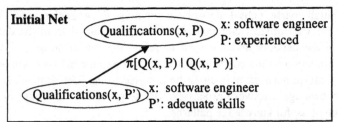

Fig. 3. An initial Causal Network with one goal and one subgoal.

Expanding the initial network by considering the database contents, we have the CN expanded to the Fig. 4:

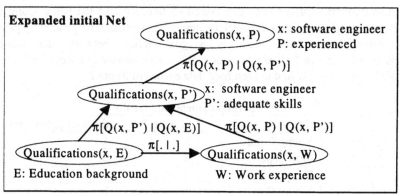

Fig. 4. An expansion of the initial Causal Network for KDD.

Note that it is the task of KDD to establish the necessary probability dependency functions on the links of the above network. According to this expanded CN, we have sub-goals: *(education background)* and *(work experience)*. Suppose an exploration of the DB involving relations *Collegian* and returns the Table 1:

Table 1. Educational data results

	College	year-grad	gpa
A1	ALBRIGHT UNIV.	3	3.5
A2	BRIAN INSTITUTE	3	3.8
A3	CARSON COLL.	2	3.1
A4	ALBRIGHT UNIV.	4	3.9
A5	BRIAN INSTITUTE	3	3.2
A6	BRIAN INSTITUTE	4	3.5
A7	DAVIDSON UNIV..	5	3.3
A8	BRIAN INSTITUTE	3	3.6
A9	CARSON COLL.	2	3.0
A10	ALBRIGHT UNIV.	2	3.4

The table reveals that the college "BRIAN INSTITUTE" is an important attribute. It is reasonable to expand the sub-goal of "education background.". Thus a goal-related sub-tree is formed as shown in Fig. 5, where EB stands for "Education background."

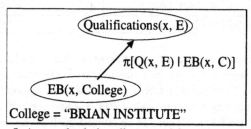

Fig. 5. A causal relation discovered from data mining

To further explore what has been discovered so fare, we take the EB(x, College) as our current sub-goal, and look for related company information by generating possible DB queries. Notice that there is a goal-relation between the sub-goals *Qualifications*(**x, E**) and *Qualifications*(**x, W**). This connection would allow us to generate DB queries and find the returned data entries of Table 2.

Table 2. Employment data results

	Company	year-on-job	times-of promotion
A2	Young Comp.	3	1
A5	Zion Super.	2	0
A6	X-ray graph.	3	1
A8	Young Comp.	4	2

The sub-goal of "work experience" now is expanded, and a goal-related sub-tree is formed as shown in Fig. 6, where "WE" stands for "Work Experience."

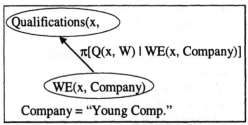

Fig. 6. Employment related sub-tree

From the above information we can discover that either company "Young Comp." employs more software engineer or more graduates from college "BRIAN INSTITUTE" were employed by company "Young Comp." Take the WE(x, Company) as our current sub-goal, we can have the following Table 3 returned after the DB query:

Table 3. Employment data results

	College	year-grad	gpa
A1	ALBRIGHT UNIV.	3	3.5
A2	BRIAN INSTITUTE	3	3.8
A4	ALBRIGHT UNIV.	4	3.9
A8	BRIAN INSTITUTE	3	3.6

This could be viewed as a partial verification that "graduates from BRIAN INSTITUTE" is an important factor in terms of qualification for a software engineer. Though the college = "ALBRIGHT UNIV." seems also acceptable, but it needs to be further verified. Any way both the node EB(x, C) and the pdf on the connection between the Q(x, E) and EB(x, C) need to be revised, such as shown in Fig. 7.

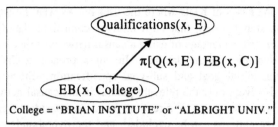

Fig. 7. Revised education background sub-tree

Further exploration will add a new node EB(x, gpa) node, as shown in Fig. 8.

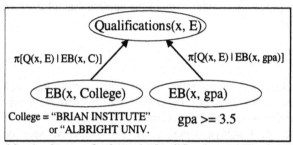

Fig. 8. Combined sub-tree of sub-goal "Qualifications(x, E) after data mining.

Of course this knowledge needs to be verified, and we will do that by further database mining. Meanwhile continuation of the above process on sub-goal *"Qualifications*(x, W) generates the relations shown in Fig. 9. In this figure we use the variables "y-o-j" and "t-o-p" to describe the related work experience, where "y-o-j" stands for "years on the job" and "t-o-p" stands for "times of promotion."

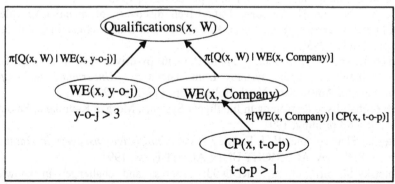

Fig. 9. Expanded sub-tree for sub-goal *"Qualifications*(x, W)" after data mining

VI. CONCLUSION

In summary, we have described a new model for KDD and an interactive, semi-automated data mining process. In this approach, a user can always provide his/her intention to guide the search of knowledge in a timely fashion. This new approach is mostly suitable to the cases of KDD where the user knows what he wants and is able to refine his goals step by step, that is, a kind of control of the KDD process is desirable to the user. An advantage of using a causal network is that it provides a way to deal with the dynamics of the database. In our approach, a CN is constructed gradually under the initial goal and sub-goal specifications. Since the knowledge propagation is goal-driven, only the relevant path(s) in the causal network need to be checked. In this way, the scope of directions need be considered can be reduced, unwanted knowledge patterns can be excluded, and the overabundance problem can be remedied. Based on the gradually refinement of the CN, the user can repeatedly search the database and retrieve the knowledge pattern in a more effective manner. Due to space limitation, some details of the approach are not included in this paper. We are now in a process to further explore the applications of the model and conduct more experiments.

REFERENCES

R. L. Blum, "Induction of causal relationships from a time-oriented clinical database: An overview of RX project," *Proceedings of Second National Conference on Artificial Intelligence*, MIT Press, Cambridge, MA, pp.355-357, 1982.

N. Cercone, and M. Tsuchiya (Guest eds.), 1993, Special issue on Learning and Discovery in knowledge-based databases, *IEEE Trans. Knowl. Data Eng.*, Vol. 5, No. 6, 1993.

G. F. Cooper and E. Herskovits, "A Bayesian method for the induction of probabilistic networks from data," *Machine Learning*, Vol. 9, No. 4, pp. 309-348, 1994..

R. G. Cowell, A. P. Dawid, and D. J. Spiegelhalter, "Sequential model criticism in probabilistic expert systems," *IEEE Transactions on Pattern Analysis and Machine Intelligence*, Vol. 15, No. 3, pp. 209-219, 1993.

J. Han, Y. Cai and N. Cercone, Data-driven discovery of quantitative rules in relational databases, IEEE Trans. Knowledge and Data Engineering, Vol. 5, No. 1, pp. 29-40, 1993.

E. Herskovits and G. F. Cooper, "Kutato: An entropy-driven system for construction of probabilistic expert systems from databases," *Uncertainty in Artificial Intelligence,* Amsterdam, North Holland, pp. 117-125, 1991

J. Pearl, Probabilistic Reasoning in Intelligent Systems. Morgan Kaufmann, Palo Alto, CA, Second printing, 1991

G. Piatetsky-Shapiro, and W. J. Frawley (eds.), *Knowledge Discovery in Databases*, Menlo Park, CA: ALBRIGHT UNIV.AI/MIT Press, 1991

G. Piatetsky-Shapiro, et, al, "KDD-93: Progress and challenges in knowledge discovery in databases,"*AI Magazine*, Vol. 15, No. 3, pp. 77-82, 1994

M. Provan and J. R. Clarke, "Dynamic network construction and updating techniques for the diagnosis of Acute Abdominal Pain," *IEEE Transactions on Pattern Analysis and Machine Intelligence*, Vol. 15, No. 3, pp. 299-307, 1993

S. K. M. Wong and P. Lingras, "Representation of qualitative user preference by quantitative belief functions," IEEE Transactions on Knowledge and Data Engineering, Vol. 6, No. 1, pp. 72-78, 1993.

From Data to Knowledge: Method-Specific Transformations *

Michael J. Donahoo, J. William Murdock, Ashok K. Goel, Shamkant Navathe, and Edward Omiecinski

Georgia Institute of Technology
College of Computing
801 Atlantic Drive
Atlanta, Georgia 30332-0280, USA

Abstract. Generality and scale are important but difficult issues in knowledge engineering. At the root of the difficulty lie two hard questions: how to accumulate huge volumes of knowledge, and how to support heterogeneous knowledge and processing? One answer to the first question is to reuse legacy knowledge systems, integrate knowledge systems with legacy databases, and enable sharing of the databases by multiple knowledge systems. We present an architecture called HIPED for realizing this answer. HIPED converts the second question above into a new form: how to convert data accessed from a legacy database into a form appropriate to the processing method used in a legacy knowledge system? One answer to this reformed question is to use method-specific transformation of data into knowledge. We describe an experiment in which a legacy knowledge system called INTERACTIVE KRITIK is integrated with an ORACLE database using IDI as the communication tool. The experiment indicates the computational feasibility of method-specific data-to-knowledge transformations.

1 Motivations, Background, and Goals

Generality and scale have been important issues in knowledge systems research ever since the development of the first expert systems in the mid sixties. Yet, some thirty years later, the two issues remain largely unresolved. Consider, for example, current knowledge systems for engineering design. The scale of these systems is quite small both in the amount and variety of knowledge they contain, and the size and complexity of problems they solve. In addition, these systems are both domain-specific in that their knowledge is relevant only to a limited class of domains, and task-specific in that their processing is appropriate only to a limited class of tasks.

At the root of the difficulty lie two critical questions. Both generality and scale demand huge volumes of knowledge. Consider, for example, knowledge systems for a specific phase and a particular kind of engineering design, namely, the

* This work was funded by a DARPA grant monitored by WPAFB, contract #F33615-93-1-1338, and has benefited from feedback from Chuck Sutterwaite of WPAFB. We appreciate the support.

conceptual phase of functional design of mechanical devices. A robust knowledge system for even this very limited task may require knowledge of millions of design parts. Thus the first hard question is this: How might we accumulate huge volumes of knowledge? Generality also implies heterogeneity in both knowledge and processing. Consider again knowledge systems for the conceptual phase of functional design of mechanical devices. A robust knowledge system may use a number of processing methods such as problem/object decomposition, prototype/plan instantiation, case-based reuse, model-based diagnosis and model-based simulation. Each of these methods uses different kinds of knowledge. Thus the second hard question is this: How might we support heterogeneous knowledge and processing?

Recent work on these questions may be categorized into two families of research strategies: (i) *ontological engineering*, and (ii) *reuse, integration* and *sharing* of information sources. The well known CYC project [Lenat and Guha, 1990] that seeks to provide a global ontology for constructing knowledge systems exemplifies the strategy of ontological engineering. This bottom-up strategy focuses on the first question of accumulation of knowledge. The second research strategy has three elements: reuse of information sources such as knowledge systems and databases, integration of information sources, and sharing of information in one source by other systems. This top-down strategy emphasizes the second question of heterogeneity of knowledge and processing and appears especially attractive with the advent of the world-wide-web which provides access to huge numbers of heterogeneous information sources such as knowledge systems, electronic databases and digital libraries. Our work falls under the second category.

[McKay et al., 1990] have pointed out that a key question pertaining to this topic is how to convert data in a database into knowledge useful to a knowledge system. The answer to this question depends in part on the processing method used by the knowledge system. The current generation of knowledge systems are heterogeneous both in their domain knowledge and control of processing. They not only use multiple methods, each of which uses a specific kind of knowledge and control of processing, but they also enable dynamic method selection. Our work focuses on the interface between legacy databases and legacy knowledge systems of the current generation.

The issue then becomes: given a legacy database, and given a legacy knowledge system in which a specific processing method poses a particular knowledge goal (or query), how might the data in the database be converted into a form appropriate to the processing method? The form of this question indicates a possible answer: *method-specific transformation* (or MST), which would transform the data into a form appropriate to the processing strategy. The goal of this paper is to outline a conceptual framework for the MST technique. Portions of this framework are instantiated in an operational computer system called HIPED (for Heterogeneous Intelligent Processing for Engineering Design). HIPED integrates a knowledge system for engineering design called INTERACTIVE KRITIK [Goel et al., 1996a, Goel et al., 1996b] with an external database represented in Oracle [Koch and Loney, 1995]. The knowledge system and the database communicate through IDI [Paramax, 1993].

2 HIPED Architecture

Figure 1 illustrates the general scheme. We describe this architecture in the following subsection by decomposing it into database, knowledge system, and user components.

2.1 Database Integration

An enormous amount of data is housed in various database systems; unfortunately, the meaning of this data is not encoded within the databases themselves. This lack of metadata about the schema and a myriad of interfaces to various database systems creates significant difficulties in accessing data from various legacy database systems. Both of these problems can be alleviated by creating a single, global representation of all of the legacy data, which can be accessed through a single interface.

Common practice for integration of legacy systems involves manual integration of each legacy schema into a global schema [Batini et al., 1986]. Clearly, this approach does not work for integration of a large number of database systems. We propose (see the right side of Figure 1) to allow the database designers to develop a metadata description, called an **augmented export schema**, of their database system. A collection of augmented export schemas can then be automatically processed by a **schema builder** to create a **partially integrated global schema**[2] which can be as simple as the actual database schema, allowing any database to easily participate, or as complicated as the schema builder can understand (See [Navathe and Donahoo, 1995] for details on possible components of an augmented export schema). A user can then submit queries on the partially integrated global schema to a **query processor** which fragments the query into queries on the local databases. Queries on the local databases can be expressed in a single query language which is coerced to the local databases query language by a **database wrapper**.

2.2 Knowledge System Integration

As with databases, a considerable number knowledge systems exist. Most knowledge systems do not provide an externally accessible description of the tasks and methods they address. We propose (see the left side of Figure 1) to allow knowledge system designers to develop a description, called a "task-method schema," of the tasks each local knowledge system can perform [Stroulia and Goel, 1995]. In this approach, a set of **knowledge systems**, defined at the level of tasks and methods, is organized into a coherent whole by a **query processor** or central control agent. The query processor uses a hierarchically organized schema of tasks

---

[2] A mechanism for complete, automated integration is unlikely.

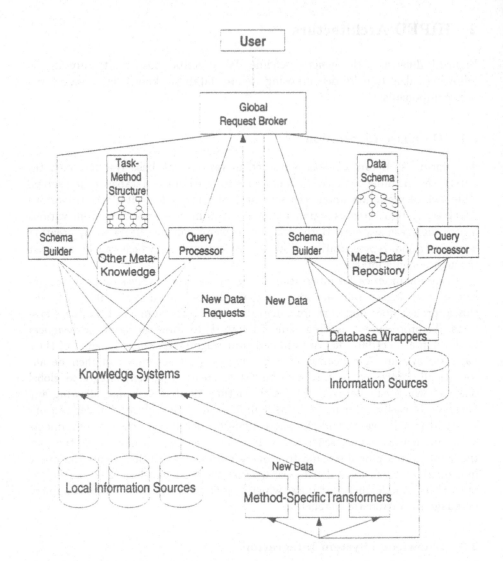

Fig. 1. The HIPED architecture (Arrowed lines indicate unidirectional flow of information; all other lines indicate bidirectional flow. Annotations on lines describe the nature of the information which flows through that line. Rectangular boxes indicate functional units and cylinders represent collections of data).

and methods as well as a collection of miscellaneous knowledge about processing and control (i.e. **other meta-knowledge**). Both the task-method structure and the other meta-knowledge may be constructed by the system designer at design time or built up by an automated **schema builder**.

2.3 Integrated Access

Transparent access to data and knowledge is important. We propose the provision of a **global request broker** which takes a query from a user, submits the query to both knowledge and database systems and returns an integrated result. Knowledge systems needing data not available in their local repositories may act as users themselves.

2.4 Method-Specific Transformation

In this paper, we are concerned with the transformation of knowledge from external sources into a form suitable for use by a knowledge system method. A naive approach involves writing a transformation function for every permutation of knowledge system and database. Clearly, this limits the overall scalability of the system.

We propose to leverage the partially integrated global representation of the knowledge and database systems by creating a method-specific transformation for each knowledge system which transforms knowledge from the partially integrated global schema into a knowledge system specific representation. The number of necessary method-specific transformations is linear with respect to the number of knowledge systems, increasing the scalability of our approach.

2.5 Information Flow

Consider a knowledge system which spawns a task for finding a design part such as a battery with a certain voltage. In addition to continuing its own internal processing, the knowledge system also submits a query to the Global Request Broker. The broker sends the query to the query processors for both integrated knowledge and database systems. The database query processor fragments the query into subqueries for the individual databases. The data derived is merged, converted to the global representation, and returned to the Global Request Broker. Meanwhile, the knowledge query processor, using its task-method schema, selects knowledge systems with appropriate capabilities and submits tasks to each. Solutions are converted to a common representation and sent to the Global Request Broker. It then passes the output from both the knowledge and database system query processors through a method-specific transformer which coerces the data into a form which is usable by the requesting knowledge system. The resulting battery may be an actual battery which satisfies the voltage specification from a knowledge or database system information source or it may be a battery constructed from a set of lower voltage batteries by a knowledge system.

3 An Experiment with HIPED

We have been conducting a series of experiments in the form of actual system implementations. Figure 2 presents an architectural view of one such experiment, in which a legacy knowledge system requests and receives information from a general-purpose database system. Since this experiment deals with only one knowledge system and only one database, we are able to abstract away a great many issues and focus on a specific question: method-specific transformation.

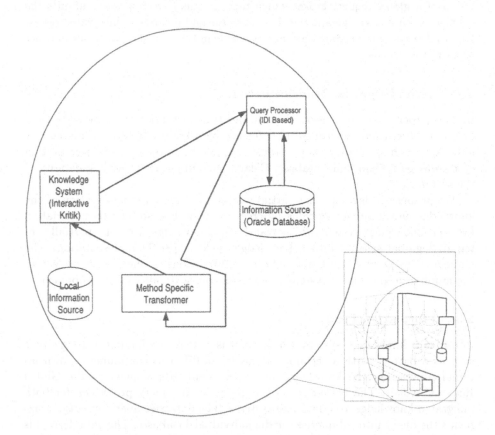

Fig. 2. The portion of the architecture relating to the proposed solution

3.1 General Method

The overall algorithm developed in this experiment breaks down into four steps which correspond to the four architectural components shown in Figure 2:

Step 1 The *knowledge system* issues a request when needed information is not available in its *local information source*.

Step 2 The *query processor* translates the request into a query in the language of the *information source.*

Step 3 The *information source* processes the query and returns data to the *query processor* which sends the data to the *method-specific transformer.*

Step 4 The *method-specific transformer* converts the data into a knowledge representation format which can by understood by the *knowledge system.*

All four of these steps pose complex problems. Executing step one requires that a knowledge system recognize that some element is missing from its knowledge and that this element would help it to solve the current problem. Performing step two requires a mechanism for constructing queries and providing communication to and from the external system. Step three is the fundamental problem of databases: given a query produce a data item. Lastly, step four is a challenging problem because the differences between the form of the data in the information source and the form required by the knowledge system may be arbitrarily complex. We focus on the fourth step: method-specific transformation. The algorithm for the method-specific transformer implemented in our experimental system is as follows:

Substep 4.1 Database data types are coerced into to knowledge system data types.

Substep 4.2 Knowledge attributes are constructed from fields in the data item.

Substep 4.3 Knowledge attributes are synthesized into a knowledge element.

3.2 Integration

The particular legacy systems which we combined in our implementation were INTERACTIVE KRITIK and a relational database system [Codd, 1970] developed under Oracle. INTERACTIVE KRITIK is a knowledge system which performs conceptual design of simple physical devices and provides visual explanations of both the reasoning processes it goes through and the design products it produces. It is an inherently multi-strategy knowledge system. It uses case-based reasoning as a general process for performing design and it also uses an assortment of model-based methods for doing specific design tasks such as diagnosis and repair.

The experimental system which we have written serves as an interface between INTERACTIVE KRITIK and our Oracle database. It is used when INTERACTIVE KRITIK is attempting to redesign a device by component substitution, one redesign strategy in its library of strategies. As a simple example, consider the situation in which the system has determined that a flashlight is not producing enough light and has decided that a more powerful bulb is needed. When the system identifies a single component whose replacement could potentially solve the design problem, it consults its library of components to see if such a replacement exists; in the example, it would check to see if it knows about a more powerful bulb and would make a substitution only if it did. In earlier implementations, the library of components was stored entirely within INTERACTIVE

KRITIK itself in the form of data structures in memory. In our experiment, these data structures are not present in memory and the request for an appropriate component takes place through our partial implementation of the pieces of the HIPED architecture illustrated in Figure 2.

INTERACTIVE KRITIK sends its request to the query processor. The request is made as a LISP function call to a function named lookup-database-by-attribute which takes three arguments: a prototype, an attribute, and a value for that attribute. An example of such a call from the system is a request for a more powerful light bulb for which the prototype is the symbol 'L-BULB which refers to the general class of light bulbs, the attribute is the symbol 'CAPACITY, and the value is the string "capacity-more" which is internally mapped within INTER-ACTIVE KRITIK to a value, 18 lumens. The query processor uses IDI to generate an SQL query as follows:

```
SELECT DISTINCT RV1.inst_name
FROM    PROTO_INST RV1, INSTANCE RV2
WHERE   RV1.proto_name = 'l-bulb'
AND     RV1.inst_name = RV2.name
AND     RV2.att_val = 'capacity-more'
```

IDI sends this query to Oracle running on a remote server. Oracle searches through the database tables illustrated in Table 1. The first of these tables, INSTANCE, holds the components themselves. The second table, PROTO_INST is a cross-reference table which provides a mapping from components to prototypes.

Table 1. The tables for the Oracle database

Table INSTANCE			Table PROTO_INST	
NAME	ATTRIBUTE	ATT_VAL	INST_NAME	PROTO_NAME
littlebulb	lumens	capacity-less	littlebulb	l-bulb
bigmotor	watts	power-more	bigmotor	motor
bigbulb	lumens	capacity-more	bigbulb	l-bulb

If Oracle finds a result, as it does in this example, it returns it via the method-specific transformer. In this case, the query generates the string "bigbulb" as the result. The prototype name and the value are also part of the result, but they are not explicitly returned by the database since they are the values used to select the database entry in the first place. The method-specific transformer converts the raw data from the database to a form comprehensible to INTERACTIVE KRITIK by using the algorithm described in Section 3.1. In Substep **4.1**, the string "bigbulb" is converted from a fixed length, blank padded string, as returned by Oracle, to a variable length string, as expected by INTERACTIVE KRITIK. In Substep **4.2**, the attributes of the new bulb are generated. The values "bigbulb" and 'L-BULB are used as the knowledge attributes **name** and **prototype-comp**; the values 'CAPACITY, 'LUMENS, and "capacity-more" are combined into a CLOS object of a class named **parameter** and a list containing this one object is created and used as the **parameters** attribute of the component being constructed. Finally, in Substep **4.3** these three attribute values are synthesized into a single CLOS object of the **component** class. The end result of this process is an object equivalent to the one defined by the following statement:

```
(clos:make-instance 'component
  :init-name      "bigbulb"
  :prototype-comp 'L-BULB
  :parameters     (list (clos:make-instance 'parameter
                          :init-name   'CAPACITY
                          :parm-units  'LUMENS
                          :parm-value  "capacity-more")))
```

These commands generate a CLOS object of the **component** class with three slots. The first slot contains the component name, the second contains the prototype of the component, and the third is a list of parameters. The list of parameters contains a single item which is, itself, a CLOS object. This object is a member of the **parameter** class and has a parameter name, the units which this parameter is in, and a value for the parameter. This object is then returned to INTERACTIVE KRITIK which is now able to continue with its processing.

4 Discussion

The complexity involved in constructing a knowledge system makes reuse an attractive option for true scalability. However, the reuse of legacy systems is non-trivial because we must accommodate the heterogeneity of systems. The scalability of the HIPED architecture comes from the easy integration of legacy systems and transparent access to the resulting pool of legacy knowledge. Sharing data simply requires that a legacy system designer augment the existing local schema with metadata that allows a global coordinator to relate data from one system to another, providing a general solution to large scale integration.

The specific experiment described in Section 3 models only a small portion of the general architecture described in Section 2. In a related experiment, we have worked with another portion of the architecture [Navathe et al., 1996]. Here, five types of queries that INTERACTIVE KRITIK may create are expressed in an SQL-like syntax. The queries are evaluated by mapping them using facts about the databases and rules that establish correspondences among data in the databases in terms of relationships such as equivalence, overlap, and set containment. The rules enable query evaluation in multiple ways in which the tokens in a given query may match relation names, attribute names, or values in the underlying databases tables. The query processing is implemented using the CORAL deductive database system [Ramakrishnan et al., 1992].

While the experiment described in this paper demonstrates method-specific transformation of data into knowledge usable by INTERACTIVE KRITIK, the other experiment shows how queries from INTERACTIVE KRITIK can be flexibly evaluated in multiple ways. We expect an integration of the two to provide a seamless and flexible technique for integration of knowledge systems with databases through method-specific transformation of data into useful knowledge.

References

[Batini et al., 1986] Batini, C., Lenzernini, M., and Navathe, S. B. (1986). A comparative analysis of methodologies for database schema integration. *ACM Computing Surveys*, 18(4):325–364.

[Codd, 1970] Codd, E. (1970). A relational model for large shared data banks. *CACM*, 13(6).

[Goel et al., 1996a] Goel, A., Gomez, A., Grue, N., Murdock, J. W., Recker, M., and Govindaraj, T. (1996a). Explanatory interface in interactive design environments. In Gero, J. S. and Sudweeks, F., editors, *Proc. Fourth International Conference on Artificial Intelligence in Design*, Stanford, California. Kluwer Academic Publishers.

[Goel et al., 1996b] Goel, A., Gomez, A., Grue, N., Murdock, J. W., Recker, M., and Govindaraj, T. (1996b). Towards design learning environments - I: Exploring how devices work. In Frasson, C., Gauthier, G., and Lesgold, A., editors, *Proc. Third International Conference on Intelligent Tutoring Systems*, number 1086 in Lecture Notes in Computer Science, Montreal, Canada. Springer.

[Koch and Loney, 1995] Koch, G. and Loney, K. (1995). *Oracle: The Complete Reference*. Osborne/McGraw Hill/Oracle, 3rd edition.

[Lenat and Guha, 1990] Lenat, D. and Guha, R. (1990). *Building Large Knowledge Based Systems: Representation and Inference in the CYC Project*. Addison-Wesley.

[McKay et al., 1990] McKay, D., Finin, T., and O'Hare, A. (1990). The intelligent database interface. In *Proc. Eight National Conference on Artificial Intelligence*, pages 677–684, Menlo Park, CA. AAAI.

[Navathe and Donahoo, 1995] Navathe, S. B. and Donahoo, M. J. (1995). Towards intelligent integration of heterogeneous information sources. In *Proceedings of the 6th International Workshop on Database Re-engineering and Interoperability*.

[Navathe et al., 1996] Navathe, S. B., Mahajan, S., and Omiecinski, E. (1996). Rule based database integration in HIPED: Heterogeneous intelligent processing in engineering design. In *Proc. International Symposium on Cooperative Database Systems for Advanced Applications*. World Scientific Press.

[Paramax, 1993] Paramax (1993). *Software User's Manual for the Cache-Based Intelligent Database Interface of the Intelligent Database Interface*. Paramax Systems Organization, 70 East Swedesford Road, Paoll, PA, 19301. Rev. 2.3.

[Ramakrishnan et al., 1992] Ramakrishnan, R., Srivastava, D., and Sudarshan, S. (1992). CORAL: Control, relations, and logic. In *Proc. International Conference of the Internation Conference on Very Large Databases*.

[Stroulia and Goel, 1995] Stroulia, E. and Goel, A. (1995). Functional representation and reasoning in reflective systems. *Journal of Applied Intelligence*, 9(1). Special Issue on Functional Reasoning.

Generalized Rules in Incomplete Information Systems

Marzena Kryszkiewicz
Institute of Computer Science
Warsaw University of Technology
Nowowiejska 15/19, 00-665 Warsaw, Poland
e-mail: mkr@ii.pw.edu.pl

Abstract. In the paper we define a notion of a generalized decision rule in a system with incomplete information. A generalized rule may be indefinite. A definite generalized rule is called certain. A rule is defined as generalized in an incomplete system if it is generalized in every completion of the incomplete system. Careful examination of the dependencies between an incomplete system and its completions allow us to state that all optimal generalized rules can be generated from the initial incomplete system. We show how to compute such rules by means of Boolean reasoning.

Keywords: Knowledge Discovery, Incomplete Information Systems, Rough Sets

1 Introduction

The problem of rules' generation from incomplete information systems (*IS*) is considered. By an incomplete system we mean a system with unknown data. Several solutions to the problem of generating decision tree from the training set of examples with unknown values have been proposed in the area of Artificial Intelligence. The simplest ones consist in removing examples with unknown values or replacing unknown values with the most common values. More complex approaches were presented in [1-2]. A Bayesian formalism is used in [1] to determine the probability distribution of the unknown value over the possible values from the domain. It is suggested in [2] to predict the value of an attribute based on the value of other attributes of the object, and the class information.

Rules' generation from incomplete systems was investigated also in the context of Rough Sets [3-7]. It was proposed in [4] to model uncertainty caused by appearance of unknown values by means of fuzzy sets. The methodology from [5] consists in transforming an incomplete system to a complete system, where each object with incomplete descriptor in the source system is represented by a set of possible subobjects in the target system. As we prove in [6], this method allows to generate the set of all optimal certain rules. Additionally, it was shown in [6] that optimal certain rules can be generated from the incomplete system by completing in an arbitrary way only the descriptor of an object-generator. All optimal certain rules supported by an object can be found if all possible descriptors of the object are considered. Different methodology was presented in [7]. It was shown there how to compute a subset of optimal generalized rules (i.e. rules with indefinite decision part in general) directly from the original incomplete decision table. The characteristic feature of such rules is that they rely only on the given knowledge and are not contradictory with unknown information about objects stored in the system.

In this paper we generalize the results we obtained in [6-7]. We define a notion of a generalized rule in an incomplete system as a rule which is generalized in every completion of the initial system (see [8]). Careful examination of the dependencies between an incomplete information system and its completions allow us to state that such a definition of generalized decision rules do not require performing the calculations in all the completions of the incomplete system. We prove that all generalized rules may be generated from the initial incomplete information system. The unique feature of the proposed method of rules' generation is its space complexity, which is $O(n)$, where n is the number of objects in the initial system.

2 Information Systems

Information system (*IS*) is a triplet $\mathcal{S} = (\mathcal{O}, AT, f)$, where $\mathcal{O}$ - is a non-empty finite set of *objects* and AT is a non-empty finite set of *attributes*, such that $f_a: \mathcal{O} \to V_a$ for any $a \in AT$, where V_a is called *domain* of an attribute a. Any attribute domain V_a may contain special symbol "*" to indicate that the value of an attribute is *unknown* (*null*). Here, we assume that an object has only one value for an attribute a, $a \in AT$, in reality. Thus, if the value of an attribute a is missing then we may conclude that the real value must be one from the set $V_a \backslash \{*\}$. System in which values of all attributes for all objects from $\mathcal{O}$ are known is called *complete*, otherwise it is called *incomplete*. Let $\mathcal{S}' = (\mathcal{O}, AT, f')$. We say that $\mathcal{S}'$ is an *extension* of $\mathcal{S}$ if $\mathcal{S}'$ is an *IS* such that if $f_a(x) \neq *$ then $f_a'(x) = f_a(x)$ for all $a \in AT$ and $x \in \mathcal{O}$. We say that $\mathcal{S}'$ is a *completion* of $\mathcal{S}$ if $\mathcal{S}'$ is a complete *IS*, which is an extension of $\mathcal{S}$. The set of all extensions of system $\mathcal{S}$ will be denoted by $EXTN(\mathcal{S})$, whereas the set of all completions of $\mathcal{S}$ will be denoted by $COMP(\mathcal{S})$. Further on, we will indicate that a notion is considered in an extension of system $\mathcal{S}$ by adding the respective upper index denoting that extension.
Let us note that null value occurring for attribute a, such that $card(V_a) = 1$, may be substituted by the unique domain value $v_a \in V_a$ without changing information capabilities of the system. From now on, without loss of generality, we will consider only systems that do not have null values for attributes a such that $card(V_a) = 1$.
In the sequel, any attribute-value pair (a,v), $a \in AT$, $v \in V_a$, will be called an *atomic property*. Any *atomic property* or its conjunction will be called *descriptor*. Conjunction of atomic properties for all attributes AT will be called *full descriptor*. Descriptor that does not possess null values for attributes $A \subseteq AT$ will be called *A-complete*. The set of objects having the atomic property (a,v), i.e. $\{x \in \mathcal{O} | f_a(x) = v\}$, will be denoted by $\|(a,v)\|$. Let us note that $\|(a,*)\| \cap \|(a,v)\| = \varnothing$, if $v \neq *$. The set of objects satisfying any descriptor t will be denoted by $\|t\|$ (or disjunction of descriptors) and will be computed in the usual way, e.g. $\|t \wedge s\| = \|t\| \cap \|s\|$ ($\|t \vee s\| = \|t\| \cup \|s\|$).

3 Indiscernibility of Objects

Let $\mathcal{S} = (\mathcal{O}, AT, f)$. Each subset of attributes $A \subseteq AT$ determines a binary *indiscernibility relation* $IND(A) = \{(x,y) \in \mathcal{O} \times \mathcal{O} | \forall a \in A, f_a(x) = f_a(y)\}$. The relation $IND(A)$, $A \subseteq AT$, is an equivalence relation and constitutes a partition of $\mathcal{O}$. Let $I_A(x)$ denote the set of objects $\{y \in \mathcal{O} | (x,y) \in IND(A)\}$. Objects from $I_A(x)$ are indiscernible with regard to their description in the system, but they may have different properties in reality, unless the system is complete.

Another *similarity relation* $SIM(A) = \{(x,y) \in \mathcal{O} \times \mathcal{O} \mid \forall a \in A, f_a(x) = f_a(y)$ or $f_a(x) = *$ or $f_a(y) = *\}$ treats two objects as similar if they may have the same properties in reality. Similarity relation is reflexive and symmetric, but may not be transitive, so it is a tolerance relation. By $S_A(x)$ we will denote the set of similar objects (i.e. possibly indiscernible) $\{y \in \mathcal{O} \mid (x,y) \in SIM(A)\}$. Of course, $SIM(A)$ and $IND(A)$, $A \subseteq AT$, are equivalent relations in a complete system.

Property 3.1

Let $B \subseteq A \subseteq AT$. Then: $I_A(x) \subseteq I_B(x)$; $S_A(x) \subseteq S_B(x)$; $I_A(x) \subseteq S_A(x)$.

Property 3.2

Let $\mathcal{S}'$ be a completion of $\mathcal{S}$ and $A \subseteq AT$. Then: $I_A'(x) = S_A'(x) \subseteq S_A(x)$.

Property 3.3

Let $A \subseteq AT$, then: $\bigcup_{\mathcal{S}' \in COMP(\mathcal{S})} I_A'(x) = S_A(x)$.

Proof. The property follows from the fact that each object $y \in S_A(x)$ is indiscernible with x with regard to attributes A in some completion of $\mathcal{S}$. $\square$

Property 3.4

If $x \in \mathcal{O}$ has A-complete descriptor, $A \subseteq AT$, in $\mathcal{S}$, then: $\bigcap_{\mathcal{S}' \in COMP(\mathcal{S})} I_A'(x) = I_A(x)$.

Property 3.5

Let $x \in \mathcal{O}$ have A-complete descriptor, $A \subseteq AT$, in $\mathcal{S}$. Let $\mathcal{S}'$ be a completion of $\mathcal{S}$ such that all null values occurring in $\mathcal{S}$ for attributes A are replaced in $\mathcal{S}'$ by respective values from A-complete descriptor of x. Then: $S_A(x) = I_A'(x)$.

4 Complete Decision Tables

Decision table (DT) is an information system $DT = (\mathcal{O}, AT \cup \{d\}, f)$, where d, $d \notin AT$ and $* \notin V_d$, is a distinguished attribute called *decision*, and the elements of AT are called *conditions*. If DT is a complete IS then DT is called *complete decision table*, otherwise it is called *incomplete decision table*. In Section 4 we will restrict our considerations only to complete decision tables.

Let us define function $\partial_A: \mathcal{O} \to \mathcal{P}(V_d)$, $A \subseteq AT$, as follows: $\partial_A(x) = \{i \mid i = d(y)$ and $y \in S_A(x)\}$. ∂_A will be called *generalized decision* in DT. If $card(\partial_{AT}(x)) = 1$ for any $x \in \mathcal{O}$ then DT is *consistent (definite)*, otherwise it is *inconsistent (indefinite)*.

4.1 Decision Rules

Decision rules we will consider will have the form: $t \to s$, where $t = \bigwedge(c,v)$, $c \in A \subseteq AT$, $v \in V_c$, and $s = \bigvee(d,w)$, $w \in V_d$. In the sequel, we will call t and s *condition* and *decision part* of a rule, respectively. A rule with a single decision value in the decision part of a rule will be called *definite*, otherwise it will be called *indefinite*.

We will say that object x, $x \in \mathcal{O}$, *supports* a rule $t \to s$ in $\mathcal{S}$ if x has both property t and s in $\mathcal{S}$. A decision rule $t \to s$ is *certain* in $\mathcal{S}$ if $t \to s$ is definite and $\|t\| \subseteq \|s\|$ in $\mathcal{S}$. A decision rule $t \rightarrow s$ is *generalized* in $\mathcal{S}$ if $\|t\| \subseteq \|s\|$ in $\mathcal{S}$. Obviously, any certain rule is generalized. A generalized decision rule $t \rightarrow s$ is *optimal* in $\mathcal{S}$ iff it is generalized in $\mathcal{S}$ and no other rule constructed from a proper subset of atomic properties occurring in t and s is generalized in $\mathcal{S}$.

Property 4.1.1

If object x, $x \in \mathcal{O}$, supports a certain rule in $\mathcal{S}$ then $I_{AT}(x) \subseteq I_{\{d\}}(x)$.

Proof. Let $t \rightarrow s$ be a rule supported by $x \in \mathcal{O}$ in $\mathcal{S}$. Let A be a set of attributes appearing in t. Since x supports rule $t \rightarrow s$ then $I_A(x) = \|t\|$ and $I_{\{d\}}(x) = \|s\|$. Additionally, since rule $t \rightarrow s$ is certain then $\|t\| \subseteq \|s\|$. By means of Property 3.1 we also have: $I_{AT}(x) \subseteq I_A(x)$. Thus, $I_{AT}(x) \subseteq I_A(x) = \|t\| \subseteq \|s\| = I_{\{d\}}(x)$ and finally $I_{AT}(x) \subseteq I_{\{d\}}(x)$. $\qquad \square$

Property 4.1.2

The decision part of an optimal generalized rule supported by object x, $x \in \mathcal{O}$, is equal to $(d,w_1) \vee (d,w_2) \vee ... \vee (d,w_n)$, where $\{w_1,w_2,...,w_n\} = \partial_{AT}(x)$.

Proof. Proposition 4.1.2 follows from the definitions of a generalized decision and an optimal generalized rule. $\qquad \square$

Property 4.1.3

Let $s = (d,w_1) \vee (d,w_2) \vee ... \vee (d,w_n)$, where $\{w_1,w_2,...,w_n\} = \partial_{AT}(x)$ for some object x. $t \rightarrow s$ is generalized if $\partial_A(x) = \partial_{AT}(x)$, where $A \subseteq AT$ is a set of objects occurring in t.

Property 4.1.4

Rule $t \rightarrow s$ is optimal generalized if $\partial_A(x) = \partial_{AT}(x)$, where $A \subseteq AT$ is a set of objects occurring in t, and for each $B \subset A$, $\partial_B(x) \neq \partial_{AT}(x)$.

Proof. Property 4.1.4 follows immediately from the definition of an optimal generalized rule and Properties 4.1.2-4.1.3. $\qquad \square$

4.2 Computing Generalized Rules

This subsection will present a method of computing all optimal generalized rules supported by an arbitrary object $x \in \mathcal{O}$. To this end, we need to introduce the useful notion of a generalized reduct for x. Set A, $A \subseteq AT$ is a *generalized reduct* for x, $x \in \mathcal{O}$, in system $\mathcal{S}$ iff A is a minimal set such that: $\partial_A(x) = \partial_{AT}(x)$. In general, object x may serve as a generator of all optimal generalized rules such that their conditional part is determined by any generalized reduct for x (see Property 4.1.4) and the decision part is determined by the generalized decision $\partial_{AT}(x)$ (see 4.1.2).

In order to compute reducts of DT we will use so called *discernibility functions* [9]. Their main properties are that they are monotonic Boolean functions and their prime implicants determine reducts uniquely. Let $\alpha_A(x,y)$ be a set of attributes $a \in A$ such that $(x,y) \notin SIM(\{a\})$. Let $\Sigma \alpha_A(x,y)$ be a Boolean expression which is equal to 1, if $\alpha_A(x,y) = \varnothing$. Otherwise, let $\Sigma \alpha_A(x,y)$ be a disjunction of variables corresponding to attributes contained in $\alpha_A(x,y)$. $\Delta_g(x)$ is a *generalized discernibility function* for $x \in \mathcal{O}$ in $\mathcal{S}$ iff

$$\Delta_g(x) = \prod_{y \in Y_g} \sum \alpha_{AT}(x,y), \text{ where } Y_g = \mathcal{O} \setminus \{y \in \mathcal{O} | \, d(y) \in \partial_{AT}(x)\}.$$

4.3 Computing Certain Rules

Certain rules are an important special case of generalized rules and they have their specific features. For instance, each object may be used as a generator of generalized rules, but only objects x satisfying the condition $I_{AT}(x) \subseteq I_{\{d\}}(x)$ (see Property 4.1.1) support certain ones. Hence, we may apply the method of computing certain rules as generalized rules, but only for objects x such that $I_{AT}(x) \subseteq I_{\{d\}}(x)$. Nevertheless, the notion of a generalized decision is superfluous in the case of certain rules. Below we present how the notions of generalized rules may be equivalently expressed in the case of certain rules:

- The decision part of an optimal certain rule is equal to $(d, d(x))$.
- A *certain reduct* for x, $I_{AT}(x) \subseteq I_{\{d\}}(x)$, in system $\mathcal{S}$ is a minimal set such that $I_A(x) \subseteq I_{\{d\}}(x)$.
- $\Delta_c(x)$ is a *certain discernibility function* for *object* $x \in \mathcal{O}$ in $\mathcal{S}$ if:

$$\Delta_c(x) = \prod_{y \in Y_c} \sum \alpha_{AT}(x, y), \text{ where } Y_c = \mathcal{O} \setminus I_{\{d\}}(x).$$

5 Incomplete Decision Tables

5.1 Decision Rules

Following the approach to incomplete information systems presented by Lipski in [8], we propose the following definition of a generalized rule: Rule $t \rightarrow s$ is *generalized in incomplete* $\mathcal{S}$ if it is generalized in every completion of $\mathcal{S}$. A generalized decision rule $t \rightarrow s$ is *optimal in incomplete* $\mathcal{S}$ iff it is generalized in $\mathcal{S}$ and no other rule constructed from a proper subset of atomic properties occurring in t and s is generalized in $\mathcal{S}$. Object $x \in \mathcal{O}$ supports a generalized rule $t \rightarrow s$ *in incomplete* $\mathcal{S}$ if x supports $t \rightarrow s$ in each completion of $\mathcal{S}$ in which $\|t\| \neq \emptyset$.

Proposition 5.1.1
$t \rightarrow s$ is generalized in $\mathcal{S}$ if it is generalized in every completion of $\mathcal{S}$ in which $\|t\| \neq \emptyset$.
Proof. By definition of a generalized rule in a complete IS, rule $t \rightarrow s$ is generalized in any completion of $\mathcal{S}$ if $\|t\| \subseteq \|s\|$. Hence, it is generalized in every completion of $\mathcal{S}$ in which $\|t\| = \emptyset$. Proposition 5.1.1 is an immediate consequence of this fact and the definition of a generalized rule. $\square$

Proposition 5.1.2
Let $DESC(Y)$ denote the set of full descriptors of all objects from Y.
Rule $t \rightarrow s$ is generalized in $\mathcal{S}$ if there is an object supporting $t \rightarrow s$ in some completion of $\mathcal{S}$ and there is no descriptor t in the set of descriptors $\bigcup_{\mathcal{S}' \in COMP(\mathcal{S})} DESC(\mathcal{O} \setminus \|s\|)$.
Proposition 5.1.2 justifies the correctness of a rules' generation approach, in which initial incomplete $\mathcal{S}$ is transformed to a complete $\mathcal{S}'$ which contains all the instances of the objects incompletely described in $\mathcal{S}$ (see [4]). Now, rules are generated from the complete system $\mathcal{S}'$. Next Propositions will justify another approach to rules' generation, which allows to compute rules from the initial incomplete system.

Proposition 5.1.3

Let $\mathcal{S}^e$ be an extension of $\mathcal{S}$ that differs from $\mathcal{S}$ only for some object x and $x \in \|t\|$ in $\mathcal{S}^e$.
Rule $t \to s$ is generalized in $\mathcal{S}$ if it is generalized in $\mathcal{S}^e$.

Immediate conclusion from Proposition 5.1.3 is that rule $t \to s$ is generalized in $\mathcal{S}$ if there exists an object $x \in \|t\|$ in some completion of $\mathcal{S}$ and $t \to s$ is generalized in all completions of $\mathcal{S}$ in which $x \in \|t\|$.

In the sequel, we will often refer to extensions of system $\mathcal{S}$ of a particular kind. Let $\mathcal{S}^e$ be an extension of $\mathcal{S}$ that differs from $\mathcal{S}$ only for an object x and x has a full complete descriptor in $\mathcal{S}^e$. The set of all extensions $\mathcal{S}^e$ of this property (i.e. extensions in which only the descriptor of an object x was fully completed) will be denoted by $C1EXTN(\mathcal{S}, x)$. Obviously, if x has a full complete descriptor in $\mathcal{S}$ then $C1EXTN(\mathcal{S}, x) = \{\mathcal{S}\}$. Otherwise $C1EXTN(\mathcal{S}, x)$ contains many extensions.

Proposition 5.1.4

Let $\mathcal{S}^e \in C1EXTN(\mathcal{S}, x)$ and $x \in \|t\|$ in $\mathcal{S}^e$.
Rule $t \to s$ is generalized in $\mathcal{S}$ if it is generalized in $\mathcal{S}^e$.

Proposition 5.1.5

Let $\mathcal{S}^e \in C1EXTN(\mathcal{S}, x)$ and $x \in \|t\|$ in $\mathcal{S}^e$.
If $t \to s$ is an optimal generalized rule in $\mathcal{S}^e$ then $s = (d, w_1) \vee (d, w_2) \vee \ldots \vee (d, w_n)$, where $\{w_1, w_2, \ldots, w_n\} = \partial_{AT}{}^e(x)$.

Proposition 5.1.6

An optimal generalized rule in $\mathcal{S}^e \in C1EXTN(\mathcal{S}, x)$ is optimal generalized in $\mathcal{S}$.

Property 5.1.1

If object x, $x \in \mathcal{O}$, supports a certain rule in $\mathcal{S}^e \in C1EXTN(\mathcal{S}, x)$ then $S_{AT}{}^e(x) \subseteq I_{\{d\}}(x)$.

Property 5.1.2

An optimal certain rule in $\mathcal{S}$ is optimal certain in all completions of $\mathcal{S}$.

5.2 Computing Generalized Rules

It is stated in Proposition 5.1.6 that optimal generalized rules supported by x may be computed in any extension $\mathcal{S}^e \in C1EXTN(\mathcal{S}, x)$. The number of different extensions $\mathcal{S}^e$ is equal to the number of different substitutions for null values in x. In order to compute the condition part of an optimal generalized rule the notion of a *generalized reduct* in $\mathcal{S}^e$ may be exploited. Set A, $A \subseteq AT$ is a *generalized reduct* for x, $x \in \mathcal{O}$, in system $\mathcal{S}^e$ if A is a minimal set such that: $\partial_A{}'(x) \subseteq \partial_{AT}{}^e(x)$ in every completion $\mathcal{S}'$ of $\mathcal{S}^e$. The definition of a generalized reduct is justified by Proposition 5.1.5.

The set of all generalized reducts of x in $\mathcal{S}$ is equal to the set-theoretical sum of all generalized reducts for x computed for in $\mathcal{S}^e$.

$\Delta_g{}^e(x)$ is a generalized discernibility function for object x in $\mathcal{S}^e$, $x \in \mathcal{O}$, iff

$$\Delta_g{}^e(x) = \prod_{\mathcal{S}' \in COMP(\mathcal{S})} \prod_{y \in Y_g^e} \sum \alpha'_{AT}(x,y), \quad Y_g{}^e = \mathcal{O} \setminus \{y \in \mathcal{O} \mid d(y) \in \partial_{AT}{}^e(x)\}.$$

All reducts of x in a $\mathcal{S}^e$ are all prime implicants of $\Delta_g{}^e(x)$.

Proposition 5.2.1

Let $x \in \mathcal{O}$. $\Delta_g^e(x) = \prod_{y \in Y_g^e} \sum \alpha_{AT}^e(x,y)$, where $Y_g^e = \mathcal{O} \setminus \{y \in \mathcal{O} \mid d(y) \in \partial_{AT}^e(x)\}$.

Proof. Let $\mathcal{S}'$ be a completion of $\mathcal{S}^e$ such that all null values occurring in $\mathcal{S}^e$ are replaced in $\mathcal{S}'$ with the respective attribute values occurring in the descriptor of x. Let $\mathcal{S}'' \neq \mathcal{S}'$ be an arbitrary completion of $\mathcal{S}^e$. One may easily notice that for each $y \in Y_g^e$, $\sum \alpha_A'(x,y) \wedge \sum \alpha_A''(x,y) = \sum \alpha_A'(x,y) = \sum \alpha_A^e(x,y)$. Since $\mathcal{S}''$ was chosen arbitrarily then we may generalize the above observation:

$$\Delta_g^e(x) = \prod_{\mathcal{S}^* \in COMP(\mathcal{S})} \prod_{y \in Y_g^e} \sum \alpha_{AT}'(x,y) = \prod_{y \in Y_g^e} \sum \alpha_{AT}'(x,y) = \prod_{y \in Y_g^e} \sum \alpha_{AT}^e(x,y). \quad \Box$$

5.3 Computing Certain Rules

According to Property 5.1.1 certain rules may be computed in an incomplete system only for objects x satisfying the condition $S_{AT}^e(x) \subseteq I_{\{d\}}(x)$. They may be computed as other generalized rules for such objects. However, we may also notice that:

- The decision part of an optimal certain rule is equal to $(d, d(x))$.
- Set A, $A \subseteq AT$ is a *certain reduct* for x, $S_{AT}^e(x) \subseteq I_{\{d\}}(x)$, in system $\mathcal{S}^e$ if A is a minimal set such that $I_A'(x) \subseteq I_{\{d\}}(x)$ in every completion $\mathcal{S}'$ of $\mathcal{S}^e$, i.e. if $S_A^e(x) \subseteq I_{\{d\}}(x)$.
- $\Delta_c^e(x)$ is a certain discernibility function for object x in $\mathcal{S}^e$, $S_{AT}^e(x) \subseteq I_{\{d\}}(x)$, if

$$\Delta_c^e(x) = \prod_{y \in Y_c} \sum \alpha_{AT}^e(x,y), \text{ where } Y_c = \mathcal{O} \setminus I_{\{d\}}(x).$$

6. Illustrative Example

Let us consider Table 6.1 which describes an incomplete decision table $\mathcal{S}$ containing information about cars. $V_{Price} = \{high, low\}$, $V_{Mileage} = \{high, low\}$, $V_{Size} = \{full, compact\}$, $V_{Max\text{-}Speed} = \{high, low\}$, $V_d = \{poor, good, excel.\}$.

Car	Price	Mileage	Size	Max-Speed	d	∂_{AT}
1	high	high	full	low	good	$\{g\}$
2	low	*	full	low	good	$\{g\}$
3	*	*	comp	high	poor	$\{p\}$
4	high	*	full	high	good	$\{g,e\}$
5	*	*	full	high	excel	$\{g,e\}$
6	low	high	full	*	good	$\{g,e\}$

Table 6.1 Car table

We will illustrate the method of generalized rules' generation by means of Proposition 5.2.1. Object 5 will be used as a rule generator. There are four possible complete descriptors of this object in reality:

1. $(P,low) \wedge (M,low) \wedge (S,full) \wedge (X,high)$,   3. $(P,low) \wedge (M,high) \wedge (S,full) \wedge (X,high)$,
2. $(P,high) \wedge (M,low) \wedge (S,full) \wedge (X,high)$,   4. $(P,high) \wedge (M,high) \wedge (S,full) \wedge (X,high)$,

where P, M, S, X stand for *Price, Mileage, Size* and *Max-Speed*, respectively.

a) Let $\mathcal{S}^e$ be an extension of $\mathcal{S}$ such that object 5 has full complete descriptor as in the case 1 in $\mathcal{S}^e$ and $\mathcal{S}^e$ differs from $\mathcal{S}$ only for object 5. We can see that:

$S_{AT}{}^e(5)=\{5\}$ and $\partial_{AT}{}^e(5)=\{excel.\}$ (though $S_{AT}(5)=\{4,5,6\}$ and $\partial_{AT}(x)=\{good,excel.\}$).
Hence, $Y_g{}^e = \mathcal{O} \setminus \{y \in \mathcal{O}| \ d(y) \in \partial_{AT}{}^e(x)\} = \mathcal{O} \setminus \{5\}$ and thus $Y_g{}^e = \{1,2,3,4,6\}$.
$\alpha_A(5,1)=\{P,M,X\}$, $\alpha_A(5,2)=\{X\}$, $\alpha_A(5,3)=\{S\}$, $\alpha_A(5,4)=\{P\}$, $\alpha_A(5,6)=\{M\}$,
so $\Delta_g{}^e(5) = (P \vee M \vee X) \wedge (X) \wedge (S) \wedge (P) \wedge (M) = PMSX$.
Thus, there is only one generalized reduct $\{P,M,S,X\}$ found for object 5 in extension $\mathcal{S}^e$, which means that only one generalized rule is supported by object 5 in $\mathcal{S}^e$, namely: $(P,low) \wedge (M,low) \wedge (Size,full) \wedge (X,high) \rightarrow (d,excel.)$.
b) Let $\mathcal{S}^e$ be an extension of $\mathcal{S}$ such that object 5 has full complete descriptor as in the case 2 in $\mathcal{S}^e$ and $\mathcal{S}^e$ differs from $\mathcal{S}$ only for object 5. We can see that:
$S_{AT}{}^e(5)=\{4,5\}$ and $\partial_{AT}{}^e(5)=\{good,excel.\}$. Hence, $Y_g{}^e = \mathcal{O} \setminus \{y \in \mathcal{O}| \ d(y) \in \partial_{AT}{}^e(x)\} = \{1,2,4,5,6\}$ and thus $Y_g{}^e = \{3\}$. $\alpha_A(5,3)=\{S\}$, so $\Delta_g{}^e(5) = S$. Thus, one generalized rule supported by object 5 is found in $\mathcal{S}^e$, namely: $(Size,full) \rightarrow (d,good) \vee (d,excel.)$.
Generalized rules for object 5 with complete descriptors as in the cases 3 and 4 may be computed in similar way. $\qquad\square$

Conclusion

Generalized rules represent certain knowledge induced from an incomplete information system $\mathcal{S}$. They are valid in every completion of $\mathcal{S}$. Certain rules constitute a subclass of generalized rules, which are definite. The main result of the paper is proving that all optimal generalized rules (and by this also all optimal certain rules) may be computed from an incomplete system. We showed how to compute such rules from the incomplete *IS* by applying Boolean reasoning. The conditional parts of optimal rules are determined by prime implicants of some Boolean functions. Hence, the problem of rules' generation is NP-hard. Nevertheless, efficient heuristics like Johnson's approximation strategy or genetic algorithms may be applied if we do not wish to generate all rules, but suboptimal ones with minimal condition parts. It is proved in [10] that suboptimal rules supported by an object may be generated in $O(kn^2)$ or $O(k^2 n \log n)$ time, where n is the number of objects and k is the number of attributes. Space complexity of our method of rules' generation is linear with regard to the number of objects in the initial incomplete system. Rules supported by different objects' descriptors may be generated in parallel.

References

[1] Kononenko I., Bratko I., Roskar E., Experiments in Automatic Learning of Medical Diagnostic Rules, Technical Report, Jozef Stefan Institute, Ljubljana, Yugoslavia, 1984.
[2] Quinlan J.R., Induction of Decision Trees, in *Readings in Machine Learning*, Shavlik J.W., Dietterich T.G. (ed.), 1990, Morgan Kaufmann Publishers, pp. 57-69.
[3] Pawlak Z., *Rough Sets: Theoretical Aspects of Reasoning about Data*, Kluwer Academic Publishers, Vol. 9, 1991.
[4] Chmielewski M.R., Grzymala-Busse J.W., Peterson N.W., Than S., The Rule Induction System LERS - A Version for Personal Computers, *Foundations of Computing and Decision Sciences*, Vol. 18 No. 3-4, 1993, pp. 181-212.
[5] Slowinski R., Stefanowski J., Rough-Set Reasoning about Uncertain Data, in *Fundamenta Informaticae*, Vol. 27, No. 2-3, 1996, pp. 229-244.
[6] Kryszkiewicz M., Rules in Incomplete Information Systems, submitted for *Journal of Information Science*.

[7] Kryszkiewicz M., Rough Set Approach to Incomplete Information Systems, *Proceedings of Second Annual Joint Conference on Information Sciences: Fuzzy Logic, Neural Computing, Pattern Recognition, Computer Vision, Evolutionary Computing, Information Theory, Computational Intelligence*, Wrightsville Beach, North Carolina, USA, 28 September - 1 October 1995, pp. 194-197; the extended version of the paper is accepted for *Journal of Information Science*.

[8] Lipski W.J., On Semantic Issues Connected with Incomplete Information Databases, *ACM Transaction on Databases Systems*, 4, 1979, pp. 262-296.

[9] Skowron A., Rauszer C., The Discernibility Matrices and Functions in Information Systems, in *Intelligent Decision Support: Handbook of Applications and Advances of Rough Sets Theory*, Slowinski R. (ed.), 1992, Kluwer Academic Publisher, pp.331-362.

[10] Nguyen S.H., Nguyen H.S., Some Efficient Algorithms for Rough Set Methods, in *Proceedings of Sixth Intl. Conference IPMU '96*, July 1-5, Granada, Espana, Vol. 3, 1996, pp. 1451-1456.

Appendix

Proof of Property 3.4

Since x has A-complete descriptor in S then $I_A(x)$ is the set of objects having the same A-complete descriptor in each completion of S. So, $\bigcap_{S' \in COMP(S)} I'\{x\} \supseteq I_A(x)$.

Let S' be any completion of S such that $S_A'(x) \setminus I_A(x) \neq \varnothing$. Let y be any object $y \in S_A'(x) \setminus I_A(x)$. Obviously, the descriptor of y in S is not A-complete. Let us remind that incomplete systems we consider do not possess null values for attributes with single domain values. Hence, among completions of S there is system S'' which differs from S' only for object x on at least one attribute from A. Thus, y has different A-complete descriptors in S'' and in S'. This means that x does not belong to the intersection of $I_A'(x) \cap I_A''(x)$, so it does not belong to $\bigcap_{S' \in COMP(S)} I_A'(x)$ either.

Arbitrariness of the choice of S' and x allow us to state that there are no objects except $I_A(x)$ that belong to the intersection of all completions of S. □

Proof of Proposition 5.1.3

Let $F(z,t)$ denote a set of all completions of S in which $z \in \|t\|$. Let x and y be arbitrary objects such that $F(x,t) \neq \varnothing$ and $F(y,t) \neq \varnothing$. Additionally, we assume that rule $t \rightarrow s$ is generalized in all systems from $F(x,t)$. Let S' be an arbitrary completion of S such that $S' \in F(y,t) \setminus F(x,t)$. This means that $x \notin \|t\|'$. On the other hand there is a completion S'' in $F(x,t)$ such that S'' differs from S' only for object x. This implies that $x \in \|t\|''$ and $\|t\|''\setminus\{x\}=\|t\|'$. So, since $\|t\|' \subset \|t\|''$ and $\|s\|$ is the same in all completions of S then $\|t\|'' \subseteq \|s\|$ implies $\|t\|' \subseteq \|s\|$. Hence, rule $t \rightarrow s$ which is generalized in S'' is also generalized in S'.

Since our choice of S' was arbitrary we may conclude that if rule $t \rightarrow s$ is generalized in all systems $F(x,t)$, then it is also generalized in all systems $F(y,t)$. Additionally, since we chose x and y arbitrarily, we can infer that if rule $t \rightarrow s$ is generalized in all systems $F(x,t) \neq \varnothing$ generated by any object x, then it is generalized in all systems $F(y,t)$ generated by all objects $y \neq x$ such that $F(y,t) \neq \varnothing$. Proposition 5.1.3 is an immediate consequence of this conclusion and Proposition 5.1.1. □

Proof of Proposition 5.1.4

Let x be an object having full complete descriptor in $\mathcal{S}^{o}$ and $x \in \|t\|$ in $\mathcal{S}^{o}$. Let $F(x,t)$ be a set of all completions of $\mathcal{S}$ in which $x \in \|t\|$. Let $G(x,t)$ be a set of all completions of $\mathcal{S}^{o}$. Since $x \in \|t\|$ in $\mathcal{S}^{o}$ then $G(x,t) \neq \varnothing$ and $G(x,t) \subseteq F(x,t) \neq \varnothing$. Additionally, we assume that rule $t{\rightarrow}s$ is generalized in $\mathcal{S}^{o}$, i.e. $t{\rightarrow}s$ is generalized in all completions from $G(x,t)$. Let $\mathcal{S}'$ be an arbitrary completion of $\mathcal{S}$ such that $\mathcal{S}' \in F(x,t) \setminus G(x,t)$. There is a completion $\mathcal{S}''$ in $G(x,t)$ such that $\mathcal{S}''$ differs from $\mathcal{S}'$ only for object x. However, $\|t\|'=\|t\|''$ and $\|s\|$ is the same in all completions of $\mathcal{S}$, so $(\|t\| \subseteq \|s\|)''$ implies $(\|t\| \subseteq \|s\|)'$. Hence, rule $t{\rightarrow}s$ which is generalized in $\mathcal{S}''$ is also generalized in $\mathcal{S}'$. Since our choice of $\mathcal{S}'$ was arbitrary we may conclude that if rule $t{\rightarrow}s$ is generalized in all systems $G(x,t)$ (i.e. if rule $t{\rightarrow}s$ is generalized in $\mathcal{S}^{o}$), then it is also generalized in all systems $F(x,t)$. Additionally, since we chose arbitrarily $\mathcal{S}^{o}$ and x, we can infer that if rule $t{\rightarrow}s$ is generalized in $\mathcal{S}^{o}$, then it is generalized in all systems $F(x,t)$ and $F(x,t) \neq \varnothing$. Proposition 5.1.4 is an immediate consequence of this conclusion and Proposition 5.1.3. □

Proof of Proposition 5.1.5

Property 4.1.2 tells us that the decision part of an optimal generalized rule r supported by object x, $x \in \mathcal{O}$, in a complete system is equal to $(d,w_1) \vee (d,w_2) \vee ... \vee (d,w_n)$, where $\{w_1,w_2,...,w_n\} = \partial_{AT}(x)$ in that system. If we remove any of (d,w_i), from $(d,w_1) \vee (d,w_2) \vee ... \vee (d,w_n)$ then rule r will not be generalized any more. Thus, we may infer that the decision part of an optimal generalized rule in an incomplete system $\mathcal{S}^{o}$ will be determined by $\partial_{AT}(x)$ in a completion $\mathcal{S}'$ of $\mathcal{S}^{o}$ such that $\partial_{AT}'(x)$ is a superset of all other generalized decision of x in other completions of $\mathcal{S}^{o}$ (otherwise rule r would not be generalized in completion $\mathcal{S}'$). Now it is sufficient to find a completion satisfying this condition.

Let $\mathcal{S}^{x}$ be a completion of $\mathcal{S}^{o}$ such that all null values occurring in $\mathcal{S}^{o}$ are replaced in $\mathcal{S}^{x}$ with the respective attribute values occurring in the full descriptor of x. Let $\mathcal{S}''$ be an arbitrary completion of $\mathcal{S}^{o}$. According to Property 3.5 we have $I_{AT}{}^{x}(x) = S_{AT}{}^{o}(x)$ and according to Property 3.2 $I_{AT}''(x) \subseteq S_{AT}{}^{o}(x)$. Hence, $\partial_{AT}{}^{x}(x) = \partial_{AT}{}^{o}(x)$ and $\partial_{AT}''(x) \subseteq \partial_{AT}{}^{o}(x)$. This means that $\mathcal{S}^{x}$ is a completion of $\mathcal{S}^{o}$ such that $\partial_{AT}{}^{x}(x)$ is a superset of all other generalized decision of x in other completions of $\mathcal{S}^{o}$. Thus, $\partial_{AT}{}^{x}(x) = \partial_{AT}{}^{o}(x)$ determines the decision part of rule $t{\rightarrow}s$. □

Proof of Property 5.1.1

Let $t{\rightarrow}s$ be a certain rule supported by $x \in \mathcal{O}$ in $\mathcal{S}^{o}$. Since object x supports a certain rule $t{\rightarrow}s$ in $\mathcal{S}^{o}$ then x supports $t{\rightarrow}s$ in every completion $\mathcal{S}'$ of $\mathcal{S}^{o}$. This means that $I_{AT}'(x) \subseteq I_{\{d\}}(x)$ (by Property 4.1.1) for each completion $\mathcal{S}'$ of $\mathcal{S}^{o}$ or equivalently $\bigcup\limits_{\mathcal{S}' \in COMP(\mathcal{S})} I'_{A}(x) \subseteq I_{\{d\}}(x)$. Additionally, according to Property 3.3, we have $S_{AT}{}^{o}(x) = \bigcup\limits_{\mathcal{S}' \in COMP(\mathcal{S})} I'_{AT}(x)$. Hence, $S_{AT}{}^{o}(x) \subseteq I_{\{d\}}(x)$. □

An Interactive Constraint-Based System for Selective Attention in Visual Search

R. Cucchiara[2], E. Lamma[1], P. Mello[2], M. Milano[1]

[1] DEIS, Univ. Bologna, Viale Risorgimento 2, 40136 Bologna, Italy
email: {mmilano, elamma}@deis.unibo.it Tel: +39 51 6443086, Fax:+39 51 6443073
[2] Dip. Ingegneria, Univ. Ferrara, Via Saragat, 41100 Ferrara, Italy
email: {pmello, rcucchiara}@ing.unife.it

Abstract. In this paper, we face the problem of model-based object recognition in a scene. Computer vision techniques usually separate the extraction of visual information from the scene from the reasoning on the symbolic data. We propose to interactively intertwine the two parts: the reasoning task on visual information is based on constraint satisfaction techniques. Objects are modeled by means of constraints and constraint propagation recognizes an object in the scene. To this purpose, we extend the classical Constraint Satisfaction Problem (CSP) approach which is not suitable for coping with undefined information. We thus propose an *Interactive CSP* model for reasoning on partially defined data, generating new constraints which can be used to guide the search and to incrementally process newly acquired knowledge.

Keywords: Computer Vision, Constraint Satisfaction.

1 Introduction

Visual search is a very popular paradigm of computer vision, relying the location and identification of a known target in a visual scene. In accordance with recent researches on attention in psychology, the process is mainly bottom-up in the earlier stages, named *pre-attentive* processes, which have the aim at extracting several basic visual features, and generating feature maps [1]. From feature maps, object features (or suitable grouping of features) are matched to target models in order to provide the correct visual search. This final process is obviously model-driven and can be carried out in many different ways according to the techniques used for describing the knowledge encoded in the model.

Since the whole visual process should deal with enormous quantities of data extracted by images, in contrast with the limited processing capabilities of the visual system, attention is a powerful mechanism endowed in the human visual system for gathering computation only in semantically significant information subsets. In particular, selective attention in psychology is the paradigm of guiding the visual process in the search of known target object on the basis of a target model. Similar concepts of *focus of attention* and attentive visual tasks are introduced also in computer vision in order to provide an efficient goal-directed visual process. [1].

This paper proposes an integrated paradigm for visual search, which exploits model-based vision techniques and concepts of selective attention for target location and identification. The paradigm is based on an original *Interactive Constraint Satisfaction Model.*

Constraint Satisfaction systems provide simple but powerful framework for solving a variety of Artificial Intelligence (AI) problems. A survey on these techniques can be found in [10]. Constraint Satisfaction Problems (CSP, for short in the following) are defined on a finite set of variables each ranging on a finite domain (numerical or symbolic) and a set of constraints. A solution to a CSP is an assignment of values to variables which satisfies the constraints.

Constraints are an expressive tool for describing visual objects in terms of visual primitives and relations between them. We propose to model visual objects in terms of CSP whose variables represent parts of the object or its suitable visual features and constraints represent spatial relations among them. Visual search is carried out by solving the CSP: the localization of an object in the scene is provided by a solution of the CSP.

The main drawback of classical CSP if used as a general purpose tool for visual search is that variable domains have to be completely defined before the constraint propagation process starts. This leads to a functional separation between the perceptive stage for computing the entire set of visual primitives present in the scene, and the further decision process guided by constraints. As a consequence, many, often very complex, visual tasks must be performed for computing useless information. Efficiency drawbacks arise especially if low-level visual primitives are used (e.g. lines, curves, corners or junctions) since their number is normally very high in images.

Therefore, we define an *Interactive Constraint Satisfaction* model which is able to guide the feature extraction by means of constraints, and request information only when needed by interaction with the vision system. Moreover it can incrementally process new information without restarting a constraint propagation process from scratch each time new information is available.

The paper is organized as follows: in section 2 we recall some ideas on CSPs and propagation algorithms. In section 3, we describe how to model visual objects in terms of CSPs and present some limitation of the classical CSP approach. In section 4.1, we propose an interactive CSP model and explain how to use it for guiding visual knowledge acquisition. Related work is described in section 5. Discussion and future work conclude the paper.

2 Preliminaries on CSP

A CSP can be defined on a set of variables $X_1, X_2, \ldots, X_n$ ranging respectively on finite domains $D_1, D_2, \ldots, D_n$. A constraint $c(X_1, \ldots X_k)$ defines a subset of the cartesian product of $D_1, \ldots, D_k$, i.e., a set of configuration of assignments which can appear in a consistent solution (if it exists). A CSP can be represented by means of a *constraint network* where each node is a variable and arcs are constraints. A CSP can be solved by means of constraint propagation. Many consistency techniques (node, arc, path consistency etc.) have been proposed (see [10] for a survey) based on the active use of constraints during the search process.

We will refer in the paper to the *arc-consistency* algorithm. An arc in the CSP representing a binary constraint $c(X_i, X_j)$ is arc-consistent iff for each value in the domain D_i for variable X_i there exists at least one value in the domain D_j for variable X_j which is consistent with the constraint $c(X_i, X_j)$. A constraint network is arc-consistent iff each arc is arc-consistent. For example, consider the constraint $X < Y$ where[3] $X :: [1..10]$ and $Y :: [1..10]$. Arc-consistency removes value 1 from the domain of Y because there does not exists in the domain of X a value which is less than 1. In the same way, value 10 is deleted from the domain of X. Arc-consistency is not complete since an arc-consistent network can be unsatisfiable. However, arc-consistency is a good tradeoff between propagation and computational cost.

A solution to a CSP is an assignment of values to variables which is consistent with constraints. A solution can be found by intertwining an arc-consistency propagation algorithm with a *labeling* strategy which performs a guess on a variable value thus exploring the solution space.

3 Modeling visual objects through constraints

In a general approach to visual search, the model of the object should be reliable and general, in order to result possibly invariant to roto-translation in 3D space, to distance object-camera and other environment factors: thus, the object model cannot be limited to a matching of measured features to absolute values previously defined, but should be based on geometric and topologic relationships between features [8, 13]. Within this extent, objects can be modeled by means of constraints and recognized by means of constraint satisfaction. Each object we want to recognize can be represented by means of a constraint graph where each object part or characterizing primitive feature is modeled by a node (variable) of the corresponding CSP and spatial or shape relations among object parts can be represented by arcs (constraints).

Specific aspects of the single primitives may be modeled as unary constraints, such as the minimum length of an object part, its color, the planarity of a surface and so on, while geometric and topologic relationships between them can be represented by binary constraints (e.g., angular relationships between contours, lines, or surfaces, or spatial relationships, such as is *connected to*, *touch*, *is contained*).

Example 1. If we want to model a rectangle, as shown in figure 1, we can identify four nodes corresponding to the four edges composing the rectangle (numbered respectively X_1, X_2, X_3 and X_4) and we impose the following symmetric constraints:

$touch(X_1, X_2)$, $touch(X_2, X_3)$, $touch(X_3, X_4)$, $touch(X_4, X_1)$,

---

[3] The notation :: associates a domain to the corresponding variable.

$no\_touch(X_2, X_4)$, $no\_touch(X_1, X_3)$, $same\_lenght(X_2, X_4)$, $same\_lenght(X_1, X_3)$, $perpendicular(X_1, X_2)$, $perpendicular(X_2, X_3)$, $perpendicular(X_3, X_4)$, $perpendicular(X_4, X_1)$, $parallel(X_2, X_4)$, $parallel(X_1, X_3)$.

Some of these constraints are redundant. This redundancy is useful when constraints are propagated by means of an incomplete algorithm such as for example arc-consistency.

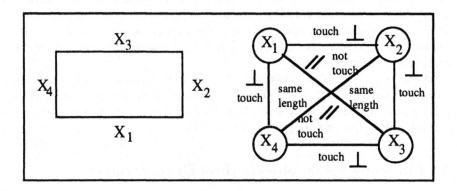

Fig. 1. Constraint-based model of a rectangle

Suppose the vision system provides all the information about the segments in the scene. Therefore, each variable ranges on a domain containing all the segments. We can perform a straightforward but inefficient backtracking algorithm in order to find a solution. Since we model objects by means of constraints, we can exploit constraint propagation in order to find a solution or at least prune the search space. Therefore, we intertwine an arc-consistency process that removes combinations of assignments which cannot appear in any consistent solution, i.e., which cannot form a rectangle, and a labeling strategy that assigns to each variable a value (a possible segment). If a solution is found, we have identified a rectangle in the scene, i.e., values for variables (four segments) which are consistent with constraints. Note that in this specific example there are symmetries in the problem, i.e., some permutation of the variables maps a solution onto another solution, [11].

The problem with this kind of representation concerns the fact that we have to acquire from the vision system all the information about segments in the scene before processing them. The segment extraction is a computationally expensive task if compared with the constraint satisfaction process. In this paper we propose an alternative approach that intertwines the vision feature acquisition with the constraint satisfaction process thus reducing the feature extraction computational cost.

4 Image Recognition through Interactive CSP

4.1 Interactive CSP

A standard CSP approach needs all the information and the knowledge on the problem at the beginning of the computation. Then it propagates constraints by removing assignments which cannot appear in any consistent solution. The interaction with a low level system and the consequent propagation requires a partial acquisition of knowledge which lasts during all the computation process. Therefore, we have to change the CSP model we use and allow the propagation algorithm to work on partially defined domains.

To this purpose, we define an *Interactive CSP* (*ICSP*) model which has to:

- cope with incomplete domain definition. Therefore, domains can be partially defined in the sense that some domain elements can be already at disposal for propagation, while other domain elements have to be acquired from the vision system in the future;
- request information when needed, thus interacting with the vision system and performing a knowledge acquisition on demand;
- guide feature extraction by means of constraints. Therefore, the CSP subsystem should generate at each computational step new constraints on the basis of already acquired knowledge;
- incrementally process new information without restarting a constraint propagation process from scratch each time new information is available.

On the basis of these requirements, we define the Interactive CSP model as follows:

Definition 1. An interactive CSP (ICSP) is defined on a finite set of variables $\{X_1, X_2, \ldots, X_n\}$ each ranging on a partially defined domain $\{D_1, D_2, \ldots, D_n\}$ where each $D_i = [Def_i \cup UnDef_i]$. Def_i represents the defined part, while $UnDef_i$ is a domain variable itself representing information which is not yet available. Both Def_i and $Undef_i$ can possibly be empty[4]. Also, for each i, $Def_i \cap Undef_i = \emptyset$. A constraint among variables defines a possibly partially defined subset of the cartesian product of variable domains.

A solution to the ICSP is, as in the case of the standard CSP, an assignments of values to variables which is consistent with constraints.

On the contrary, the constraint propagation is quite different from the standard case. Consider for the sake of clarity only binary constraints $c(X_i, X_j)$. In the more general case, in order to propagate the constraint $c(X_i, X_j)$ we have to propagate four kinds of constraints and collect the propagation results[5].

$$c(Def_i, Def_j) \cup c(Def_i, Undef_j) \cup c(UnDef_i, Def_j) \cup c(UnDef_i, UnDef_j)$$

---

[4] When both are empty an inconsistency arises.

[5] We refer, with an abuse of notation, to domains instead of variables. However, the meaning is straightforward.

The propagation between definite domains is the usual constraint propagation, while propagation on undefined domains produces new constraints. These new constraints can be used in order to guide the search and to incrementally process newly acquired knowledge from the vision system.

In the next section, we will show an example in the field of visual recognition of the use of the interactive constraint satisfaction model.

4.2 An Example on Visual Recognition

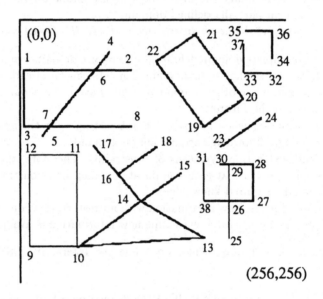

Fig. 2. Example of a visual scene

In this section, we consider an example for the recognition of (one or more) rectangles in the scene depicted in figure 2. It is an image of 256 x 256 binary valued pixel, obtained after an edge detection of a grey-level image. The rectangle model is given by means of symmetric constraints presented in section 3. We first describe how to solve the problem by means of a classical CSP approach. Then, we present an alternative solution based on the ICSP model proposed in section 4.1.

In a classical CSP model all the segments should be collected as a first step. All the segments in figure 2 can be collected in the following form: they have an associated name, the coordinates (x1, y1, x2, y2 for the two starting and ending points), the length and the angle with the horizontal axes. These characteristics are sufficient for checking the constraints on the rectangle.

In the following we will refer to a segment from a to b as (a, b). The 41 segments of figure 2 represent the domain of variables X_1, X_2, X_3 and X_4 (corresponding to the four edges of the rectangle in figure 1). Let us consider the result of an arc-consistency propagation method (see section 2). We will refer to one domain propagation only since, in this case, all constraints are symmetric. Therefore, the four variables have always the same domain during the computation and before the labeling step.

Consider segment $(1,3)$. This segment is not consistent with constraints since there does not exists in other domains a segment with the same length. Therefore, it is deleted from domain D_1. The segment $(3,8)$ is, instead, consistent since it satisfies all the constraints. Note that both constraints $touch(X_1, X_2)$ and $touch(X_4, X_1)$ are satisfied by the same segment $((1,2))$ in the domain of X_2 and X_4. The arc-consistency is an iterative algorithm which stops when the network has reached the *quiescence*, i.e., no more propagation is possible. The result of the arc-consistency consists in the following segment in variable domains: $(9, 10)$, $(10, 11)$, $(11, 12)$, $(9, 12)$, $(26, 29)$, $(27, 28)$, $(28, 29)$, $(26, 27)$, $(33, 37)$, $(33, 32)$, $(34, 36)$, $(35, 36)$, $(26, 25)$.

Note that not every segment in the remaining domain is part of a consistent rectangle since arc-consistency is not a complete propagation algorithm. In particular, segments $(33, 37)$, $(33, 32)$, $(34, 36)$, $(35, 36)$, $(26, 25)$ which are not part of any rectangle could be deleted by a more powerful constraint propagation algorithm (e.g., path-consistency). Now a labeling step starts instantiating variable X_1 to $(9, 10)$. Constraint propagation now reduces domains of other variables to $X_2 :: [(9, 12), (10, 11)]$, $X_4 :: [(9, 12), (10, 11)]$ and X_3 can be instantiated to $(12, 11)$.

Consider now the approach based on the ICSP. The main advantage is that we do not need to have all the information about segments in order to start the propagation. Therefore, we suppose that at the beginning all variable domains are undefined, i.e., the defined part is empty. Now we can ask the visual system to give us the first information about segments. This first query to the visual system can be guided in some sense if we have unary constraints on variables (e.g., find the red segments) or by means of heuristics on the problem (e.g., first we acquire segments belonging to closed figures).

In this case, we avoid this guide since we do not have neither unary constraints nor heuristics. Therefore, the system gives us the first segment for X_1, say $(1, 3)$. Therefore, the domain of X_1 is $D_1 = [(1, 3), X_1']$ where X_1' represents the undefined part of X_1. Now, since all other variables have only an undefined domain, $(1, 3)$ is consistent with constraints. However, new constraints are generated in order to check the consistency of future acquired information and to guide the search. In particular, all the constraints containing variable X_1 are "splitted" into two parts: the first results from the propagation of the undefined part of all other variables with the defined part of X_1:

$touch((1,3), X_2)$, $touch(X_4, (1,3))$, $no\_touch((1,3), X_3)$, $same\_length((1,3), X_3)$, $perpendicular((1,3), X_2)$, $perpendicular(X_4, (1,3))$, $parallel((1,3), X_3)$

the second is derived from the propagation of the undefined part of all other variables with the undefined part of X_1:

$touch(X_1', X_2)$, $touch(X_4, X_1')$, $no\_touch(X_1', X_3)$, $same\_length(X_1', X_3)$, $perpendicular(X_1', X_2)$, $perpendicular(X_4, X_1')$, $parallel(X_1', X_3)$.

The first part is used in order to guide the knowledge acquisition from the visual system. In fact, for variable X_2, we are looking for a segment that touches and is perpendicular to $(1, 3)$. Such a segment exists and is for example $(1, 2)$. Variable X_2 ranges now on the following domain: $D_2 = [(1, 2), X_2']$. Again all the constraints involving X_2 can be "splitted" by constraint propagation in two parts. Note that constraints involving the defined part of X_1 and the defined part of X_2 are solved and can be ruled out. The new constraints derived from the defined part of X_2 and the undefined part of other variables are the following:

$touch((1, 2), X_3)$, $no\_touch((1, 2), X_4)$, $same\_length((1, 2), X_4)$,
$perpendicular((1, 2), X_3)$, $parallel((1, 2), X_4)$.

Constraints involving only definite parts are:

$touch(X_1', X_2')$, $touch(X_2', X_3)$, $no\_touch(X_2', X_4)$, $same\_length(X_2', X_4)$,
$perpendicular(X_1', X_2')$, $perpendicular(X_2', X_3)$, $parallel(X_2', X_4)$.

Now, knowledge acquisition for X_3 can be driven from constraints and fails since there does not exists any segment for X_3 which touches and is perpendicular to $(1, 2)$ and does not touch and is parallel to $(1, 3)$.

A successful computation can be started when the system finds one of the segments belonging to a rectangle, such as for example $(12, 9)$. The computation can be guided by means of constraints and the attention focuses only on the part of the scene containing the rectangle.

The main advantage of the approach is that in the average case, we acquire from the visual system a fewer number of segments since we guide the extraction by means of constraints. Note also that this kind of acquisition corresponds to an a-priori application of consistency techniques since the visual system provides only consistent values with constraints. Moreover, the applied consistency is stronger than arc-consistency since we query the visual system with different constraints on many variables. For example, in the above mentioned example, when we query the system for the acquisition of a value for X_3, we ask for a segment which both touches and is perpendicular to $(1, 2)$ and does not touch and is parallel to $(1, 3)$. This corresponds to a path-consistency since the consistency check involves three variables simultaneously.

5   Related Work

Several works are related to visual search based on symbolic models for describing the *a-priori* knowledge on the target.

Different paradigms are used for target representation and model matching, in part with neural network techniques, in part with symbolic methods, such as rules [7], interpretation tree search [5] or constraint satisfaction networks [6]. This last work is closer to our work for the use of constraint satisfaction. However, it is quite different since in [6] the authors suggest the use of constraints on real number and a bound propagation, while we use finite domain constraints and an enumerative propagation.

While most of these proposals concern only the final recognition task, new trends address definition of a model which embraces all the visual process, from the visual primitive selection to the final recognition. A good example is offered by Bolle et al. proposal, [4]: it describes the use of an integrated constraint network, which is used in all levels of the visual process, starting from the extraction of local features, and assembly feature computation up to hypothesis verification. In [4] the constraint network is a hierarchical network where each node is a feature hypothesis and links between nodes represent (with continue-valued weights) conflict or agreement between hypotheses. The final scene identification is furnished by propagating the constraint network into a single globally consistent interpretation. Our approach shares with that proposal the model of constraint network, and, consequently, some advantages: a constraint network approach avoids some drawbacks due to a strictly sequential control strategy, such as that given by a tree-search; moreover it provides a unified paradigm which is general-purpose, potentially extendable also to complex visual task. However, our ICPS-based approach exhibits some differences: first, the object model is encoded in the constraint graph, where arcs represent constraints, symbolically coded in terms of geometric, topologic or metric relationships between features, represented by nodes. Second, while the control strategy in [4] is mainly data-driven, our control strategy is strongly goal-directed and model-based, in accordance with the goal of visual search. The ICSP model, whenever faces with an incompletely defined domain, i.e., whenever needs more information from the visual systems, sends a feedback to the visual system which is able to extract other visual primitives on-demand. This approach results particularly satisfactory in case of visual search conceived as a self-terminating process, in which the search, guided by the CSP, stops as soon as the target is located. In this case performing visual tasks only on-demand, and thus focusing attention only in part of the scene, makes it possible to limit the search only in those part of images where potential target may be located.

Since the constraint-based framework is general-purpose, and does not lead to specify a fixed set of visual routines, it is potentially able to cope with complex visual tasks, in accordance with the capabilities of the low-level visual operators. Therefore it can be exploited for real applications of visual search, especially in case of inspection and manipulation of object in robotic environment, whenever target object can be described by means of visual features and their relations. Clearly, constraints can be partially relaxed in order to cope with noisy and cluttered images so as to include suitable tolerances in the measured visual features. Actually this model could be not adequate for recognizing occluded objects, since occlusion may cause the lack of perception of some features. Conversely, this limitation can be useful if searching one graspable object in images containing a number of them, where the requirement of being graspable needs that the whole set of modeled features must be seen.

6 Conclusions and Future Work

We have presented a model for interactive CSP which can be applied to object recognition and identification in a visual system. Objects are modeled by means of constraints and constraint propagation is the general-purpose tool for detecting a solution. The propagation reduces the search space by pruning those assignments which cannot appear in any consistent solution, and is used to guide the search by generating new constraints at each step. Therefore, information can be acquired on-demand from the visual system thus reducing computational expensive visual tasks.

Future work concerns the extension of the system to other 2D and 3D features, such as curves, surfaces and their relationships. The second step concerns the definition of a hierarchical architecture where constraint propagation is performed at different levels of abstraction, thus considering spatial relations between objects.

7 Acknowledgments

This work has been partially supported by CNR, Committee 12 on Information Technology (Project SCI*SIA).

References

1. V. Cantoni, "Attentional Engagement in vision system", in Artificial Vision Academic Press 1997.
2. P. N. Rao, D.H.Ballard, "An active vision architecture based on iconic representations", Artificial Intelligence, 78, pp. 461-505, 1995.
3. J. Lemaire, "Use of a priori descriptions in a high level language and management of the uncertainty in a scene recognition system", Proc. of ICPR96, vol.1, pp 560-564, IEEE Press, 1996.
4. M. Bolle, A. Califano, R. Kjeldsen "A complete and extendible approach to visual recognition", IEEE Trans. on PAMI, 14, 5, 1992.
5. P.Gaston, T. Lozano Peres, "Tactile recognition and localization using object models: the case of polyhedra on a plane", IEEE Trans. on PAMI, 6, 3, 257-265, 1984.
6. I.D. Reid, J. M. Brady, "Recognition of object classes from range data" Artificial Intelligence, 78, pp. 289-365, 1995.
7. P.Pellegretti, F. Roli, S. Serpico, G. Vernazza, "Supervised learning of descriptions for image recognition purposes", IEEE Trans. on PAMI, vol. 16 n. 1, pp. 92-98 (1994).
8. B. Draper, A. Hanson, E.Riseman "Knowledge-directed vision: control, learning and integration", Proc. of IEEE, vol. 84, n. 11, pp. 1625-1681, 1996.
9. R. Baicsy "Active Perception", Proc. of IEEE, vol. 76 n. 8, pp. 996-1005, 1988.
10. V. Kumar, "Algorithms for Constraint-Satisfaction Problems: A Survey", in *AI Magazine*, vol. 13, 1992, pp. 32-44.
11. J.F. Puget, "On the Satisfiability of Symmetrical Constrained Satisfaction Problems", Tech. Report ILOG Headquarters, 1993.
12. P.Van Hentenryck, "Constraint Satisfaction in Logic Programming", MIT Press, 1989.
13. D. Vernon, "Machine Vision: Automated Visual Inspection and Robot Vision" Prentice Hall, 1991.

Abstraction of Representation for Interoperation

David A. Maluf and Gio Wiederhold

Department of Computer Science
Stanford University
Stanford, CA 94305

Abstract. When combining data from distinct sources, there is a need to share meta-data and other knowledge about various source domains. Due to semantic inconsistencies, problems arise when combining knowledge across domains and the knowledge is simply merged. Also, knowledge that is irrelevant to the task of interoperation will be included, making the result unnecessarily complex. An *algebra* over ontologies has been proposed to support disciplined manipulation of domain knowledge resources. However, if one tries to interoperate directly with the knowledge bases, semantic problems arise due to heterogeneity of representations. This heterogeneity problem can be eliminated by using an *intermediate model* that controls the knowledge translation from a source knowledge base. The intermediate model we have developed is based on the concept of *abstract* knowledge representation and has two components: a modeling behavior which separates the knowledge from its implementation, and a performative behavior which establishes context abstraction rules over the knowledge.

1 Introduction

Many designers, developers, and users realize that information in private and public databases, as on the Internet, provides increasing opportunities to enhance productivity. Understanding the content of the available information requires the use of knowledge-based systems. However, effective use of knowledge to support problem solving also requires use of multiple knowledge sources. Simply taking the union of multiple knowledge sources derived from distinct domains creates several problems. One problem is due to the differing representations of knowledge obtained from different sources. Furthermore, the terms used to represent knowledge from diverse domains will have semantic inconsistencies. These inconsistencies occur because the knowledge-content will differ both in semantics and in compositional granularity. A union of multiple knowledge bases includes irrelevant knowledge and the result will be large, and disproportionally costly to process. For interoperation, the focus should be on the intersection of the knowledge, since intersection will define the required articulations. The term *articulation* refers to the rules that are used for knowledge which provides links across domains [6]. To solve these problems, many heuristic approaches have been proposed and implemented [21]. However, these approaches have limited applicability and make it difficult to establish and maintain large knowledge bases.

We extend and generalize the identification of the articulation to a set of manipulations, such as selecting, combining, extending, specializing, and modifying components from diverse common and domain-specific ontologies. To deal with most of these issues, an algebra over ontologies has been proposed in [26] which is intended to support disciplined manipulation of knowledge resources. The representation of vocabularies and their structure is termed an *ontology* whereas the operations that combine and partition structures in a sound and well-behaved manner are termed an *ontology algebra*. The basic algebra consists of three operations, namely intersection, union and difference.

The objective of an ontology algebra is to provide the capability for interrogating many knowledge resources, which are largely semantically disjoint, but where *articulations* have been established that enable knowledge interoperability. The emergent need to define articulations between knowledge resources has been demonstrated and described in [15][27].

Although this paper does not describe the ontology algebra itself, it is motivated by it and presents two aspects, namely converting knowledge representations and partitioning.

Representation: When designing an ontology algebra for diverse ontologies and knowledge-based systems, it is important to understand the constraints that an underlying knowledge representation poses on the knowledge content. By overcoming these constraints, one can expect an increase in knowledge-sharing capabilities [21]. An early example of this approach revolves around porting ontologies from one knowledge representation language into multiple ones as done by *Ontolingua* [14]. Ontolingua is a mechanism for translating from a standard syntax into multiple-representation systems. However, directly translating entire ontologies to multiple representations leads to irrelevant knowledge, semantic inconsistencies, and disproportionally large knowledge-bases. On the other hand, imposing the ontology algebra as part of the multiple representation systems is not feasible. This can be simply demonstrated by observing that most industry standards only support declarative interfaces such as the CORBA Interface Repository [23]. In other words, the algebra requires its own workspace. Our hypothesis is that an ontology algebra to combine and partition knowledge is feasible when provided with an *intermediate* model. The intermediate model is declarative following modern concepts [20]. It establishes a rule-based environment to sustain operations envisaged by the ontology algebra.

Partitioning: In this paper, we also addresse the problem of how to abstract and entail encoded knowledge within contexts. We will formulate the foundation of knowledge abstraction as a basic problem in propositional calculus. Knowledge abstraction as used in this paper composes declarative ontological compositions, keeping their context through formal predication. These transformations will establish the *articulation axioms* for the ontology algebra. The articulation axioms represent the partitioning of a knowledge model and are maintained within an intermediate model.

The intermediate model produces the environment needed to provide users and system developers with the ability to manipulate knowledge bases and domain-specific ontologies. These manipulations will support the interoperation of descriptions of topics of interest when using the knowledge base. These descriptions are reusable by multiple applications that need to access to diverse knowledge and data sources. The descriptive formalism makes the intermediate model maintainable in rapidly changing environments.

2 Knowledge Representations and Interoperation

The development of an *intermediate* model reported in this paper is motivated by the interoperability among existing knowledge-representation formalisms. The series of knowledge representation formalisms and frameworks starting with KL-One [4] and currently culminating in systems like Classic [3] and LOOM [19] provide powerful tools and knowledge expressiveness. However, they were not intended to interoperate. How much has to be added in their infrastructure and reasoning capability to achieve knowledge interoperability is still unclear. There have been two recent efforts that open up possibilities for meaningful knowledge interoperation: the development of context logic [18] and knowledge interfaces for sharing [21]. The advance in context logic is the notion of translating encoded knowledge relative to its context. This is the approach taken in the reengineering of Cyc [17] where micro-theories confine the contextual differences [15]. Advances in knowledge sharing revolve around translating knowledge bases from one representation formalism to multiple ones. However, the problem of translating knowledge bases across different representations is difficult to implement when translation is to occur in all directions.

Most knowledge representation formalisms are bound to specialized methods of inference but a few have formats that focused on reuse rather than inferencing [16][13]. These formats provide a common denominator and support a solution for interoperability. However, manipulation of source context preserves deeper knowledge, and with the planned ontology algebra, should bring about better knowledge scalability. Abstraction in context is essential since different ontology compositions have different context granularities and hence cannot interoperate directly.

In this work we support knowledge abstraction between different knowledge compositions. We define performative rules to maintain the abstraction as part of the knowledge partitioning. The process of abstraction emphasizes the importance of separating knowledge from its implementation. The notion of separation was initially suggested in the scheme of the Agent Communication Language [12]. We realize that there is much leverage in overlaying the knowledge sources with the needed partitioning because that is where the context is best understood.

2.1 The Intermediate Knowledge Model

The intermediate model scales and partitions knowledge bases and domain ontologies given some application objectives. An intermediate model presents two facets that can operate concurrently or independently, namely a *modeling* behavior and a *performative* behavior. The modeling behavior translates the knowledge into axioms and prescribes the notion of *Articulation Axioms*. The performatives maintain the articulation axioms within contexts where *Articulation Rules* can be established. These articulation rules are used for linking knowledge across domains. To permit information from distinct sources to be accessed and operated upon, a consensus should be reached on the rules to formulate the articulation axioms. In our approach these rules are declared independently from the domain translation intermediate models. Figure 1 illustrates the two functionalities of an intermediate model: (i), the translation of knowledge from a knowledge base or knowledge repository (models A and B) to its corresponding intermediate model, and (ii), the articulation rules which are maintained through a separate intermediate model (Model C).

Most knowledge-based systems maintain knowledge models by interacting the knowledge acquisition, knowledge representation, and inference components. Similar knowledge models have a tendency to be formal in their design and involve much implicit knowledge. Correspondingly, we believe that by restricting these representations to a declarative form, we can achieve less formality, thus more abstraction. To this end, the intermediate model considers a non-formal knowledge modeling approach which has been adapted by many KBMS developments [14][29], but that we keep within a propositional calculus-capable *interlingua*. The implementation of the intermediate model employs the first-order logic Knowledge Interchange Format (KIF) [11] as its interlingua and postulates the hypothesis that the composed knowledge is independent of its representation.

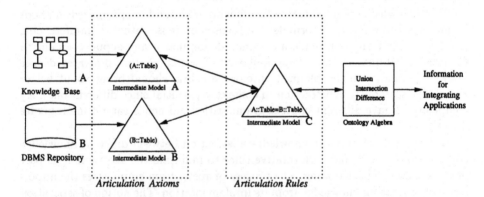

Fig. 1. When interoperation among multiple knowledge-based systems, Articulation axioms establish the partitioning of knowledge. On the other hand, articulation rules establish the links between domains and drive an ontology algebra.

Vocabulary and Relations The translation operates on a vocabulary which describes the constituents of the ontologies and contains the ontological commitments that are required for the interoperation. The vocabulary is explicitly required, since the vocabulary defines the domain knowledge. By "vocabulary" in this paper we mean an expression or a term that belongs to a dictionary. Translating the vocabulary independently of the specific base information, i.e. the current relationships among the constants, assures complete semantic coverage of the vocabulary. The vocabulary alone has no structure and is only defined by the names. This temporary decomposition of an ontology enables the agglomeration of the terms into one set of common vocabularies. A property in the implementation of the intermediate model is it performs a unification on the terms involved. "Unification" in this paper is used broadly to handle simple ontological composition details such as grammar, spelling, and word composition.

The relationships among the constants refer to the relations among the vocabulary. The relation constants establish the ground or atomic meanings within a knowledge base and apply to the predicates that maintain the relationships between the vocabulary [9].

2.2 Terminology, Definitions and Assumptions

Axioms: Predicates are the basic construct of declarative knowledge. For example, one can express the fact that a **Book** is above the **Table** by taking a relation symbol such as **Above** and defining a predicate **Above(x,y)**. Hence, for the object symbols **Book** and **Table** we can declare the proposition **Above(Book, Table)** [10]. Often, a predicate contains semantic conjunctions or disjunctions within its syntax [7] to express complex relation constructs.

To deal with the inadequacy of semantics and to conform to the syntactics of predicate logic, structured predicates are separated into simpler atomic propositions. If for example a knowledge base considers the proposition **Above(Book *and* Pen,Table)**, the intermediate model finds it is equivalent to the conjunction of the following two predicates **Above(Book, Table)** ∧ **Above(Pen, Table)**. In general, predicates are atomic and do not contain semantic operators. □

Abstraction: Abstraction is equivalent to the production of simpler approximations of domain knowledge bases driven by approximation rules. When knowledge bases involve a large vocabulary, abstraction is also the process of aggregating the knowledge model to another involving smaller vocabulary and fewer constants. Often the aggregation is performed by translating the declarative knowledge predicates and grouping the vocabulary and constants into arbitrary well-formed formulas. In [1], one can distinguish the different types of abstraction such as qualitative abstraction, quantitative abstraction, terminological abstraction and temporal abstraction. In our work, however, the notion of abstraction focuses on manipulating knowledge within context.

The principal idea in abstraction is that a knowledge base includes a number of levels of abstractions. For example, in the case of applying the relation symbol **Above** to the objects **Book** and **Table** and a third argument denoting a situation s, say {**Library, Office, Home**}. Abstraction in granularity is achieved when

the proposition **Above(Book,Table,s)** is translated into **Above(Book,Table)**.
□

Context: Context has been proposed as a means of defining the validity of a sentence relative to a situation. Formalizing contexts [18][15] develops the notion of context which allows predicate axioms for fixed situations to be "lifted" to more dynamic contexts where situations change. The context formalism is an extension to first-order logic in which sentences are valid within a context. To this end, we use the denotation of $ist(c; p)$ such that we have a formula of a proposition p which is true in a context c. For example given a context **Office**, one can write **ist(Office; Above(Book, Table))**. In this paper we drop **ist** and consider a concise and simple form as in the formulas **(c;p)**. From the previous example we may write the proposition **(Office; Above(Book,Table))**. In the implementation of the latter example, the intermediate model assumes a template pattern of the form **(AXIOM:00123 (CONTEXT Office) (RELATION Above) (OBJECT Book Table))**.

At this point it is worth noting a difference between the context logic formalism approach and the one in this paper which is that context logic defines a default coreference rule which states, that as a default, the meaning of a symbol does not change from one context to another. We consider that symbols never mean the same. The key in resolving ambiguity of meanings is in establishing and manipulating contexts. Formally we consider for every proposition p referring to a pair of objects x and y, then x is asserted as a possible context of the proposition p (*Modus ponens*) or

$$\forall x : \quad p(x, y) \Rightarrow (x; p(x, y)).$$

For instance, as one may consider the proposition **isa(Furniture,Table)**, the proposition may be reformulated and asserted as **(Furniture;isa(x,Table))** which reads **isa(x,Table)** in the context of **Furniture**. Note at this point that we assume there is no need for a proposition to refer to the object as an argument. The use of the variable **x** is to maintain the correct arity of the predicate **isa**. Similarly, the proposition **isa(Database,Table)** may be reformulated and asserted as **(Database;isa(x,Table))**. Hence **isa(x,Table)** has two contexts, namely **Furniture** and **Database**. □

Articulation Axioms: The idea of using context directly relates to the notion of abstraction in this paper. However manipulating context as an abstraction process presents another scope, namely *Articulation*. Articulations have two facets and are identified separately as *articulation axioms (AA)* and *articulation rules (AR)*. The articulation axioms are the axioms upon which these rules operate. In simple words, articulation axioms are the partitions which can be matched from one domain to another. The axioms are formulated within a domain or knowledge model whereas the rules are maintained separately from the domain [27]. □

3 Knowledge, Formulation and Rewriting

The previous sections defined a few requirements of an intermediate model. However, these requirements place no restrictions on the possible context entailment propositions can have. In this section, we explore the effect of the intermediate model first on the properties to model semantic distinctions with context.

In this section we also explore the implication of the intermediate model on translating database domain knowledge. We assume that the underlying knowledge has been translated from declarative languages which correctly conceptualized the domain knowledge as propositions. The intermediate model addresses several tasks in translating database domain knowledge, namely resolving implementation differences, interpretation and partial information.

1. *Resolving implementation differences:* As some of the work on designing databases focuses on designing data models, one can realize the different possibilities in the conceptual modeling considered in their design. For an interoperability problem such as in data integration process, one should focus on relating different data models, e.g., mapping the relational model to the object model which requires structural knowledge [25]. However, even if we consider only databases using the same data model, there are significant differences which make the task of relating the semantics of the data model difficult. These differences are due to their schema composition.

2. *Interpretation:* To permit the explicit knowledge as in the case of databases to interoperate with other sources, it is not sufficient to simply merge the information on the basis of the vocabulary. Simply matching vocabulary does not correspond to matching meanings. On the other hand, considering the ontologies of these domains would be a better tradeoff in the interoperation. For each of these domain schemas, their corresponding ontology is examined in parsing their vocabulary and the specification of their relationships. Interoperability can occur in a sound manner with propositions.

3. *Partial information:* Declarative knowledge can deal with handling incomplete information [10]. This problem in database interoperability is simply typified by the symptoms of most directed graphs which is their inability to handle partial information. For example there is no way to assert a proposition in a object hierarchy without a reference to a root object. The lack of reference in general is often found with systems that lack external schemas. Similar partial information populates most semistructured information systems, e.g., the World Wide Web.

3.1 Example: Interpreting Primitive Models

Primitive models are models that are specialized in their design. For example, one can consider a two-column tabulation as a specialized method in representing data in binary predicates. Another primitive model is the Entity Relationship (ER) model which is used in the conceptual phase of database design. Most primitive models are graphical languages although they have been expanded using an extension of the relational algebra [8][28] We will discuss their strengths and weaknesses in our setting.

We focus on the common construct in these specialized language, namely relationships. Various relationships may hold within primitive models, as taxonomic relationships, arbitrary relationships, hierarchical, cyclic, acyclic. However, the basic construct of relationships are their directed graph representation, namely labeled arcs and nodes.

One can interpret the directed graph by postulating each labeled arc with the corresponding objects into axioms. The term *interpretation* admits a formal definition in declarative knowledge and relates to a mapping process. For instance, in an object taxonomy, one may write isa(Object,Table) where Table is a subclass of Object. In a semantic network, one may write Above(Book, Table) where an arc Above relate Book to Table, etc. Formally, the declarative interpretation is taken as the implication of a performative pattern where a binary but simple proposition is formed from a relation r and terms x and y by combining them as $r(x, y)$. Figure 2.a illustrates a binary segment of a directed graph.

Context and Axioms Declarative knowledge is an excellent interlingua, however it does have its share of restrictions. In fact much of the work in declarative knowledge revolves around an assumption of one-term-one-meaning mapping. Our position is that we consider that symbols never mean the same in different contexts. This sets our approach apart from predicate logic [10] and context logic [15][5], We have two main reasons. First, when considering knowledge that has been composed using standard knowledge acquisition and concept modeling tools, one cannot expect that terms refer to the same context. For instance, Drug(Marijuana) can be administered in different contexts, namely Recreational and Medical. Secondly, when knowledge has been formulated simply as a union of multiple domains will result in a knowledge model where terms have multiple contexts and misinterpretations is likely.

Let us assume an example when a matching has occurred across domains. We consider the matching terms from two domains where specifically we focus on the resulting graph segments. The segments are "Table subclass-of Database", "Table subclass-of Furniture", "Furniture subclass-of Object" and finally "Table subclass-of Object". We formulate the corresponding binary interpretations which result in isa(Database, Table), isa(Furniture, Table), isa(Object, Furniture), and isa(Object, Table). Their corresponding implementation is shown in the following table.

VOCABULARY	RELATION CONSTANT	BINARY EXPRESSION
(OBJECT Table)	(RELATION isa)	(AXIOM:001 (nil) isa (Object Table))
(OBJECT Database)		(AXIOM:002 (nil) isa (Furniture Table))
(OBJECT Furniture)		(AXIOM:003 (nil) isa (Database Table))
(OBJECT Object)		(AXIOM:004 (nil) isa (Object Furniture))

While we can identify the vocabulary (column 1) from the relations (column 2), we can assert a set of propositions (Column 3) using the interpretation of binary relations. What is of interest in this example is that within the same model the object `Table` is asserted within two independent contexts, namely `Database` and `Furniture`. In formulating an interpretation as a binary relation, we have implicitly assumed a conjunction between the propositions in the intermediate model. However the truth of the implicit assumption is not correct. For instance, considering `isa(Furniture, Table)` ∧ `isa(Database, Table)` is syntactically but not semantically correct. To assert `isa(Furniture, Table)` and `isa(Database, Table)` concurrently we should consider a disjunction `isa(Furniture, Table)` ∨ `isa(Database, Table)`. On the other hand, a conjunction is semantically correct between `isa(Object,Table)`∧`isa(Object, Furniture)`. The difficulty in interpreting primitive models in declarative knowledge propositions, is the inability to manage the assertion of a symbol concurrently in different contexts. This simply reflects the default coreference rule which states that as default the meaning of a symbol does not change from one context to another [15]. The coreference rule is not valid when dealing with multiple domains.

Rewriting Binary Axioms The problem encountered in the previous section is not as serious as it appears. The solution is simple and lies in investigating the meaning of the directions in the graph which are considered as the argument index in the proposition.

To remedy the problem, we interpret the meaning of directions as the inheritance of *context* as for instance `Table` has `Database` as context in `isa(Database, Table)`. Once the contexts have been established on the previous example is applied, we realize that all implicit conjunctions semantically hold. The interpretation above is rewritten and asserted as `(Database; isa(x, Table))` and reads "Table subclass-of Database in context Database".

Rewriting *N*-ary Axioms The approach taken in Section 3.1, also taken by the database community, provides interpretation that formulates only binary relations. However, binary interpretations do no expose the full meaning of the terms used in the propositions. The binary interpretation of `isa(Object, Table)` does not characterize its meaning. If we reconsider the example stated in Section 3.1, `isa(Object, Table)` is true in two domain-independent contexts: `Furniture` and `Database`. `Table` unveils its context only when stated with an additional interpretation that contains `Table`, namely `isa(Furniture, Table)` or `isa(Database, Table)`.

In our approach, we generalize the problem and define the class of *N*-ary expression to include an ordering of N binary propositions. To this end, the ordering of binary expressions is performed in two possible directions, namely *spanning*, and *specializing*. *Spanning context* is the formulation of the axioms which depict the contexts a proposition has. Schematically, one can illustrate spanning context as multiple inheritance in directed graphs (Figure 2.b). On the other hand, *specializing* is the formulation of the axioms which depict for a context the propositions it relates to. For example, given the context `Object` for the proposition (Object; isa(x, Furniture)), one can specialize the context Object with (Object; isa(x, Table)). Schematically, one can illustrate a specialization as branching in directed graphs (Figure 2.c).

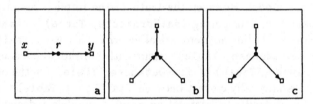

Fig. 2. Directed Graphs: Case a Shows a binary relation between two objects. Case b shows an N-ary relation where multiple objects refer to one object. Case c shows an alternative N-ary relation where one object refers to multiple ones. Note that a relation r is equivalent to the concept of arcs and in this paper this model is rather a generalization of directed graphs.

In principle, N-ary expressions are expressions which are not by default binary enforced by certain specialized primitive models. We consider the merging of binary expressions into N-ary expressions over the contexts. Hence, an N-ary expression is the logical attachment of N binary expressions where $N > 1$. For instance we may attach (Furniture; isa(Furniture, Table)) and (Object; isa(Object, Table)) into a single axiom or (Object, Furniture; isa(x, Table)) which reads that Table has two contexts: Object and Furniture. In the implementation of the intermediate model, N-ary expressions are composed by rules. The rules that formulates these N-ary expressions must be maintained separately from the domain knowledge. Illustrated graphically as in Figure 2, N-ary expressions are constructs and contain much knowledge about where different tracings and connectivities diverge. The covariancy is the N-ary set serving as articulation axioms to a contravariant set of binary expressions. This criterion strengthens the meaning of partitioning with N-ary expressions. Hence the output of implementation of N-ary expressions of the example stated in Section 3.1 extends to:

```
NARY EXPRESSION OF TYPE SPANNING

(AXIOM:005 (Object Database) isa (Table))
(AXIOM:006 (Object Furniture) isa (Table))
```

```
NARY EXPRESSION OF TYPE SPECIALIZING

(AXIOM:007 (Object) isa (Table Furniture))
```

For the added values considered by being dynamically formulated, N-ary expressions serve numerous basic roles in knowledge rewriting, as they can provide simple articulation axioms and yet afford the partitioning of a knowledge model.

3.2 Axiom Formulation and Rewriting

Our interest is in expressing axioms in the framework of propositional calculus. This interest is based on a combination of two features of the intermediate model.

First the knowledge needed can be expressed in a form more or less independent of the uses to which the knowledge might be part of. Second the reasoning performed by the partioning process involves basic but simple logical operations on these propositions.

In the implementation of the intermediate model, we specify the proposition rewriting within first-order logic and use the formalism to constrain the propositions in terms of their context. A context can be thought of as a set of terms labeling a set of propositions. Intuitively, we assume a context production rule which states that the meaning of a proposition admits the context defined by the symbols stated within the proposition. For example, the proposition **Above(Book, Table)** has as possible contexts **Book** and **Table**. Although the definition of the context production rule is not very suggestive, it is not the case when considered within the framework of propositional calculus and context logic. In general, we consider the formulas as propositions of the form

$$(c_1, ..., c_M; p_1, ..., p_N) \tag{1}$$

which are to be taken that the propositions $p_1, ..., p_N$ are true in the contexts $c_1, ..., c_M$. For example, if we consider the proposition **(Office, Book; Above(x, Table))**, then we know that predicates **Above(x, Table)** is true in the context of **Office** and **Book**. The aim of reformulation context is not to use deduction as the computational framework, but rather to integrate axioms into optimal articulation axioms when the interoperation objectives are clear.

One can get concerned with the amount of possible propositions that can be calculated from Equation 1. We simplify the problem of focusing only on the articulation needed for interoperation. Since automated inferences are potentially capable of processing the symbolic propositions, the need for rules about how to process the axioms becomes essential. Although there are no general rules in establishing the rewriting of the propositions, the intermediate model supports the two performative rules: *spanning context* and *specializing*. Both reduce the scope of the interoperation.

1. *Spanning Context:* by providing a proposition with context such as considering the conjunction of the proposition (**Database; isa(x, Table)**) to (**Object; isa(x, Table)**) from the example stated in Section 3.1 and having (**Database, Object; isa(x, Table)**). Formally we have
   $(c_1; p) \wedge (c_2; p) \Leftrightarrow (c_1, c_2; p)$
2. *Specializing:* by providing a context with propositions such as providing the proposition (**Object; isa(x, Furniture)**) to the proposition (**Object; isa(x, Table)**) and having (**Object; isa(x, Furniture), isa(x, Table)**). Formally we have
   $(c; p_1) \wedge (c; p_2) \Leftrightarrow (c; p_1, p_2)$

Since we deal with propositions, the rules of first order and context logic apply. When the number of propositions is zero ($N = 0$ in Equation 1), then the vocabulary has its own context. For instance we have the list {**Office, Table, Book**}.

Another important possibility when rewriting the axioms is that propositions are always asserted within other axioms in a recursive form. Henceforth given the general denotation of Equation 1, we have recursively $(c_i; (c_j; ., .), .)$ and subsequently (Object; (Furniture; isa(x,Table))).

In general, the achievement in recursively rewriting the context and propositions deals directly with the critical and difficult step in context abstraction and is also a contribution of this paper. Although the problem of interoperating with recursive definitions is difficult to achieve with minimal inferencing, rewriting the context recursively has two advantages. (i) it maintains the connectivity of the knowledge and (ii) it provides one way to control the context abstraction. The latter is achieved by asserting one context for each axiom. The current implementation does not support recursive definition.

Another potential interest in recursive rewriting is that it converges to the Object Extended Model (OEM) formalism which has been widely used, namely as the interlingua for The Stanford-IBM Manager of Multiple Information Sources (TSIMMIS) [30]. OEM is a self describing object model with nested identity. Every object in OEM consist of an *identifier* and a *value*. The value is either atomic, or set of objects, denoted as set of {*label, id, value*}. We refer to the *label* and *value* as context and axioms respectively.

It should be noted that one of the innovations of the intermediate model is that the proposed articulation axioms need not be static. The partitioning of the domain knowledge is dynamic where articulation axioms are asserted and retracted independently of the underlying knowledge base.

3.3 Status

The intermediate model is currently written in the 'C' Language Integrated Production System 6.0 (CLIPS) [22], a widely-available and easily portable expert system shell. Since user interface functions and data access functions are separated out into other components, the intermediate model consist mainly of rules. The wrapper that translates KIF to CLIPS facts is based on the standard KIF 'C' parser developed at Stanford University (http://logic.stanford.edu/software/kif) [11].

Figure 3 illustrates the current state of the interface of the intermediate model based on Hardy [24]. Hardy is a programmable diagramming tool. We use Hardy to assist the intermediate model in managing knowledge across domains. For the HP-Product domain (white background), a pattern matcher proposed three axioms which found in the Computer-Device domain (white background). The HP-Product and the Computer-Device domain ontologies are available from the Ontolingua server (http://www-ksl-SVC.stanford.edu:5915).

4 Conclusion

This paper presents an approach that uses context formalism in the development of standard knowledge representations and knowledge sharing and plays a role in knowledge interoperability. The context approach provides a powerful tool to define the validity of knowledge relative to a situation. This paper address the problem of how to abstract and entail encoded knowledge within contexts.

We describe an environment to interface underlying knowledge resources to the outside world. The objectives set in this paper are to establish the intermediate model needed to sustain knowledge interoperability and to produce the needed environment. Hence, users and system developers can translate knowledge bases that provide comprehensive but simple coverage of topics of interest, knowledge usability and reusability by different applications and knowledge maintenance in rapidly changing environments. The intermediate model can bring about a shift from designing knowledge base to the manipulation, enhancement, and maintenance of domain ontologies. The main objective of the intermediate model will be to handle an ontology algebra that combines and partitions structures in a sound and well-behaved manner.

The current research is a complementary approach to the current knowledge-based systems that support disciplined manipulation of knowledge resources.

5 Acknowledgments

The authors would like to thanks Oscar Firschein who carefully reviewed the draft of the document and contributed to its revised content. Input from John McCarthy at Stanford University has been particularly helpful.

References

1. M. Aben, "KADS-II CommonKADS Inferences"; Technical Report M2-UVA-041-1.0, University of Amsterdam, 1993.
2. A. Borgida, "From type systems to knowledge representation: natural semantics specification for describing logics"; Intelligent and Cooperative Information Systems, 1(1):93-126, 1992.
3. A. Borgida, R. Brachman, D. McGuinness, L. Resnick, "CLASSIC: A Structural Data Model for Objects"; SIGMOD Conference pages 58-67, 1989.
4. R. Brachman and J. Schmolze, "An Overview of the KL-ONE knowledge Representasion System"; Cognitive Science, 9(2):171-216, 1985.
5. S. Buvac and R. Fikes, "A Declarative Formalization of Knowledge Translation"; Knowledge Systems Laboratory, KSL-94-59, August 1994.
6. C. Collet, M. Huhns and W. Shen, "Resource Integration Using a Large Knowledge Base in Carnot"; IEEE Computer, 12(24), Dec. 1991.
7. K. Chang, H. Garca-Molina and A. Paepcke, "Boolean Query Mapping Across Heterogeneous Information Sources"; IEEE Transactions on Knowledge and Data Engineering, 8(4):515-521, Aug, 1996.
8. R. El-Masri and G. Wiederhold: "Data Model Integration Using the Structural Model"; Proceedings 1979 ACM SIGMOD Conference, pages 191-202.
9. J. L. Garfield (editor): "Modularity in Knowledge Representation and Natural Language Understanding"; MIT Press, 1987.
10. M. Genesereth and N. Nilsson, "Logical Foundations of Artificial Intelligence"; Morgan Kaufmann Publishers, Inc., Los Altos, CA, 1987.

11. M. Genesereth, "Knowledge Interchange Format"; Technical Report Logic-92-1, Stanford University, 1992.

12. M. Genesereth, N. Singh and M. Syed, "A Distributed and Anonymous Knowledge Sharing Approach to Software Interoperation"; Third International Conference on Information and Knowledge Management, 1994.

13. M. Gogolla, R. Herzig, S. Conrad, "Integrating the ER approach in an OO environment"; In Entity-relationship approach: Lecture notes in computer science. Springer-Verlag, Berlin; New York, 1994.

14. T. R. Gruber, "Ontolingua: A mechanism to support portable ontologies"; Technical Report, KSL-91-66, Knowledge System Laboratory, Stanford University, Stanford, CA.

15. R. V. Guha. "Context: A Formalization and Some applications"; Doctoral Dissertation, Stanford University, 1991.

16. B. L. Humphreys and D.A.B. Lindberg, "The Unified Medical Language Project: A Distributed Experiment in Improving Access to Biomedical Information"; MEDINFO 92, North-Holland, 1992, pages 1496-1500.

17. D. Lenat and R. Guha, "The Evolution of CycL, The Cyc Representation language"; Special Issue on Implemented Knowledge Representation System, Sigart, ACM, 2(3), pages 84-87, June 1991.

18. J. McCarthy, "Notes on Formalizing Context"; In proceedings of the Thirteenth International Joint Conference on Artificial Intelligence, 1993.

19. R. MacGregor and R. Bates, "The LOOM Knowledge Representation Language"; in Proceedings of the Knowledge-Based Systems Workshop, April 1987.

20. N. Singh, and M. Gisi, "Coordinating Distributed Objects with Declarative Interfaces"; in Coordination Languages and Models, Lecture Notes in Computer Science, 1061, Springer, 1996, pages 368-385.

21. R. Neches, R. Fikes, T. Finin, T. Gruber, R. Patill, T. Senator, and W. R. Swartout, "Enabling technology for knowledge sharing"; AI Magazine, 12(3):36-55, 1991.

22. G. Riley, "CLIPS: An Expert System Building Tool"; Proceedings of the Technology 2001 Conference, San Jose, CA, December 1991.

23. Sciore, Edward, Siegel, Michael, Rosenthal, Arnon, "Using semantic values to facilitate interoperability among heterogeneous information systems"; ACM Transactions on Database Systems, Vol.19, No. 2 pages 254-290, 1994.

24. J. Smart and R. Rae, "Hardy"; Technical Report Hardy User Guide, Artificial Intelligence Applications Institute, University of Edinburgh, 1995.

25. G. Wiederhold, T. Barsalou, B. S. Lee, N. Siambela and W. Sujansky, "Use of Relational Storage and a Semantic Model to Generate Objects: The PENGUIN Project"; Database '91: Merging Policy, Standards and Technology, The Armed Forces Communications and Electronics Association, Fairfax VA, June 1991, pages 503-515.

26. G. Wiederhold, "An Algebra for Ontology Composition"; Proceedings of 1994 Monterey Workshop on Formal Methods, U.S. Naval Postgraduate School, Monterey CA, pages 56-61, 1994.

27. G. Wiederhold, "Interoperation, Mediation, and Ontologies"; International Symposium on Fifth Generation Computer Systems (FGCSOB94), Workshop on Heterogeneous Cooperative Knowledge-Bases, Vol 3, pages 33-48, ICOT, Tokyo, Japan, 1994.

28. G. Wiederhold X. Qian, "Modeling Asynchrony in Distributed Databasesd"; Third IEEE Computer Society Data Engineering Conference, Los Angeles, Feb. 1987.

455

29. B. Wielinga, Walter, G.Schreiber, and H. Akkermans, "KADS-II expertise model definition document."; Technical Report M2-UVA-026-1.1, University of Amsterdam, 1993.

30. Y. Papakonstantinou, H. Garcia-Molina and J. Widom, "Object Exchange Across Heterogeneous Information Sources"; International Conference on Data Engineering, 1995.

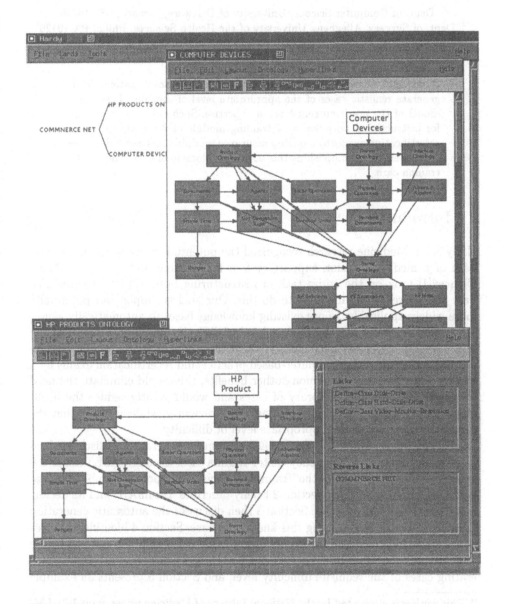

Fig. 3. The implementation of the intermediate model merged with Hardy, a programmable diagramming tool.

TraumaCASE: Exploiting the Knowledge Base of an Existing Decision Support System to Automatically Construct Medical Cases*

Sandra Carberry[1] and John R. Clarke M.D.[2]

[1] Dept. of Computer Science, University of Delaware, Newark, DE. 19716
[2] Dept. of Surgery, Allegheny University of the Health Sciences, Phila., PA 19129

Abstract. Our goal is to use existing knowledge bases to automatically generate realistic cases of the appropriate level of difficulty based on a model of the user's current level of expertise. Such cases could be used for instructional purposes by a training module or for computer-based recertification exams by a quality assurance module. This paper describes our system for accomplishing this task in the domain of emergency center trauma care.

1 Introduction

Early AI in Medicine research recognized the potential for using the knowledge base of a medical decision support system for training and testing students. Clancey[1] took on the entire task of restructuring both MYCIN's knowledge base and its reasoning methods to do this. Our goal is simpler but potentially more widely applicable: to use existing knowledge bases to automatically generate realistic cases of the appropriate level of difficulty based on a model of the user's level of expertise. Such cases could be used for instructional purposes by a training module or for computer-based practice and recertification exams by a quality assurance module. Among other benefits, this would eliminate the need to collect and pre-store a library of cases and would greatly reduce the likelihood that a selected case replicates one used previously, while ensuring that the generated cases are at the appropriate level of difficulty.

This paper describes TraumaCASE, a system for generating realistic medical cases in the domain of emergency center trauma care. TraumaCASE utilizes the extensive knowledge base of the TraumAID decision-support system[9]. The paper is organized as follows. Section 2 briefly describes TraumAID and its declarative knowledge base of rules. Section 3 then discusses the automatic generation of realistic medical cases using this knowledge base. Section 4 identifies features of the knowledge base and case generation methodology that correlate with case difficulty and describes how our system takes these features into account in generating cases of the requisite difficulty level, and Section 5 presents an example

* This work was supported by the National Library of Medicine under grant R01-LM-05764-01.

Tension_Pneumothorax(Side=S):-
- Needle_Aspiration_Chest_For_Pressure(Side=S, Result=Negative)

Tension_Pneumothorax(Side=S):-
X_Ray_Tension_Pneumothorax(Side=S, Result=Positive)

Fig. 1. Two of TraumAID's evidential rules

RO_Renal_Injury(Side=S):-
Wound(Wound-type=Gunshot, Wound-location=Abdom, Side=S)
Hematuria

Fig. 2. A TraumAID Goal-Setting Rule

---

of a case produced by our system. Section 6 describes how our system will be extended to incremental case generation that is typical of the cases presented in medical oral exams, and Section 7 discusses related work.

2 The TraumAID Knowledge Base

TraumAID[9] is a decision support system for addressing the initial definitive management of multiple trauma, currently restricted to penetrating thoraco-abdominal injuries. TraumAID's three part knowledge base is encoded declaratively and contains extensive medical knowledge related to trauma care. It consists of 1) evidential rules that derive further conclusions from existing evidence, 2) goal setting rules that post goals based on accumulated evidence, and 3) two sets of mapping rules that either map goals onto alternative procedures that can be used to satisfy the goal or map procedures onto an ordered set of actions for performing the procedure. For example, Figure 1 illustrates two TraumAID rules for drawing a conclusion of tension pneumothorax. The first indicates that the presence of a tension pneumothorax can be concluded from a non-negative needle aspiration of the chest for pressure[1] or from a positive finding of tension pneumothorax on a chest x-ray. Figure 2 illustrates one of TraumAID's goal-setting rules. It posts a goal of ruling out a renal injury when the patient has a gunshot wound in the abdomen and hematuria. Figure 3 illustrates three of TraumAID's mapping rules. The first two map goals to alternative procedures for achieving those goals, where the procedures are listed in order of preference. The last rule in Figure 3 is a TraumAID rule for mapping procedures onto an ordered set of goals and primitive actions comprising the procedure.

---

[1] A "-" preceding an antecedent in a rule indicates that the antecedent must be false and a "-%" indicates that it must be false or unknown.

Goal-Procedure Mapping Rules:

RO_Tension_Pneumothorax(Side=S):-
  Get_Needle_Aspiration_Chest_For_Pressure(Side=S)

RO_Pericardial_Tamponade:-
  Get_Ultrasound_Effusion
  Get_Needle_Aspiration_Pericardial_Sac
  Inspect_Pericardial_Sac
  Perform_Catastrophic_Chest_Wound_Procedure

Procedure-Action Mapping Rule:

Perform_Catastrophic_Chest_Wound_Procedure:-
  Endotracheal_Intubation
  Intravenous_Fluids
  Emergency_Tube_Thoracostomy(Side=Right)
  Emergency_Thoracotomy(Side=Left)

Fig. 3. Three TraumAID Mapping Rules

---

3   Automatic Case Generation

Our case generation system selects an intended overall diagnosis, such as a tension pneumothorax, and then generates a medical case consisting of a set of initial signs and symptoms, along with symptoms that can be elicited through appropriate bedside questions and results of appropriate diagnostic procedures and tests. For case generation, signs, symptoms, and test results can be seen as falling into three classes:

 - C1: those suggestive of the specified diagnosis
 - C2: those required for the specified diagnosis
 - C3: those typical of the specified diagnosis

Not only must a good case include symptoms and/or test results that lead the physician to conclude the specified diagnosis (category C2), but to be realistic it must also include features that suggest considering that diagnosis (category C1). For example, while a positive finding from a needle aspiration of the chest for pressure will produce a diagnosis of tension pneumothorax, a realistic case must also include symptoms such as a chest wound, shock, distended neck veins, and decreased breath sounds that would lead a physician to consider a tension pneumothorax and perform the needle aspiration. Thus a case generation system must identify an appropriate set of symptoms that are suggestive of the intended diagnosis. In addition, although there are many ways that a conclusion might be drawn, it is important that the case generally reflect a representative situation (category C3). For example, while one might conclude tension pneumothorax from either a positive needle aspiration of the chest for pressure or from an xray

RO_Tension_Pneumothorax(Side=S):-
    Likely_Tension_Pneumothorax(Side=S)

Likely_Tension_Pneumothorax(Side=S):-
    Wound(Location=Abdom, Side=S)
-   Distended_Abdomen
    Shock
    Distended_Neck_Veins
    Decreased_Breath_Sounds(Side=S)
-% Tension_Pneumothorax_Unlikely(Side=S)

Fig. 4. Two TraumAID Rules

---

showing a tension pneumothorax, typically physicians diagnose this condition by doing a needle aspiration of the chest; diagnosis of a tension pneumothorax by chest xray is done only through incidental finding — i.e., when an xray is done for other purposes. Thus a typical case should rely on the needle aspiration instead of the chest xray.

Our first problem was to identify how the information comprising categories C1 through C3 needed for case generation could be extracted from TraumAID's knowledge base. We found that we could identify alternative sets of findings that would suggest *considering* a particular diagnosis by starting with the TraumAID goal setting rules that post a goal of ruling out the intended diagnosis, such as the goal of ruling out a tension pneumothorax, and chain backward on the goal setting and evidential rules until we arrive at primitive elements (symptoms, findings, test results, etc.). For example, suppose that the system has selected tension pneumothorax as the intended diagnosis. The TraumAID rule for posting the goal of ruling out a tension pneumothorax, shown in Figure 4, has an antecedent of Likely_Tension_Pneumothorax. There are several alternative rules for concluding Likely_Tension_Pneumothorax, any of which can be selected by the system. One of these rules is shown in Figure 4. It contains the primitive elements of abdominal wound, distended abdomen, shock, distended neck veins, and decreased breath sounds, along with the non-primitive element Tension_Pneumothorax_Unlikely which precludes a collection of bedside questions if a definitive test has already yielded a negative result. The system enters into the case the symptoms and findings that satisfy the primitive elements. The -% setting on Tension_Pneumothorax_Unlikely indicates that this conclusion must be false or unknown. To satisfy this antecedent, we must chain on all rules that would conclude Tension_Pneumothorax_Unlikely and establish settings in the case to insure that every rule fails or does not fire.

Similarly, we found that we could identify alternative sets of findings that would warrant a particular diagnosis by starting with the TraumAid evidential rules that conclude the diagnosis and then chaining backward until we reach primitive elements. For example, if the intended diagnosis is Tension Pneumothorax, then the system could select either of the two rules shown in Figure 1; each of these rules contains a test result, and entering one of these test results into the case causes the case to warrant a conclusion of Tension Pneumothorax.

However, some methods of drawing a conclusion represent more typical cases than do others, and our system must be able to differentiate among these in constructing a case. We found that we could accomplish this by referring to TraumAID's mapping rules and its knowledge base of possible test results. Thus before selecting findings that would warrant a particular diagnosis, our system first uses the TraumAID goal-procedure and procedure-action mapping rules to identify actions that are typically performed and the test results that might be produced by those actions. So, for example, the goal-procedure mapping rule shown in Figure 3 for ruling out a tension pneumothorax specifies getting a needle aspiration of the chest for pressure[2], and this procedure consists of the action of performing the needle aspiration. Our system then accesses the knowledge base of possible results to find that this action can produce a positive, negative, or uncertain finding of air under pressure in the pleural space, represented in TraumAID by the following proposition: Needle_Aspiration_Chest_For_Pressure(Side=S, Result=?). Thus although chaining from the evidential rules will indicate that tension pneumothorax can be concluded from either a finding of tension pneumothorax on a chest xray or a non-negative finding from a needle aspiration of the chest for pressure, we can identify the needle aspiration test result as a more typical part of a tension pneumothorax case.

Our system, TraumaCASE, thus first selects an intended diagnosis, extracts the TraumAID goal-setting rules that post a goal of investigating (called *ruling out* in the medical literature) this diagnosis, and chains backward on the TraumAID evidential rules to identify symptoms and findings that would lead the physician to *consider* this diagnosis. TraumaCASE then extracts the TraumAID goal-procedure mapping rule that specifies how to go about ruling out the intended diagnosis, selects an appropriate procedure from among those given in the mapping rule, and chains on TraumAID's mapping rules to identify the actions comprising the procedure and the test results that might be produced by those actions. Finally, TraumaCASE extracts the TraumAID rule whose conclusion is the intended diagnosis and chains backwards on the TraumAID evidential rules to identify symptoms, findings, and test results that warrant the diagnosis being made. Since the system will only pursue an inference chain if the test results encountered during chaining are possible results of actions that have already been entered into the case, TraumaCASE's prior selection of an appropriate procedure and its constituent actions restricts the generated case to test results typically obtained in the given situation and thus prevents the system from generating an unrealistic case. As the system explores a path, it keeps track of the features already entered into the case and backtracks if a particular selection of rules would result in inconsistent features.

---

[2] Recall that diagnosis of a tension pneumothorax by chest xray is done only through an incidental finding.

4   Generating Cases of Different Levels of Difficulty

We utilized the expert knowledge of a trauma surgeon (J. R. Clarke) involved in the training of medical students to identify features of clinical cases that make them more complex or that require greater expertise. These features, discussed below, include not only the degree of surgical skill required but also whether the case involves multiple diagnoses, whether pursuing appropriate therapeutic procedures can reveal a more serious problem, the amount of inferencing required in managing the case, and whether the usual methods for diagnosis and treatment are available.

To generate cases requiring a low level of expertise, TraumaCASE can limit itself to common isolated problems that any third year medical student should be capable of handling. We have augmented the TraumAID knowledge base with a list of such low-level diagnoses (referred to as Level-1 cases). The case becomes more difficult if it includes two unrelated problems of different urgency with which the physician must deal. For example, TraumaCASE can select a diagnosis resulting from a chest injury and a diagnosis resulting from an abdominal injury, with the first diagnosis having a priority related to circulation and the second having a priority related to contamination, and construct a case containing independent problems. Such cases require that the user not only diagnose both independent problems but also that he or she be able to address their different priorities; these will be referred to as Level-2 cases.

For some diagnoses, such as a simple hemothorax, if the user pursues appropriate treatment and attends to the appropriate follow-up, the user will find that the problem is actually a more serious version of the original diagnosis. Such cases, which we will refer to as Level-3 cases, require greater expertise since they require attention to followup procedures and consideration of their findings.

More difficult cases can be generated by selecting from among diagnoses that are less common but which a surgical resident would be expected to handle. We will refer to these as Level-4 cases; however, if the diagnosis is suggested by some other previously diagnosed problem, then the case is part of Level-5, as discussed in the next paragraph.

One significant factor that appears to correlate with the difficulty of a case is the number of additional diagnoses that must be considered. For example, one TraumAID rule concludes that a pericardial tamponade should be investigated if the patient has a tension pneumothorax along with continued neck vein distension (i.e., neck vein distension after a needle aspiration of the chest for pressure). If the case being generated has an intended diagnosis of tension pneumothorax, we can either choose additional settings that block such rules from firing or we can choose settings that should lead the physician to consider the additional problem. Moreover, if the patient is determined to have a pericardial tamponade, then consideration of further diagnoses may be warranted. Since the TraumAID rules specify the requisite conditions both for posting a goal of considering a particular diagnosis and for concluding that the problem is present in the patient, they can be used to establish features of the generated case that control the amount of inferencing required to handle the case. The greater the amount of inferencing required, the more difficult the case becomes. Cases that require extended inferencing comprise Level-5 in our system. Level-5 cases differ significantly from Level-3 cases; in Level-3 cases, the appropriate followup actions performed in treating the original diagnosis will produce findings indicating the more serious version of the problem, whereas in Level-5 cases the original diagnosis along with other symptoms suggest consideration of a different problem that must be confirmed by further tests and inferencing.

Within each level, cases vary in difficulty depending on whether the usual methods of diagnosing and treating the case are applicable and whether they have the expected results. This is captured in TraumaCASE. When TraumaCASE is asked to generate a relatively difficult Level-i case, it can examine the TraumAID goal-procedure mapping rules and establish conditions that make the procedure of choice inappropriate or unavailable. For example, a peritoneal lavage is the procedure of choice for assessing the possibility of abdominal bleeding. However, it is contra-indicated when abdominal scarring is present (as would be suggested by the presence of a laparotomy scar); in such cases a CT scan should be performed instead. Alternatively, TraumaCASE can establish conditions indicating that a procedure did not work as expected. For example, it can have an xray following chest tube insertion indicate that the chest tube was not properly placed, forcing additional procedures. While the need to select an alternative procedure or attend to failure of a procedure does not radically change the level of difficulty of a generated case, it does affect its complexity with respect to other cases at that level.

5   Examples

TraumaCASE has been implemented in Common Lisp and runs on a Sun Sparckstation. This section works through the generation of a sample case.

Suppose that TraumaCASE is asked to produce a simple Level-5 case (all Level-5 cases are difficult, but some are more difficult than others), and it first selects an intended diagnosis of right tension pneumothorax. It must next select one of the rules whose conclusion is RO_Tension_Pneumothorax and chain backward on it to identify symptoms that should lead a physician to consider investigating a diagnosis of tension pneumothorax. There are many inference chains that could be followed, but the one selected by TraumaCASE results in the following features being entered into the case:

- Wound location is right chest
- Wound is not an open sucking chest wound
- Decreased breath sounds
- Shock
- Distended neck veins

TraumaCASE must now enter into the case appropriate actions for ruling out a tension pneumothorax. As before, it consults the TraumAID goal-procedure mapping rules. The goal-procedure mapping rule given in Figure 3 indicates that the appropriate procedure for investigating a tension pneumothorax is to get a needle aspiration of the chest for pressure, which consists of the single action of doing the needle aspiration. So it is entered into the case:

• Needle aspiration of right chest for pressure

At this point, TraumaCASE extracts the possible results of the needle aspiration from TraumAID's knowledge base. TraumaCASE must next enter into the case a set of appropriate findings and test results that would warrant a diagnosis of tension pneumothorax. TraumAID has two rules for drawing this conclusion and TraumaCASE must chain backward on one of them. However, if the system selects the rule containing an antecedent specifying a positive finding on a chest x-ray, the system will subsequently backtrack and try the other rule since a chest x-ray is not an action that has been entered into the case thus far. Thus in this instance, TraumaCASE will force generation of a case that relies on results from the procedure typically used to diagnose a tension pneumothorax. The selected rule results in the following test result being entered into the case:

• Positive needle aspiration test result on the right side

TraumaCASE must now enter appropriate actions for treating the right tension pneumothorax. Once again, it consults the mapping rules and enters the following actions into the case:

• Get a primary tube thoracostomy report
• Get a post primary chest tube xray

Since it was asked to produce a simple Level-5 case, TraumaCASE will allow inferencing to one further diagnosis; more difficult Level-5 cases could be generated by allowing further inferencing. TraumaCASE extracts those evidential rules from the TraumAID knowledge base that contain a positive finding of tension pneumothorax as one of their antecedents, and it chains forward on the TraumAID rules to identify other diagnoses that might be suggested. It selects one of these chains and attempts to establish a set of additional symptoms and findings that would suggest investigating the second diagnosis. For instance, in the example presented here, TraumaCASE selected a chain of rules that led to a goal of RO_Pericardial_Tamponade; the antecedents on this inference chain resulted in the following new findings being entered into the case (other symptoms and findings on the inference chain were already part of the generated case):

• Continued neck vein distension after needle aspiration

TraumaCASE must then select appropriate actions for investigating a pericardial tamponade. The TraumAID goal-procedure mapping rule for ruling out a pericardial tamponade (shown in Figure 3) contains four alternative procedures listed in order of preference. Since TraumaCASE was asked to generate a simple Level-5 case, it selects the most preferred procedure, namely getting an ultrasound for effusion, and enters its constituent action into the case:

- Ultrasound for Effusion

At this point, the system extracts the possible results of this diagnostic procedure from the TraumAID knowledge base. However, if TraumaCASE had been instructed to generate a more difficult Level-5 case, it might look for contraindications to the most preferred procedure; if contraindications were possible, it could establish them as part of the case and select a less preferred procedure. Next TraumaCASE selects from among the several TraumAID rules that warrant a conclusion of pericardial tamponade. As before, the system will backtrack if chaining leads to a test result that could not result from one of the actions that has been entered into the case. The system ultimately selects a set of findings that consist of an ultrasound for effusion test result along with many symptoms and findings that have already been entered into the case. Thus the only new entry at this point is

- Positive ultrasound for effusion test result

TraumaCASE then uses the TraumAID goal-procedure and procedure-action mapping rules to select an appropriate set of actions for treating the pericardial tamponade and enters them into the case, namely

- Get access to the heart
- Perform a heart repair

Since the system was asked to generate one of the simpler Level-5 cases (which are all relatively complex), further inferencing is blocked by setting the values of all other features to normal (negative).

6 Future Work

TraumaCASE is currently a stand-alone prototype system for case generation. We are currently developing an interface that will allow TraumaCASE to present a user with a stem of a case (such as a middle-aged male with a bullet wound in the right chest), respond to the user's questions (such as whether the patient has distended neck veins) and requests for actions (such as getting a chest xray), and access TraumaTIQ[6] to critique the user's handling of the case. In addition, TraumaCASE will eventually be extended to *incremental* automatic case generation in which only a stem is constructed initially and then further details are fleshed out as the user responds with bedside questions, orders for procedures and tests, etc. In this way, the case could be adjusted based on the user's degree of success in diagnosing the case thus far, with the case becoming more complex if the user is demonstrating expertise but becoming more straightforward if the user is having difficulty selecting appropriate steps. Such adjustment reflects standard practice in medical school oral exams, where the examining physician adjusts details of a case to elicit further reasoning by a student or to illustrate ramifications of a student's error.

7 Related Work

Although other researchers have investigated the generation of simulated patient cases, their knowledge bases, kinds of cases, or the focus of their work have been different. Most of these simulations, such as those described in [2, 3, 8], rely on knowledge bases that detail the manifestations associated with each disease along with their frequencies of occurrence; cases are generated by randomly selecting manifestations for inclusion in the case, with the manifestation's probability of inclusion determined by its frequency of occurrence. While these systems have produced good results, these methods of generation do not permit flexibility in generating cases of varying degrees of difficulty or facilitate incremental case generation. In contrast, we have been utilizing the knowledge base of an existing decision support system that contains rules for developing diagnostic and therapeutic plans for managing patient care, and we have been concerned with generating cases appropriate to different levels of expertise.

We recently became aware of work by Fontaine[5] that uses backward chaining on a knowledge base of rules as part of an "authoring module" for creating cases that will be presented to a student. However, the focus of their work was on assisting a human instructor in creating cases and assuring that the resultant case was consistent. Although their system has the ability to make random assignments of possible symptoms and test results, it cannot differentiate between normal and abnormal cases nor can it regulate the difficulty of the generated case. Thus it still must rely on a human instructor both to specify the desired disease or diagnosis captured by the case and to sift through all of the cases that might be generated and select those that are appropriate for the student.

Eliot and Woolf[4] developed a somewhat different approach to producing simulated cases. Their system works in the domain of cardiac resuscitation, and a simulation consists of a series of transitions between states of cardiac arrest or arrhythmias. While their system uses the probabilities of state transitions to guide the simulation, it also includes a mechanism that biases the system to enter states that provide an opportunity to teach high priority topics. However, the kind of case they produce differs from ours in that the generated case is a series of patient state transitions rather than a set of consistent symptoms, findings, actions, and test results for making a particular diagnosis.

Generating problems at the appropriate level of difficulty is also an issue for tutoring systems in non-medical domains. For example, Beck, Stern, and Woolf[1] use information from a student model to generate appropriate problems in a mathematics tutor. However, rather than devising a strategy for directly constructing good problems, they use a generate-and-test paradigm in which possible problems are randomly generated, each problem is evaluated with respect to the desired features (as indicated by the student model), and then the problem with the best evaluation is selected. Level of expertise also impacts the kinds of examples that should be used in text, as shown by the work of Mittal and Paris[7] in which they identified different features of examples in introductory texts versus advanced reference manuals.

8 Conclusion

This paper has presented TraumaCASE, a system for automatically generating medical cases of the appropriate level of difficulty by reasoning with the declarative knowledge base of an existing decision support system. By automatically generating tailored cases, our system exploits the knowledge already encoded in an existing knowledge base, eliminates the need to maintain a library of pre-stored cases, and can produce cases that are appropriate for the particular user and application. While our system is implemented in the domain of trauma care, we believe that our approach demonstrates the feasibility of automatically generating realistic cases of different levels of difficulty and that similar techniques can be applied to other decision support systems with declarative knowledge bases of rules. Our work suggests that automatic case generation may well be feasible. If so, it makes good on the promise that knowledge encoded in medical knowledge bases could be used for the training and testing of medical personnel. In the future, combining realistic case generation with realistic human figure animation may provide even more, in the form of "life-like" virtual casualties for the immersive VR training systems of the future.

References

1. Joseph Beck, Mia Stern, and Beverly Woolf. Using the Student Model to Control Problem Difficulty. In *Proc. of the Sixth International Conference on User Modeling*, pages 277–288, 1997.
2. Homer Chin and Gregory Cooper. Case-based Tutoring from a Medical Knowledge Base. *Computer Methods and Programs in Biomedicine*, 30:185–198, 1989.
3. Robert Cundick, Charles Turner, Michael Lincoln, James Buchanan, Curtis Anderson, Homer Warner, and Omar Bouhaddou. Iliad as a Patient Case Simulator to Teach Medical Problem Solving. In *Proc. of SCAMC*, pages 902–906, 1989.
4. Chris Eliot and Beverly Woolf. An Adaptive Student Centered Curriculum for an Intelligent Training System. *User Modeling and User-Adapted Interaction*, 5(1):67–86, 1995.
5. D. Fontaine, P. LeBeux, C. Riou, and C. Jacquelinet. An Intelligent Computer-Assisted Instruction System for Clinical Case Teaching. *Methods of Information in Medicine*, pages 433–445, 1994.
6. A. Gertner and B. L. Webber. A Bias Towards Relevance: Recognizing Plans Where Goal Minimization Fails. In *Proc. of the Thirteenth National Conference on Artificial Intelligence*, Portland, OR, 1996.
7. Vibhu Mittal and Cecile Paris. Generating natural language descriptions with examples: Differences between introductory and advanced texts. In *Proc. of the Eleventh National Conference on Artificial Intelligence*, pages 271–276, 1993.
8. R.C. Parker and R.A. Miller. Creation of Realistic Appearing Simulated Patient Cases Using Internist-1/QMR Knowledge Base and Interrelationship Properties of Manifestations. *Methods of Information in Medicine*, 28(4):346–351, 1989.
9. Bonnie L. Webber, Ron Rymon, and John R. Clarke. Flexible Support for Trauma Management Through Goal-Directed Reasoning and Planning. *Artificial Intelligence in Medicine*, 4:145–163, 1992.

An Intelligent System Dealing with Negative Information

Daniel Pacholczyk

LERIA, Université d'Angers, 2 Boulevard Lavoisier, F-49045 Angers Cedex 01

pacho@univ-angers.fr

Abstract: In this paper, we present an Intelligent System dealing with Linguistic Negation of Nuanced Properties. It is basically founded upon a Similarity Relation between Properties through their corresponding Fuzzy Sets. With the aid of an Interactive Choice Strategy, a User can explain more explicitly the intended meaning of the Negative Information. This Model improves the abilities in Knowledge Management in that premise or conclusion of a Rule can include Linguistic Negations.

1   Introduction

In this paper, we present an Intelligent System dealing with Affirmative or Negative Information within a Fuzzy Context. The Imprecise Information being generally evaluated in a Numerical way, our System is essentially based upon Zadeh's Fuzzy Set Theory [24]. The Model has been conceived in such a way that the User can deal with statements expressed in Natural Language, that is to say, referring to a Graduation Scale containing a finite number of Linguistic expressions. In many Domains a part of Knowledge is represented by facts, denoted as « x is A », and its Management is founded upon classical Rule, denoted as if « x is A » then « y is B ». So, their Representation can be handled with Fuzzy Sets associated with respective Properties. In previous papers [5, 6, 17] we have introduced Fuzzy Linguistic Operators f_α and Modifiers m_β allowing the User to express Knowledge having the following form « x is $f_\alpha \, m_\beta \, A$ ». Note that a Property, denoted as « $f_\alpha \, m_\beta \, A$ », which requires for its expression a list of *Nuances* (i.e. (f_α, m_β)), is called *Nuanced Property*. So, the User can introduce in his Knowledge Base an assertion like « Smith is *really very* small ». This point is briefly presented in Section 2. Indeed, he also wishes to include in a Knowledge Base a fact like « The house of Smith is *not* high » or a particular rule like if « Smith is *not* tall » then « Smith is invisible in a crowd ». More formally, we have to propose a formal Representation of « x is not A » and of « if « x is not A » then « y is B » ». Some linguists [12, 7, 14, 4, 11] have proposed methods generally dealing with precise Properties. In Section 4, we propose a Generalization of these Approaches to Negation within a Fuzzy Context. At this point, we can present linguistic Analysis of fact like « the number of buildings is *not* low ». This Negation implies the *Rejection* of « the number of buildings is low », and, a *Reference to another Nuanced Property* like « very high » in order to translate the previous Negation into the fact « the number of buildings is very high ». It can be noted that « very high » has a weak *Similarity* with « low ». Many authors have studied Similarity Relations conceived as a Reflexive, Symmetric but not Transitive Relation [23, 1, 26, 20, 15]. We have selected the « weakly transitive » Similarity Relation proposed in [15].

In this paper, we focus our attention on the Linguistic Negation of a Nuanced Property. More precisely, we complete the results obtained in the previous Model [17], and we improve it in order to deal with the previous facts or rules. In Section 3, we present the basic notions leading to the symbolic Concept of the θ_i *similarity of Fuzzy Sets*. Section 4 is devoted to the interpretation of *Linguistic Negation in a Fuzzy Context*. We generate a set of *ρ-plausible Linguistic Negations* in the domain. Then, we propose to the User a *Choice Strategy* of its interpretation of « x is not A ». In Section 5, we note that our interpretation leads to Properties intuitively connected with Negation in Common sense Reasoning. In Section 6, we present interpretation of some Rules containing Linguistic Negations.

2   The Representation of Affirmative Information [5, 6]

Let us suppose that our Knowledge Base is characterized by a finite number of concepts C_i. A set of Properties P_{ik} is associated with each C_i, whose Description Domain is denoted as D_i. The Properties P_{ik} are said to be the *basic Properties* connected with the concept C_i. As an example, basic Properties such as « thin », « big » and « enormous » can be associated with the particular « weight » concept. This Universe description can be connected with some concepts which can be found in linguistics [2, 3, 9, 10, 7, 12]. Indeed, our Concepts and their associated Properties stand for *semantic Categories* and *semantic Units*. A finite set of *Fuzzy Modifiers* m_α allows us to define *Nuanced Properties*, denoted as « $m_\alpha P_{ik}$ », whose membership L-R functions simply result from P_{ik} by using a translation and a contraction. We can select the following Modifiers set (*Cf.* Fig. 1): $M_7=\{$extremely little, very little, rather little, moderately (Ø), rather, very, extremely$\}$. In order to modify the Precision or Imprecision of each « $m_\alpha P_{ik}$ », we use a finite set of *Fuzzy Operators* f_α defining new *Nuanced Properties* « $f_\alpha m_\beta P_{ik}$ ». Their membership L-R functions simply result from the ones of « $m_\beta P_{ik}$ ». The following set F_6 gives us a possible choice of Fuzzy Operators (*Cf.* Fig. 2) : $F_6 = \{$vaguely, neighboring, more or less, moderately (Ø), really, exactly $\}$

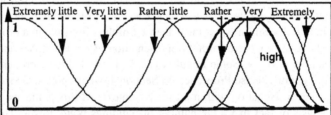

Fig. 1. A plausible set of Fuzzy Modifiers

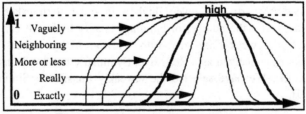

Fig. 2. A plausible set of Fuzzy Operators

In the following parts of this paper, we propose a *Generalization of the Linguistic Approach* [14, 4, 11, 7, 12] within a fuzzy context. Our Approach to « Agreement », being based upon the Similarity of Fuzzy Sets, we begin by making a presentation of the Concepts *of Nuanced Neighborhood* and *Similarity*.

3 Neighborhood and Similarity of Fuzzy Sets

Let us recall Lukasiewicz's Implication : $u \rightarrow v = 1$ if $u \leq v$ else $1-u+v$, where u and v belong to [0, 1]. The *neighborhood relation* $\mathcal{V}_\alpha$ is defined in [0, 1] as follows.

Definition 1. u and v are α-*neighboring*, denoted as $u\mathcal{V}_\alpha v$, iff Min $\{u \rightarrow v, v \rightarrow u\} \geq \alpha$.

Definition 2. Given that the *Fuzzy sets A and B are said to be α-neighboring*, and we denote this as $A \approx_\alpha B$, if and only if $\forall x, \mu_A(x) \, \mathcal{V}_\alpha \, \mu_B(x)$.

In order to define the Linguistic *Nuanced Similarity of Fuzzy Sets* we have introduced a totally ordered partition of [0, 1] : $\{I_1,..., I_7\}=[0]\cup]0, 0.25]\cup]0.25, 0.33]\cup]0.33, 0.67[\cup[0.67, 0.75[\cup[0.75, 1[\cup[1]$. We have defined a one to one correspondence between these intervals and the following totally ordered set of linguistic expressions LS $=\{\theta_1,...,\theta_7\}=\{$not at all, very little, rather little, moderately ($\varnothing$), rather, very, entirely$\}$. Now, we can put the definition of θ_i *similar Fuzzy Sets*.

Definition 3. Given $\alpha = $ Max $\{\delta \mid A \approx_\delta B\}$. Then, the Fuzzy Sets A and B are said to be θ_i *similar* if and only if α is such that $\alpha \in I_i$.

Example: In the next sections, we illustrate our argumentation by using the following example. The concept being « the number of intersection points », its associated properties will be « low », « average » and « high ». Then, a plausible interpretation of these properties is given in Figure 3.

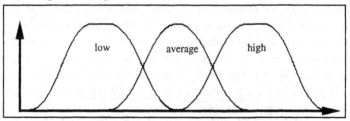

Fig. 3. A set of Basic Properties

4 A plausible Interpretation of Linguistic Negation

As already pointed out in [21], linguistically speaking, the *Affirmative Information* « x is A » implies some statements. Applying this result to Nuanced Properties, « x is A » may be interpreted as one of the following statements : « x is $\varnothing$A », « x is really A » or « x is more or less A ». As an example, the statement « x is low » corresponds to one of the following statements : « x is $\varnothing$ low », « x is really low » and « x is more or less low ». In the set of Fuzzy operators F_6, we can put : $G_1 = \{$more or less, $\varnothing$, really$\}$ and $G_2 = \{$vaguely, neighboring, exactly$\}$. So, linguistically speaking we put : « x is A »$\Leftrightarrow\{$« x is f_α A » with $f_\alpha \in G_1\}$.

Within a given field, the *Linguistic Negation* of « x is A », denoted as « x is not A », can receive the following meaning : the speaker (1), *rejects* all previous interpretations of « x is A », and (2), *refers in many cases* to a Nuanced Property P having a « weak agreement » with A, and, in such a way that « x is P » is equivalent to the statement « x is not A ». The main difficulty is then due to the fact that P is not explicitly given. In order to define a plausible Axiomatics of Linguistic Negation, we present here an *intuitive Approach to Linguistic Negation of Common Sense* within the Nuanced Property Context.

- Saying that « x is not A », the Speaker *rejects all the implicit meanings involved in « x is A »*. As an example, saying that « x is not low », we reject « x is $\varnothing$ low », « x is more or less low » and « x is really low ».

- Saying that « x is not A », *in many cases* the Speaker *refers globally* to a property P, based upon a *basic Property* defined in the same domain as A, « strongly » different from A (or « weakly » similar to A), and chosen in such a way that his Linguistic Negation means that « x is P ». Using the previous example, his implicit reference can be « average » or « high » or « extremely low ».

- Among the possible interpretations resulting from the previous global condition, the intended interpretation must be *weakly Neighboring in a local way*. More explicitly, when x satisfies « x is P » to a relatively high degree, then it satisfies « x is A » to a degree weakly neighboring from it, and conversely. Moreover, if need be this local condition of weak neighborhood must allow the User to define P as a Nuanced Property based upon A. As an exemple, he can refer to the property « really extremely low ».

- Let us suppose that more than one Property is defined in the Domain. If the *Fuzzy Property A is not marked*, then its Linguistic Negation refers to a Nuanced Property based *upon one precise basic Property P* defined in this domain. If the *Fuzzy Property A is marked*, then its Linguistic Negation is a Nuanced Property constructed upon *at least one basic Property P* (different from A) defined in this domain. In both cases, P is « weakly » similar to A. As an example (*Cf.* Fig. 4), « x is not thin » refers to « big » or « enormous ». Finally, the Fuzzy Property being *neither marked nor not marked*, then the speaker refers in many cases *to all the basic Properties* defined in the domain. As an example (*Cf.* Fig. 3), if « low » satisfies this condition, then asserting that « x is not low », the User can refer to « high », « average », and also to « low ».

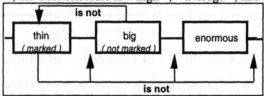

Fig. 4. The Properties associated with the concept« weight »

- In order to define the Nuanced Negation P, the Speaker uses a *Simplicity Rule*: its construction requires a small number of « Nuances ». So, he interprets « x is not low » as « x is rather high» rather than « x is more or less very little high ».

- In some particular cases, semblance of Negation is in fact an affirmative reference to a specific Nuance of a new basic Property denoted as « not-A » defined in the same domain. So, asserting « x is not A » the Speaker implicitly refers to « x is f_α not-A » with $f_\alpha \in G_1$. As an example, « Mary is not ugly » is equivalent to « Mary is $\varnothing$ not-ugly », « Mary is more or less not-ugly » or « Mary is really not-ugly ».

- In particular cases, a *Simplicity Combination Rule* is necessary to explicit Linguistic Negations. As an example, « x is not average » can be translated by « « x is very low » *or* « x is rather high » ».

In order to satisfy these intuitive properties associated with Linguistic Negation, we have defined a Concept of ρ-*plausible Negation* and constructed a *Choice Strategy of Linguistic Negation* among the all ρ-plausible solutions.

Definition 4. For a given Fuzzy Property A, let ρ be a real number such that $0.33 \geq \rho \geq 0$. If P, defined in the same domain as A, satisfies the conditions :

- $\forall f_\alpha \in G_1, P \neq f_\alpha A$ (The initial Rejection)
- P and A are θ_i-*similar* with $\theta_i <$ moderately (or $\varnothing$),   (A Global Condition)
- $\forall x, ((\mu_A(x)=\xi \geq 0.67 + \rho) \Rightarrow (\mu_P (x) \leq \xi - 0.67))$,   (A Local Condition)
- $\forall x, ((\mu_P(x)=\xi \geq 0.67 + \rho) \Rightarrow (\mu_A (x) \leq \xi - 0.67))$,   (A Local Condition)

then « x is P » is said to be a ρ-*plausible Linguistic Negation* of « x is A ».

Remark: For any Property A, the function of ρ is to increase (or not) the number of Nuanced Negations and to accept (or to reject) some Negations based upon A.

Example: Figure 5 gives us an illustration of this definition.

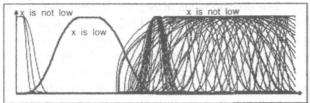

Fig. 5. 0.3-plausible Negations of « x is low »

It is obvious that the number of ρ-plausible Negations can be high (*Cf.* Fig. 5). This is due to the fact that our model accepts a great number of Operator and Modifier combinations. In order to allow the User to make his Choice from a limited number of solutions, we have constructed a *Strategy* essentially based upon a *Simplicity Rule* : he uses a very small number of terms to define a Nuanced Property. So, too often Nuanced ρ-plausible Solutions will be rejected. Firstly, we ask the User for Possibility or not of Negation based upon A. So, we can determinate a value of ρ satisfying this condition. If he does not make a Choice, we include Possibility of Negation based upon A by putting ρ=0.3. This being so, we define *sets of ρ-plausible solutions* by using the following Rules.

Simplicity Principle. Among the ρ-plausible solutions, we define **Neg (A)** the set of Nuanced Properties P based upon *at most two Nuances of a Basic Property.*

Increasing Similarity. For each Similarity degree θ_i with $\theta_i<$moderately, we define the subset S_i of **Neg (A)** whose elements P are θ_i *similar* to A.

Increasing Complexity. We constitute a partition of each S_i in subsets $S_{i P}$ where P is defined in the same Domain as A. The last subset will be $S_{i A}$. Moreover, each $S_{i P}$ is reorganized in such a way that its elements appear ordered to an increasing

Complexity extent, that is to say, the number of Nuances (different from ∅) required for their construction.

Example: The concept being « the number of intersection points », and the properties « low », « average » and « high » (*Cf.* Fig. 3), the Choice Strategy suggests the set **Neg (A)** of 0.3-plausible Linguistic Negations of « x is low » collected in Figure 6. The Choice is made among approximately 20 interpretations of « x is not low » when ρ= 0.3, and among 10 interpretations when ρ= 0.1. So, the User can choose, for any ρ, solutions as « high », « extremely high », « exactly average », « really average », and in addition, « extremely low », « really extremely low » and « exactly extremely low » for ρ= 0.3.

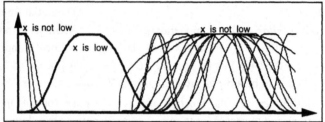

Fig. 6. Neg (A) the set of 0.3-plausible Linguistic Negations of « x is low »

Using the previous decomposition of **Neg(A)**, we can construct a *Choice Strategy* based upon the following Rules denoted **[LNi]**. This Strategy allows the User to explain his interpretation of a *particular occurrence* of the assertion « x is not A ». So, each occurrence of « x is not A » being explained with the aid of a particular Rule **[LNi]**, we associate the *mark* i to this particular occurrence. We have generalized the notion of the *marked or not marked* Property proposed in linguistics in such a way that we can manage the Fuzzy Property in a Knowledge Base. An *interactive Process* proposes to the User the following *ordered Rules*.

[LN0]: If the Negation is in fact the *logical Fuzzy Negation* denoted as ¬A, then :
- if ¬A exists as a Property defined in the same domain as A, we propose ¬A,
- if not, then for any P such that P⊂(¬A), we propose a Choice among the solutions of S_{iP}, i=1,2, ...

[LN1]: If the Negation *is based upon* A, we propose a Choice among the plausible solutions of S_{iA}, i=1,2, ...

[LN2]: If the Negation *is based upon only one* P≠A, we ask the Speaker for its basic Negation P. Then, his Choice has to be made among the plausible solutions of the previous sets S_{iP}, i=1,2, ...

[LN3]: If the Negation can be *based upon B* and C *different from A*, then the Speaker has to retain his interpretation among the solutions of S_{iB} and S_{iC} where i=1,2, ...

[LN4]: If the Negation can be based upon *one of all the basic properties*, his interpretation is one of the plausible solutions of S_{iP} where i=1,2, ... , for any P.

[LN5]: If the Negation *is in fact a New basic Property denoted as not-A*, we must ask the Speaker for its explicit meaning, and for its membership L-R function.

[LN6]: If the Negation is *simply the rejection* of « x is A », then any element of **Neg (A)** is a potential solution but he does not choose one of them.

[LN7]: If the Negation requires a *Combination based upon two basic Properties B and C,* we ask the Speaker for the adequate Linguistic Operator. So, we propose a Choice among the Simple Combination solutions of S_{1B} and S_{1C}, i=1, 2, ...

[LN8]: If no Choice is made with rules **[LN0]**, **[LN1]**, **[LN2]**, **[LN3]**, **[LN4]** or **[LN7]** then the System can propose a *Default Choice.*

Remark: Note that a lot of works on Linguistic Negation have already been achieved. Among these, the papers by Trillas, Lowen, Ovchinnokov and Esteva are not quoted here since very different points of view are considered. In the recent paper by Torra [22], one will find a closer point of view. Let us go into the comparison between our Approach and the one of Torra. Our Set **Neg(A)** of ρ-plausible Linguistic Negations and the Torra Negative Function Neg have been conceived within a Fuzzy Context in such a way that they lead to results consistent with those intuitively expected in the chosen Domain. In both cases, by using the Torra terminology, this is a function Neg from L to P(L) (and not to L), where L is a given set of Fuzzy Properties (or Linguistic Labels) and P(L) the set of parts of L. Moreover, in both Approaches the Torra Condition C2 holds, that is to say, if $x \in \text{Neg}(x')$ then $x' \in \text{Neg}(x)$. We can now point out some essential differences. Indeed, the Model of Torra concerns the sets of Linguistic Labels totally ordered. In our Approach, we refer to Fuzzy Properties for which an order relation is of no importance. This point is enforced by the fact that the Use of Fuzzy Operators in the combinations of the Basic Properties creates difficulties in making a total Order. Note that our Nuanced Properties being automatically defined, the User has not to define their L-R membership functions, he has only to supply the L-R membership functions of the Basic Properties associated with each Concept. So, the Context of our Analysis seems to be more general that the one of Torra. We can now examine the Torra Conditions C0 and C1. Linguists have pointed out that a Linguistic Negation can be simply the rejection of « x is A ». In other words, Neg(x) can be an empty Set. Moreover, the Basic Properties, associated with the concept « height », being « low », « medium » and « high », linguists accept that Neg(medium)={low, high} (in our System Nuanced Properties based upon these Basic Properties). In this case, Neg(x) is not a Convex Function. So, our analysis based upon Natural Language does not require the Torra Condition C0. We can also recall that a Linguistic Negation can induce a new Basic Property. So, the set of Linguistic Labels cannot be considered as completely defined, and it is not sure that the order can be preserved. By using the previous Basic Properties, The Linguistic Analysis accepts the following results : Neg(medium)={low, high} and Neg(low)={medium, high}. Then, if we add the following order :low<medium<high, it is obvious that the condition C1 fails in this case. Finally, it appears clearly that the Contexts of both Analyses are different, and that the Concept of Negation by Torra fulfils more restrictive conditions.

5 Common Sense Properties of the Linguistic Negation

The definitions of previous Operators, Modifiers and Linguistic Negation give us the following results.

Property 1. *The Fuzzy Operators and Modifiers have been defined in such a way that, for any property A :*

- A *and* m_α A *are at least* $\varnothing$ *similar iff* $m_\alpha \in$ {rather little, moderately, rather}.

- A *and* f_α A *are at least* $\varnothing$ *similar iff* $f_\alpha \in$ {more or less, moderately, really}.

Property 2. *Given* ρ *such that* $0.33 \geq \rho \geq 0$, *each* ρ-*plausible Linguistic Negation P is less than moderately similar to A and less than 0.33-neighboring with A.*

It is obvious that the definition of ρ-plausible negation leads to a weak global Similarity and a weak Neighborhood for the more significant values. Moreover, we have: $\mu_A(x)=1 \Rightarrow \mu_P(x) \leq 0.33$.

Property 3. *For any Fuzzy Property A, there exists a value of* ρ *such that the set of* ρ-*plausible Linguistic Negations is not empty.*

We can distinguish two cases :

- A is the only property defined in the domain. As noted before, Fuzzy Operators and Modifiers have been defined in such a way that some nuanced properties based upon A satisfy previous conditions. More precisely, it is the case when $\rho \geq 0.3$.
- At least two different Fuzzy Properties have been defined in the domain. Then, the translations and contractions have been defined in such a way that some Nuanced Properties based upon them fulfil all the conditions for any $\rho \geq 0.1$.

Finally, we can point out the fact that this Linguistic Negation satisfies *some Common sense properties of Negation.*

Property 4. *For many Fuzzy Properties A,* « *x is A* » *does not automatically define the Knowledge about* « *x is not A* ».

This property results directly from our construction Process of Linguistic Negation. Knowing exactly A does not imply, as does the Logical Negation, precise Knowledge of its Negation, since most of them require complementary information, as a mark of the property, and a Choice among possible interpretations.

Property 5. *Given Fuzzy Property A, its double Negation does not lead to A.*

Using Figure 4, the Speaker can choose « x is thin » as the interpretation of « x is not big », and « x is enormous » as the negation of « x is thin ».

Property 6. *Given the Rule* « *if* « *x is A* » *then* « *y is B* » », *we can deduce that* « *if* « *y is not B* » *then* « *z is A'* » » *where A' is a* ρ-*plausible Negation of* A.

This property results from definition of ρ-plausible Negation

Remark: Strictly speaking, the previous Approach to Linguistic Negation gives us a *Pragmatic Model* leading to results consistent with those intuitively expected. Its formal integration in Many-valued Predicate Logics is actually being examined. Our main objective is to define a new Adequate Fuzzy Negation Operator having Properties like the one proposed in a logical Approach to the Negation of Precise assertions [13, 8, 19, 18].

6 Deductive Process dealing with Linguistic Negation

As pointed out in Section 1, the User expresses some Facts or Rules with the use of Linguistic Negations. It results from previous analysis that our interactive Choice Strategy allows him to explain affirmatively their intended meanings. That is to say, the presence of such Linguistic Negations in the Knowledge Base does not generally modify the use of the existing Deductive Process.

We now illustrate this point through the Analysis of the following Rules that contain initially Linguistic Negations.

1 : if « x is not tall » then « x is not visible in a crowd »,

2 : if « x is not small » then « x is visible in a crowd », and

3 : if « x is not small » then « x is not invisible in a crowd ».

Let us suppose that :

-the properties « small », « tall » and « gigantic » are associated with the « height » concept, and

- the properties « invisible » and « visible » with the « appearance » concept.

Moreover, suppose that the User has also selected :

- « x is small » as translation of « x is not tall » (i. e. his Choice with the mark 2),

- « x is very tall » as intended meaning of « x is not small » (i. e. his Choice with the mark 3),

- « x is rather visible in a crowd » as interpretation of « x is not invisible in a crowd » (i. e. his Choice with the mark 4) and

- « x is invisible in a crowd » as linguistic negation of « x is not visible in a crowd » (i. e. his Choice with the mark 2).

Then these Choices lead to the following equivalent Rules only based upon Affirmative Information:

1': if « x is small » then « x is invisible in a crowd »,

2': if « x is very tall » then « x is visible in a crowd » and

3': if « x is very tall » then « x is rather visible in a crowd ».

It is obvious that information does not generally correspond with the Premise of Rules. As an example, the Knowledge Base can contain Facts like «x is exactly small », « x is more or less small », « x is really very tall » or « x is rather tall ». It is clear that these Rules lead to deductions in terms of Basic Properties by using the first or third Facts. But, it is not the case with the second or fourth Facts. In other words, a Deductive Process founded upon some Generalized Modus Ponens Rule (like Zadeh's [25]) creates difficulty in making useful Deductions in terms of the Basic Properties of the Discourse Universe. Note that we are actually achieving a variant of Zadeh's deductive Process *via* the previous Similarity of Nuanced Properties.

7   Conclusion

We have presented an Intelligent System dealing with Affirmative or Negative Information. Our formal Representation of Negative Information has been founded upon a particular Similarity Relation. We have proposed a Choice Strategy improving the abilities in the Management of previous Information. The User can refer to Linguistic Negations either in Facts or in Rules, since this Strategy allows him, to explain their intended meanings, and also, to exploit them by using equivalent Rules based upon Affirmative Information.

References

1.   J. F. Baldwin, B. W. Pilsworth, Axiomatic approach to implication for approx. reasoning with fuzzy logic, *Fuzzy Sets and Systems* 3, 193-219, 1980.

2.   V. Brondal, *Essais de linguistique générale*, Copenhague, 1943.

3. V. Brondal, *Les parties du discours : étude sur les catégories linguistiques*, EINAR, MUNKSGAARD, Copenhague, 1948.

4. A. Culioli, *Pour une linguistique de l'énonciation: Opérations et Représentations, Tome 1*, Ophrys 2ds., Paris, 1991.

5. E. Desmontils & D. Pacholczyk : Apport de la théorie des ens. flous à la modélisation déclarative en Synthèse d'images, *Proc. LFA'96*, 333-334, 1996.

6. E. Desmontils & D. Pacholczyk : Modélisation déclarative en Synthèse d'images: traitement semi qualitatif des propriétés imprécises ou vagues, *Proc. AFIG'96*, Dijon, 173-181, 1996.

7. O. Ducrot & J.-M. Schaeffer et al., *Nouveau dictionnaire encyclopédique des sciences du langage*, Seuil, Paris, 1995.

8. D. M. Gabbay, What is Negation in a System ? *Logic Colloquium'86*, F.R. Drake & J. K. Truss, Amsterdam, 95-112, 1988.

9. L. Hjelmslev, La catégorie des cas (1), *Acta Jutlandica*, 1935.

10. L. Hjelmslev, La catégorie des cas (2), *Acta Jutlandica*, 1937.

11. L.R. Horn, A *Natural History of Negation*, The Univ. of Chicago Press, 1989.

12. W.A. Ladusaw, Negative Concord and « Made of Judgement », *Negation, a notion in Focus*, H. Wansing, W. de Gruyter Eds., Berlin, 127-144, 1996.

13. W. Lenzen, Necessary Conditions for Negation Operators, *Negation, a notion in Focus*, H. Wansing, W. de Gruyter eds., Berlin, 37-58, 1996.

14. C. Muller, *La négation en français*, Public. romanes et françaises, Genève, 1991.

15. D. Pacholczyk, Contribution au traitement logico-symbolique de la connaissance, Thèse d'Etat, Partie C, Paris 6, 1992.

16. D. Pacholczyk, A new Approach to Vagueness and Uncertainty, *Int. Rev. CC-AI*, 9:4, 395-436, 1992.

17. D. Pacholczyk, About Linguistic Negation of Nuanced Property in Declarative Modeling in Image Synthesis, *Proc. of Int. Conf. « 5th Fuzzy in Dortmund »*, *Lecture Notes in Computer Science*, 1226 , 229-240, 1997.

18. D. Pearce, Reasoning with negative information II : Hard Negation, Strong Negation and Logic Programs, *LNAI 619*, Berlin, 63-79, 1992.

19. D. Pearce & G. Wagner, Reasoning with negative information I : Hard Negation, Strong Negation and Logic Programs, Language, Knowledge and Intentionality : Perspectives on the Philosophy of J. Hintikka, *Acta Philosophica Fennica*, 49, Helsinki, 430-453, 1990.

20. E. H. Ruspini, The Semantics of vague knowledge, *Rev. int. de Systémique*, 3:4, 387 - 420, 1989.

21. P. Scheffe, On foundations of reasoning with uncertain facts and vague concepts, *Fuzzy Reasoning and its Applications*, 189-216, 1981.

22. V. Torra, Negation Functions Based Semantics for Ordered Linguistic Labels, *Int. Jour. of Intelligent Systems*, 975-988, 1996.

23. A. Tversky, Features of Similarity, *Psychological Review*, 4, 1977.

24. L.A. Zadeh, Fuzzy Sets, *Information and Control*, 8, 338-353, 1965.

25. L.A. Zadeh, PRUF-A meaning representation language for natural languages, *Int. J. Man-Machine Studies*, 10: 4, 395 - 460, 1978.

26. L. A. Zadeh, Similarity relations and Fuzzy orderings, *Selected Papers of L. A. Zadeh*, 3, 387-420, 1987.

On Representation-Based Querying
of Databases Containing Ill-known Values

Patrick BOSC, Olivier PIVERT

IRISA-ENSSAT BP 447 22305 LANNION Cedex FRANCE
e-mail : bosc@enssat.fr, pivert@enssat.fr
tel : (33) 2 96 46 50 30, fax : (33) 2 96 37 01 99

Abstract.

In this paper, the issue of querying databases containing ill-known values is addressed. A new type of queries is introduced, based on criteria applying to the representations of ill-known data. In the regular possibilistic framework, the only authorized selection criteria concern the value that an item can take. What we propose is to enrich the query language with some concepts which are part of the possibilistic database model and which concern the qualification of imprecision/uncertainty. The representation-based querying framework defined in this paper constitutes the first step to the introduction of an explicit manipulation of the concepts of imprecision/uncertainty into a fuzzy query language.

1 Introduction

In the field of databases, numerous efforts have been made to meet new needs and requirements. In particular, a stream of research has focused on the introduction of imprecision and/or uncertainty in database management systems (DBMS's). This issue covers several different aspects, among which two striking: the expression of imprecise queries on the one hand and the storage and handling of imperfect information on the other hand.

The objective of the first aspect is to propose alternatives to the use of Boolean logic, which, in most DBMS's, remains the only way for the selection of information. An advantage of flexible queries is first to provide a reply when a classical crisp, too requiring request would have produced an empty response, and secondly to order the answers rather than to provide the user with a long list of undifferentiated elements. In [1], the fuzzy set framework is shown to be a sound scientific choice to model such queries. In particular, it is a natural basis to express the graduality involved in the notion of preference. In [2], a language called SQLf allowing for the processing of fuzzy queries addressed to regular databases is proposed. The basic idea is to enrich the SQL language which is currently used as a standard interface to current DBMS's by introducing flexible predicates interpreted in the context of fuzzy sets.

The second aspect concerns the representation of ill-known attribute values by means of possibility distributions [14]. For instance, in a database describing houses, if the size (or the price) is not perfectly known, it will be described by means of a possibility distribution (which in fact restricts the set of possible values for the size (or the price) of a particular house). This approach has been particularly developed by Umano [13], Prade [9], Prade and Testemale [10], Zemankova and Kandel [15].

In this paper, we are concerned with the querying of databases containing ill-known values represented by possibility distributions. Up to now, queries addressed to fuzzy databases have been considered to have the same form as queries addressed to crisp databases. The conditions allowed in these queries reduce to a comparison (crisp or fuzzy) between an attribute and a value, or between two attributes. What we propose is to take advantage of the specific information conveyed by possibility distributions (i.e., the information concerning the underlying levels of uncertainty) to enrich the querying of fuzzy databases. In this paper, we use the possibilistic framework, but a similar kind of approach can be envisaged for ill-known data represented in a probabilistic framework.

The paper is organized as follows. In section 2, we present the essential elements of the possibilistic framework, and we recall the principles of the querying of fuzzy databases in this framework. Section 3 is devoted to the presentation of a new type of queries, i.e., queries including conditions which explicitely refer to the qualification of imprecision/uncertainty in the data. In section 4, we compare this new querying framework with the usual possibilistic one. The paper ends with some elements of conclusion.

2 Querying of Databases Containing Ill-known Values

2.1 Representing Imperfect Data

In the possibility theory-based approach [9, 10, 11], the available information about the value of a single-valued attribute A for a tuple x is represented by a possibility distribution $\Pi_{A(x)}$ on $D \cup \{e\}$ where D is the domain of A and e is an extra-element which stands for the case when the attribute does not apply to x. If information is consistent, there should exist a value in $D \cup \{e\}$ completely possible for A(x), which leads to the normalization condition $\max_d \Pi_{A(x)}(d) = 1$. The possibility distribution $\Pi_{A(x)}$ can be viewed as a fuzzy restriction of the possible value of A(x) and defines a mapping from $D \cup \{e\}$ to [0, 1]. For instance, the information "Paul is young" will be represented by: $\Pi_{Age(Paul)}(e) = .0$ and $\Pi_{Age(Paul)}(d) = \mu_{young}(d), \forall d \in D$. Here, μ_{young} is a membership function which represents the vague predicate "young" in a given context. This approach proposes a unified framework for representing precise, imprecise, as well as vague, values of attributes, and different null value situations. Multiple-valued attributes can be dealt with in this framework too.

2.2 Matching Mechanism

When a condition of the type "attribute θ value" or "attribute1 θ attribute2" (θ being a crisp or fuzzy comparison operator) applies to imperfectly known data, the result of a query evaluation can no longer be a single value. Since we do not know the precise values of some attributes for some items, we may be uncertain about the fact that these items satisfy or not the query (to some degree). It is why two degrees attached to two points of view are used: the extent to which it is possible that the condition is satisfied and the extent to which it is certain that the condition is satisfied. From the possibility distributions $\Pi_{A(x)}$ and a subset P (ordinary or fuzzy), we can compute the fuzzy set ΠP (resp. NP) of the items whose A-value possibly (resp. necessarily) satisfies the condition P.

The membership degree of an item x to the fuzzy sets ΠP and NP are respectively given by the following formulae [5]:

$$\mu_{\Pi P}(x) = \Pi(P; A(x)) = \sup_{d \in D} \min(\mu_P(d), \Pi_{A(x)}(d)) \qquad (1)$$

$$\mu_{NP}(x) = N(P; A(x)) = 1 - \Pi(\bar{P}; A(x))$$
$$= \inf_{d \in D \cup \{e\}} \max(\mu_P(d), 1 - \Pi_{A(x)}(d)) \qquad (2)$$

Example. John's age and the predicate P (middle-aged) are represented hereafter:

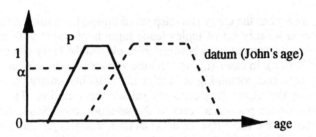

The evaluation of the condition "John's age = middle-aged" is based on the computation of the values:

$\min(\Pi_{\text{John's age}}(d), \mu_P(d))$ for which the supremum (α) will be taken to obtain the possibility degree of "John's age = middle-aged", and:

$\max(1 - \Pi_{\text{John's age}}(d), \mu_P(d))$ for which the lowest value (0) corresponds to the necessity degree of "John's age = middle-aged" (the result is 0 because there exists at least one value completely possible for John's age which does not satisfies at all the predicate "middle-aged") ◆

Selections involving disjunction, conjunction or negation of elementary conditions can be handled using basic relations of possibility theory, provided that the attribute values are logically independent [10]. Selections involving fuzzy comparators, e.g., approximate equalities, strong inequalities, can also be easily handled in this framework.

3 A New Type of Queries

3.1 Preliminary Remarks

As noted before, the selection criteria considered in the usual possibilistic framework are of the form "attribute θ value" or "attribute1 θ attribute2". In other words, the evaluation of a query consists in determining the extent to which the attribute value(s) of a tuple is compatible with a given predicate. One can observe four situations:

i) the data is precise and the criterion is Boolean (the regular case); for instance: the price of house H1 is $100,000 and we are searching for houses that cost less than $120,000;

ii) the data is precise and the predicate is vague; for instance: the price of house H1 is $100,000 and we are searching for inexpensive houses;

iii) the data is ill-known and the predicate is Boolean; for instance: the price of house H2 is described by the possibility distribution {1/100,000, .7/70,000, .7/130,000} and we are searching for houses that cost less than $120,000};

iv) the data is ill-known and the criterion is vague (the general case); for instance: the price of house H2 is described by the possibility distribution {1/100,000, .7/70,000, .7/130,000} and we are searching for inexpensive houses.

In case (i) the answer to the query is a crisp set of tuples, i.e. a usual relation. In case (ii), the answer is a fuzzy set of tuples (each tuple is provided with a satisfaction degree expressing the compatibility between the tuple and the fuzzy concept associated to the vague criterion). In cases (iii) and (iv) the answer is no longer one set of tuples but two fuzzy sets, one containing the tuples that possibly satisfy the criterion, the other containing the tuples that certainly satisfy the criterion. This uncertainty appears because of the particular form of the selection conditions: the considered criteria only concern the *value* that the data can take, which is precisely the ill-known aspect of the data. The idea is to enrich the query language with some concepts which are part of the data model and which concern the qualification of uncertainty. What we propose is to introduce a new type of queries based on criteria referring to the precise aspect of ill-known data, i.e. the *representations* of such data. For instance, one can search for houses whose size is as close as possible to a given description, corresponding for example to a fuzzy concept, e.g., small. This new type of queries is detailed hereafter.

3.2 A New Type of Conditions

The idea consists in expressing conditions which are not anymore about attribute values, but about the imprecision/uncertainty attached to attribute values, as well as predicates referring to the global representations of ill-known data. Such conditions no longer introduce uncertainty in the answer since they apply to precisely known information (i.e., the representations of ill-known data). We will first consider single-attribute conditions and then conditions involving two attributes.

Atomic Conditions Involving One Representation

Let us illustrate this new type of conditions with the help of an example. Consider a relation containing houses whose prices are possibly ill-known (i.e., represented by possibility distributions). We are interested in queries such as:

- "find the houses for which the price value $100,000 is considered more possible than the value $80,000",

- "find the houses for which all the price values {$80,000, $100,000, $150,000} are possible over a degree .8",

- "find the houses for which $100,000 is the only price value which is completely possible",

- "find the houses whose price is not precisely known".

In order to express conditions of this type, new functions must be included into the query language. Some examples of such functions are given hereafter.

Let A be an attribute, D the domain of A, and $X = \{d_1, ..., d_n\}$ a crisp subset of D. Let us denote poss(A, X) the truth value of the statement "all the values in X are possible for A". Formally, we have:

$$poss(A, \{d_1, ..., d_n\}) = min(\Pi_A(d_1), ..., \Pi_A(d_n))$$

Now let us introduce the function card_cut(A, λ) (resp. card_supp(A)) giving the number of D-values whose possibility degrees for A are greater than λ (resp. are strictly positive). We have:

$$card\_cut(A, \lambda) = |\{d \in D \mid \Pi_A(d) \geq \lambda\}|$$

$$card\_supp(A) = |\{d \in D \mid \Pi_A(d) > 0\}|$$

Using these functions, one can easily express different kinds of conditions about the uncertainty attached to attribute values, as illustrated hereafter:

i) the value a_1 is preferred to the value a_2 for attribute A

$$poss(A, \{a_1\}) \geq poss(A, \{a_2\})$$

ii) all the values $\{a_1, ..., a_n\}$ are possible over a degree λ for attribute A

$$poss(A, \{a_1, ..., a_n\}) \geq \lambda$$

iii) a_1 and a_2 are the only values completely possible for attribute A

$$poss(A, \{a_1\}) = 1 \text{ and } poss(A, \{a_2\}) = 1 \text{ and } card\_cut(A, 1) = 2$$

iv) at least n values are possible over a degree λ for attribute A

$$card\_cut(A, \lambda) \geq n$$

v) the value of attribute A is not precisely known

$$card\_supp(A) > 1.$$

These conditions being Boolean, the result of a query will be a usual relation (i.e., a relation containing non-weighted tuples). However, such criteria can also take a fuzzy form. For example, one can imagine to transform the preceding conditions into "a_1 is *much* preferred to a_2", "all the values $\{a_1, ..., a_n\}$ have a *high* degree of possibility", "*many* values are possible over a degree λ", etc. Then, the result would be a fuzzy relation i.e., a relation where a membership degree is assigned to each tuple. As a matter of fact, condition (v) can also be interpreted in a gradual way by means of a fuzzy set measure giving the extent to which the value of attribute A is ill-known.

Atomic Conditions Involving Two Representations

Several methods have been proposed to compare possibility distributions or fuzzy sets and one can distinguish two families of approaches depending on the type of comparison which is allowed between two (crisp) elements of a domain. Let $\Pi_{A(x)}$ and $\Pi_{A(y)}$ be the possibility distributions that we want to compare. Let D be the domain of attribute A. The two kinds of approaches correspond to the following cases:

i) only an identity relation is in effect on each domain of the relation concerned. In this case, one can only compare the possibility degrees $\Pi_{A(x)}(d)$ and $\Pi_{A(y)}(d)$ for each element d of the domain.

ii) the possibility-based framework is extended with some resemblance relations assumed on the domains. Formally, a tuple t of R is of the form: $t = (\Pi_{A1}, \Pi_{A2}, ..., \Pi_{An})$ with $\Pi_{Ai} \in \Pi(Di)$ and it is assumed that $res_i: Di \times Di \rightarrow [0, 1]$ is in effect available for $i = 1, ..., n$, where res_i is a resemblance relation on Di. In this context, the resemblance between two imprecise values will rely on the resemblance between possibility degrees on the one hand and on the resemblance between domain values on the other hand.

It is worth noticing that in the querying framework that we consider, we are interested in measuring the extent to which two *representations* are globally close to each other, and not the possibility degree of approximate equality between two imprecise values, contrary to what is done in several other approaches [6, 7]. For the sake of brevity, we will only study the problem of equality, but measures of inclusion can also be categorized in a similar way.

Case (i): closeness measures based on an identity relation

First, let us recall the expression of the strict equality:

$$\forall d \in D, \Pi_{A(x)}(d) = \Pi_{A(y)}(d)$$

Several authors have proposed to relax the preceding measure into a measure of approximate equality. In [12], Raju and Majumdar define the fuzzy equality measure, denoted EQ, in the following way:

$$\mu_{EQ}(\Pi_{A(x)}, \Pi_{A(y)}) = \min_{u \in D} \psi(\Pi_{A(x)}(u), \Pi_{A(y)}(u))$$

where ψ is a resemblance relation (i.e., reflexive and symmetric) over [0, 1]. Similar methods have also been advocated in [8, 10]. An alternate approach consists in defining the similarity of two fuzzy sets (two possibility distributions in our case) A and B as a function of $A \cap B$, $B - A$ and $A - B$. This approach is studied in particular in [4] where different kinds of measures of comparison are addressed.

Case (ii): closeness measure based on a resemblance relation

The preceding approaches are suitable when strict equality is the only way to compare values. Nevertheless, there are many circumstances which reveal the necessity of specifying a resemblance relation on domains. We assume here that a resemblance relation RES expressing fuzzy equality between the values of D is available. In this case, what we want to estimate is the extent to which the respective representations of $A(x)$ and $A(y)$ are interchangeable wrt the considered resemblance relation [3]. The interchangeability degree related to the pair $(A(x), A(y))$ is the degree to which $A(x)$ can be replaced with $A(y)$ (expressed in the following as $\mu_{repl}(A(x), A(y))$) and reciprocally. An imprecise value $A(x)$ can be replaced with another imprecise value $A(y)$ if, for each representative $<u/\Pi_{A(x)}(u)>$ of $A(x)$, there exists a representative $<v/\Pi_{A(y)}(v)>$ of $A(y)$ close to $<u/\Pi_{A(x)}(u)>$. The degree of closeness between these two representatives will be expressed as an aggregation of the degree of closeness between u and v on the one hand, and the degree of closeness between $\Pi_{A(x)}(u)$ and $\Pi_{A(y)}(v)$ on the other hand. The influence of a representative $<u/\Pi_{A(x)}(u)>$ on the global degree $\mu_{repl}(A(x), (A(y))$ will be all the more important as $\Pi_{A(x)}(u)$ is high.

We assume that in addition to the user-defined resemblance relation RES measuring the proximity of any two values of D, a proximity measure θ over [0, 1] is available. This measure, tied to the interchangeability measure, is defined by some norm. An intuitively reasonable choice is: $\mu_\theta(\alpha, \beta) = 1 - |\alpha - \beta|$.

Let u be a value of D such that $\Pi_{A(x)}(u) > 0$ (u belongs to the support of $A(x)$). Let us measure the extent to which there exists a representative $<v, \Pi_{A(y)}(v)>$ in $A(y)$ which can be substituted for u. The corresponding function, denoted $\mu_{s(A(x), A(y))}$, is defined hereafter:

$$\mu_{s(A(x), A(y))}(u) = \sup_{v \in supp(A(y))} \min(\mu_{RES}(u, v), \mu_\theta(\Pi_{A(x)}(u), \Pi_{A(y)}(v))).$$

As noted above, the contribution of a value u to the global degree $\mu_{repl}(A(x), A(y))$ will depend on the degree $\Pi_{A(x)}(u)$, acting as a weight. This contribution can thus be expressed as: $\max(1 - \Pi_{A(x)}(u), \mu_{s(A(x), A(y))}(u))$. Finally, a representation $A(x)$ can be replaced with $A(y)$ if all the values of the support of $A(x)$ have a substitute in $A(y)$. Thus we get:

$$\mu_{repl}(A(x), A(y)) = \inf_{u \in supp(A(x))} \max(1 - \Pi_{A(x)}(u), \mu_{s(A(x), A(y))}(u)).$$

Obviously, this function is not symmetrical since it only expresses the extent to which $A(x)$ can be replaced with $A(y)$. What we want to express now is the extent to which two representations $A(x)$ and $A(y)$ are interchangeable i.e. the extent to which $A(x)$ and $A(y)$ can be mutually replaced with each other. Using min to express the underlying conjunction, we obtain the following expression:

$$\mu_{EQ}(A(x), A(y)) = \min(\mu_{repl}(A(x), A(y)), \mu_{repl}(A(y), A(x))).$$

This measure is reflexive, symmetrical, but it is not max-min transitive in general [3]. It is worth noticing that this measure is a generalization of the one used in Raju and Majumdar's approach.

This interchangeability measure can be used to extend the fuzzy querying framework in a straightforward manner. Let us consider two ill-known data D1 and D2. In the usual fuzzy querying framework, the comparison of D1 and D2 relies on the fuzzy pattern matching method [5], which consists in computing the possibility (resp. necessity) degree of the condition "D1 = D2". In the representation-based querying framework, D1 and D2 are viewed as linguistic labels and one measures the approximate synonymy of their respective representations. This new type of condition can be expressed as: REP(D1) $\approx_i$ REP(D2), where i indicates the method chosen for comparing the values of the underlying domain (either the strict equality or a user-defined resemblance relation RES).

Up to now, we have considered that both possibility distributions involved in a representation-based comparison were describing attribute values. Another interesting case corresponds to the situation where one of the possibility distributions represents a fuzzy concept, used as a selection criterion. As a matter of fact, the definition of interchangeability given above can also be used to compare an ill-known attribute value D and a fuzzy predicate P. The basic idea is the same: we evaluate the extent to which the predicate and the value represent the same concept. For example, let us consider a possibility distribution D representing John's age and a fuzzy predicate P = "middle-aged" (represented by a fuzzy set). While the fuzzy pattern matching method [5] allows to measure the extent to which John is possibly (resp. necessary) middle-aged, the querying approach we propose can be used to measure the extent to which the representation of John's age and the fuzzy set representing the concept "middle-aged" are interchangeable. The value computed will then correspond to the synonymy of the representation of John's age and "middle-aged". Let us consider the following possibility distribution describing John's age: {.5/30, .7/35, 1/40, .7/45} and the fuzzy set associated to the concept "middle-aged": {.5/30, .7/35, 1/40, .7/45}. Since the representations are the same, the criterion "REP(age) $\approx$ REP(middle-aged)" gives the result 1 (for John), whereas the fuzzy pattern matching-based evaluation of the criterion "age = middle-aged" returns the degrees $\Pi = 1$ and $N = .5$. A measure of inclusion can be defined in a similar way in order to evaluate the extent to which a representation is more specific than another one.

4 Comparison with the Usual Possibilistic Approach

As noted before, Prade and Testemale [10] have defined some extended relational operators allowing to manipulate relations including ill-known values. The selection operation delivers a twofold fuzzy relation, i.e., a relation where each tuple is provided with two degrees Π and N (cf formulae (1) and (2)). The purpose of this section is to illustrate the fact that the expression power of the usual possibilistic framework is too limited to allow the expression of all kinds of representation-based queries. Some representation-based conditions can be expressed in the usual possibilistic framework though, but at the expense of a greater complexity in the formulation. Let us consider a relation R(X, A), X and A being sets of attributes, X being the key of relation R. Using an SQL-like language where the result of a selection is a twofold fuzzy relation, we will try to express in the regular possibilistic framework some queries considered in section 3.2.

i) the value a1 is preferred to the value a2 for attribute A

> *select * from* R *into* R1 *where* A = a₁;
> *select * from* R *into* R2 *where* A = a₂;
> *select* R1.X, R1.A *from* R1, R2 *where* R1.X = R2.X *and* R1.$\Pi \geq$ R2.Π;

ii) all the values $\{a_1, ..., a_n\}$ are possible over a degree λ for attribute A

> *select* * *from* R *into* R1 *where* A = a_1;
> ...
> *select* * *from* R *into* Rn *where* A = a_n;
> *select* R1.X, R1.A *from* R1, ..., Rn
> $\qquad$ *where* R1.X = R2.X *and* ... *and* R1.X = Rn.X
> $\qquad$ *and* R1.$\Pi \geq \lambda$ *and* ... *and* Rn.$\Pi \geq \lambda$;

iii) a_1 and a_2 are the only values completely possible for attribute A

> *select* * *from* R *into* R1 *where* A = a_1;
> *select* * *from* R *into* R2 *where* A = a_2;
> *select* * *from* R *into* R3 *where* A $\neq a_1$ *and* A $\neq a_2$;
> *select* R1.X, R1.A *from* R1, R2, R3
> $\qquad$ *where* R1.X = R2.X *and* R1.X = R3.X
> $\qquad$ *and* R1.$\Pi = 1$ *and* R2.$\Pi = 1$ *and* R3.$\Pi \neq 1$;

iv) at least n values are possible over a degree λ for attribute A

> not expressible

v) the value of attribute A is ill-known

> not expressible.

Let us consider now the second class of representation-based queries, i.e., queries involving a "syntactic" comparison of two possibility distributions. Their evaluation can be based either on the interchangeability measure defined above or on any measure of similarity of fuzzy sets. Obviously, these queries are not expressible in the regular possibilistic framework, where the comparison of ill-known values is based on fuzzy pattern matching, since their evaluation is not a matter of possibility and necessity, but a matter of "distance" between two representations.

This brief comparison shows that the expression of representation-based conditions in the regular possibilistic framework is problematical: either these conditions require multiple queries, or they are not expressible at all. This result justifies our proposal of a specific querying framework suited to this kind of selection conditions.

5 Conclusion

This paper is concerned with the querying of databases containing ill-known values represented by possibility distributions. We have introduced a new type of queries, based on criteria applying to the representations of ill-known data. These criteria can be Boolean or fuzzy. We have presented two kinds of representation-based conditions: conditions involving one representation, and conditions involving a "syntactic" comparison of two possibility distributions. In this latter case, ill-known data are viewed as linguistic labels and one can measure their approximate synonymy, or the extent to which one is more specific/general than the other. We have shown that the representation-based querying framework allows to formulate conditions that cannot be expressed in the regular possibilistic framework. This representation-based querying approach constitutes the first step to the introduction of an explicit manipulation of the concepts of imprecision/uncertainty into a fuzzy querying language. It is important to notice that the general philosophy of this approach is not specific to the case where the representation of ill-known data is of a possibilistic nature. A similar kind of approach can be envisaged for ill-known data represented in a probabilistic framework insofar as this new type of querying is not linked to a particular data model.

References

[1] Bosc P., Pivert O., Some approaches for relational database flexible querying, *International Journal of Intelligent Information Systems*, 1, pp. 323-354, 1992.

[2] Bosc P., Pivert O., SQLf: A Relational Database Language for Fuzzy Querying, *IEEE Transactions on Fuzzy Systems*, 3, pp. 1-17, 1995.

[3] Bosc P., Pivert O., On the comparison of imprecise values in fuzzy databases, *Proc. of FUZZ-IEEE'97*.

[4] Bouchon-Meunier B., Rifqi M., Bothorel S., Towards general measures of comparison of objects, *Fuzzy Sets and Systems*, 84, pp. 143-153, 1996.

[5] Cayrol M., Farreny H., Prade H., Fuzzy pattern matching, *Kybernetes*, 11, 103-116, 1982.

[6] Chen G.Q., Kerre E.E., Vandenbulcke J., A general treatment of data redundancy in a fuzzy relational data model, *Journal of the American Society for Information Science*, 43, 304-311, 1992.

[7] Cubero J.C., Vila M.A., A new definition of fuzzy functional dependency in fuzzy relational databases, *Journal of Intelligent Systems*, 9, pp. 441-448, 1994.

[8] Liu W., The fuzzy functional dependency on the basis of the semantic distance, *Fuzzy Sets and Systems*, 59, pp. 173-179, 1993.

[9] Prade H., Lipski's approach to incomplete information data bases restated and generalized in the setting of Zadeh's possibility theory, *Information Systems*, 9, pp. 27-42, 1984.

[10] Prade H., Testemale C., Generalizing Database Relational Algebra for the Treatment of Incomplete or Uncertain Information and Vague Queries, *Information Sciences*, 34, pp. 115-143, 1984.

[11] Prade H., Testemale C., Fuzzy relational databases: representational issues and reduction using similarity measures, Journal of the American Society for *Information Science*, 38, pp. 118-126, 1987.

[12] Raju K.V.S.V.N., Majumdar A.K., Fuzzy functional dependencies and lossless join decomposition of fuzzy relational database systems, *ACM Transactions on Database Systems*, 13, pp. 129-166, 1988.

[13] Umano M., FREEDOM-0: a Fuzzy Database System, *Fuzzy Information and Decision Processes*, eds M. Gupta and E. Sanchez (Amsterdam: North-Holland), pp. 339-347, 1982.

[14] Zadeh L.A., Fuzzy sets as a basis for a theory of possibility, *Fuzzy Sets and Systems*, 1, pp. 3-28, 1978.

[15] Zemankova-Leech M., Kandel A., Fuzzy Relation Data Bases — A Key to Expert Systems, (Köln: Verlag TÜV Rheinland), 1984.

Decision Value Oriented Decomposition of Data Tables *

Dominik Ślęzak

Institute of Mathematics, Warsaw University
Banacha 2, Warsaw Poland
email: slezak@alfa.mimuw.edu.pl

Abstract. The framework for decision value oriented decomposition of data tables is stated with examples of its applications to partially generalized reasoning. Operation of synthesis of information is introduced for distributed decision tables. Theoretical foundations are built on the basis of the main factors of quality of reasoning, by referring to rough set, Dempster-Shafer and statistical theories.

1   Introduction

The analogies between rough sets and other approaches to data analysis are very important in view of combining simple and intuitive rough set framework ([5]) with different models of knowledge representation (see e.g. [11],[13]). In this paper we point out what can be adopted to rough set approach to distributed data from Dempster-Shafer ([1],[9]) and statistical (see e.g. [14]) theories.

By distributed data we understand any decision table decomposed with respect to the universe of objects. Such a decomposition may be stated e.g. by mutually irrelevant sources of information with their local decision rules, where, for any new object, we synthesize them with respect to chances of its correspondence to particular sources. If such an initial knowledge about the origin of data is not given, the main task is to decompose the universe in optimal way with respect to the quality of reasoning based on synthesized decision rules (compare with [8]). For instance, in case of inconsistent decision tables, decomposition may be due to generating locally deterministic rules, which can be combined in frequential way. However, for tables with large number of possible decision values, such an approach may lead to the rules supported by too small sets of objects to be regarded as credible. We deal with this problem by considering decision value oriented decomposition methods based on adjusting the granularity of decision values. Such an approach states a tool for extracting rough set based decision rules with respect to applicability, precision and credibility (see e.g. [13],[14],[17]) as the main factors of quality analysis.

---

* This paper was supported by the State Committee for Scientific Research grant, KBN 8T11C01011.

The applicability of a decision rule is related to the chance that a new object would fit its conditions. To improve it, we can e.g. consider the rules (or groups of rules) minimal in sense of the length of conditions' pattern, keeping some degree of precision (compare with [13],[17]). In this sense applicability can be identified with credibility, since shorter decision rules are supported by larger sets of objects in data table regarded as a statistical sample. As about comparison of precision and credibility, we analyze the balance between them by adopting intervals of uncertainty ([1],[15]) for synthesized decision rules. Such a usage of Dempster-Shafer functions ([9]) can be treated as analogous to the others for rough sets applications ([6],[11]).

The paper is organized as follows. In Section 2 we introduce basic notions connected with rough sets and their approach to distributed data. Section 3 contains the model of synthesis of distributed data and methods of evaluating its quality. Section 4 is devoted to quality measures of decomposition and their properties for decision value oriented decomposition. In Section 5 we conclude with some remarks for further research.

2 Rough set approach to data

The main idea of rough sets is that, given some data, one is allowed to extract the information just from the database, without any additional knowledge. The simplest way of representing such a database is by information system - a pair $\mathbf{A} = (U, A)$, where U is non-empty, finite set of objects called the universe, and A - non-empty, finite, linearly ordered set of attributes. Each element $a \in A$ is identified with function $a : U \to V_a$, where V_a denotes the set of all values of a on objects in U. For each non-empty $B \subseteq A$ information system $\mathbf{A} = (U, A)$ induces B-information function $Inf_B : U \to \times_{a \in B} V_a$ defined by

$$Inf_B(u) = \left(a_{i_1}(u), .., a_{i_{|B|}}(u) \right) \tag{1}$$

where attributes $a_{i_j} \in B$ occur consistently with assumed linear order over A and $|B|$ denotes the cardinality of B. Objects $u_1, u_2 \in U$ are said to be indiscernible with respect to $B \subseteq A$, iff $Inf_B(u_1) = Inf_B(u_2)$. In consequence, for any subset B, we obtain the indiscernibility relation

$$IND(B) = \{(u_1, u_2) \in U \times U : Inf_B(u_1) = Inf_B(u_2)\} \tag{2}$$

Equivalence classes of $IND(B)$ (denoted by $[u]_B$ if considered with respect to given $u \in U$) are the fundamental source of knowledge about the universe U. However, we can combine it also with some irrelevant information about distribution of objects onto the set of pairwise disjoint subuniverses. Then we obtain a distributed information system $\mathbf{A} = (U, A, p)$ (compare with [3],[4]), where partition $p \in Part(U)$ is treated as the additional attribute discerning objects onto $r(p)$ subtables with universes corresponding to its equivalence classes.

In this paper we pay a special attention to distributed decision tables of the form $\mathbf{A} = (U, A, p, d)$, where $d \notin A$ is distinguished as the decision attribute and elements of A are regarded as conditions. Distributed decision table representation is convenient for extracting an inexact knowledge about decision values for new objects from information about their values on conditions. Partition corresponding to distribution of the universe splits the decision process in two steps, where the first is to examine to which subtables we should refer and the second - to synthesize local decision rules corresponding to these subtables. The degree of distribution becomes to play similar role as the representativeness condition in statistical theory ([14]), which is necessary to assume that decision rules found inside the universe remain valid outside.

In order to extract local decision rules from a given table, let us notice that each class $[u]_B$ can be identified with some vector value, equal to $Inf_B(u)$ over B. Thus, each indiscernibility relation can be written as

$$IND(B) = \left\{ Inf_B^{-1}(w_1), ..., Inf_B^{-1}(w_{|V_B|}) \right\} \tag{3}$$

for w_l belonging to the set

$$V_B = \left\{ w_l \in \times_{a \in B} V_a : \exists_{u \in U} Inf_B(u) = w_l \right\} \tag{4}$$

Now the analysis of the quality of decision rules is due to their credibility and applicability, under the admissible degree of imprecision, expressed, for fixed $B \subseteq A$, in terms of cardinalities of set values of p-generalized decision set function $\partial_{B,p} : V_B \times \{1, .., r(p)\} \to 2^{V_d}$ defined by

$$\partial_{B,p}(w_l, m) = \left\{ v_k \in V_d : \exists_{u \in Inf_p^{-1}(m)} (Inf_B(u) = w_l \wedge d(u) = v_k) \right\} \tag{5}$$

Let us conclude this section with pointing out that the above function enables to reflect the degrees of applicability and credibility as connected with, respectively, possibly short and strongly supported decision rules. The first of the following definitions, being a generalization of the notion introduced in [5] for non-distributed case, characterizes certain class of subsets of conditions as leading to relatively most applicable patterns for reasoning. The second one focuses our attention on possibly rough partitions, as giving relatively strong support to local decision rules.

Definition 1. We say that $B \subseteq A$ is a relative decision reduct in distributed decision table $\mathbf{A} = (U, A, p, d)$ iff it is minimal (with respect to inclusion), such that equality

$$\partial_{B,p}(Inf_B(u), m) = \partial_{A,p}(Inf_A(u), m) \tag{6}$$

holds for every $u \in U$ and $m = 1, .., r(p)$.

Definition 2. For each $p_1, p_2 \in Part(U)$, p_1 is said to be more detailed than p_2 (denoted by $p_1 \preceq p_2$) iff for each $u \in U$ inclusion $[u]_{p_1} \subseteq [u]_{p_2}$ holds. Moreover, p_1 is strictly more detailed than p_2 (denoted by $p_1 \prec p_2$) iff $p_1 \preceq p_2$ and there is $u \in U$ such that $[u]_{p_1}$ is a proper subset of $[u]_{p_2}$ (denoted by $[u]_{p_1} \subset [u]_{p_2}$). Given a pair $(Part(U), \preceq)$, we say that partition p is B-irreducible iff for any p' such that $p \prec p'$ there is some $w_l \in V_B$ and $u \in U$ such that

$$\partial_{B,p}(w_l, p(u)) \subset \partial_{B,p'}(w_l, p'(u)) \tag{7}$$

3 Synthesis by rough membership functions

Given distributed decision table $\mathbf{A} = (U, A, p, d)$, one can reason basing on decision rules computed over subtables to which given object is relevant. When there is more than one relevant subtable, combining corresponding decision rules is necessary. We would like to propose the two step synthesis: firstly, for a new object, we find its probability o relevance to particular subtables $\mathbf{A}_m = \left(Inf_p^{-1}(m), A, d\right)$ and next - we combine local generalized decision functions with respect to obtained conditional frequencies.

As about the first point, for a new object with value vector w_l on fixed $B \subseteq A$, we would like to state relevance probabilities as p-membership functions $\mu_{p/B} : V_B \times V_p \rightarrow [0, 1]$ such that

$$\mu_{p/B}(m/w_l) = \left|Inf_{B,p}^{-1}(w_l, m)\right| \Big/ \left|Inf_B^{-1}(w_l)\right| \tag{8}$$

Then we can represent the global knowledge by p-generalized decision set function $\partial_B^p : V_B \rightarrow \left(2^{V_d} \times [0, 1]\right)^{r(p)}$ defined by

$$\partial_B^p(w_l) = \left(\left(\partial_{B,p}(w_l, m), \mu_{p/B}(m/w_l)\right)\right)_{m=1,..,r(p)} \tag{9}$$

The following result shows that the above definition generalizes the notions of generalized decision set function $\partial_B : V_B \rightarrow 2^{V_d}$ such that

$$\partial_B(w_l) = \{v_k \in V_d : \exists_{u \in U} (Inf_B(u) = w_l \wedge d(u) = v_k)\} \tag{10}$$

as well as rough membership function $\mu_{d/B}(v_k/w_l) : V_B \times V_d \rightarrow [0, 1]$ defined by

$$\mu_{d/B}(v_k/w_l) = \left|Inf_{B,d}^{-1}(w_l, v_k)\right| \Big/ \left|Inf_B^{-1}(w_l)\right| \tag{11}$$

which were used in many rough set applications (see e.g. [11],[13]).

Proposition 3. *For each element of* $p \in Part(U)$, *given* $B \subseteq A$, *we have*

$$IND(B) \preceq p \quad \Rightarrow \quad \partial_B^p \equiv \partial_B \tag{12}$$

where the equivalence $\equiv$ *means that for each* $w_l \in V_B$ *there is* m_l *satisfying both* $\partial_{B,p}(w_l, m_l) = \partial_B(w_l)$ *and* $\mu_{p/B}(m_l/w_l) = 1$. *Moreover, there is implication*

$$IND(B) \cap p \preceq IND(B \cup \{d\}) \quad \Rightarrow \quad \partial \mu_{d/B}^p \equiv \mu_{d/B} \tag{13}$$

where $\mu_{d/B}$ *is understood as frequential distribution composed by rough membership functions given by (11) and* $IND(B) \cap p$ *denotes a partition such that for each* $u \in U$ *its equivalence class is equal to* $[u]_B \cap [u]_p$.

The above implications point out at two marginal cases, where (12) deals with partitions which do not split any of indiscernibility classes, while (13) - with those eliminating all inconsistencies with respect to decision rules induced by B. In general, one can see that taking a larger number of subtables $r(p)$ is better with respect to the precision of inference and memory necessary to store large data tables. However, handling too much detailed partitions is often in contradiction with actual situation for particular data, since local decision rules become too weakly supported. In fact, rough membership decision rules remain more precise but not so credible and, sometimes, less applicable than in case of generalized decision (see [13]). Thus, for more detailed partitions (closer to rough membership method than to generalized one) we should expect a decrease of credibility of reasoning.

Given p-generalized decision set function defined by (5), we would like to synthesize local information in terms of p-generalized membership function $\mu^p_{d/B}$: $V_B \times V_d \to [0,1]$ defined by

$$\mu^p_{d/B}(v_k/w_l) = \sum_{m:\, v_k \in \partial_{B,p}(w_l,m)} \frac{\mu_{p/B}(m/w_l)}{|\partial_{B,p}(w_l,m)|} \tag{14}$$

which combines expected chances for particular subtables in a frequential way. The following result shows in what sense such a formula can be regarded as an analogon of rough membership function.

Proposition 4. *If $B \subseteq A$, $p \in Part(U)$ and $w_l \in V_B$, then*

$$\mu^p_{d/B}(V_d/w_l) := \sum_{v_k \in V_d} \mu^p_{d/B}(v_k/w_l) = 1 \tag{15}$$

Given the number of subtables $r(p)$ as corresponding to credibility of decision table, we would like to focus on comparison of p-membership and global rough membership function computed regardless of decomposition as leading to precision analysis. For this purpose we would like to refer to Dempster-Shafer functions ([1],[9]) which have found many interesting rough set applications, e.g., by comparing them with rough approximations ([6],[11]). Let us define belief and plausibility functions $bel^p_{d/B}, pl^p_{d/B} : 2^{V_d} \times V_B \to [0,1]$ as, respectively,

$$bel^p_{d/B}(V/w_l) = \sum_{m:\, \partial_{B,p}(w_l,m) \subseteq V} \mu_{p/B}(m/w_l) \tag{16}$$

$$pl^p_{d/B}(V/w_l) = \sum_{m:\, \partial_{B,p}(w_l,m) \cap V \neq \emptyset} \mu_{p/B}(m/w_l) \tag{17}$$

The above formulas satisfy all axioms of Dempster-Shafer functions with quantities

$$\mu^p_{d/B}(V/w_l) = \sum_{m:\, \partial_{B,p}(w_l,m)=V} \mu_{p/B}(m/w_l) \tag{18}$$

as basic probability assignment function ([9]). Moreover, they generate bounds for estimation of actual dependencies between decision and conditions under given $p \in Part(U)$ (compare with [1],[15]).

Proposition 5. *Let $B \subseteq A$, $p \in Part\,(U)$ and $V \subseteq V_d$. Then we have*

$$bel^p_{d/B}\,(V/w_l) \leq \mu^p_{d/B}\,(V/w_l) \leq pl^p_{d/B}\,(V/w_l) \tag{19}$$

$$\left| \mu^p_{d/B}\,(V/w_l) - \mu_{d/B}\,(V/w_l) \right| \leq pl^p_{d/B}\,(V/w_l) - bel^p_{d/B}\,(V/w_l) \tag{20}$$

where equalities hold iff for each m the set $\partial_{B,p}\,(w_l, m)$ is included in V or $V_d \backslash V$.

Proposition 5 shows that Dempster-Shafer functions, defined respectively by formulas (16) and (17), approximate the values of p-membership function and state how they estimate the actual frequency measure. Moreover, due to (19), they can be regarded as stating the variance of p-generalized membership function as the estimator. The following result shows that for high degree of credibility expressed by $r\,(p)$ intervals of uncertainty ([1],[15]) of the form

$$\left[bel^p_{d/B}\,(V/w_l)\,, pl^p_{d/B}\,(V/w_l) \right] \tag{21}$$

can be too sharp as corresponding to admissible error of estimation. It has much in common with risk-aversity (compare with [7],[13]), since one can understand it as follows: *"If I am risk-averse, then the admissible difference in case of given decision rule should be big enough to adapt to differences from actual dependencies assumed by me."* Such a correspondence between intervals of uncertainty and precision of partially generalized rules can be compared with other rough set models (see e.g. [10],[13]).

Proposition 6. *If $p_1 \preceq p_2$ then*

$$\left(pl^{p_1}_{d/B} - bel^{p_1}_{d/B} \right) (V/w_l) \leq \left(pl^{p_2}_{d/B} - bel^{p_2}_{d/B} \right) (V/w_l) \tag{22}$$

for each $V \subseteq V_d$ and $w_l \in V_B$. Moreover,

$$\max_{V \subseteq V_d} \left\{ \left(pl^p_{d/B} - bel^p_{d/B} \right) (V/w_l) \right\} \leq 1 - \frac{\left| \{m : Inf^{-1}_{B,p}\,(w_l, m) \neq \emptyset \} \right|}{\left| Inf^{-1}_B\,(w_l) \right|} \tag{23}$$

for any $w_l \in V_B$ and $p \in Part\,(U)$.

The proof of (23) is based on noticing that, given $V \subseteq V_d$, for each p there is such p^* that its value for the left side of inequality is not lower, each partition class has at most two elements and every two-element class has exactly one object with decision value in V. The uniform bounding stated by the right side of inequality is obtained by considering partitions just with at most two-element classes.

4 Searching for optimal decomposition

Results included in Propositions 5 and 6 suggest that the analysis of intervals of uncertainty can be used in straightforward way to define a quality measure over $Part(U)$, which would enable to search for optimal decomposition with respect to any subset $B \subseteq A$. Since it is impossible to consider intervals of the form (21) for each particular pair $(V, w_l) \in 2^{V_d} \times V_B$ separately, let us introduce function $L : 2^A \times Part(U) \to [0,1]$ defined by

$$L(B,p) = \sum_{w_l \in V_B} \frac{\mu_B(w_l)}{2^{|V_d|}} \sum_{V \subseteq V_d} \left(pl^p_{d/B}(V/w_l) - bel^p_{d/B}(V/w_l) \right) \qquad (24)$$

where, as the Dempster-Shafer functions act over all possible subsets of V_d, the inner sum in formula (24) corresponds to the expected chance of the length of interval of uncertainty for given $w_l \in V_B$, over all elements of 2^{V_d}. The outer sum takes the expected chance of the inner one's value over elements of V_B, where the values of

$$\mu_B(w_l) = \left| Inf_B^{-1}(w_l) \right| / |U| \qquad (25)$$

are related to the frequential meaning of particular vector values on B over U.

The problem with function L is that it is very hard to deal with from computational point of view and one should tend to replacing it by some simpler formula. Let us introduce function $Q : 2^A \times Part(U) \to [0,1]$ defined by

$$Q(B,p) = \sum_{w_l \in V_B} \mu_B(w_l) \sum_{m \in V_p} \frac{\mu_{p/B}(m/w_l)}{2^{\left| \partial_{B,p}(w_l,m) \right| - 1}} \qquad (26)$$

which expresses aggregate precision of reasoning with particular subsets of conditions, in terms of cardinalities of generalized decision set function values. Now one can reconsider previous analysis of credibility and precision with respect to the following fact.

Proposition 7. *For each $B \subseteq A$ and $p \in Part(U)$ we have equality*

$$L(B,p) + Q(B,p) = 1 \qquad (27)$$

The above result shows that intervals of uncertainty are strictly related to precision of reasoning. Moreover, it points out at the formula Q as much easier to compute than in case of L. Let us note that, for given $p \in Part(U)$, the notion of relative decision reduct, introduced in section 2, can be expressed in terms of equality $Q(B,p) = Q(A,p)$ instead of condition (6). Thus, one of possible optimization tasks can be to maximize Q with respect to decomposition of given decision table onto some fixed number r of subtables and searching for possibly small subsets of conditions simultaneously. Then certain subclass of $Part(U)$ becomes to have a special importance.

Definition 8. We say that partition $p \in Part(U)$ is decision value oriented for $B \subseteq A$ iff for each fixed $w_l \in V_B$ value sets $\partial_{B,p}(w_l, m)$ computed over particular $\mathbf{A}_m = \left(Inf_p^{-1}(m), A, d \right)$ are pairwise disjoint for $m = 1, .., r(p)$. We denote the set of all such partitions by $Part(d/B)$.

As about intuitive meaning of the above definition, one should realize that for any $p \in Part\,(d/B)$ we can treat sets of the form $\partial_{B,p}\,(w_l, m)$ as inducing partitions over decision values (see Example 1 at the end of this section). The practical meaning is the following.

Proposition 9. *Given* $B \subseteq A$, *for each* $p \in Part\,(U)$ *there is some* B-*irreducible* $p^* \in Part\,(d/B)$ *such that* $r\,(p^*) \leq r\,(p)$ *and* $Q\,(B, p^*) \geq Q\,(B, p)$.

The above fact is very important in view of narrowing the searching space of previously stated optimization problem. In fact, knowing that for each subsets $B_1, B_2 \subseteq A$ implication

$$B_1 \subseteq B_2 \quad \Rightarrow \quad Part\,(d/B_1) \subseteq Part\,(d/B_2) \tag{28}$$

holds, it is enough to search for maxima of function Q over $Part\,(d/A)$ instead of the whole $Part\,(U)$. It enables to adopt previously developed methods for finding decision reducts ([2],[16]) by combining them with some heuristics for partitions tuning, to extract optimal pairs (B, p) under constraint $r\,(p) \leq r$.

Obviously, one could argue that such understanding of optimal decomposition is not the only possibility. Another approach is to realize that sometimes we cannot base on just one relative decision reduct which gives optimal result with respect to corresponding partition. In fact, the classification of new objects can turn out to be poorly applicable unless we handle a larger bunch of decision rules. Then the decomposition problem is to find partition of the universe with high values of Q for possibly large number of conditions subsets. In consequence, we can take any approximation of formula

$$Q\,(p) = \frac{1}{2^{|A|}} \sum_{B \subseteq A} Q\,(B, p) \tag{29}$$

as optimization measure, or we can try to search for partition with some class of corresponding condition subsets, which is enough to reason with decomposed decision table.

Example 1. Consider decision table $\mathbf{A} = (U, A, d)$ and two-class partition p as on the following picture:

A	a_1	a_2	a_3	a_4	d
u_1	0	0	0	1	1
u_2	0	1	0	0	1
u_3	1	0	0	1	2
u_4	1	0	1	1	3
u_5	0	0	0	1	1
u_6	1	1	0	0	1
u_7	0	0	0	1	3
u_8	0	0	0	1	2
u_9	0	1	1	0	3

$\mathbf{A_1}$	a_1	a_2	a_3	a_4	d
u_1	0	0	0	1	1
u_3	1	0	0	1	2
u_5	0	0	0	1	1
u_8	0	0	0	1	2
u_9	0	1	1	0	3

$\mathbf{A_2}$	a_1	a_2	a_3	a_4	d
u_2	0	1	0	0	1
u_4	1	0	1	1	3
u_6	1	1	0	0	1
u_7	0	0	0	1	3

Then, e.g. for $B = \{a_2, a_3, a_4\}$, we have $p \in Part(d/B)$. One can see that p induces the following decision value set partitions for foregoing vectors on B:

$$(0,0,1) \Rightarrow \{1,2\}_{m=1}, \{3\}_{m=2} \qquad (1,0,0) \Rightarrow \emptyset_{m=1}, \{1\}_{m=2}$$
$$(0,1,1) \Rightarrow \emptyset_{m=1}, \{3\}_{m=2} \qquad (1,1,0) \Rightarrow \{3\}_{m=1}, \emptyset_{m=2}$$

Now, for any new object with one of vector values occurring on $B = \{a_2, a_3, a_4\}$ in $\mathbf{A}$, distributions induced by p-membership functions take the form

$$\partial_B^p (0,0,1) = ((\{1,2\}, 0.8), (\{3\}, 0.2)) \quad \partial_B^p (1,0,0) = ((\emptyset, 0), (\{1\}, 1))$$
$$\partial_B^p (0,1,1) = ((\emptyset, 0), (\{3\}, 1)) \quad \partial_B^p (1,1,0) = ((\{3\}, 1), (\emptyset, 0))$$

In case of vector $(0,0,1)$ it supports the intuition that one can answer with $\{1,2\}$ because the difference between 0.8 as its frequency and 0.2 for the rest is big enough to base on, even for relatively weak representativeness of the universe, expressed by the degree of credibility $r(p) = 2$ (compare with e.g. [10],[17]). Combining with other vector values from V_B, we obtain that $Q(B,p) = 0.78$. Now, let us consider subset $B' = \{a_3\}$ for which $p \notin Part(d/B')$ and $Q(B',p)$ decreases to 0.61. By exchanging objects u_1 with u_4 and u_5 with u_7 between partition classes of p we obtain $p' \in Part(d/B')$, given by

$$Inf_{p'}^{-1}(1) = \{u_3, u_4, u_7, u_8, u_9\} \quad and \quad Inf_{p'}^{-1}(2) = \{u_1, u_2, u_5, u_6\}$$

such that $Q(B',p') = 0.83$ is better not only than $Q(B',p)$ but also than $Q(B,p)$. It suggests that condition a_3 can generate more compact and applicable decision rules itself than if taken together with the others from B. However, one should remember that it does not mean that a_3 leads to more precise rules, since we can always check modified p' for initial B. In our case it results with equality $Q(B,p') = Q(B',p')$. Since p' splits the universe onto the largest decision class in $\mathbf{A}$ and the rest, one can expect that it should behave well on average, over all subsets of conditions. Indeed, $Q(p') = 0.82$, while for comparison $Q(p) = 0.74$. Still, formal conclusion that such universal partitions have something in common with partial grouping of decision classes needs more research.

5 Conclusions

We have presented the framework for data decomposition strictly related to the main factors of reasoning quality. By analysis of intervals of uncertainty ([1],[15]) corresponding to synthesized decision rules, we have obtained the model for natural balance between credibility and applicability from one, and precision from the other hand ([13],[14]).

Due to both potential applications and properties of introduced quality measures, we have focused on decision value oriented case of decomposition. By developing the notion of a decision reduct ([5],[12]), we have stated the goal for future algorithms finding optimal distribution of data. Such algorithms can be created by combining rough set methods (see e.g. [2],[16]) with our results.

References

1. Dempster A.P., *Upper and lower probabilities induced from a multivalued mapping; Annals of Mathematical Statistics*, 38, pp.325-339, 1967.
2. Nguyen S.H., Nguyen H.S., Skowron A., *Searching for Features defined by Hyperplanes* in *Proceedings of the Ninth International Symposium on Methodologies for Information Systems ISMIS'96*, Z.W. Raś, M. Michalewicz (eds.), June, Zakopane, Poland; Lecture Notes in AI 1079, Berlin, Springer Verlag, pp.366-375, 1996.
3. Nguyen S.H., Nguyen T.T., Polkowski L., Skowron A., Synak P., Wróblewski J., *Decision Rules for Large Data Tables* in *Proceedings of Symposium on Modelling, Analysis and Simulation* vol 1, *Computational Engineering in Systems Applications CESA'96*, July 9-12, Lille, France, pp.942-947, 1996.
4. Nguyen S.H., Polkowski L., Skowron A., Synak P., Wróblewski J., *Searching for Approximate Description of Decision Classes* in *Proceedings of the Fourth International Workshop on Rough Sets, Fuzzy Sets and Machine Discovery RSFD'96*, November 6-8, Tokyo, Japan; the University of Tokyo, pp.153-161, 1996.
5. Pawlak Z., *Rough Sets. Theoretical Aspects of Reasoning about Data*, Kluwer Academic Publishers, Dordrecht, 1991.
6. Pawlak Z., Skowron A., *Rough Membership Functions; Advances in the Dempster-Shafer Theory of Evidence*, Yager R.R., Fedrizzi M., Kacprzyk J.(eds.), John Wiley & Sons, New York, pp.251-271, 1994.
7. Payne J.W., Bettman J.R., Johnson E.J., *The Adaptive Decision Maker*, Cambridge University Press, 1993.
8. Polkowski L., Skowron A., *Rough mereology: a new paradigm for approximate reasoning* in *International Journal of Approximate Reasoning*, in print.
9. Shafer G., *A Mathematical Theory of Evidence*, Princeton University Press, 1976.
10. Skowron A., *Synthesis of Adaptive Decision Systems from Experimental Data; Proceedings of the Fifth Scandinavian Conference on Artificial Intelligence SCAI-95*, Aamodt A., Komorowski J.(eds.), Amsterdam, IOS Press, pp.220-238, 1995.
11. Skowron A., Grzymała-Busse J., *From Rough Set Theory to Evidence Theory* in *Advances in the Dempster-Shafer Theory of Evidence*, Yager R.R., Fedrizzi M., Kacprzyk J.(eds.), John Wiley & Sons, New York, pp.193-236, 1994.
12. Skowron A., Rauszer C., *The Discernibility Matrices and Functions in Information Systems* in *Intelligent Decision Support. Handbook of Applications and Advances of the Rough Sets Theory*, Słowiński R.(ed.), Kluwer, Dordrecht, pp.331-362, 1992.
13. Ślęzak D., *Approximate Reducts in Decision Tables; Proceedings of Information Processing and Management of Uncertainty in Knowledge-Based Systems IPMU 96*, Granada, July 1-5, Universidad de Granada, pp.1159-1164, 1996.
14. Vapnik V., *Estimation of Dependencies Based on Empirical Data*, Springer Series in Statistics, Springer-Verlag, 1982.
15. Wasserman L.A., *Belief Functions and Statistical Inference; The Canadian Journal of Statistics Vol.18, No.3*, pp.183-196, 1990.
16. Wróblewski J., *Finding minimal reducts using genetic algorithms* in *Proceedings of the Second Annual Joint Conference on Information Sciences*, September 28 - October 1, Wrightsville Beach, NC, pp.186-189, 1995.
17. Ziarko W., *Variable Precision Rough Set Model; Journal of Computer and System Sciences*, 40, pp.39-59, 1993.

A Machine Learning Experiment
to Determine Part of Speech from Word-Endings

Jerzy W. Grzymala-Busse[1] and L. John Old[2]

[1] University of Kansas, Lawrence, KS 66045
[2] Indiana University, Bloomington, IN 47408

Abstract. A file containing the last three characters of words from Roget's Thesaurus was created. Every entry was classified as belonging to one of the five parts of speech: nouns, verbs, adjectives, adverbs, and prepositions. The machine learning system LERS induced rules from this file. The paper describes this experiment. Two interesting regularities of the English language were discovered. Moreover, using a set of rules induced by LERS it is feasible to recognize part of speech of a word on the basis of its last three characters with the expected error rate of 26.71%.

Keywords: Learning and knowledge discovery, rough set theory, Roget's Thesaurus, rule induction, classification of examples, system LERS.

1 Introduction

The data file, containing 129,797 entries, was created from Roget's Thesaurus [12]. Each entry of the file represents the last three characters of a word, and an integer between 1 and 5 showing to which part of speech the original word belonged. The file contains 71,985 nouns, 18,686 verbs, 33,859 adjectives, 5,172 adverbs and 95 prepositions. Excluded were capitalized words, foreign words and words having three letters or less; abbreviations, phrases, cross-references, and any entries which had "peculiarities". Peculiarities include, for example, interjections where the last character of the entry is an exclamation mark, or is parenthetical meta-information.

The 129,797 entries consist of 4,189 unique three-letter strings. Clearly there is a great deal of repetition. Moreover, only a small portion of the file (4.82% of the total) is consistent. This means that the remaining entries are involved in conflicts: the last three characters are the same yet original words belong to different parts of speech. Thus it is natural to process this file using rough set theory [3, 9–11, 14]. Rough set theory, originated in 1982 by Z. Pawlak, is an excellent tool for dealing with inconsistency.

2 Rule Induction by LERS

In our experiment rules were induced from the file by the LERS system (Learning from Examples using Rough Sets), see [4]. LERS assumes that an input data file is presented in the form of a table, where examples correspond to rows and columns to variables. One of the variables is a decision (in our case, the part of speech, denoted by d), while the remaining variables are attributes (in our case, the last three characters of the word, denoted by $a1$, $a2$, and $a3$). An example of such a table is presented as Table 1.

Table 1

Attributes			Decision
a1	a2	a3	d
i	n	e	1
i	n	c	1
i	n	g	1
i	n	g	3

Though Table 1 is cited here only for illustration, it contains four real entries from the input data file created from Roget's Thesaurus. In this file, 1 denotes a noun, 2 denotes a verb, 3 denotes an adjective, 4 denotes an adverb, and 5 denotes a preposition.

LERS first checks the input data file for consistency. Table 1 represents an inconsistent data set: the last two examples are conflicting. LERS uses an approach to inconsistency based on rough set theory: it computes lower and upper approximations for each concept. In Table 1 there are two concepts: $(d, 1)$ represents a noun and $(d, 3)$ represents an adjective. Rules induced from the lower approximations of the concepts are called *certain*. Rules induced from the upper approximations of the concepts are called *possible*.

The user of LERS may use one of the four algorithms to rule induction [3, 5]. In our experiment the algorithm LEM2 (Learning from Examples Module version 2) was used [2, 4]. In this algorithm, for lower and upper approximations of every concept local coverings are computed. Rules are represented by minimal complexes, from which local coverings are constructed.

Description of LEM2 is based on a few definitions. Let B be a nonempty lower or upper approximation of a concept represented by a decision-value pair (d, w). Set B *depends on a set T* of attribute-value pairs t if and only if

$$\emptyset \neq [T] = \bigcap_{t \in T} [t] \subseteq B.$$

Set T is a *minimal complex* of B if and only if B depends on T and no proper subset T' of T exists such that B depends on T'. Let $\mathbb{T}$ be a nonempty collection of nonempty sets of attribute-value pairs. Then $\mathbb{T}$ is a *local covering of B* if and only if the following conditions are satisfied:

(1) each member T of $\mathbb{T}$ is a minimal complex of B,

(2) $\bigcup_{T \in \mathbb{T}} [T] = B$, and

(3) $\mathbb{T}$ is minimal, i.e., $\mathbb{T}$ has the smallest possible number of members.

The user may select an option of LEM2 with or without taking into account attribute priorities. The procedure LEM2 with attribute priorities is presented below. The other option differs from the one presented below in the selection of a pair $t \in T(G)$ in the inner loop WHILE. When LEM2 is not to take attribute priorities into account, the first criterion is ignored. In our experiments all attribute priorities were equal to each other.

Procedure LEM2
(input: a set B,
output: a single local covering $\mathbb{T}$ of set B);
begin
    G := B;
    $\mathbb{T}$:= $\emptyset$;
    while G $\neq \emptyset$
        begin
        T := $\emptyset$;
        T(G) := $\{t \mid [t] \cap G \neq \emptyset\}$;
        while T = $\emptyset$ **or** [T] $\nsubseteq$ B
            begin
                select a pair t $\in$ T(G) with the highest attribute
                priority, if a tie occurs, select a pair t $\in$ T(G)
                such that $|[t] \cap G|$ is maximum; if another tie
                occurs, select a pair t $\in$ T(G) with the smallest
                cardinality of [t]; if a further tie occurs, select
                first pair;
                T := T $\cup$ {t};
                G := [t] $\cap$ G;
                T(G) := $\{t \mid [t] \cap G \neq \emptyset\}$;
                T(G) := T(G) – T;
            end {while}
        for each t in T **do**
            if [T – {t}] $\subseteq$ B **then** T := T – {t};
        $\mathbb{T}$:= $\mathbb{T} \cup$ {T};
        G := B $- \bigcup_{T \in \mathbb{T}}[T]$;
    end {while};
    for each T in $\mathbb{T}$ **do**
        if $\bigcup_{S \in \mathbb{T}-\{T\}}[S]$ = B **then** $\mathbb{T}$:= $\mathbb{T}$ – {T};
end {procedure}.

From Table 1 the algorithm LEM2 induces the following certain rules:

(a3, c) –> (d, 1),

(a3, e) –> (d, 1),

and the following possible rules:

(a1, i) –> (d, 1),
(a3, g) –> (d, 3).

3 Classification System of LERS

For classification of new cases LERS uses a modification of the "bucket brigade algorithm" [1, 7]. The decision as to which concept an example belongs is made on the basis of three factors: strength, specificity, and support. They are defined as follows: *Strength* is the total number of examples correctly classified by the rule during training. *Specificity* is the total number of attribute-value pairs on the left-hand side of the rule. The matching rules with a larger number of attribute-value pairs are considered more specific. The third factor, *support*, is defined as the sum of scores of all matching rules from the concept. The concept C for which the support, i.e., the value of the following expression

$$\sum_{\text{matching rules } R \text{ describing } C} \text{Strength}(R) * \text{Specificity}(R),$$

is the largest is a winner and the example is classified as being a member of C.

If an example is not completely matched by any rule, some classification systems use *partial matching*. System AQ15, during partial matching, uses the probabilistic sum of all measures of fit for rules [8]. Another approach to partial matching is presented in [13]. Holland *et al.* [7] do not consider partial matching as a viable alternative of complete matching and rely on a default hierarchy instead. In LERS partial matching does not rely on the input of the user. If complete matching is impossible, all partially matching rules are identified. These are rules with at least one attribute-value pair matching the corresponding attribute-value pair of an example.

For any partially matching rule R, the additional factor, called *matching factor*, is computed. The matching factor (R) is equal to the ratio of the number of matched attribute-value pairs of the rule R to the total number of attribute-value pairs of the rule R. In partial matching, the concept C for which the value of the following expression

$$\sum_{\text{partially matching rules } R \text{ describing } C} \text{Matching\_factor}(R) * \text{Strength }(R) * \text{Specificity}(R)$$

is the largest is the winner and the example is classified as being a member of C. All rules, induced by LERS, are preceded by three numbers: specificity, strength, and the total number of training examples matched by the rule.

Let us illustrate the classification system with an example. Say that we want to identify to which part of speech a word ending with "ing" belongs. We will use the actual possible rules induced by LERS that will apply to this pattern:

2, 4304, 8709
(a1, i) & (a2, n) –> (d, 1),

3, 80, 7118
(a1, i) & (a2, n) & (a3, g) –> (d, 2),

3, 3642, 7118
(a1, i) & (a2, n) & (a3, g) –> (d, 3),

3, 14, 7118
(a2, n) & (a1, i) & (a3, g) –> (d, 4),

3, 6, 7118
(a2, n) & (a1, i) & (a3, g) –> (d, 5).

For the concept $(d, 1)$, the support is $4,304*2 = 8,608$, for the concept $(d, 2)$ the support is $80*3 = 240$, for the concept $(d, 3)$ the support is $3,642*3 = 10,926$, for the concept $(d, 4)$ the support is $14*3 = 42$, for the concept $(d, 5)$ the support is $6*3 = 18$. Thus the winning concept is $(d, 3)$, i.e., the word was an adjective. We may reach the same conclusion computing conditional probabilities of the concept given the set of all training examples matched by the rule: for the concept $(d, 3)$ the probability is $3642/7118 = 0.517$, while the probabilities for $(d, 1)$, $(d, 2)$, $(d, 4)$ and $(d, 5)$ are $3,376/7118 = 0.474$, $14/7118 = 0.002$, $80/7118 = 0.011$, and $6/7118 = 0.001$, respectively.

One might have expected concept $(d, 2)$, a verb, to have made a stronger showing because we use verbs ending in "ing" so often in everyday speech. The catch here is that the data set is derived from a lexicon. Dictionaries and thesauri do not include entries for words which can be derived using rules, such as pluralization and verb tense (jumps, jumped, jumping), unless they follow uncommon rules (i.e., are irregular).

4 An Experiment with Roget's Thesaurus

First of all, LERS has discovered that in the file containing all the words of the Roget's Thesaurus, the hyphen cannot occur as the last character of a word or as the next to the last character of a word. Thus the hyphen may occur only on the third position, counting from the back of the word. Examples of such words are call-up, ease-up, cave-in, and drive-in.

The same is true of the character "q"—it may occur only on the third position, counting from the end of the word (e.g., antique, baroque, clique, soliloquy).

Thus the input data file could have $27*25*25 = 16,875$ different entries, yet it had only 4,189 different entries. Simply, most combinations are not characteristic for the English language.

LERS has induced from our data file 836 certain rules and 2,294 possible rules. Examples of stronger certain rules are listed below:

Rules   **Example words**

2, 331, 331
(a3, s) & (a2, c) –> (d, 1)   antics

3, 110, 110
(a3, s) & (a2, e) & (a1, i) –> (d, 1)   caries

3, 296, 296
(a3, s) & (a2, i) & (a1, s) –> (d, 1)   oasis

2, 136, 136
(a3, a) & (a2, m) –> (d, 1)   drama

2, 113, 113
(a3, a) & (a1, o) –> (d, 1)   quota

3, 18, 18
(a3, e) & (a1, y) & (a2, z) –> (d, 2)   analyze

3, 14, 14
(a2, r) & (a3, b) & (a1, o) –> (d, 2)   absorb

3, 59, 59
(a3, y) & (a2, h) & (a1, s) –> (d, 3)   trashy

2, 39, 39
(a3, y) & (a2, w) –> (d, 3)   willowy

3, 71, 71
(a3, d) & (a2, e) & (a1, u) –> (d, 3)   subdued

3, 11, 11
(a2, l) & (a3, y) & (a1, y) –> (d, 4)   shyly

3, 7, 7
(a2, l) & (a3, y) & (a1, c) –> (d, 4)   publicly

Possible rules better describe hidden regularities in the input data file because the input data file has so many conflicting entries. Stronger possible rules are the following:

2, 4304, 8709
(a1, i) & (a2, n) –> (d, 1)

(Where the 4,304 entries ending with "in*" consist of 3,376 entries ending with "ing", plus 445 ending with "ine", plus 282 with "int", and so on).

2, 5935, 6073
(a1, i) & (a2, o) –> (d, 1)

2, 2011, 5846
(a3, e) & (a1, i) –> (d, 1)

2, 5622, 6957
(a2, e) & (a3, r) –> (d, 1)

2, 6360, 7238
(a1, e) & (a2, s) –> (d, 1)

2, 2896, 3263
(a3, y) & (a2, t) –> (d, 1)

2, 2300, 4059
(a3, t) & (a1, e) –> (d, 1)

2, 2478, 3505
(a1, i) & (a2, s) –> (d, 1)

1, 9659, 12470
(a3, s) –> (d, 1)

2, 2233, 2593
(a2, c) & (a1, n) –> (d, 1)

3, 1659, 2729
(a3, e) & (a1, a) & (a2, t) –> (d, 2)

3, 633, 673
(a3, e) & (a1, i) & (a2, z) –> (d, 2)

3, 3642, 7118
(a1, i) & (a2, n) & (a3, g) –> (d, 3)

3, 1740, 2172
(a3, e) & (a2, l) & (a1, b) –> (d, 3)

3, 1278, 1635
(a3, e) & (a1, i) & (a2, v) –> (d, 3)

3, 632, 789
(a2, l) & (a3, y) & (a1, l) –> (d, 4)

3, 568, 637
(a2, l) & (a3, y) & (a1, e) –> (d, 4)

3, 560, 566
(a2, l) & (a3, y) & (a1, s) –> (d, 4)

2, 522, 907
(a2, l) & (a1, t) –> (d, 4)

Some of the possible rules are very weak, for example

3, 1, 1635
(a3, e) & (a1, i) & (a2, v) –> (d, 4)

(A single example. In this case "alive".)

3, 1, 1555
(a2, e) & (a3, d) & (a1, t) –> (d, 4)

3, 1, 800
(a3, e) & (a2, r) & (a1, u) –> (d, 4)

3, 1, 745
(a1, i) & (a3, h) & (a2, s) –> (d, 4)

3, 1, 1555
(a2, e) & (a3, d) & (a1, t) –> (d, 2)

3, 2, 2569
(a1, i) & (a3, y) & (a2, t) –> (d, 2)

3, 1, 943
(a2, a) & (a3, l) & (a1, c) –> (d, 2)

3, 1, 1052
(a1, i) & (a2, s) & (a3, m) –> (d, 2)

3, 6, 7118
(a2, n) & (a1, i) & (a3, g) –> (d, 5)

3, 1, 6811
(a1, e) & (a3, s) & (a2, s) –> (d, 5)

3, 1, 2825
(a2, n) & (a3, t) & (a1, e) –> (d, 5)

3, 3, 1675
(a3, r) & (a2, e) & (a1, t) –> (d, 5)

For validation of both rule sets: certain and possible, we assumed that the training data set is identical with the testing data set, i.e., that the same input data file was used for training and testing. This assumption is justified by circumstances: we are assuming that the input data file is complete because it was created from the entire dictionary of the English language as seen in Roget's Thesaurus.

The error rate for the certain rule set is 44.19%. The error rate for the possible rule set is 32.34%. For the possible rule set, error rates are: 8.71% for nouns, 87.66% for verbs, 20.71% for adverbs, 53.67% for adjectives, and 91.58% for prepositions. The user of system LERS may change default values of all four factors used in classification [5]. As follows from [6], one of the worst classification schemes is based on the single factor: the strength of the rule replaced by the conditional probability of the concept given the set of all training examples matched by the rule. The rule with the largest probability wins and assigns the example to the concept indicated by the right hand side of the rule. However, in our experiments on Roget's Thesaurus, this was the best classification method. For the classification method based on conditional probabilities, the error rate for the possible rule set is 26.71%. Specifically, error rates are: 11.75% for nouns, 73.58% for verbs, 19.99% for adverbs, 33.507% for adjectives, and 85.26% for prepositions.

Conclusions

LERS discovered two interesting regularities in the dictionary of the English language created from the Roget's Thesaurus: there is no English word with the hyphen or character "q" on the last or last-but-one position of the word.

Besides, using LERS and the set of all possible rules it is feasible to recognize part of speech of a word on the basis if its last three characters with the expected error rate of 26.71%.

The exclusion of words consisting of three letters or less may have been a misjudgment. Some of our most popular words, such as pronouns and the most common prepositions fall into that category. Their inclusion could radically alter the results.

Using a lexicon as a training set has the drawback that the source set, though representative of the spectrum of strings and parts of speech of the whole language, is not representative of the frequency of such combinations in written and spoken language. A tagged corpus would likely provide a more representative set of rules for recognition of the part of speech of words in, for example, on-line text files.

References

1. Booker, L. B., Goldberg, D. E., and Holland, J. F.: Classifier systems and genetic algorithms. In *Machine Learning. Paradigms and Methods.* Carbonell, J. G. (ed.), The MIT Press, 1990, 235–282.
2. Chan, C. C. and Grzymala-Busse, J. W.: On the attribute redundancy and the learning programs ID3, PRISM, and LEM2. Department of Computer Science, University of Kansas, TR-91-14, 1991, 20 pp.
3. Grzymala-Busse, J. W.: *Managing Uncertainty in Expert Systems.* Kluwer Academic Publishers, 1991.
4. Grzymala-Busse, J. W.: LERS—A system for learning from examples based on rough sets. In *Intelligent Decision Support. Handbook of Applications and Advances of the Rough Sets Theory.* Slowinski, R. (ed.), Kluwer Academic Publishers, 1992, 3–18.
5. Grzymala-Busse, J. W.: Managing uncertainty in machine learning from examples. *Proc. of the Third Intelligent Information Systems Workshop*, Wigry, Poland, June 6–11, 1994, 70–84.
6. Grzymala-Busse, J. W. and Wang, C. P. B.: Classification and rule induction based on rough sets. *Proc. of the 5th IEEE International Conference on Fuzzy Systems FUZZ-IEEE'96*, New Orleans, Louisiana, September 8–11, 1996, 744–747.
7. Holland, J. H., Holyoak K. J., and Nisbett, R. E.: *Induction. Processes of Inference, Learning, and Discovery.* The MIT Press, 1986.

8. Michalski, R. S., Mozetic, I., Hong, J. and Lavrac, N. The AQ15 inductive learning system: An overview and experiments. Department of Computer Science, University of Illinois, Rep. UIUCDCD-R-86-1260, 1986.
9. Pawlak, Z.: Rough sets. *International Journal Computer and Information Sciences* **11**, 1982, 341–356.
10. Pawlak, Z.: *Rough Sets. Theoretical Aspects of Reasoning about Data.* Kluwer Academic Publishers, 1991.
11. Ras, Z. W.: Cooperative query answering. *Proc. of the Workshop Intelligent Inf. Syst. IV*, Augustow, Poland, June 5–9, 1995, 32–41.
12. *Roget's International Thesaurus*, Thomas Y. Crowell Company, 1962.
13. Slowinski, R. and Stefanowski, J. Handling various types of uncertainty in the rough set approach. *Proc of the RKSD–93, International Workshop on Rough Sets and Knowledge Discovery*, 1993, 395–397.
14. Ziarko, W. Analysis of uncertain information in the framework of variable precision rough sets. *Found. Computing Decision Sci.* **18**, 1993, 381–396.

Learning Flexible Concepts from Uncertain Data

Mohamed Quafafou

IRIN, University of Nantes,
2 rue de la Houssiniere, BP 92208
44322, Nantes Cedex 03, France.

Abstract. Learning from examples consists of knowledge induction from training examples using an inductive learning algorithm. In practice, a preprocessing phase is necessary to transform numerical attributes into intervals (discretization), to deal with missing values, noisy data, and so forth. The major part of research efforts has proposed methods for data pre-processing but no special attention has been devoted to model and to handle the uncertainty inherent in real-world data. In this paper we introduce a preprocessing task to model uncertainty which is considered during all the learning process. In this context we formalize a notion of flexible concepts in contrast with "sharp" concepts usually represented by crisp sets. Next, we discuss an inductive learning approach based on rough set theory and we propose a method which allows the user to control both the granularity of knowledge resulting from the partition of the universe and the consistency of rules to be learned. Our proposed method is at the basis of the system Alpha which is run on real-world datasets.

1 Introduction

The learning from example problem has been widely studied by the machine learning community. The following schema (Gams et al. 1987) is generally used by a learning algorithm: (1) preprocessing of the training set: to deal with numerical attributes discretization, treatment of missing values, etc. (2) induction: to infer knowledge that is information on a higher level than the training set, and (3) test: to use the learned knowledge to deal with new and unseen events, for instance, classification of sick persons according to their symptoms.

In this paper we will focus only on points (1) and (2) and we will use 5-cross validation protocol to estimate the accuracy of our system, called Alpha. On the one hand, we use fuzzy sets to deal with continous attributes and we consider that values of both qualitative and quantitative attributes are represented by membership functions. Fuzzy sets are also used to represent flexible concepts, which are contrasted with "sharp" concepts which are usually represented by "crisp" sets. We have introduced a new uncertainty modeling task in the preprocessing phase. A teacher must specify the fuzzy sets used to define the semantics of values of a given attribute. On the other hand, we focus our discussion on learning algorithms based on rough set theory, which generally use approximations of concepts during their induction processes. Three main phases are distinguished: (1) partition of the universes, i.e., training set, (2) approximation of concepts to learn and (3) rule generation. We have extended rough set theory, called Alpha Rough Set Theory, a-RST in short, to approximate flexible concepts (Quafafou 1997a, 1997b). Consequently, we can control the granularity of knowledge which results from the partition of the universe. Finally, we can control the consistency of rules to be generated and consequently, strong rules, which are consistent enough are discovered.

In Section 2, we discuss the problems generally considered during the preprocessing phase and we introduce a new preprocessing task which consists of uncertainty modeling. Next, we show the usefulness of discovering strong rules. Section 3 is dedicated to the description of the uncertainty modeling task which leads to a transformation of the original data. Next, we introduce a general approach to induce rules using rough set theory. Section 5 shows that considering uncertainty of data leads to approximate flexible concepts instead of sharp ones. The main foundations of our learning system, are introduced in section 6. Our experimental results on two real-world bases are discussed in section 7. We conclude in section 8.

2 Data, knowledge and uncertainty

A set of training examples is generally collected and codified using a given representation language. These examples are then used by a learning algorithm to induce a description of a set of concepts, which may be incorporated in an inference engine to classify new and unseen examples. Consequently, the learning task is reduced to the induction of knowledge, i.e., description of concepts, from data, i.e., training example, using an inductive learning algorithm. In practice, a preprocessing phase is necessary to deal with numerical attributes, missing values and noisy data.

The *discretization* process (Fayyad 1992, 1993) is an important issue because most real-world applications of inductive learning involve quantitative attributes. This process replaces numerical values by intervals corresponding to qualitative terms, e.g., low, medium, high, etc. Another problem is that attribute values may be missing (Quinlan 1989). Different approaches have been developed to overcome this problem, for instance, to discard examples with missing values or to add the value "unknown" to the domain of each attribute. A value of a missing attribute may be predicted using a set of rules as proposed in (Quinlan 1986). Original data can be imprecise, i.e., only a subinterval of possible values is known instead of the precise value of a numerical attribute. On the one hand, Slowinski discusses in (Slowinski 1993) the three sources of uncertainty, which are (i) discretization of qualitative attributes, (ii) imprecise descriptors, (iii) missing values. He shows that modeling the three types of uncertainty using fuzzy sets holds them down to the problem of multiple descriptors where a finite set of attribute values is known. On the other hand, we have shown, in the context of the induction of a classifier to predicate the behavior of dynamic systems (Quafafou et al. 1995) that the conversion of numerical values into discrete intervals can increase the inconsistency of the training data, i.e., two examples are inconsistent if they have the same descriptor but belong to different classes. The major part of research efforts has proposed methods for data pre-processing but no special attention has been devoted to model and to handle the uncertainty inherent to real-world data.

The preprocessing phase results in a transformed set of training examples expressed according to a given representation language. Next, an algorithm is used to induce a set of hypotheses that describes a concept, i.e., covers all positive instances of the concept and does not cover any negative examples. However, such induction techniques are concerned only with deterministic hypotheses and generally over-fit the training data when learning concepts corrupted by noise (Bergadano and al. 1988). A non-deterministic approach to identify strong rules (Shapiro 1988) is then introduced dealing with real world data which is generally contaminated by errors and noise. Strong rules, i.e., uncertain knowledge, are partially incorrect because they can cover a proportion of negative training examples. Thus, a weight is associated with each rule and expresses the reliability of the rule, i.e., the probability that the rule gives the correct classification. Different studies have demonstrated that this approach reduces the susceptibility of inductive algorithms to noisy data (Ali et al 1993; Botta et al. 1993).

3 A pre-processing uncertainty modeling task

So far, we have underlined that learning from numerical attributes is a hard task which requires complex computations to explore large spaces and hence, to identify description of concepts, which are generally too detailed. We propose to use fuzzy sets for the discretization of continous attributes. Indeed, qualitative attributes are interpreted as linguistic variables, according to fuzzy set theory (Yager 1992; Cox 1994). Each attribute value, i.e., linguistic variable, is represented by a membership function defined by the teacher to specify how to evaluate the truth of the attribute value on the learning examples. A membership function maps a numerical domain of an attribute on the interval $[0, 1]$, i.e., the abscissa represents the values of the attribute, whereas the ordinate represents the truth value. Each value is then associated with a linguistic term and a truth value and if a numerical value is associated with several membership functions, only the one with the maximum grade is kept. Consequently, a transformation process replaces the original description vector of a training example by two vectors containing qualitative descriptions, i.e., linguistic terms, and quantitative descriptions, i.e., truth values. For instance, the vector $(100, 5, 200, good, 1265)$, the original description of the car x_i characterized by the attributes $Power, Capacity, Vibration, Interior, Weight$, is transformed into two vectors $x_{i1} = (high, medium, low, good, low)$ and $x_{i2} = (1.0, 0.76, 0.6, 1, 0.65)$. The vector x_{i1} is a qualitative description of x_i containing linguistic terms, whereas x_{i2} is a quantitative description containing degrees of possibility assigned to values of attributes appearing in x_{i1}. Remark that all attributes are continous except $Interior$; its value is $good$ with a membership degree equal to 1. Indeed, a value v of a qualitative attribute A is associated with a crisp membership function, which maps the domain of A into 0, 1 so that it takes 1 for V and none for the other values of A, i.e., $domain(A) - v$.

Each training example is then assigned a degree of possibility of its realization, which results from the aggregation of values appearing in x_{i2}. The aggregation operator may be chosen among a wide range of possible operators (Dubois and al. 1984), for instance Yager's parametrized t-norm (Yager 1979). We consider in this paper the operator min, for reasons of simplicity. Thus, the previous training example x_i is assigned a value equal to the minimum of $1.0, 0.76, 0.6, 1, 0.65$, which is 0.6.

In our approach, a concept description is induced from the pre-classified examples considering both their qualitative, i.e., x_{i1} and quantitative descriptions, i.e., x_{i2}. The resulting concepts are used to classify unseen examples predicating the price of a car according to the five previous features. As the attribute $Price$ is continous, it is associated with a set of membership functions. Using these membership functions, we transform the price of a car into a linguistic term and a truth value. For instance, the prices of $x1$, $x5$, $x8$, which are equal to 30000, 32000 and 34000 are transformed respectively into $x_{11} = high$ and $x_{12} = 0.4$, $x_{51} = high$ and $x_{52} = 0.6$, $x_{81} = high$ and $x_{82} = 0.9$. Hence, the concept $expensivecars$ is defined by $Price = high$ and cars belong to this concept with different degrees, e.g., x_1 is $slightlyexpensive$, x_5 is $moderatelyexpensive$, x_8 is $stronglyexpensive$. Thus, classical sets are not suitable for representing flexible concepts because these are not crisp. Flexible concepts are represented by fuzzy sets and they are more sensitive to data than crisp concepts.

4 A rough sets based learning strategy

Rough set theory was recently introduced by Z. Pawlak (Pawlak 1991; Pawlak et al. 1995; Grzymala-Busse 1995), offering a suitable approach to handle imperfect data. It is based on the basic notion of indiscernability and supposes that we have some information on the domain we are interested in. This information describes elements of a universe in terms of a finite set of attributes which have finite domains. Thus, each element of the universe is described by a vector of attribute values and two elements associated with the same vector are said to be indiscernable. For instance, patients with the same symptoms are indiscernible in view of the information available about them, i.e., their symptoms. The indiscernability relation, denoted I, is assumed to be an equivalence relation.

A key idea in rough set theory is the approximation of concepts using two operators which assign to each subset of the universe its two approximations called the $I - lower$ and $I - upper$ approximation. The $I - lower$ approximation of X, denoted I$-lower(X)$ is the set of elements which certainly belong to X, whereas the $I - upper$ approximation of X, denoted I$-upper(X)$ is the set of elements which possibly belong to X. Elements which are probably in X but do not certainty belong to X define a doubtful region called the boundary region, i.e., $I - upper(X) - I - lower(X)$. We say that a set X is rough (inexact) when its boundary is a non empty set: the more the size of a boundary set is small the better is the definition of the set in terms of the available knowledge.

In rough sets, a decision table in which elements are described in terms of given attributes contains one attribute called a decision or class. Each element is labeled by an expert with a class value according to its description. Different methods have been developed using a rough set framework to learn classification rules (Ziarko and al. 1993; Slowinski 1994, Grzymala-Busse 1993). The LERS (Learning from Examples based on Rough Sets) approach developed by Grzymala-Busse was applied successfully to different areas, i.e., medical (Woolery and al. 1994), natural-language (Grzymala-Busse and Than 1995a), knowledge acquisition (Grzymala-Busse and al. 1995b), and so forth. A description of a concept consists of a disjunction of complexes, where a complex is a conjunction of attribute-value pairs. Rules (minimal complexes) are directly induced from lower and upper approximations of concepts. Rules learned from the lower approximation of a concept are called certain, whereas those learned from the upper approximation are called possible. We focus our attention in this paper on a local method for induction, which consists of three main steps. The first step consists of a partition of the universe and results to granule knowledge. Next, lower and upper approximations of concepts are computed during the second step. The third step consists of generation of certain and possible rules from respectively the lower and upper approximations of each concept. Finally, these rules are used by an inference engine to deal with unseen examples, and the accuracy of the learning system is estimated.

5 Uncertain data and approximation of concepts

The indiscernability relation I is an equivalence relation defined on the equality of attributes values. The quotient set U/I contains equivalence classes which are granules of knowledge representation. However, the previous indiscernability definition is not sufficient to deal with our events, i.e., $x = (x_{i1}, x_{i2})$ because it does not take into account possibility degrees associated with values of attributes, i.e., x_{i2}. In order to cope with this problem, we introduce a parametrized relation, denoted I_α. We consider that two elements x and y are indiscernable, denoted $x\ I_\alpha\ y$, if and only if they have the same values for all attributes and if their similarity degree is greater than a given *similarity threshold* α.

$$x\ I_\alpha\ y \iff (x\ I\ y) \text{ and } (x\ S\ y \geq \alpha)$$

The relation Ia is defined on both an equivalence relation I and a similarity relation S. The relation I is similar to the classical indiscernability relation of rough set theory, i.e., $(x\ I\ y) \iff x_{i1} = y_{i1}$, and S a similarity relation (Dubois et al. 1994).

Equivalence classes are used in rough set theory to compute lower and upper approximations of a concept represented by a crisp set containing examples that belong to the concept. In order to deal with uncertainty of data and to improve the learning approach based on approximation of concepts, we propose a solution, which approximates *flexible concepts*, i.e., concepts represented by fuzzy sets using the indiscernability relation I_α . Indeed, we have shown so far that values of attributes may be vague, so an example has a value for an attribute with a given possibility degree. Consequently, an example can belong partially to a given concept, such concepts are called flexible. We have proposed a generalization of rough set theory which allows approximation of flexible concepts (Quafafou 1997a) using the parametrized indiscernability relation II_α.

Figure 1 shows eight examples, x_1, x_2, ..., x_8, having the same values for a given set of attributes, i.e., $x_{i1} = x_{j1}$ for any i and j such that $1 \le i, j \le 8$. A bold line links examples which are in the same class, whereas a solid line indicates that we consider a similarity degree of a pair of examples. The eight examples belong to the same class when the similarity threshold is equal to none ($\alpha = 0$). However, three classes arise when the value of α is equal to 0.65, the first contains examples 2, 7 and 5, the second is reduced to the singleton 4, whereas the third contains 1, 3, 6, 8. By varying the value of α to 0.90, the latter class is split into two classes containing respectively 3, 6 and 1, 8. Thus, we have defined a parametrized indiscernability relation I_α, where the similarity threshold α is a parameter in the range $[0, 1]$. The user can control the partitionning of the universe by varying α from none (coarsest partitionning) to one (finest partitionning). Note that classical rough set theory considers only the coarsest partitionning of the universe and classes are created with $\alpha = 0$.

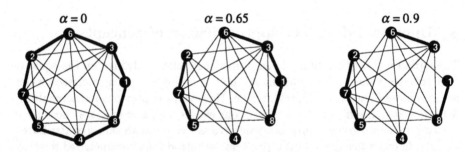

Figure 1: Evolution of the similarity graph according to α

So far we have introduced a rough set based learning strategy which uses lower and upper approximations of concepts to induce their descriptions. Approximations are computed from classes which result from the universe partitionning. We have extended the classical rough set definition of approximations to deal with fuzzy sets. Two fuzzy approximations, denoted $I_\alpha - lower(X)$ and $I_\alpha - upper(X)$, are then defined as:

$$I_\alpha - lower(X) = \bigcup_{y \in U \wedge I_\alpha(y) \subseteq X} I_\alpha(y)$$
$$I_\alpha - upper(X) = \bigcup_{y \in U \wedge I_\alpha(y) \cap X \neq \emptyset} I_\alpha(y) \cup X$$

Let us consider the following example, where the universe contains nine examples, x_1, x_2, ..., x_8, x_9, which are split into two classes according to the values of their attributes, i.e., $x_{i1} = x_{j1}$ for any i and j such that $1 \leq i, j \leq 9$. The knowledge on the domain is reduced to two classes depicted in the figure 2a. Let X be a concept to which belong the examples x_2, x_3, x_4, x_5, x_7, x_9. In classical rough set theory we deduce that this concept can not be defined according to the available knowledge, i.e., the training set, because its lower approximation is empty and its upper approximation is equal to all the universe. Moreover, the concept X is totally indefinable, i.e., no element of U belongs surely to X and all elements of U possibly belong to X. Such a situation may arise because the concept is not definable or because the data is corrupted. In this latter situation, we can explore the data controlling the granularity of knowledge by changing the value of the parameter α. For instance, four classes arise when the value of α is equal to 0.4 (figure 2b), thus the lower approximation is not empty and contains four elements: x_1, x_2, x_6, x_8. The upper approximation contains seven examples x_1, x_2, x_3, x_5, x_6, x_8, x_9. As the approximations of X are not empty, rules may be learned from them.

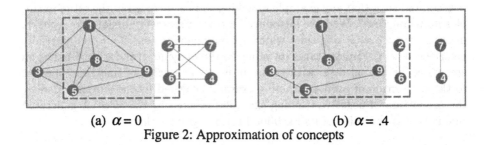

(a) $\alpha = 0$ (b) $\alpha = .4$

Figure 2: Approximation of concepts

Note that with $\alpha = 0$, i.e., the classical rough set framework, no example belongs surely to the concept X and all examples possibly belong to X. Consequently, any certain rule will be induced and all examples will be used to learn possible rules. By α varying from 0 to 1, we improve the approximation of X and consequently the rules learning process.

6 Learning flexible concepts

The learning process is carried out in three steps. First, the training examples are split into classes containing indiscernable examples. Then, lower and upper approximations are computed for each concept to learn. Finally, certain and possible rules are generated respectively from the lower and upper approximations. Such a learning process typically leads to a few reliable rules and many unreliable rules each of which is supported only by a small number of training examples; it is deterministic in nature: (1) a rule is derived if and only if it is consistent with all training examples, (2) a unique partition results from given data, unique lower and upper approximations are associated to a concept and unique set of rules are generated from each approximation, (3) no user's criteria are considered.

We have generalized rough set theory (Quafafou 1997a, 1997b) in order to substantially enhance its applicability to real-world problems. By introducing our parametrized indiscernability relation I_α , we allow a controlled partition of the universe taking into account a similarity threshold which may be introduced by a user. Consequently, the partition of the universe can be controlled by varying the value of α from none (coarsest partition) to one (finest partition. The previous example, see figure 2, shows that the similarity parameter has an influence on the indiscernability class formation and consequently the approximation of concepts. Thus, more than one partition can result from a given dataset by varying the value of α.

Once the classes are defined, the approximation process takes place considering the concepts to learn. Our extension of rough set theory allows us to approximate flexible concepts which integrate the uncertainty of the original data in their definitions. The resulting approximations are at the basis of the generation of rules. Only consistent rules are learned, indeed a rule *head* $\rightarrow$ *body* is generated such that any example matching *body* is included in the set of examples matching *head*. We have introduced a cover parameter, denoted $\alpha - cover$, in order to discover strong rules which are only enough consistent, i.e., partially incorrect. This parameter takes its values in the range $[0, 1]$ and each rule has an associated likelihood ratio with values in $[0, 1]$. The value of this ratio is equal to the proportion of positive training examples covered by the rules divided by the proportion of negative training examples covered by the rules. A generated rule is kept if the value of its likelihood ratio is greater than $\alpha - cover$.

7 Experimental results

We consider two real-world datasets, heart and pima, taken from the UCI Irvine repository[1]. We consider two situations for each dataset: (1) learning only consistent rules using the coarsest granule of knowledge i.e., $\alpha - cover = 1$ and $\alpha - sim = 0$, (2) learning enough consistent rules with finet granules of knowledge by varying $\alpha - cover$ and $\alpha - sim$ in $[0, 1]$.

The original data are transformed using only five membership functions for each attribute. indeed, the range of a continous attribute is split by hand into five intervals of approximately the same length. A membership function is then defined on each subinterval. Even if the discretization is not optimal, the performance of Alpha increases when we learn enough consistent rules with fine granules of knowledge. The accuracy of Alpha was estimated by 5-fold cross-validation. Figure 3 shows how the evolution of $\alpha - cover$ (cover parameter) influences the accuracy of Alpha on both training and test data. The value of

---

[1] anonymous ftp to ics.uci.edu

$\alpha - cover$ varies in $[0, 1]$, whereas $\alpha - sim$ is set to none. The thick grey line represents the estimated accuracy during training, and the solid line during the test. The induced model with the coarsest granule of knowledge and consistent rules, correctly predicts all training examples, i.e., its accuracy is 100% on both pima and heart, however its prediction during the test is respectively equal to 72.86% and 65.36%. By changing the values of $\alpha - cover$ in $[0, 1]$, we induce models which do not predicate correctly all training examples but they increase the accuracy of Alpha during the test phase. For instance, the accuracy of Alpha is at least equal to 77.3% when $\alpha - cover = 0.9$ or $\alpha - cover = 0.6$. The same conclusion is also valid for pima and for other datasets we have used in our experiments.

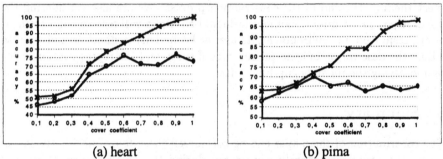

(a) heart   (b) pima

Figure 3: The estimated accuracy during training and test.

The performance of Alpha has improved in general and its accuracy has increased on both heart and pima datasets.

Table 1 shows the accuracy of Alpha considering consistent rules with the coarsest granule of knowledge ($\alpha - cover = 1$, $\alpha - sim = 0$) and enough consistent rules with a more fine granule of knowledge ($\alpha - cover < 1$, $\alpha - sim > 0$). On the heart dataset, ID3's accuracy is 72.22%, C4.5's accuracy is 77.04%, Naive-Baye's accuracy is 81.48% and Alpha's accuracy increases from 73.61% to 77.32% for $\alpha - cover = 0.4$ and $\alpha - sim = 0.3$.

	Features	Train	ID3	C4.5	Naive-Baye	$\alpha - cover$	$\alpha - sim$	Alpha
heart	13	270	72.22	77.04	81.48	1.0	0.0	73.61
						0.4	0.3	77.32
pima	8	768	71.75	72.65	75.51	1.0	0.0	65.36
						0.4	0.2	69.40

Table 1. The accuracy of ID3, C4.5, Naive-Baye and Alpha

The accuracy of Alpha is also improved on the pima dataset and increased from 65.36% to 69.40%. The values of both $\alpha - cover$ and $\alpha - sim$ were found experimentally. Other experiments not reported in the paper show that the performance of Alpha is generally improved when we control the finest of granules of knowledge, $\alpha - sim > 0$, and when we accept enough consistent rules, i.e., $\alpha - cover < 1$. The accuracy of Alpha depends also on membership functions, indeed, by changing the membership functions associated with continuos attributes of the pima dataset, the accuracy of Alpha became 74%. Consequently, a main issue we are studying currently is a fuzzy discretization process. The transformation of the original data can be automatic, i.e., the memberships are defined according to the training examples considering also the class of each example. The construction of the membership functions may be influenced by an expert, which can constrain the construction process of membership functions and inspect them at the end of the construction process. We are also considering the use of Alpha in a semi-autonomous fashion, i.e., Alpha will receive reinforcement or criticism from its environment, its user or both. This feedback will be used to adjust the description of concept, revision of rules, and the representation space by modifying the membership functions.

8 Summary

The contribution of this paper can be considered to be four-fold. Firstly, it discusses the problems generally considered during the preprocessing phase and focuses on the uncertainty modeling problem. It proposes a new preprocessing task for uncertainty modeling, which is currently based on an interactive process. Secondly, it shows that handling the uncertainty of data leads to the formalization of a notion of flexible concepts in contrast with sharp concepts, i.e., concepts represented by crisp sets. Thirdly, it considers $\alpha - RST$ framework which is a generalization of rough set theory and shows that the control of knowledge granularity improves the approximations of flexible concepts and consequently the quality of the learned rules. Lastly, it experiments the ideas developed so far with the system Alpha on two real word datasets.

References

1. Ali K.M. , Pazzani M. J. (1993). Hydra: A Noise-tolerant Relational Concept Learning Algorithm, In Proceeding of 13th International Joint Conference on Artifcial Intelligence (IJCAI'93), 1064-1070.
2. Bergadano F., Giordana A. and Saitta L. (1988).Automated concept acquisition in noisy environments. IEEE Pattern Analysis and Machine Intelligence 10.
3. Botta M., Giordana A. (1993). Smart+: A Multi-Strategy Learning Tool, In Proceeding of 13th International Joint Conference on Artifcial Intelligence (IJCAI'93), 937-943.
4. Dubois D., Prade H., (1984). Criteria aggregation and ranking of alternatives in the framework of fuzzy set theory, Studies In the Management Sciences (TIMS) Vol. 34, 1984, 326-335.

5. Dubois D., Prade H., (1994).Similarity-based approximate reasoning. In proceeding of the IEEE Symposium "computational Intelligence: Imitating Life", Orlando, FL, June 27-July 1st.

6. Chmielewski M.R., Grzymala-Busse J.W., Peterson N.W., Than S., The rule induction system LERS - A version for personal computers. Foundations of computind and decision Sciences, Vol. 18, No 3-4, pp. 181-212, 1993.

7. Clark, P., Niblett, T. (1987). Induction in noisy domains. In proceeding of the Second European Workshop on Machine Learning, 1987.

8. Cox E., The Fuzzy Systems Handbook. , Academic Press, Inc, 1994. Fayyad, U.M., Irani, K.B. (1992). On the handling of continuous-valued attributes in decision tree generation. Machine Learning, 8, 87-102, 1992.

9. Fayyad, U.M., Irani, K.B. (1993). Multi-Interval Discritization of continuous-valued attributes for classification learning, 13th International Joint Conference on Artificial Intelligence, 1022-1027.

10. Grzymala-Busse J.W. (1995). Rough Sets. Advances in imaging and physics, Vol. 94, 1995, pp 151-195.

11. Grzymala-Busse, J., Sedelow, S.Y., Sedelow, W.A. 1995a. Machine learning and knowledge acquisition, rough sets and the english semantic code. In Proceeding of the Workshop on Rough Sets and Database Mining, 23rd Annual ACM Computer Science Conference CSC'95, Nashville, TN, 91-109.

12. Grzymala-Busse, D.M., Grzymala-Busse, J. 1995b. The usefulness of a machine learning approach to knowledge acquisition. Computational Intelligence, Vol 11, No 2, 1995.

13. Pawlak Z. (1991). Rough Sets: Theoretical Aspects of Reasoning About Data. Kluwer Academic Publishers, Dordrecht, The Netherlands, 1991.

14. Pawlak Z., Grzymala-Busse J.W., Slowinski R., Ziarko W. (1995). Rough Sets. Communications of the ACM, November 1995, Vol. 38, No 11, pp 89-95.

15. Piatetsky-Shapiro, G. (1989). Discovery of Strong Rules in Databases. In Proceeding of IJCAI'89 Workshop on Knowledge Discovery in Databases, 264-274.

16. Quafafou, M., 1997a. a-RST: A generalization of rough set theory. To appear in the Fifth International Workshop on Rough Sets and Soft Computing.

17. Quafafou, M., 1997b. On the Roughness of Fuzzy Sets. To appear in the European Symposium on Intelligent Techniques.

18. Quafafou, M., Chan, C.C., A. Mekaouche (1995). An Incremental Approach for Learning Fuzzy Rules From Examples. 3th European Congress on Intelligent Techniques and Soft Computing (EUFIT'95).

19. Quinlan, J.R. (1986). Induction of Decision Trees. Machine Learning, 1, 86-106, 1986.

20. Quinlan, J. R. (1989). Unknown attribute values in induction. In proceeding of the Sixth International Workshop on Machine Learning, Morgan Kaufmann.

21. Slowinski R. (ed.) (1992). Intelligent Decision Support: Handbook of Applications and Advances of the Rough Sets Theory. Kluwer Academic Publishers, Dordrecht, 1992.

22. Slowinski R., Stefanowski J., Handling Various Types of Uncertainty in the Rough Set Approach. In proceeding of the International Workshop on Rough Sets and Knowledge Discovery, Springer-Verlag, pp 366-376.

23. Slowinski R., Zopounidis C. Rough-set sorting of firms according to bankruptcy risk. M. Parruccini (ed.), Applaying Multiple Criteria Aid for Decision to Environmental Management, 1994, pp339-357.

24. Van de Merckt, T. (1992). NFDT: A System that Learns Flexible Concepts based on Decision Trees for Numerical Attributes. In proceedings of the Ninth International Conference on Machine Learning, Morgan Kaufmann, 1992.

25. Van de Merckt, T. (1993). Decision Trees in Numerical Attributes Spaces, 13th International Joint Conference on Artificial Intelligence, 1016-1021, 1993.

26. Woolery, L.K., Grzymala-Busse, J. 1994. MachineLearning for an expert system to predict preterm birth risk. Journal of the American Medical Informatics Association, Vol.1, No 6, 1994.

27. Yager R. R. (1979). Some procedures for selecting operators for fuzzy operations, Technical Report RRY-79-05, Iona College, New Rochelle, N.Y., 1979.

28. Yager R.E., Zadeh L.H. (Eds.), An Introduction to Fuzzy Logic Applications in Intelligent Systems. Kluwer Academic Publishers, Norwell, MA, 1992.

29. Ziarko, W. Golan, R. and Edwards, D. An application of Datalogic/R knowledge discovery tool to identify strong predictive rules in stock market data. Proceedings of AAAI Workshop on Knowledge Discovery in Databases, Washington D.C., 1993, 89-101.

Determining Attribute Relevance in Decision Trees

Mirsad Hadzikadic[1] and Ben F. Bohren[2]
[1]Carolinas HealthCare System and University of North Carolina at Charlotte
[2]Speech Systems Inc.

Abstract

Concept formation, an artificial intelligence classification technique, has been used successfully by many researchers in predicting outcomes of new objects based on a decision tree built from previously seen objects. All systems based on concept formation are capable of providing outcome predictions. INC2.5, a concept formation system, goes further by (a) implementing an algorithm that identifies relevant attributes and (b) administering a test that measures system's predictive ability based on the reduced attribute set. These capabilities are important to users attempting to prove a specific feature's contribution to an outcome. This paper focuses on the algorithm for analyzing attribute relevance as opposed to the classification and prediction techniques that have been explained in previous publications.

1. Introduction

In today's high technology world the ability to collect and store data has dramatically increased. However, utilizing the data to improve future performance is more difficult than the basic collection. For example, doctors continually struggle to find patterns in patient outcomes in order to increase quality of care while decreasing cost. With the overwhelming amount of data collected in hospital everyday, researchers are looking for automated methods to find patterns in the data. Concept formation is one technology that can be of assistance.

Concept formation systems build decision trees that are then used to predict outcomes of future patients by finding similar cases within the tree. While there are numerous systems with this basic ability [1-10], INC2.5 [3-6] has been extended with an algorithm capable of searching the tree for attributes which appear to have been most influential in the formation of the tree. Using this algorithm, INC2.5 can systematically remove attributes while tracking the trees predictive ability. Upon completion, the user is presented with a list of variables in order of relevance and an 'elimination curve' showing the prediction rates as each variable was eliminated from the tree.

This approach is fundamentally different from approaches dealing with the problem of data overfitting, which arises when one "grows" a decision tree just deeply enough to perfectly classify the training examples. Overfitting can lead to difficulties when there is noise in data, or when the number of training examples is too small [12]. One way of dealing with overfitting is to prune a decision node by removing the subtree rooted at that node and replacing it with a leaf node of majority-based classification [13-15]. While pruning improves the overall performance of the decision tree, it does not help us completely remove the irrelevant attributes from the tree. Removing the unnecessary attributes from the decision making process is extremely important in, for example, healthcare, where reduced cost (fewer tests and procedures performed) and increased quality go hand in hand. The rest of this paper explains how INC2.5 eliminates attributes from the whole tree while maintaining the predictive ability of the tree itself.

Section 2 of the paper briefly reviews the classification and prediction process utilized by INC2.5. Section 3 outlines the details of the tree searching algorithm and attribute elimination/pruning process. Section 4 summarizes results of applying the algorithm to the breast cancer and general trauma data sets. The conclusion will both summarize the current progress and suggest possible directions for future research.

2. INC2.5 Example

An INC2.5 tree node (class) description contains the following data: name of the node, list of attributes and associated values, measure of cohesiveness, number of children, and number of instances stored under this class. Each node has an identical list of attributes and for each attribute the node will store all values found in its instance descriptions. A node containing a single instance may have zero or more values associated with each attribute. A class node has a structure identical to that of an instance node, but it contains the union of all instance values stored under it. When a value occurs more than once, the number of occurrences of the attribute value in that branch of the tree is recorded in the attribute list. Upon calculating the similarity between two instances, the two attribute lists are compared and a number reflecting their both distinctive and common features is returned [6].

The main components of INC2.5 are the *similarity* and *cohesiveness* modules. The similarity function [11] is used to compute the similarity between two instances or an instance and a class. The cohesiveness function is then used to calculate the average similarity of all pairs of instances contained in a class, with the new instance tentatively placed in the class. If the average similarity of this class is greater than the similarity of the same class without the new instance, then INC2.5 will permanently place the instance in the class. Otherwise, it will continue the classification process.

The following figures are snapshots of INC2.5 in the process of building a decision tree using the trauma data set. Figures 1 and 2 show incremental growth of the decision tree. Even in these early stages the tree formation shows patients with similar outcomes grouping together. In Figure 2, the fact that four patients where not grouped with any other patients does not indicate the system missed a similarity, but rather that these patients lived or died for reasons different than the grouped patients. The results in Figure 3 were achieved by using the decision tree in Figure 2 to make predictions on ten test patients. Of these ten patients the system correctly predicted eight.

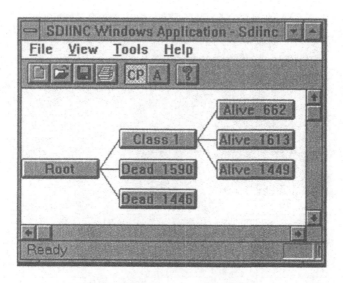

Figure 1: INC2.5 tree with 5 patients

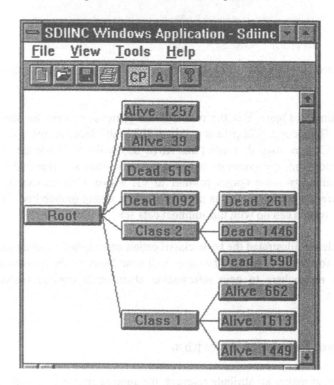

Figure 2: INC2.5 with 10 patients

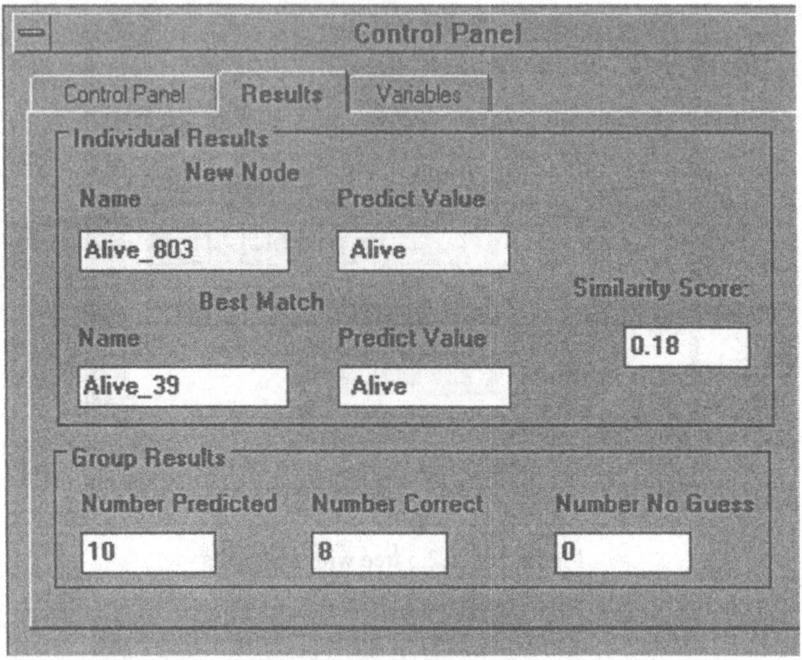

Figure 3: Prediction Results using the tree in Figure 2 and 10 randomly selected test patients.

The top frame in Figure 3 is the result of the retrieval process for the test patient Alive_803. The most similar patient to Alive_803 in the decision tree is Alive_39, thus allowing INC2.5 to correctly predict that Alive_803 will live. While the system makes a correct prediction, the similarity between the two patients is reported as only 0.18. Since the similarity score ranges from -1 to +1, where 0 means exactly half of the patients share the attributes, this is not considered a strong probability. However, it is the best the system can do with this minimal data set.

This example has illustrated the basic classification and prediction methods common to all concept formation systems. The paper will now focus on the extension of INC2.5 that allows researchers to gain information about each attribute's contribution to performance.

3. Attribute Relevance Algorithm

To define what makes an attribute relevant, the authors choose to search for attributes whose values are well separated within branches of the tree. In other words, the algorithm attempts to find attributes whose values are concentrated within one area of the tree, thereby implying those values are influential in the formation of the tree. For example, if one branch of the tree contains all tall people while another branch contains all short people, then the height attribute seems to be important. This example is obviously an extreme case in that it has a two-branch tree and perfect separation. Since the real world is filled with irrelevant, contradictory, and missing data, this ideal tree formation rarely occurs.

How should one go about determining which attributes are significant? The authors have investigated three factors for determining concentration of a feature (attribute/value pair) at any node within the tree: 1) Relative Depth of the node within the Tree (RDT), 2) Global Distribution (GD) of the feature throughout the tree, and 3) Local Distribution (LD) of the feature. Figure 4 depicts a generic INC2.5 tree. Equations 1-3 list the formulae for computing RDT, GD, and LD. Equation 4 is the combination of the three factors, yielding the degree of Feature Relevancy (FR).

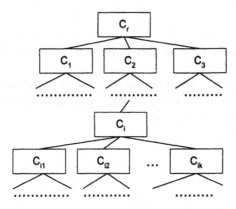

Figure 4: INC2.5 tree

$$RDT = \frac{NodeDepth}{TreeDepth} \qquad \text{Eq. 1}$$

where NodeDepth is the depth of the node in question and TreeDepth is the number of levels within the tree.

$$GD = \frac{|C_{ik}|}{|C_r|} \qquad \text{Eq. 2}$$

where C_{ik} is the node in question, C_r is the root node, and $|C|$ equals the number of singleton nodes under C that contain the feature under consideration.

$$LD = \frac{|C_{ik}|}{|C_i|}$$

Eq. 3

where C_{ik} is the same as Eq. 2 and C_i is the parent node of C_{ik} as depicted in Figure 2.

$$FR = RDT * GD * LD$$

Eq. 4

Using a tree traversal method to calculate FR at each node leads to the following algorithm for determining attribute relevance as well as any performance gains from eliminating less relevant attributes.

RelevanceTestLevel=1
Repeat
> *For each node in the tree identify features for which FeatureRelevance > RelevanceTestLevel*
> *Identify all attributes which have at least half of its features marked relevant*
> *Rebuild tree with only relevant attributes and record the prediction rate*
> *Increment RelevanceTestLevel*

Until No relevant attributes

4. Discussion

To test the algorithm the authors used two data sets, i.e. breast cancer and general trauma. The breast cancer database[1] was retrieved from the machine learning repository at University of California at Irvine, while the general trauma database was created at Carolinas Medical Center[2], Charlotte, North Carolina. The breast cancer database was chosen because of its wide spread use in testing prediction systems, while the trauma database was used to reflect actual requests that the authors received from practicing physicians.

The breast cancer database consists of 699 patients with two ideal classes, YES and NO. YES means the patient had a recurrence of breast cancer within five years, while NO means there was no recurrence during the five-year period. Within the database, 458 of the patients are benign (NO class) and 241 are malignant (YES class). In addition to the class variable, which is only used for evaluation purposes, each patient has nine associated variables (Table 1). The table also includes the highest "relevance test level" at which the variable was considered significant in the initial tree.

Table 1: A list of variables in the breast cancer domain

1.	uniform cell size	23	6.	class	17
2.	uniform cell shape	20	7.	bare nuclei	17
3.	normal nucleoli	18	8.	marginal adhesion	15
4.	single epi cell size	18	9.	bland chromatin	15
5.	clump thickness	17	10.	mitoses	14

The general trauma domain includes 284 patients evenly divided between the two classes, ALIVE and DEAD. Of the twenty-five variables listed in Table 2, the medical number and discharge status are ignored due to their uniqueness and relation to outcome variable (respectively). The class variable is used for prediction, thus leaving twenty-two variables to describe patient conditions. Again, the variables are listed with the highest relevance test level at which they were last deemed significant in the initial tree.

Table 2: A List of variables in the general trauma domain

1.	Medical Number	47	14.	length of stay	26
2.	initial hematocrit	41	15.	initial trauma score	26
3.	complication	35	16.	peritoneal lavage	25
4.	Discharge Status	31	17.	GSC motor response	25
5.	alcohol level	28	18.	GCS eye opening	25
6.	Class	28	19.	angiogram	25
7.	Age	28	20.	safety equipment	25
8.	airway management	2	21.	injury severity score	24
9.	GSC verbal response	27	22.	abdominal ct scan	24
10.	medical history	27	23.	head ct scan	23
11.	glascow coma scale	27	24.	days in ICU	23
12.	days on ventilator	26	25.	drug screen	21
13.	initial temperature	26			

While the list of attributes in Tables 1 and 2 shows the order in which the variables are deemed relevant, Figures 5 and 6 display elimination curves which track the prediction rate when less relevant attributes are eliminated. Each figure depicts the elimination curve for two randomly generated trees from which the first run results were used to build the relevant levels listed above. In both cases the runs show similar results which prove many of the attributes are unnecessary to maintain the same prediction rate. In the case of breast cancer, Figure 5, eliminating the least significant variable (mitoses) improved the performance, indicating not only did mitoses not add to predictive ability but it also hindered the system.

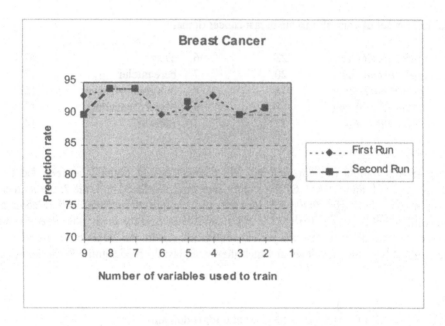

Figure 5: Elimination curve for the breast cancer data set

Another common pattern can be seen in Figure 6 where the prediction rate stays flat while (possibly redundant) attributes are eliminated. As it turns out, many of the variables are known to be correlated to each other based on the severity of the injury. Furthermore, the five most significant attributes are not included in the redundant category and once one of them was eliminated the predication ability dropped dramatically.

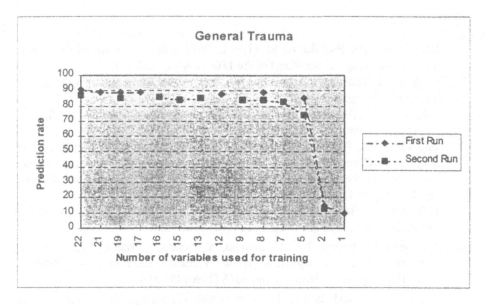

Figure 6: Elimination curve for the trauma data set

5. Conclusion

The decision tree-analysis algorithm enables INC2.5 to provide the user with a list of attributes ordered by their contribution to the tree's predictive ability. The system also provides the user with an elimination curve showing the predictive ability of the tree when less relevant attributes are pruned during the tree building process. From this curve, the researcher can determine whether the attributes are redundant (a flat curve) or a hindrance (a curve with a positive slope). Furthermore, the system helps the researcher determine the minimum set of attributes needed to accurately predict the outcomes.

While more testing is still required to demonstrate the accuracy of the tree analysis algorithm in multiple domains, the authors believe that these results are promising. Future research will include not only additional domains, but also formal methods for interpreting the output from the algorithm as well as the methods for evaluating attribute interactions within the tree.

End Notes

[1] Dr. William H. Wolberg at the University of Wisconsin Hospitals, Madison supplied the Breast Cancer database.

[2] General Surgery Department at Carolinas Medical Center, Charlotte, NC supplied the Trauma database.

References

1. Bohren, B.F. and Hadzikadic, M. (1994), Turning Medical Data into Decision-Support Knowledge. Proceedings of the 18th SCAMC, 735-739.
2. Fisher, D. H. Knowledge Acquisition Via Incremental Conceptual Clustering. In *Machine Learning*, 2, 2 (1987) 139-172.
3. Hadzikadic, M., Automated Design of Diagnostic Systems. *Artificial Intelligence in Medicine Journal*, 4 (1992a) 329-342.
4. Hadzikadic, M. Prediction Performance as a Function of the Representation Language in Concept Formation Systems. Proceedings of the Fourteenth Annual Conference of the Cognitive Science Society, 850-854, Bloomington, Indiana, July 29 - August 1, 1992b.
5. Hadzikadic, M., Bohren, B.F., "Learning to Predict: INC2.5," *IEEE Transactions on Knowledge and Data Engineering*. 9, 1 (1997) 168-173.
6. Hadzikadic, M., Bohren, B., Hakenewerth, A., Norton, J., Mehta, B., Andrews, C. "Concept Formation vs. Logistic Regression: Predicting Death in Trauma Patients." *Artificial Intelligence in Medicine Journal* 8 (1996) 493-504.
7. Hanson, S. J. and Bauer, M. Conceptual Clustering, Categorization, and Polymorphy. In Machine Learning, 3, 4 (1989) 343-372.
8. Kolodner, J. L. Retrieval and Organizational Strategies in Conceptual Memory: A Computer Model, Lawrence Erlbaum Associated, Publishers, London, 1984.
9. Lebowitz, M. Experiments with Incremental Concept Formation: UNIMEM. In *Machine Learning*, 2, 2 (1987) 103-138.
10. Michalski, R.S., and Stepp, R.E. Learning From Observation: Conceptual Clustering. In Machine Learning: An Artificial Intelligence Approach, R.S. Michalski, J.G. Carbonell, and T. M. Mitchell (eds.), Morgan Kaufmann Publishers, Inc., Lao Altos, CA, 1983.
11. Tversky, A. Features of Similarity. *Psychological Review*, 84 (1977) 327-352.
12. Mitchell, T. M. *Machine Learning*. McGraw-Hill, 1997.
13. Quinlan, J.R. *C4.5: Programs for Machine Learning*. San Mateo, CA: Morgan Kauffmann, 1993.
14. Mingers, J. An Empirical Comparison of Selection Measures for Decision-tree induction. *Machine Learning*, 3 (4) 319-342, 1989.
15. Buntine, W. and Niblett, T. A Further Comparison of Splitting Rules for Decision-tree Induction. *Machine Learning*, 8, 75-86, 1992.

A WordNet Based Rule Generalization Engine in Meaning Extraction System *

Joyce Yue Chai and Alan W. Biermann

Department of Computer Science
Box 90129, Duke University
Durham, NC 27708-0129
Internet: {chai,awb}@cs.duke.edu

Abstract. This paper presents a rule based methodology for efficiently creating meaning extraction systems. The methodology allows a user to scan sample texts in a domain to be processed and to create meaning extraction rules that specifically address his or her needs. Then it automatically generalizes the rules using the power of the WordNet system so that they can effectively extract a broad class of information even though they were based on extraction from a few very specific articles. Finally, the generalized rules can be applied to large databases of text to do the translation that will extract the particular information the user desires. A recently developed mechanism is presented that uses the strategy of over-generalizing to achieve high recall (with low precision) and then selectively specializing to bring the precision up to acceptable levels.

1 Introduction

The tremendous topics available on Internet give rise to the demand for an easily adaptable meaning extraction system for different domains. Adapting an extraction system to a new domain has proved to be a difficult and tedious process. Many research groups have taken steps towards customizing information extraction systems efficiently, such as BBN [10], NYU [6], SRI [2], SRA [7], MITRE [1], UMass [5],etc. In a rule based meaning extraction system, ideally one would like to have both unambiguous rules and generalized rules. In this way, the target information can be precisely activated by the unambiguous rules, and at the same time, the human effort involved in enumerating all the possible ways of expressing the target information can be eliminated by the generalized rules. However, practically, it's very hard to achieve both.

We have proposed a rule generalization approach and implemented it in our trainable meaning extraction system. The system allows the user to train on a small amount of data in the domain and creates the specific rules. The rule generalization routines will generalize the specific rules to make them general for the new information. In this way, rule generalization makes the customization

---

* This work has been supported by a Fellowship from IBM Corporation.

for a new domain easier by eliminating the effort in creating all the possible rules.

This paper describes the automated rule generalization method and the usage of WordNet [8]. First, it gives a brief introduction to WordNet and investigates the possibility of using WordNet to achieve generalization; then it presents experimental results based on the idea of generalization; finally, it illustrates an augmented generalization method for controlling the degree of generalization based on the user's needs.

2 Overview of System

The system contains three major subsystems which, respectively, address training, rule generalization, and the scanning of new information. First, each article is partially parsed and segmented into Noun Phrases, Verb Phrases and Prepositional Phrases. An IBM LanguageWare English Dictionary and Computing Term Dictionary, a Partial Parser [2], a Tokenizer and a Preprocessor are used in the parsing process. The Tokenizer and the Preprocessor are designed to identify some special categories such as e-mail address, phone number, state and city etc. In the training process, the user, with the help of a graphical user interface(GUI) scans a parsed sample article and indicates a series of semantic net nodes and transitions that he or she would like to create to represent the information of interest. Specifically, the user designates those noun phrases in the article that are of interest and uses the interface commands to translate them into semantic net nodes. Furthermore, the user designates verb phrases and prepositions that relate the noun phrases and uses commands to translate them into semantic net transitions between nodes. In the process, the user indicates the desired translation of the specific information of interest into semantic net form that can easily be processed by the machine. For each headword in a noun phrase, WordNet is used to provide sense information. For headwords with senses other than sense one, the user needs to identify the appropriate senses, and the Sense Classifier will keep the record of these headwords and their most frequently used senses. When the user takes the action to create the semantic transitions, a Rule Generator keeps track of the user's moves and creates the rules automatically. These rules are specific to the training articles and they need to be generalized in order to be applied on other articles in the domain. The rule generalization process will be explained in the later sections. During the scanning of new information, with the help of a rule matching routine, the system applies the generalized rules to a large number of unseen articles from the domain. The output of the system is a set of semantic transitions for each article that specifically extract information of interest to the user. Those transitions can then be used by a Postprocessor to fill templates, answer queries, or generate abstracts [3].

---

[2] We wish to thank Jerry Hobbs of SRI for providing us with the finite-state rules for the parser.

Original Training Sentence:

DCR Inc. is looking for C programmers.

Semantic Transition Built by the User through GUI:

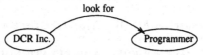

Specific Rule Automatically Created by the Rule Generator:

[DCR Inc., NG, 1, company], [look_for, VG, 1, other_type], [programmer, NG, 1, other_type] ⟶
ADD_NODE(DCR Inc.), ADD_NODE(programmer), ADD_RELATION(look_for, DCR Inc., programmer)

Fig. 1. Semantic Transition and Specific Rule

3 Rule Generalization

3.1 Rules

In a typical information extraction task, the most interesting part is the events and relationships holding among the events [2]. These relationships are usually specified by verbs and prepositions. Based on this observation, the left hand side (LHS) of our meaning extraction rules is made up of three entities. The first and the third entities are the target objects in the form of noun phrases, the second entity is the verb or prepositional phrase indicating the relationship between the two objects. The right hand side (RHS) of the rule consists of the operations required to create a semantic transition–ADD_NODE, ADD_RELATION. ADD_NODE is to add an object in the transitions. ADD_RELATION is to add a relationship between two objects. A semantic transition and its corresponding specific rule are shown in Fig. 1.

The specific rule in Fig. 1 can only be activated by a sentence with the same pattern as "DCR Inc. is looking for C programmers ... ". It will not be activated by other sentences such as "IBM Corporation seeks job candidates in Louisville, KY with HTML experience". Semantically speaking, these two sentences are very much alike. Both are expressing a fact that a company seeks professional people. However, without generalization, the second sentence will not be processed. So the use of the specific rule is very limited.

3.2 WordNet and Generalization

Introduction to WordNet WordNet is a large-scale on-line dictionary developed by George Miller and colleagues at Princeton University [8]. The most useful feature of WordNet to the Natural Language Processing community is its attempt to organize lexical information in terms of word meanings, rather than word forms. Each entry in WordNet is a concept represented by a list of synonyms–the synset. The information is encoded in the form of semantic networks. For instance, in the network for nouns, there are "part of", "is_a", "member of".... relationships between concepts. The hierarchical organization of

An Abstract Specific Rule:

$(w_1, c_1, s_1, t_1), (w_2, c_2, s_2, t_2), (w_3, c_3, s_3, t_3)$

$\longrightarrow$ ADD_NODE(w_1), ADD_NODE(w_3), ADD_RELATION(w_2, w_1, w_3)

A Generalized Rule:

$(W_1, C_1, S_1, T_1) \in Generalize(sp_1, h_1), (W_2, C_2, S_2, T_2) \in Generalize(sp_2, h_2),$

$(W_3, C_3, S_3, T_3) \in Generalize(sp_3, h_3)$

$\longrightarrow$ ADD_NODE(W_1), ADD_NODE(W_3), ADD_RELATION(W_2, W_1, W_3)

Fig. 2. Sample Rules

WordNet by word meanings [8] [9] provides the opportunity for automated generalization. With the large amount of information in semantic classification and taxonomy provided in WordNet, many ways of incorporating WordNet semantic features with generalization are foreseeable. At this stage, we only concentrate on the Hypernym/Hyponym feature.

A hyponym is defined in [8] as follows: " A noun X is said to be a hyponym of a noun Y if we can say that *X is a kind of Y*. This relation generates a hierarchical tree structure, i.e., a taxonomy. A hyponym anywhere in the hierarchy can be said to be "a kind of" all of its superordinates. ..." If X is a hyponym of Y, then Y is a hypernym of X.

Generalization From the training process, the specific rules contain three entities on the LHS as shown in in Fig. 2. Each entity (sp) is a quadruple, in the form of (w, c, s, t), where w is the headword of the trained phrase; c is the part of the speech of the word; s is the sense number representing the meaning of w; t is the semantic type identified by the preprocessor for w.

For each $sp = (w, c, s, t)$, if w exists in WordNet, then there is a corresponding synset in WordNet. The hyponym/hypernym hierarchical structure provides a way of locating the superordinate concepts of sp. By following additional Hypernymy, we will get more and more generalized concepts and eventually reach the most general concept, such as {*entity*}. Based on this scenario, for each concept, different degrees of generalization can be achieved by adjusting the distance between this concept and the most general concept in the WordNet hierarchy.The function to accomplish this task is *Generalize(sp,h)*, which returns a synset list h levels above the concept sp in the hierarchy.

The process of generalizing rules consists of replacing each $sp = (w, c, s, t)$ in the specific rules by a more general superordinate synset from its hypernym hierarchy in WordNet by performing the *Generalize(sp, h)* function. The degree of generalization for rules varies with the variation of h in *Generalize(sp, h)*.

A generalized rule is shown in Fig. 2. The $\in$ symbol signifies the subsumption relationship. Therefore, $a \in b$ signifies that a is subsumed by b, or, in WordNet terms, concept b is a superordinate concept of concept a. The generalized rule states that the RHS of the rule gets executed if *all* of the following conditions hold:

– A sentence contains three phrases (not necessarily contiguous) with headwords W_1, W_2, and W_3.

- The quadruples corresponding to these headwords are (W_1, C_1, S_1, T_1), (W_2, C_2, S_2, T_2), and (W_3, C_3, S_3, T_3).
- The synsets, in WordNet, corresponding to the quadruples, are subsumed by *Generalize(sp₁, h₁)*, *Generalize(sp₂, h₂)*, and *Generalize(sp₃, h₃)* respectively.

During the scanning process, the generalized rules are used to create semantic transitions for new information.

3.3 Experiments and Discussion

We have conducted a set of experiments based on seven levels of generalization. We set the MAX_DEPTH to 6. At degree 0, if entity one and/or entity three in the rule occurred lower than depth 6 in the WordNet hierarchy, we generalized them to their hypernym at depth 6. At degree 1, two object entities that appear lower than depth 5 in the hierarchy were generalized to their hypernym at depth 5. At degree $i (0 \leq i \leq 6)$, the object entities in the rules with depths greater than $(MAX\_DEPTH - i)$ were generalized to their Hypernymy at depth $(MAX\_DEPTH - i)$.

The system was trained on three sets of articles from the *triangle.jobs* USENET newsgroup, with emphasis on the following seven facts:

- Company Name. Examples: IBM, Metro Information Services, DCR Inc.
- Position/Title. Examples: programmer, financial analyst, software engineer.
- Experience/Skill. Example: 5 years experience in Oracle.
- Location. Examples: Winston-Salem, North Carolina.
- Benefit. Examples: company matching funds, comprehensive health plan.
- Salary. Examples: $32/hr, 60K.
- Contact Info. Examples: Fax is 919-660-6519, e-mail address.

The first training set contained 8 articles; the second set contained 16 articles including the first set; and the third set contained 24 articles including those in the first two sets. For rules from each training set, seven levels of generalization were performed. Based on the generalized rules at each level, the system was run on 80 unseen articles from the same newsgroup to test its performance on the extraction of the seven facts.

The evaluation process consisted of the following step: first, each unseen article was studied to see how many facts of interest were present in the article; second, the semantic transitions produced by the system were examined to see if they correctly caught any facts of interest. Precision is the number of transitions correctly conveying certain semantic information out of the total number of transitions produced by the system; recall is the number of facts correctly embodied in the transitions out of the total number of facts present in the articles.

Precision decreases from 96.1% to 68.4% for the first training set as the degree of generalization increases from 0 to 6. The first set of eight training articles has better performance on precision than the other two sets. For the third training set of 24 articles, recall increases from 48.2% to 76.1% as generalization degree increases. As expected, the third training set out-performed the other two training sets on recall. The overall performance of recall and precision is defined by F-measurement [4], which is

$$\frac{(\beta^2 + 1.0) * P * R}{\beta^2 * P + R}$$

where P is precision, R is recall, $\beta = 1$ if precision and recall are equally important. The F-measurement with respect to the degree of generalization on three different training sets is shown in Fig. 3. The F-measurement for the second and the third training sets reaches its peak when generalization degree is 5, which suggests that more generalization doesn't necessarily provide better performance.

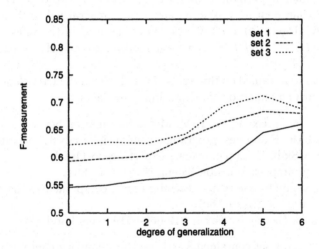

Fig. 3. F Measurement vs. generalization degree

The amount of training affects the performance too. Fig. 4 shows the F-measurement with respect to the amount of training. The outermost curve is for generalization degree 6, and the innermost curve is for degree 0. It shows that, for a specific domain, by applying the generalization approach, an enormous amount of training is not absolutely necessary. There will be a certain threshold for the F-measurement.

The effect of generalization degree on individual facts is shown in Fig. 5. For different fact extractions, generalized rules performed differently. The degree of generalization had the biggest impact in the extraction of *position/title*. The recall jumped from 31.6% to 82.5% when degree increased from 0 to 6. Some other facts such as *salary* were not changed much by the generalization. The recall did increase, but not greatly, only from 20% to 26.7%. This indicates the effect of generalization varies among different facts. It is more effective in extracting the

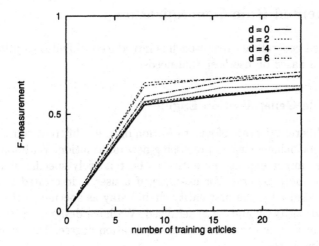

Fig. 4. recall vs. training set at different degree

fact, such as *position/title*, that is expressed in a learnable, comparably small set of pattern structures, with variations on the contents of the structures.

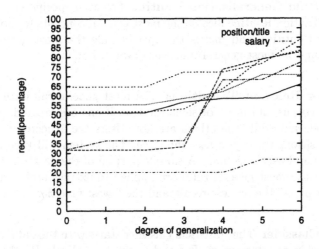

Fig. 5. recall of extracting individual fact vs. degree of generalization

Moreover, with the increase in the degree of generalization, precision tends to fall while recall tends to increase. The question that arises here is: What degree of generalization gives us the best compromise between precision and recall? If the user prefers high recall and doesn't care too much about the precision, or vice-versa, is there any way to control the generalization level in order to meet the user's needs?

4 Augmented Rule Generalization

An augmented generalization approach is introduced to find the optimal level of generalization based on user's special needs.

4.1 Tunable Generalization Engine

Rules with different degrees of generalization on their different constituents will have a different behavior when processing new information. Within a particular rule, the user might expect one entity to be relatively specific and the other entities to be more general. For example, if a user is interested in finding all DCR Inc. related jobs, the first entity should stay as specific as that in Fig. 1, and the third entity should be generalized. We have designed a Tunable Rule Generalization Engine to control the generalization degree. The engine consists of the following parts:

- Complete Rule Generalization Routine.
- Interface for Relevant Transitions.
- Statistical Classifier
- Rule Tuner

Complete Rule Generalization Routine For each specific rule, Complete Rule Generalization Routine locates the most general concepts for both the first and the third entities, and makes the specific rule the most general rule. A specific rule and its most general rule are shown in Fig. 6.

Interface for Relevant Transitions The most general rules are applied to the training corpus and a set of semantic transitions are created. Some transitions are relevant while the others are not. Users are expected to select the relevant transitions through a user interface. The system will keep a database of transitions and user selections. A sample portion of the database is shown in Fig. 6. When the most general rules are applied to extract useful information, the system achieves the highest recall, and the lowest precision.

Statistical Classifier The statistical classifier starts with the database of transitions and relevant information. For each most general rule R_i, the statistical classifier will calculate the following probabilities:

$$Relevancy\_Rate(R_i) = \frac{number\ of\ relevant\ transitions\ created}{total\ number\ of\ transitions\ created}$$

$$Object\_1\_Relevancy\_Rate(R_i) = \frac{number\ of\ relevant\ object\_1\ created}{total\ number\ of\ object\_1\ created}$$

$$Object\_2\_Relevancy\_Rate(R_i) = \frac{number\ of\ relevant\ object\_2\ given\ relevant\ object\_1}{total\ number\ of\ relevant\ object\_1\ created}$$

$Relevancy\_Rate(R_i)$ is the measure of how well the most general rule R_i performs on extracting the relevant information. Very high $Relevancy\_Rate(R_i)$

Specific Rule:

[degree, NG, 3, other_type], [in, PG, 0, other_type], [field, NG, 3, other_type]
    ADD_NODE(degree), ADD_NODE(field), ADD_RELATION(in, degree, field)

Most General Rule:

$(W_1, C_1, S_1, T_1) \in \{abstraction\}, (W_2, C_2, S_2, T_2) \in \{in\}, (W_3, C_3, S_3, T_3) \in \{psychological\_feature\}$
    ADD_NODE(W_1), ADD_NODE(W_3), ADD_RELATION(W_2, W_1, W_3)

Database of Transitions Created by the Most General Rule:

index	obj1	obj1 relevant	relation	obj2	obj2 relevant	count
1	quality	no	in	technical issues	no	1
2	instruction	no	in	instruction program	no	1
3	one degree	yes	in	health related field	yes	1
4	BS	yes	in	technical discipline	yes	2
5	your resume	no	in	graphical preference	no	1
6	BS	yes	in	science	yes	1

Fig. 6. Database of Transitions

such as 97% suggests that the most general rule R_i does not produce much over-generation in this domain. It implies that R_i can bring very high recall, but is not responsible for the low precision. This rule can be kept in the rule base for future use without further tuning.

If the *Relevancy_Rate* is low and beyond the user's tolerance, some actions should be taken to make the rule less general. If *Object_1_Relevancy_Rate*(R_i) is lower than the user's tolerance, the first entity in the rule needs to be tuned. If *Object_2_Relevancy_Rate*(R_i) is lower than the user's tolerance, the third entity in the rule needs to be tuned. The tuning will be done by Rule Tuner.

Rule Tuner For each entity in the most general rule that has been identi-fied for tuning by Statistical Classifier, Rule Tuner will make it more specific to the user's interests. For example, in Fig. 6, the Statistical Classifier decides that {abstraction} in the most general rule is too general, then the Rule Tuner will start to put constraints on this entity by decreasing the generalization de-gree of the original specific concept {degree}. Since {instruction}, {quality}, {resume} are irrelevant concepts, we need to find a most general hypernym of {degree}, which is not the hypernym of {instruction},{quality} and {resume}. From the hypernym hierarchy as shown in Fig. 7, {approval, commendation} is the desired hypernym. The concept {approval,commendation} will replace con-cept {abstraction} in the most general rule to form the optimally generalized rule. The concept such as {approval, commendation} in the example is more general than the original specific concept, and at the same time, is not respon-sible for the over-generation. We call this concept *Uppermost Relevant Concept*. For each entity in the rule which needs to be tuned, Rule Tuner will go through all the corresponding objects and find the *Uppermost Relevant Concept* for that entity and replace the original most general concept with the *Uppermost Rele-*

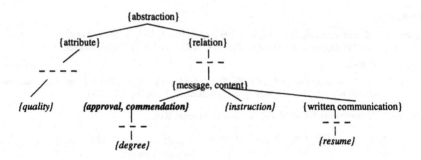

Fig. 7. Hypernym Hierarchy

vant Concept . After Rule Tuner examines every entity in every rule, a set of optimally generalized rules are created. The generalization level is different on each entity based on the user's interests.

4.2 Experiments and Results

We applied the optimally generalized rules created by the Tunable Generalization Engine on extracting *position/title* information from *triangle.job* newsgroup. The system was trained on 32 articles from the domain and 19 specific rules were created. Then we passed the rules to the Tunable Rule Generalization Engine and created a set of optimally generalized rules. We applied this set of optimal rules to 130 unseen articles.

Three more experiments were conducted to compare the results. One was to apply the specific rules to the unseen articles, another one was to apply the most generalized rules to the unseen articles, the third one was to apply the rules we manually generalized without the use of the Tunable Generalization Engine. The result is shown in Table 1, where precision is the number of relevant transitions out of the total number of transitions; recall is the number of *position/title* correctly fetched out of the total number of *position/title* that should be fetched.

When the specific rules were applied, the system reached the highest precision at 100%, but the lowest recall at 39%. When the most general rules were applied, the system achieved the highest recall at 70%, but the lowest precision at 27%. By using Tunable Generalization Engine, the optimized rules pushed up precision by 50% and only sacrificed 1% recall. Automatically optimized rules performed better than the manually optimized rules.

5 Conclusion and Future Work

This paper describes a generalization approach based on WordNet. The rule generalization makes it easier for the meaning extraction system to be customized to a new domain. Tunable Generalization Engine makes the system adaptable to the user's needs. The idea of first achieving the highest recall with low precision,

Table 1. Performance Comparison

	Specific Rules	Most General Rules	Manually Optimized Rules	Automatically Optimized Rules
Recall	39%	70%	65%	69%
Precision	100%	27%	75%	77%
F-Measure	56%	39%	70%	73%

then pushing up the precision while keeping the recall comparably steady has been successful. We are currently studying how to enhance the system performance by further refining the generalization approach.

References

1. Aberdeen, John, et al.: Description of the *ALEMBIC* System Used for MUC-6, *Proceedings of the Sixth Message Understanding Conference (MUC-6)*, pp. 141-155, November 1995.
2. Appelt, Douglas E., et al.: SRI International: Description of the FASTUS System Used for MUC-6, *Proceedings of the Sixth Message Understanding Conference (MUC-6)*, pp. 237-248, November 1995.
3. Amit Bagga, Joyce Chai: A Trainable Message Understanding System, *to appear at ACL Workshop on Computational Natural Language Learning*, 1997.
4. Chinchor, Nancy: MUC-4 Evaluation Metrics, *Proceedings of the Fourth Message Understanding Conference (MUC-4)*, June 1992, San Mateo: Morgan Kaufmann.
5. Fisher, David, et al.: Description of the UMass System as Used for MUC-6, *Proceedings of the Sixth Message Understanding Conference (MUC-6)*, pp. 127-140, November 1995.
6. Grishman, Ralph.: The NYU System for MUC-6 or Where's the Syntax? *Proceedings of the Sixth Message Understanding Conference (MUC-6)*, pp. 167-175, November 1995.
7. Krupka, George R.: Description of the SRA System as Used for MUC-6, *Proceedings of the Sixth Message Understanding Conference (MUC-6)*, pp. 221-235, November 1995.
8. Miller, G.A., et al.: *Five Papers on WordNet*, Cognitive Science Laboratory, Princeton University, No. 43, July 1990.
9. Resnik, Philip: Using Information Content to Evaluate Semantic Similarity in a Taxonomy.*Proceedings of IJCAI-95*
10. Weischedel, Ralph.: BBN: Description of the PLUM System as Used for MUC-6, *Proceedings of the Sixth Message Understanding Conference (MUC-6)*, pp. 55-69, November 1995.

Representing and Reasoning on SGML Documents

Diego Calvanese, Giuseppe De Giacomo, and Maurizio Lenzerini

Dipartimento di Informatica e Sistemistica
Università di Roma "La Sapienza"
Via Salaria 113, 00198 Roma, Italy
{calvanese,degiacomo,lenzerini}@dis.uniroma1.it

Abstract. In this paper, we address the issue of representing and reasoning about documents for which an explicit structure is provided. Specifically, we devise a framework where Document Type Definitions (DTDs) expressed in the Standard Generalized Markup Language (SGML) are formalized in an expressive Description Logic equipped with sound, complete, and terminating inference procedures. In this way, we provide a general reasoning mechanism that enables various reasoning tasks on DTDs, including the verification of typical forms of equivalences between DTDs, such as strong equivalence and structural equivalence, as well as parametric versions of these equivalences. Notably, this general reasoning mechanism allows for verifying structural equivalence in worst case deterministic exponential time, in contrast to the known algorithms which are double exponential. As a whole, the study in this paper provides some of the fundamental building blocks for developing articulated inference systems that support tasks involving the intelligent navigation of large document databases such as the World Wide Web.

1 Introduction

In this paper, we address the issue of representing and reasoning on documents for which an explicit structure is provided. The possibility of representing and reasoning on the document structure is advocated by research in both Knowledge Representation and Databases. In particular, the view of the World Wide Web as a large information system constituted by a collection of interconnected documents, and the increasing popularity of private intranets among large companies or institutions for keeping documentation online, is stimulating much work on information retrieval from large document databases (see for example [9,13,10,11]).

This work points out that being able to represent and reason on the structure of documents placed in document databases helps in several tasks related to information retrieval. For example, it enables to improve both the precision of the information retrieved by providing flexible additional selection criteria, and the efficiency of the retrieval process, by allowing for retrieving just a short description of a large document to decide its relevance, instead of the document itself [8,12,1,6,14,13].

```
<!DOCTYPE Mail [
  <!ELEMENT Mail    (From, To, Subject, Body)>
  <!ELEMENT From    (Address)>        <!ELEMENT To   (Address)+>
  <!ELEMENT Subject (#PCDATA)>        <!ELEMENT Body (#PCDATA)>
  <!ELEMENT Address (#PCDATA)> ]>
```

Fig. 1. DTD M for mail documents

The structure of a document is typically made explicit by using special tags to mark its various parts. One of the most prominent formalisms for defining marked-up documents is the *Standard Generalized Markup Language* (SGML) [7]. In SGML, the structure of marked-up documents is described by means of *Document Type Definitions* (DTDs) which assert the set of "rules" that each document of a given document type must conform to. SGML DTDs have been used to define wide range of document types, from very general ones, such as generic HTML documents, to very specific ones, e.g. a specific form of email messages.

In this paper, we show a formalization of SGML DTDs in terms of an expressive Description Logic, $\mathcal{DL}$, equipped with sound, complete, and terminating inference procedures. This logic includes non-first-order constructs, such as reflexive-transitive closure and well-foundedness, which play a crucial role in the formalization. The inference procedures for such logic provide us with a general reasoning mechanism that enables effective reasoning tasks on DTDs. These include the verification of typical forms of equivalences between DTDs [17,15], such as: strong equivalence, i.e. whether two DTDs define the same sets of marked-up documents; structural equivalence, a weaker form of equivalence abstracting from tag names in the documents; and parametric versions of these equivalences. Notably, this general reasoning mechanism allows for verifying structural equivalence in worst case deterministic exponential time, in contrast to the known algorithms which are double exponential.

The paper is organized as follows. In Section 2, SGML DTDs and documents are introduced. In Section 3, the basic reasoning tasks on DTDs are defined. In Section 4, the Description Logic $\mathcal{DL}$ is presented and the formalization of DTDs (and related reasoning tasks) within $\mathcal{DL}$ is developed. Finally in Section 5 some conclusions are drawn.

2 SGML DTDs and Documents

An SGML document consists of an SGML prologue and a marked-up document. The prologue includes a *Document Type Definition (DTD)*, which is constituted by a set of *element type definitions* defining the generic structure of the various components of the marked-up document. The logical components of a document are called *elements*.

The fundamental characteristics of DTDs can be formalized by means of Extended Context Free Grammars (ECFGs) [17]. Marked-up documents are seen as *syntax trees* constructed according to the grammar, where the tree structure is determined by the various *tags* that occur in the document and that constitute the markup. An ECFG is a tuple $(\mathbf{E}, \mathbf{T}, \mathbf{P}, I)$, where $\mathbf{E}$ is an alphabet of *nonterminal symbols*, $\mathbf{T}$ is an alphabet of *terminal symbols*, $\mathbf{P}$ is a set of *production rules*, and $I \in \mathbf{E}$ is the initial symbol of the grammar. The nonterminal symbols are the elements defined in the DTD, and the start symbol is the element that specifies the document type. The terminal symbols are the basic types of SGML, such as #PCDATA, which represent generic (unmarked) strings with no associated structure within the DTD. In the following, with the term *symbol*, denoted by the letter S, we mean a generic terminal or nonterminal symbol in $\mathbf{E} \cup \mathbf{T}$. Each production rule $E \to \alpha$ of the ECFG corresponds to an element type definition. E is the defined element, and α, called *content model*, is an expression over the symbols of the grammar constructed according to the following syntax:

$$\alpha ::= S \mid \varepsilon \mid \alpha_1, \alpha_2 \mid \alpha_1 | \alpha_2 \mid \alpha^*.$$

In fact, α is a regular expression with "," denoting concatenation and "|" denoting union. When no ambiguity may arise, we identify α with the set of words generated by the regular expression that α represents. Additionally, in content models, the following standard abbreviations are used:

$$\alpha_1 \& \alpha_2 = (\alpha_1, \alpha_2) | (\alpha_2, \alpha_1) \qquad \alpha? = \varepsilon | \alpha \qquad \alpha^+ = \alpha, \alpha^*.$$

We observe that while "?" and "+" pose no particular problem, expanding "&" may in the worst case lead to an exponential increase in the size of the DTD.

Figure 1 shows an example of a DTD M for a simple mail document, expressed in SGML syntax. It is straightforward to derive the set of ECFG productions corresponding to the various element type definitions.

DTDs contain in fact also other aspects that are not directly related to the document structure. An example is the possibility to associate to each element a set of properties by means of a so called *attribute list*. In the following, for the sake of simplicity, we do not consider those additional aspects. We remark, however, that the representation of DTDs in terms of Description Logics provided in Section 4, makes it easy to take also these aspects into consideration.

Let $\mathcal{D} = (\mathbf{E}, \mathbf{T}, \mathbf{P}, I)$ be a DTD. We assume without loss of generality that for each element $E \in \mathbf{E}$, $\mathbf{P}$ contains at most one element type definition $E \to \alpha$ where E appears on the left hand side. We also assume that for each element E appearing in $\mathbf{P}$, there is an element type definition $E \to \alpha$ in which E is the symbol on the left hand side. In fact, if such condition is not satisfied, the grammar can easily be transformed in polynomial time into one that generates the same set of marked-up documents, and in which the condition holds.

The set $docs(\mathbf{P}, S)$ of *marked-up documents* generated by $\mathbf{P}$ starting from a symbol S is inductively defined as follows:

- If S is a terminal, then $docs(\mathbf{P}, S) = S$.
- If S is an element and $(S \to \alpha) \in \mathbf{P}$, then $docs(\mathbf{P}, S)$ is the set of sequences $<S> d_1 \cdots d_k </S>$, where $<S>$ and $</S>$ are the start and end tags associated

to the element S, and $d_1, \ldots, d_k$ are documents generated by an instance of the regular expression α. Formally

$$docs(\mathbf{P}, S) = \{ \texttt{<S>} d_1 \cdots d_k \texttt{</S>} \mid \exists \sigma \in \alpha \text{ such that } \sigma = S_1 \cdots S_k$$
$$\text{and } d_i \in docs(\mathbf{P}, S_i), \text{ for } i \in \{1, \ldots, k\}\}$$

The set of marked-up documents generated by a DTD $\mathcal{D} = (\mathbf{E}, \mathbf{T}, \mathbf{P}, I)$ is given by $docs(\mathbf{P}, I)$.

3 Basic Reasoning Tasks on DTDs

Given two DTDs, a fundamental problem is to determine whether they are equivalent in some sense, i.e. whether they define the same sets of documents [17,15]. Here, we consider a more general problem, which is that of checking various forms of language inclusion (instead of equivalence). The most basic form of inclusion (equivalence) is inclusion (equality) of the sets of marked-up documents generated by the two DTDs. Formally, let $\mathcal{D}_1 = (\mathbf{E}, \mathbf{T}, \mathbf{P}_1, I_1)$ and $\mathcal{D}_2 = (\mathbf{E}, \mathbf{T}, \mathbf{P}_2, I_2)$ be two DTDs[1]. We say that $\mathcal{D}_1$ is *strongly included* in $\mathcal{D}_2$, denoted with $\mathcal{D}_1 \preceq_s \mathcal{D}_2$, if $docs(\mathbf{P}_1, I_1) \subseteq docs(\mathbf{P}_2, I_2)$. For determining strong inclusion, the names of the start and end tags that constitute the markup of the two documents play a fundamental role.

In some cases, however, the actual names of the tags may not be relevant while the document structure imposed by the tags is of importance. The form of inclusion obtained by ignoring the names of tags and considering only their positions is called *structural inclusion* [17]. One DTDs is structurally included into another if, when we replace in every document generated by the DTDs all start and end tags with the unnamed tags <> and </> respectively, the resulting sets for the two DTDs are one included into the other.

Structural equivalence of two DTDs is decidable, but the known algorithms take time doubly exponential in the size of the two DTDs [17]. This complexity bound holds if one does not consider the "&" operator, which, if expanded may lead to an additional exponential blowup.

While the restrictions imposed by strong inclusion may be too strict in some cases, structural inclusion, which ignores completely all tag names, may be too weak. A natural generalization of these two concepts is obtained by considering a spectrum of possible inclusions, of which strong and structural inclusion are just the two extremes. The different forms of inclusion are obtained by considering certain tag names as equal, and others as different, when confronting documents. This allows us to parameterize inclusion (and therefore equivalence) of DTDs with respect to an equivalence relation on the set of tag names.

Formally, we consider an equivalence relation $\mathcal{R}$ on the set $\mathbf{E}$ of nonterminal symbols. For an element $E \in \mathbf{E}$, we denote by $[E]_\mathcal{R}$ the equivalence class of E with respect to $\mathcal{R}$. Given a DTD $\mathcal{D} = (\mathbf{E}, \mathbf{T}, \mathbf{P}, I)$ and such an equivalence

---

[1] In general, when comparing DTDs we assume without loss of generality that they are over the same alphabets of terminals and elements.

Concepts C	Syntax	Semantics
concept name	A	$A^{\mathcal{I}} \subseteq \Delta^{\mathcal{I}}$
top	$\top$	$\Delta^{\mathcal{I}}$
bottom	$\bot$	$\emptyset$
negation	$\neg C$	$\Delta^{\mathcal{I}} \setminus C^{\mathcal{I}}$
conjunction	$C_1 \sqcap C_2$	$C_1^{\mathcal{I}} \cap C_2^{\mathcal{I}}$
disjunction	$C_1 \sqcup C_2$	$C_1^{\mathcal{I}} \cup C_2^{\mathcal{I}}$
universal quantif.	$\forall R.C$	$\{o \mid \forall o' : (o,o') \in R^{\mathcal{I}} \rightarrow o' \in C^{\mathcal{I}}\}$
existential quantif.	$\exists R.C$	$\{o \mid \exists o' : (o,o') \in R^{\mathcal{I}} \wedge o' \in C^{\mathcal{I}}\}$
qualified number	$\exists^{\leq n} Q.C$	$\{o \mid \#\{o' \mid (o,o') \in Q^{\mathcal{I}} \wedge o' \in C^{\mathcal{I}}\} \leq n\}$
restrictions	$\exists^{\leq n} Q^-.C$	$\{o \mid \#\{o' \mid (o,o') \in (Q^-)^{\mathcal{I}} \wedge o' \in C^{\mathcal{I}}\} \leq n\}$
well-founded	$wf(R)$	$\{o_0 \mid \forall o_1, o_2, \dots \text{(ad infinitum)} \ \exists i \geq 0 : (o_i, o_{i+1}) \notin R^{\mathcal{I}}\}$
Roles R	**Syntax**	**Semantics**
role name	P	$P^{\mathcal{I}} \subseteq \Delta^{\mathcal{I}} \times \Delta^{\mathcal{I}}$
union	$R_1 \cup R_2$	$R_1^{\mathcal{I}} \cup R_2^{\mathcal{I}}$
concatenation	$R_1 \circ R_2$	$R_1^{\mathcal{I}} \circ R_2^{\mathcal{I}}$
inverse	R^-	$\{(o,o') \mid (o',o) \in R^{\mathcal{I}}\}$
refl. trans. closure	R^*	$(R^{\mathcal{I}})^*$
identity	$id(C)$	$\{(o,o) \mid o \in C^{\mathcal{I}}\}$

Table 1. Syntax and semantics of $\mathcal{DL}$ concept and role constructs.

relation $\mathcal{R}$, we inductively define the set $docs_{\mathcal{R}}(\mathbf{P}, S)$ of $\mathcal{R}$-*marked-up documents* generated by $\mathbf{P}$ starting from a symbol S as follows:

- If S is a terminal, then $docs_{\mathcal{R}}(\mathbf{P}, S) = S$.
- If S is an element and $(S \rightarrow \alpha) \in \mathbf{P}$, then

$$docs_{\mathcal{R}}(\mathbf{P}, S) = \{<[S]_{\mathcal{R}}> d_1 \cdots d_k </[S]_{\mathcal{R}}> \mid \exists \sigma \in \alpha \text{ such that } \sigma = S_1 \cdots S_k$$
$$\text{and } d_i \in docs_{\mathcal{R}}(\mathbf{P}, S_i), \text{ for } i \in \{1, \dots, k\}\}$$

The set of $\mathcal{R}$-marked-up documents generated by a DTD $\mathcal{D} = (\mathbf{E}, \mathbf{T}, \mathbf{P}, I)$ is given by $docs_{\mathcal{R}}(\mathbf{P}, I)$.

For two DTDs $\mathcal{D}_1 = (\mathbf{E}, \mathbf{T}, \mathbf{P}_1, I_1)$ and $\mathcal{D}_2 = (\mathbf{E}, \mathbf{T}, \mathbf{P}_2, I_2)$ and an equivalence relation $\mathcal{R}$ on $\mathbf{E}$, we say that $\mathcal{D}_1$ is $\mathcal{R}$-*included* in $\mathcal{D}_2$, denoted with $\mathcal{D}_1 \preceq_{\mathcal{R}} \mathcal{D}_2$, if $docs_{\mathcal{R}}(\mathbf{P}_1, I_1) \subseteq docs_{\mathcal{R}}(\mathbf{P}_2, I_2)$.

Observe that, if we choose for $\mathcal{R}$ the equivalence relation in which all equivalence classes are singletons, we obtain strong inclusion. On the other hand, if $\mathcal{R}$ contains a single equivalence class constituted by the whole set $\mathbf{E}$, we obtain structural inclusion.

4 Description Logic for DTDs

Let us introduce the logic $\mathcal{DL}$ which we use for formalizing DTDs and which is a simplified version of the formalisms in [5,4]. The syntax and semantics of $\mathcal{DL}$ are shown in Table 1, where we denote concept names by A, arbitrary concepts by C, role names by P, and arbitrary roles by R, all possibly with subscripts. The semantics of the $\mathcal{DL}$ constructs is the standard one, except for the construct $wf(R)$, called *well-founded*, which is interpreted as those objects that are the initial point of only finite R-chains.

A $\mathcal{DL}$ *knowledge base* is a set of assertions of the form

$$C_1 \sqsubseteq C_2,$$

where C_1 and C_2 are arbitrary concepts without any restrictions. We use also $C_1 \equiv C_2$ as an abbreviation for the pair of assertions $C_1 \sqsubseteq C_2$ and $C_2 \sqsubseteq C_1$.

An interpretation $\mathcal{I}$ *satisfies* the assertion $C_1 \sqsubseteq C_2$ if $C_1^{\mathcal{I}} \subseteq C_2^{\mathcal{I}}$. An interpretation is a *model* of a knowledge base $\mathcal{K}$ if it satisfies all assertions in $\mathcal{K}$[2]. Typical reasoning services (i.e. subsumption, satisfiability, logical implication) in $\mathcal{DL}$ are EXPTIME-complete [5,4].

Let $\mathbf{D} = \{\mathcal{D}_1, \ldots, \mathcal{D}_k\}$ be a finite collection of DTDs. We assume without loss of generality that all DTDs in the collection share the same alphabets $\mathbf{T}$ of terminals and $\mathbf{E}$ of elements, i.e. that $\mathcal{D}_i = (\mathbf{E}, \mathbf{T}, \mathbf{P}_i, I_i)$, for $i \in \{1, \ldots, k\}$. We describe now how to construct from $\mathbf{D}$ a $\mathcal{DL}$ knowledge base $\mathcal{K}$ capable of fully capturing the various structural aspects of the DTDs in $\mathbf{D}$. The knowledge base $\mathcal{K}$ is constituted by three parts, called $\mathcal{K}_0, \mathcal{K}_1$ and $\mathcal{K}_2$, respectively, which we now describe.

Independently from the particular collection of DTDs, $\mathcal{K}_0$ contains special assertions that model general structural properties of marked-up documents:

$$\texttt{DStruc} \equiv \forall(\mathtt{f} \cup \mathtt{r}).\texttt{DStruc} \sqcap \exists^{\leq 1}\mathtt{f}.\top \sqcap \exists^{\leq 1}\mathtt{r}.\top \sqcap \exists^{\leq 1}(\mathtt{f} \cup \mathtt{r})^-.\top \sqcap wf(\mathtt{f} \cup \mathtt{r})$$

$$\texttt{Tag} \sqsubseteq \texttt{DStruc} \sqcap \forall(\mathtt{f} \cup \mathtt{r}).\bot$$

$$\texttt{Terminal} \sqsubseteq \texttt{DStruc} \sqcap \forall(\mathtt{f} \cup \mathtt{r}).\bot \sqcap \neg\texttt{Tag}$$

Every instance of DStruc represents an SGML document. Every instance of **Tag** represents a tag in $\mathbf{D}$, either a start or an end tag. Finally, every instance of **Terminal** represents a terminal symbol in $\mathbf{D}$.

The concept DStruc is defined in terms of the roles $\mathtt{f}$ and $\mathtt{r}$ (standing for "first" and "rest" respectively). The components of a document are found by following the $(\mathtt{f} \cup \mathtt{r})^+$-links. More precisely, the first component of a document d is its $\mathtt{f}$-filler, the second component is its $(\mathtt{r} \circ \mathtt{f})$-filler, the third component is its $(\mathtt{r} \circ \mathtt{r} \circ \mathtt{f})$-filler, and the last component is its $\mathtt{r}^h$-filler, for some $h > 0$[3].

Observe that the definition of DStruc imposes that $\mathtt{f}$ and $\mathtt{r}$ are functions, and that every instance of DStruc has at most one $(\mathtt{f} \cup \mathtt{r})$-predecessor, hence enforcing a binary tree structure on the $(\mathtt{f} \cup \mathtt{r})^*$-connected components in the models of the knowledge base. Notably, the use of the well-foundedness construct is essential to impose finiteness and acyclicity of such connected components.

$\mathcal{K}_1$ is used to represent the specific tags and terminal symbols appearing in $\mathbf{D}$. In particular,

---

[2] This means that we adopt *descriptive semantics* for cycles.

[3] $\mathtt{r}^h$ denotes $\mathtt{r} \circ \cdots \circ \mathtt{r}$ (h times).

– For each terminal $F \in \mathbf{T}$, $\mathcal{K}_1$ contains an assertion

$$F \sqsubseteq \texttt{Terminal}.$$

– For each element $E \in \mathbf{E}$, $\mathcal{K}_1$ contains two assertions

$$\texttt{Start}E \sqsubseteq \texttt{Tag} \qquad\qquad \texttt{End}E \sqsubseteq \texttt{Tag},$$

where $\texttt{Start}E$ and $\texttt{End}E$ represent start and end tags.

$\mathcal{K}_2$ encodes the knowledge about the various production rules in $\mathbf{D}$. In particular, for each $\mathcal{D}_i \in \mathbf{D}$, and for each element E, such that $(E \to \alpha) \in \mathbf{P}_i$, $\mathcal{K}_2$ contains the assertion:

$$E_{\mathcal{D}_i} \equiv \texttt{DStruc} \sqcap \exists \mathtt{f}.\texttt{Start}E \sqcap \exists(\mathtt{r} \circ \tau(\alpha)).\texttt{End}E$$

with $\tau(\alpha)$ defined inductively as:

$$\begin{aligned} \tau(\varepsilon) &= id(\top) & \tau(S) &= id(\exists \mathtt{f}.cn(\mathcal{D}_i, S)) \circ \mathtt{r} \\ \tau(\alpha_1 | \alpha_2) &= \tau(\alpha_1) \cup \tau(\alpha_2) & \tau(\alpha_1, \alpha_2) &= \tau(\alpha_1) \circ \tau(\alpha_2) \\ \tau(\alpha^*) &= \tau(\alpha)^* \end{aligned}$$

where $cn(\cdot, \cdot)$ is a mapping that associates to each pair constituted by a DTD $\mathcal{D}_i$ and a symbol S a concept name as follows:

$$cn(\mathcal{D}_i, S) = \begin{cases} E_{\mathcal{D}_i} & \text{if } S = E \text{ for an element } E \in \mathbf{E} \\ F & \text{if } S = F \text{ for a terminal } F \in \mathbf{T} \end{cases}$$

Note that the first component (the $\mathtt{f}$-filler) of every instance of $E_{\mathcal{D}_i}$ is its start tag, whereas the last component (the $\mathtt{r}^h$-filler) is its end tag. The remaining components (the $(\mathtt{r}^k \circ \mathtt{f})$-fillers, with $k < h$) are determined by the complex role $\tau(\alpha)$. Indeed $\tau(\alpha)$ reflects the structure imposed by α on the parts of a document that are defined by $E \to \alpha$, and can be explained in terms of an encoding of the tree representing the marked-up document into a binary tree.

Observe that for each element E we have introduced two concept names $\texttt{Start}E, \texttt{End}E$ representing its tags. Thus, for each tag in the collection $\mathbf{D}$ of DTDs there is a unique pair of corresponding concepts in $\mathcal{K}$. On the contrary, the information about the DTD a given element belongs to is explicitly carried out in the knowledge base. Indeed, there is one concept $E_{\mathcal{D}_i}$ in $\mathcal{K}$ for each DTD $\mathcal{D}_i$ in $\mathbf{D}$ containing the definition of an element E.

We stress that in each model of $\mathcal{K}$, the extension of every $E_{\mathcal{D}_i}$ is completely determined by the extension of the concepts representing tags and terminal symbols. In other words, given a model $\mathcal{M}$ of $\mathcal{K}$, it is possible to determine whether an object o is an instance of $E_{\mathcal{D}_i}$ by taking into account only the structure of the $(\mathtt{f} \cup \mathtt{r})^*$ connected component of $\mathcal{M}$ containing o. This property, which is ensured by the well-foundedness construct in the assertion on $\texttt{DStruc}$, is essential in order to obtain the desired correspondence between reasoning on the DTDs in $\mathbf{D}$ and reasoning on $\mathcal{K}$.

$$\begin{aligned}
\texttt{Mail}_M &\equiv \texttt{DStruc} \sqcap \exists\texttt{f.StartMail} \sqcap \exists(\texttt{r} \circ id(\exists\texttt{f.From}_M) \circ \texttt{r} \circ id(\exists\texttt{f.To}_M) \circ \texttt{r} \\
&\quad \circ id(\exists\texttt{f.Subject}_M) \circ \texttt{r} \circ id(\exists\texttt{f.Body}_M) \circ \texttt{r}).\texttt{EndMail} \\
\texttt{From}_M &\equiv \texttt{DStruc} \sqcap \exists\texttt{f.StartFrom} \sqcap \exists(\texttt{r} \circ id(\exists\texttt{f.Address}_M) \circ \texttt{r}).\texttt{EndFrom} \\
\texttt{To}_M &\equiv \texttt{DStruc} \sqcap \exists\texttt{f.StartTo} \sqcap \\
&\quad \exists(\texttt{r} \circ id(\exists\texttt{f.Address}_M) \circ \texttt{r} \circ (id(\exists\texttt{f.Address}_M) \circ \texttt{r})^*).\texttt{EndTo} \\
\texttt{Subject}_M &\equiv \texttt{DStruc} \sqcap \exists\texttt{f.StartSubject} \sqcap \exists(\texttt{r} \circ id(\exists\texttt{f.\#PCDATA}) \circ \texttt{r}).\texttt{EndSubject} \\
\texttt{Body}_M &\equiv \texttt{DStruc} \sqcap \exists\texttt{f.StartBody} \sqcap \exists(\texttt{r} \circ id(\exists\texttt{f.\#PCDATA}) \circ \texttt{r}).\texttt{EndBody} \\
\texttt{Address}_M &\equiv \texttt{DStruc} \sqcap \exists\texttt{f.StartAddress} \sqcap \exists(\texttt{r} \circ id(\exists\texttt{f.\#PCDATA}) \circ \texttt{r}).\texttt{EndAddress}
\end{aligned}$$

Fig. 2. The $\mathcal{K}_2$ part of the knowledge base $\mathcal{K}$ derived from the DTD M

Figure 2 shows the $\mathcal{K}_2$ part of the knowledge base $\mathcal{K}$ corresponding to the DTD M described in Figure 1. One can easily derive the $\mathcal{K}_0$ and $\mathcal{K}_1$ parts of $\mathcal{K}$.

The knowledge base $\mathcal{K}$ corresponding to a collection $\mathbf{D}$ of documents can directly be used to determine strong inclusion between DTDs belonging to $\mathbf{D}$.

Theorem 1. *Let $\mathcal{D}_i$ and $\mathcal{D}_j$ be two DTDs in $\mathbf{D}$, and $\mathcal{K}$ the $\mathcal{DL}$ knowledge base derived from $\mathbf{D}$ as specified above. Then $\mathcal{D}_i$ is strongly included in $\mathcal{D}_j$ if and only if $cn(\mathcal{D}_i, I_i)$ is subsumed by $cn(\mathcal{D}_j, I_j)$ in $\mathcal{K}$.*

The knowledge base $\mathcal{K}$ can also be extended in order to verify the other forms of inclusions introduced in Section 2. Let $\mathcal{R} = \{\{E_1^1, \ldots, E_{n_1}^1\}, \ldots, \{E_1^m, \ldots, E_{n_m}^m\}\}$ be an equivalence relation on the set $\mathbf{E}$ of elements. We obtain the knowledge base $\mathcal{K}_{\mathcal{R}}$ from $\mathcal{K}$ by adding for each equivalence class $\{E_1^j, \ldots, E_{n_j}^j\}$ and for each element E_i^j, with $i \in \{1, \ldots, n_j-1\}$, the assertions:

$$\texttt{Start}E_i^j \equiv \texttt{Start}E_{i+1}^j \qquad\qquad \texttt{End}E_i^j \equiv \texttt{End}E_{i+1}^j$$

With these assertions we are essentially imposing the equivalence of all the concepts representing tags of elements belonging to each set $\{E_1^j, \ldots, E_{n_j}^j\}$. Therefore, when reasoning on $\mathcal{K}_{\mathcal{R}}$ the differences between the various tags associated to equivalent elements are ignored, coherently with the notion of $\mathcal{R}$-inclusion.

Theorem 2. *Let $\mathcal{D}_i$ and $\mathcal{D}_j$ be two DTDs in $\mathbf{D}$, $\mathcal{R}$ an equivalence relation on $\mathbf{E}$, and $\mathcal{K}_{\mathcal{R}}$ the $\mathcal{DL}$ knowledge base derived from $\mathbf{D}$ as specified above. Then $\mathcal{D}_i$ is $\mathcal{R}$-included in D_j if and only if $cn(\mathcal{D}_i, I_i)$ is subsumed by $cn(\mathcal{D}_j, I_j)$ in $\mathcal{K}_{\mathcal{R}}$.*

From decidability in deterministic exponential time of logical implication in $\mathcal{DL}$ [5] we obtain as an immediate consequence an EXPTIME upper bound for $\mathcal{R}$-inclusion and $\mathcal{R}$-equivalence between DTDs. This results also in an exponential improvement over previously known algorithms for checking structural equivalence.

Corollary 3. *$\mathcal{R}$-inclusion and $\mathcal{R}$-equivalence between two DTDs can be verified in deterministic exponential time in the size of the DTDs.*

5 Conclusions

Several recent papers dealing with the problem of retrieving information from a document database such as the World Wide Web argue that the current techniques for representing and reasoning on document structures should be improved. We have provided a view of DTDs as concepts of the expressive Description Logic $\mathcal{DL}$, and we have demonstrated that this approach is indeed very effective for both faithfully representing document structures, and answering some open questions regarding DTD equivalence checking. By exploiting the constructs of $\mathcal{DL}$, we are able to integrate into the structure of documents also aspects related to the semantics of the information contained in them. For example, attribute lists of DTD elements can be modeled easily in $\mathcal{DL}$. As another example, if part of a document (corresponding to a terminal symbol T in the DTD) includes a table with information about, say, departments and employees, this can be represented by adding suitable properties to the concept corresponding to T. We can also represent links to other documents, such as those typically found in the Web, by means of a special concept with suitable roles for the name of the link and the associated anchor. Obviously, by means of suitable assertions we can constrain the anchor to point to a document of a specific DTD.

The framework presented in this paper for representing and reasoning on structured documents provides a notable example of handling objects composed of different parts. The *part-whole* relation is seen as having a special importance in several applications [6,3,12]. $\mathcal{DL}$, by means of the reflexive-transitive closure and the well-foundedness constructs, is able to capture fundamental aspects of the part-whole relation [12,2,16] as shown in [5].

Two further research directions are worth pursuing. On the one hand, further aspects of DTDs could be captured in order to represent, for example, other properties of documents, exceptions (as described in [17]), and constraints on the number of occurrences of a certain pattern in an element definition. On the other hand, the deductive power of $\mathcal{DL}$ allows one to study new types of reasoning on DTDs, such as further forms of parameterized equivalence (e.g. abstracting from the definition of a specified element) and document classification (infer which is the DTD that best matches a given marked document among a set of candidates).

References

1. J. Åberg. Creating a description logics knowledge base for world wide web documents. Technical Report LiTH-IDA-Ex-9641, Department of Computer and Information Science, Linköping University, Sweden, 1996.
2. A. Artale, E. Franconi, and N. Guarino. Open problems with part-whole relations. In *Proc. of the 1996 Description Logic Workshop (DL-96)*, number WS-96-05, pages 70–73. AAAI Press, 1996.
3. A. Artale, E. Franconi, N. Guarino, and L. Pazzi. Part-whole relations in object-centered systems: An overview. *Data and Knowledge Engineering*, 20:347–383, 1996.

4. D. Calvanese. Finite model reasoning in description logics. In *Proc. of the 5th Int. Conf. on the Principles of Knowledge Representation and Reasoning (KR-96)*, pages 292–303. Morgan Kaufmann, 1996.

5. D. Calvanese, G. De Giacomo, and M. Lenzerini. Structured objects: Modeling and reasoning. In *Proc. of the 4th Int. Conf. on Deductive and Object-Oriented Databases (DOOD-95)*, number 1013 in LNCS, pages 229–246. Springer-Verlag, 1995.

6. V. Christophides, S. Abiteboul, S. Cluet, and M. Scholl. From structured documents to novel query facilities. In R. T. Snodgrass and M. Winslett, editors, *Proc. of the ACM SIGMOD Int. Conf. on Management of Data*, pages 313–324, 1994.

7. International Organization for Standardization. *ISO-8879: Information processing – Text and office systems – Standard Generalized Markup Language (SGML)*, October 1986.

8. T. Kirk, A.Y. Levy, Y. Sagiv, and Divesh Srivastava. The Information Manifold. In *Proceedings of the AAAI 1995 Spring Symp. on Information Gathering from Heterogeneous, Distributed Enviroments*, pages 85–91, 1995.

9. Craig Knoblock and Alon Y. Levy, editors. *Proceedings of the AAAI 1995 Spring Symp. on Information Gathering from Heterogeneous, Distributed Enviroments*, number SS-95-08, Menlo Park (U.S.A.), 1995. AAAI Press/The MIT Press.

10. D. Konopnicki and O. Shmueli. W3QS: A query system for the World Wide Web. In *Proc. of the 21th Int. Conf. on Very Large Data Bases (VLDB-95)*, pages 54–65, 1995.

11. L. Lakshmanan, F. Sadri, and I. N. Subramanian. A declarative language for querying and restructuring the Web. In *Proc. of the 6th Int. Workshop on Reasearch Issues in Data Enginnering: Interoperability of Nontraditional Database Systems*. IEEE Computer Science Press, 1996.

12. P. Lambrix. *Part-Whole Reasoning in Description Logic*. PhD thesis, Dep. of Computer and Information Science, Linköping University, Sweden, 1996.

13. A. Mendelzon, G. A. Mihaila, and T. Milo. Querying the World Wide Web. *International Journal on Digital Libraries*, 1(1):54–67, 1997.

14. D. Quass, A. Rajaraman, I. Sagiv, J. Ullman, and J. Widom. Querying semistructured heterogeneous information. In *Proc. of the 4th Int. Conf. on Deductive and Object-Oriented Databases (DOOD-95)*, pages 319–344. Springer-Verlag, 1995.

15. D. R. Raymond, F.W. Tompa, and D. Wood. From data implementation to data model: Meta-semantic issues in the evolution of SGML. *Computer Standards and Interfaces*, 1995.

16. U. Sattler. A concept language for an engineering application with part-whole relations. In A. Borgida, M. Lenzerini, D. Nardi, and B. Nebel, editors, *Working Notes of the 1995 Description Logics Workshop*, Technical Report, RAP 07.95, Dipartimento di Informatica e Sistemistica, Università di Roma "La Sapienza", pages 119–123, Rome (Italy), 1995.

17. D. Wood. Standard Generalized Markup Language: Mathematical and philosophical issues. In Jan van Leeuwen, editor, *Computer Science Today, Recent Trends and Developments*, number 1000 in LNCS, pages 344–365. Springer-Verlag, 1995.

Conceptual Modelling of the "Meaning" of Textual Narrative Documents

Gian Piero Zarri

Centre National de la Recherche Scientifique
54, boulevard Raspail
75270 PARIS Cedex 06, France
zarri@cams.msh-paris.fr

Abstract. A considerable amount of "useful" information is buried into natural language "narrative" documents. In these, the information content (the "meaning") consists mainly in the description of "facts" or "events" relating the real or intended behaviour of some (not necessarily human) "actors". In this paper, we suggest that at least some directions for establishing a standard methodology to accurately represent this meaning could be found in the solutions adopted in NKRL (acronym of "Narrative Knowledge Representation Language"), a conceptual modelling language which has a long history of successful, concrete applications.

1   Introduction

A considerable amount of important, "economically relevant" information is buried into natural language (NL) texts : this is true, e.g., for most of the corporate knowledge documents (memos, policy statements, reports, minutes etc.), as well as for the vast majority of information stored on the Web. A fundamental subset of this useful NL information is then formed by the so-called "narrative" documents. In these, the main part of the information content consists in the description of "facts" or "events" which relate the real or intended behaviour of some "actors" (characters, personages, etc.) : these try to attain a specific result, experience particular situations, manipulate some (concrete or abstract) materials, deliver or receive messages, etc. Please note that, in this sort of texts, the actors or personages are not necessarily human beings ; we can have narrative documents concerning the vicissitudes in the journey of a nuclear submarine (the "actor" or the "personage") or the various avatars in the life of a commercial product.

Being able to represent the semantic content of narrative information — i.e., its key "meaning" — in a general, accurate, and effective way is then both conceptually relevant and economically interesting. We can remark that, even if the formal properties of this sort of meaning has been studied for decades in the NL and AI communities (see also the discussion in Section 4., "Conclusion"), the problem of its correct, **standard** representation has not, apparently, yet been solved. For example, some current proposals for describing and indexing WWW NL documents like Meta Content Framework, Semantic Header or Dublin Core, see, e.g., (Weibel *et al.* 1995) concern only the "external" identification framework of these documents (subject, author, title, language, creation date ...), neglecting then the representation of their "internal" semantic content. On the other hand, the knowledge sharing initiatives like KIF or Ontolingua (Gruber 1993) seem unable, in the so-called "ontological" domain, to go beyond the representation of data structures which have the traditional form of bundles of attribute / value relations : their utility for representing narrative situations, where more complex data structures are needed to take into account also the "role" the different entities play within an event, is then subject to caution.

In this paper, we suggest then that at least some directions for formally establishing a standard vehicle for representing the semantic content of narrative information could be found in the solutions adopted in a conceptual language like NKRL (acronym of "Narrative Knowledge Representation Language") for describing (and actually exploiting) narrative documents. The (pragmatic) representation principles used in NKRL have, in, fact, a long history of successful, concrete applications which go back to the Seventies ; recent implementations have been realised in the framework of two European projects : NOMOS, Esprit P5330, and COBALT, LRE P61011.

2 The architecture of NKRL

NKRL is a two layer language.

2.1 The lower layer

The lower layer of NKRL consists of a set of general representation tools which are structured into several integrated components, four in our case.

The definitional component of NKRL supplies the tools for representing the "important notions" (concepts) of a given domain ; in NKRL, a concept is, therefore, a definitional data structure associated with a symbolic label like *physical_entity*, *human_being*, *taxi_* (the general class including all the taxis, not a specific cab), *city_*, etc. These definitional data structures are, substantially, frame-like structures ; moreover, all the NKRL concepts are inserted into a generalisation/specialisation (tangled) hierarchy that, for historical reasons, is called H_CLASS(es), and which corresponds well to the usual "ontologies" of terms.

To give rise to well-formed ontologies of NKRL concepts, the original notions must be conceived in terms of sets and subsets — where, as usual, asserting that *a* pertains to the set *A*, (*a* : *A*) is equivalent to assert that *a* is characterised by the type *A*. Moreover, no confusion is allowed between "subsets" — giving rise to standard H_CLASS concepts, like *european_city* which is a specialisation of the concept *city_* — and "instances", like paris_. Instances are still, of course, directly associated as terminal symbols with particular H_CLASS terms, but they are in the domain of another NKRL component, the enumerative component, see below. Moreover, a fundamental assumption about the organisation of H_CLASS concerns the differentiation between "notions which can be realised (instantiated) directly into enumerable specimens", like "chair" (a "physical object") and "notions which cannot be instantiated directly into specimens", like "gold" (a "substance") — please note that a notion like "white gold" is a specialisation (subset) of gold, not an instance. The two high-level branches of H_CLASS stem, therefore, from two concepts that — adopting the terminology used in (Guarino, Carrara and Giaretta 1994) — we have labelled as *sortal_concepts* and *non_sortal_concepts*, see also Fig. 5 in subsection 3.2 below. The specialisations of the former, like *chair_*, *city_* or *european_city*, can have direct (immediate) instances (chair_27, paris_), whereas the specialisations of the latter, like *gold_*, or *colour_*, can admit further specialisations, see *white_gold* or *red_*, but do not have direct instances.

The enumerative component of NKRL concerns then the formal representation of the instances (concrete examples, see lucy_, wardrobe_1, taxi_53, paris_, not subsets) of the sortal concepts of H_CLASS. In NKRL, their formal representations take the name of "individuals". Individuals are characterised by the fact of being countable (enumerable), of being associated with a temporal dimension (and, often, with a spatial dimension), and of possessing unique symbolic labels (lucy_, wardrobe_1, taxi_53) ; see, below, subsection 3.1 for the representation of "collections" of instances. Throughout this paper, we will use the italic type style to represent a "*concept_*", the roman style to represent an "individual_".

We can note immediately that, in NKRL, the concepts and their instances (individuals) are kept conceptually distinct even if they are represented using the same data structures. The main reason for adopting this type of organisation is linked with the very different epistemological status of concepts — which define a generic, abstract mould for some useful notions to be taken into consideration in a given domain — with respect to the individuals, which represent specific entities occurring in the context of some concrete events of the domain. In this respect, concepts are permanent, at least in the context of a given application ; individuals represent, on the contrary, unpredictable, randomly-occurring entities stored sequentially into an NKRL-like system according to their order of arrival in the environment of this system. Please note that, see before, individuals are also linked with the concept hierarchy, where they appear as the "leaves" of particular sortal concepts ; they are, therefore, indexed by the H_CLASS hierarchical structure.

The "events" proper to a given domain — i.e., the dynamic processes describing the interactions among the concepts and individuals that play a "role" in the contest of these events — are represented by making use of the "descriptive" and "factual" tools.

The descriptive component concerns the tools used to produce the formal representations (called predicative templates) of general classes of narrative events, like "moving a generic object", "formulate a need", "having a negative attitude towards someone", "be present somewhere". In the context of the descriptive component, the events taken into consideration must be "structured events", i.e., they must be characterised by the explicit mention of an actor, an object, an instrument, etc. Correspondingly — and in opposition to the binary data structures used for concepts and individuals — predicative templates are characterised by a threefold format where the central piece is a semantic **predicate**, i.e., a named relation that exists among one or more **arguments** introduced by means of **roles** :

$$(Pi\ (R1\ a1)\ (R2\ a2)\ ...\ (Rn\ an)) ,$$

see the examples in subsection 3.1. Presently, the predicates pertain to the set {BEHAVE, EXIST, EXPERIENCE, MOVE, OWN, PRODUCE, RECEIVE}, and the roles to the set {SUBJ(ect), OBJ(ect), SOURCE, DEST(ination), MODAL(ity), TOPIC, CONTEXT}. Please note that, in NKRL, predicates and roles express only some functional relationships strictly necessary for the full appraisal of the "meaning" to be represented. In this sense, our roles, e.g., are more similar to the "correlators" of Ceccato's operational linguistics, see (Ceccato 1967) — where to each correlator corresponds a set of language-independent, mental operations — than to the (syntactically constrained) Jackendoff's thematic roles (Jackendoff 1990), which are strongly influenced by the search for some form of optimal correspondence between the semantic contents and the surface form these contents can assume in a particular natural language. Templates are structured into an inheritance hierarchy, H_TEMP(lates), which corresponds, therefore, to a "taxonomy (ontology) of events".

The instances ("predicative occurrences") of the predicative templates, i.e., the NKRL representation of single, specific events like "Tomorrow, I will move the wardrobe", "Lucy was looking for a taxi", "Mr. Smith has fired Mr. Brown", "Peter lives in Paris" are in the domain of the factual component. The reasons for distinguishing between descriptive and factual component are identical to those already examined in a definitional/enumerative context .

2.2 The upper layer

The upper layer of NKRL consists of two parts. The first is a "catalogue" which gives a complete description of the formal characteristics and the modalities of use of the well-formed, "basic templates" (like "moving a generic object" mentioned above) associated with the language. Presently, the basic templates are more than 150, pertaining mainly to a (very general) socio-economico-political context where the main characters are human beings or social bodies. By means of proper specialisation operations it is then possible to obtain from the basic templates the (specific) "derived" templates that could be concretely needed to implement a particular, practical application — e.g., "move an industrial process" — and the corresponding occurrences — e.g., "move, in a well-defined spatio-temporal framework, this particular industrial production". In NKRL, the set of legal, basic templates included in the catalogue can be considered, at least in a first approach, as fixed (see Section 4, "Conclusion", for the advantages of this solution). Please note, however, that the possibility (if need be) of inserting new basic elements in the catalogue is not excluded, and new templates can (carefully) be created on the model of the existing ones.

The second part of the upper layer is given by the general concepts which pertain to the upper levels of H_CLASS — such as *sortal_concepts*, *non_sortal_concepts*, *physical_entity*, *modality_*, *event_*, etc., see also Fig. 5 below. They are, as the upper levels of H_TEMP, invariable, i.e., they are not subjected to change when another application in a different domain is taken into account. These concepts form a sort of upper-level, invariable ontology to be compared with Bateman's "Generalized Upper Model" (Bateman, Magnini and Fabris 1995), even if our selection criteria are, once again, functional more than linguistically motivated.

3 Examples of characteristic NKRL features

3.1 Descriptive/factual components

Fig. 1 supplies a simple example of factual NKRL code. It translates a fragment of fictitious, COBALT-like news story : "Yesterday, the spokesman said in a newspaper interview that his company has bought three factories abroad", which is represented according to the rules for encoding "plural situations" in NKRL, see (Zarri 1995).

Two occurrences (factual component), identified by the symbolic labels c1 and c2 and instances of basic NKRL templates, bring out the main characteristics of the event. The arguments human_being_1, company_1, newspaper_1, interview_1, purchase_1, factory_99, abroad_ are individuals ; yesterday_ is a fictitious individual introduced here, for simplicity's sake, in place of real or approximate dates, see, e.g., (Zarri 1992) for some details about the representation of temporal information in NKRL. *spokesman_* and *cardinality_*, that pertain both to the *property_* subtree of the H_CLASS hierarchy, are concepts. The attributive operator, SPECIF(ication), is one of the NKRL operators used to build up structured arguments (or "expansions"), see (Zarri and Gilardoni 1996) ; the SPECIF lists, with syntax (SPECIF e_1 p_1 ... p_n), are used to represent some of the properties which can be asserted about the first element

e_1, concept or individual, of the list. e.g., *human_being* and *chairman_* in c1. The arguments, and the templates / occurrences as a whole, may be characterised by the presence of particular codes, "determiners" or "attributes", which give further details about their significant aspects. For example, the "location attributes", represented as lists, are linked with the arguments by using the colon (":") operator, see c2.

```
c1)   MOVE   SUBJ      (SPECIF human_being_1 (SPECIF spokesman_
                            company_1))
             OBJ       #c2
             DEST      newspaper_1
             MODAL     interview_1
             date-1:   yesterday_
             date-2:

c2)   PRODUCE  SUBJ    company_1
               OBJ     (SPECIF purchase_1 (SPECIF factory_99
                          (SPECIF cardinality_ 3))): (abroad_)

[ factory_99
       InstanceOf  :  factory_
       HasMember   :  3 ]
```

Figure 1 - An example of NKRL code.

The non-empty HasMember slot in the data structure explicitly associated with the individual factory_99 makes it clear that this last, mentioned in c2, is referring in reality to several instances of *factory_*. Individuals like factory_99 are "collections" rather then "sets", given that the extensionality axiom (two sets are equal iff they have the same elements) does not hold here. In our framework, two collections, say factory_99 and factory_100, can be co-extensional, i.e., they can include exactly the same elements, without being necessarily considered as identical if created at different moments in time in the context of totally different events, see also (Franconi 1993). In Fig. 1, we have supposed that the three factories were, *a priori*, not sufficiently important in the context of the news story to justify their explicit representation as specific individuals, e.g., factory_1, factory_2, factory_3 ; please note that, if not expressly required by the characteristics of the application, a basic NKRL principle suggests that we should try to avoid any unnecessary proliferation of individuals.

Going on now with some information about the descriptive/factual structures, we reproduce in Fig. 2 the (tripartite), basic template of H_TEMP that gives rise to the occurrence c2 of Fig. 1. In this figure, optional elements are in round brackets (see, e.g., the role SOURCE which introduces the possible "origin" of the situation). In the corresponding occurrences, see c2, the variables (x, y, u, etc.) are replaced by concepts or individuals according to the associated constraints, expressed as combinations of concepts pertaining to the H_CLASS upper levels.

Fig. 3 is a schematic representation of the H_TEMP hierarchy, where only the branches BEHAVE, MOVE and PRODUCE have been developed to some, very limited extent. In this figure, the syntactic description of the templates is particularly sketchy : e.g., all the symbolic labels have been eliminated, and the templates are discriminated only through the associated natural language comments. For a more realistic picture of a template, see Fig. 2 above. The codes "!" and "≠" mean, respectively, "mandatory" and "forbidden" (e.g., in the "transmit an information to someone" template, MOVE sub hierarchy, the presence of a DEST(ination) role is expressly required).

```
{ PRODUCE3.1 ; 'acquire, buy'

    IsA : PRODUCE3 ; 'perform a task or action'

    PRODUCE  SUBJ       x : [<location_>]
             OBJ        (SPECIF y e l { e }+)
             (SOURCE    u : [<location_>])
             (DEST      v : [<location_>])
             (MODAL     w
             (CONTEXT   z)
             ({'modulators'})
             [date-1: <date_>, 'initial date' l 'observed date']
             [date-2: <date_>, 'final date']

    x  =  <human_being_or_social_body>
    y  =  <purchase_> ; e = <valuable_entity>
    u  =  <human_being_or_social_body>
    v  =  <human_being_or_social_body>
    w  =  <modality_> l 'symbolic label of predicative occurrence'
    z  =  <situation_framework>}
```

Figure 2 - An example of basic template.

We can conclude the discussion of Fig. 1 by noticing that the MOVE construction at the origin of $c1$ is necessarily used to translate any event concerning the transmission of an information ("the spokesman said ..."). The corresponding template makes use of what is called a "completive construction". Accordingly, the filler of the OBJ(ect) slot in the occurrences (here, $c1$) which instantiates the transmission template is always a symbolic label ($\#c2$) which refers to another predicative occurrence, i.e., the occurrence bearing the information content to be spread out ("the company has bought three factories abroad ..."), see also Fig. 3.

As a second example of descriptive/factual structures, we give now, Fig. 4, an NKRL interpretation of the narrative sentence : "We have to make orange juice" which, according to Hwang and Schubert (Hwang and Schubert 1993: 1298), exemplifies several interesting semantic phenomena. To translate the general idea of "acting in order to obtain a given result", we use :

i) A (predicative) occurrence ($c3$ in Fig. 4), instance of a basic template pertaining to the BEHAVE branch of H_TEMP, and corresponding to the general meaning of "focusing on a result". This occurrence is used to express the "acting" component, i.e., it allows us to identify the SUBJ of the action, the temporal co-ordinates, possibly the MODAL(ity) or the instigator (SOURCE), etc.

ii) A second predicative occurrence, $c4$ in Fig. 4, which contains a different NKRL predicate (e.g., PRODUCE in Fig. 4) and which is used to express the "intended result" component. Please note that, for all the "focus on..." constructions, the reference time is the timestamp ("observed date" in Fig. 4) linked with the first occurrence (BEHAVE). The second occurrence, which happens "in the future", is necessarily marked as hypothetical, i.e., it is always characterised by the presence of a "uncertainty validity attribute", code "*".

. **H_TEMP** ("hierarchy of predicative templates")

.. **BEHAVE templates** ; predicate : BEHAVE

... "external manifestation of the subject" ; ≠OBJ
.... "acting in a particular role" : MODAL < role_ [ex: *rugby_player*] >
.... "manifest a particular quality" ; MODAL < *quality_* >

... "focus on a result"; ≠ OBJ, DEST, TOPIC; ≠mod. "against, for"; !GOAL bind. struct.
.... "act explicitly to obtain the result" ; ≠modulator "ment"
.... "wishes and intentions" ; ! modulator "ment"

... "concrete attitude toward someone/s.thing"; !OBJ, MODAL; ≠DEST, GOAL; ≠"ment"

.. **EXIST templates** ; predicate : EXIST ; !location of the SUBJ ; ≠DEST

.. **EXPERIENCE templates** ; predicate : EXPERIENCE ; !OBJ ; ≠DEST

.. **MOVE templates** ; predicate : MOVE

... "moving a generic entity" ; OBJ < *entity_* >
.... "move a material thing" ; OBJ < *physical_entity* >
..... "change the position of something" ; ≠DEST (ex: "move the wardrobe")
..... "transfer something to someone" ; !DEST (ex: "send a letter to Lucy")

... "generic person displacement"; SUBJ = OBJ = <*human_being*> ; !loc. of SUBJ, OBJ

... "transmit an information to someone" : !DEST
.... "transmit a generic information" ; OBJ < *type_of_information* [ex: *message_*] >
.... "transmit a structured information" ; OBJ "label of binding/predicat. occurrence"

.. **OWN templates** ; predicate : OWN ; !OBJ ; ≠DEST

.. **PRODUCE templates** ; predicate : PRODUCE ; !OBJ

... "conceive a plan or idea" ; !modulator "ment"

... "creation of material things" ; OBJ < *physical_entity* > ; ≠modulator "ment"

... "perform a task or action" ; OBJ < *action_name* >
.... "acquire, buy" ; OBJ < *purchase_* >
.... "sell" ; OBJ < *sale_* >

... "relation involvem." ; SUBJ (COORD); OBJ *mutual_agreem.* MODAL <*relationsh._*>

... "production of events by an active cause" ; SUBJ < *active_cause* > ; OBJ < *event_* >

.. **RECEIVE templates** ; predicate : RECEIVE ; !OBJ ; ≠DEST

Figure 3 - Schematic H_TEMP hierarchy (ontology of events).

iii) A "binding occurrence", c5, linking together the previous predicative occurrences and labelled with GOAL, an operator pertaining to the "taxonomy of causality" of NKRL. Binding structures, templates or occurrences — i.e., lists where the elements are symbolic labels, c3 and c4 in Fig. 4 — are second-order structures used to represent the logico-semantic links which can exist between (predicative) templates or occurrences.

```
c3)   BEHAVE SUBJ  (COORD informant_1 (SPECIF human_being
                                       (SPECIF cardinality_ several_)))
             [oblig, ment]
             date1:  observed date
             date2:

c4)  * PRODUCE  SUBJ  (COORD informant_1 (SPECIF human_being
                                          (SPECIF cardinality_ several_)))
               OBJ   (SPECIF orange_juice (SPECIF amount_))
               date1: observed date + i
               date2:

c5)   (GOAL c3 c4)
```

Figure 4 - Representation of "wishes and intentions".

The general schema for representing the "focusing on an intended result" domain in NKRL, see also Fig. 3, is then :

c_α)   BEHAVE   SUBJ   <human_being_or_social_body>

c_β)   * <predicative_occurrence>, with any syntax

c_γ)   (GOAL c_α c_β)

In Fig. 4, "oblig" and "ment" are "modulators", see (Zarri 1995), i.e., particular determiners used to refine or modify the primary interpretation of a template or occurrence as given by the basic "predicate — roles — argument" association. "Ment(al)" pertains to the "modality" modulators. "Oblig(atory)" suggests that "someone is obliged to do or to endure something, e.g., by authority", and pertains to the "deontic modulators" series. Other modulators are the "temporal modulators", "begin", "end", "obs(erve)", see again (Zarri 1992). Modulators work as global operators which take as their argument the whole (predicative) template or occurrence. When a list of modulators is present, as in the occurrence c3 of Fig. 4, they apply successively to the template/occurrence in a polish notation style to avoid any possibility of scope ambiguity. In the constructions for expressing "focus on ...", see Fig. 3, the absence of the "ment(al)" modulator in the BEHAVE occurrence means that the SUBJ(ect) of BEHAVE takes some concrete initiative (acts explicitly) in order to fulfil the result ; if "ment" is present, as in Fig. 4, no concrete action is undertaken, and the "result" reflects only the wishes and desires of the SUBJ(ect). several_, see c3 and c4, is used conventionally in NKRL to represent the cardinality of sets of totally undefined size, like those corresponding to a generic plural referent, as in "men" or "books", see (Zarri and Gilardoni 1996). In c4, "i" is conventionally used to denote an unknown time increment with respect to the timestamp that characterises c3.

3.2   Definitional/enumerative components

Fig. 5 gives a very sketchy representation of the upper level of H_CLASS (hierarchy of concepts, definitional component). Please note, in this figure, the presence of a sortal concept event_. As already stated, the events represented by means of templates and occurrences must be structured events, i.e., they must be characterised by the specific indication of an actor, an object, etc. If we only want to explicitly mention an event (e.g., president_clinton_interview_49), without giving all its structural details, we will simply make use of a particular individual, i.e., of an instance of *event_*. We can also remark, in this figure, that *substance_* and *colour_* are regarded in NKRL as examples of non sortal concepts. For their generic terms, *pseudo_sortal_concepts* and *characterising_concepts*, we have adopted here again the terminology of (Guarino, Carrara and Giaretta 1994).

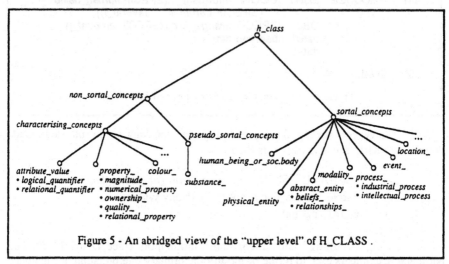

Figure 5 - An abridged view of the "upper level" of H_CLASS .

The data structures used for concepts and individuals are essentially frame-based structures, and their design is relatively traditional. These structures are composed of an OID (object identifier, the generic symbolic label of the concept to be defined, or the specific name of the individual to be created), and of a set of characteristic features (slots). Slots are distinguished from their fillers ; three different types of slots are used, "relations", "attributes", and "procedures", see, e.g., (Zarri 1995a) for some details.

4   Conclusion

As already mentioned, see the "Introduction", the problem of the conceptual representation of narrative texts is certainly not a new one. Several (at least partly) implemented formalisms exist that claim to be able to represent extensive chunks of natural language semantics — see Conceptual Graphs (Sowa 1984), SNePS (Shapiro and Rapaport 1992), CYC (Lenat and Guha 1990), LILOG (Herzog and Rollinger 1991), Episodic Logic (Hwang and Schubert 1993), etc. Moreover, since Schank's work (Schank 1973), several authors have tackled the specific problem of representing structured events see, e.g., the recent Park's proposal (Park 1995), where a set of primitives for modelling the dynamic aspects ("events") of a domain is provided.

In defence of the introduction of the NKRL formalism, we can however put forward (at least) the two following arguments :

- Making use of a relatively simple, intuitive and easily manageable formalism, NKRL offers some interesting solutions to very hard problems concerning the "practical" aspects of the knowledge representation endeavour. We can also note that the architecture of NKRL allows us to distinguish exactly between a (possibly very detailed) representation of events *per se* — as instances of the structures (templates) proper to the event ontology — and the customary use of reified events as instances linked with the *event_* subtree of the concept ontology. A fundamental (and apparently unique) characteristic of NKRL is represented by the fact that the catalogue of basic templates, see subsection 3.1 above and Fig. 3, can be considered as part and parcel of the definition of the language. This approach is particularly important for practical applications, and it implies, in particular, that : i) a system-builder does not have to create himself the structural knowledge needed to describe the events proper to a (sufficiently) large class of narrative texts and documents ; ii) it becomes easier to secure the reproduction or the sharing of previous results.

References

Bateman, J. A., Magnini, B., and Fabris, G.: The Generalized Upper Model Knowledge Base : Organization and Use, in Towards Very Large Knowledge Bases - Knowledge Building and Knowledge Sharing. Amsterdam: IOS Press, 1995.

Ceccato, S.: Concepts for a New Systematics, Inf. Storage and Retriev. 3 (1967) 193-214.

Franconi, E.: A Treatment of Plurals and Plural Quantifications Based on a Theory of Collections, Minds and Machines 3 (1993) 453-474.

Gruber, T.R.: A Translation Approach to Portable Ontology Specifications, Knowledge Acquisition 5 (1993) 199-220.

Guarino, N., Carrara, M., and Giaretta, P.: An Ontology of Meta-Level Categories, in Proc. of the 4th Int. Conf. on Principles of Knowledge Repres. and Reasoning. San Francisco: Morgan Kaufmann, 1994.

Herzog, O., and Rollinger, C.-R., eds.: Text Understanding in LILOG - Integrating Computational Linguistics and Artificial Intelligence. Berlin: Springer-Verlag, 1991.

Hwang, C.H., and Schubert, L.K.: Meeting the Interlocking Needs of LF-Computation, Deindexing and Inference : An Organic Approach to General NLU, in Proc. of the 13th Int. Joint Conf. on Art. Intelligence. San Francsico: Morgan Kaufmann, 1993.

Jackendoff, R.: Semantic Structures. Cambridge (MA): The MIT Press, 1990.

Lenat, D.B., and Guha, R.V.: Building Large Knowledge Based Systems. Reading (MA): Addison-Wesley, 1990.

Park, B.J.: A Language for Ontologies Based on Objects and Events, in Proc. of the IJCAI'95 Workshop on Basic Ontological Issues in Knowledge Sharing, 1995.

Schank, R.C.: Identification of Conceptualizations Underlying Natural Language, in Computer Models of Thought and Language. San Francisco: W.H. Freeman, 1973.

Schank, R.C., and Abelson, R.P.: Scripts, Plans, Goals and Understanding. Hillsdale (NJ): Lawrence Erlbaum, 1977.

Shapiro, S.C., and Rapaport, W.J.: The SNePS Family, in Semantic Networks in Artificial Intelligence. Oxford: Pergamon Press.

Sowa, J.F.: Conceptual Structures : Information Processing in Mind and Machine. Reading (MA): Addison-Wesley, 1984.

Weibel, S., Godby, J., Miller, E., and Daniel, R.: OCLC/NCSA Medatada Workshop Report. Dublin (Ohio): OCLC Online Computer Library Center, 1995.

Zarri, G.P.: Encoding the Temporal Characteristics of the Natural Language Descriptions of (Legal) Situations, in Expert Systems in Law. Amsterdam: Elsevier Science, 1992.

Zarri, G.P.: Representing and Querying Complex Conceptual Structures in the Framework of NKRL, in Suppl. Proc. of the 3rd Int. Conf. on Conceptual Structures. Berlin: Springer-Verlag, 1995

Zarri, G.P., and Gilardoni, L.: Structuring and Retrieval of the Complex Predicate Arguments Proper to the NKRL Conceptual Language, in Foundations of Intelligent Systems, ISMIS'96. Berlin: Springer-Verlag.

Intelligent Computation of Presentation Documents

Joseph D. Oldham and Victor W. Marek and Mirosław Truszczyński

Department of Computer Science, University of Kentucky, Lexington, KY 40506,
{oldham,marek,mirek}@cs.engr.uky.edu

Abstract

Intelligent presentation of data requires flexibility of expression based on user needs and data content, both of which evolve. This flexibility is not offered by the current generation of database management systems. To address this problem systematically we are developing editing tools to quickly build intelligent, user-tailored presentation systems for databases.

Our presentation systems are called *computational registers* (registers). We describe registers as an architecture for generating documents that summarize data with a particular class of user in mind. A system to manage creation and maintenance of registers is a *register system*. We describe DEXTER, our own register system currently under development.

1 Introduction

There are groups of users who do not have sufficient access to information from databases for the following reasons:
1. Insufficient ability to use the standard database front end.
2. Inadequate presentation of the data for the user's specialized needs.
3. Lack of familiarity with the scheme of the database at hand.
In hospitals, for example, physicians, nurses and payment agents all need access to pieces of medical records, all have distinct perspectives on the data (beyond database views), and often lack skills and time to overcome the limitations of the presentation capabilities of database systems.

The problem is an impedance mismatch between users and data management systems. Intelligent presentation of data requires flexibility of expression based on user needs and data content, both of which evolve. This flexibility is not offered by the current generation of database management systems. To address this problem systematically we are developing editing tools to quickly build intelligent, user-tailored presentation systems for databases [5, 1].

Specialized presentation software is often written to present data to a particular kind of user. Our goal is to move toward automating this process. Our method is to describe an architecture for presentation, which we call *computational registers* (registers.) We are developing software tools for specifying, building, coordinating and maintaining registers. We refer to these tools as a *register system*. In this paper we will discuss registers, and DEXTER (Data EXpression Through Edited Registers), a register system we are developing.

Here is an example of data and a desired expression of this data in a form customized for a particular class of users. We will consider this example throughout the paper.

Example 1. Suppose our database contains the following data:

NAME	COURSE	Asn1	Poss1	Wt1	Asn2	...	Asn12
Joe Marek	CS121	91	100	0.1	0	...	-1
Victor Oldham	CS121	80	100	0.1	80	...	-1

The summary we want is a "midterm grade report" to be sent to a student. We assume that our register operates on the data on a tuple by tuple basis. Outputs for these tuples might be as follows:

```
To: Joe Marek
Re: CS 121 Mid term grade report
Your mid term grade, based on a weighted average of 74.5 on due
assignments, is C.  PLEASE NOTE that homework 2 is missing.
Your score is based on the following homework scores: 91, 0, 84,
and a midterm score of 94.
```

```
To: Victor Oldham
Re: CS 121 Mid term grade report
Your weighted average of 85.4 on due assignments earns a mid term
grade of B.  Your score is based on the following homework scores:
90, 90, 90 and a midterm score of 80.
```

We assume that the database record contains all the essential information on which we would base our report. A database stores a lowest common denominator form of data. The fundamental task of a register is to restore to the data a semantics that reflects the user's perspective on the data. To achieve this functionality in an intuitive way, registers take advantage of conventions and language familiar to the user. For any register the range of expression is constrained. A report for a different purpose would be generated differently, hence would require a distinct register. Registers related by applicability to the same data, which also exist under the same register system, may share resources.

2 Registers and Register Systems

Computational registers are designed to generate, from a record of known structure (as in a database), a summary document (including multimedia) represented in a language such as HTML or SGML ([10, 15, 16].) *Register* describes an approach to presentation without regard for specifics of how that approach is implemented.

Specifically, a *computational register* consists of:
1. *Register domain description*: ontology, vocabulary and vernacular
2. *Register processing specification*: field, mode and tenor mappings.

Registers are processed by a *register execution engine*. This is a a register-independent program that interprets field, mode and tenor specifications and creates output documents on the basis of external database records.

To facilitate building registers, we need a set of tools that will allow rapid development of register components. This set of tools together with the register execution engine will be called a *register system*. Thus, a *register system* consists of:

1. An *authoring system* designed to allow creation and modification of registers

2. A *register execution engine* to process registers developed in the authoring system.

In the discussion that follows we always keep in mind that our end goal is not a register, but a register system. A register system should allow the register author to focus on data presentation rather than programming details, and allow resources for a set of registers to be shared and kept up to date.

2.1 Register Domain Description

Register domain description components specify information that must be available to the register for coherent management of presentations.

Ontology refers to a set of classes, including both system and author-defined classes within the register system, sufficient to represent database information within the register. Objects of these classes are the *terms* of the register.

Example 2. We should be able to represent data about a student for the report in some intuitive way in the ontology:

```
Class Student
        StudentName     Name
        Homework[n]     Homeworks
        Exam            MidTermExam
        Character       CurrentGrade
        . . .
```

The register *vocabulary* is a dictionary of strings . In a register system, a register vocabulary is a subset of the system wide vocabulary. Vocabulary entries for register systems carry semantic information. In an attempt to represent data with user-appropriate semantics registers rely on conventions of language and presentation common in the targeted user group. While this language is powerful, it can be subject to misunderstanding. Online definition of terms supports both user trust and authoring coherence.

Example 3. The vocabulary of the register for the midterm-grade example must contain an entry for the string "midterm grade". It might look as follows:

```
MIDTERM GRADE (noun: count, singular) Pertinent classes: STUDENT.
Synonyms: GRADE, CURRENT GRADE.
A letter GRADE assigned based on performance on work ....
```

The last component of a register's domain description is called *vernacular*. The vernacular is a collection of *register phrases*, which: express relationships on facts established by the register field; are used to form the document outline by the register mode; and are given expression in the register tenor.

Example 4. Here is an example of a phrase definition for a text phrase:

```
Phrase    SCOREEARNS( WA, G )
          1. your midterm grade, based on a weighted average of
             $WA$ on due assignments, is $G
          2. your weighted average of $WA on due assignments earns
             a midterm grade of $G
```

This phrase will yield one of the texts listed in its definition as a possible way of expressing the relation between the weighted average and the mid-term grade. We treat phrase definitions as text templates. There are other possibilities.

2.2   Register Processing Description

Register processing consists of field, mode and tenor processing. *Field processing* uses the field specification of a register, e.g. a set of rules, to transform a record in the original database scheme into a record in another scheme, called the *internal scheme*. The internal scheme is defined in terms of the classes of register's ontology. The transformation determined by the field is a database mapping, which may disregard some information, may synthesize new attributes from several original ones, and may break old attributes into several new ones.

All access to the original data occurs in field processing. If field processing is completed before the other phases are allowed to begin, then mode and tenor processing will be based on a fixed instance of the internal scheme.

(Re)modeling the original data via a field mapping has two chief purposes:
1. The data is cast in a form appropriate for direct use while building presentations for a particular class of users.
2. Mediating ([14]), i.e. finding a common representation, if a register needs to access data from several sources, or for register reuse, especially register ontology reuse.

Example 5. As the result of field processing in our running example of mid-term grading reports, we might obtain the following term of class **Student**:

```
Name = "Joe Marek"          CurrentScore = 74.5
CurrentGrade = 'C'          MissingAssignments = 'Hw 2'
Hw[] = 91, 0, 84            MidTermGrade = 94
```

Mode processing operates on the internal representation of the original data. The two main tasks for mode processing are to: define content by selecting phrases from the vernacular that describe relationships between facts; establish the structure of the final document. Mode processing relies only on data in the instance of the internal scheme, as determined by the register field. The result of mode processing is a *document outline*.

Example 6. Here is a document following our running example:

```
Grade Report : GREETING(Name, Course)
               SCOREEARNS(CurrentScore, CurrentGrade)
Exceptional Circumstance : MISSINGWARNING( MissingAssignments )
Grade Support : SCOREBASE( Hw[], MidTermGrade )
```

The goal of register processing is a document that is consistent in meaning and always user appropriate, but variable in expression, word choice and, when necessary, phrasing and structure. Both document structure and phrase selection are variable in the mode. Variability in phrase expression, synonym substitution for terms, and so on, are handled at the tenor level.

Tenor processing executes a procedure for each phrase and builds the final presentation, for instance an HTML document.

2.3   Register Systems

Our main goal is to automate the process of register development by creating a register system. A register system should provide:

1. Authoring tools supporting definition and maintenance of a register domain and processing descriptions.

2. A register processor to convert the definitions defined in the above system into executable code.

A register system will allow register developers to create reliable document generating software. Consequently, they can focus more on domain issues and less on programming details. It will also help with software maintenance and, in many cases, will allow meta tags carrying semantic information to be added to documents automatically. Finally, such a system supports sharing and reuse of resources.

3   The DEXTER Register System

We will now briefly describe the DEXTER Register System which we are developing. Following a brief description of DEXTER's authoring subsystem, our focus will be on DEXTER's approach to field and mode processing. We will discuss neither DEXTER's register execution engine nor its tenor processing in this paper.

The authoring subsystem consists of a suite of editors specialized to support the register author's various tasks. There is also a library of classes and methods to support the details of presentation. The form of ontology classes definable by the author is restricted. The aggregation hierarchy for these classes must be acyclic and general methods are not allowed. Connectivity to only one database, *Mini SQL* ([17]) is supported, and any database meta data needed is expected to be supplied by the author. Since processing in DEXTER is specified by rules, editors for each phase of processing must support creation of the appropriate rule forms. As all access to the external database occurs during field processing the query editing component is a subcomponent of the field editor. Text phrases in DEXTER are specified by templates, defined by the register author.

3.1 Field in DEXTER

DEXTER's field processing is described as a set of rules. DEXTER assumes null values are legal in either the external or internal scheme. We will use the following notation to describe these rules. A tuple in the external database scheme will be denoted t. An attribute in the external scheme is denoted a_i. Thus $t.a_i$ is the ith coordinate of tuple t. The subset of t attributes known to be non-null is denoted by $\hat{t}$. The internal scheme is noted analogously, with s b_j, and $\hat{s}$ replacing t, a_i and $\hat{t}$ respectively. The s_j are register terms, to which field rules assign value. Terms must be assigned in some order, and $s_{1 \leq i < k}$ denotes the set of terms assigned prior to assignment to $s.b_k$. Whether coordinates of s and t have values or not is necessary but not sufficient information to write rules. We must also be able to define relations on those coordinate values. Thus, $\mathcal{R}$ denotes a relation over $\hat{t}$ and $\hat{s}$, the non-null coordinates of s and t. Finally, E_j are expressions over $\hat{t}, \hat{s}$ and constants, evaluating to a type compatible with the $s.b_j$. A general form of a field rule in DEXTER is:

IF $(t.a_1 = Null \wedge \ldots \wedge t.a_k = Null \wedge t.a_{k+1} \neq Null \wedge \ldots \wedge t.a_p \neq Null)$
$\wedge\, s.b_1 = Null \wedge \ldots \wedge s.b_l = Null \wedge s.b_{l+1} \neq Null \wedge \ldots \wedge s.b_q \neq Null)$
$\wedge\, (\mathcal{R}(\hat{t}, \hat{s}))$
THEN $s.b_{q+1} = E_{q+1}(\hat{t} \cup \hat{s} \cup s_{1 \leq i < q+1})\,, \ldots,\, s.b_{q+r} = E_{q+r}(\hat{t} \cup \hat{s} \cup s_{1 \leq i < q+r})$

Note that these are epistemic rules; rule applicability depends on what we do and do not know. Here is a simple example of such a rule:

IF $(t.AltGradeOption = Null \wedge t.ACut \neq Null \wedge t.BCut \neq Null)$
$\wedge(s.CurrentGrade = Null \wedge s.score \neq Null)$
$\wedge(t.BCut \leq s.Score < t.ACut)$
THEN $s.CurrentGrade = Bgrade$

The fact that rules may depend on values assigned to a tuple s earlier in the process makes the order of rule evaluation important.

3.2 Mode in DEXTER

DEXTER breaks mode processing into two distinct steps: *content determination* and *structure instantiation*. Both are managed with a rule based approach. Here is an example of a *DEXTER Content Rule*:

IF $(s.MissingAssignments \neq Null)$
THEN *Include* $MISSINGWARNING(s.MissingAssignments\,)$

The above rule can be generalized to epistemic rules of the form:

IF $(s.b_1 = Null \wedge \ldots \wedge s.b_k = Null \wedge s.b_{k+1} \neq Null \wedge \ldots \wedge s.b_n \neq Null)$
THEN *Include* $P_1(\sigma_1) \wedge \ldots \wedge P_r(\sigma_r)$

where the $s.b_i$ and $\hat{s}$ are as above, P_j are phrases, and σ_j is an ordered subset of $\hat{s}$ forming an argument list for P_j. Order of evaluation does not matter for these rules.

DEXTER structure rules determine which sections of a document are opened or closed. A section must be opened for writing before a phrase can be expressed in that section. Here is a simple structural rule.

IF $(Open(Body) \wedge \neg Open(GradeSupport) \wedge$
$Included(SCOREBASE(X, Y)) \wedge$
$\neg Included(MISSINGWARNING(X)))$
THEN $Open(GradeSupport) \wedge Assert(SCOREBASE(X, Y))$

Included(phrase) holds if *phrase* appears in the output of the content rules. Notice that the applicability of this rule depends on absence of information about a grade warning and that these rules are again order dependent.

The general form of a structural rule follows. The Σ_i are document sections. If $Open(\Sigma_i)$ holds then it is legal to place phrases into Σ_i, and to open or close subsections of Σ_i. Further, $P_j(x_j)$ is a phrase P_j with arguments x_j.

IF $(Open(\Sigma_{m+1}) \wedge \ldots \wedge Open(\Sigma_n)) \wedge$
$(\neg Open(\Sigma_{n+1}) \wedge \ldots \wedge \neg Open(\Sigma_q)) \wedge$
$(Included(P_1(x_1)) \wedge \ldots \wedge Included(P_l(x_l))) \wedge$
$(\neg Included(P_{l+1}(x_{l+1})) \wedge \ldots \wedge \neg Included(P_r(x_r))))$
THEN $Open(\Sigma_\alpha) \wedge Assert(\pi_I) \wedge Close(\sigma_{A,O})$

Note that x_j and x_k may overlap. This means phrases may share variables. For instance, $Included(P_j(x_j))$ is true when the phrase (with associated variables) can be unified with some phrase included by the mode content rules. Thus to satisfy this condition some unification on shared variables (but with no function symbols) must occur. When the rule condition is satisfied then three actions may be taken:
1. A single section, Σ_α, is opened and marked as the current section.
2. Members of a possibly empty subset of included phrases, (π_I), are placed in the current section for later expression.
3. Members of a possibly empty set of sections which were previously open, $\sigma_{A,O}$, are marked as no longer open.

4 Additional Benefits of Register Generated Documents

The principal use for registers is to present data to the user in a way that takes into account the semantics that the user applies to the data. However, there are other applications of registers and register systems. Many have to do with the capacity of these systems to support meta data with very low overhead. To indicate the potential in this area we will briefly discuss the approach to meta data we take in DEXTER, which we call *semantic tags*. (This is distinct from the same term in [2].)

By a *semantic tag* we mean a tag (as in HTML) which, for some part of a document, indicates that part's *content* in the sense of its meaning. Families of registers, controlled by a register system with a common vocabulary, offer advantages in this area. A dictionary of tags used in a register system can be published for appropriate communities. Since the purpose of a register is to systematically transform data into a document representation, registers can add semantic tags to documents automatically. Beyond consistency, the principal benefit of register tagging is that it is a low overhead operation, taking advantage of already necessary work. As semantic tagging via registers is clearly possible, we will now discuss some applications of registers and register systems which make it clear that this form of systematic tagging of content is useful. This implies several directions for further research.

1. *Searching* for patterns with multiple meanings is inefficient. Register generated documents can be automatically and consistently tagged for content with a level of specificity that is prohibitive for hand-written documents. The tagging scheme used in the register system may be published and thus may support search for patterns (tags) with agreed upon meanings.

2. We can say that a database must: store data, allow searching on that data, and allow viewing of search results. Consider a collection of documents that are semantically tagged. Content is represented consistently and hence searchable as above. Tags can guide data expression. Hence, a collection of semantically tagged documents may be viewed as a *virtual database*. Such a virtual database might stand alone, or we might have several such databases on top of a standard database, acting as front ends for several user communities.

3. There are implications for *information synthesis and control*. With untagged documents we can ask the question "Is there a document that describes process X?" With a set of tagged documents we can ask if it is possible, from this document set, to *construct* a document that describes process X. We can ask if our collection makes a complete set of facts publicly available.

4. There is a point at which a document is not yet generated, but its content and structure are determined. This can serve as a form of document *compression*. Assuming that a register can be executed at the client side, documents can be encoded either by the underlying external data, its internal representation or the document outline, whichever is more compact.

5   Related Work

A fundamental problem that the register author must solve is referred to in [7, 6] as the *the writer's problem*. Specifically, how does an author proceed, given some facts, in using background knowledge and communicating those facts with some end in mind? Our current focus is on text presentations. Thus, generating coherent, reliable text is critical. The works of McKeown [13], Paris [5] and Bateman and Paris [1] are related. In DEXTER, however, we take a simpler approach, borrowing from descriptive linguists ([9] among others.) IVORY [3] is a tool developed at Stanford University to assist the physician in writing progress notes. In this case the approach to text generation in a single DEXTER register is similar, but DEXTER's phrases are not hardwired.

The advent of the World Wide Web has resulted in intense scrutiny of automation and authoring support for documents, e.g. [11]; creating documents that are more content accessible via automated means, e.g. [16]. Mapping SGML document type definitions into object oriented database schema is considered in [4]. The problem of analyzing and representing data has been considered, e.g. [12] and the TSIMMIS project [8, 14]. As in TSIMMIS we assume self describing internal representations of data in our systems. Our approaches differ as our goals differ.

6 Conclusions

There is a legitimate need to increase the functional power of systems to support information access. Computational registers as described here support information access by attempting to restore to data some of the semantics expected by particular groups of users in a natural way. Continuing to write *ad hoc* code to accomplish this task is not sufficient. That the task of writing data presentation software is common, and usually achievable, implies that we can understand and should try to automate the process. The end goal is to clarify and support or automate the process of writing registers such that the register author can focus more on meeting user expectation, and less on manipulating background systems. Our system, DEXTER, is a step in that direction.

DEXTER's register architecture allows for substantial register reusability. An ontology developed for the needs of a register to build presentations of medical data can be used for a number of other registers working with possibly different databases. Given such a register, to make it usable with yet another database requires only the development of an appropriate field specification. Similarly, if a modification of a presentation of the same data is required, only the tenor must be changed. Consequently, DEXTER's architecture maximizes reusability in the context of changing requirements.

Acknowledgements

This work was supported by USARO contract DAAH-04-96-1-0398. Helpful discussions with Professor Raphael Finkel and Anthony Borchers are gratefully acknowledged.

References

1. J. A. Bateman and C Paris. Phrasing text in terms a user can understand. In *Proceedings of IJCAI*, 1989.

2. P. Buitelaar. A Lexicon for Underspecified Semantic Tagging. Available via Computation and Language EPrint Archive, http://xxx.lanl.gov/cmp-lg/ as paper 9705011, 1997

3. K.E. Campbell, K. Wickert, L.M. Fagan, and M.A. Musen. A computer-based tool for generation of progress notes. In *Proceedings of the Sixteenth Annual Symposium on Computer Applications in Medical Care*, 1993.

4. V. Christophides, S. Abiteboul, S. Cluet, and M. Scholl. From structured documents to novel query facilities. In *Proceedings of SIGMOD 94*. ACM, 1994.

5. Paris C.L. *The Use of Explicit User Models in Text Generation: Tailoring to a User's Level of Experience*. PhD thesis, Columbia University, 1987. also technical report CUCS-309-87.

6. D. Estival and F. Gayral. A nlp approach to specific types of texts: Car accident reports. In *Proceedings of Workshop on Context in Natural Language Processing IJCAI 95*, 1995.

7. D. Estival and F. Gayral. A study of context(s) in a specific type of texts: Car accident reports. Available via Computation and Language EPrint Archive, http://xxx.lanl.gov/cmp-lg/ as paper 9502032, 1995.

8. H. Garcia-Molina, J. Hammer, Y. Ireland, K. and Papakonstantinou, and J. Ullman. Integrating and accessing heterogeneous information sources in tsimmis. In *Proceedings of the AAAI Symposium on Information Gathering*, 1995.

9. M. Gregory and S. Carroll. *Language and Situation: Language Varieties and Their Social Contexts*. Routledge And Keegan Paul, Ltd., 1978.

10. E. van Herwijen. *Practical SGML*. Kluwer Academic Publishers, 1990.

11. K. Jones. Tops on-line – automating the construction and maintenance of html pages. In *Electronic Proceedings of Second World Wide Web Conference 94: Mosaic and the Web*, 1994. Electronic Publication: http://www.ncsa.uicu.edu/SDG/IT94/Proceedings/Autools/jones/jone.html.

12. R.E. Kent and C. Neuss. Creating a web analysis and visualization environment. In *Electronic Proceedings of Second World Wide Web Conference 94: Mosaic and the Web*, 1994. http://www.ncsa.uicu.edu/SDG/IT94/Proceedings/Autools/kent/kent.html.

13. Kathleen R. McKeown. *Text Generation*. Cambridge University Press, 1985.

14. Y. Papakonstaninou, H. Garcia-Molina, and J. Ullman. Medmaker: A mediation system based on declarative specifications. In *Proceedings ICDE 96*, 1996. available via ftp://www-db.stanford.edu/pub/papkonstantinou/1995/medmaker.ps.

15. D. Raggett. HTML 3.2 reference specification. Electronic Publication: http://www.w3.org/pub/WWW/TR/REC-html32.html, 1997.

16. C.M. Sperberg-McQueen and R.F. Goldstein. Html to the max a manifesto for adding sgml intelligence to the world-wide web. In *Electronic Proceedings of Second World Wide Web Conference 94: Mosaic and the Web*, 1994. Electronic Publication: http://www.ncsa.uicu.edu/SDG/IT94/Proceedings/Autools/sperberg-mcqueen/sperberg.html.

17. Hughes Technologies. Hughes technologies library. Published Electronically at http://Hughes.com.au/library/. Contains documentation on miniSQL.

Flexible Database Querying Based on Associations of Domain Values

Troels Andreasen

Roskilde University, Computer Science Department,
Intelligent Systems Laboratory
P.O.Box 260, DK-4000 Roskilde, Denmark
email: troels@ruc.dk

Abstract

In this paper we present an approach to database querying based on fuzzy evaluation of queries. In the approach a dedicated mining for domain knowledge is involved. The result of this is a special kind of associations between values and is represented in fuzzy networks. Such a network is used to relax queries and to relate objects in the database. The network exploit the database, in the sense that it is obtained by pure statistical means from mining the database for associations between domain values. It is a special variant of a projection of, or a orthogonal view on, data in the database.

The approach described here has been implemented and applied in an experiment on a "real-world" library database. In this application associations are modeled between keywords used in librarians descriptions of books in the database. Examples and conclusions are partly based on the results of this experiment.

1. Introduction

We present below preliminary ideas and results from a research project on flexible querying in connection with bibliographic databases. General ideas and principles applied are not specific for library data. However it has turned out that library data often is of very high quality partly because competent "domain experts" – namely librarians – examine, adjust and complement descriptions using standardized, systematic domains before objects are added to the database. The high quality is valuable when doing experiments with non-standard query-answering and is in fact a premise when establishing domain knowledge from mining data.

During evaluation a context for the query is established by flexible interpretation in two respects. Partly by a applying fuzzy evaluation of each single criteria stated and partly by applying a tolerant interpretation of the compound query by adjusting the connection of all single criteria within a range, taking disjunction as the least and conjunction as the most restrictive connection.

The context for a query leads to objects related to, but not in the direct answer to the query and the interpretation in general leads to a ranking of objects as candidates to the answer of the query. Based on this it is possible to narrow or broaden the query and thus obtain an answer of a suitable size. Furthermore the more general answer is a good basis for browsing or navigating in the entire database.

To obtain the possibility to apply fuzzy evaluation to non-ordered domains a special semantic network is consulted. The network relates keywords such that a given word can be expanded to a set of words that are associated.

2. Fuzzy Logic and Fuzzy Query Evaluation

The approach described in this paper is based on fuzzy evaluation of queries, that involves a fuzzy logic rather than a classical Boolean logic interpretation of queries. Fuzzy logic generalizes Boolean logic and may be seen as the extreme result of extending from two-valued, over multi-valued to infinite-valued logic. Truth values are in fuzzy logic denoted from the interval [0,1], with 0 denoting false, 1 denoting true and values within]0,1[denoting true to some degree. While classical logic is based on classical set-theory, fuzzy logic is based on fuzzy set-theory. In classical set-theory we can only have an element as either fully a member or else not at all a member of a given set. In fuzzy set-theory an element may be member of a given set to a degree, usually denoted by a value in the interval [0, 1], with degree 0 corresponding to not at all member and degree 1 to fully member, while e.g. 0.5 corresponds to member to some degree.

I natural language we often use words and concepts that are better modeled with fuzzy logic than with classical two-valued logic. For instance to express that a book is new, using only two-valued logic, it is necessary to decide on an exact limit on age, to distinguish "new book", say, books published within the latest 3 years are new, and books older than that are not new. Using fuzzy logic it is possible to get a lot closer to the intention with the concept. We could decide on a simple function as shown in figure 1, to express that, books published within the latest two years are new, books published within two years and four years ago are new to some degree, and books older than that, are not new.

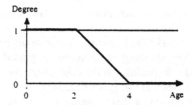

Fig. 1. The concept "new book" modeled as a fuzzy set. The function shown is called the membership function for the concept.

Apart from introducing new concepts, we can use fuzzy logic to generalize equality into similarity. For instance the expression "equal to 3" can be relaxed into "around 3" and the expression "between 2 and 4" can be relaxed into "around 2 to 4" as shown in the two membership functions below.

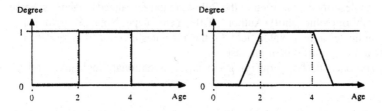

Fig. 2. Relaxing equality into similarity.. The expression "between 2 and 4" relaxed into "around 2 to 4" : Shown are membership functions for the two expressions.

In fuzzy querying one important logical aspect is this kind of similarity for elements of a given domain.

For domains with a natural order it is straight-forward to define similar values for a given value; these are the values closest to the given value according to the order.

Problems arise when the domain in question is without ordering. In that case similarity must be explicitly defined in some kind of network relating similar elements. Of major interest in our approach, among domains without ordering, are domains of words used in describing properties of objects. In a library database these may be authors keywords, librarians keywords, words appearing in titles, notes, abstracts or other textual attributes attached to objects.

In general we can distinguish two types of similarity notions on domains of words; thesaurus-like and association-like similarity.

A thesaurus as figure 3a relates words in a network, that to a given word points to other words that are similar with respect to meaning. Likewise we can have associations explicitly expressed in a network like figure 3b that relates words in a manner, where a given word points to other words that are similar with respect to the context they are applied in.

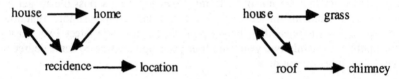

Fig. 3.   **(a): a thesaurus structure, (b): an association structure**

We call these kind of networks under one, for semantic networks. Obviously we obtain a generalization when allowing relations to be graded, that is, when allowing for fuzzy semantic networks. Especially in the case where domain knowledge involves some kind of statistics, it is relevant to grade relations.

We apply in our approach a fuzzy semantic network, denoting a special interpretation of associations. A network of this kind is illustrated in figure 5 below. For each word the network defines a fuzzy membership function for the constraint X=w. For instance for X=Childhood, the word Childhood is member to degree 1, Children is member to degree 0.9 and Education is member to degree 0.2.

3.   Fuzzy Querying in a Bibliographic Database

The bibliographic databases used in this project are of quite complex database schemes, however our main focus has only been a subset extracted from the schemes. This can be described simplified in the following unnormalized database scheme:

bibliographic_entity(Author*, Title, Year, Type, Note*, Keyword*)

where * indicates a multi-value field. Of the attributes mentioned especially the multi-value attribute Keyword is of interest.

Our approach to fuzzy querying extends conventional Boolean querying in two respects:

- a fuzzy connection of constraints in a compound query, relaxing conjunction "as much a necessary" down toward disjunction
- fuzzy interpretation of single constraints, weakening such that similar, but non-matching values are considered (fuzzy semantic networks are used here)

The former leads to a tolerant aggregation of constraints, whereas the latter is about relaxing a single constraint into a more tolerant counterpart based on predefined parameters delimiting the fuzzyfication.

We present below first the fuzzy interpretation of a compound query. We introduce then a special semantic network applied in the prototype, which is purely based on statistics on the state of the database. Finally we describe the overall principle of query evaluation and give examples of queries evaluated against the small database used in the experiment with the implemented prototype.

3.1. Simple Weakening of a Compound Query

The implemented prototype is prepared for general fuzzy aggregation of query constraints. However to keep calculations simple and easy to check, we use only simple arithmetic average for aggregation. Further studies need to be done in order to investigate the influence of more advanced aggregation on the capability to compute good answer to queries.

The principle of aggregation of a compound query is as follows.

Given a compound query Q with n single constraints $C1, ..., Cn$. Suppose that an object O in the database satisfies the constraint Ci to the degree $Ci(O)$. Then the object O satisfies the query Q to the degree

$$Q(O) = C1(O) + ... + Cn(O)) / n$$

Thus the truth value of "O satisfies Q" is the average of the n single truth values of "O satisfies Ci".

Notice that this principle of query evaluation may be applied without any other kind of weakening. If all single constraints are crisp (can take only the values true or false, that is, 1 or 0), then the interpretation becomes: n satisfied constraints is considered better (is graded with a better truth value) than $n-1$ satisfied constraints, which in turn is considered better than $n-2$ satisfied constraints, etc.

Even though this principle is simple it may appear quite powerful in practice. It supports a new and better means for users querying the database. It is no longer necessary to minimize the set of constraints posed in a query as normally done by users who prefer non-empty answer. Suddenly it becomes fruitful to express all potentially relevant constraints describing the users intention, since the process of minimizing usually performed by the user is so to say replaced by the simple weakening performed by the system.

3.2. A Semantic Network based on Keyword Indexing in the Actual Database State

The most important domain in the bibliographic database is the set of words used in different descriptions of objects in the database, e.g. in titles, abstracts, notes, related keywords and even author.

Our main interest is the association type of relation of words and a major issue in the project is how to establish such association networks. Since we did not have access to any useful manually created association networks apart from the available classification systems and since these constitute only very sparse networks (networks with only very few edges), we started early to focus on automatically discovery of associations by, so to say, mining data in the database. We have discussed an analyzed a range of different ways to perform such a task, but we do by no means consider our analysis as exhaustive. A lot more work has to be done in this direction. However we did deduce rules of thumb during discussion and experiments with controlled data mining for semantic networks.

For the experiment discussed in this paper we have chosen to build a network based on librarian keywords with no influence on associations from words as used in other fields describing objects. Thus even titles are ignored when associating words.

We have chosen a simple function that relates two words A and B based on the frequencies with which they appear in descriptions of objects in the database. The function is asymmetric and is based on the frequencies:

#(A): number of objects described by word A

#(B): number of objects described by word B

#(A and B): number of objects described by word A and by word B

The word A relates to B to the degree:

#(A and B) / (#(A) + 1)

B relates to A similarly by:

#(A and B) / (#(B) + 1)

We should emphasize here that this function has been chosen as an ad hoc first solution and that further studies has to be done to investigate this problem of statistical association. The intention, that should be captured by the function is; the more frequent B appears wherever A appears, the more is B related by A. Further we don't want any word, but A itself, that is related fully (degree 1) from A. This restriction is expressed in a simple adhoc-fashion by the "+ 1" in the denominator.

Thus with the frequencies of the words A and B, as shown in figure 4a, that is, #(A) = 7, #(B) = 19 and #(A and B) = 4, we obtain the association from A to B as #(A and B) / #(A) = 4 / (7+1) = 0.5 and the association from B to A as #(A and B) / #(B) = 4 / (19+1) = 0.2.

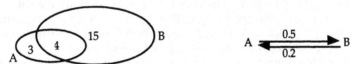

Fig. 4. (a): Frequencies of A and B, (b): Resulting associations

As an example of what this means of associating words might lead to, consider the following small section of the semantic network, derived from the database in the experiment:

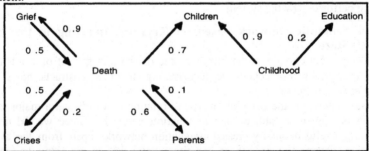

Fig. 5. A small section of the network of associations derived from the bibliographic database in the experiment

The approach described in this paper is, as far as softening of words as query constraints are concerned, solely based on semantic networks as described above. So an important question is of course: What are these kind of associations and how can their meaning be described?

The intention is to capture relations that resemble aspects of human associations. As compared to the other extreme to achieve this; knowledge acquisition by interviewing an expert in the domain in question, one major drawback appears to be obvious. Words that are closely related by association may also be closely related by meaning, as for instance parent and mother. When two words are closely related by meaning the typical description will include only one of these words, and therefore we obtain no or only a weak association between the two words in this case.

However since our semantic networks are based only on the set of attached librarian keywords and since each word in this set is carefully chosen to be with a distinct meaning, this drawback have only little influence on the quality of the resulting network.

3.3. Overall Fuzzy Evaluation of Queries

The evaluation of queries applied in this approach is basically a general fuzzy evaluation. However we have deliberately chosen to narrow to a simplistic variant in the experiments carried out, because the main focus is not to obtain the best possible solution, but rather to reveal the extend to which automatically derived domain knowledge might correspond to real world human knowledge about a domain, and to indicate the power of applying such knowledge in cooperative query evaluation. The simplistic approach is the following.

A query is restricted to be conjunctive, thus of the form Q

$$Q = \text{and } Q1 \text{ and } \ldots \text{ and } Qn.$$

The general form of a simple query constraint Qi is $Ai \, \emptyset i \, Vi$, where Ai is a database attribute, $\emptyset i$ is a comparison operator and Vi a value. However we shall, to keep things simple, ignore constraints other than on the attribute "keyword" using the "="-operator and then take each Qi to be just a value for keyword.

A query, such as

$$V1 \text{ and } V2 \text{ and } V3 \text{ and } V4$$

is evaluated under two threshold values. A threshold TA that delimits the extend to which the aggregation can be relaxed and a threshold TC that delimits the extend to which a single constraint can be relaxed. With TA=1 and TC=1 the query is interpreted as a Boolean query. Keeping TC=1 and lowering TA to say 0.75, matching objects will include those that meet only 3 out of the 4 constraints, while TA=0.5 accept 2 out of the 4 constraints.

The influence of lowering TC is as follows. If we set TC=α then each constraint Vi is relaxed to be matched by the set $r(Vi) = \{(Vi,1), (Vi1,\sigma1), \ldots (Vik,\sigma k)\}$ including all values Vij that Vi associates to, to a grade $\sigma j \geq \alpha$.

Thus for the query

$$Q = \text{Death and Childhood}$$

we get, when referring to figure 4 with TC=0.8

$$r(\text{Death}) = \{(\text{Death},1), (\text{Grief}, 0.9)\}$$
$$r(\text{Childhood}) = \{(\text{Childhood},1), (\text{Children}, 0.9)\}$$

while TC=0.6 leads to

$$r(\text{Death}) = \{(\text{Death},1), (\text{Grief}, 0.9), (\text{Children}, 0.7), (\text{Parents}, 0.6)\}$$
$$r(\text{Childhood}) = \{(\text{Childhood},1), (\text{Children}, 0.9)\}$$

Since we use average as aggregation we get objects satisfying Q to the grades:

Category	Grade	Subsets of objects keywords
1	1.00	{Death,Childhood}
2	0.90	{Death,Children} {Grief,Childhood}
3	0.85	{Grief,Children} {Children,Childhood}
4	0.80	{Parents,Childhood}
etc.		
N	0.50	{Death},{Childhood}
N+1	0.45	{Grief},{Children}
etc.		

Fig. 6. Average aggregation over objects described by keywords including one of the subsets shown

Now setting thresholds TA = 1 and TC = 1 results in only Category 1 objects. Keeping TA=1 and lowering TC does not change anything since TA delimits the aggregation, which is average and thus falls below 1, when one constraint is satisfied below 1. Keeping TC=1 and setting TA=0.5 corresponds to the simple weakening principle described above and leads to an answer consisting of Category 1 and Category N objects. Setting TA=0.85 and setting TC=0.7 or lower leads to Category 1, 2 and 3 objects in the answer.

To give an impression of how this works in practice an answer to the query Q = Death and Childhood is shown in figure 7 below. The query is evaluated on the about 6000 objects database, which is also the basis for the fuzzy semantic network shown in figure 5. Without relaxing the query, thus with TA=1 and TC=1, the answer is empty. For the answer shown the chosen thresholds are TA=0.80 and TC=0.80. Only titles and query grades for the books are listed.

1	0.95	Only a broken heart knows
2	0.95	Baby's death – "life's always right"
3	0.95	We have lost a child
4	0.95	Loosing a child
5	0.95	Cot death
6	0.95	When parents die
7	0.95	To say good-bye
8	0.95	We have lost a child
9	0.95	A year without Steve
10	0.95	Taking leave
11	0.95	Grief and care in school
12	0.89	Can I die during the night
13	0.89	Children's grief
14	0.89	Children and grief

Fig. 7. The answer to the query Q = Death and Childhood, when evaluated on the database in the experiment.

We should emphasize that the database used in the experiment is not fake. The content is descriptions of "real world" books on issues related to children, school and education. All descriptions are made by librarians, that have carefully examined the books and in this connection chosen distinct, describing keywords from a standardized classification system (DK5).

The resulting network is really the work of the librarians. However they are not aware that they have been doing this work. What they see is only their description. The network however, is so to say a description of their descriptions.

4. Concluding Remarks

We have presented above ideas and preliminary results from an ongoing research project on applying fuzzy query evaluation based on domain knowledge derived from the database state, by mining for "statistical associations". The functions used for grading objects in the answer and for building the networks are deliberately chosen as simple and naive, partly because we want the principles to be as easily comprehendible as possible, and partly because further research has to be done to reveal properties that make functions suitable and more accurate.

In this paper we have shown only one example of a query result. However, we have developed a system, which is frequently tested by and discussed with librarians, whom agree that the relaxation applied in general leads to relevant additional objects.

We will claim that results of our experiments shows that under certain assumptions on quality of data, mining for associations will lead to results that can support better answers to queries. Also we consider the resulting semantic networks as valuable additional information, that may be of interest not only to the casual user of the system, but also potentially to the professionals with insight knowledge of the domain, because the network constitute a kind of inversion of data and therefore may exploit patterns that are otherwise hidden even from experts.

Finally we should like to thank the Danish Library Center, a company who supplies all Danish libraries with bibliographic data, for their collaboration and financial support to the project, from which this paper emerges.

References

1. Andreasen T and Pivert O. Improving answers to failing fuzzy queries. in Proc. VI IFSA World Congress, Sao Paulo, Brazil, 1995.
2. Andreasen T and Pivert O. On the weakening of fuzzy relational queries. in Proceedings ISMIS '94, EIGHT INTERNATIONAL SYMPOSIUM ON METHODOLOGIES FOR INTELLIGENT SYSTEMS. 1994. Charlotte, North Carolina: Springer Verlag, Lecture Notes in Artificial Intelligence.
3. Andreasen T. Dynamic Conditions, Datalogiske Skrifter, nr. 50, 1994, Roskilde University
4. Andreasen T. On flexible query answering from combined cooperative and fuzzy approaches. in Proc. VI IFSA World Congress, Sao Paulo, Brazil, 1995.
5. Christiansen, H., Larsen H L and Andreasen T, Proceedings of the second workshop on Flexible Query-Answering Systems. Datalogiske Skrifter no. 62. 1996, Roskilde University.
6. Henrik Legind Larsen and Ronald R. Yager: Query Fuzzification for Internet Information retreival. *Datalogiske Skrifter* No. 60, 1996. To appear in *Fuzzy-Set methods in Information Engineering: A Guided Tour of Applications,* John Wile & Sons.
7. Klir G.J. and Volger T.A., *Fuzzy Sets, Uncertainty, and Information.* 1988, Printice Hall.

8. Larsen H L and Andreasen T, Proceedings of the first workshop on Flexible Query-Answering Systems. Datalogiske Skrifter no. 58. 1995, Roskilde University.
9. Larsen, H.L., and Yager, R.R.: An approach to customized end user views in information retrieval. In J. Kapcprzyk and M. Fredrissi, Eds., *Multiperson Decision Making Using Fuzzy-sets and Possibility Theory,* Kluwer Academic Publishers, pp.128–139, 1990.
10. Larsen, H.L., and Yager, R.R.: The use of fuzzy-relational thesauri for classificatory problem solving in information retrieval and expert systems. *IEEE J.on System, Man, and Cybernetics* 23(1):31–41, 1993.
11. Larsen, H.L.: Recognition of implicit concepts in unstructured queries. Proc. VI IFSA World Congress, Sao Paulo, Brazil, 1995, Vol. 1, pp. 233-236.

A Modal Logical Framework for Security Policies

Frédéric Cuppens and Robert Demolombe

ONERA-CERT, 2 Avenue E. Belin, 31055, Toulouse Cedex, France,
email: {Frederic.Cuppens,Robert.Demolombe}@cert.fr

Abstract. It turns out that security becomes more and more important in many information systems. In this paper, we are more specifically interested in confidentiality requirement. In this context, we show how knowledge representation technique based on formal logic can be used to propose a faithful model of confidentiality. Our approach is to develop a modal logic framework which combines doxastic and deontic logics. This framework enables to specify confidentiality policies –in particular, multilevel security policies– and express various types of security constraints including consistency, completeness and inference control constraints.

1 Introduction

A new interesting application domain for modal logic modelling is multilevel security policies for data base management systems (DBMS). To define these kinds of policies one has to assign a classification level to sentences used to represent data base content and a clearance level to users who can access the data base. Both classification and clearance are taken from a set of security levels which generally has the structure of lattices. Here we focus on the problem of confidentiality of data and the general idea for the definition of a policy is:

A user can access some data only if the user's clearance level is greater or equal to the classification level of this data.

In [1] Denning shows that to define a complete model of the security constraints which have to be enforced by a data base management system, it is convenient to decompose the confidentiality into two sub-problems:

1. To control information flow inside the DBMS. If this problem is solved we are guaranteed that a user can get information from the DBMS only if he has permission to get it, in the context of the multilevel security policy. Several formal security models have been proposed to deal with this problem, for instance non-interference [2], non-deducibility [3] or causality [4].
2. To control derived information. If this problem is solved we are guaranteed that a user cannot infer, from the information obtained from the DBMS, information he is not permitted to know. Several techniques have been proposed to detect special cases of inference, for instance by analyzing dependencies within a relational database schema [5], or through second path analysis [6]. More recent works are also interested in detection of partial inferences [7]. However, we are not aware of a general model for inference control.

The modal logic framework we suggest is general enough to model both sub-problems. However, in this paper, we are more interested in the second sub-problem, which is usually called the "inference problem". But, from a theoretical point of view, the separation between the two foregoing problems is not tight; this is because it is difficult to control information flow inside a given DBMS without analyzing what information a user can derive from the information he explicitly gets from the database (in particular, see sections 4.3 for a short discussion of the non-interference, non-deducibility and causality models).

Most of the difficulties in reasoning about this kind of security policies come from the fact that security policies may be incomplete, in the sense that, for some data, the policy do not explicitly say if users are permitted or not to access these data. Another source of technical difficulties is the fact that the set of data that have a given security level is not necessarily a consistent set. To overcome these difficulties we have designed an appropriate modal logic framework which combines doxastic logic and deontic logic[1]. Notice that the objective of this paper is to find a precise formalization of concepts involved in security policies but it is not our purpose here to design an efficient implementation of the modal logic framework.

Our approach is a continuation of the work presented in [9]. In [9], we suggested a logical framework specially designed to reason within a multilevel security policy. We have defined a semantics and an axiomatics which is sound and complete with respect to this semantics. However, this semantics was quite complex and hard to intuitively understand. In this paper, we present, in section 2, a general logical framework and show that this framework may not only apply to multilevel security policy but also to other kinds of confidentiality policy, for instance the Chinese Wall security policy [10]. In fact, we mainly focus on semantics and we guess that this semantics provides better understanding than [9]. Section 3 then shows how multilevel security policy may be represented as a special case of our general logical framework. Finally, section 4 suggests a formalization of the notions of security policy consistency and completeness, and different kinds of security constraints to prevent inference problems due to deductive reasoning or to abductive reasoning.

2 The modal logical framework

2.1 Knowledge and Beliefs

We assume that the database content is represented by a consistent set db of sentences of a language L of Propositional Calculus. It is not assumed that sentences in db are true in the world. This means that db is considered a set of beliefs.

To analyze confidentiality problems that may occur when accessing a database, we first need to represent how users interact with the database. For this

---

[1] It is assumed that the reader is familiar with basic concepts of modal logic. These can be found in [8].

purpose, we shall define, for each database user i, a modality KB_i which applies to sentences of L. Formulae of the form KB_ip, where p is a sentence of L, are to be read: "user i knows that the database believes p".

In a structure M, modality KB_ip is interpreted by the relation R_i which is defined on $W \times W$, where W is the set of possible worlds in structure M. Therefore, the semantics of KB_ip is defined as follows:

$$M, w \models KB_ip \text{ iff } \forall w'(wR_iw' \Rightarrow M, w' \models p)$$

For convenience the set $\{w' : wR_iw'\}$ will be denoted by $R_i(w)$. The set of worlds where p is true is denoted by $\|p\|$. We shall also assume that if p is a satisfiable[2] sentence of L then $\|p\| \neq \emptyset$. Using these notations, the above semantics of KB_ip can be equivalently stated as follows:

$$M, w \models KB_ip \text{ iff } R_i(w) \subseteq \|p\|$$

We shall assume that relation R_i is serial, that is $\forall w \in W, R_i(w) \neq \emptyset$. This means that modality KB_i obeys the axioms of a KD logic [8].

2.2 Permission and Prohibition to know

We are interested in databases which contain some sensitive data. In this context, some users may be not permitted to access the overall database. What part of the database an individual is permitted to access is defined by a *confidentiality policy*.

Our formalization of a given confidentiality policy is based on the concept of role [11, 12]. Intuitively, each user is associated with a set of roles which represents the behavior this user is playing in a given situation. In each role are defined the permissions, obligations and prohibitions laid upon the role-holder.

In the context of a confidentiality policy, one wants to regulate user's *knowledge*. For this purpose, we shall define, for each role r, two modalities PKB_r and FKB_r which apply to sentences of L. Formulae of the form PKB_rp (resp. FKB_rp) are to be read: " any agent who plays the role r is permitted (resp. forbidden) to know that the database believes p".

In a structure M, modality PKB_rp is interpreted by two accessibility relations D_r and R_{xr} which are both defined on $W \times W$. Intuitively, D_r is the deontic accessibility relation which characterizes the set of ideal [13, 14] mental states of an agent xr who plays the role r. We shall assume that relation D_r is serial. R_{xr} is a doxastic accessibility relation which characterizes xr's mental state, that is the set of xr's beliefs. R_{xr} is also a serial relation.

Using these two accessibility relations, the semantics of PKB_rp is defined as follows:

$$M, w \models PKB_rp \text{ iff } \exists w'(wD_rw' \text{ and } \forall w''(w'R_{xr}w'' \Rightarrow M, w'' \models p)$$

or equivalently:

$$M, w \models PKB_rp \text{ iff } \exists w'(wD_rw' \text{ and } R_{xr}(w') \subseteq \|p\|) \tag{1}$$

---

[2] Here "satisfiable" means satisfiable in Classical Propositional Calculus.

Permission is traditionally interpreted as a "possibility" modality. This explains the existential quantifier in definition (1). As usual, prohibition is then defined as negation of permission. Therefore, we have: $FKB_rp \stackrel{def}{=} \neg PKB_rp$.

Notice that we can also define, for each role r, a function F_r from W into 2^W and use this function to define PKB_r as follows:

$$M, w \models PKB_rp \text{ iff } \exists X(X \in F_r(w) \text{ and } X \subseteq \|p\|) \tag{2}$$

We can easily show that definitions (1) and (2) are equivalent, provided the following three conditions hold for all $w \in W$:

- $F_r(w) \neq \emptyset$
- $\emptyset \notin F_r(w)$
- $\forall X(X \in F_r(w) \Leftrightarrow \exists w', (wD_rw' \text{ and } R_{xr}(w') = X)$

Notice also that we might define a third modality OKB_r for obligation to know as follows:

$$M, w \models OKB_rp \text{ iff } \forall w'(wD_rw' \Rightarrow R_{xr}(w') \subseteq \|p\|)$$

However, since we are only interested in confidentiality, this modality will not be used in this paper.

2.3 Properties of Permission and Prohibition to know

From this semantics, we have shown in [9] that modalities PKB_r and FKB_r have the following properties:

Property 1: $\models p \rightarrow q \Rightarrow \models PKB_rp \rightarrow PKB_rq$.
Property 2: $\models p \rightarrow q \Rightarrow \models FKB_rq \rightarrow FKB_rp$.

Properties 1 and 2 show that the set of sentences that an agent playing the role r is permitted to know is extended by their logical consequences whereas the set of sentences that this agent is forbidden to know is extended by their logical implicants.

We also have the following properties.

Property 3: $\not\models PKB_rp \wedge PKB_rq \rightarrow PKB_r(p \wedge q)$.
Property 4: $\not\models FKB_r(p \wedge q) \rightarrow (FKB_rp \vee FKB_rq)$.

The intuitive meaning of property 3 is that it may happen that p can be derived from a given permitted mental state of xr and that q can be derived from another permitted mental state of xr, whereas there is no permitted mental state of xr that enables to derive $p \wedge q$.

For instance, if, in a model M, we have: $F_r(w) = \{\|a\|, \|b\|\}$, then we have $M, w \models PKB_r(a) \wedge PKB_r(b)$, whereas we have not $M, w \models PKB_r(a \wedge b)$. This corresponds to a "Chinese wall" type of regulation [10], where the conjunction of two sentences may be strictly more sensitive than each term in the conjunction.

Property 4 is simply the converse of property 3. Its intuitive meaning is that it is possible that an agent playing the role r is forbidden to know $p \wedge q$, whereas this agent is neither forbidden to know p nor forbidden to know q. In fact, it may happen that neither p nor q independently enables the derivation of a sensitive sentence, whereas their conjunction enables to derive it.

3 Multilevel security policies

3.1 Two different approaches

Intuitively, a given multilevel policy assigns a classification level to some sentences of the language used to represent the database content and a clearance level to database users. Sentence classifications and user's clearances are both taken in a set of *security levels*. For instance, the *sensitivity levels* Top Secret (TS), Secret (S), Confidential (C), and Public (P) may be used as security levels. In this case, the set of sensitivity levels is associated with a total order, viz. $P < C < S < TS$. However, it is also possible to define more complex security policies where $<$ is a partial order (see [15]).

In order to formally represent a given multilevel security policy, we shall define a function which assigns a classification level to some formulas of language L. To formalize this classification function, we define, for each security level l, a modality [l], and formulae of the form [l]p are to be read: "formula p is classified at level l". For instance, the sentence [S]Salary(Smith, 5000) denotes the fact that the classification level of the formula *Smith's salary is 5000* is secret.

We shall assume that the classification function is not necessarily complete: some sentences in L may not be classified. On the other hand, the set of sentences to which a given classification has been assigned should not be confused with the set of sentences actually stored in the database. More precisely, we shall assume that the classification function may be defined independently from the multilevel database content:

1. A sentence may be classified without being stored in the database. This enables to take into account some general classification rules such as: Smith's salary is secret (and this does not depend on the actual value of Smith's salary stored in the database). In this case, every formula of the form Salary(Smith, sal$_i$), where sal$_i$ is a possible salary value would be classified at secret. But, if we assume that Smith's salary is unique and for instance equal to 5000, then only formula Salary(Smith, 5000) will be actually stored in the database.

2. Conversely, a database might wrongly behave, for instance by providing some sentence classified at secret to a user whose clearance is confidential. We do not *a priori* exclude this kind of situation. This will be the purpose of security constraints (see section 4) to decide which situations are satisfactory or not.

For reasons of formalization convenience, instead of modalities [l]p, we shall actually consider modalities $[\leq l]$ and $[\overline{\leq l}]$ (for each security level l). These modalities may apply to any finite (not necessarily consistent) set of formulae in L. Intuitively, formulae of the form $[\leq l](p1, ..., p_n)$ (resp. $[\overline{\leq l}](p_1, ..., p_n)$) are to be read: "$p_1$, ..., p_n is the set of all formulae classified at a level lower or equal (resp. classified, but not at a level lower or equal) to l".

In a structure M, these modalities are interpreted by functions C_l (resp. $C_{\bar{l}}$) from W into 2^W. Intuitively if, in world w, a given formula p is classified at a level lower or equal to l, then $\|p\|$ belongs to $C_l(w)$. And if, in world w, a given formula p is classified but not at a level lower or equal to l, then $\|p\|$ belongs to

$C_{\bar{l}}(w)$. We shall assume that, if $l_1 < l_2$, then, for every $w \in W$, $C_{l_1}(w) \subseteq C_{l_2}(w)$ and $C_{\bar{l_2}}(w) \subseteq C_{\bar{l_1}}(w)$.

Using these functions, the semantics of $[\leq l](p1, ..., p_n)$ and $[\overline{\leq l}](p_1, ..., p_n)$ are respectively defined as follows:

$M, w \models [\leq l](p_1, ..., p_n)$ iff $C_l(w) = \{\|p_1\|, ..., \|p_n\|\}$

$M, w \models [\overline{\leq l}](p_1, ..., p_n)$ iff $C_{\bar{l}}(w) = \{\|p_1\|, ..., \|p_n\|\}$

Our next objective is to define permission and prohibition to know from these classification functions. The key point is actually to notice that we can propose two different attitudes.

The first attitude is to consider that a database user is permitted to know every formula whose classification level is lower or equal to user's clearance level. We shall call this first attitude *explicit permission*. It is presented in section 3.2. Prohibition to know is then defined by duality; it corresponds to the notion of *implicit* prohibition.

The second attitude is to consider that a database user is prohibited to know every formula whose classification level is not lower or equal to the user's clearance level. We shall call this second attitude *explicit prohibition*. It is presented in section 3.3. By duality, we can define the notion of *implicit permission*.

It must be clear that these two attitudes are generally distinct. This is because we have no guarantee that the classification function is defined in such a way that explicit prohibition would coincide with the negation of explicit permission.

That is why in [9], we have introduced two modal operators for permission and prohibition which are not complementary. By contrast, here permission and prohibition are complementary but we have distinguished two kinds of permission which correspond to explicit and implicit permission.

3.2 Explicit permission

To represent explicit permission in a multilevel security policy, we shall define, for each security level l, a modality PKB_l^1. Formulae of the form $PKB_l^1 p$ are to be read: "an agent cleared at level l is explicitly permitted to know that the multilevel database believes p".

As explained in section 2.2, to define the semantics of modality PKB_l^1 we have simply to define a function F_l^1 from W into 2^W. The definition of F_l^1 is derived from function C_l as follows:

$F_l^1(w) = \{X : \exists X_1 \exists X_2 ... \exists X_m$
$\quad (\quad X_1 \in C_l(w) \text{ and } X_2 \in C_l(w) \text{ and } ... X_m \in C_l(w) \text{ and}$
$\quad \quad X = X_1 \cap X_2 \cap ... \cap X_m \text{ and } X \neq \emptyset)$

If we denote by f_X a formula such that $\|f_X\| = X$, then, the constraint on X intuitively means that $\vdash f_X \leftrightarrow f_{X1} \wedge ... \wedge f_{X_m}$ and f_X is not a contradiction, that is, f_X is equivalent to the conjunction of a consistent subset of formulae whose classification levels are less or equal to l.

We have $FKB_l^1 p \stackrel{\text{def}}{=} \neg PKB_l^1 p$. $FKB_l^1 p$ represents implicit prohibition at level l.

3.3 Explicit prohibition

To represent explicit prohibition in a multilevel security policy, we shall define, for each security level l, a modality FKB_l^2. Formulae of the form $FKB_l^2 p$ are to be read: "an agent cleared at level l is explicitly forbidden to know that the multilevel database believes p".

To define the semantics of modality FKB_l^2 we shall define a second function F_l^2 from W into 2^W. Using function $C_{\bar{l}}$, our function F_l^2 is defined by:

$$F_l^2(w) = \{X \ : \ X \subseteq W \text{ and } \forall Y(Y \in C_{\bar{l}}(w) \Rightarrow X \not\subseteq Y)\}$$

Condition $X \not\subseteq Y$ means $\not\vdash f_X \to f_Y$. Then, the constraint on X means that from f_X we cannot infer any sentence f_Y whose classification level is not less or equal to l.
We have $PKB_l^2 p \overset{\text{def}}{=} \neg PKB_l^2 p$. $PKB_l^2 p$ represents implicit permission at level l.

4 Security Constraints Modelling

4.1 Consistency of a multilevel security policy

We first present a security constraint to guarantee the confidentiality policy consistency. This constraint is satisfied in a given situation, that is in a given world w of a model M, if there is no sentence p and no security level l such that a user cleared at level l is both explicitly permitted to know p and explicitly forbidden to know p. The formal representation of this constraint is:

$$M, w \models \neg(PKB_l^1 p \wedge FKB_l^2 p)$$

This may be equivalently stated as follows:

$$M, w \models PKB_l^1 p \to PKB_l^2 p$$

It is easy to prove that this constraint is enforced if the following condition is satisfied in model M:

$$\forall X \in F_l^1(w), \exists X' \in F_l^2(w), X' \subseteq X$$

Enforcing the policy consistency constraint is mandatory in every multilevel security policy. This means that the agent who is in charge of defining a multilevel security policy should always verify that this policy is consistent.

4.2 Completeness of a multilevel security policy

We may also require that the multilevel security policy is complete. Completeness in a given world w of a model M means that, for every sentence p and security level l, any user cleared at level l should be explicitly permitted to know p or explicitly forbidden to know p. The formal representation of this constraint is:

$$M, w \models PKB_l^1 p \vee FKB_l^2 p$$

This may equivalently be stated as follows:

$$M, w \models PKB_l^2 p \to PKB_l^1 p$$

Notice that this is the converse of consistency constraint. It is also easy to prove that this constraint is enforced if model M satisfies the following condition:

$$\forall X \in F_l^2(w), \exists X' \in F_l^1(w), X' \subseteq X$$

If the multilevel security policy is both consistent and complete, then the definitions given in sections (3.2) and (3.3) would actually be equivalent. This means that explicit permission would coincide with implicit permission. However, we do not guess that enforcing the completeness constraint is mandatory. This means that you may accept that some sentences are neither explicitly permitted nor explicitly prohibited. But, you will have to make a choice for these sentences. You will be *restrictive* if you actually decide to refuse the access to these sentences and *permissive* if you take the opposite decision. In the next section, we shall show how our model enables to represent these two approaches.

4.3 Deductive channels

General constraint Another general security constraint which has to be satisfied says that, in a given world of a model M, if a user i, who plays the role r, knows that the database believes some sentence p, then this is permitted for users who play the role r. This constraint is represented by:

$$M, w \models KB_i p \rightarrow PKB_r p \tag{3}$$

where i denotes any agent playing the role r.

It is easy to prove that this constraint is enforced if model M satisfies the following condition:

$$\exists X \in F_r(w), X \subseteq R_i(w)$$

In the case of a multilevel security policy, we can actually derive two different constraints from this general constraint. The first constraint called *restrictive* is based on explicit permission, whereas the second constraint called *permissive* is based on explicit prohibition. We shall first present the permissive approach and then the restrictive approach.

Permissive approach Let us consider a situation where a given user i, cleared at level l, gets some data p from the database. According to the permissive attitude, this situation is satisfactory if p is not explicitly prohibited for i (i.e., $\neg FKB_l^2 p$). In our logic, this first attitude corresponds to the following constraint:

$$M, w \models KB_i p \rightarrow PKB_l^2 p$$

This attitude is the one which is used in every database which contains some sensitive data and tries to provide users who are not cleared to know the sensitive data with some statistics about them. In this case, this constraint says that a given situation is satisfactory if a given user is provided with data which do not allow him to derive sensitive data.

In [16], we show that this attitude corresponds to the approaches of both non-interference [2] and non-deducibility [3] models.

Restrictive approach According to this second attitude, a given situation is satisfactory if every user only knows explicitly permitted data. In our logic, this second attitude corresponds to the following constraint:

$$M, w \models KB_i p \rightarrow PKB_l^l p$$

where l represents user i's clearance level. This second attitude is actually the one which is used in every currently available multilevel database management system: a given user is only permitted to access some data if this data is really classified at a lower level than user's clearance level. We shall call this constraint restrictive.

In [16], we show that this attitude corresponds to the approach of the causality model [4]. However, it is interesting to note that this constraint does not necessarily prevent a user from knowing (actually deriving) some data classified at a higher level that this user's clearance, that is the restrictive attitude does not always imply the permissive attitude. For this purpose, the policy consistency constraint has to be enforced. In this case, it is indeed trivial to prove that, if the policy is consistent, then the restrictive attitude is a stronger attitude than the permissive one.

4.4 Abductive channels

Even if security constraints about deductive channels are enforced, there may be a risk of security policy violation. Indeed, let us consider a situation where agent i knows that the data base believes p and i has permission to know this fact. In this case there is no problem with respect to deductive channels. However, if there exists a sentence h such that p and h implies q (i.e. $h \rightarrow (p \rightarrow q)$) and agent i is not permitted to know that the data base believes q (i.e. $\neg PKB_r q$), and there is a risk that agent i knows h without accessing the data base, then there is a risk of violation for sentence q.

It is the role of the designer of the security policy to estimate, for a given h, whether the risk of knowing h independently of the data base has to be taken into account, but it is the role of some automated reasoning process to determine which sentence h the designer has to consider.

For this purpose we have formally defined in [9] the predicate Abd(p,h,q). Abd(p,h,q) holds iff we have $h \rightarrow (p \rightarrow q)$ and, to remove trivial cases, the set {p,h} is consistent and we have $\not\vdash h \rightarrow q$. Then, the security constraints that prevents abductive channels in a world w of a model M is expressed by:

$$M, w \models KB_i p \wedge Abd(p, h, q) \rightarrow PKB_r q \tag{4}$$

where i denotes any agent playing the role r and h is a sentence for which there is a significant risk that agent i knows h without accessing the data base.

It is worth noting that, according to the definition of Abd(p,h,q), the weakest information agent i has to know to infer q from p is $p \rightarrow q$. Then, from a practical point of view, before to provide agent i with the answer to a query that allows i to infer p, it has to be checked whether there exists some sentence q such that $\neg PKB_r q$, and $p \rightarrow q$ may be known by agent i.

According on whether we are restrictive or permissive, we can then derive from general constraint (4) two different security constraints to prevent abductive channels in the context of a multilevel security policy.

5 Conclusion

We have presented a modal logical framework which can be used to model non trivial security policies. We have seen that security constraints require a fine analysis of two possible attitudes in regard to the regulation; both of them have been formalized in this logic.

The logical framework has been presented from a model theoretic point of view. In [9] we have defined an associated axiomatics which has been proved to be sound and complete if language L contains a finite number of atomic sentences.

Further investigations may go in several directions. The first one is to define efficient strategies for reasoning in this logic in order to design a realistic implementation. This may require to restrict language L to definite Horn clauses.

Another direction is to extend the expressive power of the logic by splitting modalities PKB and FKB into two independent modalities; the first one for permission and prohibition and the second one for knowledge. This extension may be useful to define regulation about access to the regulation itself. For instance, in some applications there is a need for constraints of the form: "agents who play the role r_1 are forbidden to know that agents who play the role r_2 are permitted to know p"; these constraints may be fulfilled using "cover stories" to hide some data (see [17]).

Finally, let us notice that it is sometimes assumed that the security classification of data is determined by the security clearance of users who insert data. In particular, this assumption is present in information flow-based definitions of secrecy such as non-interference, non-deducibility or causality. For instance in the causality model, a user is permitted to know any information deducible from the data this user has inserted in the database. It would be interesting to study how to extend the model we present in this paper to represent this kind of assumption. For this purpose, we may need to combine deontic modalities with action modalities. This would also enable to consider more general security policies, especially those which combine confidentiality and integrity requirements.

Acknowledgement

This work was partially supported by the ESPRIT Basic Research Action MEDLAR 2.

References

1. D. Denning. *Cryptography and Data Security.* Addison-Wesley, 1982.
2. J. Goguen and J. Meseguer. Unwinding and Inference Control. In *IEEE Symposium on Security and Privacy*, Oakland, 1984.
3. D. Sutherland. A Model of Information. In *Proceedings of the 9th National Computer Security Conference*, 1986.
4. P. Bieber and F. Cuppens. A Logical View of Secure Dependencies. *Journal of Computer Security*, 1(1):99–129, 1992.
5. X. Qian, M. Stickel, O. Karp, T. Lunt, and T. Garvey. Detection and Elimination of Inference Channels in Multilevel Database Systems. In *IEEE Symposium on Security and Privacy*, Oakland, 1993.
6. L. Binns. Inference Through Secondary Path Analysis. In *Database Security, 6: Status and Prospects.* North-Holland, 1993. Results of the IFIP WG 11.3 Workshop on Database Security.
7. J. Hale, J. Threet, and S. Shenoi. A Practical Formalism for Imprecise Inference Control. In *Eighth Annual IFIP WG 11.3 Working Conference on Database Security*, Bad Salzdetfurth, Germany, 1994.
8. B. F. Chellas. *Modal Logic: An Introduction.* Cambridge University Press, 1988.
9. F. Cuppens and R. Demolombe. A Deontic Logic for Reasoning about Confidentiality. In M. Brown and J. Carmo, editors, *Deontic Logic, Agency and Normative Systems*, Workshops in Computing. Springer, 1996.
10. D. Brewer and M. Nash. The Chinese wall security policy. In *IEEE Symposium on Security and Privacy*, Oakland, 1989.
11. F. Cuppens. Roles and Deontic Logic. In A. J. I. Jones and M. Sergot, editors, *Second International Workshop on Deontic Logic in Computer Science*, Oslo, Norway, 1994.
12. I. Pörn. *Action Theory and Social Science; Some Formal Models*, volume 120 of *Synthese Library.* D. Reidel, Dordrecht, 1977.
13. J. Carmo and A. I. J. Jones. Deontic database constraints and the characterization of recovery. In A. J. I. Jones and M. Sergot, editors, *Second International Workshop on Deontic Logic in Computer Science*, Oslo, Norway, 1994.
14. A.J.I. Jones and I. Pörn. Ideality, Sub-ideality and Deontic Logic. *Synthese*, 65, 1985.
15. C. Landwehr. Formal models for computer security. *ACM Computing Surveys*, 3:247–278, September 1981.
16. F. Cuppens. A Logical Analysis of Authorized and Prohibited Information Flows. In *IEEE Symposium on Security and Privacy*, Oakland, 1993.
17. F. Cuppens and R. Demolombe. Normative Conflicts in a Confidentiality Policy. In *ECAI'94 Workshop on Artificial Normative Reasoning*, Amsterdam, The Netherlands, 1994.

Completeness for Linear Regular Negation Normal Form Inference Systems *

Reiner Hähnle[1], Neil V. Murray[2], Erik Rosenthal[3]

[1] Department of Computer Science, University of Karlsruhe, 76128 Karlsruhe, Germany, reiner@ira.uka.de, +49-721-608-4329
[2] Department of Computer Science, State University of New York, Albany, NY 12222, USA, nvm@cs.albany.edu, (518) 442-3393
[3] Department of Mathematics, University of New Haven, West Haven, CT 06516, brodsky@charger.newhaven.edu, (203) 932-7463

Abstract. Completeness proofs that generalize the Anderson-Bledsoe excess literal argument are developed for calculi other than resolution. A simple proof of the completeness of regular, connected tableaux for formulas in conjunctive normal form (CNF) is presented. These techniques also provide completeness results for some inference mechanisms that do not rely on clause form. In particular, the completeness of regular, connected tableaux for formulas in negation normal form (NNF), and the completeness of NC-resolution under a linear restriction, are established.

Keywords: *Logic for Artificial Intelligence, completeness, tableau method, resolution, non-clausal inference, negation normal form*

1 Introduction

Robinson developed semantic tree arguments to provide completeness proofs for resolution and related inference systems; these arguments are not entirely transparent. The excess literal technique discovered by Anderson and Bledsoe [1], which is strictly syntactic, was a considerable simplification. Their technique, which is essentially an induction on the size of the formula, was the basis for the first completeness proofs of certain refinements of resolution. Their technique has been considered by other authors but has seldom been applied to non-resolution systems. (There have been some non-resolution applications: Baumgartner and Furbach [2], where a similar technique is applied to model elimination, and Letz [7], where such an induction is made implicitly. Bibel's connection graph resolution completeness result [3] uses a related technique.)

Reducing the size of the search space is an important consideration in most automated deduction systems. With resolution, this is often done with subsumption checking and with the linear restriction. Analogously, the search space for the tableau method can be reduced using regularity and connectivity. The

---

* This research was supported in part by the National Science Foundation under grants CCR-9404338 and CCR-9504349.

first proof that the tableau method is complete with these restrictions is due to Letz [7] (proofs for closely related systems were presented previously in [6, 8]; other restrictions have been investigated by Wallace and Wrightson [15]). While elegant and insightful, Letz' proof is not the easiest to follow. The proof presented here provides a slight generalization by disallowing extensions by unit clauses, while at the same time being considerably shorter and simpler. The slight generalization is not the focus of this paper; the proof technique, which may be of interest in other settings, and the results for negation normal form are.

Effective proof methods that do not rely on conjunctive normal form (CNF) are often desirable for AI applications since reliance on clause form can create an exponential blow-up even before inference procedures are applied. Efficient clause form translations commonly used in theorem provers preserve unsatisfiability but not logical equivalence. Thus, any system — for example, the diagnosis system reported in [12], based on Reiter's theory [13] — that depends on logical equivalence cannot use these translations. One difficulty with non-clausal proof methods is that relatively few refinements have been developed for restricting the search space. Among the many refinements for CNF based systems, *linear* restrictions are of considerable importance.

In this paper, the Anderson-Bledsoe technique is adapted to paradigms that employ negation normal form (NNF). Completeness is proved for NNF inference techniques under a kind of linearity restriction as well as with a regularity condition, while preserving the simplicity and elegance of their technique. In particular, the completeness of *connected tableaux* and *connected regular tableaux* for NNF formulas (defined below) and the completeness of linear non-clausal resolution are established. Several proofs are omitted for lack of space and can be found in [5].

In Section 2 the Anderson-Bledsoe excess literal technique for proving completeness of resolution is described; it is generalized and applied to prove the completeness of linear resolution. An alternative generalization is used to demonstrate the completeness of regular connected tableaux with CNF input. The completeness of non-clausal tableaux and of linear non-clausal resolution is discussed in Section 3.

2 Conjunctive Normal Form

Recall that a *clause* is a disjunction of literals, and that a formula in *conjunctive normal form* (CNF) is a conjunction of clauses. Such a conjunction is often referred to as a *set* of clauses. A *link* is a complementary pair of literals occurring in different clauses, and a literal occurrence is said to be *pure* if it is not linked to any literal in the clause set. It is easy to verify the *Pure Rule*:

Lemma 1. (Pure Rule) If a clause set with a pure literal is unsatisfiable, then so is the set of clauses produced by removing the clause containing the pure literal. □

2.1 Resolution

The work described here was inspired by the Anderson-Bledsoe [1] excess literal proof of the completeness of resolution, and we begin with that proof.

Theorem 2. (Anderson-Bledsoe) Binary resolution (with merging) is refutation complete for propositional logic.

Proof: Let $S = \{C_1, C_2, \ldots, C_m\}$ be an unsatisfiable set of clauses. We must show that there is a refutation of S using resolution. Let n be the number of *excess literals* in S, i.e., the number of literals in S minus the number of clauses in S, and proceed by induction on n. If $n = 0$, then every clause is a unit clause. Since S is unsatisfiable, there must be two clauses consisting of complementary literals. Since they are unit clauses, their resolvent is the empty clause.

Suppose now that there is a resolution proof of any unsatisfiable clause set with at most n excess literals, and suppose that S has $n + 1$ excess literals. At least one clause, say C_1, contains at least two literals. Let C_1' be the result of removing one literal, say p, from C_1, and let S' be the result of replacing C_1 by C_1' in S. Since any satisfying interpretation for S' would satisfy S (i.e., if C_1' is *true*, so is C_1), S' must be unsatisfiable. Since S' has n excess literals, there exists a resolution proof of S'. That proof produces the empty clause from S'. Thus, if it is applied to S, it will either produce the empty clause or a clause containing only the literal p. That clause may contain several copies of p, but they can be merged to create the clause $\{p\}$.

We now have a set of clauses containing $S'' = \{\{p\}, C_2, C_3, \ldots, C_m\}$, which is unsatisfiable since any satisfying interpretation would satisfy S. Finally, S'' has fewer excess literals than S, so there is a proof of S''; the two proofs together provide a proof of S. $\qquad\qquad\square$

An interesting variation of this proof can be obtained by applying the induction to the number of distinct atoms that appear in S. This can be demonstrated by proving that resolution with the linear restriction is complete. Formally, a resolution proof is *linear* if one parent of each resolvent, except for the first, is the most recently derived clause. We require the following two lemmas. The first is [8, Lemma 2.3.2, p.63], and the second is a variant.

Lemma 3. Let S be a minimally unsatisfiable set of clauses, let B be a subset of the clause $C \in S$, and let $S' = (S - \{C\}) \cup \{B\}$. Then S' contains a minimally unsatisfiable set of clauses that includes B (and does not include C). $\qquad\square$

Lemma 4. Let $S = \{C_0, C_1, C_2, \ldots, C_k\}$ be a minimally unsatisfiable set of clauses, and suppose $C_0 = \{p\} \cup \{q_1, \ldots, q_n\}$, where $n \geq 0$. Obtain S' from S by deleting every occurrence of p in S, and obtain S'' by applying the Pure Rule to S', i.e., by deleting clauses containing $\bar{p}$. Let $C_0' = \{q_1, \ldots, q_n\}$. Then

1. S' is unsatisfiable;
2. S'' is unsatisfiable;

3. C_0' is a member of any minimally unsatisfiable subset of $\mathcal{S}'$;

4. C_0' is a member of any minimally unsatisfiable subset of $\mathcal{S}''$. □

Theorem 5. Linear binary resolution (with merging) is refutation complete for propositional logic.

Let $\mathcal{S} = \{C_1, C_2, \ldots, C_m\}$ be an unsatisfiable set of clauses. We assume that $\mathcal{S}$ is minimally unsatisfiable; otherwise, restrict attention to a minimally unsatisfiable subset. We must show that there is a refutation of $\mathcal{S}$ using linear resolution. We will prove the following slightly stronger result: There is a refutation of $\mathcal{S}$ in which any clause may be used as the top clause, i.e., the one used in the first step.

We proceed by induction on the number of distinct atoms in $\mathcal{S}$. If there are none, then $\mathcal{S}$ contains the empty clause, and we are done. Otherwise, suppose that all unsatisfiable sets of clauses with at most n atoms can be refuted with linear resolution, and assume that $\mathcal{S}$ has $n + 1$ atoms including the atom p. If $\mathcal{S}$ contains the unit clause $\{p\}$, fine; otherwise, remove all occurrences of p from $\mathcal{S}$. This formula is unsatisfiable since any satisfying interpretation would also satisfy $\mathcal{S}$. Consider a minimally unsatisfiable subset; by Lemma 4, every clause that had contained p in $\mathcal{S}$ is in this set. Also, since no occurrence of $\bar{p}$ is linked, no clause containing $\bar{p}$ is present. By the induction hypothesis, there is a refutation $\mathcal{R}_p$ by linear resolution. Note that if that refutation is applied to $\mathcal{S}$ — call the resulting refutation $\mathcal{R}_p'$ — none of the clauses containing $\bar{p}$ are resolved upon, and that the result is either the empty clause[4] or the clause $\{p\}$; (merging several copies of p may be required). This clause is of course the last resolvent.

Analogously, if we begin by deleting $\bar{p}$, a proof $\mathcal{R}_{\bar{p}}$ can be found that, when applied to $\mathcal{S}$ — let the resulting proof be $\mathcal{R}_{\bar{p}}'$ — will produce the empty clause or the clause $\{\bar{p}\}$. If either $\mathcal{R}'$ or $\mathcal{R}_{\bar{p}}'$ did produce the empty clause, then we are done. Otherwise, we may assume that the latter proof began with a clause C containing $\bar{p}$. The two proofs are linear, and we can put them together, maintaining linearity, by resolving $\{p\}$ and C. This proof may still produce the unit clause $\{\bar{p}\}$ because of multiple occurrences of $\bar{p}$. However, by resolving with the unit $\{p\}$, linearity is maintained and the empty clause is produced. □

The above induction is somewhat reminiscent of the Davis-Putnam procedure [4]. Refutations are obtained from the induction hypothesis by removing all occurrences of a given atom. Completeness for connected CNF tableaux can be proved with this technique. Below the size-based induction of Theorem 2 is adapted to obtain Letz' result [7] (with a slight strengthening) that completeness also holds when a regularity restriction is imposed along with connectivity. In subsequent sections, these induction techniques are employed to prove completeness for various non-clausal systems.

---

[4] In fact, this cannot happen because of minimality, but this is not really relevant.

2.2   Analytic Tableaux

Definition. A *tableau proof tree* for a set (conjunction) S of clauses is a tree labeled with formulas, constructed as follows:

1. The tree consisting of the single node S is a tableau; this tree is the *initial* tableau.
2. Suppose T is a tableau containing a node on the branch Θ labeled C, the conjunction of $C_1, C_2, \ldots, C_n$, (each of which is a clause). Then a tableau is obtained by replacing the node labeled C with n new nodes labeled $C_1, C_2, \ldots, C_n$ on the branch Θ. This is the *alpha rule*; it is applied automatically to nodes labeled with conjunctions.
3. Suppose T is a tableau containing a node labeled C, a clause containing the literals $l_1, l_2, \ldots, l_n$. Then a tableau is obtained by extending any branch Θ below C by appending n new leaves to Θ labeled $\{l_1\}, \{l_2\}, \ldots, \{l_n\}$. This is the *beta rule*; it is sometimes referred to as a *beta extension*.

A tableau is *closed* if each branch contains a pair of nodes labeled with complementary literals. In this case we speak of a *proof* or a *refutation* of S.

Observe that, for a set of clauses, the alpha rule is applied exactly once: to the initial tableau. Many authors choose to omit alpha rules, thus simplifying the definition of a tableau proof tree. We employ the alpha rule because it makes CNF tableaux and the definitions in the next paragraph special cases of NNF tableaux. Also, there is a slight technical advantage: All unit clauses are placed (by the first and only alpha step) on the initial branch and therefore need never be used for extensions.

A tableau proof tree with CNF input is *weakly connected* if each time a beta rule extends a branch, the formula to which the rule has been applied is linked to a node along the branch. (This property is present in the fully condensed proof trees of [11], but its presence is not sufficient for a proof tree to be fully condensed.) The tableau is *connected* if immediately prior to the extension the node to which the selected formula is linked appears after the last branch point. Note that after the first beta extension of a non-unit clause, this link must be to a leaf. Insisting that tableaux be connected is similar to the linear restriction for resolution.

A tableau proof tree with CNF input is *regular* if no branch contains distinct nodes labeled with identical *literals*. Observe that even a clause set with two identical clauses can have a regular tableau proof tree. This is the only way in which a regular (thus alpha) step can introduce repeated formulas on a branch when the input is in CNF. Such repeated formulas can be introduced much more easily with NNF input. In fact, repetitions along a branch due to alpha rules cannot be avoided in NNF. However, obvious ones such as repeated clauses can: If a conjunction (or disjunction, for that matter) has identical arguments, all but one can simply be deleted. Henceforward we assume all formulas have been so condensed.

It is interesting to note that regularity excludes extensions by unit clauses. This is no problem. Indeed, this is desirable: No closure is ever enabled by such an

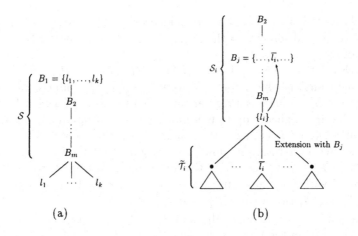

Fig. 1. Tableau T and forest $\tilde{T}$ from the proof.

extension since all such unit clauses label nodes on every branch in the tree. This effect is produced by the first (and only) alpha step. The formal inclusion of the alpha rule also makes possible connected proofs that are free of (unnecessary!) unit extensions. As with Theorem 5, it is essential that we work with a *minimally* unsatisfiable set of clauses.

The next theorem demonstrates that Letz' result can be obtained in a straightforward manner by adapting the induction argument from Theorem 2. Theorem 6 slightly enhances Letz' in that extensions with unit clauses are disallowed.

Theorem 6. The tableau method restricted to regular connected tableaux, free of unit extensions, is complete for unsatisfiable (finite) sets of (ground) clauses.

Proof: Let S be an unsatisfiable set of clauses. We assume that S is minimal; otherwise, restrict attention to a minimal subset. We will prove the following slightly stronger result: Given any (non-unit) clause in S, there is a closed tableau for S in which that clause is the first to which a beta rule is applied. We proceed by induction on the number n of literal occurrences in S.

If $n = 0$, the result is trivial. The case $n = 1$ is not possible by minimality. If $n = 2$, there must be two unit clauses containing complementary literals, no beta rule is necessary, and again the result is trivial. Observe, again because of minimality, that this is the only case in which S contains only unit clauses.

Assume now that there is a closed regular connected tableau for every unsatisfiable formula with at most n literal occurrences, and let $S = \{B_1, B_2, \ldots, B_m\}$ be a minimally unsatisfiable clause set with $n + 1$ literal occurrences ($n \geq 2$). Suppose that $B_1 = \{l_1, l_2, \ldots, l_k\}$ is the (non-unit) clause in S selected for the first extension step; let T be the resulting tableau — see Figure 1a.

Observe that T is both regular and connected: Were T irregular, some branch would have duplicate literals, which is to say, for some $i, 1 \leq i \leq k$, S contains the unit clause $\{l_i\}$. But that clause would subsume B_1, contrary to minimality. That T is connected follows for the same reason: Were B_1 not linked, it would be unnecessary.

For each i, let $\mathcal{S}_i = (\mathcal{S} - \{B_1\}) \cup \{\{l_i\}\} = \{\{l_i\}, B_2, \ldots, B_m\}$. By Lemma 3, any minimally unsatisfiable subset of $\mathcal{S}_i$ contains $\{l_i\}$. The induction hypothesis applies to each $\mathcal{S}_i$, so there is a regular connected tableau T_i for each $\mathcal{S}_i$. In each T_i, beta rules are applied only to non-unit clauses in a minimally unsatisfiable subset. Furthermore, l_i is linked to a clause B_j in that subset. If B_j is not a unit, the induction hypothesis allows us to assume that the first application of a beta rule in T_i is to B_j. Let $\tilde{T}_i$ be the forest obtained from T_i by deleting the nodes labeled with the clauses from $\mathcal{S}_i$ — see Figure 1b. If B_j is a unit, i.e., if $B_j = \{\overline{l_i}\}$, then T_i closes with $\{l_i\}$, and $\tilde{T}_i$ is empty.

We expand T by, for every i, adjoining $\tilde{T}_i$ to the branch whose leaf is labeled $\{l_i\}$; i.e., the roots of the forest $\tilde{T}_i$ become the children of the leaf $\{l_i\}$. Observe that, if $\tilde{T}_i$ is empty, then l_i is linked to the unit clause $\{\overline{l_i}\}$; so the branch whose leaf is $\{l_i\}$ is closed in T. Thus, since every T_i is closed, T is a closed tableau for $\mathcal{S}$. Since there are no unit extensions in T, the proof will be complete if we show that T is regular and connected.

T is regular since the initial extension of B_j is regular and each T_i is regular. Finally, T is connected because the extension of B_j is connected and each l_i either closes its branch or is linked to the non-unit of the first extension in T_i.

$\square$

3 Non-Clausal Methods

The techniques illustrated in the previous section can be used in non-clausal settings. The proofs are somewhat involved and are omitted here for lack of space; see [5].

We begin by recalling that a formula is in *negation normal form* (NNF) if the only connectives are conjunction, disjunction, and negation, and if all negations are at the atomic level. The tableau method works with NNF formulas as well as with formulas in clause form. In the NNF context, the phrase *set of formulas* means the conjunction of the formulas in the set. In particular, we assume the formulas in the set to be either disjunctions or literals.

We now define NNF tableaux. Since only atoms are negated, and since conjunction and disjunction are the only other logical operators, the rules for constructing an NNF tableau are the obvious generalization of the alpha and beta rules for CNF tableaux and are quite simple. The alpha rule, which applies to conjunctions, does not increase the number of branches and is applied automatically; the beta rule, which applies to disjunctions, does increase the number of branches and should not be applied automatically.

Definition. A *tableau proof tree* for an NNF formula $\mathcal{S}$ is a tree labeled with formulas and constructed as follows:

1. The tree consisting of a single node labeled $\mathcal{S}$ is a tableau; this tree is the *initial* tableau.

2. If T is a tableau, and if N is a node in T labeled with $\mathcal{S} = \wedge_{i=1}^{n} \mathcal{S}_i$, where each $\mathcal{S}_i$ is a disjunction or a literal, then N is replaced by n new nodes on the same branch labeled $\mathcal{S}_1, \mathcal{S}_2, \cdots, \mathcal{S}_n$. This is the *alpha rule* and is applied automatically to any node labeled with a conjunction.

3. If T is a tableau, and if N is a node in T labeled with $\mathcal{S} = \vee_{i=1}^{n} \mathcal{S}_i$, where each $\mathcal{S}_i$ is a conjunction or a literal, then a tableau may be obtained by appending n new nodes below any branch Θ containing N; each new node is uniquely labeled with some $\mathcal{S}_i$, $1 \leq i \leq n$. This is the *beta rule* and we say that Θ has been *beta-extended* by $\mathcal{S}$.

A tableau is *closed* if each branch contains a node labeled *false* or contains a pair of nodes labeled with complementary literals. The next theorem provides completeness for the tableau method with NNF formulas; the proof uses the Davis-Putnam style induction.

Theorem 7. The tableau method is a complete refutation procedure for unsatisfiable (finite) sets of (ground) NNF formulas. □

A tableau proof tree is *weakly connected* if each time a beta rule extends a branch, the formula to which the rule has been applied is linked to a node along the branch. The tableau is *connected* if immediately prior to the extension the node to which the selected formula is linked appears after the last branch point. This amounts to saying that the link is to a leaf or to a node created by an alpha rule applied to a leaf.

The next theorem strengthens Theorem 7 with a connectedness restriction; the proof is a reasonably straightforward adaptation of the proof of Theorem 7.

Theorem 8. Connected tableaux are a complete inference procedure for finite sets of ground NNF formulas. □

There are two problems with Theorem 8: No notion of regularity is enforced, and unit extensions are not excluded. The following example shows that unit extensions cannot be excluded if we demand a connected tableau. Let $\mathcal{S}$ be the conjunction of the two unit clauses $\{\overline{p}\}$ and $\{\overline{q}\}$ and the formula $B = (l \wedge (p \vee q)) \vee p$. After the first alpha rule application, the only possible non-unit extension is with B. To complete the proof tree without unit extensions, $(p \vee q)$ must be extended, and connectivity cannot be maintained.

Observe that both p and q are linked to unit clauses in $\mathcal{S}$. Therefore, violating connectivity (at least in this example) would seem to be both necessary and harmless. We shall see that this situation is more than fortuitous.

We say that the beta extension of a node labeled $\mathcal{F}$ is *u-connected* if every link in $\mathcal{F}$ is to a node labeled with a literal. A *tableau is u-connected* if every beta extension is either connected or u-connected. Note that u-connectivity for tableaux is a bit weaker than connectivity but stronger than weak connectivity.

In order to generalize CNF regularity to the NNF case in a useful way, both semantic and proof theoretic issues must be considered. Insufficient space precludes a detailed discussion, but the definition below is a generalization of the definition of regularity for CNF tableaux. Since nodes labeled by conjunctions are automatically replaced by the alpha rule, the nodes of an NNF tableau are always labeled by either literals or disjunctions.

Suppose we have a node labeled $\mathcal{F} = (\mathcal{F}_1 \vee \mathcal{F}_2 \vee ... \vee \mathcal{F}_n)$ on a branch Θ in an NNF tableau. Suppose further that we beta-extend Θ to create n new branches $\Theta_1, ..., \Theta_n$, where $\Theta_i = \Theta \cup \mathcal{F}_i$. Note that if $\mathcal{F}_i$ is a literal, then it labels the single new node on Θ_i; otherwise, $\mathcal{F}_i = \mathcal{F}_{i1} \wedge \mathcal{F}_{i2} \wedge ... \wedge \mathcal{F}_{iq}$, the alpha rule applies, and each $\mathcal{F}_{ij}$ labels a new node on Θ_i. We say that this beta extension is *irregular* if for some Θ_i, the new nodes on Θ_i are a subset of the nodes on Θ; i.e., the extension is irregular if for some $\mathcal{F}_i$, every node produced by the application of the alpha rule to $\mathcal{F}_i$ is labeled with a formula identical to that labeling some node on Θ. The step is *regular* if it is not irregular. Observe that all alpha steps are regular. A tableau proof tree is regular if every extension is regular.

Theorem 9. The tableau method restricted to regular u-connected tableaux free of unit extensions is a complete refutation procedure for unsatisfiable (finite) sets of (ground) NNF formulas. □

We now consider NC-resolution and begin by providing a precise definition (in the ground case). Let $\mathcal{F}$ and $\mathcal{G}$ be arbitrary unnormalized ground formulas, where $\mathcal{H}$ occurs as a subformula of both $\mathcal{F}$ and $\mathcal{G}$. If $\beta = true$ or $\beta = false$, we denote by $\mathcal{F}[\beta/\mathcal{H}]$ the result of replacing all occurrences of $\mathcal{H}$ in $\mathcal{F}$ by β and of performing truth-functional simplifications. Then the formula

$$\mathcal{F}[true/\mathcal{H}] \vee \mathcal{G}[false/\mathcal{H}]$$

is an NC-resolvent of $\mathcal{F}$ and $\mathcal{G}$ on the subformula $\mathcal{H}$. For the remainder of this paper we will consider only the case where $\mathcal{H}$ is a literal. Note that NC-resolution is defined for completely unnormalized formulas and does not require NNF. Here we restrict attention to NNF, so that the results of Section 3 can be employed.

The definition of linear NC-resolution is completely analogous to that of ordinary linear resolution. Formally, an NC-resolution proof is *linear* if one parent of each resolvent, except for the first, is the most recently derived formula.

Theorem 10. Linear non-clausal resolution is a complete inference procedure for finite sets of ground NNF formulas. □

References

1. Anderson, R., and Bledsoe, W., A linear format for resolution with merging and a new technique for establishing completeness, *J. ACM* 17(3) (1970), 525 – 534.
2. Baumgartner, P. and Furbach, U. Model elimination without contrapositives. *Proc. 12th Conference on Automated Deduction CADE, Nancy/France.* In *Lecture Notes in Artificial Intelligence*, (Bundy, Ed.), Springer-Verlag, Vol. 814, 87-101.
3. Bibel, W., On matrices with connections, *J. ACM* 28 (1981), 633 – 645.
4. Davis, M. and Putnam, H. A computing procedure for quantification theory. *J.ACM* 7, 1960, 201-215.
5. Hähnle, R., Murray, N.V. and Rosenthal, E. On proving completeness. Tech. Rep. TR 96-6, Dept. of Comp. Sci., SUNY Albany, NY, December, 1996.
6. Kowalski, R. and Kuehner D., Linear Resolution with Selection Function. *Artificial Intelligence*, 2(3), (1971), 227–260.
7. Letz, R., *First-order calculi and proof procedures for automated deduction*, Ph.D. dissertation, TU Darmstadt.
8. Loveland, D.W., *Automated Theorem Proving: A Logical Basis*, North-Holland, New York (1978).
9. Murray, N.V., and Rosenthal, E., Inference with path resolution and semantic graphs. *J. ACM* 34,2 (1987), 225–254.
10. Murray, N.V., and Rosenthal, E. Dissolution: Making paths vanish. *J.ACM* 40,3 (July 1993), 504-535.
11. Oppacher, F. and Suen, E. HARP: A tableau-based theorem prover, *Journal of Automated Reasoning* 4 (1988), 69–100.
12. Ramesh, A. and Murray, N.V. An application of non-clausal deduction in diagnosis. *Proceedings* of the *Eighth International Symposium on Artificial Intelligence*, Monterrey, Mexico, October 17-20, 1995, 378–385.
13. Reiter, R., A theory of diagnosis from first principles. *A.I. Journal*, **32** (1987), 57-95.
14. Smullyan, R.M., *First-Order Logic* (2nd Edition), Dover Press, 1995.
15. Wallace, K. and Wrightson, G. Regressive merging in model elimination tableau-based theorem provers, *Journal of the Interest Group in Pure and Applied Logics*, (Special Issue: Selected Papers from Tableaux'94), **3** (Oct. 1995), 921-938.

Renaming a Set of Non-Horn Clauses

Xumin Nie[1] and Qing Guo[2]

[1] Department of Computer Science
Wichita State University
Wichita, Kansas 67260
E-mail: nie@cs.twsu.edu

[2] Department of Computer Science
State University of New York
Albany, New York 12222
E-mail: guo@cs.albany.edu

Abstract. Several extensions of the logic programming language Prolog to non-Horn clauses use case analysis to handle non-Horn clauses. In this paper, we present analytical and empirical evidence that, by making a set of clauses less "non-Horn" using predicate renaming, the performance of these case-analysis based procedures can be improved significantly. In addition, we will investigate the problem of efficiently constructing a predicate renaming that reduces the degree of "non-Hornness" of a clause set by the maximum. We will show that the problem of finding a predicate renaming to achieve minimal "non-Hornness" is NP-complete.

1 Introduction

Intelligent systems require programming languages that are expressive, efficient and possess clear semantics. The logic programming language Prolog [2] based on Horn clause logic [6, 5] has become a popular candidate for such a language. Though Horn clause logic is quite expressive and of universal computing power, it can not handle negation in a satisfactory way. Therefore, it is natural to consider extensions of Prolog style Horn Clause logic programming to non-Horn clauses. Some examples of such extensions are [1, 8, 9, 15, 16]. The design philosophy of these extensions is to extend the underlying procedure of Prolog while retaining as many as possible the structural properties of Prolog. This philosophy is reflected in the fact that all the extensions use Prolog style back chaining and behave exactly the same as Prolog when only Horn clauses are used. They differ in their device for handling non-Horn clauses.

Several extensions in the literature are procedures based on case-analysis [9, 15, 16]. These procedures are characterized by the use of positive implication form for clauses and the limited use of contrapositives, in contrast to some procedures that require the use of all contrapositives [8]. The basic device for handling non-Horn clauses in these case-analysis based procedures is the *case analysis rule*, or the *splitting rule*, which allows one to prove the unsatisfiability of non-Horn clause set by proving the unsatisfiability of a collection of Horn set cases. It has been shown that the performance of the case-analysis based procedures is heavily influenced by how "non-Horn" a set of clauses is [12, 13, 14]. These procedures can efficiently handle Horn sets just as Prolog does. However, when the clause sets become increasingly non-Horn, the performance of these procedures will degrade. This suggests the possibility of improving the performance of these procedures by transforming a non-Horn clause set to one that is less non-Horn.

In this paper, we investigate the application of predicate renaming to reduce the degree of non-Hornness of a clause set in order to improve the performance of case-analysis based procedures. Predicate renaming is a simple and satisfiability-preserving transformation of a clause set by switching the signs of some predicates in the clause set. We will show that, by structural analysis and experimental result, we could significantly improve the performance of some case-analysis based procedures by reducing the degree of how non-Horn a clause set is using predicate renaming. In addition, we will investigate the problem of efficiently constructing a predicate renaming that reduces the degree of non-Hornness of a clause set by the maximum.

The rest of the paper is organized as follows. We provide some preliminary definitions in section 2. In section 3, we show how predicate renaming can improve performances by examining two case-analysis based procedures. In section 4, we present some experimental results to further demonstrate the potential for performance improvement. In section 5, we examine the general problem of renaming a clause set so that it is "minimally non-Horn". We conclude the paper in section 6.

2 Preliminaries

We define the terms *term, atom, literal, clauses, Horn clauses*, and *non-Horn clauses* in the usual way. We will use a reserved literal *false* to represent absurdity. Let L, L_i and H_i denote atoms, we use a *program clause* $L{:-}L_1, L_2, \ldots, L_n$ to represent a Horn clause $L \vee \neg L_1 \vee \neg L_2 \cdots \neg L_n$, a *goal clause* $false{:-}L_1, L_2, \ldots, L_n$ to represent an all negative clause $\neg L_1 \vee \neg L_2 \cdots \neg L_n$, and a *multi-head program clause* $H_1; \ldots; H_k{:-}L_1, L_2, \ldots, L_n$, to represent a non-Horn clause $H_1 \vee \cdots H_k \vee \neg L_1 \vee \neg L_2 \cdots \vee \neg L_n$. For example, the Horn clause $P \vee \neg Q \vee \neg R$ is represented as $P{:-}Q, R$, the all negative clause $\neg P \vee \neg Q \vee \neg R$ as $false{:-}P, Q, R$, and the non-Horn clause $P \vee Q \vee \neg R$ as $P; Q{:-}R$.

Definition 1. A *sequent* is a formula of the form $\Gamma \to L_0$ where Γ, called the *assumption*, is a set of literals and L_0 is a literal. Logically, a sequent $\Gamma \to L_0$ is interpreted as $\Gamma \supset L_0$. We will abbreviate $\emptyset \to L_0$ to $\to L_0$. We use the term *goal* or *subgoal* to refer to the sequents encountered during the proof process. The term *top-level goal* refers to the sequents of the form $\Gamma \to false$. A proof system is a *sequent style proof system* if all the inference rules of the proof system are of the form

$$\frac{\Gamma_1 \to L_1, \Gamma_2 \to L_2, \ldots, \Gamma_n \to L_n}{\Gamma \to L_0}$$

which specifies that one can infer $\Gamma \rightarrow L_0$ if all $\Gamma_i \rightarrow L_i$ ($i = 1, 2, \ldots, n$) have been proven. $\Gamma_i \rightarrow L_i$ ($i = 1, 2, \ldots, n$) can be regarded as subgoals of $\Gamma \rightarrow L_0$.

Example 1. The inference system of Prolog, which is complete for Horn clauses [6, 5], can be represented as a sequent style proof system where, for each Horn clause $L_0:-L_1, L_2, \ldots, L_n$, there is an inference rule

$$\frac{\rightarrow L_1, \ \rightarrow L_2, \ldots, \ \rightarrow L_n}{\rightarrow L_0}.$$

We shall measure how non-Horn a set of clauses is by its *non-Horn factor*.

Definition 2. Let s be a clause and h be the number of positive literals in s ($0 \leq h \leq |s|$). The *non-Horn factor* of s, denoted by $nHf(s)$, is $max(0, k - 1)$. Given a set of clauses $S = \{s_1, s_2, \ldots, s_n\}$, the non-Horn factor of S, denoted by $nHf(S)$, is the summation of the non-Horn factors of all clauses in S. That is, $nHf(S) = nHf(s_1) + nHf(s_2) + \cdots + nHf(s_n)$.

3 Predicate Renaming

Intuitively, a predicate renaming switches the signs of some predicates in a set of clauses. It is formally defined below.

Definition 3. Let S be a set of clauses over a set of propositional variable X, A be a subset of X, s be a clause in S and l be a literal. $r_A(l)$ is the complement of l if the variable of l is in A; otherwise it is l. $r_A(s) = \{r_A(l) \mid l \in s\}$. $r_A(S) = \{r_A(s) \mid s \in S\}$. We say $r_A(S)$ is a *renaming* of S using A. For brevity, we say that A is a renaming.

Example 2. Suppose $S = \{P \vee Q \vee R, P \vee \neg Q \vee R, \neg P \vee Q, \neg P \vee \neg Q, \neg R\}$ and $A = \{R\}$. $r_A(S) = \{P \vee Q \vee \neg R, P \vee \neg Q \vee \neg R, \neg P \vee Q, \neg P \vee \neg Q, R\}$.

It is easy to see that a renaming preserves the satisfiability of a set of clauses. That is, given a set of clauses S and a renaming A, S is satisfiable if and only if $r_A(S)$ is.

To examine the effect of predicate renaming on the performance of proof procedures, let us consider two closely related procedures. They are near-Horn Prolog [9] and simplified problem reduction format [15]. Both procedures are based on case analysis and have been shown to be structurally very similar [17]. They only differ in the ordering on reduction and the format of proofs constructed. Both proof procedures use the same set of sequent style inference rules, which are generated for each input clause. For each Horn clause $L_0:-L_1, L_2, \ldots, L_n$, we have a *reduction rule*

$$\frac{[\Gamma \rightarrow L_1], [\Gamma \rightarrow L_2], \ldots, [\Gamma \rightarrow L_n]}{\Gamma \rightarrow L_0}.$$

For each non-Horn clause $H_1; \ldots; H_k{:}{-}L_1, L_2, \ldots, L_n$, we have the *case analysis rule*, or the *splitting rule*

$$\frac{[\Gamma \rightarrow L_1], \ldots, [\Gamma \rightarrow L_n], [\Gamma, H_1 \rightarrow U], \ldots, [\Gamma, H_k \rightarrow U]}{\Gamma \rightarrow U}.$$

We also have the *assumption axiom*, or the *cancellation rule*

$$\Gamma \rightarrow L \quad \text{if} \quad L \in \Gamma.$$

If a clause set contains only Horn clauses, both procedures behave exactly like Prolog. If a clause set contains non-Horn clauses, the proof procedures recursively break the clause set into several clause sets which have fewer non-Horn clauses than the original set by using the case analysis rule. This is valid since for a set of clause $S = S' \cup \{H_1; \ldots; H_k{:}{-}L_1, L_2, \ldots, L_n\}$ is unsatisfiable if $S_i = S' \cup \{H_i{:}{-}L_1, L_2, \ldots, L_n\}$ is unsatisfiable for some i $(1 \le i \le k)$ and $S' \cup \{H_j\}$ are unsatisfiable for all j $(i \ne j, 1 \le j \le k)$.

Example 3. Let us consider the following two sets of clauses S_1 and S_2, both of which are unsatisfiable. It is easy to see that $S_2 = r_A(S_1)$ where $A = \{R\}$. We also note that the non-Horn factor of the clause set is reduced after renaming, that is, $nHf(S_1) = 3$ and $nHf(S_2) = 1$.

$$S_1 = \{\; 1.\;\; P; Q; R. \qquad\qquad S_2 = \{\; 1.\;\; P; Q{:}{-}R.$$
$$2.\;\; P; R{:}{-}Q. \qquad\qquad\qquad 2.\;\; P{:}{-}Q, R.$$
$$3.\;\; Q{:}{-}P. \qquad\qquad\qquad\quad 3.\;\; Q{:}{-}P.$$
$$4.\;\; false{:}{-}P, Q. \qquad\qquad\quad 4.\;\; false{:}{-}P, Q.$$
$$5.\;\; false{:}{-}R. \qquad\qquad\qquad 5.\;\; R.$$
$$\} \qquad\qquad\qquad\qquad\qquad \}$$

Fig. 1 and Fig. 2 show the proofs for S_1 and S_2 respectively using the sequent style inference rules. Some goals are labeled by a number in parentheses to indicate the inference rules on the goals. Goals without a label have the form $\Gamma \rightarrow L$ where $L \in \Gamma$, which are established by the assumption axiom, or the cancellation rule.

$$\frac{\dfrac{R \rightarrow R}{R \rightarrow false(5)} \quad \dfrac{P \rightarrow P \quad \dfrac{P \rightarrow P}{P \rightarrow Q(3)}}{P \rightarrow false(4)} \quad \dfrac{Q \rightarrow Q \quad \dfrac{P, Q \rightarrow P \quad P, Q \rightarrow Q}{P, Q \rightarrow false(4)} \quad \dfrac{P, R \rightarrow R}{P, R \rightarrow false(5)}}{Q \rightarrow false(2)}}{\rightarrow false(1)}$$

Fig. 1. Proof for S_1

As we can see, the proof from S_1 is more complicated than the proof from S_2. 14 goals are needed for S_1 and 11 for S_2. If we construct the proofs for S_1 and

$$\frac{\displaystyle -R(5) \quad \frac{P \to P \quad \dfrac{P \to P \quad \dfrac{Q \to Q \quad Q \to R(5)}{Q \to P(2)} \quad Q \to Q}{P \to Q(3) \qquad Q \to P(2)}}{P \to false(4) \qquad\qquad Q \to false(4)}}{\to false(1)}$$

Fig. 2. Proof for S_2

S_2 in the format required by near-Horn Prolog, the proof for S_1 has 16 steps and the proof for S_2 has 13. The main reason for the variation in the complexity of proofs is that S_1 is more non-Horn than S_2 and, as a result, more applications of the case analysis rule are needed for S_1 to complete the proof. To prove the unsatisfiability of S_1, it is broken into three clause sets $S_{11} = \{P, (2), (3), (4), (5)\}$, $S_{12} = \{Q, (2), (3), (4), (5)\}$, and $S_{13} = \{R, (2), (3), (4), (5)\}$ by the case analysis rule from the non-Horn clause $P; Q; R$. Each of S_{11}, S_{12} and S_{13} is a non-Horn set and possibly requires further application of the case analysis rule from the non-Horn clause $P; A:-Q$. On the other hand, to prove the unsatisfiability of S_2, it is broken into two Horn sets $S_{21} = \{P, (2), (3), (4), (5)\}$ and $S_{22} = \{Q:-R, (2), (3), (4), (5)\}$ by the case analysis rule from $P; Q:-R$. In general, as the number of non-Horn clauses increases or the number of positive literals in the non-Horn clauses increases, the process of breaking a non-Horn set into subsets containing fewer non-Horn clauses will produce more and more subsets, effectively increasing the complexity of the proofs. This also suggests that we can improve the performance of the two procedure procedures by reducing the number of non-Horn clauses and/or the number of positive literals in the non-Horn clauses, that is, by the reducing the non-Horn factor of a clause set. In example 3, the non-Horn factor of S_1 is reduced by a predicate renaming $A = \{R\}$.

4 Experimental Results

We have shown that if we can, by predicate renaming, transform a set of clauses to one which is equivalent but less non-Horn, the performance of some procedures based case analysis could be improved. In order to confirm this observation, we have performed some experiments using a theorem prover that implements a proof procedure [16] which is a variant of the simplified problem reduction format with certain mechanism built in to control the applications of case analysis rules.

We have constructed two sets of problems, the *original set* and the *renamed set*. The original set contains 100 instances of random 3-SAT problems generated using the fixed clause-length model [11]. The renamed set contains the problems obtained from those in the original set by predicate naming. The renaming is incrementally constructed by successively picking a propositional variable such that, if we rename this variable, the non-Horn factor of the set of clauses is reduced by the maximum. Ties are broken at random. This greedy process continues until no propositional variable can be renamed to reduce the non-Horn factor of clause set.

We have run the theorem prover on problems in both the original set and the renamed set. The experimental results are summarized in Table 1. We can see that the performance of the theorem prover is greatly improved. The average running time is reduced over 22% and the average inferences performed is reduced by almost 17%. It is also interesting to note that proof length does not seem to increase very much after renaming. Although the experiment is only performed on a theorem prover based on one proof procedure, we can expect similar performance gain for near-Horn Prolog and possibly for restart model elimination [1].

Table 1: Experimental Results Summary			
Problem Set	Run Time	Inferences	Proof Length
original set	31.51	488.73	18.45
renamed set	24.47	406.48	17.55
improvement	22.3%	16.8 %	4.9%

5 Mininum non-Horn Factor Problem

We have demonstrated in the previous sections that we can use predicate renaming to reduce the non-Horn factor of a set of clause and, as a result, the performance of some proof procedures can be improved. Given a clause set, there are many different renamings. It is natural that we would like to choose one that reduces the non-Hornness of the clause set by the maximum. The best we can hope for, of course, is to find a renaming which transforms the clause set into a Horn set.

It has been shown that a remaining that transforms a set of clauses into a Horn set can be constructed efficiently, if one such renaming exists at all [7, 10]. The question remains that, given a set of clauses S, if S can not be transformed into a Horn set by predicate renaming, can we efficiently find a renaming A such that the non-Horn factor of $r_A(S)$ is minimized? We will show below that this problem is NP-complete.

The problem can be slighted reformulated as follows: Given a set of clauses S and an integer k ($k \geq 0$), find a renaming A such that the non-Horn factor of $r_A(S)$ is at most k. We will refer to this problem as the *Minimum non-Horn Factor problem*.

Definition 4. The Minimum non-Horn Factor problem (MinNH) is defined as follows:

INSTANCE : A set of clauses S over a set of propositional variables X and an integer $k \geq 0$.
QUESTION : Is there a renaming A ($\subset X$) for S such that $nHf(r_A(S)) \leq k$?

We will prove the NP-completeness of minimum non-Horn factor problem by reducing to it the Maximum 2-Satisfiability problem (MAX2SAT), which is NP-complete [3, p. 259]. The proof is based on a bijection between the truth assignments of a set of two-literal clauses and its renamings, which is established below in lemma 7 and lemma 8. We first need to define the notion of truth assignments.

Definition 5. Let $S = \{s_1, s_2, \ldots, s_m\}$ be a set of clauses over propositional variables $X = \{x_1, x_2, \ldots, x_n\}$. A *truth assignment* is a complete mapping $X \to \{T, F\}$. Let V be a truth assignment, l be a literal and s be a clause. V can be extended to literals and clauses as follows:

$$V(l) = \begin{cases} T \text{ if } l = x_i \text{ and } V(x_i) = T; \\ T \text{ if } l = \neg x_i \text{ and } V(x_i) = F; \\ F \text{ otherwise.} \end{cases}$$

$V(s) = T$ if and only if there is a literal l in s such that $V(l) = T$.

Definition 6. The Maximum 2-Satisfiability (MAX2SAT) problem is defined as follows:

INSTANCE : A set X of propositional variables, a set S of clauses over X such that each clause contains exactly two literals, and a positive integer $p \leq |S|$.
QUESTION : Is there a truth assignment for X that simultaneously satisfies at least p clauses in S?

Lemma 7. *Let $S = \{s_1, s_2, \ldots, s_m\}$ be a set of clauses over propositional variables $X = \{x_1, x_2, \ldots, x_n\}$. Each clause in S contains two literals. Given a truth assignment $V : X \to \{T, F\}$, we define a renaming*

$$A = \{x_i \mid V(x_i) = T\}.$$

For any clause s_i in S, if $V(s_i) = T$, then $r_A(s_i)$ is a Horn clause.

Proof. Let s_i be a clause in S. There are three cases to consider:

1. $s_i = \{x_{i_1}, x_{i_2}\}$. Since $V(s_i) = T$, we know that either $V(x_{i_1}) = T$ or $V(x_{i_2}) = T$. Suppose $V(x_{i_1}) = T$, then $x_{i_1} \in A$ and $r_A(s_i) = \{\neg x_{i_1}, r_A(x_{i_2})\}$ is a Horn clause.

2. $s_i = \{x_{i_1}, \neg x_{i_2}\}$. Since $V(s_i) = T$, we know that either $V(x_{i_1}) = T$ or $V(x_{i_2}) = F$. If $V(x_{i_1}) = T$, then $x_{i_1} \in A$ and $r_A(s_i) = \{\neg x_{i_1}, r_A(\neg x_{i_2})\}$; if $V(x_{i_2}) = F$, then $x_{i_2} \notin A$ and $r_A(s_i) = \{r_A(x_{i_1}), \neg x_{i_2}\}$. In both cases, $r_A(s_i)$ is a Horn clause.

3. $s_i = \{\neg x_{i_1}, \neg x_{i_2}\}$. Since $V(s_i) = T$, we know that either $V(x_{i_1}) = F$ or $V(x_{i_2}) = F$. Suppose $V(x_{i_1}) = F$, then $x_{i_1} \notin A$ and $r_A(s_i) = \{\neg x_{i_1}, r_A(\neg x_{i_2})\}$ is a Horn clause. $\square$

Lemma 8. *Let $S = \{s_1, s_2, \ldots, s_m\}$ be a set of clauses over propositional variables $X = \{x_1, x_2, \ldots, x_n\}$. Each clause in S contains two literals. Given a renaming A, we define the following truth assignment $V : X \to \{T, F\}$:*

$$V(x_i) = \begin{cases} T \text{ if } x_i \in A \\ F \text{ if } x_i \notin A \end{cases}$$

For any clause s_i in S, if $r_A(s_i)$ is a Horn clause, then $V(s_i) = T$.

Proof. Let s_i be a clause in S. There are three cases to consider:

1. $s_i = \{x_{i_1}, x_{i_2}\}$. Since $r_A(s_i)$ is a Horn clause, we have either $x_{i_1} \in A$ or $x_{i_2} \in A$. Suppose $x_{i_1} \in A$, then $V(x_{i_1}) = T$, consequently $V(s_i) = T$.
2. $s_i = \{x_{i_1}, \neg x_{i_2}\}$. Since $r_A(s_i)$ is a Horn clause, we have either $x_{i_1} \in A$ or $x_{i_2} \notin A$. According to the definition of V, if $x_{i_1} \in A$, then $V(x_{i_1}) = T$; if $x_{i_2} \notin A$, then $V(x_{i_2}) = F$. In both cases, $V(s_i) = T$.
3. $s_i = \{\neg x_{i_1}, \neg x_{i_2}\}$. Since $r_A(s_i)$ is a Horn clause, we have either $x_{i_1} \notin A$ or $x_{i_2} \notin A$. Suppose $x_{i_1} \notin A$, then $V(x_{i_1}) = F$. According to the definition of V, $V(s_i) = T$. $\quad\square$

Theorem 9. *The Minimum non-Horn Factor problem is NP-complete.*

Proof. It is straight forward to show that MinNH is in NP. To show that MinNH is NP-complete, let an instance of MAX2SAT consist of a set of two-literal clauses $S = \{s_1, s_2, \ldots, s_m\}$ over a set of propositional variables $X = \{x_1, x_2, \ldots, x_n\}$ and a positive integer $p \le m = |S|$. The corresponding instance of MinNH consists of the same set of clauses S over X and $k = m - p$.

Suppose there is a truth assignment $V : X \to \{T, F\}$ which satisfies at least p clauses in S. Based on lemma 7 we can find a renaming A for S such that there are at least p Horn clauses in $r_A(S)$. Since each clause in $r_A(S)$ contains two literals, the non-Horn factor of each clause is either 0 or 1, and the non-Horn factor of $r_A(S)$ is the number of non-Horn clauses in $r_A(S)$. Because there are m clauses in $r_A(S)$ and at least p of them are Horn clauses, $nHf(r_A(S)) \le k$, where $k = m - p$.

Suppose there is a renaming A for S such that $nHf(r_A(S)) \le k$. Then there are at most k non-Horn clauses in $r_A(S)$ and at least p Horn clauses in $r_A(S)$ where $k = m - p$, because each clause in $r_A(S)$ has two literals and $nHf(r_A(S))$ is equal to the number of non-Horn clauses in $r_A(S)$. Based on lemma 8, there is a truth assignment V for MAX2SAT which satisfies at least p clauses in S. $\quad\square$

6 Related Works

A detailed analysis is given in [14, 12] on how the non-Hornness of a clause set can affect the search space and efficiency of several extensions of Prolog to non-Horn clauses. It is suggested in [4] that predicate renamings be used to transform a clause set into a Horn set so that unit resolution can be used. In [7, 10], it is shown that if a predicate renaming exists that transforms a clause set S into a Horn set, that is, S is *renamable Horn*, we can find such a renaming in polynomial time. The case of the renamable Horn is a special case of the MinNH problem where $k = 0$. The bijection between the truth assignments of a set of two-literal clauses and its renamings established in lemma 7 and lemma 8 is a generalization of the bijection established in [7] between the models of a set of two-literal clauses and the Horn renamings.

7 Conclusions

We have presented analytical and empirical evidence that, by transforming a set of clauses into one that is less "non-Horn" by predicate renaming, we can significantly improve the performance the case-analysis based procedures that extend Horn clause logic programming to non-Horn clauses. We have also investigated the general problem of finding a predicate renaming to transform a clause set into one that is minimally non-Horn. We have shown that this problem is NP-complete.

References

1. P. Baumgartner and U. Furbach, Model elimination without contrapositives and its application to PTTP, *Journal of Automated Reasoning* **13** 339 – 359 (1994).
2. W.F. Clocksin and C.S. Mellish, *Programming in Prolog*, Springer-Verlag (1981).
3. M.R. Garey and D.S. Johnson, *Computers and intractability: A guide to the theory of NP-completeness*, W.H.Freeman and Company (1979).
4. L. Henschen and L. Wos, Unit refutations and Horn sets, *Journal of ACM* **21** (4) (1974) 590 – 605.
5. J.W. Lloyd, *Foundations of logic programming*, Springer-Verlag (1987).
6. R.A. Kowalski, Predicate logic as a programming language, *Information Processing*, pp. 569 – 574, North Holland, Stockholm (1974).
7. H.R. Lewis, Renaming a set of clauses as a Horn set, *Journal of ACM* **25** (1) (1978) 134-135.
8. D.W. Loveland, A simplified format for the model elimination theorem-proving procedure, *Journal of ACM* **16** (3) 349–363 (1969).
9. D.W. Loveland, Near-Horn Prolog and beyond, *Journal of Automated Reasoning* **7** (1) 1–26 (1991).
10. H. Mannila and K. Mehlhorn, A fast algorithm for renaming a set of clauses as a Horn set, *Information Processing Letter* 21 269-272 (1985).
11. D. Mitchell, B. Selman and H. Levesque, Hard and easy distributions of SAT problems, *Proceeding of AAAI-92*, pp. 459 – 465 (1992).
12. X. Nie, Complexities of non-Horn clause logic programming, *Methodologies for Intelligent Systems* **5**, Z. Ras, M. Zemankova, and M. Emrich, eds. 539–544 (North-Holland, 1990)
13. X. Nie, How well are non-Horn clauses handled, 6th *International Symposium on Methodologies for Intelligent Systems*, Lecture Notes in Computer Science 542, 580–588 (Springer-Verlag, 1991).
14. X. Nie, A note on non-Horn clause logic programming, *Artificial Intelligence*, in press.
15. D.A. Plaisted, A simplified problem reduction format, *Artificial Intelligence* **18** 227-261 (1982).
16. D.A. Plaisted, Non-Horn clause logic programming without contrapositives, *Journal of Automated Reasoning* **4** (3) (1988) 287-325.
17. D.W. Reed and D.W. Loveland, A comparison of three Prolog extensions, *Journal of Logic Programming* **12** 25 – 50 (1992).
18. D. W. Reed and D.W. Loveland, Near-Horn Prolog and the ancestry family of procedures, *Annals of Mathematics and Artificial Intelligence* **14** (1995).

Constraints, Causal Rules and Minimal Change in Model-based Update

Yan Zhang

Department of Computing
University of Western Sydney, Nepean
Kingswood, NSW 2747, Australia
E-mail: yan@st.nepean.uws.edu.au

Abstract. We consider knowledge base update while the domain constraints are explicitly taken into account. We argue that the traditional constraint form is problematic to capture the causality of the domain, and ignoring this point may lead to difficulties in knowledge base updates. To handle this problem properly, it is necessary to describe the causal rules of the domain explicitly in the update formalism. Unlike other researchers viewing causal rules as some kind of inference rules, we distinguish causal rules between defeasible and non-defeasible cases. It turns out that a causality-based update theory in our formalism can be specified as a Reiter's closed default theory while defeasible causal rules correspond to closed normal defaults and non-defeasible causal rules correspond to closed defaults without justification. By using Lukaszewicz's model default theory, we provide a formal semantics for our causal rules. We then propose a causality-based minimal change approach for representing update, and show that our approach provides plausible solutions for model-based updates. We also investigate the properties of our approach and show that our approach generalizes the classical PMA update theory [4] and a recent causality-based update method [2].

1 Introduction

We consider knowledge base update while the domain constraints are explicitly taken into account. Traditionally, the properties of a domain are characterized by logical formulas which we call *domain constraints*. A knowledge base, eg. a set of logical formulas or the conjunction of these formulas, is viewed as a description of the real world. The knowledge base needs to be updated if new knowledge about the world occurs, and any change to the knowledge base must be consistent with the domain constraint [4, 5].

However, it is obvious that not every domain property can be captured by a logical formula. For instance, a sentence like "heavy rainfall *causes* floods" represents some causal relation between "heavy rainfall" and "floods". For example, if we know that there is a heavy rainfall, we would expect to have floods. From a semantical point of view, a causal rule is different from a logical implication. Suppose we use logical formulas to represent causal relations, then the causal relation "heavy rainfall causes floods" would be likely represented by a logical formula *heavy-rainfall* ⊃ *floods*. Therefore, if *heavy-rainfall* is true, then from this formula, it follows that *floods* is true. However, note that *heavy-rainfall* ⊃ *floods* is also logically equivalent to the formula ¬*floods* ⊃ ¬*heavy-rainfall*. It is also the case that ¬*heavy-rainfall* is followed from ¬*floods*. But it would not be normally regarded that no flooding is a *cause* of the absence of rain.

In many of current formulations of knowledge base updates, properties about the domain are normally characterized by a set of logical formulas called *domain constraints*, and there is no difference between general logical constraints and causal rules. Any changes to the knowledge base must be consistent with the domain constraint. However, as we will see next, ignoring such difference may result in difficulties in knowledge base updates.

Consider the simplified stuffy room example [4]. There is a constraint about the room which says that if both ducts in the room are blocked, then the room becomes stuffy. This constraint is expressed by the following formula:

$$blocked(duct_1) \wedge blocked(duct_2) \supset stuffy(room). \tag{1}$$

Suppose the initial knowledge base[1] ψ is

$$\psi \equiv \neg blocked(duct_1) \wedge blocked(duct_2) \wedge \neg stuffy(room) \wedge (1).$$

Now suppose that we update ψ with $blocked(duct_1)$ (i.e., the $duct_1$ becomes blocked) using Winslett's PMA [4][2]. Informally, the PMA updates the knowledge base by updating every possible models of this knowledge base, and the change of models obey the rule of minimal change with respect to model inclusion. In this example, ψ has exactly one model S:

$$S = \{\neg blocked(duct_1), blocked(duct_2), \neg stuffy(room)\}.$$

Therefore, we get the following resulting knowledge base ψ' by the PMA:

$$\psi' \equiv blocked(duct_1) \wedge (blocked(duct_2) \wedge stuffy(room) \vee \\ \neg blocked(duct_2) \wedge \neg stuffy(room)) \wedge (1).$$

which corresponds to two models:

$$S_1 = \{blocked(duct_1), blocked(duct_2), stuffy(room)\}, \text{ and}$$
$$S_2 = \{blocked(duct_1), \neg blocked(duct_2), \neg stuffy(room)\},$$

S_1 says that after updating ψ with $blocked(duct_1)$, the $duct_2$ still stays blocked and the room then becomes stuffy, while S_2 implies that updating ψ with $blocked(duct_1)$ may lead to $duct_2$ unblocked. But intuitively, only S_1 represents our desired solution while S_2 is quite implausible in some sense – why does the change of $duct_1$ to blocked cause the $duct_2$ to be unblocked?

As constraint (1) is also logically equivalent to the following formula:

$$blocked(duct_1) \wedge \neg stuffy(room) \supset \neg blocked(duct_2), \tag{2}$$

---

[1] Traditionally, a knowledge base is viewed as a set of logical formulas, or the conjunction of these formulas.

[2] We will review the PMA formally in section 3.

it is not difficult to see that both S_1 and S_2 are forced by (1) and (2) respectively to have minimal differences with S. But semantically, (1) is not simply a logical implication. It should represent a causal relation between $blocked(duct_1)$, $blocked(duct_2)$ and $stuffy(room)$ – the fact that $duct_1$ and $duct_2$ blocked *causes* the fact that the room becomes stuffy, which, as the sentence "heavy rainfall *causes* floods" shows, is *not* logically equivalent to formula (2).

From the above discussion, we argue that to describe the update correctly, we need to specify the causality of the domain explicitly, which should have different semantics from general constraints. The goal of this paper is then to formalize causal rules in knowledge bases and show how this solves the problem as described above. The paper is organized as follows. Section 2 defines causal rules and causal theories formally, and uses Lukaszewicz's default model theory to provide formal semantics for causal theories. Section 3 then proposes a new principle for update called the *causality-based minimal change*. A formulation of update based on this principle is also developed. Section 4 illustrates a further example to show how our approach provides and also investigates relations between our approach and other related work. Finally, section 5 concludes the paper with some remarks.

2   Causal Rules as Defaults

Let $\mathcal{L}$ be a first order language with equality and two additional symbols $\leadsto$ and $\Rightarrow$ which we will use to express causal rules. A *causal rule* is any expression of the form $A \leadsto B$ or $A \Rightarrow B$, where A and B are closed first order formulas of $\mathcal{L}$. Specifically, an expression $A \leadsto B$ is read "the fact that A *normally causes* the fact that B", while an expression $A \Rightarrow B$ is read "the fact that A *causes* the fact that B". For both cases, we will call A a *cause* of $A \leadsto B$ (or $A \Rightarrow B$) and B an *effect* of $A \leadsto B$ (or $A \Rightarrow B$).

The above two forms of expressions $A \leadsto B$ and $A \Rightarrow B$ represent *defeasible* and *non-defeasible* causal rules respectively in our problem domain. For example, consider a causal rule which says that "the fact that a match has been struck normally causes the fact that it has lit". However, if the match is wet and we know that striking a wet match normally does not light, then this causal rule should not be triggered during our reasoning. So this causal rule is defeasible. On the other hand, a statement that "the fact that some one is dead causes the fact that this person is not walking" should not be defeasible from our commonsense.

A *causal theory* CT is defined as a pair $(\mathcal{A}, \mathcal{C})$, where $\mathcal{A}$ is a set of closed first order formulas of $\mathcal{L}$ and $\mathcal{C}$ a set of causal rules[3]. Both $\mathcal{A}$ and $\mathcal{C}$ need not be finite but are at most countably infinite. Intuitively, a causal theory represents knowledge about a domain while $\mathcal{A}$ is viewed as basic facts or invariant properties of the domain, and $\mathcal{C}$ represents the causality about the domain.

Now we try to provide a model theoretic semantics for the causal theory. In fact, we can treat our causal rules as defaults in Reiter's default logic [3]. In

---

[3] Note that $\mathcal{C}$ includes both forms of causal rules as we described earlier.

particular, a defeasible causal rule $A \leadsto B$ can be viewed as a normal default $A : B/B$, while a non-defeasible causal rule $A \Rightarrow B$ is viewed as a default $A : /B$ (i.e. a closed default without justification). Therefore, a causal relation like *heavy-rainfall* $\leadsto$ *floods* can be also interpreted as "if there is a heavy rainfall and it is consistent to believe that there are floods, then one may believe that there are floods caused by a heavy rainfall". Hence, in our formalism, causal reasoning turns out to be a kind of default reasoning, and a causal theory corresponds to a closed default theory [3].

Treating causal theories as closed default theories, we then can use the model default theory originally proposed by Etherington and extended by Lukaszewicz [1] to provide formal semantics for our causal theories.

Let Φ be a class of first order interpretations of language $\mathcal{L}$ and A a closed first order formula. $\Phi(A) = \{\varphi \mid \varphi \in \Phi$ and $\varphi \models A\}$. Φ is called *elementary* iff Φ is the class of all models of some set of closed first order formulas $\mathcal{F}$.

Definition 1. Let Φ be a class of first order interpretations of language $\mathcal{L}$ and Π a set of closed first order formulas. The pair $< \Phi, \Pi >$ is called a *structure* iff

(i) Φ is elementary;
(ii) For every $A \in \Pi$, $\Phi(A) \neq \emptyset$.

Definition 2. Let Φ be an elementary class of first order interpretations of language $\mathcal{L}$ and $c = A \leadsto B$ or $c = A \Rightarrow B$ be a causal rule. We say that c is *applicable* with respect to Φ iff

(i) $\varphi \models A$ for every $\varphi \in \Phi$;
(ii) If $c = A \leadsto B$, there is some $\varphi \in \Phi$ such that $\varphi \models B$.

Definition 3. Let $< \Phi, \Pi >$ be a structure. The *characteristic function* f_c of a causal rule $c = A \leadsto B$ or $c = A \Rightarrow B$ with respect to $< \Phi, \Pi >$ is defined as follows:

$$f_c(< \Phi, \Pi >) = \begin{cases} < \Phi(B), \Pi \cup \{B\} > & \text{if } c = A \leadsto B \text{ and is applicable} \\ & \text{with respect to } \Phi \\ < \Phi(B), \Pi > & \text{if } c = A \Rightarrow B \text{ and is applicable} \\ & \text{with respect to } \Phi \\ < \Phi, \Pi > & \text{if } c \text{ is not applicable} \\ & \text{with respect to } \Phi \end{cases}$$

Definition 4. Let $< \Phi, \Pi >$ be a structure and let $\mathcal{C}$ be a set of causal relations. We say that $< \Phi, \Pi >$ is *stable* with respect to $\mathcal{C}$ iff

$$f_c(< \Phi, \Pi >) = < \Phi, \Pi > \text{ for all } c \in \mathcal{C}.$$

Definition 5. Let $< \Phi, \Pi >$ be a structure and $< c_i >$ a sequence of causal relations. By $f_{<c_i>}(< \Phi, \Pi >)$ we denote:

$$f_{<c_i>}(< \Phi, \Pi >) = \begin{cases} < \Phi, \Pi > & \text{if } < c_i > = <> \text{ (the empty sequence)} \\ < \bigcap \Phi_i, \bigcup \Pi_i > & \text{otherwise} \end{cases}$$

where $< \Phi_0, \Pi_0 > = < \Phi, \Pi >$, and for $i = 0, 1, \cdots$

$$< \Phi_{i+1}, \Pi_{i+1} >= f_{c_i}(< \Phi_i, \Pi_i >).$$

Definition 6. Let $< \Phi, \Pi >$ be a structure, Ψ be an elementary class of first order interpretations of language $\mathcal{L}$. Suppose $< c_i >$ is a sequence of causal relations. We say that $< \Phi, \Pi >$ is $f_{<c_i>}$-accessible from Ψ iff $< \Phi, \Pi >= f_{<c_i>}(< \Psi, \emptyset >)$. We say that $< \Phi, \Pi >$ is *accessible* from Ψ with respect to $\mathcal{C}$ iff there is a sequence (possible empty) $< c_i >$ of causal relations from $\mathcal{C}$ such that $< \Phi, \Pi >$ is $f_{<c_i>}$-accessible from Ψ.

Now we are ready to give the definition of the class of models of a causal theory[4].

Definition 7. Let $CT = (\mathcal{A}, \mathcal{C})$ be a causal theory, $Models(\mathcal{A})$ the class of all models of $\mathcal{A}$, and Θ the set of all subclasses of $Models(\mathcal{A})$ such that for each $\Phi \in \Theta$, there exists a set of closed first order formulas Π satisfying

(i) $< \Phi, \Pi >$ is a structure;
(ii) $< \Phi, \Pi >$ is stable with respect to $\mathcal{C}$;
(iii) $< \Phi, \Pi >$ is accessible from $Mod(\mathcal{A})$ with respect to $\mathcal{C}$.

Then, the class of all models of CT, denoted as $Models(CT)$, is defined as

$$Models(CT) = \bigcup_{\Phi \in \Theta} \Phi$$

Note that it has been proved in [1] that the set of all models of CT coincides with the union of sets of models for all extensions of default theory CT (recall that CT is also a Reiter's default theory).

Example 1. Consider a causal theory

$$CT = (\{heavy\text{-}rainfall\}, \{heavy\text{-}rainfall \rightsquigarrow floods\}).$$

Obviously, from Definition 7, we have

$$Models(CT) = \{\{heavy\text{-}rainfall, floods\}\}.$$

3 Causality-based Minimal Change

3.1 Preliminaries

We will first introduce some preliminary concepts and review the PMA (*possible models approach* [4]) – a classical minimal change based approach for update. We represent a *knowledge base* by a closed first order formula ψ. $Models(\psi)$ denotes the set of all models of ψ. We also consider *domain constraints* about the world. Let $\mathcal{D}$ be a satisfiable closed first order formula that represents all

---

[4] A detailed explanation of the following definition is referred to Lukaszewicz's work [1].

state constraints about the world[5]. Thus, for any knowledge base ψ, we require $\psi \models \mathcal{D}$. Let I be an interpretation of $\mathcal{L}$. We say that I is a *state* of the world if $I \models \mathcal{D}$. A knowledge base ψ can be treated as a *description* of the world, where $Models(\psi)$ is the set of all *possible states* of the world with respect to ψ.

Let ψ be a knowledge base and μ a closed first order formula which is regarded as a new knowledge (information) about the world. Then informally, the general question of updating ψ with μ is how to specify the new knowledge base after combining the new knowledge (information) μ into the current knowledge base ψ (we also call μ as the *update effect*).

In the PMA, the knowledge base update is achieved by updating *every possible state* of the world with respect to ψ with μ, and such update is constructed based on the *principle of minimal change* on models. Formally, let I_1 and I_2 be two interpretations of $\mathcal{L}$. We say that I_1 and I_2 *differs* on a ground atom l if l appears in exactly one of I_1 and I_2. $Diff(I_1, I_2)$ denotes the set of all different ground atoms between I_1 and I_2. Let I be an interpretation and $\mathcal{I}$ a set of interpretations. We define the set of all *minimal different interpretations* of $\mathcal{I}$ with respect to I as follows:

$$Min(I, \mathcal{I}) = \{I' \mid I' \in \mathcal{I}, \text{ and there does not exist other}$$
$$I'' \in \mathcal{I} \text{ such that } Diff(I, I'') \subset Diff(I, I')\}.$$

Let S be a state of the world, i.e., $S \models \mathcal{D}$, and μ a closed first order formula. Then the PMA [4] defines the set of possible resulting states as follows:

$$Res^{\mathcal{D}}(S, \mu) = Min(S, Models(\mathcal{D} \wedge \mu)).$$

Definition 8. Let ψ be a knowledge base and μ a closed first order formula. $\psi \diamond_{pma} \mu$ denotes the update of ψ with μ by the PMA[6], where the set of all models of $\psi \diamond_{pma} \mu$ is defined by
$$Models(\psi \diamond_{pma} \mu) = \bigcup_{S \in Models(\psi)} Res^{\mathcal{D}}(S, \mu).$$

3.2 Updating States

Taking the causality into account, we need to consider the effect of update that is related causality of the domain. Here we propose a *causality-based minimal change principle*. Similarly to the PMA, in our approach, the knowledge base update is also achieved by updating every models (or state) of this knowledge base. So we first consider the state update.

The basic idea is: during state change, the minimal change principle is applied generally but with exception on the *causal effects* of the update. For instance, in

---

[5] Usually, we use a set of formulas to represent domain constraints. In this case, $\mathcal{D}$ is viewed as a conjunction of all such formulas. In the rest of the paper, we will alternatively denote $\mathcal{D}$ as a set of formulas or a conjunction of these formulas if it does not cause confusion.

[6] Here we only consider the *well-defined* update, that is, μ is consistent with the state constraint $\mathcal{D}$.

the simplified stuffy room example, suppose that we replace the constraint (1) with a causal relation:

$$blocked(duct_1) \land blocked(duct_2) \Rightarrow stuffy(room), \tag{3}$$

and the current knowledge base corresponds to the unique state:

$$S = \{\neg blocked(duct_1), blocked(duct_2), \neg stuffy(room)\}. \tag{4}$$

If we update S with $blocked(duct_1)$, intuitively, we would expect the resulting state to be

$$S' = \{blocked(duct_1), blocked(duct_2), stuffy(room)\}.$$

To derive this intuitive resulting state from S, we may use the minimal change principle on ground atom $blocked(duct_2)$ but with exception on literal $\neg stuffy(room)$.

The reason is that since $blocked(duct_2)$ is consistent with the update effect $blocked(duct_1)$, according to the minimal change principle, $blocked(duct_2)$ should persist during the state change. On the other hand, because of the causal rule (3), we know that from $blocked(duct_1)$ and $blocked(duct_2)$, we should *causally* derive $stuffy(room)$. That is, $stuffy(room)$ is an causal effect of the update. So, the minimal change principle should *not* apply to literal $\neg stuffy(room)$. Now we are ready to formalize the idea described above. The following two definitions give the formal description of the state update in the causality-based minimal change approach.

Definition 9. Let C and D be the sets of causal relations and constraints of the domain respectively, S a state of the world, and μ a closed first order formula. Let δ be a maximal subset of S such that

1. $D \cup \{\mu\} \cup \delta$ is consistent,
2. for any $A \leadsto B$ or $A \Rightarrow B$ in C, $\delta \not\models \neg B$,
3. if there s no such δ satisfying conditions 1 and 2 above, let $\delta = \emptyset$.

The set of all such maximal subsets of S is denoted as $Max(S, \mu)$.

Definition 10. Let C, D, S, μ, δ and $Max(S, \mu)$ be defined as above. A causal theory $CT^\mu_{S,\delta}$ is specified as follows:

$$CT^\mu_{S,\delta} = (A, C), \text{ where } A = D \cup \{\mu\} \cup \delta, \text{ and } \delta \in Max(S, \mu).$$

Then the set of all possible resulting states from updating S with μ, $Res^{C,D}(S, \mu)$, is defined as

$$Res^{C,D}(S, \mu) = \bigcup_{\delta \in Max(S,\mu)} Min(S, Models(CT^\mu_{S,\delta})). \tag{5}$$

In Definition 9, δ is the maximal subset of S with respect to μ such that (1) δ is consistent with domain constraints $\mathcal{D}$ and the direct effect of μ, and (2) δ is also consistent with the effect of each causal rule in $\mathcal{C}$. Obviously, condition (1) is the basic requirement for a state change. Condition (2) means that those facts in δ together with $\mathcal{D}$ and μ *may* causally derive some causal effects according to some causal rules in $\mathcal{C}$. In this case, if negations of these causal effects are entailed by S, they should be changed after this update. To make such causal reasoning successfully, it is necessary to require that δ be consistent with the effect B of any causal relation $A \rightsquigarrow B$ or $A \Rightarrow B$ in $\mathcal{C}$. Note that condition (3) is necessary since if we have a causal rule like $A \Rightarrow False$ then there does not exist a δ satisfying conditions (1) and (2). In this case, we assign $\delta = \emptyset$.

The derivation of causally indirect effects of μ with respect to $\mathcal{C}$ is achieved by specifying a causal theory $CT^{\mu}_{S,\delta}$ in Definition 10 and obtaining all models $Models(CT^{\mu}_{S,\delta})$ of $CT^{\mu}_{S,\delta}$[7]. Then we specify the set of final possible resulting states to be the union of those models in $Models(CT^{\mu}_{S,\delta})$ for any $\delta \in Max(S,\mu)$, such that models in $Mod(CT^{\mu}_{S,\delta})$ have minimal differences with the the initial state S.

Let us continue with the stuffy room example presented above where $\mu \equiv blocked(duct_1)$, initial state S is (4) and the only causal rule is (3). From Definition 9, $Max(S,\mu) = \{\delta\} = \{\{blocked(duct_2)\}\}$, and from Definition 10, we have

$$CT^{\mu}_{S,\delta} = (\{blocked(duct_1),\ blocked(duct_2)\},\ \{(3)\}), \text{ and}$$

$$\begin{aligned} Res^{\mathcal{C},\mathcal{D}}(S,\mu) &= Min(S, Models(CT^{\mu}_{S,\delta})) \\ &= \{\{blocked(duct_1), blocked(duct_2), stuffy(room)\}\}, \end{aligned}$$

which gives the desired solution as we expect.

3.3 Updating Knowledge Bases

So far, based on the state update presented above, we can formally define our knowledge base update operator. As presented previously, in our formalism, we distinguish the constraints and causal rules of the domain explicitly. In particular, we will use a causal theory to represent our knowledge base where both domain constraints and causal rules are represented clearly. Formally, a *knowledge base* Ω is a causal theory defined as $\Omega = (\{\psi\} \cup \mathcal{D}, \mathcal{C})$, where ψ is a closed first order formula, $\mathcal{D}$ is a set of closed first order formulas representing the domain constraints, and $\mathcal{C}$ is a set of causal rules above the domain.

Let $\Omega = (\{\psi\} \cup \mathcal{D}, \mathcal{C})$ be a knowledge base, and ϕ a closed first order formula. We say that Ω *causally entails* ϕ, denoted as $\Omega \models_{\mathcal{C}} \phi$, if for every $m \in Models(\Omega)$[8], $m \models \phi$. For example, if $\Omega = (\{blocked(duct_1) \wedge blocked(duct_2)\}, \{blocked(duct_1) \wedge blocked(duct_2) \Rightarrow stuffy(room)\})$, then $\Omega \models_{\mathcal{C}} stuffy(room)$.

---

[7] The class of all models of a causal theory is defined in Definition 7.

[8] Again, the class of all models of a causal theory is defined by Definition 7.

Definition 11. Let $\Omega = (\{\psi\} \cup \mathcal{D}, \mathcal{C})$ be a knowledge base, and μ a closed first order formula that is consistent with $\mathcal{D}$. We define the update of Ω with μ by using the causality-based minimal change approach, denoted as $\Omega \diamond_{cmc} \mu$, as follows:

$$\Omega \diamond_{cmc} \mu = (\{\psi'\} \cup \mathcal{D}, \mathcal{C}), \text{ where } Models(\Omega \diamond_{cmc} \mu) = \bigcup_{S \in Models(\Omega)} Res^{\mathcal{C}, \mathcal{D}}(S, \mu).$$

Let us consider the stuffy room example presented above once again. In our formalism, suppose the current knowledge base is $\Omega = (\{\psi\}, \{(3)\})$, where $\mathcal{D} = \emptyset$ and $\psi \equiv \neg blocked(duct_1) \wedge blocked(duct_2) \wedge \neg stuffy(room)$. Ignoring the detail, it is not difficult to see that

$$\Omega \diamond_{cmc} \mu = (\{\psi'\}, \{(3)\}), \text{ where } \psi' \equiv blocked(duct_1) \wedge blocked(duct_2),$$

from which we have $\Omega \diamond_{cmc} \mu \models_{\mathcal{C}} stuffy(room)$.

4 Related Work

We first discuss the relation between our approach and the PMA [4]. In fact, it is not difficult to see that if $\mathcal{C} = \emptyset$, our approach is exactly the same as the PMA. This is shown by the following theorem.

Theorem 12. $Res^{\mathcal{D}}(S, act) = Res^{\emptyset, \mathcal{D}}(S, act)$.

Recently, McCain and Turner proposed a causality-based method to represent state update, where a state is an interpretation of a propositional language [2][9]. Differently from our approach presented here, in their formalism, a causal rule is presented as an (non-defeasible) inference rule. For instance, expression $A \Rightarrow B$ indicates a causal relation between propositional formulas A and B[10]. Let $\mathcal{C}$ be a set of such causal rule, Γ a set of propositional formulas. Γ is *closed under* $\mathcal{C}$ if for every $A \Rightarrow B \in \mathcal{C}$, if $A \in \Gamma$ then $B \in \Gamma$. For any formula A, $\Gamma \vdash_{\mathcal{C}} A$ denotes that A belongs to the *smallest* set of formulas containing Γ that is closed with respect to propositional logic and closed under $\mathcal{C}$. Then the set of possible states resulting from updating S with μ, $Res^{\mathcal{C}}(S, \mu)$, is specified to be the set of interpretations such that

$$Res^{\mathcal{C}}(S, \mu) = \{S' \mid S' = \{l \mid (S \cap S') \cup \{\mu\} \vdash_{\mathcal{C}} l\}\}^{11}. \tag{6}$$

Note that in McCain and Turner's method, the possible resulting states are defined by satisfying a fixpoint condition with respect to the inference relation $\vdash_{\mathcal{C}}$.

---

[9] In fact, it is easy to extend McCain and Turner's method of state update to knowledge base update with the same way of the PMA and our approach defined by Definitions 8 and 11 respectively.

[10] In order to compare our approach with McCain and Turner's consistently, we slightly modify some notations in McCain and Turner's formulation.

[11] Note that l is a propositional literal.

Example 2. The light-power domain. Consider a domain with following two causal rules:

$$off(switch) \vee \neg power \Rightarrow \neg light, \tag{7}$$

$$True \Rightarrow on(switch) \wedge \neg off(switch) \vee \neg on(switch) \wedge off(switch), \tag{8}$$

$$True \Rightarrow on(switch) \supset light. \tag{9}$$

Then the set of causal rules $\mathcal{C}$ consists of (7), (8) and (9). Now suppose the initial state S_1 is $\{light, on(switch), \neg off(switch), power\}$. Consider the update of S_1 with $\mu_1 \equiv \neg power$. Then we will have the solution $Res^{\mathcal{C}}(S_1, \mu_1) = \emptyset$. This solution seems highly arguable: why can the power not be cut off?

Let us consider another initial state $S_2 = \{\neg light, \neg on(switch), off(switch), \neg power\}$. Similarly, updating S_2 with $\mu_2 \equiv on(switch)$ will lead to another unintuitive solution: $Res^{\mathcal{C}}(S_2, \mu_2) = \emptyset$.

From the above example, we can see that distinguishing causal rules as defeasible and non-defeasible seems more natural and flexible than just representing them as unified non-defeasible inference rules. In fact, restricting our approach to the propositional case, the following result shows that McCain and Turner's method can be treated as a special case in our system.

Theorem 13. *Let $\mathcal{C}$ be a set of causal rules in which every causal relation has the form $A \Rightarrow B$, S a state, and μ a propositional formula. Then $Res^{\mathcal{C}}(S, \mu) = Res^{\mathcal{C}, \emptyset}(S, \mu)$.*

5 Conclusion

In this paper, we proposed a new approach for model-based update. We have seen that to specify indirect effects of an update properly, we need to represent the domain causality explicitly in the formalism, and distinguishing causal rules as defeasible and non-defeasible cases does provide us more flexible capabilities to handle problems of update.

References

1. W. Łukaszewicz, *Non-Monotonic Reasoning.* Ellis Horwood, 1990.
2. N. McCain and H. Turner, A causal theory of ramifications and qualifications. In *Proceedings of 14th International Joint Conference on Artificial Intelligence (IJCAI'95).* Morgan Kaufmann Publisher, Inc. (1995) 1978–1984.
3. R. Reiter, A logic for default reasoning. *Artificial Intelligence* **13** (1980) 81–132.
4. M. Winslett, Reasoning about action using a possible models approach. In *Proceedings of the Seventh National Conference on Artificial Intelligence (AAAI'88).* Morgan Kaufmann Publisher, Inc. (1988) 89–93.
5. Y. Zhang and N.Y. Foo, Updating knowledge bases with disjunctive information. In *Proceedings of the Thirteenth National Conference on Artificial Intelligence (AAAI-96),* pp562-568. AAAI/MIT Press. Portland, August 1996.

Knowledge Revision for Document Understanding

Floriana Esposito   Donato Malerba   Giovanni Semeraro   Stefano Ferilli

Dipartimento di Informatica - Università degli Studi di Bari
Via E. Orabona 4 - 70126 Bari, Italy
{esposito, malerba, semeraro, ferilli}@lacam.uniba.it

Abstract. A key issue in the area of knowledge revision is the definition of efficient and effective (*ideal*) refinement operators. The paper presents a closed loop incremental learning system, called INCR/CSL, that implements two ideal operators for upward (generalization) and downward (specialization) refinement. It is employed as the knowledge maintenance engine in an intelligent agent for the automated processing of paper documents. Experimental results in the area of document understanding for semantic indexing of documents in a digital library service show that INCR/CSL is able to cope effectively and efficiently with this real-world learning task.

1 Introduction

In the context of knowledge revision, a key issue from both the efficiency and the effectiveness points of view is the definition of *ideal* (that is to say, *locally finite*, *proper* and *complete*) refinement operators. Theoretical results concerning this subject have demonstrated that, under the classical framework of θ-subsumption in a full first-order Horn clause logic, the search space does not allow us to have such a kind of operators, while these desirable properties can be achieved when the *Object Identity* assumption (and the notion of θ_{OI}-subsumption) [12] is adopted in the space of Datalog programs. Nevertheless, it can be proved that this constraint does not limit the expressive power of the adopted representation language.

Two ideal operators, one for the upward and one for the downward refinement, have been defined and implemented in a learning system, called INCR/CSL, which acts as Rule Refiner in a typical incremental architecture. It has been employed as the knowledge maintenance engine in an intelligent agent for the automated processing of paper documents: This aims at handling large databases of documents in digital form allowing the information extraction and the retrieval of documents by semantic indexing.

This paper aims at presenting the above system and the experimental results obtained by using it. In the next section, the logical language used to represent both the learned knowledge and the examples used is introduced. Section 3 briefly recalls the basic notions about refinement operators and the conditions that they should satisfy to be considered *ideal*. Section 4 presents the learning system INCR/CSL. Section 5 explains the experiments run on the problem of document understanding, and compares the results with those obtained by a batch system.

2 Ideal Refinement Operators under θ_{OI}-subsumption

When a logical theory fails in classifying new evidence which becomes available, it needs to be changed in order to restore the properties of completeness and consistency with respect to (wrt) all the examined positive and negative examples, respectively. This task can be performed in a *batch* way (i.e., by starting again from scratch in constructing a new theory from the whole set of examples) or in an *incremental* way (i.e., by only modifying the clauses of the existing theory causing the failure). In the latter case, *refinement operators* have to be used, which give rise to the question of what are the desirable properties they have to meet for the purposes of efficiency and effectiveness.

Most of the current research has recognized the answer to this question in the concept of *ideality* [13]. Informally, a refinement operator is *ideal* when it is *locally finite* (i.e., it succeeds in performing its task in a finite number of steps), *complete* (i.e., it is able to reach all the possible refinements of the clause it is applied to) and *proper* (i.e., it avoids considering as a refinement the clause itself, or a clause that is logically equivalent to the original one, so avoiding useless and computationally expensive loops).

A formal presentation of the above concepts is given in [4], where also definitions and results are available showing the importance of ideal refinement operators for the purposes of efficiency and effectiveness in the context of knowledge revision and their non-existence in the search space induced by the classical θ-subsumption ordering. Moreover, two operators have been defined meeting the conditions for ideality in the search space of the Datalog clauses restricted by the *Object Identity* assumption (within a clause, terms denoted with different symbols must be different [12]): One for the upward refinement, and its dual for the downward refinement.

3 The Representation Language

Henceforth, we refer to [9] for what concerns the basic definitions of a *substitution*, *positive* and *negative literal*, *clause*, *definite* and *program clause*, and *normal program*. We will indifferently use the set notation and the Prolog notation for clauses. Given a first-order clause ϕ, *vars*(ϕ), *consts*(ϕ) and $|\phi|$ denote respectively the set of the variables, the set of the constants and the number of literals occurring in ϕ. By *logical theory* we mean a set of *hypotheses*, by *hypothesis* we mean a set of program clauses with the same head. In the paper, we are concerned exclusively with logical theories expressed as *hierarchical programs*, that is, as programs for which it is possible to find a *level mapping* [9] such that, in every program clause $P(t_1, t_2,...,t_n) \leftarrow L_1, L_2,...,L_m$, the level of every predicate symbol occurring in the body is less than the level of P. Another constraint on the representation language is that, whenever we write about clauses, we mean *Datalog* (i.e., function-free) *linked* clauses. A definition of linked clause can be found in [8]. An instance of a linked clause is $C = P(x) \leftarrow Q(x, y), Q(y, z), \neg R(x, v)$. Conversely, the clauses $D = C - \{Q(x, y)\}$ and $F = C \cup \{\neg R(v, w)\}$ are not linked.

The differences existing between examples and hypotheses are the following.

- Each example is represented by one *ground* clause with a unique literal in the head.
- Each hypothesis is a set of program clauses with the same *head*.

An *example E* is *positive* for a hypothesis *H* if its head has the same predicate letter and sign as the head of the clauses in *H*. The example *E* is *negative* for *H* if its head has the same predicate, but opposite sign. Thus, more precisely, a negative example is a *generally Horn clause* [7]. Furthermore, we adopt the *negation-as-failure* rule [2] to define the meaning of a negated literal in the body of a program clause.

Generally, the canonical inductive paradigm requires the fulfilment of the properties of completeness and consistency for the learned rules.

A *theory T* is *inconsistent* iff at least one of its hypotheses is inconsistent wrt some negative example. In turn, a *hypothesis* is *inconsistent* wrt a negative example *N* iff at least one of its clauses is inconsistent wrt *N*. A *clause C* is *inconsistent* wrt *N* iff there exists a substitution σ that is compliant wrt the object identity assumption and such that the following conditions are satisfied:

$$1) \; body(C).\sigma \subseteq body(N), \qquad\qquad 2) \; \neg \, head(C).\sigma = head(N)$$

where *body(φ)* and *head(φ)* denote the *body* and the *head* of a clause φ, respectively. If at least one of the two conditions above is not met, we say that *C* is *consistent* wrt *N*.

As to the incompleteness, we say that a *theory T* is *incomplete* iff one of its hypotheses is incomplete wrt some positive example. A *hypothesis* is *incomplete* wrt a positive example *P* iff each of its clauses does not θ_{oi}-subsume *P*. Otherwise it is *complete* wrt *P*.

Now, we can introduce the notions of commission and omission error.

Given a theory *T* and an example *E*, *T* makes a *commission error* if there exists a clause *C* in a hypothesis of *T* that is inconsistent wrt *E*. *T* makes an *omission error* if there exists a hypothesis of *T* that is incomplete wrt *E*.

When a commission error occurs, it becomes necessary to specialize the inconsistent clause *C* so that the new clause *C'* restores the consistency property of the theory. When an omission error occurs, it becomes necessary to generalize the incomplete hypothesis *H* so that the new hypothesis *H'* restores the completeness property of the theory.

4 Incremental Learning for Knowledge Revision: INCR/CSL

Incremental learning is necessary when either incomplete information is available at the time of initial theory generation or the nature of the concepts evolves dynamically. The latter situation is the most difficult to handle since time evolution needs to be considered. In any case, it is useful to consider learning as a *closed loop* process, where feedback about performance is used to activate the knowledge revision phase [1].

In Fig. 1 the general architecture of a classical closed loop learning system is given. The process of hypothesis refinement consists of a number of functions related to each other by a closed loop information flow. The system takes from the *Expert/Environment* a set of examples of the concepts to be learned. This set can be subdivided into three subsets, namely *training, tuning* and *test examples*, according to the way in which examples are exploited during the learning process. Specifically, training examples, previously classified by the Expert, are exploited by the *Rule Generator* in a batch mode in order to generate a first version of the knowledge that is able to explain the provided examples.

The Rule Generator implements a *model-driven* inductive learning algorithm, called INDUBI/CSL [10]. It is a multiple predicate learner, that is to say, it can learn several

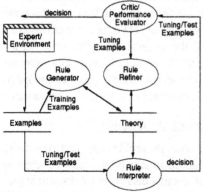

Fig. 1. The architecture of an incremental learning system.

concepts, even though they depend on each other. Specifically, differently from most learning systems, INDUBI/CSL does not make the assumption that concepts to be learned are independent of one another. Nonetheless, in order to deal with concept dependencies, it requires the user to be able to specify a *dependency hierarchy*, that takes the form of a directed acyclic graph (*dag*), whose nodes represent concepts to be learned. The order in which concepts are learned by INDUBI/CSL is completely defined by the dependency hierarchy. In particular, the concepts at the lowest level of a dependency hierarchy have to be learned first, since their definition does not depend on other concepts (*minimally dependent* concepts).

Subsequently, the theory is used by the *Rule Interpreter* in order to verify that rules continue to be valid also when new examples become available. The Rule Interpreter takes in input the set of rules (inductive hypotheses) and a tuning/test example and produces a decision. The *Critic/Performance Evaluator*, that may be a human expert or a computer program, compares the decision produced by the Rule Interpreter to the correct one and decides whether firing the rule refinement process or simply communicating the decision. Besides this, the Critic takes care of locating the cause of the wrong decision and choosing the proper kind of correction. In such a case, tuning examples are exploited incrementally by the *Rule Refiner* to modify incorrect rules according to a data-driven strategy. The Rule Refiner is INCR/CSL, consisting of two distinct modules, a *Rule Generalizer* and a *Rule Specializer*, which attempt to correct incomplete and inconsistent hypotheses, respectively. Test examples are exploited to put to the proof the predictive capabilities of the theory, intended as the behaviour of the theory on previously unclassified observations.

The Rule Generalizer adopts an operator which is inspired to the Interference Matching proposed by Hayes-Roth and McDermott. Briefly, given a generalization G and an example E not covered by G, both expressed as linked Horn clauses, it decomposes $body(G)$ into two conjunctions, $G_1=L_1 \wedge L_2 \wedge ... \wedge L_i \wedge .. \wedge L_n$ and G_2, such that each L_i contains the maximum non-null number of variables not appearing in $L_1 \wedge L_2 \wedge ... \wedge L_{i-1}$ while G_2 is the conjunction of the remaining literals of $body(G)$. Then, the set of all possible substitutions such that G_1 matches against E is built. Such a set is exploited in order to generate some generalizations of E and G by dropping literals in G_2. Since G_1 is not always uniquely determined, several sets of generalizations can be built. At the end of this process of generation of candidate generalizations, the best one is chosen according to a preference criterion. The generalizations produced by such an operator are *linked* and comply with the bias of *object identity*.

The specializing operator implemented in the Rule Specializer of INCR/CSL is based on the negation. In particular, it adds the negation of one or more literals of a misclassified example to the Horn clause representation of an *inconsistent* hypothesis, after having properly turned constants into variables. The search for the literals to be added is firstly performed in a set named *reduced base of consistent specializations* and, in case of failure, it is extended to the *augmented base of consistent specializations*. Indeed, two theorems prove that clauses generated by adding literals in the former set preserve the consistency property and are most general specializations of the inconsistent hypothesis. On the contrary, the consistency property of clauses generated by adding literals in the latter set has to be checked on the misclassified example. The search strategy takes advantage of the structure of the set of the linked Horn clauses, L, ordered by the generality relation($\leq$).

5 Use in the Context of Digital Document Processing

We successfully employed this learning system to solve the problems related to the tasks of document classification and understanding [3]. Indeed, a major bottleneck in developing technologies for an electronic system dealing with documents lays in the document pre-processing phase, and in particular, in the transformation of data presented on paper into an effective electronic representation to be used in the system's database. Since the pixel representation of a document image is far from being considered effective, it is necessary to process the bitmap in order to extract an abstract representation of the content of the document itself.

In this context, the learning systems can be employed to perform the *information capture* (i.e., the task of setting information free of the physical medium on which they are stored) and *semantic indexing* (which will be then used by a system dealing with the document database). This kind of indexing will allow our system to go far beyond the simple functions currently offered by the available systems, by making an *information retrieval* based not only on the classical information stored about the documents, but also on the documents' content which can be inferred from the layout of the document (which is a major innovation in this field).

It is important to note that the use of intelligent techniques allows to process equally well different kinds of paper documents, provided that they have some typing standard.

Information capture through document processing can take place at several levels of abstraction. The lowest level (*document analysis*) aims at extracting the geometric (or *layout*) structure of a document, that is, a hierarchical organization of layout areas with content of different categories (text, image or graphics). For example, in this level the document image is segmented into rectangular blocks associated with only one category (*primitive tokens*), which are then grouped in order to form larger and meaningful layout component [5]. The layout structure associates the content of a document with a *hierarchy of layout objects* (such as text lines, vertical/horizontal lines, graphic elements and images): In the resulting *layout tree*, the leaves are the basic blocks (typically rectangular areas delimiting portions of contents on the presentation medium), the internal nodes are composite objects (obtained by grouping together basic blocks as well as composite objects of lower level) and the root is the whole document. In multi-page documents, a composite object can represent a set of pages (rectangular areas corresponding to units of the presentation medium); all other internal blocks (*frames*) correspond to rectangular areas within a page. An example of hierarchical layout structure of a document can be found in Fig. 2.

The next level, after detecting the layout structure, is *document understanding*, in which the logical constituents of a document (such as author, title and sections of a paper) can be identified. The logical objects, too, can be arranged in another hierarchical structure (*logical structure*, shown in Fig. 3), which is the result of repeatedly dividing the content of a document into increasingly smaller parts, on the basis of the human-perceptible meaning of the content, so that *basic logical objects* (leaves of the logical tree) can concur in the formation of *composite* ones (internal nodes of the logical tree). Of course, while the layout objects are the same regardless of the document type, the logical objects strictly depend on the application (for example, a business letter will contain parts which are different from those of a scientific paper). This is the central and most powerful level, since it is straightforward to note that knowing the logical function of a part of the document (which means entering the semantics field) is the key to knowing where to search the information the user needs (or the conditions he gives in the query).

A typical ability of humans is that of associating a possible meaning to some tokens basing only on the spatial organization of blocks in the page layout, without reading their content (i.e., a mapping can be found from the layout in the logical structure); nevertheless, it may become difficult finding all correct mappings when the document processing

624

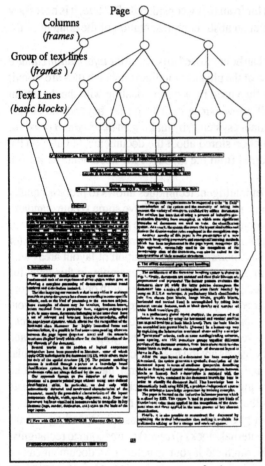

Page

Columns
(*frames*)

Group of text lines
(*frames*)

Text Lines
(*basic blocks*)

Fig. 2. The hierarchical layout structure of a document.

system has to deal with a variety of layout and logical structures: In this case, the problem can be simplified in that of *document classification*, which consists in simply classifying the documents into a set of distinct classes characterized by certain standard layout and logical structures.

The first issue in organizing the page layout is the association of a semantic primitive concerning the type of content to the set of tokens detected by the segmentation process. We defined five basic categories of blocks (text, picture, graphic, horizontal and vertical solid black line), allowing us to distinguish larger layout components (paragraphs, tables, line drawings, halftone images and formulas), each of which is described by the numerical features automatically produced by the segmentation process (height, length, area, eccentricity of the block, etc.) concerning global properties of the block and not the configurations of pixels within them.

The next step is building meaningful groupings of blocks basing on both perceptual/spatial criteria and on knowledge about typesetting conventions, in order to reduce the computational complexity of the subsequent recognition process. The output of the whole process is a set of layout objects organized in five distinct levels: *basic blocks, lines, sets of lines, first frames,* and *second frames*.

As to the document understanding, the adopted strategy consists of a hierarchical model fitting, which limits the range of labelling possibilities: The page layout is described by means of a first-order logic language, and such a description is first matched against models of classes of documents and then against models of the single logical components of interest for that class (an example of a document along with its first-order language description is given in Fig. 4). All models are expressed in the same language used to describe the page, and have been induced from some training documents, each associated with a class and a set of labelled layout components.

Therefore, we faced two learning problems: The former, regarding the classes of documents (document classification), and the latter, concerning the logical structures of each class (document understanding). In particular, learning models of the logical components of a document involves a further problem with respect to inducing models

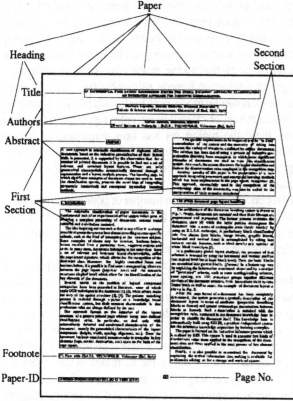

Fig. 3. The hierarchical logical structure of a document.

of the classes of documents, because the logical components may be related to each other (e.g., in standard scientific papers, the author's affiliation is above the abstract and under the title). Indeed, taking into account these relations in the dependence graph caused the system to generate more accurate and comprehensible models.

For our experiments, we considered a database of 30 single-page documents (Olivetti letters), in each of which we labelled the components obtained by the layout analysis phase with the corresponding logical meaning (*logotype*, *signature*, *body*, *ref*, *sender*, *date*, and *receiver*) in order to obtain the clauses representing the examples. Each labelled object is a positive example for the component it is associated to and, at the same time, is a negative example for all the other components.

The experiments have been run first with, and then without, the assumption of

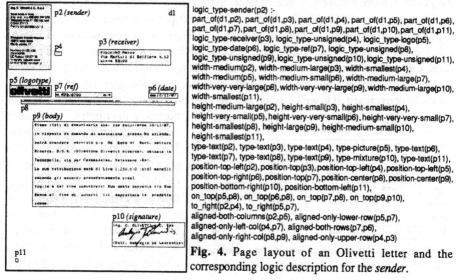

```
logic_type-sender(p2) :-
part_of(d1,p2), part_of(d1,p3), part_of(d1,p4), part_of(d1,p5), part_of(d1,p6),
part_of(d1,p7), part_of(d1,p9), part_of(d1,p10), part_of(d1,p11),
logic_type-receiver(p3), logic_type-unsigned(p4), logic_type-logo(p5),
logic_type-date(p6), logic_type-ref(p7), logic_type-unsigned(p8),
logic_type-unsigned(p9), logic_type-unsigned(p10), logic_type-unsigned(p11),
width-medium(p2), width-medium-large(p3), width-smallest(p4),
width-medium(p5), width-medium-small(p6), width-medium-large(p7),
width-very-very-large(p8), width-very-very-large(p9), width-medium-large(p10),
width-smallest(p11),
height-medium-large(p2), height-small(p3), height-smallest(p4),
height-very-small(p5), height-very-very-small(p6), height-very-very-small(p7),
height-smallest(p8), height-large(p9), height-medium-small(p10),
height-smallest(p11),
type-text(p2), type-text(p3), type-text(p4), type-picture(p5), type-text(p6),
type-text(p7), type-text(p8), type-text(p9), type-mixture(p10), type-text(p11),
position-top-left(p2), position-top(p3), position-top-left(p4), position-top-left(p5),
position-top-right(p6), position-top(p7), position-center(p8), position-center(p9),
position-bottom-right(p10), position-bottom-left(p11),
on_top(p5,p8), on_top(p6,p8), on_top(p7,p8), on_top(p9,p10),
to_right(p2,p4), to_right(p5,p7),
aligned-both-columns(p2,p5), aligned-only-lower-row(p5,p7),
aligned-only-left-col(p4,p7), aligned-both-rows(p7,p6),
aligned-only-right-col(p8,p9), aligned-only-upper-row(p4,p3)
```

Fig. 4. Page layout of an Olivetti letter and the corresponding logic description for the *sender*.

dependence between the concepts, and in both cases they have been replicated ten times, by randomly splitting the database of 30 documents into two subsets, namely a *learning* set and a *test* set, with dimension 20 and 10, respectively. In turn, the learning set has been subdivided into *training* set and *tuning* set, with dimension 5 and 15, respectively, and has been exploited in two distinct ways, according to the mode - batch or incremental - adopted to learn the Datalog programs. For the batch mode, this set has been entirely given to INDUBI/CSL as its input. For the incremental mode, only the training set has been used by INDUBI/CSL in order to produce the set of classification rules representing the first version of the knowledge base; then, the tuning set has been exploited to correct incrementally omission and commission errors, if any, through the two refining operators. Lastly, the test set has been exploited to evaluate the predictive accuracy of the inferred programs on unclassified components.

Table 1 reports the information concerning the mean number of positive and negative examples in the experimental sets during the different phases. The main interest is that of comparing the performance of the batch system to the incremental one, under the assumptions of independence/dependence of the learned concepts.

Fig. 5a shows the results concerning the experimentation under the independence assumption, while Fig. 5b refers to those under the dependence assumption. These diagrams compare the theory learned in batch mode with that learned incrementally along two dimensions, namely their predictive accuracy on the test set and the computational time taken by the learning system to produce the rules. Specifically, the *batch time* is relative to the training set for the batch mode, while the *incremental time* is computed as the sum of the computational time concerning the training set for the incremental mode plus the time concerning the tuning set. Values concerning the predictive accuracy are percentages, while those concerning the time are expressed in seconds. All the reported figures refer to the average of the ten replications.

Tables 2a and 2b illustrate the results of two statistical methods exploited to evaluate the significance of the observed differences as to predictive accuracy (*P.A.*) and time (*Time*) for each component, namely the paired t test (parametric) and the Wilcoxon test (non parametric). More precisely, Table 2a refers to the independence assumption among the various concepts, while Table 2b concerns the case of dependent concepts. For a thorough explanation of the two statistical tests, refer to [11]. The t test has been performed as two-sided test at a 0.01 level of significance, while the Wilcoxon test both at 0.05 and at 0.01 level. Each entry in the table contains the t value and the corresponding significance value for the t test, the W value and the corresponding critical value, along with the sample sizes, for the Wilcoxon test. It is well-known that the t test requires that the population data be normally distributed, when used with small sample sizes (less than 30). Conversely, the Wilcoxon test does not make any assumption on the distribution of the population data. In our setting, the sample size is 10, i.e. the number of replications, thus the t test might seem to be unsuitable. However, we performed preventively a normality

	Learning set (batch) #pos+#neg	Training set (incr.) #pos+#neg	Tuning set #pos+ #neg	Test set #pos+ #neg
logotype	20+220	5+55	15+165	10+110
signature	19+221	4+56	15+165	10+110
body	20+220	5+55	15+165	10+110
ref	31+209	8+52	23+157	15+105
sender	23+217	6+54	17+163	12+108
date	24+216	6+54	18+162	12+108
receiver	24+216	6+54	18+162	12+108

Table 1. Sizes of the example sets in the experiments conecrning the problem of document understanding.

Fig. 5. Experimental results obtained with INCR/CSL: (a) independent concepts; (b) dependent concepts.

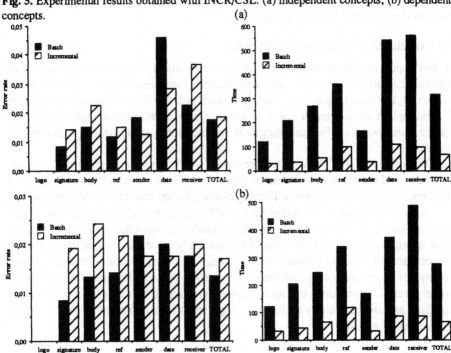

test in order to establish whether the population data are normally distributed. Such a test allows us to state that the population is normally distributed at a 0.01 level of significance.

Table 2 (a): independent concepts

Independence assumption	t test batch vs. incremental				Wilcoxon test batch vs. incremental							
	P.A.		Time		P.A.				Time			
	t value	sign. value	t value	sign. value	W value	crit. value =0.05	crit. value =0.01	sample size	W value	crit. value =0.05	crit. value =0.01	sample size
logo	-	-	33.242	.0001	-	-	-	10	55	38	45	10
signature	1.3	.2259	13.322	.0001	18	24	28	7	55	38	45	10
body	1.353	.2091	8.946	.0001	22	33	38	8	55	38	45	10
ref	.318	.7577	8.287	.0001	2	24	28	7	55	38	45	10
sender	2.332	.0445	8.002	.0001	-22	24	28	7	55	38	45	10
date	-1.848	.0975	8.879	.0001	-20	24	28	7	55	38	45	10
receiver	1.788	.1109	14.141	.0001	-5	19	21	6	55	38	45	10

(a)

Table 2 (b): dependent concepts

Dependent concepts	t test batch vs. incremental				Wilcoxon test batch vs. incremental							
	P.A.		Time		P.A.				Time			
	t value	sign. value	t value	sign. value	W value	crit. value =0.05	crit. value =0.01	sample size	W value	crit. value =0.05	crit. value =0.01	sample size
logo	-	-	23.123	.0001	-	-	-	10	55	38	45	10
signature	1.941	.842	14.848	.0001	22	28	32	8	55	38	45	10
body	2.448	.0388	16.843	.0001	16	15	15	5	55	38	45	10
ref	1.079	.3092	10.488	.0001	8	19	21	6	55	38	45	10
sender	-.712	.4945	7.912	.0001	-10	28	32	8	55	38	45	10
date	-.418	.6848	14.805	.0001	5	24	28	7	55	38	45	10
receiver	.557	.5911	7.706	.0001	-2	10	10	4	55	38	45	10

(b)

Table 2. Statistical results: (a) independent concepts; (b) dependent concepts.

Figures 5a and 5b show that the batch-learned programs outperform the incrementally-learned ones for all the classes, with the exception of *sender* and *date*, as regards the predictive accuracy; on the contrary, as to the computational times the incremental system outperforms the batch one in all cases. According to the test results, however, the *t* test reveals no difference between the predictive accuracies, but a significant difference in the case of computational time, both in the independence and in the dependence cases (shaded boxes). According to the Wilcoxon test the results are the same, excluding a difference in the predictive accuracies regarding the component *body* in the case of dependent concepts (shaded box in Table 2b).

6 Conclusions and Future Work

In this paper, the importance of having ideal refinement operators in the context of incremental knowledge revision has been recalled. The operators have been defined by restricting the search space of Datalog clauses ordered by the classical relation of θ-subsumption to the search space of Datalog clauses interpreted under the Object Identity assumption, i.e., by weakening the θ-subsumption ordering to the θ_{OI}-subsumption ordering.

The system INCR/CSL has been presented, which implements these concepts and operators, and performs an incremental refinement of multiconcept hierarchical logical theories, expressed in the form of Datalog clauses, on the ground of new examples.

The machine learning system has been used for acquiring and revising the knowledge of an intelligent agent able to build the logical models of paper documents starting from their layout structure. The possibility of automatically associating geometric regions of a document with semantic labels allows an easy information capture and an efficient retrieval of document portions by semantic indexing. These techniques allow to process equally well different kinds of paper documents, provided that they have some typing standard, and are particularly useful in the organization of a digital library of documents in electronic form [6].

References

1. Becker J.M., *Inductive learning of decision rules with exceptions: methodology and experimentation*, B.S. dissertation, Department of Computer Science, University of Illinois at Urbana-Champaign, Urbana, Illinois, UIUCDCS-F-85-945, August 1985.

2. Clark K.L., *Negation as failure* in Logic and Databases, H. Gallaire and J. Minker (eds.), Plenum Press, New York, 293-321, 1978.

3. Esposito, F., Malerba, D., and Semeraro, G., Multistrategy Learning for Document Recognition, *Applied Artificial Intelligence: An International Journal*, Vol.8, No.1, 33-84, 1994.

4. Esposito F., Laterza A., Malerba D. and Semeraro G., *Locally Finite, Proper and Complete Operators for Refining Datalog Programs*, in Foundations of Intelligent Systems, Lecture Notes in Artificial Intelligence 1097, Z.W. Ras and M. Michalewicz (Eds.), Springer, 468-478, 1996.

5. Esposito F., Malerba D. and Semeraro G., *From Machine Perception to Machine Learning: generating models of visual objects*, in Machine Learning and Perception, 139-148, G. Tascini, F. Esposito, V. Roberto and P. Zingaretti (Eds.), Singapore: World Scientific, 1996.

6. Esposito F., Malerba D., Semeraro G., Fanizzi N., and Ferilli, S., Adding Intelligence to Digital Libraries: IDL, *IJCAI-97 Workshop on AI in Digital Libraries - Moving From Chaos to (More) Order*, 1997.

7. Grant, J., & Subrahmanian, V.S., Reasoning in Inconsistent Knowledge Bases, *IEEE Transactions on Knowledge and Data Engineering*, Vol.7, N.1, 177-189, 1995.

8. Helft, N., Inductive Generalization: A Logical Framework, in *Progress in Machine Learning*, I. Bratko & N. Lavrac (Eds.), Sigma Press, Wilmslow, 149-157, 1987.

9. Lloyd, J.W., *Foundations of Logic Programming*, Second Edition, Springer-Verlag, New York, 1987.

10. Malerba, D., Semeraro, G., and Esposito, F., A multistrategy approach to learning multiple dependent concepts. In *Machine Learning and Statistics: The Interface*, C. Taylor and R. Nakhaeizadeh (Eds.), Wiley, London, pp. 87-106, 1997.

11. Orkin M. and Drogin R., *Vital Statistics*, McGraw-Hill, 1990.

12. Semeraro G., Esposito F. and Malerba D., *Ideal Refinement of Datalog Programs*, in Logic Program Synthesis and Transformation, Lecture Notes in Computer Science 1048, M. Proietti (Ed.), Springer, 1996.

13. van der Laag P.R.J. and Nienhuys-Cheng S.-H., *A Note on Ideal Refinement Operators in Inductive Logic Programming*, ILP-94, S. Wrobel (Ed.), GMD-studien Nr. 237, 247-260, 1994.

Author Index

Lecture Notes in Artificial Intelligence (LNAI)

Lecture Notes in Computer Science